'This book offers a significant contribution towards understanding the gains, limits and limitations of India's economic policies since 1991. The volume, with generous inputs from leading scholars, is an excellent guide for academics and practitioners alike. The chapters included in this volume review the role of these policies towards social inclusion and social transformation. They also discuss new ideas that can help India fight poverty and inequality and embark on the path of growth and sustainability.'

Kunal Sen, *Director, UNU-WIDER and Professor of Development Economics, University of Manchester, UK*

'Rajesh Raj S. N. and Komol Singha have put together a must-read handbook for understanding the ongoing economic policy changes and their complex consequences that India has undertaken over the last 30 years. Integrating 27 original chapters by 37 authors, the book is an essential reading for all those who are interested in India's economic and social development since 1991.'

Ira Gang, *Professor of Economics, Department of Economics, Rutgers University, USA*

THE ROUTLEDGE HANDBOOK OF POST-REFORM INDIAN ECONOMY

This handbook presents a comprehensive study of the post-reform Indian economy, three decades after the economic liberalization started in the early 1990s.

It studies the broad range of changes that were introduced in the reforms era, assessing their impact on sectors like manufacturing, agriculture, banking and finance, among others. It also assesses the performance of these sectors amid globalization and the socio-economic shifts in the country. The volume evaluates the contribution of the reforms to social transformation, social inclusion, sustainability and human development, and deliberates on the gains, blind spots and limitations. With contributions from scholars across the country, case studies and comparative analyses that draw on data analysis, econometric evidence and historical sensibility, this is an authoritative volume on the reforms of the 1990s and their impact on the Indian economy and people.

Topical and the first of its kind, the book will be a useful resource for scholars and researchers of economics, development studies, political economy, management studies, public policy and political studies.

Rajesh Raj S. N. is Associate Professor at the Department of Economics, Sikkim University, Gangtok, India. His research spans Industrial Economics, Firm Dynamics, Efficiency and Productivity Analysis and Informal Labour. He is Associate Editor of the *Journal of South Asian Development*. His books include *Out of the Shadows? The Informal Manufacturing in Post-Reform India* and *Small Firm Ownership and Credit Constraints in India*. He is a co-editor of *Productivity in Indian Manufacturing: Measurement, Methods and Analysis*. He is the recipient of the Dr. V K R V Rao Prize in Economics for the year 2014 by the ISEC, Bangalore, and ICSSR, New Delhi.

Komol Singha is Associate Professor at the Department of Economics, Sikkim University, Gangtok, India, where he teaches development economics. His research interests broadly cover Development Economics, Institutional Economics, Social Sector, etc. Prior to this present institution, he was with the Institute for Social and Economic Change, Bengaluru.

THE ROUTLEDGE HANDBOOK OF POST-REFORM INDIAN ECONOMY

Edited by Rajesh Raj S. N. and Komol Singha

LONDON AND NEW YORK

First published 2022
by Routledge
2 Park Square, Milton Park, Abingdon, Oxon OX14 4RN

and by Routledge
605 Third Avenue, New York, NY 10158

Routledge is an imprint of the Taylor & Francis Group, an informa business

British Library Cataloguing-in-Publication Data
A catalogue record for this book is available from the British Library

Library of Congress Cataloging-in-Publication Data
A catalog record has been requested for this book

ISBN: 978-0-367-42870-9 (hbk)
ISBN: 978-1-032-11145-2 (pbk)
ISBN: 978-0-367-85574-1 (ebk)

DOI: 10.4324/9780367855741

Typeset in Bembo
by Deanta Global Publishing Services, Chennai, India

Rajesh Raj S. N. dedicates this book to

Amma, Indira, Tanya

CONTENTS

FIGURES

TABLES

CONTRIBUTORS

Ishan Anand is Assistant Professor, Jindal Global Law School, O P Jindal University, Sonipat, Haryana.

Pinaki Chakraborty is Professor, National Institute of Public Finance and Policy, New Delhi.

Rishab Das is MBA Student, Post Graduate Programme, Indian Institute of Management Indore, Madhya Pradesh.

Aparajita Dhara is Associate Professor of Economics, Rishi Bankim Chandra Evening College, Naihati, West Bengal.

Abhijit Dutta is Professor of Commerce, Department of Commerce, Sikkim University, Gangtok, Sikkim.

Bishwanath Goldar is Former Professor, Institute of Economic Growth, New Delhi.

Haripriya Gundimeda is Professor of Economics, Department of Humanities and Social Sciences, Indian Institute of Technology Bombay, Powai, Mumbai, Maharashtra.

Manish Gupta is Assistant Professor, National Institute of Public Finance and Policy, New Delhi.

Gopal Kadekodi is Honorary Professor, Centre for Multidisciplinary Research, Dharwad. Karnataka.

Vinish Kathuria is Professor of Economics, SJM School of Management, Indian Institute of Technology (IIT) Bombay, Powai, Mumbai, Maharashtra.

Mausumi Kar is Associate Professor of Economics, Women's Christian College, Kolkata, West Bengal.

Saibal Kar is Professor of Economics at the Centre for Studies in Social Sciences, Calcutta (CSSSC), India and a Research Fellow of the Institute for Labor Economics (IZA) in Bonn, Germany.

C. Nalin Kumar is Associate Professor, School of Management, Presidency University, Rajanukunte, Bengaluru, Karnataka.

Sweta Lahiri is Faculty Member, Heramba Chandra College, Kolkata, West Bengal.

Sudhansu Sekhar Mahapatra is Professor of Commerce, Department of Commerce, Sikkim University, Gangtok, Sikkim.

Soumya Manjunath is Mahalanobis Fellow, Centre for Economic Policy and Public Finance, Asian Development Research Institute, Patna, Bihar.

Sanghita Mondal is Assistant Professor, IIFT Kolkata Campus, Kolkata, West Bengal.

R. Nagaraj is Professor of Economics, Indira Gandhi Institute of Development Research, Mumbai, Maharashtra.

Aviral Pandey is Assistant Professor, A. N. Sinha Institute of Social, Patna, Bihar.

R. Rijesh is Assistant Professor, Institute for Studies in industrial Development, New Delhi.

Marina Rai is PhD Scholar, CSRD-JNU, New Delhi.

Rajesh Raj S. N. is Associate Professor of Economics, Sikkim University, Gangtok, Sikkim.

Gaurang Rami is Professor of Economics, Veer Narmad South Gujarat University, Surat, Gujarat.

Pratik Rumba is PhD Scholar, Centre for Informal Sector and Labour Studies, Jawaharlal Nehru University, New Delhi.

B. Satheesha is PhD Scholar, Department of Humanities and Social Sciences, Indian Institute of Technology Delhi, New Delhi.

Indrani Sengupta is PhD Scholar, Zakir Husain Centre for Educational Studies, Jawaharlal Nehru University, New Delhi.

Partha Pratim Sengupta is Professor, Department of Humanities and Social Sciences, National Institute of Technology Durgapur, West Bengal.

Dawa Sherpa is PhD Scholar, Centre for Economic Studies and Planning, Jawaharlal Nehru University, New Delhi.

Madhabendra Sinha is Assistant Professor of Economics, Department of Economics & Politics, Visva-Bharati University, Santiniketan, West Bengal 731235, INDIA.

Aparajita Singh is PhD Scholar, Department of Humanities and Social Sciences, Indian Institute of Technology Bombay, Powai, Mumbai. Maharashtra.

Loitongbam Bishwanjit Singh is Post-doctoral Fellow, Department of Economics, Manipur University, Imphal, Manipur.

Nidhi Singh is Scientist C, Department of Health Research, Ministry of Health and Family Welfare, Government of India, New Delhi.

Sushant Kumar Singh is Assistant Professor of Economics, K. P. College, Murliganj, Bihar.

Komol Singha is Associate Professor of Economics, Sikkim University, Gangtok, Sikkim.

Malini L. Tantri is Assistant Professor of Economics, Institute for Social and Economic Change, Bengaluru, Karnataka.

Anjana Thampi is Assistant Professor, Jindal Global Law School, O. P. Jindal Global University, Sonepat, Haryana.

Jayan Jose Thomas is Associate Professor of Economics, Indian Institute of Technology Delhi, New Delhi.

PREFACE

India launched its market-oriented reforms in 1991. Recognizing the importance of international competitiveness in an increasingly interdependent and globalizing world economy, the country's economic reforms specifically targeted the largely restrictive trade and industrial policies. They included a gradual reduction of industrial licensing, removal/reduction of import duties for almost all manufactured intermediate and capital goods, tariff reduction and relaxation of rules for foreign investment, etc. The post-reforms period also witnessed a series of fiscal, monetary and financial sector reforms. The fundamental objective of these measures was to bring about a rapid and sustained improvement in the quality of life of the people of India through sustained growth in income and productive employment.

These structural reforms in the Indian economy are now almost 30 years old. But scholars and analysts have offered divergent views on the impact of these reforms on various sectors of the economy. While some economists and analysts have highlighted the significant gains in terms of acceleration of growth, trade and market expansion, and industrial competitiveness, there are many critics who vehemently argued that the reforms have not produced expected outcomes in economic and social indicators. These sceptics point to the surging inequality in income, low rate of employment generation and sluggishness in agriculture to question the much-touted success of the 1991 reforms. They aver that it is no secret that the country witnessed its slowest social improvement during this period and that, specifically, educational and health indicators grew at a substantially slower rate than before.

In this context, the Department of Economics, Sikkim University, Gangtok, organized a two-day national conference on 'India after a Quarter Century of Economic Reforms: The Benefits and Costs' from 5 to 6 October 2018. The seminar was sponsored by the Directorate of Economics, Statistics, Monitoring and Evaluation (DESM&E), Government of Sikkim, Sikkim, India. The conference brought together policy makers, academicians, researchers and leading social scientists within the country. The seminar through its papers deliberated on the transformation of the Indian economy in the past two-and-a-half decades of economic reforms and also discussed new ideas that can help India reduce poverty and inequality, and embark on the path of growth and sustainability in the next 25 years. This edited volume is an outcome of this seminar and comprises several papers presented at the conference, selected based on their relevance to the theme, critical approach and strength of their suggestions. The findings, as arrived at by different contributors in various chapters, highlight the critical issues related to the implementation of reforms and their impact on various sectors of the economy and further the debate on the theme. All the chapters included in this volume present new material based on current research and have been subjected to rigorous internal reading and external refereeing. We do hope that this will be useful to the academia, research scholars, undergraduate and postgraduate courses in the disciplines of economics, commerce, management, economics, geography, development studies and other social sciences.

We are thankful to all the contributors. We are grateful to Sikkim University for providing the infrastructure and other support for the workshop. We gratefully acknowledge the generous financial support from DESM&E, Government of Sikkim (GoS), without which it would not have been possible for us to organize the seminar. We are also thankful to the reviewers who reviewed the manuscript. We also thank Prabin Chauhan Chhetri for the excellent research assistance. Finally, we thank the editorial team at Routledge, without whose continuous support, this volume would not have seen the light of day.

Gangtok, India
4 January 2021

Rajesh Raj S. N.
Komol Singha

INTRODUCTION

Rajesh Raj S. N. and Komol Singha

India launched its market-oriented reforms in 1991. These reforms represented a clear departure from the strongly inward-looking trade policy regime followed in India until then. Recognising the importance of international competitiveness in an increasingly interdependent and globalising world economy, the economic reforms specifically targeted the largely restrictive trade and industrial policies. They included a gradual dismantling of industrial licensing, removal of import licensing for nearly all manufactured intermediate and capital goods, tariff reduction and relaxation of rules for foreign investment (Srinivasan, 2000). The period also witnessed a series of fiscal reforms and monetary and financial-sector reforms. While fiscal reforms strove to attain fiscal discipline, the monetary reforms mainly aimed to eliminate interest rate distortions and rationalise the structure of lending rates. The fundamental objective of these measures was to bring about rapid and sustained improvement in the quality of life of the people of India through sustained growth in income and productive employment.

These reforms are now almost 30 years old. But views on the impact of these structural reforms on various sectors of the Indian economy are divergent. While some economists and analysts highlight the significant gains in terms of acceleration of growth, trade and market expansion and industrial competitiveness (Panagariya, 2008; Ahluwalia, 2019), among other things, there are others who vehemently argue that the reforms have not produced expected outcomes in social indicators. These sceptics point to the surging inequality in income, low rate of employment generation and sluggishness in agriculture to question the much-touted success of the 1991 reforms (Jha, 2004; Himanshu, 2019; Kannan and Raveendran, 2009; Thomas, 2012; Balakrishnan, 2000). These critics aver that it is no secret that the country witnessed its slowest social improvement during this period, and that, specifically, educational and health indicators grew at a substantially slower rate than earlier (Ray, 2008). The recent slump in growth and a greater tendency towards protectionism have further strengthened their arguments. Despite these conflicting views, a serious deliberation on the benefits and costs of reforms has not happened. Time is now far riper than ever to discuss and deliberate on the gains, limits and limitations of these reforms.

Some of the important policy events that unfolded with the formation of the National Democratic Alliance (NDA) government at the Centre since 2014 are also likely to influence, adversely or positively, the development of various sectors of Indian economy. They include the end of Inspector Raj for small and medium firms; 23 years after India got rid of Licence Raj

 DOI: 10.4324/9780367855741-101

in 1991, welfare schemes targeted mainly at women (Ujjwala scheme that began in 2016) and several other policies, including demonetisation, GST system, programmes to enhance banking to the poor (Pradhan Mantri Jan-Dhan Yojana), Direct Benefit Transfer scheme and so on. In addition, some of the initiatives undertaken during the NDA regime that are worth mentioning include Make in India, scrapping of Foreign Investment Promotion Board, Smart Cities mission and The Arbitration and Conciliation (Amendment) Act. An array of similar reforms were effected in the agricultural sector too and includes Paramparagat Krishi Vikas Yojana (PKVY), Pradhan Mantri Kisan Samman Nidhi Yojana (PMKSNY), Pradhan Mantri Fasal Bima Yojana (PMFBY) and Pradhan Mantri Sinchai Yojana, among others.[1] Some amendments that were observed in the financial sector include Finance Act (2016) and The Insolvency and Bankruptcy Code.[2]

Although the direct impact of these reforms is hard to capture, the large-scale implications of such amendments cannot be overlooked. For instance, bilateral ties have a direct bearing on Foreign Direct Investment (FDI) flows (both inward and outward) and trade. Similarly, various schemes initiated in the agriculture sector might explain the recent trends in agricultural production and productivity. While some of the nuances of such initiatives taken by the NDA government in recent years have been highlighted in the book, there is less focus on the implications of these initiatives on various macro issues such as poverty, income distribution, gender welfare, GDP and so on. The lack of adequate attention to the recent initiatives mainly emanates from the fact that these new initiatives or schemes started by the NDA government is fairly new and, therefore, its impact may not be clearly evident in such a short time period. However, the book has largely tried to provide a comprehensive understanding of the Indian economy in the post-reform period with statistical evidence, as and when available.

This handbook is conceived to fill this obvious gap in the literature and aims to provide a perspective on how the new policies adopted since 1991 have changed the economic landscape of India. Besides providing an easily accessible summary of a broad range of changes that took place in the reforms era, the chapters included in the volume also evaluate the contribution of these policies to social inclusion and social transformation through the lens of land reforms, food security, poverty reduction and overall human development. The chapters also discuss new ideas that can help India reduce poverty and inequality and embark on the path of growth and sustainability. Due care was taken during the selection of the chapters to ensure that the volume does not seem like a random collection of essays. Most of the contributions were drawn from scholars who are experts in their respective areas. In doing so, we were gently dirigiste in getting contributions that could be grouped under six main topics: 'Agrarian Reforms and Agriculture', 'Trade and Manufacturing', 'Financial Sector Developments', 'FDI, R&D and Innovation', 'Social Sector in India' and 'Sectoral and Regional Issues'. We are fairly successful in obtaining chapters that offer a serious and critical discussion on each of the above topics.

The first section consisting of five chapters (Chapter 1–5) is on the theme 'Agrarian Reforms and Agriculture'. While economic growth has certainly picked up in the post-reforms period, not every sector has been a part of the growth story. The agricultural sector is one such laggard. In their chapter, Thomas and Satheesha probe this issue and examine the trends in growth of incomes and output in Indian agriculture. Along with examining the performance at the state level, the study also investigates how the state-level differences in growth influence the pattern of growth in rural labour markets. They find that the agricultural growth in India has not been consistent and marked by large temporal and spatial variations. The agricultural incomes in India grew faster during the 1980s but registered a sharp decline during the 1990s and the first half of the 2000s. The sector then witnessed a revival during the period 2004–2005 to 2011–2012, only to report a fall again after 2011–2012. However, the growth performance varied across the

Indian states. According to the study, Uttar Pradesh, Punjab and Haryana continue to lead the way with respect to food grain production though the growth of food grain production seems to have attained some degree of saturation in these states. The study also finds significant shift of the labour force away from the agriculture since the mid-2000s, and the major reasons for this were the emergence of employment opportunities in rural construction, cropping pattern and emergence of employment opportunities in the non-agricultural sectors.

The next chapter by Anand chimes in well with the first chapter. He undertakes a careful investigation of the sources of agricultural growth and the distributional aspect of this growth process in the reforms period. In particular, the study traces the sources that contributed to the recovery of agricultural growth post-2004–2005 period. Anand attributes the growth revival to favourable terms of trade, farm diversification, increase in public spending and intensified input use as indicated by a rise in the sale of tractors, fertiliser consumption and credit availability. The rise in output price and yield too contributed to the recovery of agricultural growth in the mid-2000 period. A related question explored by the chapter is the distributional outcomes of agrarian changes prompted by the growth revival. Based on evidence collected from National Sample Survey Office (NSSO) surveys, Anand maintains that the agricultural growth in India has not only been promoting inequality, but it has also been immiserising for the bottom 20 percent of farmer households. He contends that the fruits of agricultural growth have largely been cornered by large land holders. Considering the economic conditions of small holders and their reliance on oppressive sources of credit, the author envisages further worsening of India's agrarian crisis and calls for greater government intervention to provide reprieve to the peasantry who are in distress notwithstanding the high growth.

Redistributive land reform and agrarian reforms since the introduction of new economic policies gradually changed the agrarian structure and the associated class relations in India. Focusing on the issue of 'redistributive land reform' in the context of neoliberal globalisation, Rumba in his chapter argues that agrarian structure has witnessed a substantial change during the post-reforms period. One such change noticed by the author is the movement of landowning households from the farm sector to the non-farm sector. This has led to the emergence of larger proportion of landowning but non-cultivating households who otherwise used to be the permanent supplier of land in the land lease market. This coupled with declining job opportunities in the agricultural sector has forced the labour supplying households to enter the tenancy market despite the steep land rental price. Along with the increase in the inequities in access to land, the chapter by Rumba also highlights the rise of the 'land hunger class', who are willing to cultivate and pay high rent in the land lease market, in the post-reform period. The chapter emphasises that the agrarian structure in neoliberal India comprises two types of households: who are eager to cultivate land but are landless or own small plots of land and the other who owns land but does not want to do any cultivation.

In the next chapter, Manjunath investigates the nexus between infrastructure and agriculture in rural areas in the context of the Indian state of Karnataka. The emphasis is on the role of economic and institutional infrastructure and human capital on agricultural growth. Using a composite index of quality of rural infrastructure, the study examines the availability, quality and utilisation of infrastructure in rural areas and its subsequent effect on agricultural income. Based on the field survey data collected from 20 districts, his study suggests substantial inter-district disparity in access to and quality of rural infrastructure in the state. He then establishes that such disparities in infrastructural quality do explain the inter-district differences in agricultural income. The finding of positive nexus between infrastructural quality and agricultural growth, according to him, reveals how important it is to enhance the quality of infrastructure in rural areas. The study emphasises that rather than focusing on mere provision of infrastructure with regard to quantity, the stress should be on efficiency and quality of such provisions.

Environmental sustainability is the area where the progress is less evident. In fact, all important indicators relating to environmental sustainability demonstrate steady deterioration. Though its relevance is increasingly recognised in policy-making circles, there exists very limited research examining whether the economic reforms have succeeded in attaining environmental sustainability. The last chapter in this section attempts to fill this void in the literature. The authors analyse the trends in the macro- and micro-level economic indicators that measure the well-being of the people and assess the impact of these indicators on the environment. They agree that India has witnessed significant economic achievements in the post-reforms period. Along with the increase in gross domestic product, there has been substantial improvement in social indicators too. However, this demographic and economic growth has put considerable pressure on agriculture, forests, subsoils and air and water resources leading to resource degradation. They establish that pollution levels and environmental degradation have increased due to increased consumption levels and extraction of resources. According to the authors, 'Increase in the corporations, changes in consumption patterns with higher environmental foot prints, along with the extraction of resources with little regard for sustainability of the resources has put India's environmental and social sustainability at stake'. They argue that it is high time for India to move to a new phase of environmentally inclusive reforms. Which means the focus must be on enhancing human capabilities and minimising the impact on environment through sustainable use of natural resources, proper waste management and by reducing environmental pollution.

The chapters in the second section are concerned with 'Trade and Manufacturing'. The section has six chapters and most of these chapters examine how these reforms, especially the substantial liberalisation in trade policy, impacted the performance of the manufacturing sector. These chapters are expected to spur wider discussion on whether the manufacturing sector has performed to its potential in the past two-and-a-half decades of economic reforms or, as argued in one of the chapters, whether we need to re-invent industrial policy keeping in view the long-term national goals.

Nagaraj examines India's industrial performance in the aftermath of 1991 reforms and attempts to draw lessons from this performance for the future. He stresses that the liberal economic reforms carried out over the last quarter century has not benefitted the manufacturing sector, despite faster economic growth and output diversification. In his view, India failed to catch up with its Asian peers to cement its reputation as a successful industrialised nation with rising manufactured exports even after a quarter century of the market-oriented reforms. What explains the underperformance of India's industrial sector? He dismisses the contention of the protagonists of reforms that incomplete reforms have hobbled industrialisation in India. Debunking the claim of labour market rigidity as a reason for industrial stagnation, he states that recent experiences suggest that 'hire and fire' policy effectively rules the organised labour market today. Evidence on the employment of non-permanent workers in large numbers by large enterprises points to the fact that the seemingly rigid laws do not apply to a growing segment of organised workers. Rather his reasons for industrial stagnation post reforms lie in 'structuralist economic view of India's long-term constraint as one with low agriculture productivity (compared to global average), poor public infrastructure and extreme energy import dependence'. While suggesting the solutions to step up industrialisation, he emphasises the importance of extensive state intervention to accelerate domestic savings and public investment. He also stresses the need to locate industries and products in which imports are succeeding on account of easy credit and those which require productivity improvement.

Goldar analyses the reasons for a slide in labour incomes in India's organised manufacturing sector since the 1990s. In his chapter, he is particularly interested in investigating the role of India's trade reforms on labour income share in organised manufacturing. The analysis is carried out for the period 1990–1991 to 2014–15, a period encompassing approximately a quarter century of economic reforms in India, using industry and plant-level panel data. His study finds a clear downward trend in labour income share in the post-reform period till 2007–08, and an upward trend thereafter. The finding of downward trend in labour income share during 1990–91 to 2007–08 and the post-2007 trend reversal are also visible among two-digit industries. While looking at the factors that contributed to the decline in labour income share, the econometric analysis points to the significant role played by trade reforms. The study finds that import liberalisation contributed heavily to the fall in labour income share which led to the widening of the gap between growth of labour productivity and growth of real product wages. Apart from trade reforms, increase in capital intensity and increase in total factor productivity also contributed to the declining share of labour income. Finally, the chapter also tries to locate the factors that explain the trend reversal in labour income share in manufacturing after 2007. The analysis reveals that the prime explanation lies in the significant rise in the growth rate of real wages in agriculture. Goldar argues that faster growth in real wages in agriculture drove up the wages in manufacturing which led to an increase in labour income share.

The next chapter in this section focuses on the export competitiveness of Indian manufacturing sector since the onset of trade liberalisation reforms in the early 1990s. The chapter by Rijesh noted a sharp decline in the levels of trade protection in the post-reform era. In particular, the peak tariff on manufactures has declined from 400 percent in the early 1990s to less than 10 percent in the recent period. At the same time, there has been a significant improvement in goods trade in the post-liberalisation period; both exports and imports have registered double-digit growth rates. Along with strong trade performance, the study also finds a noticeable shift in trade composition towards technology-intensive products like machinery and chemical sectors. While exploring the link between trade liberalisation and export competitiveness, the study concludes that trade liberalisation policy alone is not sufficient to achieve higher export competitiveness in the international market. Instead, it is important to focus more on investing in technology and knowledge-based assets to reduce production cost and improve the quality of the exported products. To achieve this, 'creating a well-functioning institutional apparatus, improved physical infrastructure, and environment for the development of innovative production capabilities' are in order.

One cannot deny the important role of services sector in influencing manufacturing growth. Given that manufacturing performance depends critically on the state of service inputs, Mausumi Kar argues that services sector might have played a key role in the success of the Indian manufacturing sector, especially in the post-reforms period. Kar maintains that the reforms of the 1990s have greatly transformed the services sectors, thereby allowing foreign and domestic competition with greatly improved regulation. She goes on to state that such improvements have enhanced firms' ability to invest in new business opportunities and better production technology as well as to exploit economies of scale. In her chapter, she probes whether such rapid improvements in service-led activities had a positive spillover effect on its manufacturing counterpart. Her econometric investigation at the state-level reveals that all round expansion of services trade may not necessarily augment productivity performance of manufacturing sector. On the contrary, the manufacturing sector is more likely to experience lower labour productivity and income, if there is too large an expansion of services trade. She therefore contends that limitless growth of services trade is unlikely to be a promising strategy for a country like India which advances inclusive growth as its long-run developmental goal.

The liberalisation of trade regime in the 1990s has led to substantial increase in the inflow of FDI to India. This has led to a huge surge in studies looking at the role of FDI spillover effects on productivity and export performance of Indian manufacturing firms. The next chapter by Mondal contributes to this burgeoning literature by examining the role of FDI spillover effects on export performance. As a departure from the existing studies, her study classifies firms into different categories based on their technology intensity to find out if the role of FDI spillover effects on export performance varies across the technology category sectors. Following the Organisation for Economic Co-operation and Development (OECD) definition, the study classifies the firms into four technology intensity sectors, namely, High Technology (HT), Medium High Technology (MHT), Medium Low Technology (MLT) and Low Technology (LT) sectors. Her empirical analysis based on data for 6,000 Indian firms suggests limited role for FDI spillovers in influencing export decision or export activity of the Indian firms. The study, on the other hand, finds that export performance of firms crucially hinges on in-house R&D activity and technology import. Mondal, therefore, stresses the need for encouraging more in-house R&D activities and skill enhancement through proper training.

Over the years, there has been an increased attention towards easing the procedural hassles in doing business and conducting cross-border trade over time. The last chapter in this section by Nalin Kumar discusses the effect of such reform measures on India's agri-food trade sector. He then examines the distractive effects of reforms induced by the ease of doing business. His analysis is based on two sectors, namely, marine products and spices export sectors, the sectors where non-tariff barriers are highly prevalent and the ones which face severe competition from leading exporters. His analysis reveals that the lack of co-evolution of institutions in implementing trade policy reforms resulted in a scenario in which reforms do not trickle down to a sector. On the one hand, continued trade policy reforms failed to tackle issues related to standards, non-tariff barriers and the burden of documentation for India's agri-food exports. On the other hand, the reforms induced by the ease of doing business distract the very basic institutional and infrastructural reforms the sector deserves.

The third section titled 'Financial Sector Developments' basically deals with the structural changes that have occurred in the Indian financial system in the post-reforms era. It reflects upon various dimensions of the Indian financial system such as resource sharing, trends in inflation following the globalisation process, firm portfolio and financing behaviour of non-financial corporations (NFCs) and shadow banking, among others. While the first chapter in the section is descriptive in nature, the remaining three chapters employ econometric exercises to fulfil their objectives.

The first chapter in this section brings into light the issues involved with using the census population of 1971 as the criterion for sharing resources among Indian states. The authors argue that in order to have a fair and equitable resource sharing, a more recent population census must be chosen as the base. They vouch for the replacement of 1971 population estimate with the most recent population census, that is, 2011. In the process, they also question the fundamental idea of using population size as a resource-sharing criterion among Indian states and talk about designing an appropriate grant mechanism that can actually reward better performing states rather than penalise them by increasing their fiscal burden. In the next chapter, the authors explore yet another dimension of reforms that was undertaken in the early 1990s and examines the association between globalisation and rate of inflation in India. The use of the latest Reserve Bank of India (RBI) database from 1991–92 to 2018–19 adds significantly to the literature on this topic. The study reveals that there exists a unidirectional causality between globalisation and rate of inflation. Using trade openness and FDI inflow as the indicators of globalisation, they conclude that globalisation and money supply have a positive impact on inflation in India.

Sushant Kumar Singh in his chapter analyses the changes that the firm portfolio and financing behaviour of the NFCs have undergone in India in the post-reforms period, using firm-level data drawn from the Centre for Monitoring Indian Economy (CMIE) prowess database. He outlines the changing behaviour of NFCs and articulates the interrelations between financialisation and corporate decisions in the post-reform era. The study closely scrutinises the sector-wise consolidated annual financial statements of firms to identify the investment behaviour of Indian firms. The study finds that the process of financialisation is mainly taking place through expansion of the stock market and the derivative market. The study also finds sharp evidence of changes in investment behaviour of firms during this period. The firms are increasingly investing in financial assets and paying out huge chunk of their profits to financial agents. His analysis also points to a declining trend in the creation of new physical assets indicating a fall in the growth of real accumulation process and financial activities.

The last chapter by Dawa Sherpa resonates well with the previous chapter and provides an overview of financial system in India in general and shadow banks in particular. Like the previous chapter, this chapter too relies on the CMIE prowess database to depict the rise of shadow banks in Indian financial system in the post-reforms period with partial emphasis on gold loan. Basically, the study highlights the systemic risks shadow banks poses to the overall financial system in India. The study shows that although shadow financial institutions have become more interconnected with other parts of the financial system, in the process, they have also become more sophisticated in terms of their activities and risk-taking positions. Due to its excessive dependency on bank borrowings, a gold loan Non-Banking Financial Company (NBFC) is vulnerable to funding shocks, liquidity shocks and its asset quality being deteriorated overtime. He therefore argues for increasing the regulation of the gold loan NBFCs and controlling their reliance on banks.

The fourth section deals with FDI, R&D and innovation. This section has three chapters. One of the prominent developments in the post-liberalisation years is the substantial rise in FDI. This surge in FDI in India is largely aided by relaxation of policies on investment, such as investment incentives, and the reduction or elimination of capital controls and other forms of barriers to investment. There is a very general agreement that FDI inflows aid the growth and development of the economies of host countries through employment generation, expansion of supply of goods and increased revenue generation through rise in exports. In addition, there can also be spillover effects associated with FDI originating from foreign companies, which can help in the provision of new skills and technologies for domestic producers. Have the benefits from the rise in FDI inflows trickled down? The chapters in this section attempt to provide an answer to this question.

A highly crucial aspect of external sector liberalisation is the proliferation of bilateral investment treaties between countries. These treaties safeguard the rights of investments of foreign firms through an array of investors' rights, and in most cases, allow the investors to take to legal course if the rights are violated. It is argued that bilateral investment treaties boost the credibility of host countries and results in increased investment. The impact of such treaties on FDI has been the focus of many existing studies. Majority of these studies in the context of developing countries, however, have focused on the role of bilateral investment treaties on attracting FDI while its role on stimulating outward FDI has been barely studied in the literature. In his chapter, Kathuria concentrates on this aspect and studies the role of bilateral investment treaties on outward FDI from India. His study is based on the outward FDI data from India to 140 countries over the period 2007–2014. In terms of outward FDI stock, India is currently the 11th largest economy among all emerging markets, according to the study. The study also reports that signing and ratification of bilateral investment treaties was an important activity in the post-liberalisation period. However, the analysis by Kathuria does not find any role for such treaties in influencing outward foreign direct investment (OFDI). His panel data analysis shows that outward FDI from India is not influenced by bilateral investment treaties. On the other hand, it is the economic growth, per capita income and size of the country that have induced outward FDI.Though aggregate OFDI may not have gone up with bilateral investment treaties, Kathuria believes that investor protection clause in such treaties may still have enhanced the effects of other types of investment policies.

The next chapter by Bishwanjit Singh examines the impact of foreign ownership and Intellectual property rights (IPR) protection on innovation activities. He writes that the market shares of Multinational companies (MNCs) witnessed a significant upsurge following the trade liberalisation of 1991 and patent policy changes thereafter. This is particularly more evident in the Indian pharmaceutical industry. He argues that the expansion of foreign ownership in Indian pharmaceutical firms is likely to augment R&D activities in these firms. His study for the period 1999 to 2014 using the annual census data of 552 firms investigates this possibility in the Indian pharmaceutical industry. The findings confirm this possibility and suggest that foreign ownership encourages domestic firms to undertake R&D activities. It is also found that the relationship is more robust among exporting firms. However, the study finds little evidence to support the role of patent policy changes on R&D activities.

In the last chapter in this section, Nidhi Singh traces the system building activities of molecular diagnostic industry in the aftermath of economic liberalisation programme initiated in the 1990s. By adopting a system framework and using both secondary and primary survey data, the study finds that trade liberalisation has mostly favoured the foreign firms while domestic players have hardly benefitted from the trade reforms. The study shows the heavy reliance on imports and equipment from abroad by the actors in this industry as direct implications of trade liberalisation policy regime initiated since the 1990s. Even the innovative capabilities in terms of production, technology and investment are found to be highly concentrated in the hands of few MNCs. On the other hand, the domestic industrial base has a nascent presence and the young start-up firms serve the bulk of indigenous product development that meets the severe health care problems of the wider society. According to the study, since the development of the industrial base has a transformative effect on the present healthcare diagnostic system, there is a need to address the system-based challenges and issues for developing a socially responsible molecular diagnostic industrial base in the country.

The fifth section of this compendium focuses on the broader theme 'Social Sector in India'. The five chapters in this section touch upon the basic dimensions of human development and reflect the current scenario with respect to health, nutrition and education in India. The first chapter in this section traces the nexus between agriculture and nutrition status in India. The next two chapters focus on the performance of public distribution system and compare the two conventional approaches, namely universal approach and targeted Public Distribution System (PDS) approach. The fourth chapter briefly highlights the silent withdrawal of government which has paved the way for the private players to flourish and further widen the inequality in the education sector. It emphasises on the role of government to address the issue. The last chapter deals with the methodological issues involved in calculating the Human Development Index.

Despite high economic growth, nutritional deficiencies have loomed darkly in the Indian health sector affecting infants, children, men and women in India. Scholars argue that progress in nutritional status have not been able to keep pace with the country's impressive success in hastening economic growth in last few decades. This forms the crux of Chapter 19 by Pandey where he investigates the relationship between agriculture and nutrition status in India. Here, he argues that one of the solutions to food and nutrition security lies in agricultural growth as improved agriculture leading to better household food security can ensure adequate dietary intake and nutritional status. According to the study, malnutrition is present in most of the states of India. Besides the agrarian states of Bihar, Uttar Pradesh, Jharkhand and Madhya Pradesh, the study reports higher levels of malnutrition in high-income states of Maharashtra, Karnataka and Gujarat too, belying the general belief that high-income states tend to have low level of malnutrition. By employing an econometric analysis, the study further probes the link between agriculture and nutrition and gives credence to the significant role of agricultural performance in explaining the difference between levels of malnutrition across the states of India. The analysis also underscores the important role of agriculture diversification, household amenities and child-care practices on nutritional status. The findings from the study persuade the author to emphasise the need to increase farmers' income in order to address the issue of malnutrition.

Rising expenditure on non-food essentials has pushed poorer sections of the society into a nutritional trap. Shining a light on this issue, the next chapter by Anjana Thampi examines the state-level variations in nutrition and the role of PDS in mitigating any nutritional deficiency. To be precise, she compares the state-level variations in the incidence of hunger and undernutrition using Global Hunger Index and examines the nutritional impact of PDS in India. She highlights the extent to which PDS has been successful in bridging the nutritional gap among the poor population, especially in rural areas. The study finds that PDS has turned out to be a positive and successful step to tackle hunger and undernutrition situation in India.

Corroborating on the point that poorer section needs due attention, Marina Rai compares the efficiency of the two approaches (universal approach versus targeted approach) of PDS in India, with particular reference to two major states viz. West Bengal and Tamil Nadu. Using NSSO survey data, this study provides a succinct overview of the performance of PDS in these two states (one following the universal approach while the other following the targeted approach) in both rural as well as urban areas during the period 1993–94 to 2009–10. The study concludes that universal approach is more effective especially due to higher participation, lower targeting errors of excluding the needy and greater benefits to the poor which improve nutritional outcomes among the beneficiaries.

The chapter by Sengupta explores the interplay between two forces (public and private) in the education market in India and seeks to identify the determinants of private tuitions in India. Using NSSO data (42nd and 71st rounds), the chapter flags the issue of silent withdrawal by the government from the education sector (through reduced investment) which has paved the way for the private players to flourish and capitalise the sector. It is well-known that the probability of attending tuition is more for the privileged children (belonging to the higher income group and forward caste) than the underprivileged. Keeping this in mind, any backward step (here, withdrawal from the education market) taken by the government will further widen the gap between the haves and the have-nots. The study suggests that instead of carving out an escape plan and thereby reinforcing inequality in the society in terms of access to education, the government must take up a pro-active role and look for an alternative form of market in education which is exclusively based on 'ability to pay'.

The final chapter in this section brings to light new evidence in difference in the value of HDI that arises solely due to changes in methodology in calculating Human Development Index (HDI). Using 2010 as the focal point, the study shows that a shift from the old methodology (prior to 2010) to a new methodology (after 2010) has cost India's HDI progress by around one decade. Using deterministic regression model, the study shows that during 1990–2014, education index has contributed more in increasing HDI value than health index and income index. The study also performs an out-sample forecasting and finds that India is expected to enter into High HDI (HHDI) by 2037 and Very High HDI (VHHDI) by 2048.

The last section in this compendium focuses on the theme 'Sectoral and Regional Issues'. The four chapters in this section highlight some of the relevant issues at the sectoral and sub-national level that have received less attention in the existing scholarly literature. The North Eastern Region (NER) of India is considered as the vital cog in the Act East Policy. Therefore, it becomes extremely important to have a comprehensive understanding of the growth dynamics of the region and the first chapter exactly does that. Using secondary data between 1980 and 2010, the study analyses the state-wise and sector-wise performance of the NER and highlights the dominance of tertiary sector over primary and secondary sector in the region. In other words, the study finds that there is a constant rise in the share of tertiary sector and a fall in the share of primary sector during the period. The study further reveals that the tertiary sector is turning out to be the driving force for economic growth in the region in recent decades.

The next chapter deals with the structural transformation of the rural economy in the post-reform period in India. In this chapter, Dhara employs the Employment and Unemployment Survey data of the NSSO for the period 1990–2010 to examine whether growth in rural non-farm employment is 'distress driven' or 'growth driven'. In other words, it analyses the determinants of rural non-farm employment in India by taking into account the push and pull factors operating behind rural occupational transformation. She examines this question separately for male and female workforce and finds clear gender-wise differences in factors influencing the employment transition. While the transition from agricultural to non-agricultural sectors for male workforce is driven by growth-related forces, such transitions are mostly distress-driven for female workers.

The next chapter studies the implications of oil price shocks on employment and wages of workers in the transport sector of India. In this study, Saibal Kar and Sweta Lahiri employ a general equilibrium model to address this issue. Using unit level data from three rounds of NSSO viz. 61st round (2003–04), 66th round (2009–10) and 68th round (2011–12), the study concludes that oil price rise is likely to affect the wages of the workers negatively which is mainly due to potential mobility of such workers from formal to informal sub-sectors within the transport sector. While higher educational qualification helps to raise the real wages, reforms in the labour market may increase wages of informal workers in the event of oil price shocks.

The final chapter in this theme tries to capture the gender element of trade expansion in the plantation sector in India. The study makes use of seven rounds of occupational wage survey of the plantation industry during 1958–2016 to locate the changing composition of the workforce based on gender differences across industries and occupations in the sector with a special focus on post-liberalisation period. The study lends strong support to the endogenous growth model and concludes that the impact of trade liberalisation on gender is highly sector specific and may further widen the gap between males and females, particularly in terms of equality and wages.

The chapters included in this handbook together constitute the largest single collection of evidence on the impact of reforms on the Indian economy and the people. The wide-angled vision, historical sensibility, data analysis and econometric evidence contained in these chapters offer a more nuanced and granular picture of economic liberalisation. In doing so, it also questions some adventurist narratives on the recent economic history of the country. The chapters in this collection ought to be of interest to students, teachers and researchers of Indian economy, particularly due to its comprehensive coverage on the impact of reforms on various aspects of the economy since the start. In our opinion, this collection provides a 'one solution' to many serious and contentious issues that have revolved around reforms in India.

Notes

1 All these schemes were within the ambit of the National Sustainable Agriculture Mission (NSAM) which basically aimed to boost agricultural production, increase farmer's income and provide safety nets to small and marginal farmers, thereby providing relief to the agriculture sector.
2 Similar initiatives were undertaken in other sectors too, which we do not discuss here.

References

Ahluwalia, M.S. (2019), India's Economic Reforms: Achievements and Next Steps, *Asian Economic Policy Review*, 14: 46–62.

Balakrishnan, P. (2000), Agriculture and Economic Reforms: Growth and Welfare, *Economic and Political Weekly*, 35(12): 999–1004.

Himanshu. (2019), Inequality in India: A Review of Levels and Trends, *WIDER Working Paper* 2019/42, UNU-WIDER, Helsinki, Finland.

Jha, R. (2004), Reducing Poverty and Inequality in India: Has Liberalization Helped?, in Cornia, G.A. (Ed.), *Inequality Growth and Poverty in an Era of Liberalization and Globalization*, Oxford University Press, Oxford.

Kannan, K.P. and Raveendran, G. (2009), Growth Sans Employment: A Quarter Century of Jobless Growth in India's Organised Manufacturing, *Economic and Political Weekly*, 44(10): 80–91.

Panagariya, A. (2008), *India: The Emerging Giant*, Oxford University Press, Oxford.

Ray, A.K. (2008), India's Social Development in a Decade of Reforms: 1990–91/1999–2000, *Social Indicators Research*, 87: 409–425.

Srinivasan, T.N. (2000), *Eight Lectures on India's Economic Reforms*, Oxford University Press, Delhi.

Thomas, J.J. (2012), India's Labour Market during the 2000s: Surveying the Changes, *Economic and Political Weekly*, 47(51): 39–51.

PART I

Agrarian reforms and agriculture

1

AGRICULTURE AND RURAL LABOUR MARKETS IN INDIA

Jayan Jose Thomas and B. Satheesha

Introduction

In India, agriculture and allied sectors employ approximately 42.0 per cent of the country's total workforce. According to the Periodic Labour Force Survey (PLFS), National Statistical Office (2019), there were 197.3 million people engaged in agriculture and its allied sectors, out of a total estimated workforce of 471.3 million in 2017–18. However, the combined share of these sectors in the country's gross domestic product (GDP) was only 14.8 per cent in 2017–18. The aim of this chapter is to understand, first, the broad trends in the growth of the agricultural sector in India and, second, the implications of this growth for the country's rural labour markets. Agricultural production depends on a number of factors, importantly area under cultivation, changes in the cropping pattern, and growth of yield. In India, there is increasing demand for land for non-agricultural purposes, mainly due to growing urbanization, expansion of housing, and rise in the numbers of commercial and industrial enterprises. The area under cultivation in India has been registering a decline over time (Bhalla and Singh 2009). There have been important variations in the cropping pattern in the country, over time and across regions. In 2014–15, production of food crops, importantly rice and wheat, occupied approximately 70 per cent of the area under cultivation in the northern region, which includes Uttar Pradesh, Haryana, and Punjab. Similarly, eastern and central-eastern regions also have relatively large shares of cultivable area under food grain production. On the other hand, in the western and southern parts of the country, there has been a marked shift in the cropping pattern towards non-food grain production.

As shown above, 41.9 per cent of the workforce in India is engaged in agriculture and allied activities, and the proportion is higher in the rural areas. However, the size and composition of the agricultural workforce varies considerably across Indian states. Similarly, there are regional variations in the growth of non-agricultural employment in rural areas. Understanding this background, this chapter examines how the changes in the nature and growth of the agricultural sector influence the pattern of growth of rural labour markets across Indian states.

This chapter is divided into five sections. The second section of the chapter analyses the broad trends in the growth of incomes and output in Indian agriculture. The discussion mainly highlights the different phases of growth of Indian agriculture. The third section examines the structure and growth of agricultural production across Indian states. The chapter argues that

 DOI: 10.4324/9780367855741-1

there exist large variations across Indian states with respect to the growth and structure of agricultural production. The fourth section discusses rural labour market outcomes in India during the recent periods. Further, we attempt to associate rural labour market outcomes across Indian states with the changes in the agricultural sector. The fifth section concludes the chapter by summarizing the major findings of the study.

Data sources and methodology

This chapter has used crop-wise data (three-year averages) on the area under cultivation, production, and labour use for major crops. These data have been obtained from the Directorate of Economics and Statistics, Ministry of Agriculture and Farmers Welfare, Government of India. The data on employment and labour markets used in this chapter have been based on the employment and unemployment surveys carried out by the National Sample Survey Office (NSSO). The period of analysis in this chapter is between 1981–82 and 2017–18.

Growth of incomes and output in Indian agriculture: broad trends

Some of the long-standing hurdles to the growth of Indian agriculture have been well discussed in the literature. These include, most importantly, the existence of a high degree of inequalities in rural areas, most importantly in the ownership of land and other assets. Daniel Thorner (1956) argued that the concentration of economic power in the rural economy in the hands of a small number of absentee landholders slowed down productivity growth in the Indian countryside (also see Harris 2013).

The growth of agriculture and food production in India accelerated with the Green Revolution launched during the mid-1960s. The early phase of the Green Revolution, roughly from the mid-1960s to the late 1970s, benefitted only a limited number of regions – western Uttar Pradesh, Punjab, and Haryana. The major gainers during this phase were the relatively rich peasants in the above-referred regions as they could afford to invest in the new technologies. It is argued that the gains were more widely spread during the late phase of the Green Revolution during the 1980s. Rice cultivation in Tamil Nadu, Andhra Pradesh, and West Bengal benefitted from the technological improvements during this phase. More importantly, small cultivators too could participate in and gain from the transformations in the countryside. The increased availability of credit to the agricultural sector, following the nationalization of major commercial banks in 1969, was a factor that aided this process (Rao 1994; Ramachandran and Rawal 2010).

As is well known, India began wide ranging economic reforms in 1991. However, the impact of the reforms on the agricultural sector has not been very positive. The growth of incomes from agriculture and allied activities decelerated during the 1990s and through the first half of the 2000s compared to the growth during the previous decade (see Table 1.1). Several reasons have been attributed to the deceleration in agricultural growth after the 1990s. First, there has been a decline in investment, especially public investment, in agriculture, particularly during the 1990s (Ramachandran and Rawal 2010). Roy (2017) showed that although private investment in agriculture in India began rising rapidly from the late 1990s onwards, the growth of public investment in agriculture recovered only by the mid-2000s. The slowdown in public investment had a particularly negative impact on the expansion of irrigated area and agricultural research, which is important for productivity improvements.

Another factor for the slow progress in agricultural growth from the 1990s onwards has been a reversal in some of the policies linked to rural banking, including importantly a reduction in

Table 1.1 Average annual growth of agricultural gross domestic product (GDP) and overall GDP, India, 1981–82 to 2017–18 (in per cent)

Sectors	*1981–82 to 1991–92*	*1991–92 to 2004–05*	*1991–92 to 1999–2000*	*1999–00 to 2004–05*	*2004–05 to 2011–12*	*2011–12 to 2017–18*
Agriculture and allied activities	3.0	2.8	3.5	1.7	3.8	2.7
Overall GDP	5.2	6.1	6.5	5.8	8.5	6.9

Source: *Handbook of Statistics on Indian Economy*, Reserve Bank of India (RBI).
Note: The GDP figures for the years from 1981–82 to 2011–12 are at constant 2004–05 prices. The GDP figures for the years after 2011–12 are based on the revised GDP series with 2011–12 as the base year. Growth rates have been calculated using semilogarithmic regression.

the number of rural bank branches. The share of credit disbursed to agriculture declined during the 1990s relative to the 1980s. Although this share of credit to agriculture increased again during the 2000s, this increase was not so much on account of lending to small cultivators, but more due to an increase in indirect finance to agriculture, which benefitted agribusiness companies and large cultivators (Ramakumar and Chavan 2007). The decline in agricultural prices following the liberalization of agricultural trade, which included the removal of quantitative restrictions on agricultural imports, also dampened the growth of agricultural incomes during the first half of the 2000s.

The revival of agricultural growth in India from the mid-2000s onwards is linked to the faster growth of agricultural investment during the same period (Chand and Parappurathu 2012; Sen 2016). Public expenditures on agriculture and allied activities increased after the mid-2000s. The government also stepped up expenditures on a major public works employment programme – Mahatma Gandhi National Rural Employment Guarantee Act (MGNREGA) – during the late 2000s, which helped to revive rural incomes and wages.

The pattern over time of the growth of the production of food grains and of some other crops has been similar to that of the growth of agricultural incomes (outlined above). The production of food grains in India grew at an annual average rate of 2.8 per cent during the 1980s but this growth declined to 1.1 per cent only during the 1990s and through the first half of the 2000s. In fact, food grain production in the country recorded negative rates of growth during the first half of the 2000s (1999–2000 to 2004–05). However, food grain production and overall agricultural incomes revived impressively in growth after 2004–05 (see Table 1.2).

The growth of the production of oilseeds had slowed down in India during the 1990s relative to the 1980s, but this growth revived impressively from the early 2000s. In the case of the production of cotton, there has been an impressive revival in growth in the country from the early 2000s onwards (see Table 1.2).

Finally, it is striking that there has been a distinct deceleration in the growth of agricultural and overall incomes in India since 2011–12. This is evident from a comparison of the growth rates during the periods 2004–05 to 2011–12 and 2011–12 to 2017–18 (see Table 1.1). Compared to the 2004–05 to 2011–12 period, there was a sharp downward drift during the 2011–12 to 2016–17 period in the growth of the production of food grains, oilseeds, cotton, and sugar cane (see Table 1.2).

Table 1.2 Compound annual rates of growth of production (various crops) in India, 1981–82 to 2016–17 (in per cent)

Crops	*1981–82 to 1991–92*	*1991–92 to 2004–05*	*1991–92 to 1999–2000*	*1999–00 to 2004–05*	*2004–05 to 2011–12*	*2011–12 to 2016–17*
Food grains	2.8	1.1	2.3	-0.7	3.3	0.5
Oilseeds	4.4	2.1	1.4	3.3	2.9	–2.6
Cotton	2.1	4.1	2.2	7.3	11.5	–0.4
Sugar cane	3.1	–0.5	2.1	–4.6	6.2	0.1

Source: Directorate of Economics and Statistics (1982, 1992, 2000, 2012, 2015), Ministry of Agriculture and Farmers Welfare.

Structure and growth of agricultural production: across Indian states

This section examines State-wise variations across India with respect to the structure and growth of the agricultural sectors. It is important to note that such differences affect labour market outcomes, especially in rural areas.

In India, food grain crops account for a dominant share of the gross cropped area, although this share declined from 73.1 per cent in 1981–82 to 62.7 per cent in 2014–15. Within food grains, rice is the crop that is cultivated most extensively, followed by wheat. These crops accounted for 22.2 per cent and 15.9 per cent respectively of the total gross cropped area in the country in 2014–15. Coarse cereals accounted for the highest share of total gross cropped area in the country of 24.0 per cent in 1981–82, but this share declined substantially over the years, to 12.7 per cent in 2014–15. It is clear that there has been a diversification away from the cultivation of coarse cereals. On the other hand, the area under cultivation of oilseeds increased over the years, from 10.7 per cent of the total (cropped area) in 1981–82 to 14.4 per cent in 2004–05. According to Bhalla and Singh (2009), favourable prices and programmes such as the Technology Mission on Oil Seeds launched in 1986 helped to increase the area under cultivation and production of oilseeds. Over the years, there has been a marginal increase in the area under cultivation of non-food crops such as cotton and sugar cane, as well as in the area under horticulture cultivation in India (see Table 1.3).

Three northern states, that is, Uttar Pradesh, Punjab, and Haryana, continue to be leaders in the country with respect to agricultural production, particularly food grain. These three states had a combined share of 32.3 per cent in India's total food grain production in 2014–15, much higher than that of the national level, which was estimated at 20.9 per cent in 2011 (see Table 1.4). Tables 1.5 and 1.6 provide a picture of the relative importance of various crops in cultivation and total agricultural production across Indian states.

Statistics related to the gross cropped area indicate that the intensity of agricultural operations in the three states referred to above is relatively high. The three states had a combined share of 20.5 per cent in India's total gross cropped area (in 2014–15), whereas they comprise only 10.2 per cent of the total geographical area of the country (see Table 1.4).

Nevertheless, it appears that Punjab, Haryana, and Uttar Pradesh have reached some degree of saturation in growth with respect to food grain production since 2011–12. In 2011–12, Uttar Pradesh produced 50.3 million tonnes of food grains, and Punjab another 28.4 million tonnes. The combined share of Uttar Pradesh, Punjab, and Haryana in total food grain production in the

Table 1.3 Shares of various crops to gross cropped area in India (in per cent)

	1981–82	*1991–92*	*1999–2000*	*2004–05*	*2011–12*	*2014–15*
Rice	23.0	23.4	24.0	21.9	22.5	22.2
Wheat	12.5	12.7	14.6	13.8	15.3	15.9
Coarse cereals	24.0	18.3	15.6	15.2	13.5	12.7
Pulses	13.5	12.4	11.2	11.9	12.5	11.9
Food grains	73.1	66.9	65.3	62.8	63.7	62.7
Oilseeds	10.7	14.2	12.9	14.4	13.4	12.9
Cotton	4.6	4.2	4.6	4.6	6.2	6.5
Sugar cane	1.8	2.1	2.2	1.9	2.6	2.6
Plantation	–	–	–	–	2.6	2.9
Horticulture	–	4.6	5.2	6.2	8.0	7.9

Source: Same as Table 1.2.

country was 37.2 per cent in 2011–12. However, by 2014–15, food grain production declined to 39.6 million tonnes in Uttar Pradesh and 26.7 million tonnes in Punjab. With respect to the rate of growth of food grain production, Punjab was distinctly above the Indian average during the period from 1981–82 to 2004–05, but below the Indian average during the period from 2004–05 to 2011–12 (see Figure 1.1).

While Punjab, Uttar Pradesh, and Haryana seem to have already crossed their prime, two other states in the north-central belt of the country have made significant improvements with respect to food grain production from the 2000s onwards. These are Madhya Pradesh and Rajasthan. In Madhya Pradesh, food grain production more than doubled between 2004–05 and 2014–15: from 14.1 million tonnes to 28.7 million tonnes (see Tables 1.6 and 1.7).

In the case of West Bengal, which is another major agricultural producer in the country, the growth of food grain production had been the fastest during the 1980s. However, the growth of food grain production in West Bengal stagnated somewhat after 2004–05. It appears that West Bengal did not gain as much as the rest of the country during the period from 2004–05 to 2011–12, which was a period of general revival in the growth of agricultural production in the country as a whole (see Table 1.6).

In Bihar and Jharkhand, food grain production grew at impressive rates between 2004–05 and 2011–12, but the growth decelerated during the period from 2011–12 to 2014–15. The southern states of Tamil Nadu, Karnataka, and Andhra Pradesh are also major producers of food grains, with a combined share of 15.7 per cent in India's food grain production in 2014–15. These states experienced fast growth between 2004–05 and 2011–12, and deceleration after that (see Table 1.6).

In the case of Punjab, Uttar Pradesh, Uttarakhand, and Himachal Pradesh, cultivation of food grains accounts for 75 per cent or more of the gross cropped area of these states. This has also been the case with Bihar, Jharkhand, and Chhattisgarh. However, there has been considerable diversification away from food grain cultivation in the agricultural sectors of a number of other states, including Maharashtra, Gujarat, Andhra Pradesh, Karnataka, Tamil Nadu, West Bengal, Rajasthan, and Madhya Pradesh (see Tables 1.5 and 1.7).

In Madhya Pradesh and Rajasthan and to a lesser extent in Gujarat and Maharashtra, there has been rapid growth over the years in the production of oilseeds. Much of the impressive increase in the production of oilseeds occurred in India after the 2000s (from 20.7 million tonnes in 1999–2000 to 29.8 million tonnes in 2011–12). Similarly, the production of cotton increased

Table 1.4 Distribution of net sown area, gross cropped area, and total food production, across Indian states, 2014–15 (in per cent)

	Net sown area	*Gross cropped area*	*Total geographical area*	*Food grain production*	*Population, 2011*
Andhra Pradesh	4.5	3.9	5.0	4.2	4.1
Karnataka	7.2	6.2	5.8	4.8	5.0
Kerala	1.5	1.3	1.2	0.2	2.8
Tamil Nadu	3.4	3.0	4.0	3.8	6.0
Telangana	3.1	2.7	3.4	2.8	2.9
South, total	19.6	17.1	19.3	15.8	20.7
Maharashtra	12.4	11.8	9.4	4.5	9.3
Gujarat	7.4	6.4	6.0	2.8	5.0
West, total	19.8	18.4	15.4	7.4	14.4
Haryana	2.5	3.3	1.3	6.0	2.1
Himachal Pradesh	0.4	0.5	1.7	0.6	0.6
Jammu & Kashmir	0.5	0.6	3.1	0.5	1.0
Punjab	2.9	4.0	1.5	10.6	2.3
Rajasthan	12.5	12.2	10.4	7.8	5.7
Uttar Pradesh	11.8	13.2	7.4	15.7	16.5
Uttarakhand	0.5	0.6	1.6	0.6	0.8
North, total	31.2	34.3	27.1	41.8	29.0
Bihar	3.8	3.9	2.9	5.2	8.6
Jharkhand	1.0	0.8	2.4	1.9	2.7
West Bengal	3.7	4.9	2.7	6.6	7.5
East, total	8.5	9.5	8.0	13.7	18.9
Chhattisgarh	3.3	2.9	4.1	3.0	2.1
Madhya Pradesh	11.0	12.0	9.4	11.4	6.0
Odisha	3.9	4.5	4.7	3.6	3.5
Central-east, total	18.2	19.4	18.2	17.9	11.6
Assam	2.0	2.1	2.4	2.2	2.6
North-east, total	3.3	3.2	8.0	3.3	3.8
India	100	100	100	100	100

Source: Same as Table 1.2, Census of India 2011.

significantly from fewer than 2 million tonnes in 1999–2000 to close to 6 million tonnes by 2011–12 – almost a threefold increase during this ten-year period. Gujarat and Maharashtra have been the major beneficiaries of the growth of cotton cultivation (see Tables 1.8 and 1.9).

Labour market changes

This section tries to understand the labour market implications of the changes described in the previous sections.

Data from the National Sample Survey Office (NSSO) suggest that overall employment in India increased impressively, by 59.4 million, during the five years between 1999–2000 and 2004–05. However, during the next seven years, that is, between 2004–05 and 2011–12, overall employment in India increased by only 14.7 million (see Table 1.10). It will appear easy to conclude from the above that the Indian economy's ability to generate jobs reduced drastically during the second half of the 2000s. The problem with such a conclusion, however, is that it

Table 1.5 Shares of various crops in gross cropped area, in India and selected Indian states, 2014–15 (in per cent)

	Rice	*Wheat*	*Coarse cereals*	*Pulses*	*Food grains*	*Oilseeds*	*Horticulture*	*Other*
Andhra Pradesh	31.1	0	6.8	13.6	51.5	13.9	17.2	17.4
Arunachal Pradesh	42.5	1.3	24.7	3.8	72.4	11.7	35.8	0.5
Assam	61.1	0.6	0.8	3.6	66.1	7.5	15.7	10.6
Bihar	42.5	28.1	9.5	7.5	87.7	1.5	15.3	3.5
Chhattisgarh	66.5	1.7	4.5	15.8	88.4	5.1	11.6	0.6
Gujarat	6.2	8.7	8.1	4.6	27.6	19.9	13	23.6
Haryana	19.7	39.8	7.3	1.3	68	7.8	6.8	11.4
Himachal Pradesh	7.9	36	35	3.4	82.2	1.3	34.6	0.2
Jammu & Kashmir	23.5	27.2	28.5	2.1	81.3	5	34.4	0.1
Jharkhand	–	–	–	–	–	–	–	–
Karnataka	10.8	1.6	27.3	18.9	58.7	11.2	16.3	20.2
Kerala	7.6	0	0	0	7.6	0	51.9	57.9
Madhya Pradesh	9	25.2	7.5	23.1	64.9	29.7	5.5	2.8
Maharashtra	6.6	4.5	23.1	14.5	48.8	18.1	7.2	23.1
Manipur	58.6	0.6	6.8	8.4	74.5	9.6	25.4	1.7
Meghalaya	32.1	0.1	6.1	2.3	40.7	4	36.1	7.5
Mizoram	25.5	0	3.9	2.9	32.4	1.5	96.5	8.4
Nagaland	39	0.6	15.9	7.4	62.9	13	18.2	1.3
Odisha	46.2	0	1.9	9.2	57.3	2.4	15.1	4.1
Punjab	36.8	44.6	1.7	0.6	83.8	0.6	4.1	6.5
Rajasthan	0.7	13.7	24.7	13.9	53	18.4	6	2
Sikkim	8.1	0.3	34.6	4.6	47.6	5.8	46.7	0
Tamil Nadu	29.9	0	14.3	14.7	59	6.9	23.1	20.3
Telangana	26.6	0.1	14.7	7.7	49.2	9.3	12.7	32.2
Tripura	53.2	0	0.9	2.4	56.6	1.8	29.4	3.3
Uttar Pradesh	22.5	37.7	7.7	9	76.8	4.3	6.7	8.2
Uttarakhand	23.9	31.7	20.2	6.1	81.8	2.9	28.8	9.3
West Bengal	55.5	3.5	1.7	2.6	63.2	8	18.5	2.2
Goa	26.6	0	0	5.4	32	1.4	66.8	54.9
India	22.2	15.9	12.7	11.9	62.7	12.9	11.8	11.7

Source: Same as Table 1.2.
Note: (a) Gross cropped area in India/an Indian State = 100 per cent. (b). In a few states, notably Arunachal Pradesh, Bihar, Chhattisgarh, Himachal Pradesh, Jammu & Kashmir, Madhya Pradesh, Manipur, Mizoram, and Uttarakhand, total area under different crops is more than gross cropped area. This could be due to the effect of mixed cropping in these states (c) Other major crops which are cultivated in India but data on which are not reported in this table include cotton, sugar cane, and plantation.

is based on an analysis of the growth of *overall employment,* which is the sum of employment generated in agriculture and the non-agricultural sectors. Arthur Lewis, who won the Nobel Prize for his work in the area of development economics, had famously predicted during the 1950s that employment in agriculture would decline with economic progress (Thomas 2012; Thomas 2015).

Curiously, however, workers employed in agriculture and allied activities in India increased by 17.4 million during the first half of the 2000s. In fact, employment in agriculture accounted for almost a third of the overall generation of employment in the country

Table 1.6 Production of food grains, across Indian states, in various years (in million tonnes)

States	*1981–82*	*1991–92*	*1999–2000*	*2004–05*	*2011–12*	*2014–15*
Andhra Pradesh	11.4	11.7	13.7	13.4	18.4	10.5
Karnataka	7.3	7.9	9.9	10.5	12.1	12.1
Tamil Nadu	7.4	8.2	9.0	6.2	10.2	9.6
Telangana						7.1
South, total	27.5	29.0	33.3	30.7	41.2	39.9
Gujarat	5.1	3.4	4.1	5.3	8.9	7.1
Maharashtra	10.6	8.4	12.7	10.5	12.5	11.3
West, total	15.8	11.9	17.0	16.0	21.5	18.6
Haryana	6.0	9.1	13.1	13.1	18.0	15.2
Punjab	13.3	19.6	25.2	25.7	28.4	26.7
Rajasthan	7.2	8.0	10.7	12.2	19.5	19.6
Uttar Pradesh	24.3	35.5	45.6	37.8	50.3	39.6
North, total	53.1	75.0	97.4	93.6	121.1	105.4
Bihar	8.2	10.6	14.4	7.7	14.0	13.2
Jharkhand	0.0	0.0	0.0	2.3	4.2	4.8
West Bengal	6.6	12.9	14.9	16.1	16.0	16.5
East, total	14.8	23.5	29.3	26.1	34.2	34.5
Chhattisgarh	0.0	0.0	0.0	5.0	6.9	7.5
Madhya Pradesh	12.8	15.5	21.3	14.1	20.4	28.7
Odisha	5.4	8.3	5.6	6.9	6.4	9.0
Central-east, total	18.3	23.8	26.9	26.0	33.7	45.1
Assam	2.4	3.4	4.0	3.6	4.7	5.5
North-east, total	3.5	5.0	5.8	5.7	7.4	8.2
India	133.3	168.4	209.8	198.4	259.3	252.0

Source: Same as Table 1.2.

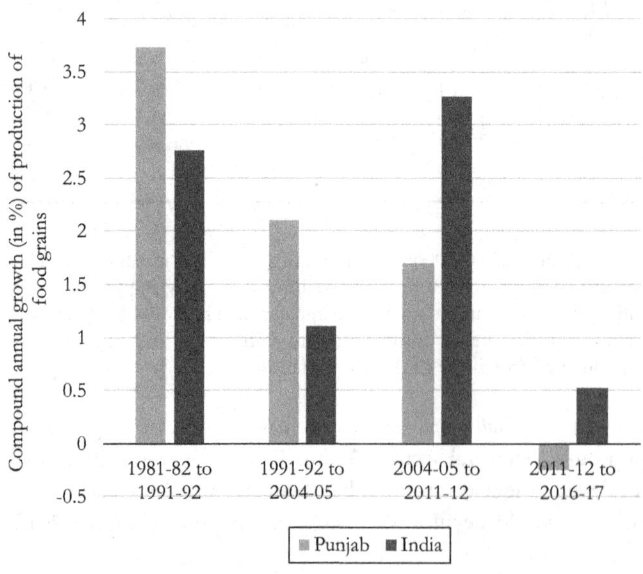

Figure 1.1 Compound annual growth (in per cent) of production of food grains, Punjab and India, 1981–82 to 2016–17. *Source*: Directorate of Economics and Statistics, Ministry of Agriculture and Farmers Welfare, Government of India.

Table 1.7 Production of selected crops, in various Indian states, 2014–15 (in million tonnes)

	Rice	*Wheat*	*Coarse cereals*	*Pulses*	*Food grains*	*Oilseeds*	*Cotton (lint)*	*Sugar cane*
Andhra Pradesh	7.2	0.0	2.3	1.0	10.5	0.6	0.5	10.0
Karnataka	3.5	0.3	6.9	1.4	12.1	1.0	0.4	43.8
Kerala	0.6	0.0	0.0	0.0	0.6	0.0	0.0	0.2
Tamil Nadu	5.7	0.0	3.1	0.8	9.6	1.0	0.1	28.1
Telangana	4.4	0.0	2.4	0.3	7.1	0.6	0.6	3.3
South, total	21.5	0.3	14.8	3.4	39.9	3.2	1.6	85.4
Gujarat	1.8	3.1	1.6	0.6	7.1	4.9	1.8	14.3
Maharashtra	2.9	1.3	5.0	2.1	11.3	2.9	1.2	84.7
West, total	4.9	4.4	6.7	2.6	18.6	7.7	3.0	99.1
Haryana	4.0	10.4	0.8	0.1	15.2	0.7	0.4	7.2
Himachal Pradesh	0.1	0.6	0.6	0.0	1.4	0.0	0.0	0.0
Jammu & Kashmir	0.5	0.3	0.4	0.0	1.2	0.0	0.0	0.0
Punjab	11.1	15.1	0.5	0.0	26.7	0.1	0.3	7.0
Rajasthan	0.4	9.8	7.5	2.0	19.6	5.3	0.3	0.4
Uttar Pradesh	12.2	22.4	3.6	1.4	39.6	0.8	0.0	133.1
Uttarakhand	0.6	0.7	0.3	0.1	1.6	0.0	0.0	6.2
North, total	28.9	59.3	13.7	3.6	105.4	7.0	0.9	153.9
Bihar	6.4	4.0	2.4	0.5	13.2	0.1	0.0	14.0
Jharkhand	3.4	0.3	0.5	0.6	4.8	0.2	0.0	0.5
West Bengal	14.7	0.9	0.7	0.2	16.5	0.9	0.0	2.1
East, total	24.4	5.3	3.5	1.3	34.5	1.2	0.0	16.6
Chhattisgarh	6.3	0.1	0.3	0.7	7.5	0.2	0.0	0.1
Madhya Pradesh	3.6	17.1	3.1	4.8	28.7	7.7	0.3	4.6
Odisha	8.3	0.0	0.2	0.4	9.0	0.1	0.1	0.7
Central-east, total	18.2	17.2	3.6	6.0	45.1	8.0	0.4	5.3
Assam	5.2	0.0	0.1	0.1	5.5	0.2	0.0	1.1
North-east, total	7.4	0.0	0.5	0.2	8.2	0.4	0.0	1.7
India	105.5	86.5	42.9	17.2	252.0	27.5	5.9	362.3

Source: Same as Table 1.2.

(of 59.4 million) during that period. On the other hand, between 2004–05 and 2011–12, employment in agriculture and allied activities in India fell by 33.3 million, while employment in the non-agricultural sectors increased by 48.0 million. As a result, overall employment increased only modestly, by 14.7 million, during the seven years after 2004–05 (see Table 1.10, also see Thomas 2015).

But why did agricultural employment increase during the first half of the 2000s and fall subsequently? It is pertinent to note here that these changes in employment occurred largely in the case of females. Therefore, one possibility is that these changes simply reflect the ways in which the NSSO investigators defined self-employment of females in agriculture over the various survey rounds (Thomas 2015).

At the same time, some scholars argue that the increase in employment in agriculture in 2004–05 was indeed real. It was a case of female members turning to self-employment as a

Table 1.8 Production of oilseeds, across Indian states, in various years (in million tonnes)

	1981–82	*1991–92*	*1999–2000*	*2004–05*	*2011–12*	*2014–15*
Andhra Pradesh	1.5	2.5	1.4	2.2	1.3	0.6
Tamil Nadu	1.3	1.6	1.5	1.1	1.1	1.0
Telangana	0.0	0.0	0.0	0.0	0.0	0.6
Gujarat	2.5	1.6	1.7	3.0	5.0	4.9
Maharashtra	1.2	1.1	2.7	2.7	4.5	2.9
Haryana	0.2	0.8	0.6	0.8	0.8	0.7
Rajasthan	0.7	2.7	3.4	5.5	5.7	5.3
Uttar Pradesh	1.7	1.4	1.3	1.0	0.9	0.8
West Bengal	0.2	0.5	0.4	0.7	0.7	0.9
Madhya Pradesh	0.8	3.0	5.8	4.8	7.7	7.7
India	12.1	18.6	20.7	24.4	29.8	27.5

Source: Same as Table 1.2.

Table 1.9 Production of cotton, across Indian states, in various years (in million tonnes)

	1981–82	*1991–92*	*1999–2000*	*2004–05*	*2011–12*	*2014–15*
Andhra Pradesh	0.1	0.2	0.3	0.4	0.8	0.5
Karnataka	0.1	0.1	0.1	0.1	0.2	0.4
Telangana	0.0	0.0	0.0	0.0	0.0	0.6
Gujarat	0.4	0.2	0.4	0.8	2.0	1.8
Maharashtra	0.2	0.2	0.5	0.5	1.2	1.2
Haryana	0.1	0.2	0.2	0.4	0.5	0.4
Punjab	0.2	0.4	0.2	0.4	0.4	0.3
Rajasthan	0.1	0.1	0.2	0.1	0.2	0.3
Madhya Pradesh	0.1	0.0	0.1	0.1	0.3	0.3
India	1.3	1.7	2.0	2.8	6.0	5.9

Source: Same as Table 1.2.

last-ditch effort to support their families given the general distress in rural areas and the falling household incomes at that time (Abraham 2009; Thomas 2015).

By the same token, the argument goes, the withdrawal of female workers from agriculture as seen in the NSSO's 2011–12 survey was partly a reflection of the improvement in conditions in rural India by that time. In fact, for rural India, the second half of the 2000s was characterized by a modest improvement in agricultural growth and the creation of employment by public works programmes, mainly MGNREGA (Mahatma Gandhi National Rural Employment Guarantee Act). There was a clear upturn in rural wages in India during the second half of the 2000s as compared to the first half (Thomas 2012; Thomas 2015).

To summarize, the slowdown in the growth of overall employment in India during the second half of the 2000s is on account of a massive withdrawal of workers from the agricultural sector. The latter is, in turn, an outcome driven largely by some positive changes in rural India, including a significant expansion of enrolment in educational institutions and the opening up of new opportunities, mainly in construction.

At the same time, the slow growth of job opportunities in the manufacturing and services sectors is a continuing concern for the Indian economy. Of the net increase of 48 million new non-agricultural jobs in India between 2004–05 and 2011–12, 24 million or half of the total increase was on account of jobs in the construction sector, which is characterized by low wages and poor working conditions (See Tables 1.10 and 1.11; also see Thomas 2015).

Rural labour market outcomes across Indian states

There are large variations across Indian states with respect to the size and composition of the agricultural workforce. Among Indian states, the size of the workforce in agriculture is the largest in Uttar Pradesh (35.4 million in 2011–12). The other states with relatively large agricultural workforce include Maharashtra (24.1 million), Andhra Pradesh (21.0 million), Bihar (17.6 million), Madhya Pradesh (16.3 million), and Rajasthan (13.8 million). In each of these states, workers engaged in agriculture and allied activities as a share of the total workforce is higher than the Indian average. The relative size of the agricultural workforce is higher than the Indian average also in Himachal Pradesh, Odisha, Chhattisgarh, Assam, and Meghalaya. On the other hand, there has been substantial diversification of the workforce away from agriculture in Kerala, Tamil Nadu, Tripura, and Goa (see Table 1.12).

Table 1.10 Estimates of the number of agricultural and non-agricultural workers in India, 1983 to 2011–12 (in millions)

Time-periods	*Agricultural workers*	*Non-agricultural workers*	*All workers*
Net increase in number of workers, 1983 to 1993–94	32.4	38.7	71.1
Net increase in number of workers, 1993–94 to 2004–05	18.2	65.2	83.4
Net increase in number of workers, 1999–2000 to 2004–05	17.4	41.9	59.4
Net increase in number of workers, 2004–05 to 2011–12	−33.3	48.0	14.7
Number of workers in 2011–12	224.4	248.1	472.5

Source: Thomas (2015).
Notes: Estimates based on NSSO and Census of India. Agricultural workers also include workers engaged in activities allied to agriculture such as livestock, fishing, and forestry and logging.

Table 1.11 Estimates of the number of workers in agriculture and allied activities and construction, 2004–05 to 2011–12 (in millions)

	Agriculture and allied activities	*Construction*
2004–05	257.7	26
2011–12	224.4	49.9
Net increase, 2004–05 to 2011–12	−33.3	23.9

Notes and *source*: Same as Table 1.10.

Table 1.12 Workers in agriculture and allied activities, across Indian states, 2011

	Census, 2011		*NSSO, 2011–12*		*NSSO, 2011–12*	
	As per cent of all workers		*As per cent of all workers*	*As per cent of all rural workers*	*Estimates of workers, in 100,000 numbers*	
	Cultivators	*Agricultural workers*	*Workers in agriculture and allied activities*	*Workers in agriculture and allied activities*	*Workers in agriculture and allied activities*	*All Workers*
India	24.6	30.0	47.5	64.1	2244.6	4725
Andhra Pradesh	16.5	43.1	52.5	69.4	210.2	400.6
Tamil Nadu	12.8	29.2	33.5	51.2	108.1	322.5
Karnataka	23.7	25.8	48.5	70.2	126.3	260.6
Kerala	6.0	11.2	20.4	31.3	25.9	127.0
South, total	16.0	31.3	42.4	61.4	470.5	1110.7
Maharashtra	25.5	27.3	49.1	77.3	241.0	490.4
Gujarat	21.8	27.4	46.9	74.7	119.9	255.9
Goa	0.0	0.0	3.8	4.6	0.2	5.2
West, total	24.1	27.2	48.1	76.1	361.1	751.5
Uttar Pradesh	29	30.2	52.0	63.5	353.7	680.8
Rajasthan	45.5	16.4	49.9	60.8	138.4	277.6
Punjab	19.2	16.2	35.8	52.2	39.4	110.1
Haryana	28.1	16.9	40.9	58.2	35.8	87.5
Jammu & Kashmir	27.9	11.6	40.3	50.5	20.1	49.9
Uttarakhand	41.0	10.3	46.6	61.5	17.1	36.7
Himachal Pradesh	58.3	5.6	58.3	62.8	21.1	36.2
North, total	31.7	22.1	48.9	61.2	625.6	1278.8
Bihar	20.7	52.7	61.6	67.6	175.5	284.8
West Bengal	14.7	29.3	36.8	53.3	133.5	362.5
Jharkhand	29.0	33.6	49.4	60.6	57.7	116.7
East, total	19.5	40.0	48.0	60.6	366.7	764
Madhya Pradesh	31.0	38.6	57.8	72.2	163.3	282.7
Odisha	23.4	38.3	54.9	62.2	96.0	175.0

Chhattisgarh	32.8	41.8	71.8	85.2	85.7	119.3
Central-east, total	29.4	39.2	59.8	71.7	345.0	577.0
Assam	34.2	15	54.3	62.2	57.2	105.4
North-east, total	35.9	14.9	50.4	58.8	71.7	142.3

Source: Census of India 2011 and NSSO (2013).

The share of the rural workforce engaged in agriculture (in 2011–12) was relatively high in the central and western states, including Chhattisgarh (85.2 per cent), Madhya Pradesh (72.2 per cent), Maharashtra (77.3 per cent), and Gujarat (74.6 per cent). The other states which have a relatively large share of the rural workforce engaged in agriculture include Bihar (67.7 per cent), Karnataka (70.2 per cent), and Andhra Pradesh (69.4 per cent). On the other hand, this share was relatively low in Kerala (31.4 per cent), Tamil Nadu (33.5 per cent), Punjab (52.4), West Bengal (53.2 per cent), and Haryana (57.9 per cent) (see Table 1.12). It needs to be noted that rural wages are relatively high in states in which there has been a diversification of the rural workforce away from agriculture and low in states in which this diversification has been slow. Therefore, rural wages are relatively high in Kerala, Tamil Nadu, Punjab, and Haryana, whereas rural wages are relatively low in Chhattisgarh, Madhya Pradesh, Maharashtra, and Gujarat (Thomas and Satheesha 2017).

Similarly, there exist substantial variations with respect to the composition of the agricultural workforce among the Indian states. The share of agricultural labourers in the total agricultural workforce is relatively high in some of the southern and eastern states, including Andhra Pradesh, Tamil Nadu, Bihar, and West Bengal. On the other hand, the share (in the total workforce) of cultivators is relatively high in Maharashtra, Rajasthan, Uttarakhand, Himachal Pradesh, Assam, Meghalaya, and Manipur (see Table 1.12).

The Ministry of Agriculture and Farmers Welfare provides information on the type of labour used in agriculture, that is, family labour, attached labour and casual labour (see Table 1.13).

Table 1.13 Family labour and casual labour as shares of total human labour hours in agriculture, across Indian states, 2014–15 (in per cent)

	Family labour hours as per cent of total hours in agriculture	*Casual labour hours as per cent of total hours in agriculture*
Andhra Pradesh	34.6	62.9
Assam	82.6	16.9
Bihar	51.1	48.4
Chhattisgarh	73.9	26.1
Gujarat	47.3	52.5
Haryana	59.9	38.4
Himachal Pradesh	93.7	5.6
Jharkhand	52.7	47.3
Karnataka	35.7	64.2
Kerala	11.2	88.8
Madhya Pradesh	66.1	32.2
Maharashtra	45.3	52.6
Odisha	69.4	28.9
Punjab	40.6	49.7
Rajasthan	75.5	24
Tamil Nadu	34.8	64.1
Uttar Pradesh	61.7	38.2
Uttarakhand	88.3	11.5
West Bengal	42.5	57.5
India	53.5	46.5

Source: Directorate of Economics and Statistics (2015), Ministry of Agriculture and Farmers Welfare.

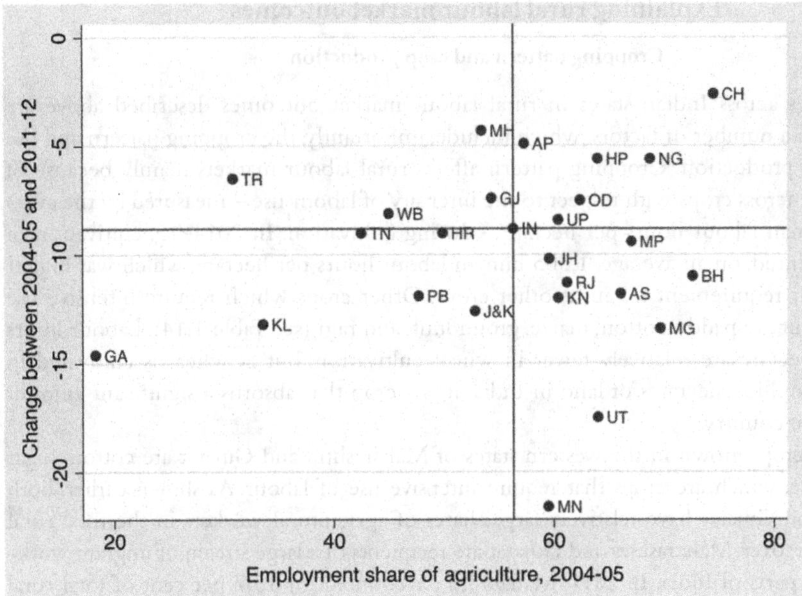

Figure 1.2 Shares (in per cent) of employment in agriculture in 2004–05 and change in shares (in percentage points) of employment in agriculture between 2004–05 and 2011–12, across Indian states (rural+urban). *Source:* Authors' computation based on NSSO(2006) and NSSO (2013).

According to this data, states which have recorded a relatively large share of casual labour hours in total agricultural labour hours include Andhra Pradesh, Bihar, Tamil Nadu, Gujarat, Maharashtra, and West Bengal. These are also the states in which agricultural workers account for relatively large proportions of the total workforce engaged in agriculture (which include agricultural workers as well as cultivators). On the other hand, the proportion of family labour hours in total labour hours in agriculture is relatively high in the states of Himachal Pradesh, Uttarakhand, Assam, and Rajasthan. These are also the states, which have recorded relatively high proportions of cultivators in the agricultural workforce (see Table 1.12 and 1.13).

The period from 2004–05 to 2011–12 is marked by a decline in the size of the workforce engaged in agriculture and related activities, in absolute numbers, in most Indian states. There were only two states in which agricultural employment recorded an increase during this period: Chhattisgarh and Tripura. Figure 1.2 is a scatter plot of Indian states with shares of the workforce engaged in agriculture and allied activities in 2004–05 on the X-axis and the change (in percentage points) between 2004–05 and 2011–12 in the shares of the agricultural workforce on the Y-axis. Bihar, Rajasthan, Uttar Pradesh, Madhya Pradesh, Jharkhand, and Karnataka are states which have relatively large shares of their workforce engaged in agriculture. At the same time, each of these states also experienced a sharp decline in the share of the agricultural workforce between 2004–05 and 2011–12. On the other hand, states which experienced a relatively slow decline in the share of the agricultural workforce even while beginning with a relatively large agricultural workforce in 2004–05 include Chhattisgarh, Himachal Pradesh, Andhra Pradesh, and Maharashtra (Figure 1.2).

Explaining rural labour market outcomes

Cropping pattern and crop production

The differences across Indian states in rural labour market outcomes described above are associated with a number of factors, which include, importantly, the cropping pattern and the nature of crop production. Cropping pattern affects rural labour markets mainly because of the differences across crops with respect to the intensity of labour use – measured by the average use of human labour hours per hectare – during cultivation. In 2014–15, cultivation of sugar cane required, on an average, 1,505 human labour hours per hectare, which was higher than the labour requirement for most other crops. Other crops which require intensive use of human labour are paddy, cotton, maize, groundnut, and ragi (see Table 1.14). Labour hours required per hectare are relatively fewer in wheat cultivation, but as wheat is cultivated in more than 30 million hectares of land in India, it is a crop that absorbs a significant amount of labour in the country.

The major crops grown in the western states of Maharashtra and Gujarat are cotton, sugar cane, and maize, which are crops that require intensive use of labour. As shown earlier, both Maharashtra and Gujarat have relatively large shares of agricultural workers in the total rural workforce. Moreover, Maharashtra and Gujarat are recipients of a large stream of migrant workers from other parts of India. In 2011, Maharashtra accounted for 15.7 per cent of total rural migrants in the country (Census of India 2011).

In 2011–12, approximately 70 per cent of all rural workers in Andhra Pradesh and Karnataka were dependent on agriculture and allied activities for their livelihood (as discussed earlier, see Table 1.12). The high reliance on agriculture for rural employment is linked to the cropping

Table 1.14 Average human labour (man hours/hectare) used in different crops, across Indian states, 2014–15

	Paddy	*Wheat*	*Maize*	*Pulses*	*Groundnut*	*Other oilseeds*	*Cotton*	*Sugar cane*
Andhra Pradesh	614	–	537	276	537	245	873	1,616
Bihar	633	389	529	324	–	–	–	–
Chhattisgarh	502	–	–	361	–	–	–	–
Gujarat	845	366	823	572	677	466	1,015	–
Haryana	561	268	–	245	–	213	531	–
Jharkhand	649	–	662	235	–	–	–	–
Karnataka	720	–	509	326	569	233	796	1,192
Kerala	473	–	–	–	–	–	–	–
Madhya Pradesh	518	285	395	322	–	283	810	–
Maharashtra	1,333	427	844	487	735	394	930	1,800
Odisha	1,046	–	–	344	–	–	978	–
Punjab	346	124	368	–	–	–	640	–
Rajasthan	–	462	534	221	540	323	803	–
Tamil Nadu	582	–	663	257	792	–	1,016	1,731
Uttar Pradesh	797	393	441	377	–	314	–	1,184
West Bengal	1,055	–	–	–	–	627	–	–
India	710	370	608	334	688	318	839	1,505

Source: Same as Table 1.2.

pattern in these states. The major crops grown in these states include rice, cotton (in Andhra Pradesh), sugar cane, and maize (in Karnataka), all of which require high labour inputs. Further, Andhra Pradesh and Karnataka receive a relatively large stream of migrant workers. These states accounted for 9 per cent and 6.1 per cent respectively of all rural migrant workers in India in 2011 (Census of India 2011).

Studies have recorded that in some regions in western and southern India, there has been an increase in demand for migrant labourers, especially for female migrants, for work in crops such as cotton and sugar cane (Mazumdar et al. 2013). Shiralkar et al. (2019) found that workers from the Marathwada region and from some drought-prone districts in Maharashtra migrate to the sugar cane growing regions in western Maharashtra during periods of sugar cane harvesting.

As already noted, the northern states including Punjab, Haryana, Uttar Pradesh, and Rajasthan are some of the leading producers of food grains in India. Uttar Pradesh is also a major producer of sugar cane. The cultivation of labour-intensive crops is one of the reasons for the relatively large share (64 per cent in 2011–12) of agricultural workers in the total rural workforce of Uttar Pradesh. However, the shares of the workforce engaged in agriculture are relatively low in Haryana and Punjab despite the fact that these states grow labour-intensive crops such as paddy (see Table 1.12). A possible reason could be the relatively high levels of mechanization of agricultural operations in these states (see Table 1.14). Studies also showed that the extensive mechanization of agricultural operations in Punjab and Haryana has resulted in a decline in the demand for labour (Jodhka 2014; Tiwana and Singh 2017).

The central-eastern states of Madhya Pradesh, Odisha, and Chhattisgarh mainly cultivate food grains such as rice, wheat, and pulses. Since the 1990s, there has been a substantial increase in the area allocated for the cultivation of oilseeds, importantly soybeans, in Madhya Pradesh. In 2014–15, 30 per cent of the gross cropped area in Madhya Pradesh was under the cultivation of oilseeds. Madhya Pradesh alone accounts for 28 per cent of India's total production of oilseeds (see Tables 1.5 and 1.6). In 2011–12, the proportions of the rural workforce engaged in agriculture were 85.2 per cent, 72.2 per cent, and 62.2 per cent respectively in Chhattisgarh, Madhya Pradesh, and Odisha (see Table 1.12).

In Bihar, the major crops grown are rice, wheat, and maize, which are all crops requiring high labour inputs. The proportion of the rural workforce engaged in agriculture is relatively large in Bihar. West Bengal is one of the leading rice producers in India. Nevertheless, the share of the rural workforce engaged in agriculture is below the Indian average in this State (see Table 1.12).

Growth of non-farm employment

An important factor that contributed to the shift of the workforce away from agriculture in India during the second half of the 2000s was the relatively fast growth of non-farm employment, particularly in the construction sector. Between 2004–05 and 2011–12, states such as Bihar, Madhya Pradesh, Uttar Pradesh, and Rajasthan recorded fast growth of employment in the construction sector, mostly in rural areas of these states (Thomas 2015).

Given the above-discussed context, we shall refer here to an important methodological issue: an apparent divergence between the Census and NSSO with respect to the diversification of employment outside agriculture. The NSSO surveys show that the size of the workforce engaged in agriculture and related activities declined in most Indian states between 1999–2000 and 2011–12. On the other hand, the Census data indicates that the population engaged in agriculture (cultivators and agricultural labourers combined) increased in absolute numbers in most Indian states between 2001 and 2011. Marginal agricultural labourers (especially males) contributed the most to the growth of the agricultural workforce in India during the 2000s, according to the Census. The Census recorded fast growth of marginal agricultural labourers between 2001 and 2011 in a few states, which included Bihar, Odisha, Madhya Pradesh, and Rajasthan (Thomas and Jayesh 2016).

At the same time, estimates based on the NSSO suggest that, after the mid-2000s, there was a large increase in construction jobs in rural India, especially in the states of Bihar, Madhya Pradesh, Uttar Pradesh, and Rajasthan. According to NSSO, almost half of the incremental non-agricultural employment generated in India between 2004–05 and 2011–12 (23.9 million out of 48 million) was in construction, and an overwhelming proportion of the increase in construction jobs (20.5 million out of the net increase of 23.9 million) occurred in rural areas (See Tables 1.10 and 1.11; also see Thomas 2015; Thomas and Jayesh 2016).

A possible reason for the discrepancies between estimates from the Census and the NSSO is that the Census might have counted some workers who had been identified as construction workers by the NSSO as marginal agricultural labourers. This could have happened particularly in states such as Bihar, Odisha, Madhya Pradesh, and Rajasthan. The discrepancies also highlight a problem associated with India's employment statistics, especially with regard to measuring short-term migration among workers (Thomas and Jayesh 2016).

The recent village survey-based studies found that the growth of non-farm employment accelerated the shift of the workforce away from agriculture in rural areas. Heyer (2013) found that expansion of the knitwear industry in Tiruppur, Tamil Nadu had resulted in a fall in employment in agriculture and contributed to the rise of agricultural wages in that State. In Bihar, occupational diversification away from agriculture has been driven by an increase in migration to non-agricultural occupations outside the village (Sharma and Rodgers 2015). A long-term longitudinal village study carried out in Palanpur (in Moradabad district of Uttar Pradesh) identified the growth of non-farm activities in nearby towns as a key driver of change (Himanshu et al. 2018).

MGNREGA and rural employment

Mahatma Gandhi National Rural Employment Guarantee Act (MGNREGA), launched by the Central government during the mid-2000s, has produced a substantial impact on rural employment and rural wages in India. In 2011–12, 6.7 million casual workers were engaged in public works in the country, of which 2.9 million were employed through the MGNREGA (Thomas 2015). Thomas (2014) showed that casual employment in public works accounted for 69 per cent of the incremental non-agricultural employment for rural females in the country between 2004–05 and 2011–12. Chand and Srivastava (2014) note that the impact of MGNREGA on total labour supply in rural India may have been limited, but the rural employment scheme played a major role in raising real wages in the country's rural areas after the mid-2000s. Studies indicate that the implementation of MGNREGA has only been of limited success in Bihar, Gujarat, Jharkhand, and Uttar Pradesh, whereas the programme has been relatively successful in Odisha, Himachal Pradesh, Rajasthan, Andhra Pradesh and Tamil Nadu (Khera and Nayak 2009; Khera 2011).

Summary and conclusions

One of the major achievements made by independent India has been in the area of food production. Total food grain production in India increased from 133.3 million tonnes in 1981–82 to 198.4 million tonnes in 2004–05, and to 252.0 million tonnes in 2014–15. The growth of agricultural incomes in India has been at relatively fast rates during the 1980s but slowed down sharply during the 1990s and the first half of the 2000s. The growth of agricultural and overall incomes revived impressively in India during the period from 2004–05 to 2011–12, but agricultural growth appears to have slowed down again after 2011–12.

There are significant differences in agricultural growth across Indian states. Uttar Pradesh, Punjab, and Haryana continue to be leaders in the country with respect to food grain production. But the growth of food grain production seems to have reached some degree of saturation in these three states as well as in Tamil Nadu, Andhra Pradesh, and West Bengal, which are the states that gained the most during the 'Green Revolution' years from the 1960s through the 1980s. At the same time, the growth of food grain and other agricultural production revived after the 2000s in the case of some other states. These include Madhya Pradesh, Rajasthan, Chhattisgarh, and Odisha. The growth in the production of oilseeds and cotton in the country was particularly impressive after the mid-2000s.

An important feature of India's labour market has been the marked shift of the labour force away from agriculture from the mid-2000s onwards. There have been both 'push' and 'pull' factors behind such diversification of the workforce. A major 'pull' factor has been the emergence of employment opportunities in rural construction during the period from 2004–05 to 2011–12.

The behaviour of rural labour markets has been influenced by a number of factors, including the cropping pattern and the rate of growth of employment opportunities in the non-agricultural sectors. The share of agricultural workers in the total rural workforce is high in a number of states, notably Maharashtra, Gujarat, Andhra Pradesh, and Karnataka. The high reliance on agriculture for rural employment in these states is linked to their cropping pattern. The major crops grown in these states include rice, cotton, sugar cane, and maize, all of which require high labour inputs.

NSSO data suggests that between 2004–05 and 2011–12, the growth of construction jobs was particularly fast in the rural areas of states such as Bihar, Madhya Pradesh, Uttar Pradesh, and Rajasthan. This has contributed to the shift of the workforce away from agriculture in these states. At the same time, data from the Census of India suggests that there was, in fact, an increase in marginal agricultural workers in these very states between 2001 and 2011. The discrepancies between the two data sources suggest that short-term migration may have played an important role in the diversification of the rural workforce in some of the northern and eastern states. Studies show that MGNREGA has also played a major role in influencing labour market outcomes in rural India, helping to raise real wages in rural areas after the mid-2000s.

References

Abraham, Vinoj. 2009. "Employment Growth in Rural India: Distress Driven?" *Economic and Political Weekly* 44 (16): 97–104.

Bhalla, Gurmail Singha and Gurmail Singh. 2009. "Economic Liberalisation and Indian Agriculture: A Statewise Analysis." *Economic and Political Weekly* 44 (52): 34–44.

Census of India. 2011. Office of the Registrar General and Census Commissioner, Government of India.

Chand, Ramesh and Shinoj Parappurathu. 2012. "Temporal and Spatial Variations in Agricultural Growth and Its Determinants." *Economic and Political Weekly* 47 (26&27): 55–64.

Chand, R. and S. K. Srivastava. 2014. "Changes in the Rural Labour Market and Their Implications for Agriculture." *Economic and Political Weekly* 49 (10): 45–53.

Directorate of Economics and Statistics. 2015. *Cost of Cultivation/Production & Related Data.* New Delhi: Ministry of Agriculture and Farmers Welfare.

Directorate of Economics and Statistics. (1982, 1992, 2000, 2012, 2015). *Area, Production and Yield Statistics.* New Delhi: Ministry of Agriculture and Farmers Welfare.

Harris, John. 2013. "Does 'Landlordism' Still Matter? Reflections on Agrarian Change in India." *Journal of Agrarian Change* 13 (3): 351–364.
Heyer, Judith. 2013. "Integration into a Global Production Network: Impacts on Labour in Tiruppur's Rural Hinterlands." *Oxford Development Studies* 41 (3): 307–321.
Himanshu, Peter Lanjouw and Nicholas Stern. 2018. *How Lives Change: Palanpur, India and Development Economics*. United Kingdom: Oxford University Press.
Jodhka, Surinder S. 2014. "Emerging Ruralities: Revisiting Village Life and Agrarian Change in Haryana." *Economic and Political Weekly* 49 (26–27): 5–17.
Khera, Reetika (eds). 2011. *The Battle for Employment Guarantee*. Delhi: Oxford University Press.
Khera, Reetika and Nandini Nayak. 2009. "Women Workers and Perceptions of the National Rural Employment Guarantee Act." *Economic and Political Weekly* 44 (43): 49–57.
Mazumdar, I., N. Neetha and I. Agnihotri. 2013. "Migration and Gender." *Economic and Political Weekly* 48 (10): 54–64.
National Statistical Office. 2019. *Periodic Labour Force Survey (PLFS)*. Annual Report (July 2017–June 2018) New Delhi: Ministry of Statistics and Programme Implementation.
NSSO. 2006. *Employment and Unemployment Situation in India 2004–05*. Parts I and II [61st Round (July 2004–June 2005), Report No. 515] New Delhi: National Sample Survey Organization, Ministry of Statistics and Programme Implementation.
_______. 2013. *Employment and Unemployment Situation in India 2009–10*. [68th Round (July 2011–June 2012)] New Delhi: National Sample Survey Organization, Ministry of Statistics and Programme Implementation.
Ramachandran, V. K. and V. Rawal. 2010. "The Impact of Liberalization and Globalization on India's Agrarian Economy." *Global Labour Journal* 1 (1): 56–91.
Ramakumar, R. and P. Chavan. 2007. "Revival of Agricultural Credit in the 2000s: An Explanation." *Economic and Political Weekly* 42 (5): 57–63.
Rao, J. Mohan. 1994. "Agricultural Development under State Planning." In *The State, Development Planning and Liberalisation in India*, edited by Terence J. Byres, 220–264. Delhi: Oxford University Press.
Roy, Shantanu De. 2017. "Economic Reforms and Agricultural Growth in India." *Economic and Political Weekly* 52 (9): 67–72.
Sen, Abhijit. 2016. "Some Reflections on Agrarian Prospects." *Economic and Political Weekly* 51 (8): 12–15.
Sharma, Alakh and Gerry Rodgers. 2015. "Structural Change in Bihar's Rural Economy: Findings from a Longitudinal Study." *Economic and Political Weekly* 50 (52): 45–53.
Shiralkar, Kumar, Mukta Kulkarni, Vivek Ghotale and Sominath Gholwe. 2019. "Migrant Labour in Maharashtra's Sugar Industry." *Economic and Political Weekly* 54 (20): 36–43.
Tiwana, Balwinder Singh and Paramjit Singh. 2017. "Changes in Production Structure and Class Composition in Agriculture: An Analysis of Agrarian Question Based on Punjab Experience." In *Changing Contours of Indian Agriculture: Investment, Income and Non-farm Employment* edited by S. Bathla and A. Dubey, 113–132. Singapore: Springer.
Thomas, Jayan Jose. 2012. "India's Labour Market during the 2000s: Surveying the Changes." *Economic and Political Weekly* 47 (51): 39–51.
Thomas, Jayan Jose. 2014. "The Demographic Challenge and Employment Growth in India." *Economic and Political Weekly* 49 (6): 15–17.
Thomas, Jayan Jose. 2015. "India's Labour Market during the 2000s: An Overview." In *Labour, Employment and Economic Growth in India*, edited by K. V. Ramaswamy, 21–56. New Delhi: Cambridge University Press.
Thomas, J. J. and M. P. Jayesh. 2016. "Changes in India's Rural Labour Market in the 2000s: Evidence from the Census of India and the National Sample Survey." *Review of Agrarian Studies* 6 (1): 81–115.
Thomas, J. J. and B. Satheesha (unpublished). 2017. *Wages, Internal Migration and Labour Markets: An Analysis of Indian States*. Background paper for International Labour Organization (ILO), New Delhi.
Thorner, Daniel. 1956. *The Agrarian Prospect in India*. New Delhi: University Press for the Delhi School of Economics.

2

AGRICULTURAL GROWTH AND DISTRESS IN INDIA'S POST-LIBERALIZATION ERA

Ishan Anand

Introduction

Over three decades have passed since India adopted the policies of economic liberalization. India emerged as one of the fastest growing economies in the world in the past decade (IMF 2014) before the slowdown gripped the economy in 2017. However, agricultural growth in the post-reform period has remained significantly lower than the non-agricultural sectors, worsening sectoral inequalities. A NSSO survey revealed that 40 per cent of agricultural households in 2002–03 disliked farming and given a choice, they would take up another profession. The main reasons for this were reported to be low profitability and the risks involved. While there is considerable evidence of persistent distress in the agrarian economy, there have been significant temporal and regional variations in agricultural growth performance. The post-reform period witnessed years when agricultural growth plummeted after a robust performance during the 1980s as well as a phase when the output growth was unprecedented.

Chand and Parappurathu (2012) report statistical breaks in the GDP of the agricultural sector. They show a decline in trend growth of agricultural GDP and a sharp fall in growth rate for the value of output of crop groups like cereals, oilseeds and fibres during 1995–96 to 2004–05. There has been a gradual weakening of green revolution-induced technology in the era of liberalization. Policy changes induced a reduction in the flow of formal credit and slowed down public expenditure on agriculture. The withdrawal of state support and liberalization of agricultural markets resulted in a rise in input costs and fluctuations in output prices, which led to the widespread agrarian crisis in the countryside (Reddy and Mishra 2009). The severity of the crisis is reflected in the fact that more than 3 lakh farmers and agricultural labourers committed suicide during the post-reform period (Basu, Das and Misra 2016).

Agricultural growth picked up after a prolonged slump in 2004 and Chand and Parappurathu (2012) refer to the years 2004–05 to 2010–11 as the 'period of recovery'. The period between 2004–05 and 2013–14 also saw the implementation of the rural employment guarantee scheme, unprecedented hikes in the minimum support price and farm loan waiver. The period of economic liberalization hence presents contrasting phases of Indian agriculture; the first period (1996–97 to 2004–05) was marked by retrogression in agricultural growth and the second (2005–06 to 2013–14) witnessed accelerating growth rates. Years 2014–15 and 2015–16 were affected by El Niño, and two consecutive drought years saw a fall in output growth. Demonetization in

DOI: 10.4324/9780367855741-2

2016 was a jolt to the economy which also had a severe impact on the rural and agrarian sector. Several regions saw massive farmer protests in 2018 over demands such as farm loan waivers and a large protest in 2020–21 over the farm laws aimed at deregulation of agricultural markets.

The phase of low agricultural growth in the 1990s and early 2000s, its causes and consequences for the welfare of cultivators is well-documented in the literature (Reddy and Mishra 2009; Haque 2016). The recovery of agricultural growth and the changes in welfare outcomes in the second period are yet to be fully addressed (Lerche 2013). This chapter contributes to the literature by presenting an analysis of the trends and sources of agricultural growth, and the distributional outcomes of this growth process in the post-liberalization period. The growth performance is divided into two sub-periods – period 1 (1996–97 to 2004–05) and period 2 (2005–06 to 2013–14). The empirical analysis in this chapter is largely based on these two sub-periods. One important limitation of the study is the unavailability of recent data. The latest official data on farm household income is available for 2013 and data on consumer expenditure is available for 2011–12. The change in growth and distributional outcomes in Indian agriculture after 2014 have been discussed briefly. It is argued that notwithstanding the spell of decent growth performance after the mid-2000s, the crisis of profitability, low productivity and indebtedness continues to plague Indian agriculture, and underlines the need for state intervention to protect the interests of the vulnerable peasantry.

Growth performance of the agricultural sector

After low growth in the first sub-period (1996–97 to 2004–05), agricultural GDP registered a trend growth rate of 3.7 per cent per annum during the second sub-period (2005–06 to 2013–14) (Table 2.1). The period 2005–06 to 2013–14 was also good for other sectors and the overall GDP grew at more than 7 per cent per annum. While manufacturing grew at 7 per cent, the highest growth was registered by services like trade, hotel and restaurants, transport and communication and finance, insurance and real estate. GDP per capita growth increased from 3.8 per cent in the first period (1996–97 to 2004–05) to 5.5 per cent in the second (2005–06 to 2013–14). The share of agriculture in the GDP fell from 26.6 per cent in 1993–94 to 15.7 per cent in 2018–19, when its share in employment was 42.5 per cent

Table 2.1 Trend growth rates of GDP and its components at constant (2004–05) prices

Sector	*Period 1* *1996–97 – 2004–05*	*Period 2* *2005–06 – 2013–14*	*Overall* *1996–97 – 2013–14*
Agriculture	1.8	3.7	2.9
Agriculture and allied	1.9	3.7	3.0
Manufacturing	4.9	7.0	7.0
Construction	7.8	6.4	8.4
Trade, hotel and restaurants	7.4	10.1	8.8
Transport and communication	10.7	11.0	11.1
Finance, insurance and real estate	7.2	10.7	9.2
GDP factor cost	5.7	7.2	7.0
Per capita income	3.8	5.5	5.2

Source: calculated from the Handbook of Statistics on the Indian Economy, RBI.

Table 2.2 Agriculture's share in GDP and employment

	1993–94	*1999–2000*	*2004–05*	*2011–12*	*2018–19*
Share in employment (%)	64.6	61.7	58.5	48.9	42.5
Share in GDP (%)	26.6	22.3	17.7	17.0	15.7

Source: World Development Indicators; NSS EUS and PLFS.

(Table 2.2). The workforce that left agriculture has largely taken to jobs that are informal in nature and bereft of social security benefits. This development has been referred to as the stunted structural transformation (Binswanger-Mkhize 2013). The imbalance between agricultural GDP and employment has led to an increase in differences between per capita income of agricultural and non-agricultural sectors.

Table 2.3 Trend growth rates of area, production and yield for major crops

	1996–97 – 2004–05			*2005–06 – 2013–14*		
Crop	*Production*	*Area*	*Yield*	*Production*	*Area*	*Yield*
Bajra	1.7	–0.7	2.3	1.8	–2.8	4.6
Maize	3.7	2.2	1.5	5.9	2.0	3.9
Total coarse cereals	0.5	–0.9	1.4	2.7	–1.9	4.6
Rice	0.0	–0.6	0.6	1.8	–0.1	2.0
Wheat	0.0	–0.3	0.3	4.0	1.6	2.4
Total cereals	0.1	–0.6	0.7	2.8	–0.1	2.9
Tur	–0.6	0.1	–0.7	2.2	1.7	0.5
Gram	–1.9	–1.6	–0.3	6.4	3.6	2.8
Total pulses	–0.8	–0.2	–0.6	4.6	1.2	3.4
Total food grains	0.0	–0.5	0.6	2.9	0.1	2.8
Groundnut	–2.4	–2.6	0.3	0.4	–2.9	3.3
Soyabean	0.9	2.5	–1.6	5.7	4.6	1.2
Rapeseed & mustard	0.9	–2.1	2.9	0.8	–0.7	1.5
Total oilseeds	–0.6	–1.0	0.4	2.5	0.0	2.6
Jute & Mesta	0.2	–1.7	1.9	0.5	–1.1	1.6
Cotton	0.7	–1.6	2.3	8.2	4.6	3.5
Sugar cane	–2.0	–0.4	–1.5	1.7	1.2	0.6
Tobacco	–2.1	–3.8	1.7	5.1	3.4	1.7
Potato	1.1	0.6	0.5	8.9	4.5	4.4
Onion	4.8	2.8	1.9	10.9	7.9	3.0
Non-food*	–1.6	–0.8	–0.8	3.9	2.3	1.9
All crops*	–0.6	–0.6	0.0	3.5	1.2	2.5

Source: Calculated using data from Directorate of Economics and Statistics.
Note: *Calculated from index of area, production and yield provided by the Handbook of Statistics on the Indian Economy, RBI.

Area, yield and production

The trend growth rates of area, yield and production for major crops and crop groups are presented in Table 2.3. In the first sub-period (1996–97 to 2004–05), there was a stagnation in the production of food as well as non-food components of the crop economy. Food and non-food output started to rise from the mid-2000s and reached unprecedented levels in later years. Despite a dip in production during the drought years 2009–10, 2014–15 and 2015–16, the overall trend in the second period of the post-liberalization era is that of increasing production levels. The index numbers of the area for food grains show a stagnating trend in the study period (Figure 2.1). The index of the area of non-food was initially lower than that of food, caught up during the mid-2000s and has been higher than the area of food since then. This suggests a change in cropping pattern.

While almost all crop groups registered a negative or close to zero per cent output growth in the first period (1996–97 to 2004–05), the production growth was 4.8 per cent for onion and 3.7 per cent for maize. Output growth increased for all crops and crop groups in the second period. While the output growth rate for 'all crops' was around 3.5 per cent, the same for cotton, potato and onion were above 8 per cent. The trend growth of yield for food grains was around 0.5 per cent per annum in the first sub-period. For 'all-crops', the yield growth was 0.01 per cent per annum in the first sub-period. In the second period (2005–06 to 2013–14), there was a rise in yield growth rates for almost all crop groups. In this period, the rates of growth of yield for coarse cereals, horticulture crops, cotton and some oilseeds were higher than the yield growth rate of major food crops like wheat and paddy. The area growth for coarse cereals, rice, oilseeds and jute and mesta was negative.

Sources of agricultural growth

Agricultural growth is determined by the interplay of existing agrarian structure, technology and production practices, input use and state policy. In this section, the chapter discusses the changes in select price and non-price factors that have been used extensively in the literature to explain changes in agricultural outcomes.

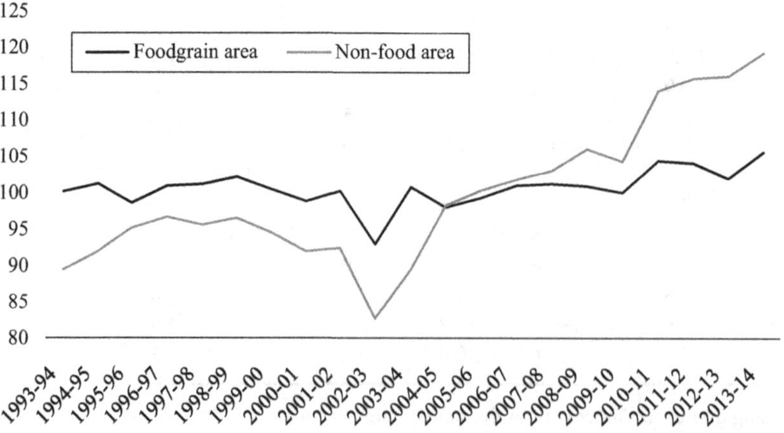

Figure 2.1 Index number of area of food and non-food. *Source*: Handbook of Statistics on the Indian Economy, RBI.

Terms of trade

Some recent studies have highlighted the contribution of favourable terms of trade (TOT) in the revival of agricultural growth (Chand and Parappurathu 2012, World Bank 2014). The Ministry of Agriculture constituted a working group in 2012 to revisit the methodology to calculate the terms of trade. The new methodology has separated the terms of trade for the agricultural sector (farmers and agricultural labourers) and for farmers. Labour power sold has been included in the list of services sold from agriculture to non-agriculture. The committee also changed the base year for calculating the TOT from triennium ending (TE) 1990–91 to TE 2011–12 (Dev and Rao 2015). Table 2.4 shows the index of the price paid (IPP) by the agricultural sector, the index of price received by agriculture (IPR), the ratio of the two and the Index of Terms of Trade (ITOT), which is a weighted index of IPP and IPR. The old series (Table 2.4) shows a rise in ITOT during 1996–97 to 1998–99 and a decline thereafter. The new series (Figure 2.2) shows a favourable price movement for agriculture and for farmers after 2005–06, which stagnated after reaching a peak in 2010–11. This improvement in agriculture's terms of trade after 2005–06 played an important role in the revival of agricultural growth (Sen 2016). There is a divergence between the ITOT for agriculture and non-agriculture, and farmers and non-farmers after 2010–11. This is indicative of a divergence in the performance of farm and non-farm rural economy in recent years.

Public expenditure on agriculture

The inadequacy of public expenditure has been highlighted as an important reason for poor outcomes in agriculture (Haque 2016). The expenditure on the rural economy increased from 1.9 per cent of the GDP in the 1970s to 2.8 per cent in the 1980s (Jha and Acharya 2011). This trend changed after the onset of neoliberal reforms and rural expenditures have shown a declining trend from the early 1990s (Jha and Acharya 2011). Figure 2.3 shows the trends in combined budgetary allocations of the centre and the states for the agricultural sector as a percentage of development expenditure and total expenditure. The share of budgetary allocation for the agricultural sector as a percentage of development expenditure fell from 16 per cent in 1998–99 to 11.8 per cent in 2003–04. This share started increasing after 2003–04 and reached the peak of 15.1 per cent in 2008–09, before declining again. A similar trend can be seen in the

Table 2.4 Index of terms of trade between agriculture and non-agricultural sector, old series

year	*IPP*	*IPR*	*Ratio*	*ITOT*
1996–97	184.9	190.6	0.97	103.1
1997–98	194.9	205.9	0.95	105.6
1998–99	209.8	220.8	0.95	105.2
1999–2000	214.0	219.8	0.97	102.7
2000–01	223.0	225.0	0.99	100.9
2001–02	229.0	235.3	0.97	102.8
2002–03	239.2	247.9	0.96	103.6
2003–04	248.7	251.2	0.99	101.0
2004–05	257.5	258.2	1.00	100.3

Source: Price Policy for Kharif Crops, 2013–14, CACP.
Note: IPP – index of prices paid; IPR – index of prices received; ratio – the ratio of IPR and IPP; ITOT – index of terms of trade.

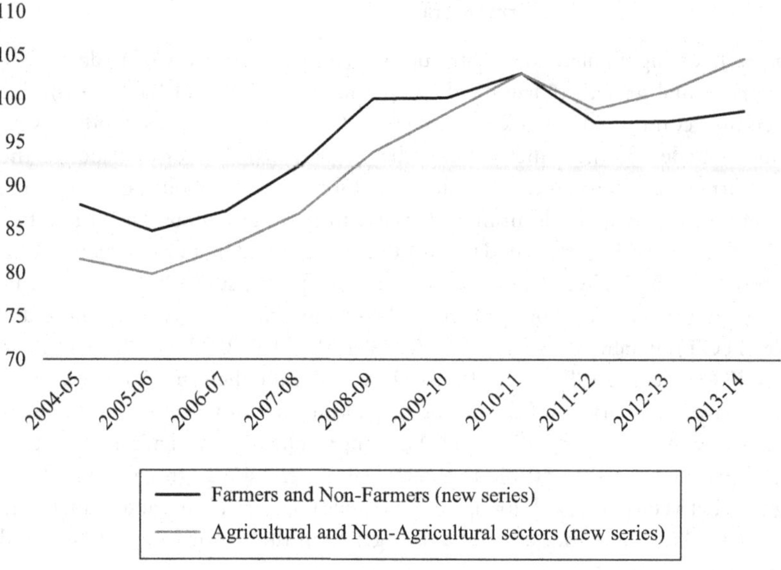

Figure 2.2 Index of terms of trade (new series). *Source*: Directorate of Economics & Statistics, DAC&FW.

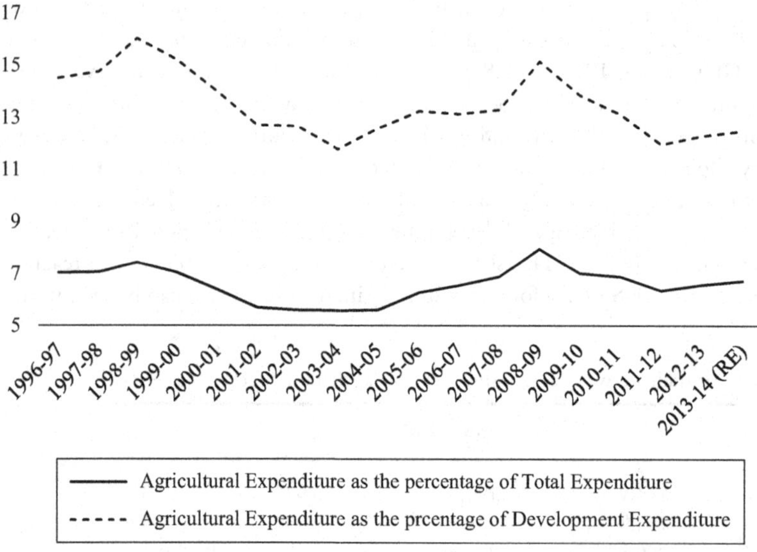

Figure 2.3 Share of agriculture expenditure in the aggregate combined expenditure of the centre and the states (revenue plus capital). *Source*: Indian Public Finance Statistics, various issues.

share of the agricultural sector in the total expenditure. A significant proportion of development expenditure on agriculture falls under revenue expenditure and goes towards subsidies for fertilizers, power and irrigation, etc.

The share of subsidy on fertilizer and power, irrigation and flood control as a proportion of development expenditure is depicted in Figure 2.4. While there was a hike in fertilizer subsidy during 2000–01, the general trend is that of stagnation and decline in the first period (1996–97

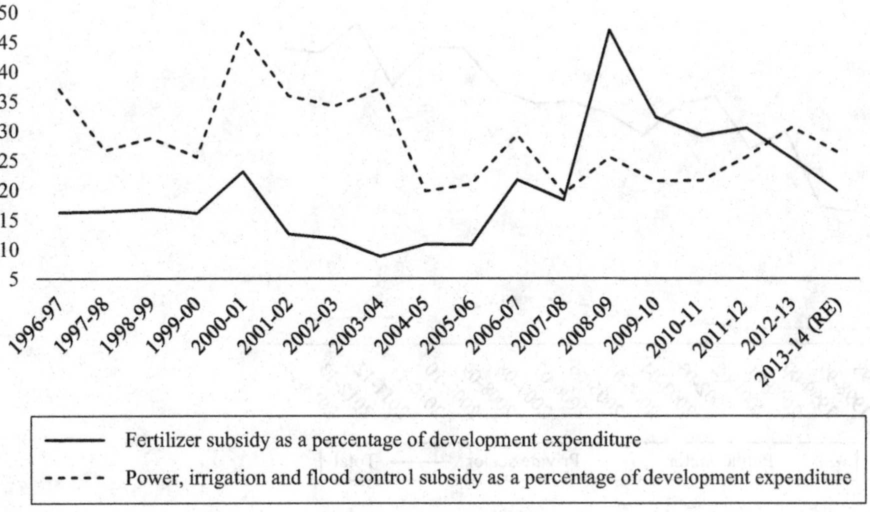

Figure 2.4 Fertilizer and power, irrigation and flood control subsidy as percentage of development expenditure. *Source*: Indian Public Finance Statistics, various issues.

to 2004–05). The share of fertilizer subsidy as a percentage of development expenditure declined from 16 per cent in 1996–97 to its lowest in the study period at 8.7 per cent in 2003–04, rose to 46.9 per cent in 2008–09 and fell again. The subsidy on power, irrigation and flood control displays a declining trend in the overall period but fluctuates across the years. The Department of Fertilizers introduced the nutrient-based subsidy (NBS) scheme in 2010 to keep the rising fertilizer subsidy in check. Under the NBS scheme, a fixed amount of subsidy was to be provided on each grade of Phosphatic & Potassic (P&K) fertilizers depending on its nutrient content. P&K fertilizers were deregulated and the result of this was an immediate rise in the price of these fertilizers. Not only did the deregulation and the NBS scheme not help in checking the fertilizer subsidy, it also ended up worsening the NPK ratio and contaminating soil health (Himanshu 2015).

Capital formation in agriculture

Although capital formation is undertaken by both the private and the public sector, an important distinction exists between these two. Public capital formation usually takes the route of non-excludable large-scale investments in infrastructure and irrigation projects. Public capital formation declined throughout the 1980s (Balakrishnan, Golait and Kumar 2008). Figure 2.5 plots Gross Capital Formation (GCF) in the agricultural sector and the share of public and private sectors as a share of agricultural GDP. The total GCF as a share of agricultural GDP increased from 7 per cent in 1996–97 to 14 per cent in 2001–02. This rise in the total capital formation can be attributed to the rise in private investment as the share of public sector GCF as a percentage of agricultural GDP fell from 2.4 per cent in 1996–97 to 1.8 per cent in 2000–01. Total GCF stagnated during 2000–01 to 2007–08 as a result of a fall in private sector GCF. The new GDP series (2011–12) shows a fall in GCF between 2011–12 and 2013–14. Gross capital formation in agriculture has largely been dominated by private investment in the entire period. Figure 2.6 plots the contribution of the public sector in the total GCF. The share of the public sector in total GCF fell from 27.5

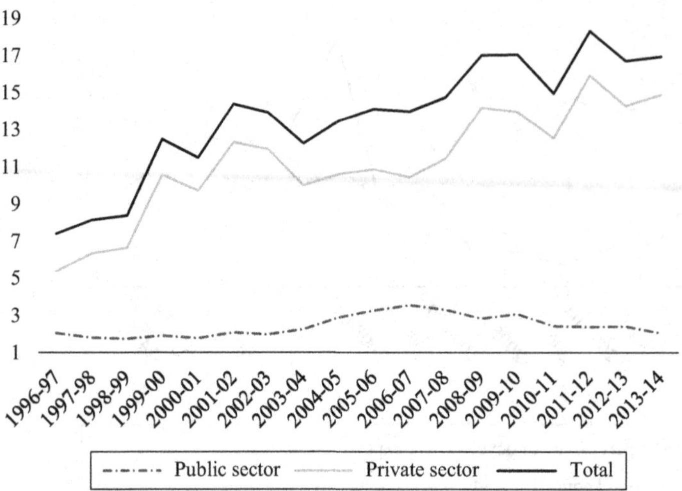

Figure 2.5 Gross capital formation in agriculture as a share of agricultural GDP (%). *Source*: National accounts statistics, CSO.

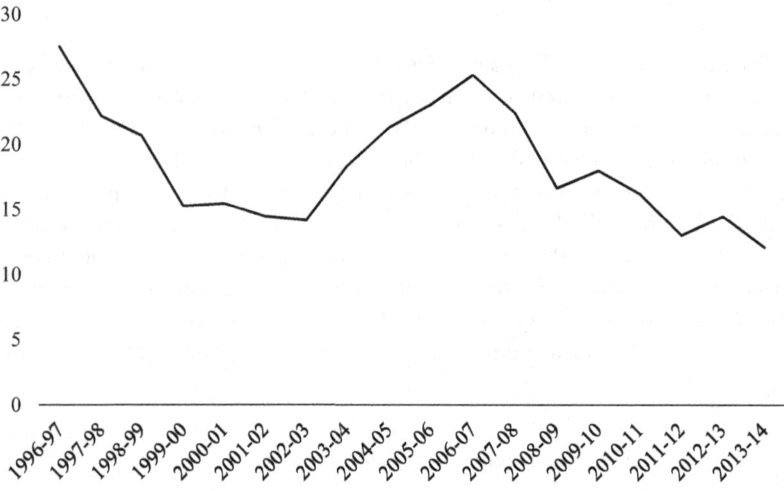

Figure 2.6 Share of public sector GCF in total GCF in agriculture (%). *Source*: National accounts statistics, CSO.

per cent in 1996–97 to 14.2 per cent in 2002–03, started rising thereafter, reached the peak of 25.3 per cent in 2006–07 and declined again.

Irrigation, fertilizer consumption and mechanization

The net sown area depicts a stagnant trend in the study period (Table 2.5). There was a sharp decline in the net sown area during the 2002–03 drought, resulting in a loss of about 10 million hectares during that year. The net irrigated area (NIA) has increased from 55.1 million hectares in 1996–97 to 68.1 million hectares in 2013–14. The average annual growth rate for NIA was 0.97 in the first sub-period (1996–97 to 2004–05), which improved marginally to 1.6 per cent in the second period (2005–06 to 2013–14). The main driver of irrigation growth in recent

Table 2.5 Net sown area, net irrigated area and fertilizer consumption

year	*Net irrigated area (million hectares)*	*Net sown area (million hectares)*	*Net irrigated area as a % of net sown area*	*Fertilizers consumption (NPK), lakh tonnes*
1996–97	55.1	142.9	38.6	143.1
1997–98	55.2	142.0	38.9	161.9
1998–99	57.4	142.8	40.2	168.0
1999–2000	57.5	141.1	40.8	180.7
2000–01	55.2	141.3	39.1	167.0
2001–02	56.9	140.7	40.5	173.6
2002–03	53.9	131.9	40.9	160.9
2003–04	57.1	140.7	40.6	168.0
2004–05	59.2	140.6	42.1	184.0
2005–06	60.8	141.2	43.1	203.4
2006–07	62.7	139.8	44.9	216.5
2007–08	63.2	141.0	44.8	225.7
2008–09	63.6	141.9	44.9	249.1
2009–10	61.9	139.2	44.5	264.9
2010–11	63.7	141.6	45.0	281.2
2011–12	65.7	141.0	46.6	277.9
2012–13	66.1	139.9	47.2	255.4
2013–14	68.1	141.4	48.2	244.8

Source: RBI handbook of statistics on Indian economy.

times has been groundwater irrigation (World Bank 2014). However, reliance on groundwater use through pumps has depleted water levels and this raises a serious question of sustainability (World Bank 2014).

The data provided by Land Use Statistics (LUS) suggest that the area under irrigation for sugar cane (not shown in the graph) is very high. After sugar cane, the highest proportion of area under irrigation is for the crop groups spice and condiments and fruits and vegetables (Figure 2.7). During the study period, the rate of increase of area under irrigation was also higher for these two crop groups. The area under irrigation for food grains stagnated during 1999–00 to 2004–05 but increased after that to reach 52 per cent in 2013–14. The percentage of area irrigated for oilseeds and cotton seems to have stagnated after 2006–07.

India's fertilizer consumption stagnated during 1999–2000 to 2004–05 but rose after that, reached a peak of 281 million tonnes in 2010–11 and declined thereafter (Table 2.5). The data on the sale of tractors suggest a decline during 1999–00 to 2002–03 but a sharp rise after that (Figure 2.8). The number of tractors sold increased from around 173,000 in 2002–03 to approximately 697,000 in 2013–14. This sharp rise in the sale of tractors, along with a rise in the consumption of fertilizers during most of the second sub-period (2004–05 to 2013–14) is indicative of increasing mechanization and intensifying input use in Indian agriculture.

Growth decomposition

Table 2.6 gives the share of major crops and crop groups in the total cropped area and in the total value of the output of agriculture. The area share of rice, total cereals and total pulses declined marginally during 1996–97 to 2013–14, while the share of wheat in the total area increased. The area share of total fibres and cotton decreased during 1996–97 to 2004–05, but

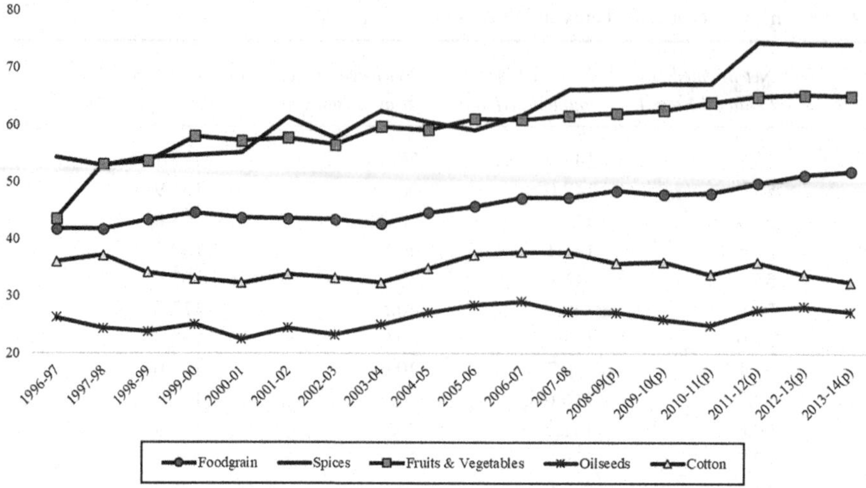

Figure 2.7 Area under irrigation (percentage). *Source*: Land Use Statistics 2013–14

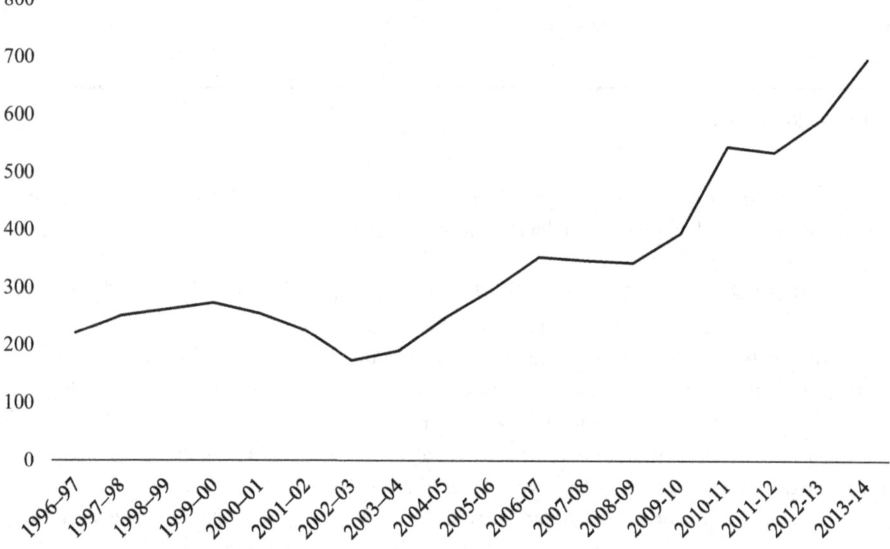

Figure 2.8 Number of tractors sold (in thousands). *Source*: Agricultural Statistics at a Glance 2018 and Sarkar (2013).

increased in the later years. The area share also increased for fruits and vegetables. In terms of the value of output, there has been a steady decline in the share of food grains (cereals and pulses). The share of oilseeds and sugar cane has declined, whereas there has been a marginal rise in the share of cotton and condiments and spices. The most prominent rise has been in the share of fruits and vegetables, which increased by around 5 percentage points during 1996–97 to 2013–14. Cotton, condiment and spices, and fruits and vegetables increased their share in both area and output in the study duration. From the previous section, it is known that the yield growth improved for food as well as non-food crops during the second period. The data also suggests

Table 2.6 Share of crops in total cropped area and agriculture's value of output

Crops	*Share in area (%)*			*Share in VO (%)*		
	1996–97	*2004–05*	*2013–14*	*1996–97*	*2004–05*	*2013–14*
Rice	23.0	22.3	22.1	18.3	15.7	14.7
Wheat	13.7	14.1	15.6	12.1	10.3	9.3
Total cereals	53.7	51.7	50.5	35.5	30.1	27.9
Total pulses	12.3	12.5	11.8	5.7	4.3	4.5
Total oilseed	14.8	15.6	15.0	11.4	10.0	8.0
Sugar cane	2.4	2.3	2.8	6.4	6.1	6.1
Cotton	4.9	4.7	5.9	4.2	3.7	5.5
Total fibre	5.5	5.3	6.4	4.8	4.0	5.8
Condiments and spices	1.5	1.6	1.6	3.5	3.4	3.8
Potato	0.7	0.7	1.0	1.8	2.0	2.6
Onion	0.2	0.3	0.6	0.5	0.8	1.6
Total fruits and veg	26.0	26.8	28.3	20.6	25.0	25.4

Source: Calculated from Land Use Statistics and National Accounts Statistics.
Note: 2013–14 figures are provisional, VO – Value of Output

that after an unfavourable trend during 1998–99 to 2005–06, the terms of trade for agriculture improved. A decomposition method has been used to quantify the contribution of these sources to total agricultural growth.

Aggregate output growth can be decomposed into changes in the area, yield, prices and cropping pattern (Birthal, et al. 2014). The decomposition method is as follows:

If A*i* is the area under crop *i*, Y*i* is the yield of crop *i* (kilogram per hectare), P*i* is the real price of crop *i* (rupees per kilogram), the gross value of output (GVO) from *n* crops can be written as:

$$GVO = \sum_{i=1}^{n} A_i Y_i P_i$$

A*i*, the area under crop *i*, can be expressed as its share in the total cropped area, a*i*=A*i*/∑A*i*. Using this we get:

$$GVO \cong \sum_{i=1}^{n} a_i Y_i P_i \sum_{i=1}^{n} A_i$$

Taking derivate on both sides, the equation can be written as:

$$d(GVO) \cong \left(\sum_{i=1}^{n} a_i Y_i P_i\right) d\left(\sum_{i=1}^{n} A_i\right) + \left(\sum_{i=1}^{n} A_i\right) d\left(\sum_{i=1}^{n} a_i Y_i P_i\right)$$

The second term on the right-hand side can be further expanded to the following equation:

$$d(GVO) \cong \left(\sum_{i=1}^{n} a_i Y_i P_i\right) d\left(\sum_{i=1}^{n} A_i\right) + \left(\sum_{i=1}^{n} A_i\right)\left(\sum_{i=1}^{n} a_i Y_i dP_i\right) + \left(\sum_{i=1}^{n} A_i\right)\left(\sum_{i=1}^{n} a_i dY_i P_i\right) + \left(\sum_{i=1}^{n} A_i\right)\left(\sum_{i=1}^{n} da_i Y_i P_i\right)$$

The left-hand side term represents the change in real GVO over the previous period. The first term on the right-hand side represents the change in GVO due to change in cropped area, the second term represents the changes in GVO due to change in price, the third term shows the impact of the change in yield and the fourth term shows the impact of diversification or changes in cropping pattern. The diversification term will be zero if there are no changes in the cropping pattern or if the value of output per hectare is the same for all crops. A positive contribution of the diversification term represents the change in GVO due to a shift in the cropping pattern towards high-value crops. The share of each component can be calculated by dividing both sides by the change in GVO. The change in GVO is approximately equal to the contribution of area, yield, prices and diversification because of the presence of an interaction term.

Implicit prices are generated by dividing the crop-wise value of output by output quantities. Prices are then deflated using the Wholesale Price Index (WPI). Crops that have been included in the decomposition exercise are: cereals (rice, wheat, bajra, ragi, barley, small millets, jowar, maize), pulses (gram, urd, moong, masoor, tur, horsegram, other pulses), oilseeds (sunflower, safflower, linseed, seasmum, nigerseed, groundnut, castor, soyabean, rapeseed & mustard, coconut) and other crops which include spices and horticulture crops (arecanut, banana, onion, potato, sweet potato, tapioca, sugar cane, cotton, jute, mesta, senhemp, guarseed, pepper, cardamom, chillies, coriander, garlic, ginger and turmeric).

The decomposition result is shown through the monetary contributions of area, yield, price and diversification in Figure 2.9. The slow growth during the first period (1996–97 to 2004–05) was driven by declining prices and a fall in area. The decline in area can be explained by a spell

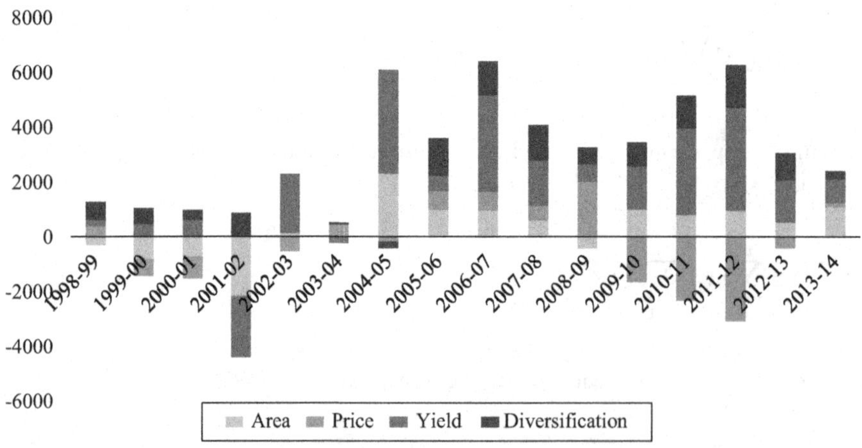

Figure 2.9 Contribution of area, yield, price and diversification components to growth in GVO (Crore rupees). *Source*: Calculated using data from Directorate of Economics and Statistics, Ministry of Agriculture and CSO.

of poor monsoon during that period, and the inability of farmers to cope with it given the slow growth of irrigation and shrinking public investment. The contribution of yield to aggregate growth was modest during 1996–97 to 2000–01. The rise in the contribution of yield in the later period can be attributed to improvements in the availability of agricultural credit, fertilizers and better quality seeds. Price contributed negatively in a number of years during 1999–00 to 2004–05. As the terms of trade turned in favour of agriculture, the contribution of price to aggregate growth became positive and significant. From 2005–06 onwards, all components contributed positively and the performance of yield and prices improved significantly. The decline in output price contributed negatively to growth for most years after 2010–11. The diversification component contributed positively towards changes in GVO for most of the years in the study period, indicating a shift in the cropping pattern towards high-value crops.

Distributional outcomes of the growth process

This section analyses the changes in distributional outcomes and well-being of the peasantry in the era of liberalization. The 1990s was referred to as the 'lost decade' for poverty reduction (Sen and Himanshu 2004). It has been argued that the 1990s saw a sharp decline in the growth of consumption expenditure for poor farmers, even though rich farmers improved their relative position; this phenomenon has been described as 'immiserizing growth' (Vakulabharanam and Motiram 2011). In this section, I present the analysis of changes in distributional outcomes and the level of well-being of the peasantry using large sample survey data and a review of existing studies.

Farmer suicides

The National Crime Records Bureau (NCRB) presents the data on farmer suicide in its annual reports titled Accidental Deaths and Suicides in India (ADSI). This data suggests more than 3 lakh farmers were driven to suicide during 1995–2015 (Table 2.7). It has been argued that these numbers might be underestimates (Sainath 2014). In 2015, Bihar, Goa, Himachal Pradesh, Jammu & Kashmir, Jharkhand, Mizoram, Nagaland, Uttarakhand, West Bengal and all seven Union Territories

Table 2.7 Farmer suicides reported in India, 1995–2015

Year	*No. of suicides*	*Year*	*No. of suicides*
1995	10720	**2006**	17,060
1996	13729	**2007**	16,632
1997	13622	**2008**	16,196
1998	16015	**2009**	17,368
1999	16082	**2010**	15,964
2000	16603	**2011**	14,027
2001	16415	**2012**	13,754
2002	17971	**2013**	11,772
2003	17143	**2014**	12,360
2004	18241	**2015**	12,602
2005	17131	**1995–2015**	321,407

Source: Mishra (2014); ADSI, 2015, NCRB.

reported zero incidences of farmers'/cultivators' suicides. Despite what seems to be a clear case of underreporting, 12,602 suicides were recorded in the official data in 2015. In 2015, indebtedness accounted for 39 per cent of the suicides whereas crop failure was behind 19 per cent of suicides.

Income of agricultural households: evidence from NSS data

The Situation Assessment Survey of Farmers (SASF) was carried out by the NSSO in the 59th round. The survey covered 51,170 households in visit 1 (January to August 2003) and 51,105 of these households were surveyed in visit 2 (September to December 2003). The survey collected information on income from various sources, indebtedness, consumption, access to resources, farming practices and access to modern technology. In the 70th round (2013), the NSSO conducted the Situation Assessment Survey of Agricultural Households (SASAH) and covered a total of 35,200 households in visit 1 (January to July 2013) and 34,907 households in visit 2 (August to December 2013). These two surveys differ in a number of ways. The SASF had kept outside its scope all agricultural activities of households which did not possess or operate any land. The SASAH dispensed with the criterion of possession or operation of agricultural land. A new criterion was adopted by the SASAH and those households which earned a minimum of Rs 3,000 per annum from agricultural activities and had at least one member self-employed in agriculture were considered as eligible for the survey. Unlike the SASF, the SASAH considered only the out of pocket expenditures and imputations were not made for inputs received for free or out of home stock.

Following a previous study (Chandrasekhar and Mehrotra 2016), certain adjustments have been made for the two datasets to be comparable. Using the consumer price index for agricultural labour (CPIAL) as the deflator, it is found that the household income cut-off criterion of Rs 3,000 for the 2013 survey is equivalent to Rs 1,382 in 2003. Only those households from the 2003 survey whose annual income was above Rs 1,382 were considered. The sample was also restricted to households whose main source of income was cultivation, wage labour, livestock or non-farm income, as the income data is collected only for these sources. Households whose main source of income was pensions, remittances, interest and dividends or other sources were not considered. It is believed that these changes allow for a meaningful comparison of the two datasets.

Income of agricultural households

The analysis of household incomes is presented for quantiles of household income and by size-class of land possessed. The households were divided into five quintiles (Q1 being the bottom 20 per cent and Q5 the richest 20 per cent) of total income – an aggregate of net returns from cultivation, wage, livestock income and returns from non-farm activities (Table 2.8). The average monthly crop income for the bottom 40 per cent of agricultural households in 2013 was less than Rs 1,000. The overall monthly returns from crop cultivation increased 1.3 times during the ten year period. The data provide evidence of immiserization of the bottom 20 per cent of the households, as both crop incomes and total income for the first quintile is lower in 2013. The crop income for the second quintile remained almost the same during the two rounds. The increase in average crop income and total income was highest for the topmost quintile. The Q5/Q1 ratio for both crop and total income increased in 2013, indicating a rise in between-group inequality.

Households were categorized into five groups by size of land possessed, from households possessing less than 1 hectare of land to those possessing more than 6 hectares (Table 2.9). The

Table 2.8 Average real monthly income (Rs) by income quintile

	2003		2013		Ratio	
	Crop income	Total income	Crop income	Total income	Crop	Total
Q1	530	695	404	372	0.8	0.5
Q2	969	1,857	998	2,279	1.0	1.2
Q3	1401	3,242	1,730	3,896	1.2	1.2
Q4	2216	5,406	2,782	6,528	1.3	1.2
Q5	7028	15,516	9,931	19,555	1.4	1.3
All	2428	5,342	3,167	6,521	1.3	1.2

Source: Calculated using unit level record, 59th and 70th round, NSSO.
Note: Figures have been rounded to zero decimal places.

Table 2.9 Average real monthly income (Rs.) by land size-group

Land (ha)	2003		2013		Ratio	
	Crop income	Total income	Crop income	Total income	Crop	Total
Marginal (<1)	1,039	4170	1,401	4,744	1.3	1.1
Small (1–2)	2,902	5,339	4,202	7,323	1.4	1.4
Semi-medium (2–4)	5,118	7,599	7,628	10,975	1.5	1.4
Medium (4–6)	8,522	10,914	13,677	17,450	1.6	1.6
Large (>6)	14,508	17,860	21,881	27,437	1.5	1.5
All	2,428	5,342	3,167	6,521	1.3	1.2

Source: Calculated using unit level record, 59th and 70th round, NSSO.

average income for marginal farmers was less than Rs 1,500 per month in 2013. The rise in crop income and total income has been the lowest for marginal farmers. The ratio for crop incomes for large (>6 hectares) and marginal (<1 hectares) farmers was 14 in 2003 and 15.6 in 2013. The same ratio for total income was 4.3 in 2003 and 5.8 in 2013. Between-group disparity has increased between these two rounds and the large landowners have further improved their relative position vis-à-vis the smallholders in the latest round of the survey.

State-wise analysis of agricultural incomes

Table 2.10 shows the average returns from crop cultivation for major states for the two rounds and the ratio of incomes for 2013 and 2003. The overall average real crop income increased 1.3 times during 2003 and 2013. The states where the average real income is lower in 2013 from the previous round include Bihar, West Bengal and Uttarakhand. The variations in state-wise average incomes also show the regional disparity in the returns from crop cultivation. The average income in Punjab was 11 times higher than that in West Bengal in 2013. Table 2.10 also shows the percentage of households that reported negative income or losses from crop cultivation. While the proportion of households reporting a loss from crop cultivation varies across states, Andhra Pradesh and Tamil Nadu recorded losses from crop cultivation for close to 20 per cent

Table 2.10 Returns to crop cultivation, total income and proportion of households reporting negative crop incomes

	2003–13 Ratio		*Households (%)*	
	Crop	*Income*	*2003*	*2013*
Himachal Pradesh	1.3	1.1	6.7	5.4
Punjab	1.2	1.3	0.3	3.8
Uttaranchal	1.0	0.8	1.2	1.0
Haryana	1.8	1.7	3.8	3.1
Rajasthan	1.9	1.4	26.9	8.3
Uttar Pradesh	1.3	1.1	3.4	2.3
Bihar	0.8	0.8	1.5	5.0
Assam	1.1	1.0	0.2	0.4
West Bengal	0.6	0.9	2.3	7.1
Jharkhand	0.9	1.1	0.4	1.2
Odisha	2.0	2.0	5.8	2.8
Chhattisgarh	2.2	1.5	7.0	1.2
Madhya Pradesh	1.3	1.3	4.8	2.0
Gujarat	1.2	1.3	5.2	3.5
Maharashtra	1.5	1.4	6.6	11.1
Andhra Pradesh	1.5	1.4	19.6	17.0
Karnataka	1.8	1.5	12.5	12.4
Kerala	1.5	1.4	2.9	5.5
Tamil Nadu	1.1	1.3	19.3	20.3
All India	1.3	1.2	7.0	6.3

Source: Calculated from the unit level data, NSSO.
Note: Crop – average real crop income; Income – total real household income (aggregate of net returns from crop cultivation, livestock, non-farm and wages); Households – the percentage of households reporting negative crop incomes.

of the households in both rounds. At the all-India level, the proportion of households reporting negative incomes from crop cultivation was 7 per cent in 2003 and 6.3 per cent in 2013.

Evidence on indebtedness for the SAS data

Table 2.11 gives the incidence of indebtedness among agricultural households by size-class of land cultivated from the SASAH 2013. About 52 per cent of farmers reported being in debt in 2013. While 31.6 per cent of farmer households reported taking loans from institutional sources, 33.5 per cent of households reported being in debt from non-institutional sources. Non-institutional debt from moneylenders and traders usually comes with oppressive conditions and high rates of interest. Data disaggregated by size-class of farmers show that a smaller proportion of smallholders (marginal and small farmers) have access to institutional credit in comparison to the medium and large farmers. Incidence of indebtedness is extremely high in the southern states of India (Table 2.12). The high incidence of indebtedness in the southern states is driven by both institutional and non-institutional credit, with the exception of Kerala. High incidence of debt from non-institutional sources points to the limitations of farm loan waivers, which usually take only formal debt into consideration.

Table 2.11 Incidence of indebtedness among agricultural household by size-class

Size-class	*Indebted*	*Institutional*	*Non-institutional*
Marginal (0–1 ha)	47.6	24.3	34.0
Small (1–2 ha)	55.7	41.1	30.4
Semi-medium (2–4 ha)	66.5	53.2	34.6
Medium (4–10 ha)	76.3	65.0	37.0
Large (>10 ha)	78.7	73.3	36.1
Total	51.9	31.6	33.5

Source: computed from SASAH 2013.

Table 2.12 Incidence of indebtedness among agricultural household by state

	Institutional	*Non-institutional*	*Total*
Assam	4.9	13.5	17.5
Himachal Pradesh	21.7	12.6	28.0
Jharkhand	5.3	25.0	29.0
Chhattisgarh	16.5	23.5	37.3
Haryana	32.1	21.2	42.3
Bihar	13.0	34.5	42.6
Gujarat	30.3	16.6	43.0
Uttar Pradesh	24.2	26.4	43.7
Madhya Pradesh	25.2	28.9	45.7
Uttaranchal	30.3	25.6	51.1
West Bengal	25.8	38.6	51.6
Punjab	36.9	28.8	53.2
Orissa	29.5	37.0	57.6
Maharashtra	43.3	26.6	57.6
Rajasthan	32.3	44.7	62.0
Karnataka	59.3	53.3	77.1
Kerala	71.9	24.0	77.4
Tamil Nadu	60.7	51.6	82.6
Telangana	73.9	69.7	89.1
Andhra Pradesh	72.0	72.3	92.9
All India	31.6	33.6	52.0

Source: computed from SASAH 2013.

Recent changes in agricultural growth and distributional outcomes

Agricultural growth declined to 2.9 per cent between 2014–15 and 2018–19. The rate of growth of production for major crops in this period was lower than during 2004–05 to 2013–14 (Himanshu 2019). The post-2013–14 years were marked by falling output prices, stagnating minimum support price growth, worsening terms of trade for agriculture and stagnation in real rural wages. Demonetization also affected the largely informal agrarian economy by severely impacting demand. There was a hike in MSP in 2018 and the introduction of a direct cash transfer scheme PM-KISAN in 2019, but these measures seem inadequate given the scale of the agrarian crisis. Although no official data source is available for accessing the state of a farmer's income or indebtedness after 2013, several indicators suggest a worsening of welfare in recent years. The leaked data from the consumer expenditure survey of 2017–18 showed a fall in food expenditure in rural areas and indicated a rise in rural poverty. The Periodic Labour Force Surveys indicate a massive rise in unemployment rates in recent years. The pandemic and the recession in 2020–21 are bound to inflict severe economic pain, and reports suggest that the earlier gains in poverty reduction over the years may be reversed. In the midst of the pandemic in 2020, three farm laws were introduced in Parliament despite widespread protests. In essence, farm laws are aimed at deregulating agricultural markets and facilitating the entry of private capital into agricultural trade and contract farming. The move seems to be an aggressive pursuit of laissez-faire policies and further withdrawal of the state from providing direct support to the peasantry through the creation of agricultural markets and infrastructure.

Discussion and conclusion

This chapter has reviewed the evidence on the agricultural growth and distributional outcomes in the post-liberalization era. The major findings that emerge from this analysis, and their implications, are discussed in this section. The growth performance of the agricultural sector recovered between 2005–06 and 2013–14, after a dismal performance in 1996–97 and 2004–05. However, the growth momentum could not be maintained and seems to have faltered after 2014. Data suggests that the recovery in agriculture post-2004–05 was aided by favourable terms of trade, increase in public spending and intensified input use as indicated by a rise in the sale of tractors, fertilizer consumption and credit availability. A decomposition of GVO suggests that price and yield contributed to the recovery of agricultural growth between 2005–06 and 2013–14. The changes in the area and share in the value of output also suggest a positive role of diversification to higher value crops in agricultural growth. However, the terms of trade for agriculture started to turn unfavourable from 2010 and the decline in public investment post-2008–09 does not augur well for productivity enhancement.

The evidence from two rounds of NSS surveys suggests that agricultural growth has not only been inequality-inducing, it has also been immiserizing for the bottom 20 per cent of the agricultural households. The income levels of agricultural households, particularly for smallholders, remain abysmally low and growth in farm income has been sluggish. Data on indebtedness shows the reliance of smallholders mainly on oppressive sources of credit. This highlights the need to improve farm loan waiver schemes to include informal loans in order to provide greater relief to the peasantry.

The evidence presented here indicates that notwithstanding the brief period of high agricultural growth between 2005 and 2013, structural issues continue to hinder the growth and well-being of a large majority of agricultural households. Small farm sizes, low income and productivity levels, and dependence of a disproportionately large segment of the population on agriculture highlights the need for active state intervention through price and non-price measures to protect the interests of the peasantry.

References

Balakrishnan, P., Golait, R., & Kumar, P. (2008). *Agricultural Growth in India Since 1991*. Reserve Bank of India, Department of Economic Analysis and Policy, Mumbai.

Basu, D., Das, D., & Misra, K. (2016, May 21). Farmer Suicides in India: Trends across Major States, 1995–2011. *Economic & Political Weekly, 51*(21), 61–65.

Binswanger-Mkhize, H. P. (2013, June 27). The Stunted Structural Transformation of the Indian Economy. *Economic & Political Weekly, 48*(26–27), 5–13.

Birthal, P. S., Joshi, P. K., Negi, D. S., & Agarwal, S. (2014, February). Changing Sources of Growth in Indian Agriculture. *IFPRI Discussion Paper 01325.*

Chand, R., & Parappurathu, S. (2012, June 30). Temporal and Spatial Variations in Agricultural Growth and Its Determinants. *Economic & Political Weekly, 47*(26–27), 55–64.

Chandrasekhar, S., & Mehrotra, N. (2016, April 30). Doubling Farmers' Incomes by 2022: What Would It Take? *Economic & Political Weekly, 51*(18), 10–13.

Dev, S. M., & Rao, N. (2015, April 11). Improved Terms of Trade for Agriculture. *Economic & Political Weekly, 50*(15), 19–22.

Directorate of Economics and Statistics. (2019). *Agricultral Statistics at a Glance 2018.* Ministry of Agriculture & Farmers Welfare, Government of India, Department of Agriculture, Cooperation & Farmers Welfare.

Haque, T. (Ed.). (2016). *Agrarian Distress in India: Causes and Remedies.* New Delhi: Concept Publishing Company Private Limited.

Himanshu. (2015, April 1). India's Flawed Fertilizer Policy. *Live Mint.* Retrieved from http://www.livemint.com/Opinion/XCCJwEzbzwiyWFYfK1wRdO/Indias-flawed-fertilizer-policy.html

Himanshu. (2019, April 12). India's Farm Crisis: Decades Old and with Deep Roots. *Ideas for India.*

International Monetary Fund. (2014). *World Economic Outlook.* Washington, DC.

Jha, P., & Acharya, N. (2011, July-December). Expenditure on the Rural Economy in India's Budgets since the 1950s: An Assessment. *Review of Agrarian Studies, 1*(2), 134–156.

Lerche, J. (2013, July). The Agrarian Question in Neoliberal India: Agrarian Transition Bypassed? *Journal of Agrarian Change, 13*(3), pp. 382–404.

National Crime Records Bureau. (2016). *Accidental Deahs and Suicides in India 2015.* Ministry of home Affairs, New Delhi.

Reddy, D. N., & Mishra, S. (2009). Agriculture in Reforms Regeime. In D. N. Reddy, & S. Mishra, *Agrarian Crisis in India.* New Delhi: Oxford University Press.

Sainath, P. (2014, August 1). *How states fudge the data on declining farmer suicides.* Retrieved from Rediff.com: http://www.rediff.com/news/column/p-sainath-how-states-fudge-the-data-on-farmer-suicides/20140801.htm

Sarkar, A. (2013). Tractor Production and Sales in India, 1989–2009. *Review of Agrarian Studies, 3*(1), 55–72.

Sen, A. (2016, February 20). Some Reflections on Agrarian Prospects. *Economic and Political Weekly, 51*(8), 12–15.

Sen, A., & Himanshu. (2004, September 18). Poverty and Inequality in India-I. *Economic and Political Weekly, 39*(38).

Vakulabharanam, V., & Motiram, S. (2011). Political Economy of Agrarian Distress in India Since the 1990s. In S. Ruparelia, S. Reddy, J. Harriss, & S. Corbridge, *Understanding India's New Political Economy: A Great Transformation?* London and New york: Routledge.

World Bank. (2014, May 21). *Republic of India : Accelerating Agricultural Productivity Growth.* Washington, D.C.

3

REDISTRIBUTIVE LAND REFORM IN THE NEO-LIBERAL PHASE OF THE INDIAN ECONOMY

Pratik Rumba

Introduction

The last few decades have seen the integration of the Indian economy into the world economy. In the absence of egalitarian land redistribution, which constrained the home market and the economy as a whole, the state was forced to maintain deficit financing of a high magnitude that inevitably led to the problem of fiscal deficit and balance of payments in the 1980s. This in turn acted as a proximate factor in determining external pressure for embarking on a process of economic reform since the mid-1980s. Initially, economic reform did not make specific reference to the agricultural sector; however, in terms of its share in the workforce and the intimate relationship with other sectors through input–output and consumption linkages, the macroeconomic and other changes were bound to have a significant impact on the sector (Ghosh and Chandrasekhar 2003).

The critical change that has been brought about with the implementation of new economic policies has caused direct or indirect impacts on the agrarian structure and the associated class relations in India. The agrarian sector in the post-reform period is hit by stagnation and a class of nouveau poor is burgeoning. The significant proportions of farmer households are in debt and millions of farmers have committed suicide (Nagaraj et al. 2014). The available literature on agrarian studies maintains the declining importance of the agricultural sector in the overall project of nation building, i.e., industrialisation (Lerche et al. 2013). The development trajectory of most of the developed economies was such that the agricultural sector played a vital role in generating and siphoning off surpluses for industrialisation. However, in the present path of economic development it is argued that the required capital is freely available in the world economy (Bernstein 1996; 2004; 2006). Hence, the contemporary developing economies may proceed with or without the transformation of the agricultural sector. In other words, the classic 'agrarian questions' have become irrelevant in the era of neo-liberal globalisation.

The present chapter is an attempt to understand the issue of 'redistributive land reform' in the context of neo-liberal globalisation. The denial of the need for a resolution of agrarian question(s) is also a refutation of the programme of land reform. Land reform was at the core of the agrarian reform to dismantle the feudal production relations in the countryside. At a time of 'independence' the majority of the population were attached to agriculture. The share of agriculture in the Gross Domestic Product (GDP) at factor cost was highest, followed

DOI: 10.4324/9780367855741-3

by the service and industrial sectors. India needed industrialisation in which agriculture could have played a pivotal role. However, the agrarian structure of the economy was dominated by the rentier, usury and merchant classes that acted as a barrier to agricultural investment and the development of productive forces. Therefore, the task at hand was to completely dismantle these parasitic classes.

The method in which almost all developed economies tried to weaken or completely abolish feudal or pre-capitalist relations was through a programme of agrarian land reform, despite variations in the form and path (Byres 1991). In addition, the building up of cooperative farming and communes would have substantially led to a higher increase in the production of agricultural goods which in turn would have further generated the market for industrial goods (Ghosh 2009). The agricultural surplus could have been outsourced in augmenting capital for the building industry which would have again generated a market for agricultural goods. The development of the industrial sector would have absorbed the surplus labour arising in agriculture (Lewis 1954), leading to the formation of a home market (Lenin 1964) and facilitating all-round economic and social development.

The term 'land reform' is generally understood to mean a compulsory takeover of land, usually by the state, from the biggest landholder with or without (partial) compensation. Redistributive land reform aims to empower poor peasants and alter the agrarian and class structure of rural society (Jacobs 2010). Moreover, redistributive land reform 'implies a change in power relationships towards greater participation of the rural poor in decision making at all levels and especially in decisions directly affecting their livelihood. It, therefore, has revolutionary implications' (Barraclough 1991). Land reform continues to remain an important agrarian agenda of the left parties in India, whilst the resolution of the agrarian question(s) is seen as 'the axis of the people's democratic revolution' (Ramachandran 2011).

In light of the neo-liberal onslaught of the Indian economy and the current concerns that the 'classic agrarian question' has either been 'resolved' or 'bypassed', this chapter examines the issue of redistributive land reform. Is land reform still relevant in the present path of economic development? It also looks at several interrelated themes such as: How has agriculture fared in the post-reform period? What types of classes have been emerging in the agrarian structure? Can agricultural growth occur without the necessary structural transformation? How far has capitalism progressed in agriculture and what are the hurdles to it in contemporary times? The chapter attempts to critically evaluate the underlying theoretical framework of existing literature to arrive at a nuanced understanding of the issue, i.e., redistributive land reform.

The present study is based on the successive rounds of the National Sample Organisation Survey. The analysis of the performance of the agricultural sector is based on the data from the Directorate of Economics and Statistics, Department of Agriculture and Cooperation. Changes in the occupational structure in the rural area were studied by using the NSS survey of 'Household assets and liabilities' (Report nos. 500 and 570). For the rural labour market, the NSS survey of employment and unemployment for the years 1993–94, 1999–2000, 2004–05, 2009–10 and 2011–12 has been used. The various rounds of NSS survey reports (48th, 59th and 70th) have been used to analyse the changes in the agrarian structure. A unit-level analysis of the NSS data was done whenever it was necessary. The chapter also makes use of some of the major findings of the scholars in the field. The NSS uses criteria based on land owned or operated to classify rural households, which makes class analysis of agrarian structure quite difficult. Nevertheless, scholars have used an average size class of ownership holdings as a proxy to determine class positions of farm households (Mishra 2007). Moreover, the result from the aggregate level data is complemented by the finding from the village studies in recent years.

Agrarian transition and land reform

The transformation of agrarian structure in an economy dominated by pre-capitalist relations of production meant the transformation of a landlord dominated economy to an economy based on capitalist relations of production. The domination of the landlord constrains the actual producer to carry out reinvestment of capital as much of the surplus generated is transferred to the landlord for the 'use of land' (Smith 1976). In the capitalist social formation the generated surplus is reinvested back into agriculture. There may be a landlord but the capitalist rent would constitute a small segment of the total surplus produced. Therefore, the transformation of agrarian structure means transformation in the form of surplus production and abstraction which are conducive to a high rate of investment (Patnaik 1995).

The manner in which landlordism has been abolished in economies where capitalist transformation has been successful is through the process of land reform. The politics of land reform has taken a different form depending on time, space and specific features of the various economies (Byres 1991). In the People's Republic of China the landed property of rentiers was confiscated followed by free and egalitarian distribution to the peasants. The economically backward China transformed itself into a strong, self-reliant China within a very short span of time. In the early 1950s extensive and successful land reforms were carried out in Japan, Taiwan and South Korea. The land reforms in these countries were instituted due to pressure by the USA in order to tackle the growing influence of communists in the continent. In Latin America, land reform was carried out with similar intent; the US government saw land reform with individual family tenure as the 'perfect package', a solution that would increase rural incomes, boost industrialisation processes and calm peasant unrest (Deere and Leon, 1987; Thiesenhusen, 1995; cf. Jacobs, 2010). However, at the level of theoretical abstraction one may observe two paths to capitalist transition: (1) American Path or transition from below; (2) Prussian path or transition from above. In the former case, the landlord estate is distributed among the landless and erstwhile tenants allowing capitalist development 'from below' through the process of peasant differentiation. While in the latter, the landlord economy is slowly transformed into a capitalist economy.

The historical experience of some of the economies suggests that the 'former' guarantees the development of capitalism while the 'latter' may or may not guarantee the same. The classic example has been Japanese land reform. In the post-Meiji restoration (the late 1860s) the landlord turned capitalist farmer experimented with capitalist production by hiring-in wage labourers, but later when they witnessed high profitability in the tenancy market they simply chose to remain landlords. It was only in the post–World War II period that land reform in Japan completely abolished the landlord estate and the economy picked up quickly. Post-war Japanese land reform is considered one of the most successful projects in the history of agrarian reform in the world (Kawagoe 2016).

Agricultural development in the pre- and post-reform periods

Agriculture in the pre-reform period

Agrarian transition remained a central concern of the policy makers in a newly formed independent India. A significant proportion of the population lived in the countryside and the majority of them were attached to agriculture as a source of livelihood. The agrarian structure of the economy was dominated by rentiers, usury and the merchant classes (Ghosh 2009) that acted as a barrier to agricultural investment, long-term growth and the development of productive forces. Egalitarian redistribution of land would have overcome much of this barrier.

However, India pursued a rather more conservative path of land reform. The ruling elite conveniently remained oblivious to the task of transforming the pre-capitalist relations as it was antithetical to the interests of landlords and other parasitic classes (Diwakar 1994). The Indian big bourgeois class meanwhile continued to rely on foreign capital in its efforts to strengthen and consolidate its class position; while an attempt to overcome the problem of home market constraint was sought through large-scale state expenditure. The land reform that sought to benefit only a handful of rich peasantry and the landlord class at the expense of the vast majority of the agrarian rural population was the worst failure that the 'post-independence' era ever witnessed. Rather than putting effort into creating technical capabilities, there was heavy dependence on the mercy of other developed nations for technologies and capital that in turn had much political and military repercussion.

Notwithstanding the absence of egalitarian land reform, the state did try to curtail the influence of the parasitic classes by imposing a ceiling and protecting tenants. The zamindari system was abolished and through legislation land rent was regulated. Banking networks were promoted to take control of money lenders and efforts were made to increase irrigation and power facilities. Despite the conservative land reform, the post green revolution phase of the Indian economy witnessed a sharp increase in agricultural output, capital investment, mechanisation and commodification of agricultural products. Some of these macro indicators suggested a 'tendency' towards a capitalist form of production relations. The village-level studies (Patnaik 1972a; 1972b; 1986) showed the same results.

Agriculture in the post-reform period

This section reviews the performance of agriculture in the post-reform period. Table 3.1 to Table 3.3) for the pre-reform period show the changes in cropping pattern and growth story between the two different regimes.

Agricultural production, yield and area

It is interesting to note that the period between 1980–81 and 1989–90 observed a relatively higher growth both in production and yield of all major crops (Table 3.1 to Table 3.3). During the same period low or negative growth in area was observed for the majority of crops, reflecting the fact that production was mainly spurred through the increase in yield.

The area under rice cultivation increased annually by 0.41 per cent while the production and yield witnessed an impressive growth rate of 3.62 per cent and 3.19 per cent respectively. In the case of wheat, growth in production grew at a rate of 3.57 per cent and yield showed a splendid growth of 3.10 per cent. The area under wheat grew at a rate of 0.46 per cent. Despite negative growth in area, coarse cereals witnessed an increase in production and yield registering an annual growth rate of 0.40 per cent and 1.62 per cent, respectively. Pulses also recorded high growth in production and yield despite negative growth in area. Despite the decline in area growth, the production of food grain was as high as 2.85 per cent, which was due to a yield growth of 2.74 per cent.

In the case of non-food grains, the oilseeds registered an impressive growth of 5.2 per cent and 2.43 per cent in production and yield, respectively. Similarly, despite the negative growth in area, cotton witnessed high growth in both production (2.80) and yield (4.10). Sugar cane witnessed growth in area (1.44), production (2.70) and yield (1.44) throughout the decade. The production of non-food grew at a rate of 3.77 per cent per annum, attributable to an area growth of 1.12 per cent and yield growth of 2.31 per cent. Hence, the principal crops recorded

Table 3.1 Compound growth rates of area of principal crops

Years	*Rice*	*Wheat*	*Coarse cereals*	*Total cereals*	*Pulses*	*Total food grain*	*Oilseeds*	*Sugar cane*	*Cotton*	*Non-food grain*	*All principal crops*
1980–81/1989–90	0.41	0.46	−1.34	−0.26	−0.09	−0.23	1.51	1.44	−1.25	1.12	0.1
1990–91/1999–00	0.68	1.72	−2.12	0.04	−0.6	−0.07	−0.86	−0.07	2.71	1.18	0.27
2000–01/ 2009–10	−0.1	1.28	−0.75	0.09	1.62	0.37	2.14	1.12	2.6	2.16	0.91

Table 3.2 Compound growth rates of production of principal crops

Years	*Rice*	*Wheat*	*Coarse cereals*	*Total cereals*	*Pulses*	*Total food grain*	*Oilseeds*	*Sugar cane*	*Cotton*	*Non-food grain*	*All principal crops*
1980–81/1989–90	3.62	3.57	0.4	3.03	1.52	2.85	5.2	2.7	2.8	3.77	3.19
1990–91/1999–00	2.02	3.57	–0.02	–0.02	0.59	2.02	1.63	2.73	2.29	2.69	2.29
2000–01/2009–10	1.51	2.16	2.8	2.01	3.35	2.12	4.6	1.64	13.8	3.67	2.5

Table 3.3 Compound Growth Rates of Yield of Principal Crops

Years	*Rice*	*Wheat*	*Coarse cereals*	*Total cereals*	*Pulses*	*Total food grain*	*Oilseeds*	*Sugar cane*	*Cotton*	*Non-food grain*	*All principal crops*
1980–81/1989–90	3.19	3.1	1.62	2.9	1.61	2.74	2.43	1.24	4.1	2.31	2.56
1990–91/1999–00	1.34	1.83	1.82	1.59	0.93	1.52	1.15	1.05	–0.41	1.09	1.33
2000–01/2009–10	1.61	0.87	4.24	3.19	1.9	2.89	3.59	0.52	10.91	2.49	3.25

Source: Directorate of Economics and Statistics, Department of Agriculture and Cooperation; *Growth rates are based on fourth advance estimates 2010–11 released on 19.07.2011; (Base: T.E.1981–82 = 100).

an unprecedented growth rate of 3.19 per cent that was due solely to a yield growth of 2.56 per cent per annum as the area growth grew by a mere 0.1 per cent.

However, the fruit of the green revolution could not last long as the growth in production for the majority of crops could not be sustained during the 1990s. The overall food grain production growth declined to 2.02 per cent. Interestingly, production growth for rice and wheat were sustained during this period mostly with an increase in area growth (0.68 per cent for rice and 1.72 per cent for wheat) as the growth in yield was lower than the previous decade. In the case of non-food grain crops, oilseeds and sugar cane recorded a decline in area and yield in addition to negative or stagnant growth in production. Even though the area under cotton increased (2.71), the growth in production declined compared to the previous year and the growth in yield shows a negative growth rate (–0.41) which in the earlier decade registered an annual growth of 4.1 per cent. Therefore, it is of no surprise that millions of cotton grower farmers committed suicide in different parts of the country. With the decline in both the production of food grains and non-food grain crops, the principal crops grew at an annual rate of 2.29 per cent in the 1990s.

The decade of the 2000s witnessed a slight improvement over the previous decade. There was a sharp increase in the production of pulses, which registered an annual growth rate of 3.35 per cent. Both yield and area contributed to higher growth in production. However, rice witnessed a decline in production and area growth while the yield growth improved marginally compared to the 1990s. As for wheat, the decade of the 2000s saw a decline in area, production and yield. However, coarse cereals and pulses recorded an impressive growth both in production and yield, leading to an improvement in overall food grain production (2.12) which was attributable mostly to an increase in the growth of yield (2.89). As for non-food grains, crops that witnessed respectable growth in production were oilseeds (4.6) and cotton (13.8). The production growth was attributable to an increase in both yield and area growth. The principal crops grew at a rate of 2.5 per cent which was an improvement over the previous decade but much lower than the growth recorded under the previous regime. Also, the regime change facilitated a shift in the cropping pattern from food grain to non-food grain that later showed an increase in annual area growth rate compared to the pre-reform period.

Gross capital formation in Indian agriculture

Capital formation through investment enables the farmers to improve the stock of equipment, tools and productivity of resources employed, which in turn helps them to use their resources, particularly land and labour, more productively. In India, Central Statistical Organization (CSO) compiles estimates on investment with the breakup of public and private investments. Investment by the public sector includes mostly irrigation, and private investment comprises (a) farm households – equipment, machinery, irrigation, land reclamation and land improvement –and (b) private corporate investment.

The public investment in agriculture as a percentage of public sector gross capital formation (Table 3.4) increased from 14.71 per cent in the 1960s to 16.85 per cent in the 1970s (Bhatla 2014). However, after the 1980s its share started to fall. The first decade of economic reform recorded a share as low as 6.3 per cent. The public investment showed some improvement after the 2000s. Public expenditure has always complemented private expenditure in agriculture. However, private sector investment as a percentage of total private investment improved marginally in the 1970s followed by a continuous decline in the era of economic reform. As a consequence of this, the contribution of agriculture in the total Gross Domestic Capital Formation (GDCF) declined from 15.02 per cent to 7.47 per cent between 1980–90 and 2000–08.

Table 3.4 Percentage share of private and public GCFA in total GDCF, GCFA in GDPA and GCFA in GDCF

Investment	*1980–90*	*1990–00*	*2000–10*
GCFA/GDPA	9.36	8.29	16.83
GCFA/GDCF	15.02	9.3	7.47
Public GCFA/GDCF	9.71	6.3	7.10
Private GCFA/GDCF	21.09	11.06	8.23

Source: Bhatla 2014; Planning Commission, Govt. of India, 2014; GCFA: Gross Capital Formation in Agriculture, GDPA: Gross Domestic Product in Agriculture; GDCF: Gross Domestic Capital Formation.

From the perspective of long-term agricultural growth, the ratio of Gross Capital Formation in agriculture (GCFA) to Gross Domestic Product from agriculture itself is important. The ratio reflects the investment rate in agriculture and the increase in the ratio is reflective of the fact that the investment is being ploughed back into the sector. The ratio increased from 7.89 in the 1960s to 11.23 in the 1970s followed by a decline over the next two decades (9.36 and 8.29). However, as agricultural growth improved in the 2000s, the ratio improved to 16.83, which was induced by an expansion in public expenditure. Therefore, the data from the production and investment in agriculture shows the crisis-like situation in the initial phase of economic liberalisation. However, the agriculture sector has been recovering since the 2000s.

Changing agrarian structure

In the process of the development of capitalism one may expect an increase in the importance of agricultural labour households. This may become possible only when the cultivator household converts itself into a class of agricultural labourer. It may happen through a continuous process of differentiation and separation from the fundamental means of production which, in agriculture, is land. Hence, the change in the pattern of landholding remains at the core of the analysis of agrarian transformation. In India, the National Sample Survey Organization (NSSO) provides data on the change in the pattern of landholding every ten years.

Dominance of small-scale producer

The household ownership holding of NSS data (Table 3.5) shows that the proportion of landless households increased initially from 9.64 per cent in 1971–72 to 11.33 per cent in 1982 per cent and then started to decline throughout the next three decades. Scholars, however, have criticised this narrow definition of landlessness, since 90 per cent of the land of a household having less than 0.41 hectares is used for the homestead (Rawal 2008). The proportion of marginal households increased steadily from 52.98 per cent in 1971–72 to 75.41 per cent in 2012–13. A proportion of small households witnessed a marginal decline while semi-medium households saw a considerable decline over a period of economic reform. The households that have witnessed a substantial decline in the last five decades are large landholding (medium and large) households. The proportion of medium households declined from 7.88 per cent in 1971–72 to 1.93 per cent in 2012–13, while the large households share dropped from 2.12 per cent to 0.24 per cent during the same period.

The trend in households share corresponds to a trend in the share of area owned (Table 3.5). The percentage share of large landholder households declined continuously from 53.64

Table 3.5 Share of household and area owned by size class holding (in ha.)

Year	*Percentage of Households*					
	Landless	*Marginal*	*Small*	*Semi-medium*	*Medium*	*Large*
1971–72	9.64	52.98	15.49	11.94	7.88	2.12
1982	11.33	55.31	14.7	10.78	6.45	1.43
1992	11.25	60.63	13.42	9.28	4.54	0.88
2003	10.04	69.63	10.81	6.03	2.96	0.53
2012–13	7.41	75.41	10	5.01	1.93	0.24
Percentage distribution of area owned						
1971–72	0	9.76	14.68	21.92	30.73	22.91
1982	0	12.22	16.49	23.58	29.83	18.07
1992	0	16.93	18.59	24.58	26.07	13.83
2003	0.01	23.05	20.38	21.98	23.08	11.55
2012–13	0.01	29.76	23.54	22.07	18.83	5.81

Source: NSS report no. 491; report no. 571;
landless <=0.002 ha; marginal 0.002–1.000; small 1.000–2.000; semi-medium 4.000–10.000; large> 10.000

per cent in 1971–72 to 25 per cent in 2012–13. The semi-medium households have managed to maintain their share over the decades. The proportion share of small households has increased substantially. They accounted for only 14.68 per cent of total land in 1971–72 while in 2012–13 the share went up to 23.54 per cent. The marginal households also witnessed a phenomenal increase in their area share as the data shows in 1971–72 they owned 9.76 per cent of total land and in 2012–13 the proportion was 29.76 per cent. Therefore, the permanent feature that has come to dominate the Indian agrarian structure is the increasing importance of small-scale producer both in terms of number and area owned. The findings from village studies also suggest the increasing importance of small-scale producers in recent years (Sharma 2005; Ramanamurthy 2014).

However, the increase in proportionate share does not necessarily improve the conditions of their existence since household size has also increased. Even though the proportion of large landholder households declined, the average area per household is still substantial (Figure 3.1).

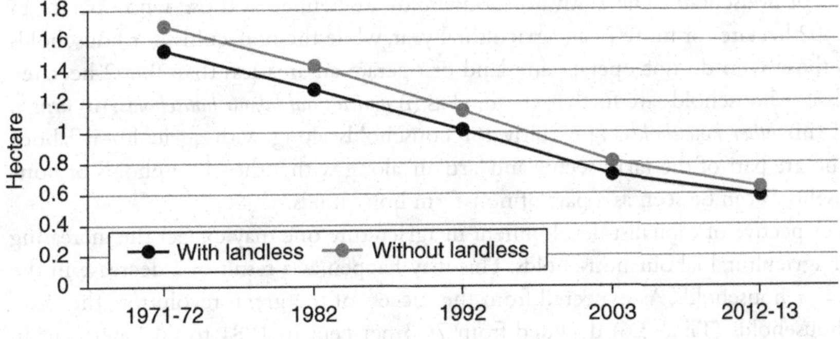

Figure 3.1 Average area owned per household. *Source*: NSS Report No. 571

Furthermore, another important feature as well as the concern of the agrarian scene in India is the decline in the average size of landholdings. The average area owned per household excluding landless households was 1.69 in 1971–72 which fell to 0.64 by 2012–13.

Based on the analysis of some of these trends at the aggregate level, Basu and Basole (2011a) have argued the dominant production relations as capitalist in Indian agriculture. The declining size and share of the large landholder has led some scholars like Harriss (2013) to argue the decline in the importance of landlordism in the countryside. Das and Basu (2013), based on the declining trend in an average area (per household), suspect the possibility of redistributive land reform in contemporary India.

Does the claim fulfil the Marxian criteria of agrarian 'transformation'? To what extent can the decline in the size of large households (area owned) be equated to a decline in 'landlordism'? In the Marxian political economy framework 'landlord' is defined as a 'class' constituting rural households that appropriate surplus from the tenant household. It is true that, 'traditionally', landlord as a class possessed large landholdings and derived substantial income in the form of 'rent'; nonetheless, the size of the landholding is neither a necessary nor sufficient condition to define a 'landlord class' in the Marxian political economy.

One of the preconditions for the development of capitalist relations in agriculture is the formation of a labour market. Basole and Basu (2011a), in an attempt to trace out the dominant production relation in Indian agriculture, use a category called 'effectively landless household' which they closely equate with the existence of 'free wage labour' in the capitalist sense. It is true that land poor peasant households including some lower strata of middle peasant households may work for wages as agricultural labour in contemporary Indian agriculture but they can hardly be seen as similar to the class of 'free wage labour' used in the classical Marxian framework. What distinguishes free wage labour from the effectively landless household is their continuing relationship to the land, and their resistance to being totally dependent upon wage earning for their subsistence. The possibility of the transformation of land poor peasant households into the class of agricultural or rural proletariat cannot be denied. However, such possibility exists, as described by Lenin (1972) in the 'Development of Capitalism in Russia', only when the developing capitalist relations guarantees a better existence through wage labour than tilling a parcel of land. Does such a possibility exist in the contemporary farm and non-farm sector? The next section explores the changing occupational structure of rural households.

Changing occupational structure

The NSS survey on 'household asset and liabilities' provides some information on the changing occupational structure of rural households in India. The survey classifies households as cultivator and non-cultivator households. The cultivator households are defined as those who operate an area of land 0.002 hectares or more in an agricultural year, while the non-cultivator households are defined as those who do not operate any land or operate an area less than 0.002 hectares. The non-cultivator households are further classified as (i) *agricultural labour households*, (ii) *artisan households* and (iii) *other households*. The cultivator households along with agricultural labour households who are part of the farm sector and 'artisan' along with 'other' households of non-cultivator households can be seen as a part of non-farm households.

From the perspective of capitalist development in agriculture one may expect the increasing importance of agricultural labour households. This may happen as a result of a decrease in the share of cultivator households. As expected from the success of the green revolution, the share of cultivator households (Table 3.6) declined from 76.3 per cent in 1981 to 66.1 per cent in 1991. The cultivator households further declined by 11 per cent in 2002. However, the share

Table 3.6 Percentage Distribution of Rural Households by Occupational Category during 1981, 1991, 2002 and 2012

Households Occupational category	*Percentage of households*			
	1981	*1991*	*2002*	*2013**
Cultivators	76.3	66.1	59.7	62
Agricultural labour	11.3	14.2	14.4	10.1
Artisans	1.6	3.8	5.2	nf
Others	10.8	15.8	20.7	nf
Non-cultivators	23.7	33.9	40.3	38
All households	100	100	100	100
Sectorial distribution of rural household				
Farm sector	87.6	80.3	74.1	72.1
Non-farm sector	12.4	19.7	25.9	27.9

Source: NSS Report No. 500; nf refers to data not found * Bhue and Vijay (2016) calculation based on unit-level data from 70th round.

increased from 59.7 per cent in 2002 to 62 per cent in 2012–13. On the other hand, the share of agricultural labour households increased from 11.3 per cent in 1981 to 14.2 per cent in 1991. Their share witnessed a marginal increase of 1.4 per cent; however, the share drastically declined from 14.4 per cent in 2002 to 10.1 in 2013. The increase in the share of cultivator households and the decline in the share of agricultural labour households in the last two rounds of the NSS household survey stand in striking contrast to the processes of classical agrarian transition as discussed much in Marxian political economy discourse (Hilton 1976).

The common feature that has been identified from the historical experience of developed economies is the increase in the importance of the non-farm sector in the process of development. Even though there has been a significant shift in the income structure, the shift in the occupational structure has not been very impressive from the farm to the non-farm sector. The non-farm sector increased its income share (Table 3.6) from 12.4 per cent in 1981 to 19.7 per cent in 1991and further to 25.9 per cent in 2002 and to 27.9 per cent in 2013.

Employment growth in rural India actually witnessed a decline in the post–economic reform period (Table 3.7). Employment growth in the farm sector grew at a rate of 1.35 per cent while in the post-reform period employment declined drastically and turned negative in the last decade. Employment growth in the non-farm sector more or less stagnated in the entire neo-liberal phase of the economy. Employment growth marginally increased in the first decade of economic liberalisation followed by a decline in the next decade. In rural areas, employment grew at an average rate of 2.02 per cent between 1983 and 1993; however, the decade following the economic reform witnessed a decline in employment growth to 1.83 per cent between 1993 and 2004 and to 1.5 per cent between 1999 and 2010. Employment growth within the non-farm sector either stagnated or declined for all sectors except the construction sector. It was the construction sector that witnessed impressive employment growth within the non-farm sector.

The inter-sectorial variation in workers' productivity among various sectors determines the workforce movement (Table 3.8). Productivity in industry is highest followed by the service sector and agriculture. Therefore, rural households should have actually moved to either industry or the service sector where productivity is highest. However, this did not happen as one may observe that the movement has actually occurred in the construction sector where productivity

Table 3.7 Sectorial growth of rural employment (in %)

Sector	*1983/1993–94*	*1993–94/200 4–05*	*1999–00/2009–10*
1	3	4	5
Farm sector	1.35	0.67	–0.13
Non-farm sector	3.36	3.64	3.61
Within non-farm sector			
Mining & quarrying	3.24	–0.08	2.7
Manufacturing	2	3.17	1.95
Utilities	5.58	–1.86	2.11
Construction	5.67	7.19	9.72
Trade, hotelling, etc.	3.77	5.24	2.54
Transport & communication, etc.	3.39	5.16	3.68
Financing, insurance, real estate & business services	3.58	7.23	7.68
Community, social and personal services	3.91	0.4	1.85
Total	2.02	1.84	1.5

Source: NSSO Employment and Unemployment: Report no. 409, 458, 515 and 554.

Table 3.8 Sectorial productivity (at 1986–87 prices, NDP in Rs/employed workers)

Sector	*1993–04*	*2009–10*	*CGR*
Agriculture	5,349	8,448	2.9
Industry	8,693	24,666	6.7
Construction	14,067	13,821	–1
Services	18,302	42,016	5.3
Total	7,476	15,863	4.8

Source: Chand and Srivastava, 2014.

has been recorded as relatively the lowest and negative. Therefore, one may argue that it is not the 'pull' factor but the 'push' factor that is at work in the countryside.

Who are moving away from the farm sector?

The only paper that has attempted to engage inter-sectorial labour flow, empirically at the aggregate level, in recent years is by Eswaran et al. (2009). By using NSS employment data of various rounds, they disaggregate the entire population into cohorts of eight years age intervals for the purpose of understanding the age groups that are most mobile. In their empirical exercises they found that shift from the farm sector was primarily associated with education. It was the young males, and to a lesser extent young females, in the age group 18–26 years that actually moved away from the farm sector. The employment structure for other cohorts did not change much over time. In the case of the illiterate male workforce, the entire shift happened in the construction sector since the sectorial distribution of employment (see Table 3.6 to Table 3.7) in all other sectors remained virtually unchanged. Using regression analysis they showed that the non-farm sector has generated employment for educated workers rather than for illiterates and primary school graduates. They argue that the non-farm sector demands a wage premium over what a worker with certain age and education characteristics can get in the farm sector. The wage premium associated with education were growing over time which was Rs 86 for literate workers over illiterate, Rs 197 for those who attended middle school and Rs 696 for graduates.

Binswanger-Mkhize (2013) argues the absorption of labour into the urban economy has been slow, and rural–urban migration has been far less than what could have been expected in a rapidly growing economy. The reason for relatively slow rural–urban migration in India is a consequence of the low share of manufacturing in employment. By using the REDS data, Binswanger-Mkhize (2013) argues that self-employment in the rural non-farm sector has become dynamic. Between 1999 and 2007, the number of households engaged in non-farm self-employment more than doubled. If rural to urban migration is less and self-employment in the non-farm sector has become more dynamic then which segment of farm households has access to the non-farm sector? According to the World Bank (2007), households in the farm sector with required human capital and also investable surplus gain have access to non-farm opportunities. For Binswanger-Mkhize (2013) it was those who are educated and some segments of farmer households that had access to the non-farm opportunities.

Village studies in recent years shed some light on the mobility of farm households. Rawal (2006), based on fieldwork from two villages (Dhamar and Birdhana of Haryana), suggests there is an entry barrier to the non-farm sector for agricultural labour households. Vijay (2012), based on a survey of nine villages in Andhra Pradesh, suggests there is a movement of land-owning households from the farm to the non-farm sector. There are other village-level studies (Ramanamurthy 2014; Vakulabhranam et al. 2011) that also support the hypothesis of movement of landowning households to non-farm activities or to urban areas.

The empirical evidence from aggregate data and case studies suggest that (i) rural–urban migration has been very slow, (ii) there is an entry barrier in the non-farm sector, and (iii) farm households with some level of education and farm assets (such as land) with investable surplus have moved away from the farm sector. If these are the recent developments then one may be interested in understanding the survival strategy of '*labour supplying households*' and '*land poor households*' within the farm sector? The answer may lie in the rising importance of tenancy relations in the post-reform period.

Increasing importance of tenancy

The tenancy is one of the oldest institutions that facilitate the '*reproduction of labour*'. One of the limitations of the tenancy arrangement is the constraint that it puts on the '*re-investment of capital*' back to agriculture as the agreement is time specific. Smith (1976) argues that even when the tenant does some level of investment on his leased land, the landlord demands more rent for the 'augmented' land at the time of renewal of present contract as if the investment had been made from his own pocket. Therefore, in classical political economy discourse the gradual disappearance of tenancy relations is seen as an indicator of developing capitalist production relations in agriculture.

Basole and Basu (2011a) characterise production relations, as 'capitalist' places of considerable importance to the changing nature of tenancy relations. The NSS landholding data (Table 3.9) except for the year 1990 shows a declining trend in tenancy relations both in terms of percentage of household participation (25 per cent in 1971–72 to 10.1 per cent in 2003) and

Table 3.9 Share of leased-in (Ln) areas and households (HHs) to total operated (Op.) area, pure tenant in total leased-in land

Year	*1991–92*	*2002–03*	*2012–13*
Share Ln to total Op. area*	8.52	6.5	10.25
Share of HH Ln to total operating HH *	11	10.10	12.26
Share of pure tenants to total tenants*	12.1	25.29	30.49
Share of pure tenant in total Ln land**	dnf	3.1	15.1

Source: NSS 59th and 70th Rounds unit-level data; dnf means data not found
*Murali et al. (2017) calculation based on NSS unit-level data, 59th and 70th rounds-land and livestock reports (visit 1); **calculation is based on the NSS unit-level data – 59th and 70th round by the author.

proportion of leased-in to the total operated area (12 per cent in 2071–72 to 6.5 per cent in 2003). However, it would be a mistake to characterise the trend as a permanent feature of Indian agriculture for two reasons: (i) the 70th NSS survey on 'household ownership and operational holding' data shows an increase in the participation of households (12.26 per cent) and operated land under tenancy (10.25 per cent), and (ii) the 59th round survey was carried out in a drought year (2003) which may have influenced the proper functioning of the tenancy market as the land leased market is an annual contract.

The state-level analysis of incidence of tenancy (Table 3.10) shows that the majority of the state seems to have followed a similar national trend except for Gujarat, Haryana, Odisha and Uttar Pradesh in terms of tenant holding. As opposed to the national trend in states like Gujarat and Odisha, the tenant holding increased in 2003 and declined in 2013 whereas Haryana and Uttar Pradesh witnessed a continuous decline. In terms of land under tenancy in total operated area (Table 3.10), states like Madhya Pradesh, Tamil Nadu, Rajasthan and Karnataka followed the national trend whereas Uttar Pradesh showed the opposite trend. For all other states tenancy increased continuously except for Assam, Haryana and Maharashtra that witnessed continuous decline.

It is interesting to observe (Table 3.10) that the share of pure tenants in the total tenant households, between 2003 and 2013, increased for the majority of states except for Gujarat, Karnataka, Kerala, Maharashtra, Punjab and Odisha. At the national level, the proportion of pure tenants increased from 12.1 per cent in 2003 to 25.29 per cent in 2003 and further to 30.49 per cent in 2012–13. The state of Andhra Pradesh had the highest proportion of pure tenant households (47.05) while Punjab had the lowest (3.56). Even though the proportion of pure tenants in Odisha declined, it still had higher (39.65) than the national average. The evidence (Table 3.10) also shows that the land under pure tenancy in total leased-in the area increased significantly from 3.1 per cent in 2003 to 15.1 per cent in 2012–13.

In terms of the category of operational holding (Table 3.11), the share of marginal households in total leased-in the area increased significantly from 16.3 per cent in 1991–92 to 30.26 per cent in 2012–13. Small and semi-medium households maintained their share in the last three NSS surveys. The share of medium households declined (14.6) in 2003 and increased (18.14) again in 2013. The percentage share of large land holders in the total leased land has been declining continuously over the decades. Following Mishra (2007), if we consider poor peasantry as consisting of marginal and small landholders, middle peasantry as semi-medium and rich peasantry as medium landholders, then one may argue that the tenancy market is domi-

Table 3.10 State-wise share of tenant household, pure tenant household and leased-in are in total operated area

State	*% of tenant household*				*% pure tenant in total tenant household ***		*% of leased-in area*			
	1981–82	*1991–92*	*2002–03*	*2012–13*	*2003*	*2013*	*1981–82*	*1991–92*	*2002–03*	*2012–13*
(1)	*(2)*	*(3)*	*(4)*	*(5)*	*(6)*	*(7)*	*(8)*	*(9)*	*(10)*	*(11)*
Andhra Pradesh*	13.08	14.1	13.2	25.21	27.48	47.05	6.2	9.6	9.24	26.66
Assam	12.9	10.1	6.7	7.12	19.12	39	6.4	8.9	5.86	4.28
Bihar	19.7	5.6	12.38	12.45	27.27	29.55	10.3	3.9	9.19	16.14
Gujarat	4.8	3.7	6.13	5.67	58.71	14.41	2	3.3	5.3	5.69
Haryana	25.9	17.1	12.85	11.87	4.81	12.98	18.2	33.7	16.98	16.01
Karnataka	10.7	8	4.99	8.18	36.34	9.39	6	7.4	3.71	7.34
Kerala	6.7	5.2	4.68	12.11	45.2	18.93	2.6	2.9	4.82	8.74
Madhya Pradesh*	8	9	6.48	7.68	24.9	32.68	3.6	6.3	3.74	6.3
Maharashtra	10.6	6.9	6.6	8	29.65	20.34	5.2	5.5	4.85	3.43
Odisha	18.2	16.9	17.13	15.5	49.47	39.65	9.9	9.5	14.47	17.44
Punjab	21.3	15.9	12.2	14.69	5.83	3.56	16.1	18.8	19.71	26.34
Rajasthan	7.1	6.5	3.42	8.67	16.96	19.03	4.3	5.2	3.4	6.83
Tamil Nadu	24.7	15.3	9.3	12.2	24.75	46.27	10.9	10.9	6.78	14.37
Uttar Pradesh*	20.5	15.5	12.93	10.18	16.9	18.9	10.2	10.5	10.64	7.89
West Bengal	23.1	14.4	13.7	16	31.32	33.22	12.3	10.4	10.54	14.69
All India	15.2	11	10.12	12.26	25.29	30.49	7.2	8.52	6.5	10.25

Source: NSS Report no. 571; Round Report No. 407.
Entries in 2002–03 and 2012–13 are based on visit no.1; ** calculation by Murali and Vijay (2017) based on unit-level data; * the entries for newer state have been considered as part of older state for the ease of comparison.

Table 3.11 Percentage of area leased-in by category of operational holdings across last three LHS surveys of NSS

Category of Operational holdings (land size in ha)	*1991–92*		*2002–03*		*2012–13*	
	% area leased-in	*% share in total leased-in area*	*% area leased-in*	*% share total in leased area*	*% area leased-in*	*% share total in leased area*
(1)	(2)	(3)	(4)	(5)	(6)	(7)
Marginal	8.7	16.3	8.6	30.3	10.73	30.26
Small	8.5	19.3	6.8	22.1	9.85	22.31
Semi-Medium	7.4	21.6	6.3	21.8	10.01	22.01
Medium	6.9	22	4.2	14.6	9.52	18.14
Large	11.4	20.9	6.1	11.2	12.25	7.28
All	8.5	100	6.5	100	10.25	100

Source: NSS Report No. 571; Report No. 407; Report No. 492 *Figure corresponds to the period July 2012–December 2012

nated by the poor peasant household. What is the implication of increasing participation of the labour-supplying households in the agrarian transition? It may imply a problem in the formation of the labour market which is the pre-requisite for capitalist development in agriculture.

The evidence from village studies overwhelmingly conforms to aggregate level data. Ramachandran et al. (2010) in their study of Ananthavaram village in an irrigated (Guntur) district of Andhra Pradesh found that the tenant household increased from 18 per cent to 37 per cent and operated land under tenancy from 22 per cent to 67 per cent between 1974 and 2004–05. Subramanian's (2000) survey of three villages in Andhra Pradesh found 29.1 per cent of land (in a tank irrigated village), 27.6 per cent of land (in a village under canal water) and 22.8 per cent (in a village under pump reservoir) under tenancy. Rawal and Osmani (2009) reports a high incidence of tenancy in Harevli (western Uttar Pradesh) and Birdhana (Haryana). A study of Palakurichi village, which otherwise had no history of tenancy relations, in Tamil Nadu by Surajit (2014), reports 43 per cent of land under tenancy. There are a few other village-level studies that found considerable decline or little evidence of tenancy relations (Harris et al. 2010; Sharma 2005).

According to Vijay and Sreenuvasulu (2013), in his study of nine villages in Andhra Pradesh the poor peasants dominated the land leased market. Rawal and Osmani (2009) in a study of three villages – Ananthavaram (Andhra Pradesh), Harevli (Uttar Pradesh) and Birdhana (Haryana) – found that the limited employment opportunity and the low earning from casual labour forced landless and poor peasant households to enter into tenancy relations offering sky rocketing rental prices for land.

In the classical political economy discourse, share cropping is considered as a pre-capitalist arrangement where its decline is taken as positive development from the perspective of long-term agricultural growth. As evident from Table 3.12, hare cropping has always been the dominant form of lease contract in Indian agriculture. However, the recent NSS survey (2012–13) shows fixed money (41) as the most prevalent form of tenancy arrangement followed by share cropping (28.7) and fixed produce (17).

Table 3.12 Trend in percentage distribution of leased-in operated area by terms of lease across the last five LHS surveys of NSS

Terms of Lease	*Percentage distribution of leased-in operated area*				
	1970–71	*1981–82*	*1991–92*	*2002–03*	*2012–13*
(1)	(2)	(3)	(4)	(5)	(6)
Fixed money	15.4	10.9	19	29.5	41.1
Fixed produce	11.6	6.3	14.5	20.3	17
Share of produce	47.9	41.9	34.4	40.3	28.7
Others	25.1	40.9	32.1	9.9	12.9
All terms	100	100	100	100	100

Source: NSS Report No. 571

However, given the diversity and complexity of the Indian economy, the terms of lease also varied across the regions. The state-wise data on terms of lease shows that for the majority of states (and union territories) share cropping was still the prevalent form of lease contract followed by fixed money. It is also interesting to note that the states where fixed money dominated the lease arrangement also showed a decline in the share of land under tenancy and the proportion of pure tenant households (Table 3.10) except for states like Tamil Nadu and Andhra Pradesh. This may imply a dynamic form of capitalist development in progress in some of these states (Table 3.13).

The 'withering away' of redistributive land reform: reconsideration

Redistributive land reform arises from the presence of the burden of rent on tenants, which acts as a barrier for reinvestment back into agriculture. The failure of neo-liberal reform in terms of the generation of enough non-farm employment opportunities has led to large numbers of the rural workforce being trapped in the farm sector. The manufacturing sector has more or less stagnated since economic reform has shut down every possibility of movement of surplus labour from the farm sector. The absence of enough employment opportunity in urban areas and the entry barrier into the non-farm sector has forced rural households to enter into the tenancy market as a survival mechanism. Landless and poor peasant households pay high rent (Ramachandran 2011) to the landlord. They have been exploited not only in the land leased market but also the interlinked factor market (Vakulabhranam et al. 2011).

The decline in the share of agricultural labour households (Table 3.4) and increase in the share of cultivator households may mean that agricultural labour households are entering into the tenancy market as cultivators instead of the labour market. This is because the share of pure tenant households has significantly increased in recent years and the tenancy market is dominated by labour-supplying households (landless and land poor households). The entry of the labour-supplying households as cultivator and their dominance in the tenancy market is opposed to the 'classical transition' trajectory experienced by developed economies. The increase in the proportion of pure tenant households and other land poor households (marginal and small) in the land leased market also implies the emergence of a '*land hunger class*' in Indian agriculture today.

Table 3.13 Percentage distribution of leased-in operated area by terms of lease for major states

State	*Fixed money (FM)*	*Fixed produce (FP)*	*Share of produce (SP)*	*Relatives under no specific terms (RTs)*	*Others (OTH)*	*Dominant terms of lease*
Andhra Pradesh	60.9	25	9.1	4.6	0.4	FM
Assam	13.4	9.8	67	6.1	3.4	SP
Chhattisgarh	24.1	36.5	35.1	0.3	4	FP
Gujarat	24.9	0	48.6	25.7	0.8	SP
Haryana	79.5	7.8	2.1	9.7	1	FM
Himachal Pradesh	28.5	2.1	6.5	52	11	RTs
Jharkhand	15.4	33.6	31.7	0	0	FP
Karnataka	17	14.7	63.4	2.7	2.1	SP
Madhya Pradesh	14.4	9.8	42.5	16.9	16.5	SP
Maharashtra	54.7	1.8	27.3	7.6	8.5	FM
Odisha	6.9	24.3	45.2	5.3	13.8	SP
Punjab	94.5	1	1.9	1.2	1.4	FM
Rajasthan	29.5	13.2	36.9	5.6	17.3	SP
Tamil Nadu	63.2	7.4	6.9	20.7	1.7	FM
Telangana	65.6	6.6	27.2	0.6	0	FM
Uttar Pradesh	26.9	13.2	36.9	5.6	17.3	SP
West Bengal	24.7	15.5	49.1	5.6	5	SP
Jammu and Kashmir	0	0	11.2	19.3	53.6	OTH
Kerala	39.8	11.5	6.5	36.4	5.9	FM
N E States	25.2	23	25.3	17.9	8.7	SP
Groups of UTs	7.8	6.7	63	22.3	0.2	SP
All India	41.1	17	28.7	7.6	5.3	FM

Source: NSS Report No. 571 (2015).

Another important feature of the agrarian sector is that the share of the 'land owning non-cultivating household' (lnNCH) increased from 6.3 per cent in 2003 to 11 per cent in 2013. However, the proportion of lnNCHs in the total non-cultivating households has recently declined from 40.3 per cent to 38 per cent. The decline in the share may imply that either the lnNCHs have moved back to agriculture as cultivators, since the proportion of cultivator households have increased in a recent NSS survey (Table 3.4), or they have moved to urban areas. There exists no empirical evidence of lnNCHs shifting back to agriculture households (Bhue et al. 2016). There exists some empirical evidence on the movement of landowning households in urban areas (Surajit 2014; Ramanamurthy 2014; Vijay 2012; Vakulabhranam et al. 2011). Furthermore, Bhue et al. (2016) further argue that the non-cultivating household may have been diverting agricultural land for non-agricultural purposes since cultivable land owned by landowning non-cultivating households has declined from 5.5 per cent to 3.5 per cent between 2002 and 2012.

The NSS 'household asset and liabilities' (2015) survey data shows that 94 per cent of rural households held land in rural areas and only 1 per cent owned some land in urban areas, whereas in the case of urban households 57 per cent of households had land in urban areas and as high as

Table 3.14 Proportion of urban households reporting rural land in each household asset holding class

Household asset holding class	*Average area per ha.*	*Average area (ha.) per reporting hhs*	*% of households reporting*
1	0	0	0
2	0	0	0.9
3	0.021	0.208	10.1
4	0.039	0.247	15.8
5	0.064	0.388	16.5
6	0.1	0.676	14.8
7	0.126	0.685	18.4
8	0.173	0.836	20.7
9	0.278	1.198	23.2
10	0.681	2.432	28
All	0.148	0.993	14.9

Source: NSS Report 570 (2015), 70th Round, pp. 29.

15 per cent owned land in rural areas (Table 3.14). The proportion increases to more than 20 per cent from the eighth decile onwards. Apart from the first decile class of asset holding households, almost all households possessed some land in rural areas. The household in the highest decile class owned the largest area in both urban and rural areas.

The average landholding (Figure 3.1) may have declined over the last few decades but simultaneously we have also witnessed the rise of a '*land hunger class*' in the agrarian structure. The landless and the land poor have entered into the land leased market as cultivators, instead of the labour market, and pay exorbitant rents for land. Another defining feature of contemporary Indian agriculture is the increasing importance of non-cultivating households who own land but do not cultivate it. In agrarian transition discourse, landowning non-cultivating households are termed as 'landlord classes'. The significance of the landowning non-cultivating households (including absentee landlords) in the agrarian structure is that they form the permanent 'supply side' component in the land lease market. In other words, there are households who want to cultivate land but are landless or own a small plot of land and there are households who own land but do not want to cultivate it that may be either leasing it out or diverting land for non-agricultural purposes. Given the declining size of the average landholding, redistributive land reform may look difficult or impossible but the policy makers of India would not be able to breathe a sigh of freedom in the presence of an increasing land hunger class in rural India.

Conclusion

The chapter is solely based on various national sample survey organisations data (NSSO) to understand the various trends in agrarian structure. These surveys are conducted every ten years. The latest survey on important variables with respect to agrarian structure such as ownership holding, assets and liabilities was conducted in 2012–13 and was made available to researchers and scholars for analysis only in 2015. Hence, data on other aspects of farm sectors are deliberately taken till 2012–13. After the 2014 general election, the National Democratic Front led by the Bharatiya Janata Party came into power; however, there has not been a single policy related to the agricultural sector that may have revolutionised the production conditions and structure of the farm economy. In fact, the latest farm bill/law which the central government is trying to implement and which farmers are already opposing in the streets may worsen the pace of capitalist development in Indian agriculture. The discussion on the latest development at the policy level and its implications for the agrarian class demands a separate analysis.

The agrarian transition in India has been very slow. The sector is dominated by the small-scale producer. Indian agriculture may have to wait for quite some time to witness large-scale capitalist farming. The recent literature on land prices suggests that over the last few decades India has permanently entered a 'new land price regime' with extremely high prices (Chakravorty 2013). For Chakravorty (2013) the new land price regime is driven by an increasing supply of money, high income inequalities and scarcity of land. Bhalla and Singh (2009) also contend that the growth of land productivity has slumped with the onset of neo-liberal reform. According to Jodhka (2014), an acre of land which could be sold for around 3 lakhs sometime in the late 1980s sold for 25 to 30 lakh rupees or even more in 2008–09 in two villages of Haryana. Vakulabhranam et al. (2011) in their field visit to coastal Andhra Pradesh found that over the last 15 years, land prices had escalated by more than 10–20 times, which according to them is the cause of the rebirth of absentee landlordism and tenancy. In India, land is characterised as an inactive market where 'the extent of land entering into the land market depends on supply side factors i.e., distress condition faced by the landholding households in the rural areas' (Bhaduri 1973; Basu 1986). The mounting land price and inactive land market may act as a barrier to the growth of the rich peasantry in agriculture.

Even though the agriculture sector witnessed some improvement at the beginning of the century, there has not been much movement of labour-supplying households from farm to non-farm sector. One may argue that growth can continue without the necessary structural transformation in the agrarian structure. Even though there are village-level studies that tend to show the peasant differentiation under process in agriculture (Ramachandran et al. 2011), there are also studies which suggest that capital accumulation is taking place not on the production site but in the circulation (Harriss-White 2008; Banerjee 2009).

Entry to the non-farm sector has been difficult for the illiterate and landless poor peasant households. The only sector where they have found seasonal employment is the construction sector as manual labour. The construction sector is characterised as having low productivity and less job security. The construction sector witnessed a boom particularly in the second half of the last decade while all other sectors virtually created no jobs. Now, a matter of concern is what if there is an end to the construction boom?

There is empirical evidence of the movement of landowning households from the farm to non-farm farm sector as well as from rural to urban areas. The proportion of non-cultivating land owing households has increased over the last few decades. Urban households own a considerable amount of land in rural areas. The landowning non-cultivating households and the absentee landlord, who otherwise are termed as landlords in classical political economy literature, form the permanent suppliers of land in the land lease market. On the other hand, the absence of negative employment growth in agriculture and the inability of the non-farm sector to create enough employment opportunities have impelled labour-supplying households to enter into tenancies despite exorbitant rental prices for land. The entry of the labour-supplying households in the land lease market may further impede the capitalist development in Indian agriculture. Since the formation of labour market is a pre-requisite for the development of capitalism.

Therefore, one of the most important developments that have taken place in the neo-liberal phase of the Indian economy is the rise of the 'land hunger class' in the agrarian structure. The rental income from land may not be the only income or form a significant proportion of the landlord's total income. But from the perspective of the land hunger tenant the rental income may constitute a significant part of his total income. Furthermore, the empirical evidence shows that landowning non-cultivating households are also diverting agricultural land for non-agricultural purposes. Thus we have a situation in which there are households who are eager to cultivate land but are landless or own small plots of land and there are households who own land but do not want to cultivate it. Redistributive land reform may look difficult or impossible but it is true that there exists a demand for it from the land hunger class.

References

Banerjee, A. (2009). "Peasant Classes, Farm Incomes and Rural Indebtedness: An Analysis of Household Production Data from Two States." Working Paper No. 410, Centre for Development Studies, Trivandrum.

Barraclough, S. (1991). *An End to Hunger?* London: Zed Books.

Basole, A. and Basu, D. (2011a). "Relations of Production and Modes of Surplus Extraction in India: Part I-Agriculture", *Economic and Political Weekly*, Vol. 46, No. 14, pp. 63–79.

Basu, D. and Das, D. (2013). "The Maoist Movement in India: Some Political Economy Considerations", *Journal of Agrarian Change*, Vol. 13, No. 3, pp. 365–381.

Basu, K. (1986). "The Market for Land: Analysis of Interim Transaction", *Journal of Development Economics*, Vol. 20, No. 1, pp. 163–177.

Bathla, S. (2014). "Public and Private Capital Formation and Agricultural Growth in India: State Level Analysis of Interlinkages during Pre and Post Reform Periods", *Agricultural Economics Research Review*, Vol. 27, No. 1. pp. 19–36.

Bernstein, H. (1996). "Agrarian Question Then and Now", in Bernstein, H. and Brass, T. (eds.), *Agrarian Question: An Essay in Appreciation of T.J. Byres* (pp. 22–59). London: Frank Cass.

Bernstein, H. (2004). "Changing before Our Very Eyes: Agrarian Questions and the Politics of Land in Capitalism Today", *Journal of Agrarian Change*, Vol. 4, No. 2, pp. 190–225.

Bernstein, H. (2006). "Is There an Agrarian Question in the 21st Century?", *Canadian Journal of Development Studies*, Vol. 27, No. 4, pp. 449–460.

Bhaduri, A. (1973). "A Study of Agricultural Backwardness under Semi-Feudalism", *The Economic Journal*, Vol. 83, No. 329 (Mar.), pp. 120–137.

Bhalla, G. S. and Singh, G. (2009). "Economic Liberalisation and Indian Agriculture: A Statewide Analysis", *Economic and Poitical Weekly*, Vol. XLIV, No. 52, pp. 34–44.

Bhue, C. and Vijay, R. (2016). "Importance of Landowning Non-cultivating Households: Some More Evidence", *Economic and Political Weekly*, Vol. LI, No. (25), pp. 19–21.

Binswanger-Mkhize, H. P. (2013). "The Stunted Structural Transformation of the Indian Economy: Agriculture, Manufacturing and the Rural Non Farm Sector", *Economics and Political Weekly*, Vol. 48, No. 26 & 27 (June), pp. 5–13.

Byres, T. J. (1991). "The Agrarian Question and Differing Form of Capitalist Agrarian Transition: An Essay with Reference to Asia", in Breman, J. and Mundle, S. (eds.), *Rural Transformation in Asia* (pp. 3–76). New Delhi: Oxford University Press.

Chakravorty, S. (2013). "A New Price Regime: Land Market in Urban and Rural India", *Economic and Political Weekly*, Vol. XLVIII, No. 17, pp. 45–54.

Chand, R. and Srivastava, S. K. (2014). "Changes in the Rural Labour Market and Their Implication for Agriculture", *Economic and Political Weekly*, Vol. 49, No. 10 (March), pp. 47–54.

Deere, C. D. and Leon De Leal, M. (eds.). (1987). "Introduction", in Derre, C. D., Leon De Leal, M. (eds.), *Rural Women and State Policy* (pp. 1–17). Boulder, CO: Westview Press.

Diwakar, D. M. (ed.). (1994). *India: A Semi Feudal Semi Colonial State*. New Delhi: Manak Publication.

Eswaran, M., Kotwal, A., Ramaswami, B. and Wadhwa, W. (2009). "Sectorial Labour Flows and Agricultural Wages in India, 1983–2004: Has Growth Trickled Down?", *Economic and Political Weekly*, Vol. 44, No. 2, pp. 46–55.

Ghosh, J. and Chandrasekhar, C. P. (2003). *The Market that Failed: A Decade of Neoliberal Economic Reforms in India*. New Delhi: Left Word Books.

Ghosh, S. K. (2009). *Naxalbari: Before and After, Reminiscences and Appraisal*. Kolkata: New Age Publisher.

Harriss, J. (2013). "Does 'Landlordism' Still Matter? Reflections on Agrarian Change in India", *Journal of Agrarian Change*, Vol. 13, No. 3, pp. 351–364.

Harriss-White, B. (2008). *Rural Commercial Capital: Agricultural Markets in West Bengal*. New Delhi: Oxford Universty Press.

Hilton, R. (1976). *The Transition from Feudalism to Capitalism*. London: New Left Books.

Jacobs, S. (2010). "Agrarian Reform", *Sociopedia.isa*. http://www.sagepub.net/isa/resources/pdf/agrarian%20Reform.pdf.

Kawagoe, T. (2016). *Agricultural Land Reform in Postwar Japan: Experiences and Issues*. World Bank Policy Research Working Paper No. 2111. https://elibrary.worldbank.org/doi/abs/10.1596/1813-9450-2111

Lenin, V. I. 1899 (1964). "The Development of Capitalism in Russia", *Collected Works*, 4th edition, ,Vol 3, pp. 552–600. Moscow Publication.

Lerche, J., Shah, A. and Harriss-White, B. (2013). "Introduction: Agrarian Questions and Left Politis in India", *Journal of Agrarian Change*, Vol. 13, No. 3, pp. 337–350.

Lewis, W. A. (1954). "Economic Development with Unlimited Supplies of Labour", *The Manchester School of Economics and Social Studies*, Vol. 22, No. 2, pp. 139–191.

Mishra, S. K. (2007). "On Agrarian Transition in West Bengal", *The Marxist*, Vol. 13, No. 2, pp. 1–22.

Murali, D. A. and Vijay, R. (2017). "Revival of Agriculture Sector and Increasing Tenancy in India", *Economic and Political Weekly*, Vol. LII, No. 31, pp. 18–21.

Nagaraj, K., Sainath, P., Rukmani, R., and Gopinath, R. (2014). "Farmers' Suicides in India: Magnitudes, Trends, and Spatial Patterns, 1997–2012", *Review of Agrarian Studies*, Vol. 4, No. 2, pp. 53–83.

Patnaik, U. (1972a). "Development of Capitalism in Agriculture-I", *Social Scientist*, Vol. 1, No. 2 (Sep.), pp. 15–31.

Patnaik, U. (1972b). "Development of Capitalism in Agriculture-II", *Social Scientist*, Vol. 1, No. 2 (Sep.), pp. 3–19.

Patnaik, U. (1986). "The Agrarian Question and Development of Capitalism in India", *Economic and Political Weekly*, Vol. 21, No. 18 (May), pp. 781–793.

Patnaik, U. (1995). "The Economic Ideas of Mao Zedong on Agricultural Transformation and Its Relation to Capital Formation and Industrialisation", *China Report*, Vol. 31, No. 1, pp. 23–45.

Ramachandran, V. K. (2011). "The State of Agrarian Relations in India Today", *The Marxist*, Vol. 27, No. 1–2, pp. 51–90.

Ramanamurthy, R. V. (2014). "Conditions of Petty Commodity Reproduction and Agrarian Transition in Rural Andhra Pradesh: A Study in Three Villages", Paper presented at the conference *The Return of the Land Question: Dispossession, Livelihoods, and Contestation in India's Capitalist Transition*, co-organized by the Faculty of Arts and the Australia India Institute, University of Melbourne, the Institute of Development Studies Kolkata, and the Indian Institute of Management, Calcutta (*IDSK* March 4–6, 2014).

Rawal, V. (2006). "The Labour Process in Rural Haryana (India): A Field-Report from Two Villages", *Journal of Agrarian Change*, Vol. 6, No. 4 (Oct.), pp. 538–583.

Rawal, V. (2008). "Ownership Holdings of Land in Rural India: Putting the Record Straight", *Economic and Political Weekly*, Vol. 43. No. 10, pp. 43–47.

Rawal, V. and Osmani, Siddique. (2009). *Economic Policies, Tenancy Relations and Household Incomes: Insights from Three selected villages in India*. Social and Policy Research Institute, Univesity of Ulster. http://archive.indianstatistics.org/misc/vrosmani2009.pdf

Rawal, V., Ramachandran, V. K. and Swaminathan, M. (2010). *Socio Economic Survey of Three Villages in Andhra Pradesh*. New Delhi: Tulika Books.

Sharma, A. N. (2005). "Agrarian Relations and Socio-Economic Change in Bihar", *Economic and Political Weekly*, Vol. 40, No. (Mar. 5–11, 2005), pp. 960–972.

Smith, A (1776) 1976. *An Inquiry into the Nature and Cause of Wealth of Nation*. London: Oxford University Press.

Subramanyam, S. (2000). "Agricultural Tenancy in India: Growth Promoting or Growth Retarding", *Artha Vijnana*, Vol. XLII, No. 4, pp. 360–366.

Surjit, V. (2014). "Tenancy and Distress in Thanjavur Region, Tamil Nadu", in V.K. Ramachandran and M. Swaminathan (eds.), *Agrarian Studies 3: Dalit Households in Village Economies*. New Delhi: Published by Tulika Books.

Thiesenhusen, W. (1995). *Broken Promises: Agrarian Reform and the Latin American Campesino*. Boulder, CO: Westview Press.

Vakulabharanam, V., Prashad, N. P., Laxminarayan, K. and Sudheer, K. (2011). "Understanding the Andhra Crop Holiday Movement", *Economic and Political Weekly*, Vol. 46, No. 50, pp. 13–16.

Vijay, R. (2012). "Structural Retrogression and Rise of New Landlords in Indian Agriculture: An Empirical Exercise", *Economic and Political Weekly*, Vol. 47, No. 5, pp. 37–45.

Vijay, R. and Sreenuvasulu, Y. (2013). "Agrarian Structure and Land Lease Arrangement: An Investigation in Nine Villages in Andhra Pradesh", *Economic and Political Weekly*, Vol. 48, No. 26 & 27 (July), pp. 42–49.

World Bank. (2007). *India: Land Policies for Growth and Poverty Reduction*. New Delhi: Oxford University Press.

Reports

National Sample Survey Organisation, Ministry of Statistics and Programme, Government of India –

– (1992). "Land and Livestock Holding Survey", Report No. 407.

– (1997). "Employment and Unemployment in India, 1993–94", Report No. 409.

– (2001). "Employment and Unemployment in India, 1999–2000", Report No. 458 (55/10/2).

– (2005). "Household Assets and Liabilities", Report No. 500.

– (2006). "Employment and Unemployment in India, 2004–05", Report No. 515 (61/10/1).

– (2006). "Household Ownership Holdings in India", Report No. 491.

– (2011). "NSS KI (66/10) Key Indicators of Employment and Unemployment in India 2009–10".

– (2014). "Employment and Unemployment in India, 2011–12", Report 554 (68/10/1).

– (2015). "Household Assets and Liabilities", Report No. 570.

– (2015). "Household Ownership and Operational Holdings in India", Report No. 571.

4

IMPACT OF QUALITY INFRASTRUCTURE ON AGRICULTURE IN KARNATAKA

Soumya Manjunath

Introduction

The Indian economy has experienced high economic growth rates in the period of post reforms, largely fuelled by non-agricultural growth, averaging more than 6 per cent in the previous decade. However, the pertinent question of equity and distribution remain quite evident in the stark rural–urban divide. Improvement in agricultural production continues to be one of the major developmental concerns of emerging economies such as India in the era of neo-liberalization. The relevance of agriculture stems not only from the fact that it addresses the food security needs of the growing population but also that it contributes to the industrial sector, helps in earning foreign exchange and assists in poverty reduction (Bolt 2004; Byerlee et al. 2005). The potential that agriculture holds needs to be made use of at the optimum level so that the entire economy benefits. However, the persistence of regional disparities in the agricultural sector and low agricultural incomes are of serious concern (Bhalla and Singh 2012). Despite significant efforts by the state, the agricultural sector remains trapped in the vagaries of nature and market risks (Jain and Parshad 2007).

The performance of agricultural sector, in general, is constrained by factors such as the vagaries of rainfall, insufficient credit support, inefficient markets, market risks, inadequate infrastructure, low capital formation, institutional bottlenecks, knowledge deficits and paradoxes of policy initiatives (Rao 2008). Degradation of natural resources and lack of adequate infrastructure can diminish the potential of agriculture (OECD 2006). Development economics has highlighted the importance of investing in agriculture and the creation of infrastructure and institutions to facilitate growth in the agricultural sector (Schultz 1964; Timmer 2002; Straub and Terada-Hagiwara 2011, O'Gorman 2015). Infrastructure has been identified as one of the crucial factors. Infrastructure assists not only in productivity improvements in agriculture but also in reduction of regional imbalances in growth (Binswanger et al. 1989; Thorat et al. 2003; Fan and Zhang 2004; Birthal et al. 2014). To maximize the multiplier effects that agriculture offers, strengthening of infrastructure facilities and institutional mechanisms become crucial. The provision of appropriate and adequate infrastructure in rural areas is crucial to accelerate agricultural growth and reduce disparities across the regions (Fan and Zhang 2004).

In the context of a faster, inclusive, and sustainable growth strategy exemplified in the Twelfth Five Year Plan, the development of agriculture in Karnataka assumes greater importance for the

DOI: 10.4324/9780367855741-4

growth of the rest of the economy. Endowed with rich natural and human resources, Karnataka is in the south-western region of India, spanning an area of 1,91,976 square kilometres, covering about 5.84 per cent of the total geographical area of India. Karnataka's agriculture is monsoon dependent as its dry land is second only to Rajasthan (Karnataka Human Development Report 2006). Problems continue to plague Karnataka's agriculture because of degrading natural resources, inefficient land holdings, low-value agriculture, institutional bottlenecks and so on (Deshpande 2006). Rao (2008) has highlighted that agriculture in the state of Karnataka is carrying the burden of policies marked by the neglect of backward areas and the poor, encouragement of wasteful use of water, electricity and other scarce inputs, dysfunctional subsidies, and negligence towards infrastructure and investments.

Against the backdrop of the failure of the economy to be inclusive in nature, as seen by the presence of disparities in developmental parameters, the need for the establishment and expansion of such facilities in rural areas has become imperative. Therefore, it is vital to understand the factors that determine/delimit the agricultural performance of the regions. When measured by the quantity/volume of provisions, infrastructure is seen as contributing to productivity improvements in agriculture. However, a pertinent question that arises is, despite provisions and creations of new facilities in rural areas, why is the agricultural performance not registering a corresponding improvement. Despite more investments, the outcomes of rural areas have not been encouraging. One plausible answer could be the differences in the quality of provisions and services of infrastructure. The deficiency in the utilization of the available services could possibly be attributed to the differences in information access and quality in provisions which can decrease the actual benefits of these structures (Chong and Calderon 2001). Like Hazell and Ramasamy (1991) stressed, improving access to quality provisions can spur agricultural growth.

Along with infrastructure assets, the viability of agriculture depends on its profitability and interaction among the region-specific features, village dynamics and other socio-economic factors. A study at the ground level on socio-economic, institutional and infrastructural constraints faced by farmers in pursuing farming profitably can throw light upon the interrelations between infrastructure and agriculture. In this regard, the present chapter seeks to understand how differences in quality and quantity of infrastructure influence the utilization of rural infrastructure assets for the benefit of agriculture.

Development and infrastructure quality: a brief review

Development literature recognizes the importance of expanding infrastructure provision for promoting growth in the economy. The review of empirical studies suggests that deficiencies in the provision of infrastructure are detrimental to the growth of the economy. The existing studies establish that investment in infrastructure helps in increasing farmers' access to input and output markets and increases consumer demand in rural areas, thereby facilitating the integration of less developed areas into national and international economies (Fan and Zhang 2004; Fan et al. 1999). In recent years, the role of infrastructure in development has gone beyond a mere understanding in terms of volumes and quantities in influencing economic growth. The quality of infrastructure offered also needs to be considered while evaluating its performance in propelling growth and development. This is in lieu of the fact that, despite significant additions to quantities of infrastructure provisions, it has not really translated into significant effects on growth. There has been a growing understanding of the distributive effect that infrastructure services achieve growth rather than the mere creation of new structures. Recent literature on infrastructure development has gone beyond mere explanations of infrastructure with regard to their quantity, to also include efficiency and quality of provisions. In this regard, the focus should also be on understanding differences in infrastructure quality which can possibly offer explanations for differences in economic growth across regions.

Most of the empirical studies have focused on the quantity or volume of infrastructure facilities while analysing the linkages between infrastructure and growth. International experience also shows that good infrastructure management means more than increasing the number of infrastructure stocks; it also involves improving the quality of infrastructure (World Bank 1994). The quality of infrastructure investments plays a crucial role in influencing agricultural output and growth. Demonstrating the importance of providing high-quality roads, Fan and Chan-Kang (2005) stress that differences in the quality of road infrastructure have implications for pro-poor growth. Thorat and Sirohi (2004) emphasized that besides providing an adequate quantity of infrastructure, ensuring the quality of provisions is a key to influencing productive activities. Escribano et al. (2010) describe infrastructure quality as having a pervasive influence on all areas of an economy and that low-quality infrastructure would limit production and access to markets, effectively causing adverse effects on the performance of the economy. The study assessed the impact of infrastructure quality on the TFP of African manufacturing firms by employing econometric techniques and found that poor quality electricity provisions and water outages affected the allocative efficiency of poor countries. Therefore, it is evident that providing better quality infrastructure has significant positive effects across different sectors of the economy. In relation to power infrastructure, it was noticed that the quality of electricity varies considerably, with outer regions suffering regular black-outs (World Bank 2008). Calderón and Servén (2004) provide an empirical estimation of the impact of infrastructure on economic growth, considering both quantity and quality measures of infrastructure using different specification tests, and concluded that income inequalities decline with higher quantities and better quality of infrastructure. Economic returns to total GDP were higher for investments in low-quality roads and additional investment in high-quality roads has fewer effects on poverty reduction than in low-quality roads (Fan and ChanKang 2005).

The effect of quality infrastructure was also studied in relation to income distribution in a few studies, however with mixed results (Calderón and Servén 2004; Senevirante and Sun 2013). For instance, Calderón and Servén (2004) showed that while infrastructure stocks had a significant effect, the association between quality of infrastructure and economic growth was less robust; while Senevirante and Sun (2013) found that better quality and quantity of infrastructure have a positive association with income distribution. Further, quantity and quality of provisions are not a substitute for one another, rather are important for the distribution of income. Bogetic and Fedderke (2005) stressed that poorer income groups had extremely limited access to infrastructure facilities. About 40 per cent of the growth differentials between low and high growth countries were due to differences in the effective use of infrastructure resources (Hulten 1996). The World Development Report (1994) establishes the linkages between infrastructure and development in the context of developing countries. The report points out that the policy focus should not only be on the quantity of infrastructure investment but also on the quality of investment. The report identifies that the basic cause of poor past performance has been inadequate institutional incentives for the provision of infrastructure.

Further, most studies in the Indian context have looked at the construction of aggregate indices of infrastructure to examine the impact of infrastructure on agricultural development. However, using these indices to explore the relationship with agricultural productivity has received relatively less attention from scholars. Earlier studies on agricultural development in India in general, and in Karnataka in particular did not adequately capture rural infrastructure as a growth promoting variable. Also, most studies examining the role of infrastructure on productivity have focused mainly on specific types of infrastructures exclusively in order to examine their influences on agriculture. Thus, the present paper attempts to look at the impact of the quality of rural infrastructure on agricultural productivity at a district level using a comprehensive list of rural infrastructure indicators by employing empirical specifications.

Conceptualizing infrastructure quality

Disentangling the concept and measurement of quality in analysing economic principles of infrastructure development is a challenging one. Generally, an analysis of infrastructure has been explained from the adequacy point of view. Provisions of infrastructure and additional investments by themselves are instruments of economic development. What has not been discussed much in empirical literature is the creation of infrastructure assets as per the needs of the region and how they are being used to reach the desired level of agricultural outcomes. Chong and Calderon (2001) found a significant association between increases in infrastructure stock and quality to a more equitable distribution of income, especially in developed countries. Gunatilaka (1999) pointed out that the effectiveness and utilization of an infrastructure asset would depend on characteristics such as quality, reliability and quantity. Fitzsimmons and Fitzsimmons (1994) emphasized that the location of service facilities was an important determinant of access to infrastructure services. Setting up infrastructure in rural areas requires huge investments and there is a trade-off between building new infrastructure to improve accessibility and upgrading the quality of existing infrastructure (Gibson and Olivia 2010).

When the quality of infrastructure is said to be important for it to be utilized optimally, the concept of quality attains both objective and subjective dimensions (Payson 1994). Objectively, the quality of infrastructure or service is its ability to perform its intended function at an optimum level. For example, the quality of irrigation would mean the physical status of canals, regularity of water supply and sufficiency of water supply. While there can be a way to ascertain the quality of canal construction, whether the irrigation regularity and quantity meets the needs of the farmers can be only obtained through a subjective evaluation of the farmers.

A similar situation is encountered in assessing the quality of other infrastructures. Each infrastructure, due to its very nature, would have different measures of quality since their purposes and the modalities in which they fulfil their purposes are different. The subjective perception of the quality of individual infrastructures is important in ensuring the optimum utilization of the facility/service. In the ideal world, the objective quality of a physical infrastructure and the perception of the beneficiaries regarding the quality of the service delivery will correspond. However, this may not be the case on the ground since the perception of the service delivery changes due to a variety of individual and socio-economic factors (Gabrysch and Campbell 2009).

All this makes the assessment of quality, especially of the different categories of infrastructure, a formidable challenge. An attempt is made to understand how utilization of the existing infrastructure might be enhanced from the quality dimension. It may also point to a direction whereby further studies and analysis can gravitate towards making infrastructure more impactful in boosting agricultural development. This chapter considers both objective factors that make up the quality of infrastructure/service delivery and subjective assessment of the farmers regarding the perceived quality of the infrastructure.

Dimensions of infrastructure assessment

In general, the chapter considers infrastructure as those facilities and services which not only facilitate improvements in agricultural production but also help farmers to better their welfare.

The purpose of the analysis is to understand the different aspects that govern a farmer to use the infrastructure services in the village for improving agricultural production. The paper attempts to include dimensions of availability, accessibility and quality as the basic set of parameters determining the utilization of infrastructure assets and services in rural areas.

Availability of infrastructure

Availability of infrastructure facilities is a prerequisite for access to infrastructure facilities and services. The provisions or the expansions of facilities by the government need to take into consideration the needs of the region where they are being provided. The availability of productivity-improving infrastructure enables the farmers to make appropriate farming decisions.

Accessibility of infrastructure

Accessibility to these facilities largely depends on physical access, affordability and access to information. It is important to note that availability does not ensure access to these facilities. The physical accessibility would refer to the distance to these provisions like travel time and waiting time to access these services. Stifel and Minten (2008) note that besides the quality of infrastructure, the distance between the market and farm would lead to productivity differences among farmers. Location of the facility and capability of infrastructure to deliver for the purposes it was created is an important determinant of accessibility. Another aspect that determines access is affordability such as travel costs, transaction costs or other charges. Accessibility has several key dimensions, including physical, information and economic accessibility (Osmani 2010). Access to services, however, cannot be ensured despite the expansion of facilities and services as it depends also on the farmer's ability and other socio-economic factors.

Quality of infrastructure

There is no consensus on the definition of what constitutes quality in literature. Since the nature of infrastructure is varied, a uniform understanding of quality may not be feasible. Quality infrastructure could mean those facilities/services which maximize the welfare or utility of the farmer. Quality is that property of infrastructure without which the full potential of the provisions cannot be realized. It is the level to which an infrastructure is capable of delivering the intended results in actual conditions, relative to its full potential. Quality is the capacity of service or facility to fulfil its intended purpose consistently with operational efficiency. In other words, infrastructure quality can be understood as the services or assets that can function effectively as a whole, and where the incompetence or absence of any one of the dimensions can adversely influence their utilization, thereby affecting the agriculture performance. Quality of service itself would determine the kind of utilization of infrastructure facilities. The foundational parts of infrastructure, therefore, need to include dimensions of accessibility, affordability, and certain quality standards for their effective utilization.

Utilization of infrastructure

Utilization refers to the use of the available infrastructure facilities to achieve the desired objective. Utilization is the extent to which the intended users use the infrastructure facility for maximizing agricultural development. This depends on the availability, accessibility, affordability, quality of services. For instance, longer distances, travel time and higher costs can limit the use of these services. Further, awareness or information about the provisions and the skills to use the provisions determine the utilization of the provisions.

Thus, the chapter considers assessing the quantity and quality of the infrastructure such as irrigation, electricity, transport, telecommunication, extension services, market, and credit institutions. For instance, the distance to different facilities such as credit institutions, regulated markets and public transport stations is taken as an indicator because it defines the farmer's ability to access and utilize various other associated infrastructures which are beneficial for agriculture. Even as providing better physical infrastructure in the market is crucial, so is the need to provide proper storage infrastructure which is important for post-harvest management. Usage of telecommunication services has been included for agricultural purposes as an important variable explaining access to information that is helpful in making agricultural decisions. The importance of extension services on farming activities is seen through indirect effects. Evenson and Mwabu (1998) noted that extension services would impact on the unobserved productive aspects of farmers leading to gains in agricultural productivity.

Database and methodology

The focus of the analysis was on public provisions of infrastructure which would influence changes in agricultural performance in the context of Karnataka's economy. It was crucial to capture the complex factors that determine agricultural performance at the ground level. Such an understanding could be achieved through a primary survey which would give information not only at the village level but also from the perspective of farmers. The farmer questionnaire sought quantifiable data on different aspects of agricultural development starting from a general socio-economic profile of the farmers, agricultural information and, most importantly, aspects of rural infrastructure in the village. The parameters that were included are the availability of infrastructure, affordability, accessibility and quality of infrastructure needed for their utilization. The estimated effect of rural infrastructure needs to account for quality differences that could possibly explain differences in agriculture development.

The districts of Mandya and Bijapur were chosen in the sample based on various developmental indicators of agricultural and infrastructural development. The analysis attempts to provide an assessment of the quality and quantity of selected infrastructure available to 20 villages in these districts during the year 2013–14. The selection of villages and farmer households was carried out using stratified random sampling methodology. From each district, two taluks were selected based on their access to canal water and distance to district headquarters. Based on the distance from taluk headquarters, two clusters of villages were selected to include ten villages in total from each taluk. Further, from each village, ten representative farmers were selected based on random sampling to represent different classes of farming categories. In total, 20 villages and 200 farmers formed the sample of the study to explore the association between agriculture and infrastructure in the districts of Mandya and Bijapur.

The focus of the primary data analysis was on capturing the socio-demographic profile of the farmers, their access to infrastructure facilities and services in the village and quality differences in infrastructure provisions across the different districts. Descriptive analysis has mostly been used for the analysis of data. To arrive at an index of quality of rural infrastructure, principal component analysis was used to aggregate the quality parameters. The sub-indices of irrigation, electricity, transport, telecommunication, market, credit and extension services were obtained using principal component analysis, which were added up to arrive at the overall quality index. Thus, the farmer household analysis included assessing the quantity and quality of infrastructure provisions in the village in relation to agricultural development.

Composite index of quality of rural infrastructure

The present study considered infrastructure facilities to include irrigation, electricity, road transport, telecommunication, market, credit, extension services to measure their qualitative aspects through a primary survey. The sub-indices of each infrastructure type were arrived at using max–min normalization method. The basic formula for scaling a variable from 0 to 1 is as follows:

$$\frac{X_i - X_{min}}{X_{max} - X_{min}}$$

Once the variables were converted to scale free values, the scale free indicators of infrastructure development were combined into sub-indices of quality of rural infrastructure using principal component analysis. The overall quality index was obtained by aggregating the sub-indices of infrastructure quality.

The paper examines the association between availability, quality and utilization of infrastructure in rural areas in relation to agricultural development which is proxied by using the measure of agricultural income per acre. Using the data obtained from the individual farmers, the relationship of perceived quality of infrastructure to its utilization and the income of farmers is assessed. The quality of this infrastructure based on the perception/opinions of the respondents is also being examined.

Discussion of field survey results

For analysing the impact of differences in quantity and quality of infrastructure provisions in rural areas, the study surveyed 200 farmers in 20 villages of the districts of Mandya and Bijapur and included eight types of infrastructure to include irrigation, electricity, road transport, telecommunication, market, formal credit institutions and extension services. The present section discusses the results of the primary survey used to analyse the quality aspects of rural infrastructure. The distribution of economic and institutional infrastructure facilities has been presented as per taluks.

The general socio-economic profile of the sample farmers is presented in Table 4.1. The farmer households were divided into five categories such as marginal farmers (less than 2.5 acres), small farmers operating between 2.5 and 5 acres, medium farmers with holdings between 5.01 and 10 acres and large farmers with landholding above 10 acres. Of the total 200 farmer households, marginal and small holdings accounted for the relatively large proportion (73 per cent) of the farmer households. Large farmer households constituted only 10 per cent in Mandya district while accounting for 48 per cent in Bijapur. The age distribution of the farmers surveyed is more biased towards the middle age group, 41 to 50 years, constituting about 31 per cent. As per the field survey, 40 per cent of the farmers had no formal education and about 42 per cent of the farmers reported having undergone primary and secondary years of schooling.

Overall, the survey revealed that the regions have displayed differential access and quality performances across infrastructure types. Mandya district seemed to enjoy greater access to quality of infrastructure provisions while some Bijapur districts suffered mainly due to lack of adequate access to irrigation, electricity, transport networks and credit. It is thus clear that the ground-level understanding of infrastructure quality indicates the need for local planning as the needs and characteristic features of each region are different. Besides developing only objective measures of quality such as the number of facilities, the perceptions of farmers in accessing

Table 4.1 General profile of the farmer households

Particulars	*Category*	*Mandya*	*Nagamangala*	*Bijapur*	*Badami*	*Total*
Type of farmer	Marginal (<2.5 acres)	24 (48)	19 (38)	6 (10)	8 (16)	57 (28)
	Small (2.5–5 acres)	19 (38)	28 (56)	20 (40)	24 (48)	91 (45)
	Medium (5.0–10 acres)	3 (6)	2 (4)	8 (16)	10 (20)	23 (12)
	Large (>10.00 acres)	4 (8)	1 (2)	16 (32)	8 (16)	29 (15)
Age (years)	Up to 40 years	11 (22)	12 (24)	15 (30)	20 (40)	58 (29)
	41 to 50 years	21 (42)	7 (14)	20 (40)	15 (30)	63 (31)
	51 to 60 years	13 (26)	12 (24)	12 (24)	11 (22)	48 (24)
	Above 60 years	5 (10)	19 (38)	3 (6)	4 (8)	31 (16)
Education	Illiterate	33 (66)	10 (20)	16 (32)	21 (42)	80 (40)
	Primary	5 (10)	11 (22)	6 (12)	12 (24)	34 (17)
	Secondary/ High Secondary	9 (18)	12 (24)	19 (38)	10 (20)	50 (25)
	PUC	1 (2)	7 (14)	6 (12)	3 (9)	17 (8)
	Diploma/Degree and above	2 (4)	10 (20)	3 (6)	4 (8)	19 (10)
Farming experience (years)	Up to 10 years	3 (6)	5 (10)	2 (4)	4 (8)	14 (7)
	11 to 20 years	7 (14)	7 (14)	15 (30)	22 (44)	51 (25)
	21 to 30 years	15 (30)	9 (18)	18 (36)	11 (22)	53 (27)
	Above 30 years	25 (50)	29 (58)	15 (30)	13 (26)	82 (41)
Social group	SC/ST	10 (20)	15 (30)	21 (42)	21 (42)	67 (34)
	OBC	9 (18)	9 (18)	22 (44)	18 (36)	58 (29)
	General	31 (62)	26 (52)	7 (14)	11 (22)	75 (38)
Annual agricultural income per acre (Rs)	Up to 20000	35 (70)	48 (96)	29 (58)	33 (66)	145 (72)
	20001 to 40000	8 (16)	1 (2)	5 (10)	15 (30)	29 (15)
	40001 to 60000	0	1 (2)	11 (22)	2 (4)	14 (7)
	Above 60000	7 (14)	0	5 (10)	0	12 (6)

Source: Field Survey, 2013–14.
Note: Figures in parentheses indicate percentages.

and utilizing the infrastructure need to be considered (Diener and Suh 1997). Therefore, the perceptions of farmers on availability, access and quality of infrastructure have been considered in measurable quantifiable terms and combined into a composite index of infrastructure quality so that the surveyed villages can be assessed with regard to their infrastructure development levels (Ahmed and Donovan 1992). The overall quality of infrastructure index was constructed combining individual infrastructure indices consisting of both quantity and quality measures.

This section analyses the determinants of agricultural incomes across the sample villages in a simple linear regression framework. Table 4.2 provides the descriptive statistics of the variables used in the regression analysis. The infrastructure considered for analysing the quantity and quality parameters comprise of irrigation, electricity, road, telecommunication, market, credit and extension services. Further, an overall index of infrastructure quality has also been computed to capture their influences on agricultural income. All the infrastructure quality indices are taken

Table 4.2 Descriptive statistics of variables used in regression analysis

Variable	*Observations*	*Mean*	*Std. Dev*	*Min*	*Max*
Ln Agricultural income per acre	200	9.87	0.75	8.21	13.02
Infrastructure quantity and quality indices					
Ln Irrigation index	200	0.31	0.46	0	1.27
Ln Electricity index	200	0.57	0.38	–0.43	1.07
Ln Road index	200	-0.21	0.41	–1.18	0.36
Ln ICT index	200	0.55	0.64	–0.58	1.62
Ln Market index	200	–1.91	1.34	–3.94	0.99
Ln Credit index	200	0.69	0.29	–0.14	1.02
Ln Extension index	200	0.23	0.33	–0.29	1.01
Ln Overall infrastructure index	200	2.11	0.30	1.25	2.82
Other Variables					
Years of education	200	6.90	5.62	0	17
Type of farmer (1= Medium or large, 0, otherwise)	200	0.26	0.44	0	1
Regional dummy (1=South, 0 otherwise)	200	0.50	0.50	0	1

Source: Author's calculation.

in their logarithmic forms while years of education are taken as the actual number of years of formal education. Dummy variables were considered for type of farmer and regions, where 1 indicates medium or large farmer and 1 indicates those farmers belonging to the southern district of Karnataka to factor in the region-specific features, respectively.

The estimates of the regression framework for the determinants of agricultural income with infrastructure variables as the main set of explanatory variables are presented in Table 4.3. The multivariate analyses find supporting evidence for infrastructure quality as significantly influencing agricultural income. The coefficient of determination in the model was 54 per cent suggesting that the explanatory variables explain 54 per cent of the variability on the utilization of infrastructure facilities in the farmer's household in the study area.

Infrastructure factors significantly influencing agricultural income per acre were road extension facilities. The regression estimates show that the coefficient of extension services was positive and highly significant at 1 per cent. Extension services in the village are essential for the acceleration of farm incomes, thereby suggesting that there is a need to focus on providing agricultural oriented training and demonstrations by extension personnel. The regional dummy variable is statistically significant at 5 per cent, indicating that southern regions have better farm incomes. The coefficient of type of farmer was significant and had a positive relationship with income, indicating that medium and large farmers can produce more, diversify their agricultural operations, store and sale without having to go for distress sales, leading to greater marketable surplus and incomes.

The elasticity coefficient of electricity index was 0.15, suggesting that providing better quality of electricity in terms of greater reliable hours of supply and fewer voltage fluctuations

Table 4.3 Regression estimates of determinants of agricultural income

Dependent Variable: Agricultural income per acre

Variables	*Coefficient*
Log irrigation	0.07 (0.66)
Log electricity	0.15 (1.52)
Log road	0.19 (1.85)*
Log ICT	0.07 (1.11)
Log market	–0.02 (–0. 67)
Log credit	0.06 (0.47)
Log extension	0.44 (3. 77)***
Regional dummy (1=South, 0 otherwise)	0.26 (2. 47)**
Type of farmer (1=medium or large; 0, otherwise)	1.18 (12. 51)***
Constant	9.15 (65. 3)***
No of observations	200
R2	0.54
F (9, 190) = 25.15	Prob> F= 0.000

Source: Author's calculation.

Note: Figures in parentheses indicate t values.

***, ** and * denote significance at 1%, 5% and 10% levels, respectively.

increases agricultural incomes by about 15 per cent. Because increasing commercialization of agriculture and growing dependency on mechanization for farming operations, improvements in village access to reliable electricity will have a positive impact on household income. The coefficient value of 0.07 of the irrigation index suggests that better access and reliability in the supply of water for irrigation is positively associated with household income from agriculture. However, the coefficient of irrigation index was not significant. The coefficient of road condition although insignificant, had a positive effect on farm incomes. It is well understood that good quality roads always create better access to markets, credit and other services and a lack of the same can lead to greater transport costs, and act as a constraint in seeking benefits from market reforms. The coefficient of telecommunication, formal credit infrastructure had a positive relationship with farmers' income. It is crucial to have easy access to credit as an easy credit flow always assists in meeting the working capital requirements of the farmer.

Determinants of agricultural income using the overall index of infrastructure

The empirical results of the determinants of agricultural income using the overall index of infrastructure quality are presented in Table 4.4. The results of the regression model reveal that the

Table 4.4 Regression estimates of agricultural income using index of infrastructure
Dependent Variable: Agricultural income

Variables	*Coefficient*
Log overall infrastructure index	0.48
	(3.84)***
Education years	–0.02
	(–2.34)*
Regional dummy	0.15
(1=South, 0 otherwise)	(1.81)***
Type of farmer	1.17
(1= Medium or large, 0, otherwise)	(12.62)**
Constant	8.59
	(32.17)***
No. of observations	200
R2	0.53
F (4, 195) = 55.24	Prob>F=0.000

Source: Author's calculation.
Note: Figures in parentheses indicate t values.
***, ** and * denote significance at 1%, 5% and 10% levels, respectively.

quality of the overall infrastructure has a positive and significant effect on agricultural income per acre of the farmer. Further, years in formal schooling has been taken to explain agricultural income per acre. The elasticity of years of education is negative and significant at 10 per cent level; probably suggesting that with better access to formal education, people may seek non-agricultural employment. A farmer with better educational attainment may tend to look towards employment opportunities in urban centres.

The elasticity coefficient for regional dummy was positive and significant at 1 per cent level indicating that southern regions have better incomes than the northern taluks. The coefficients of farm size as indicated by type of farmer had a positive relationship with agricultural income per acre. In the estimated income model, the coefficient of determination was 53 per cent, implying that the power of independent variables explained variation in agricultural incomes of farm households. The overall index of infrastructure quality has a robust relationship with agricultural income.

Determinants of utilization of rural infrastructure

Besides constructing indices of individual infrastructure types such as irrigation, electricity, transport, market and so on, the variables defining different dimensions of assessment of quality were combined. For this purpose, the access, quality and utilization variables of all types of infrastructure were combined to arrive at sub-indices such as infrastructure access index, quality index and utilization index. Firstly, variables were made scale free by using the min–max method and then aggregated the transformed variables into sub-indices of quality of rural infrastructure. The main purpose behind this exercise was to understand the extent to which quality played its role in the utilization of the available facilities and services. Then, these quality indices were incorporated in a regression framework to examine each of their effects on agricultural incomes.

Table 4.5 Correlation between infrastructure indices

Indices	*Access Index*	*Quality Index*	*Utilization Index*
Access index	1		
Quality index	0.16	1	
Utilization index	0.49	0.43	1

Source: Author's calculation.

Table 4.6 Determinants of utilization of infrastructure in rural areas

	Dependent Variable: Utilization index of infrastructure
Variables	*Coefficient*
Ln Access index	0.49 (6.67) ★★★
Ln Quality index	0.25 (6.37) ★★★
Ln Income	0.01 (0.16)
Years in education	0.001 (0.39)
Type of farmer (1= Medium or large, 0, otherwise)	0.03 (0.48)
Constant	8.59 (0.21)
No. of observations	200
R2	0.35
F (5, 194) = 22.07	Prob>F=0.000

Source: Author's calculation.
Note: Figures in parentheses indicate t values.
★★★, ★★ and ★ denote significance at 1%, 5% and 10% levels, respectively.

The association between different dimensions of infrastructure such as access, quality and utilization indices was determined using correlation analysis. Pearson correlation coefficients were used to compute the correlation coefficients of different dimensions of infrastructure. As shown in Table 4.5, the correlation coefficients suggest that there is a relatively strong association between infrastructure access and utilization. Infrastructure quality and utilization had a correlation of 0.43, indicating that areas with better quality facilities showed better usage of services. The strong association between the different dimensions of infrastructure indices only suggests their stability.

An analysis was carried out to examine the role played by infrastructure access and quality in determining utilization. The results of the regression for the determinants of utilization of infrastructure facilities are given in Table 4.6. The explanatory variables consist of infrastructure access, infrastructure quality, income, years in education and type of farmer. The coefficient of access index was 0.49 and significant at 1 per cent level, suggesting that improved access to facilities and services determines utilization of services. Better access to services in rural areas would simply imply greater mobility, better outcomes and greater engagement in productive activities. The coefficient of infrastructure quality was positive and significant at 1 per cent, indicating that improvements in the quality of infrastructure would mean greater utilization of these services. The explanatory power of the model was 35 per cent. The other variables such as income, years in education and type of farmer showed a positive association, though were not significant.

Conclusion

A wide variety of socio-economic and political factors govern the actual development of the agricultural sector in India. Despite rapid strides in improving agricultural performance in recent decades, the analysis has shown that a wide disparity in access to markets, inefficiency in the use of existing infrastructural provisions and poor formal credit availability can cripple agricultural productivity. The vast dry areas, varying climatic conditions and market risks can limit the growth potential of the agricultural sector in Karnataka. The analysis reveals that a lack of access and poor quality of infrastructure hinder the growth in agricultural incomes of rural households in Karnataka. Therefore, supporting infrastructure and policy can go a long way in stabilising agricultural productivity.

Overall, it is evident that infrastructure is a key driver of agricultural growth in Karnataka. When the results are analysed using both indicators of quantity and quality across different types of economic, institutional and social infrastructures, and the findings highlight that not only volume and access but also the quality of provisions play a significant role in utilization of the existing structures to achieve higher levels of development. The analysis of the impact of infrastructure on agricultural development confirms and reinforces that investments in rural areas are crucial to accelerate productivity growth in agriculture. The investment in rural areas has largely been demand driven and the public authorities have generally not created excess capacities in case of any further need. The neo-liberal period has witnessed an explicit recognition of the role of agriculture with the rest of the economy along with the need to provide a favourable investment climate to absorb the benefits of technological progress and accelerate the pace of modernization of agriculture. However, significant stagnation or low yield in selected food grains has weakened the pace of agricultural productivity growth in Karnataka leading to widening disparities. Therefore, efficient utilization of the infrastructure provisions is crucial and can act as a good stimulus for achieving greater productivity and minimizing regional disparities.

Optimal utilization of existing infrastructure is a result of a combination of factors. Utilization of some infrastructure is conditional on the availability and quality of other infrastructure and it is possible that the lowest common denominator determines the overall utilization of infrastructure. Thus, the link between access and quality with their utilization is positive and statistically significant, reiterating that quality plays a crucial role in influencing utilization. Improvement in the quality of existing infrastructure should also be on the policy agenda to ensure adequate utilization rather than the mere creation of new facilities. However, it is important to note that infrastructure provision is not a surrogate for better quality of infrastructure resources. Since infrastructural facilities have long-term impacts that go beyond immediate requirements, it is crucial to prioritize investments to augment the development process over time. The issues that arise from inadequacies of infrastructure are complex in nature and thus require well-planned, region-specific, people-centred system-level planning.

References

Ahmed, Raisuddin, and Cynthia Donovan. 1992. *Issues of Infrastructural Development: A Synthesis of the Literature* (Vol. 1). Washington, DC: International Food Policy Research Institute (IFPRI).

Bhalla, Gurdarshan Singh, and Gurmail Singh. 2012. *Economic Liberalization and Indian Agriculture: A District Level Study*. New Delhi: Sage Publications.

Binswanger, Hans P., Shahidur R. Khandekar, and Mark R. Rosenzweig. 1989. *How Infrastructure and Financial Institutions Affect Agricultural Output and Investment in India.* Working Paper Series 163. Washington, DC: World Bank.

Birthal, Pratap S., Digvijay S. Negi, Awadesh K. Jha, and Dhiraj Singh. 2014. "Income Sources of Farm Households in India: Determinants Distributional Consequences and Policy Implications." *Agricultural Economics Research Review* 27 (1): 37–48.

Bogetic, Zeljko, and Johannes Fedderke. 2005. "Infrastructure and Growth in South Africa: Benchmarking, Productivity and Investment Needs." In Paper presented at Economic Society of South Africa (ESSA) Conference. Durban, South Africa, September 17. 1–58.

Bolt, Richard. 2004. *Accelerating Agriculture and Rural Development for Inclusive Growth: Policy Implications for Developing Asia.* ERD Policy Brief No. 29. Manila: Asian Development Bank.

Byerlee, Derek, Xinshen Diao, and Chris Jackson. 2005. *Agriculture, Rural Development, and Pro-Poor Growth: Country Experiences in the Post-Reform Era.* Agriculture and Rural Development Discussion Paper 21. Washington, DC: World Bank.

Calderón, César, and Luis Servén. 2004. *The Effects of Infrastructure Development on Growth and Income Distribution.* World Bank Policy Research Working Paper No. 3400. Washington, DC: World Bank. doi:10.1596/1813-9450-3400.

Chong, Alberto, and César Calderón. 2001. *Volume and Quality of Infrastructure and the Distribution of Income: An Empirical Investigation.* Working Paper. Washington, DC: Inter-American Development Bank, Research Department No.450.

Deshpande, R. S. 2006. *Karnataka's Agricultural Policy 2006.* Bangalore: Department of Agriculture and Horticulture, Government of Karnataka.

Diener, Ed, and Eunkook Suh. 1997. "Measuring Quality of Life: Economic, Social, and Subjective Indicators." *Social Indicators Research* 40 (1): 186–216.

Escribano, Alvaro, Luis J. Guasch, and Jorge Pena. 2010. *Assessing the Impact of Infrastructure Quality on Firm Productivity in Africa: Cross-Country Comparisons Based on Investment Climate Surveys from 1999 to 2005.* Policy Research Working Paper 5191. Washington, DC: World Bank.

Evenson, Robert E., and Germano Mwabu. 1998. *The Effects of Agricultural Extension on Farm Yields in Kenya.* Center Discussion Paper No. 798. Economic Growth Center, Yale University, Economic Growth Center, New Haven, CT.

Fan, Shenggen, and Connie Chan-Kang. 2005. "Is Small Beautiful? Farm Size, Productivity, and Poverty in Asian Agriculture." *Agricultural Economics* 32: 135–146.

Fan, Shenggen, Peter Hazell, and Sukhadeo Thorat. 1999. *Linkages between Government Spending, Growth, Poverty in Rural India.* Washington, DC: International Food Policy Research Institute.

Fan, Shenggen, and Xiaobo Zhang. 2004. "Infrastructure and Regional Economic Development in Rural China." *China Economic Review* 15 (2): 203–214.

Fitzsimmons, JamesA., and Mona J. Fitzsimmons. 1994. "Service Facility Location." In *Service Management for Competitive Advantage*, 130–157. New York: McGraw Hill .

Gabrysch, Sabine, and Oona M. Campbell. 2009. "Still Too Far to Walk: Literature Review of the Determinants of Delivery Service Use." *BMC Pregnancy and Childbirth* 9 (34): 1–18. doi:10.1186/1471-2393-9-34.

Gibson, John, and Susan Olivia. 2010. "The Effect of Infrastructure Access and Quality on Non-Farm Enterprises in Rural Indonesia." *World Development* 38 (5): 717–26. https://doi.org/10.1016/j.worlddev.2009.11.010.

Gunatilaka, Ramani. 1999. "Rural Infrastructure Programmes for Poverty Reduction: Policy Issues from the Sri Lankan Experience." In Paper prepared for the Regional Consultation on WDR2001 for South Asia on Poverty Reduction and Social Progress: New Trends and Emerging Lessons. Rajendrapur, Bangladesh, April 4–6.

Hazell, Peter B. R., and C. Ramaswamy. 1991. *The Green Revolution Reconsidered: The Impact of High-Yielding Rice Varieties in South India.* Baltimore: Johns Hopkins University Press.

Hulten, Charles R. 1996. *Infrastructure Capital and Economic Growth: How Well You Use It May Be More Important than How Much You Have.* NBER Working Paper No. 5847. Cambrdige, MA: National Bureau of Economic Research. 1–37.

Jain, R., and M. Parshad. 2007. *The Working Group on Risk Management in Agriculture for the Eleventh Five Year Plan (2007–2012).* New Delhi: Government of India, Planning Commission.

OECD. 2006. *Promoting Pro-Poor Growth: Agriculture*. Paris: Organisation for Economic Co-operation and Development (OECD).

O'Gorman, Melanie. 2015. "Africa's Missed Agricultural Revolution: A Quantitative Study of the Policy Options." *The BE Journal of Macroeconomics* 15 (2): 561–502.

Osmani, Siddiqur R. 2010. "Realising the Right to Development in Bangladesh: Progress and Challenges." *The Bangladesh Development Studies* XXXIII (1 and 2): 25–90.

Payson, Steve. 1994. *Quality Measurement in Economics: New Perspectives on the Evolution of Goods and Services*. Aldershot: Edward Elgar Publishing.

Rao, Vidyananda Mohan. 2008. *Sustainability of Indian Agriculture: Towards an Assessment*. Working Paper No.193. Bangalore: Institute for Social and Economic Change.

Schultz, Theodore W. 1964. *Transforming Traditional Agriculture*. New Haven: Yale University Press.

Seneviratne, Dulani, and Sun Yan. 2013. *Infrastructure and Income Distribution in ASEAN-5: What are the Links?* IMF Working Paper No. 13/41. Washington: International Monetary Fund.

Stifel, David, and Bart Minten. 2008. "Isolation and Agricultural Productivity." *Agricultural Economics* 39 (1): 1–15. doi:10.1111/j.1574-0862.2008.00310.x.

Straub, Stéphane, and Akiko Terada-Hagiwara. 2011. "Infrastructure and Growth in Developing Asia." *Asian Development Review* 28 (1): 119–156.

Thorat, Sukhadeo, Ramesh Chand, and G. Bhalla. 2003. *Rural Public Investment in India: Lessons for Growth and Poverty Reduction*. New Delhi: International Food Policy Research Institute.

Thorat, Sukhadeo, and Smita Sirohi. 2004. "State of the Indian Farmer: A Millennium Study." Vol. 6, in *Rural Infrastructure*. New Delhi: Government of India, Ministry of Agriculture and Academic Foundation.

Timmer, C. Peter. 2002. "Agriculture and Economic Development." Vol. 2A, in *Handbook of Agricultural Economics-Agriculture and its External Linkages*, edited by Bruce L. Gardner and Gordon C. Rausser. Amsterdam: Elsevier Science Publishers.

World Bank. 1994. *World Development Report 1994: Infrastructure for Development*. New York: Oxford University Press.

World Bank. 2008. *Spending for Development: Making the Most of Indonesia's New Opportunities*. Washington, DC: World Bank.

5

ENVIRONMENTAL SUSTAINABILITY OF ECONOMIC REFORMS IN INDIA

Haripriya Gundimeda, Gopal Kadekodi and Aparajita Singh

Introduction

Reforms, the world over, are part of human evolution for welfare, starting from looking for fire for cooking and heating, clearing land for agriculture to produce food, languages for communication and so on. The process always involved the deployment of resources such as labour, man-made capital and natural resources. Human history is full of instances of reforms on skill development of labour, conversion and use of natural resources such as forests, minerals, fossil fuels, water, air, biodiversity, wildlife and many such natural and environmental endowments, the creation of man-made capital along with institutionalizing nation states and laws of governance on all resources (Westphal Treaty of 1648). The process took on a new dimension about three centuries ago, by incorporating 'development' in addition to welfare. At every stage in this history of reforms, 'sustainability' of human welfare has been the main criterion, constantly mentioned and deliberated. But in the most recent period, mankind has added environmental and ecological concerns as a warning to push the idea of development and sustainable development further.

The written documentary evidence shows that Kautilya distinguished between land and forest and proposed several sustainability criteria for better management almost 1850 years ago. His model of sustainable development was based on the ability to manage natural resources based on the assimilation of idealist, moral and realistic values of human life. The classification proposed by Kautilya echoes with the present-day literature on the use and non-use values of environmental resources. The great Chinese thinker, Confucius in 550 BC mentioned reform in price and management by talking about value and price and suggested a large number of producers but few thrifty consumers and suggested that the true price of the natural resource should be offered, and the modern thinking of sustainability reforms dwells on this model. The father of economics, Adam Smith, proposed a balanced approach between moral philosophy and economic development and called for balancing self-interest with social justice as part of his concept of sustainable development of the environment and society. J.S. Mill proposed the idea of a just 'stationary state' to accommodate both a utilitarian and model growth theory of private property, but with constraints and obligations of social, economic and ecological coexistence.

However, driven by neoclassical thinking, the last century witnessed economic growth-oriented development, with the key emphasis on balancing capital and labour as the main driver

 DOI: 10.4324/9780367855741-5

of sustainable growth (not development). This viewpoint was stressed by the earlier growth theory literature that growth rate was determined by the savings ratio and the capital–output ratio. Harrod (1939), Domar (1946), Solow (1974, 1986) showed that, depending on the labour capital substitution and diminishing returns of the inputs and technological progress, economics conditionally converge to a certain per capita income. These models did not pay much regard to the status of natural capital. The general viewpoint has been that technical progress can offset declining natural capital (Stiglitz 1974, Hartwick 1977, 1995, Dixit 1980, Baumol 1996). The importance of embodied knowledge and human capital in triggering economic growth has been emphasized by Barro and Sala-i-Martin (1995) and Romer (1990). However, none of the above theories recognized the role of natural capital.

During the 1970s, the publication of *Silent Spring* and *Limits to Growth* by Meadows et al. (1972) and the energy crisis indicated the limits to growth due to scarcity of natural resources. This led to the emergence of new growth theories with natural capital and environmental disamenities like pollution. Connor (1997) argues that today's environment problems are primarily because of world-scale expansion, industrial production, mass consumption, rapid transport and communication. The mounting environmental problems led to the discourse on sustainable development after the Brundtland commission and Rio Earth Summit, which caught the attention of policymakers as a panacea to resolve the environmental problems. Sustainable development is the 'development that meets the needs of the present without compromising the ability of future generations to meet their own needs' (Brundtland 1987). The United Nations has given targets to all countries to reach the millennium development goals, which were soon replaced by sustainable development goals. The need for measuring sustainable development has shifted the attention from GDP growth as a measure of welfare to the changes in comprehensive wealth and inclusive wealth (Dasgupta 2001, Arrow et al. 2012, UNU-IHDP and UNEP 2012, 2014, Urban Institute and UNEP 2018), which accounts for all capital –produced, natural, human and social capital.

Driven by a severe balance of payments crisis by the end of the 1990s, India embarked on a path of economic liberalization and carried out a series of reforms as part of the structural adjustment programme, and has emerged as one of the fastest growing economies of the world. The average growth rate in India during the period 1990–2018 can be categorized into three phases: the 1990s maintained an average decadal growth of 5.6%; average decadal growth increased to 6.8% during the 2000s; and then India experienced a slight deceleration in growth from 2010 resulting from poor industrial growth and global slowdown (see Figure 5.1). In terms of the social indicators, India's performance has been better post 1991. India has also successfully lifted people above the poverty line as the number of poor reduced from 45.3% in the 1990s to 21.9% in 2011–12 (according to the last census of 2011) (Compendium of Environment Statistics 2016b). The latest research projects show that India has drastically reduced its poverty to around 3% by the end of 2019 and India will be out of the list of top ten countries with extreme poverty by 2030 (Gupta 2019).

There is little doubt that the reforms have paid off as the economic performance improved. However, higher GDP does not necessarily translate into a higher quality of life. Have these reforms help sustain environmental resources, in pollution reduction or imbibing environmental policies? And have these reforms helped in improving the quality of life when viewed from the perspective of environment and human health? The relationship between increasing national income and sustainable development is not straightforward (Tisdell 2001).

GDP does not measure the impact of production activities on the quality of the environment and natural resources and thus on human well-being. Substituting natural capital to achieve higher growth can impact the health of people which could impact human capital, and thus

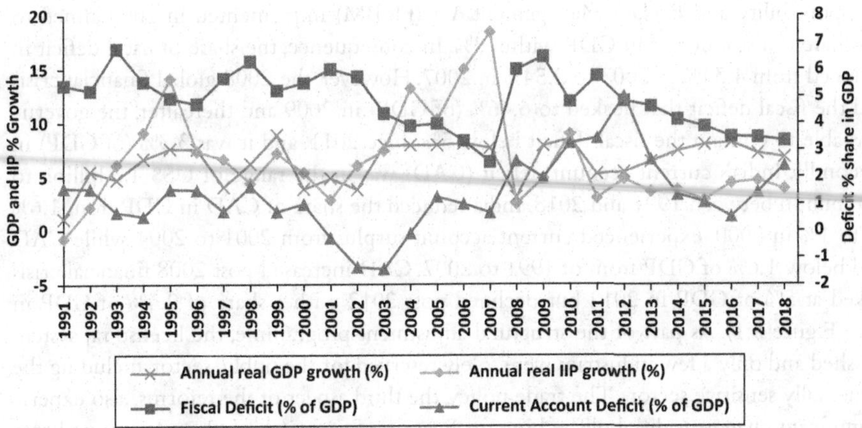

Figure 5.1 Trends in growth of real GDP, real IIP, fiscal deficit and current account deficit from 1991 to 2018. *Source*: Author's creation based on data from World Bank and Reserve Bank of India (RBI) Handbook of Statistics.

produced capital (Gundimeda 2018). As it has been three decades since globalization in India it is interesting to study whether the economic reforms have improved the quality of life viewed from the sustainability perspective of the environment and human health. Or has the growth been 'crowded out' by degrading environmental quality?

The objective of this chapter is to look into whether the reforms have succeeded in attaining environmental sustainability which is one of the major development policy challenges for the country. The chapter is structured as follows: the second section describes the recent trends in the macro- and micro level economic indicators. Most of them, directly and indirectly measure the well-being of people. The third section focuses on the interactions between these economic indicators and the environment. The fourth section discusses various policy approaches currently in place for environmental sustainability and how these issues might be challenging to economic growth and the fifth section provides the conclusion.

Economic reforms and their impact on economic performance

India has recorded good economic achievements in the last three decades. This period has witnessed two distinct types of economic reforms in India. For the sake of convenience, the first one will be termed macroeconomic reforms. Substantially, this refers to the June 1991 announcements of economic reforms in India, often labelled as liberalization, Privatization and Globalization. The second will be termed micro reforms like the decentralized development programs or the energy sector reforms. This can be basically dated as the 1992 (73rd and 74th Amendments)[1] Constitutional Amendment to institute decentralized developmental rural and urban institutions, and the 2006 Constitutional amendments introducing the Employment Guarantee Scheme, empowering people to be entitled to employment for up to 100 days per year (Ministry of Rural Development 2013).

GDP has increased 5.5 times since 1991. The average growth rate in India was 5.6% between 1991 and 2000, 6.75% between 2001 and 2010 and 6.82% between 2011 and 2018. The prime reason for reforms being initiated in India was to reduce the fiscal deficit. Figure 5.1 shows that the share of fiscal deficit in GDP was above 5% between 1991 and 2002. The

Fiscal Responsibility and Budget Management Act (FRBM) implemented in 2003 aimed to limit the share of fiscal deficit in GDP within 3%. In consequence, the share of fiscal deficit in GDP reduced from 4.34% in 2003 to 2.54% in 2007. However, the 2008 global financial crisis increased the fiscal deficit that peaked to 6.46% (of GDP) in 2009 and thereafter, the government was able to contain the fiscal deficit below 5% since 2011, and it was 3.3% (of GDP) in 2018. Secondly, India's current account deficit (CAD) was in the range of US$ 4.3 billion to US$ 65.6 billion between 1991 and 2018. India reduced the share of CAD in GDP from 1.6% in 1991 to 1% in 2000, experienced current account surplus from 2001 to 2004 while CAD remained below 1.6% of GDP from of 1991 to 2007. CAD increased post 2008 financial crisis and peaked at 5% of GDP in 2012 but declined post 2012 with a share of 2.4% of GDP in 2018 (See Figure 5.1). As part of the structural adjustment programme, the license raj system was abolished and only a few industries were solely reserved for the public sector, including the environmentally sensitive sectors. The trade policy, the third aspect of the reforms, also experienced significant change. India abolished import licensing for capital goods and intermediates, eased quantitative restrictions and switched to a flexible exchange rate regime. The liberalization policies boosted India's trade which increased steadily from 14% of GDP in 1991 to 20% in 2001. The share of trade in GDP increased progressively post 2000 from 20% (in 2001) to a peak of 43% in 2008. However, the 2008 financial crisis and continued global slowdown affected Indian exports, and the total trade share in GDP had reduced to 30% in 2018 (see Figure 5.2), typically dominated by the oil, gems and jewellery, service sector, petroleum products and industrial components. The fourth important aspect of the reform was to lift control on foreign exchange inflow in India. Many sectors were placed under the automatic approval route for FDI, especially after 2000. There was an increase in the share of foreign direct investment (FDI) in GDP from 0.02% in 1991 to the highest of 3.6% in 2008. The 2008 financial crisis also affected the foreign inflow, whose share in GDP reduced post 2008 to 1.59% in 2018, as can be seen from Figure 5.2.

As income increases, the role of the primary sector declines and India is no exception. The share of agriculture in GDP has decreased steadily from 26.9% in 1990 to 21.6% in 2000 and the decline continued to 17% in 2010 and to 14.6% in 2019 owing to service-led growth in India (World Bank Data). However, approximately 43.21% of the workforce are still engaged in the sector. The Kuznets curve shows that as per capita income increases, inequality initially

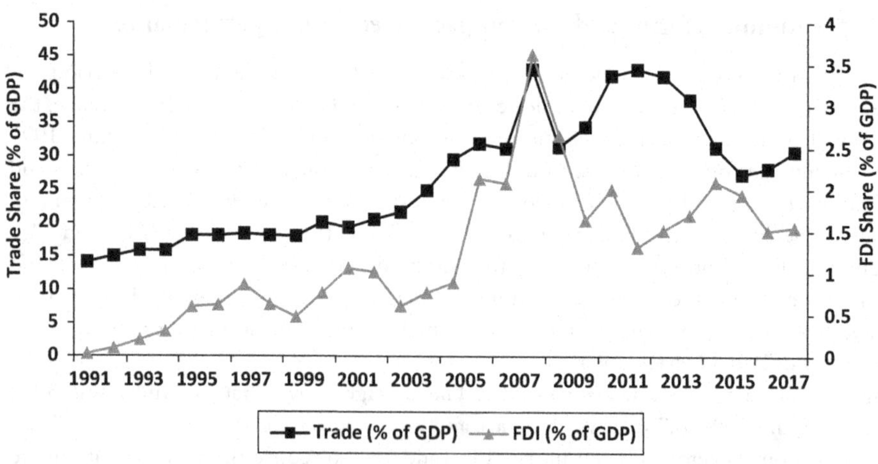

Figure 5.2 Flow of trade and FDI (% of GDP) from 1991 to 2018. *Source:* World Bank Data.

widens and later decreases. It remains to be seen whether we have reached the point of influx yet as the economic disparity seems to be widening; 77.4% of India's wealth is concentrated in the hands of the top 10% of the population (Samuel 2019). India's Gini coefficient for wealth increased to 0.74 in 2012 from 0.65 in 1991 (Dang and Lanjouw 2018). Although India has shown some improvement in gender disparity ratio from 2006 to 2018 (see Table 5.1), there is still a lot of potential as India ranks 109 out of 149 countries in the global gender gap, having a global gender gap index of 0.61 (World Economic Forum 2018).

At the start of the reforms in 1991, India lacked in several social indicators (Dreze and Sen 1999). But post liberalization, India improved on its social indicators. India's adult literacy rate changed from 48.2% in 1991 to 74.3% in 2018. The Human Development Index (HDI) improved from 0.43 in 1990 to 0.64 in 2018. However, Figure 5.3 shows that India's HDI performance is not significant in comparison to other developing countries.

Talking of decentralized development as major economic reform in India, several major policy developments can be listed. Firstly, financial devolution was permitted up to the level

Table 5.1 Global gender gap of India between 2006 and 2018

	2006		*2018*	
	rank	*score*	*rank*	*score*
Global gender gap score	98	0.601	108	0.665
Economic participation and opportunity	110	0.397	142	0.385
Educational attainment	102	0.819	114	0.953
Health and survival	103	0.962	147	0.94
Political empowerment	20	0.227	19	0.382
Rank out of 149 countries	115		149	

Source: World Economic Forum 2018.

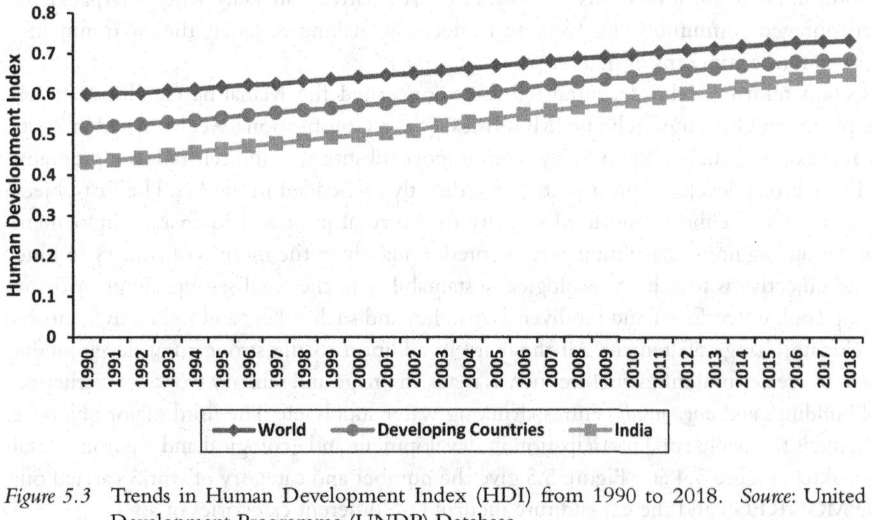

Figure 5.3 Trends in Human Development Index (HDI) from 1990 to 2018. *Source*: United Nations Development Programme (UNDP) Database.

Table 5.2 Annual budgetary allocation to Ministry of Panchayati Raj (MoPR)

Year	*Total budget allocation*	*MoPR allocation*	*MoPR share in total*
2004–05	477829	31	0.01
2005–06	514344	50	0.01
2006–07	563991	3826	0.68
2007–08	680521	4771	0.70
2008–09	750884	4781	0.64
2009–10	1020838	4781	0.47
2010–11	1108749	5171	0.47
2011–12	1257729	5251	0.42
2012–13	1490925	5350	0.36
2013–14	1665297	7000	0.42
2014–15	1794892	7000	0.39
2015–16	1777477	94	0.01
2016–17	1978060	768	0.04
2017–18	2146735	791	0.04
2018–19	2442213	825	0.03
2019–20	2786349	871	0.03
2020–21	3042230	900	0.03

Source: Indiabudget.gov.in.
Note: Figure in parenthesis denotes the percentage value of the total budget expenditure in that year.

of Gram Panchayat, to undertake developmental activities at the rural and urban levels. The Ministry of Panchayati Raj (MoPR) was created in 2004 and central budgetary allocations to the Ministry of Panchayat Raj to the tune of Rs 900 crore constituting 0.03% of the total central budget has been allocated as given in Table 5.2. However, in 2015–16, the budget declined drastically due to the slashing of funds for the Backward Region Grant Fund (BRGF) scheme, so the budget has decreased considerably since 2015. Among the 29 major functions identified and assigned to the panchayats, environmental sustainability is one of the tasks. Some examples are minor irrigation, social forestry, drinking water, fuel and fodder, non-conventional energy and such others. There are several success stories of participative leadership where 'Sarpanch' of villages encouraged community involvement in decision-making to tackle the environmental and socio-economic concerns of their areas.

The second reform at the decentralized level concerned the Mahatma Gandhi National Rural Employment Guarantee Scheme (MGNREGS) as a Constitutional Act launched in 2006, and under 'Make in India' program (early as an import substitution and self-reliance program) in 2015. Three broad development objectives are directly embedded in the Act. The first objective is to guarantee livelihood and food security to the rural poor and to create employment opportunities during non-agricultural periods, predominantly in the months of January to June. The second objective is to achieve ecological sustainability in the rural settings by prioritizing rejuvenating land, water, forest and biodiversity patches and such others and indirectly contributing to climate change abatement. All these are in addition to the strong rural development component to create rural infrastructure such as roads, drainage and sanitary works, construction of school buildings and *anganwadi* centres, drinking water supply etc. The third major objective of the scheme is to enable rural participation in development and ecological and environmental decision-making. Figure 5.4 and Figure 5.5 give the number and category of works carried out under the MGNREGS and the expenditure incurred on different categories of assets.

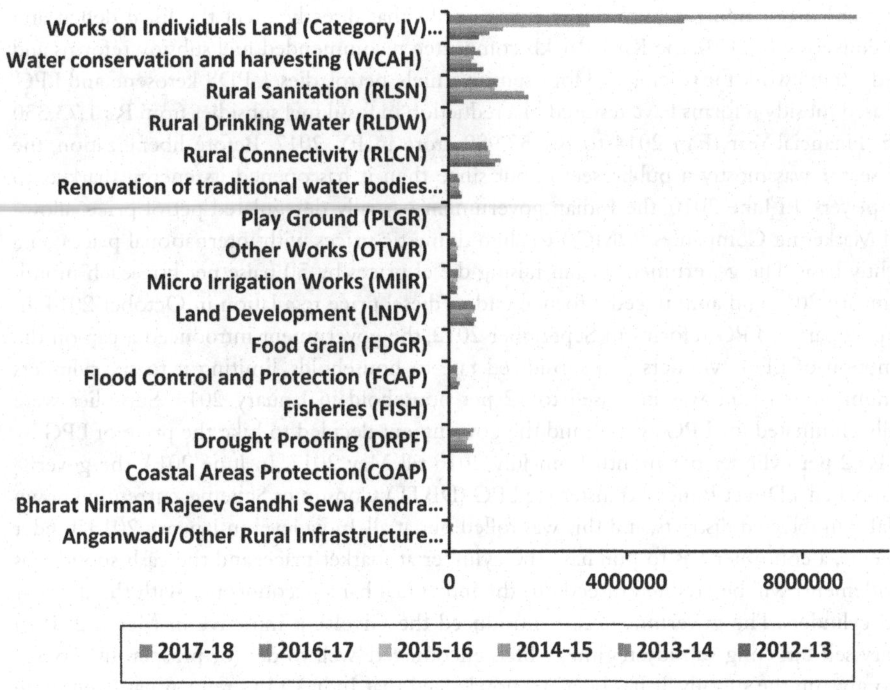

Figure 5.4 Number of works carried out under MNREGS from 2012–13 to 2017–18. *Source*: Lokhande and Gundimeda (2018).

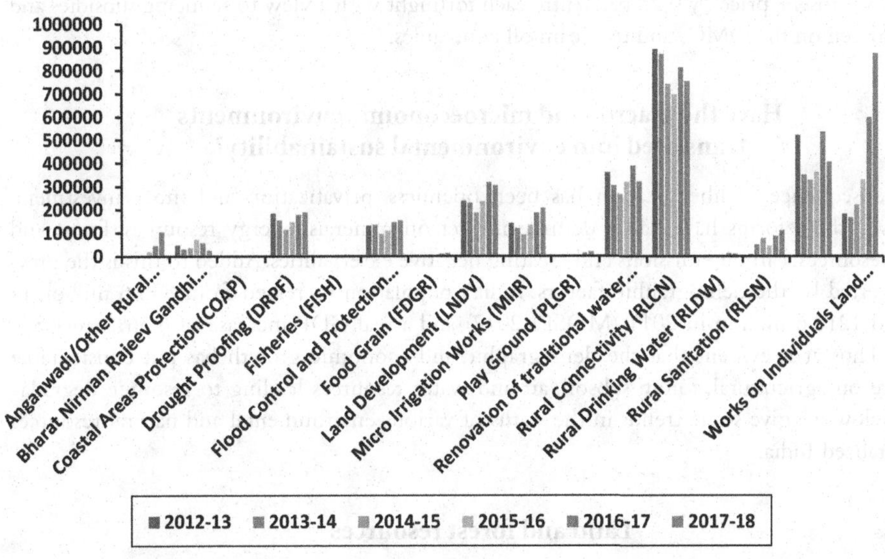

Figure 5.5 Expenditure (in Lakhs) incurred towards creation of various works under MGNREG scheme. *Source*: (Lokhande and Gundimeda, 2018).

The third major reforms were the energy reforms that directly affect the fiscal deficit and carbon emissions. In 2010, the Kirit Parikh committee recommended fuel subsidy reforms and outlined a framework for pricing the four sensitive fuels, petrol, diesel, PDS kerosene and LPG. The phased subsidy reforms have resulted in a reduction in fossil fuel subsidies from Rs.1,73,330 crore in Financial Year (FY) 2014 to Rs. 52,980 crore in FY 2017. Before liberalization, the energy sector was mostly a public sector, but since then it has opened its energy markets to private players. In June 2010, the Indian government partially deregulated petrol price, allowing Oil Marketing Companies (OMCs) to align domestic prices with international prices on a fortnightly basis. The government began raising diesel prices by 50 paise per litre each month from January 2013 and announced a formal end to diesel price regulation in October 2014. In addition, as part of LPG reforms in September 2012, the government introduced a cap on the consumption of LPG cylinders at a subsidized rate to households, limiting it to six cylinders per annum, which later was increased to 12 per household in January 2014. Subsidies were gradually eliminated for LPG as well, and the government decided to hike the price of LPG by nearly Rs.2 per cylinder per month from July 2016 till May 2017. In June 2013, the government launched a Direct Benefit Transfer for LPG (DBTL) Consumer Scheme, currently known as PaHaL,[2] in selected districts, and this was rolled out at all-India level in January 2015. Under this scheme, a consumer has to purchase the cylinder at market price, and the cash subsidy (as per entitlement) will be credited directly to the individual bank accounts per with the delivery of LPG cylinders. The government also introduced the GiveItUp initiative in March 2015, a voluntary self-targeting subsidy regime, which encouraged 'well to do' (or prosperous) households to give up the subsidy. It has been acknowledged that India's LPG reform has been quite successful and has reduced leakages and increased fiscal savings to the government. Increased penetration of LPG and electricity led the government in February 2015 to free the sale of non-PDS kerosene from regulated control. Further, in July 2016, OMCs were allowed to hike the PDS kerosene price by 0.25 paisa/litre each fortnight with a view to reducing subsidies and their burden on the OMCs and upstream oil companies.

Have the macro- and microeconomic environments translated into environmental sustainability?

The consequence of liberalization has been openness, privatization and more investment. However, the reforms have had a definite impact on minerals, energy resources, forest and water resources, carbon emissions and creating negative externalities. Added to this is the pressure exerted by the demographic factors. India's population increased from 838.6 million in 1991 to 1210.6 million in 2011 (MOSPI 2017) and a real GDP increase of 6.36% since the 1990s. Thus, it is evident that the demographic and economic growth has put considerable pressure on agricultural, forest, subsoil, air and water resources leading to resource degradation. Below we give some trends in the status of various environmental and natural resources in liberalized India.

Land and forest resources

In the pre-liberalization era, around 66% of the population was dependent on agriculture, forestry and fisheries as their source of livelihood. However, a shift towards industry and services has resulted in 43% of people making their living from the primary sector in 2018 (World Bank Data). The gross cropped area in the country increased from 182.24 million hectares in 1991 to 200.86

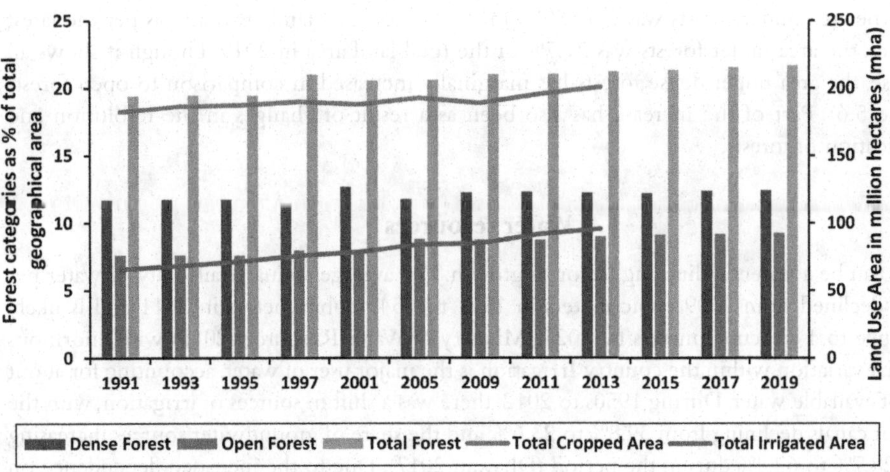

Figure 5.6 Land use in India from 1991 to 2013 and categories of forest from 1991 to 2019. *Source*: Compendium of Environment Statistics 2016a for Land Use data and various reports of Forest Survey of India for data on area under forest categories.

million hectares in 2013 (see Figure 5.6). The gross irrigated area increased from 65.68 million hectares to 95.77 million hectares from 1991 to 2013 (Compendium of Environment Statistics 2016a). The water and input intensity of Indian agriculture increased due to the green revolution, and agricultural yields initially jumped and then more or less stabilized. However, this agricultural intensification has come with a cost. According to the ISRO report 2016, there was an increase of 1.87 million hectares in area of degraded land area between 2003 and 2011 with a total degraded area of 96.4 million hectares in 2011 (SAC 2016), mostly due to water erosion and vegetation degradation (see Figure 5.7). According to the Indian Institute of Remote Sensing Report 2015, estimated soil erosion in India has affected 147 million hectares. India's soil is eroding at a rate of 16 tonnes per hectare annually thrice more than the permissible limit (Awasthi 2015). India requires an additional 100 million tons of food production to meet its food security by 2020 but irrigated agriculture can contribute only 64 million tons as water depletion has become a serious concern (Dhawan 2017). In

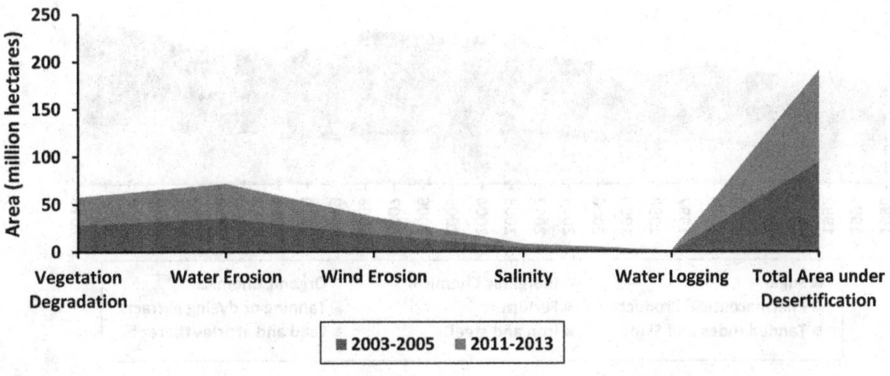

Figure 5.7 Desertification and land degradation status in India. *Source*: Space Application Centre (SAC) 2016.

1990, the area under forests was 6,39,390 km² (19.4% of total land area) and as per the latest statistics, the area under forests was 21.7% of the total land area in 2019. Though it shows an increase, the area under dense forests has marginally increased in comparison to open forests (Figure 5.6). Part of the increase has also been as a result of changes in the resolution and classification of forests.

Water resources

Water can be a potential limiting factor to growth. The average annual availability of water per capita declined from 2209 cubic meters in 1991 to 1545 cubic meters in 2011 and is likely to reduce to 1486 cubic meters by 2021 (Ministry of Water Resources 2015) with enormous regional variation within the country. Irrigation is the major user of water, accounting for about 84% of available water. During 1950s to 2012, there was a shift in sources of irrigation, with the share of canals declining from 39.8% to 23.6%, and the share of groundwater sources increasing from 28.7% to 62.4% during the period (Dhawan 2017). Due to the increased dependence on groundwater, there have been instances of groundwater overexploitation, and around 39% of wells are showing a decline in groundwater levels (Dhawan 2017). The siltation of reservoirs has been a significant issue due to soil erosion arising out of deforestation. Currently, around 65% of reservoirs are running dry, with Maharashtra being one of the most affected areas (Earth Observatory 2019). Besides, though the number of people who lack access to basic drinking water has declined from 21% to 7% from 2000 to 2017 (World Bank Data), still more than 100 million people live in poor water quality areas and around 54% of the population is facing high to extremely high water stress (Dhawan 2017).

Pollution

India's pollution problem has been growing rapidly. The water, land and air have been contaminated. Major investment has been in the manufacturing sector that includes 17 highly polluting industries that are on the CPCB's (Central Pollution Control Board) 'Red List'. The share of the most polluting sectors in India's exports increased dramatically from 10% in 1990 to 16% in 2018, suggesting that India could be emerging as a net exporter of pollution-intensive commodities (see Figure 5.8). The significant increase has been in shares of polluting industries of

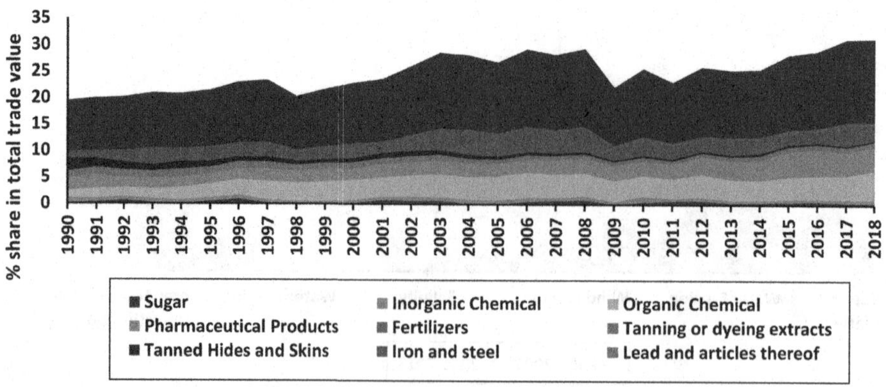

Figure 5.8 Share of dirty industries in total exports of India from 1990 to 2018. *Source*: UN Comtrade Data.

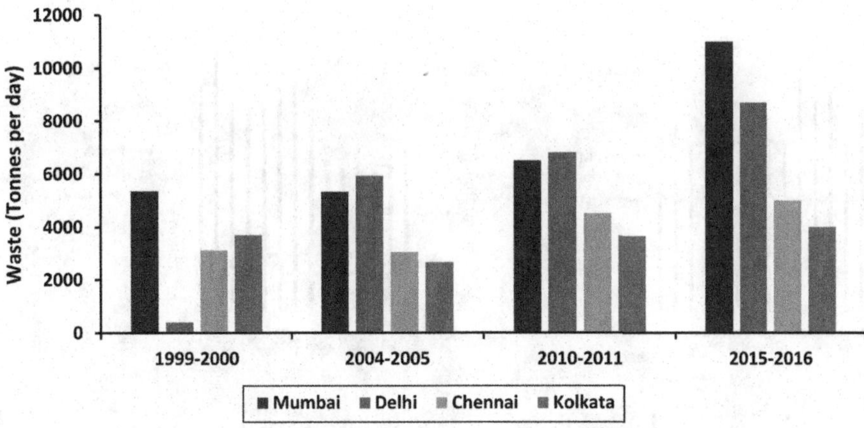

Figure 5.9 Waste generation in metropolitan cities in India for specific years. *Source*: Ministry of Statistics and Programme Implementation, Govt. of India. (ON1964) *Note*: Data taken from India Stata.

organic chemicals, pharmaceuticals and iron and steel among the industries considered. The waste generated from various cities has also increased over time as seen from Figure 5.9. These trends indicate the need for greater investment in environmental management. Most of the surface and ground water resources in India have been seriously polluted due to industrial effluents and discharging sewage water into water bodies. There has been an increase in the number of polluted rivers from 302 to 351 while that of critically polluted rivers increased from 34 to 45 over two years from 2015 to 2017 (Koshy 2018).

Air pollution

Air pollution in the bigger cities is a growing hazard to health and quality of life; 14 of the 15 Indian cities figure in the top 15 polluted cities of the world (World Health Organization (WHO) 2016). The average PM10 in metropolitan cities is much above the prescribed annual mean standard of 60 μg/m^3 as seen in Figure 5.10, and the concentration is increasing for Delhi and Mumbai. For air pollutant nitrogen dioxide, the concentration has been below the prescribed annual mean standard of 40 μg/m^3 for cities Mumbai and Chennai, while it is increasing and above the prescribed standard for Delhi and Kolkata (see Figure 5.10). In addition to particulate matter, vehicular pollution and industrial emissions are major pollutants in the country. In addition, indoor air pollution is a major source of pollution in India, largely due to the burning of biomass and poorly ventilated conditions. There has been a higher incidence of respiratory illnesses among children and the elderly in India since the 1990s as seen from Figure 5.11.

One good aspect post liberalization is the availability of clean fuels and a shift to non-biomass based energy sources. Figure 5.12 shows an increase in the share of renewables in total energy production from 0% in the 1980s to 5.36% in 2015. This is also because of India's commitment to reduce carbon emissions by 2020.

Environmental health

India is malnutritional in terms of health and poor health can lead to decreased productivity and lower quality of life. The risk is higher now more than before because of the contamination of surface and river water. Figure 5.13 shows the concentration of Dissolved Oxygen

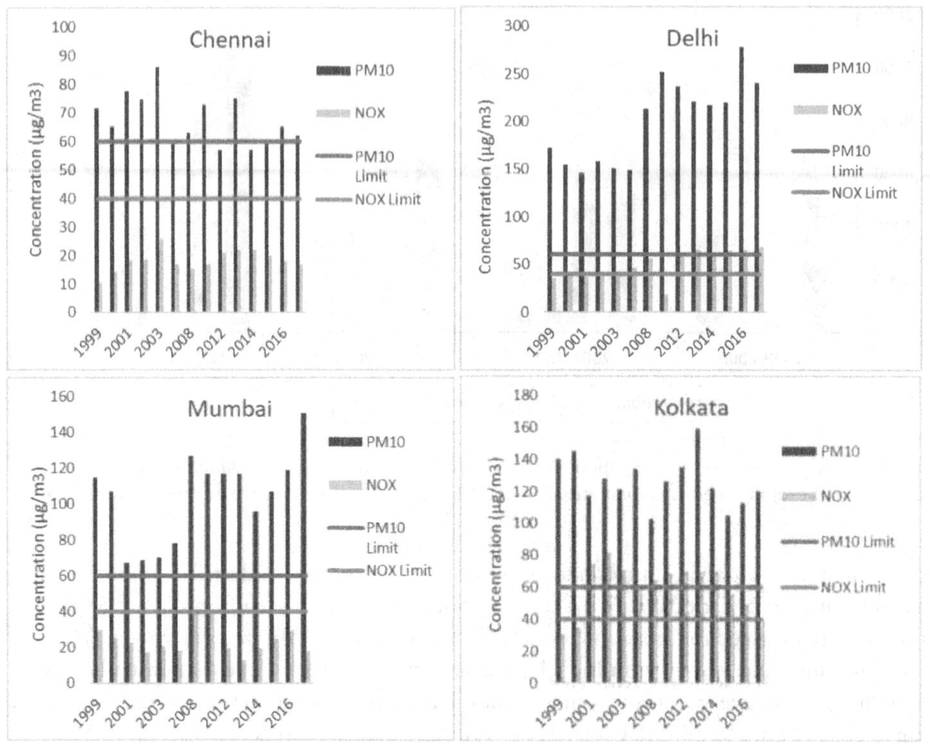

Figure 5.10 Trends in annual average concentration of PM10 and NOX for metropolitan cities in India. *Source*: Figure created based on data from Ministry of Statistics and Programme Implementation, Govt. of India. (ON1964) & Past Issues and taken from IndiaStat.

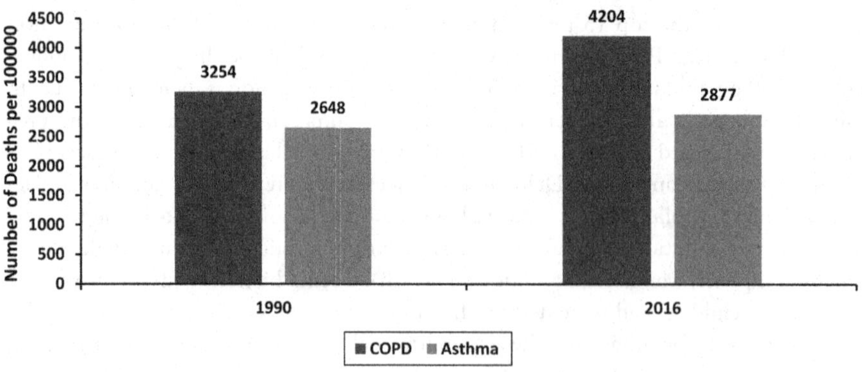

Figure 5.11 Reported cases of airborne diseases (COPD and asthma) in India between 1990 and 2016. *Source*: Salvi et al. 2018 *Note*: COPD=chronic obstructive pulmonary disease.

(DO) (minimum level) and Biological Oxygen Demand (BOD) (maximum level) for two of the important rivers of India – Ganga and Yamuna. The minimum permissible limit of DO is 5mg/l for safe drinking water but the DO concentration has been lower than the limit for both rivers, indicating that the river water is polluted. The maximum permissible limit of BOD is 3 mg/l for safe drinking water but BOD concentration has been higher for Ganga and Yamuna,

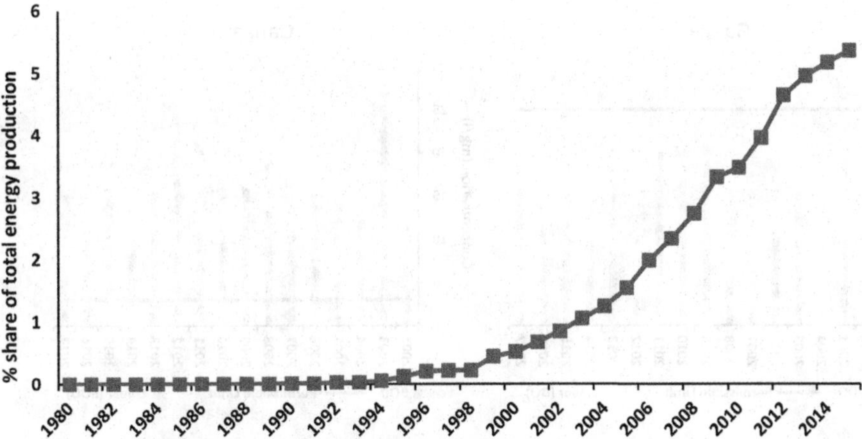

Figure 5.12 Percentage share of renewable sources (excluding hydroelectric) in total energy production. *Source*: Figure created based on World Bank Data.

indicating polluted water. However, the quality of water from the Yamuna has been worsening in comparison to Ganga over time (Figure 5.13). The number of water-related diseases is on the rise and a number of children die each year due to various water-related diseases. Figure 5.14 shows reported cases of major waterborne diseases from 2013 to 2017.

Climate change

Post 1991, climate change has emerged as a major threat and India is especially highly vulnerable due to high levels of poverty, population and dependence on natural resource-based sectors. India is already experiencing changes in climate as the mean annual temperature in India changed from 24.28 in 1991 to 26.29 degrees Celsius in 2017 (see Figure 5.15). India has also been experiencing greater variability of rainfall and increased frequency and severity of droughts, floods and cyclones.

India is the third largest emitter of CO_2 gas emissions globally but, in terms of CO_2 per capita emissions, India stands at 130th position in the world. India's average emissions per capita is around 2 tCO_2/person as against 17 tCO_2/person in the USA and 7t CO_2/person in China and 6.7 tCO_2/person in European Union. However, in terms of absolute emissions, China tops the list with 10,065 $MtCO_2$ followed by the USA at 5416 $MtCO_2$. India's absolute emissions are at 2654 $MtCO_2$ for the year 2018. As shown in Figure 5.16, India's carbon emissions are on the rise as GDP has grown, but the emissions per capita and GDP per capita have converged. Initially, emissions per capita were higher than GDP per capita, indicating that India's emphasis on renewable energy sources and improving energy efficiency has yielded results.

Is this trend a concern or could India soon reach a point of inflection and reduce pollution? Should we be concerned about the initial environmental degradation that occurs as countries grow/industrialize, but that would subsequently decline during the later stages of growth (Grossman and Krueger 1991)? As countries grow, initially, environmental quality deteriorates due to scale effect (use of higher inputs), composition effect (increase in the share of pollution-intensive goods) and technique effect (emphasis on the cleaner production process at a later stage). So, there is an inverted U-shaped relationship between growth and environmental degradation. Some researchers have tried

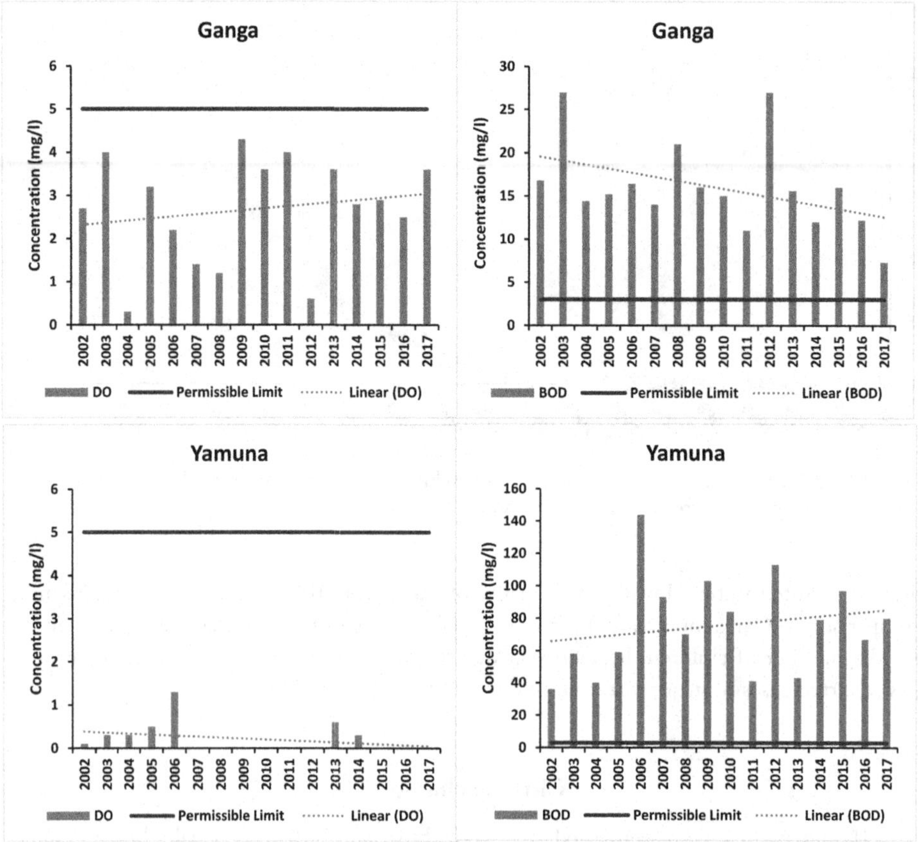

Figure 5.13 Annual mean trends in BOD (maximum value) and DO (minimum value) concentration (mg/l) of Ganga and Yamuna from 2002 to 2017. *Source*: Figure created based on data from Central Pollution Control Board *Note*: The minimum DO limit of Yamuna from 2007–2012 was zero.

to explore whether EKC (Environmental Kuznets Curve) is valid in the Indian context for some of the pollutants. If there is evidence of inverted U, we could conclude that environmental degradation would automatically be addressed. Managi and Jena (2008) examined the relation between the environmental productivity of three pollutants – SO_2, nitrogen dioxide (NO_2), suspended particulate matter – and income using state-level industrial data from 1991 to 2003. The results showed that in India, the scale effect dominated the technique effect, and that the combined effect of income on environmental productivity was negative. Mythili and Mukherjee (2011) denied the EKC kind of relationship between river effluents and per capita net state domestic product (NSDP) when dealing with three river effluents such as BOD, DO and pH, during the period 1990–91 to 2005–06 in 14 Indian states. This is due to a lack of policy ordinance implementation in different states. Barua and Hubacek (2008) examined the relation between BOD, Chemical Oxygen Demand (COD) and income using watershed level data of 12 states and found the EKC relationship in only four states out of the 12.

What do these indicators mean for the sustainability of Indian states? There has been no study that has looked at pre and post liberalization but the study by IFMR (2011) constructed

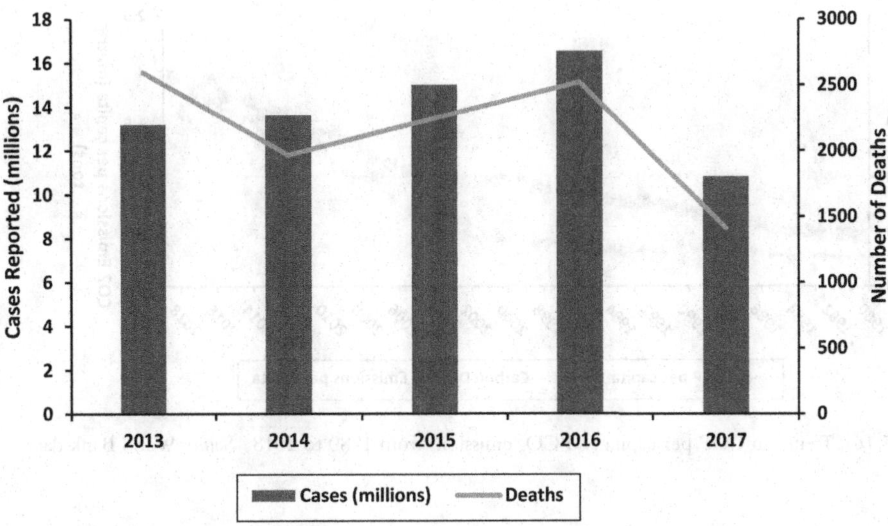

Figure 5.14 Number of cases reported from waterborne diseases. *Source*: Figure created by authors based on Lok Sabha; data taken from India Spend 2018. *Note*: Diseases include cholera, typhoid, viral hepatitis, and acute diarrhoeal diseases.

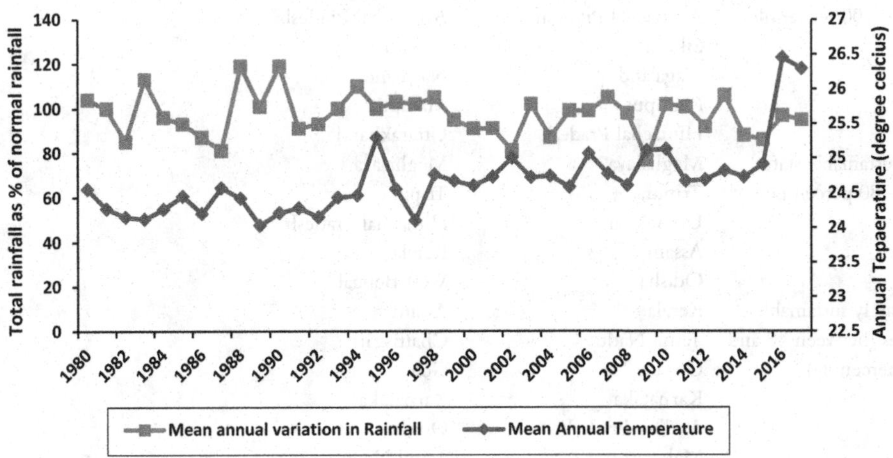

Figure 5.15 Annual temperature and annual variation in rainfall from 1980 to 2017. *Source*: Temperature data taken from data.gov.in and rainfall data from Indiastat.

an environmental sustainability index for two years, 2009 and 2011, and checked which of the states were sustainable. The environmental sustainability index is a composite index of 41 indicators selected using the DPSIR framework – drivers (driving forces that extract from and pollute), pressures (depletion and pollution), state (present condition of the environment), impact (impact on ecosystem and health), response (societal efforts to reduce the pollution) (DPSIR) framework. The results are given in Table 5.3.

While the indicator approach gives a diagnostic tool, it does not consider the impact on all forms of capital. Gundimeda (2018) assessed the links between economic growth and different

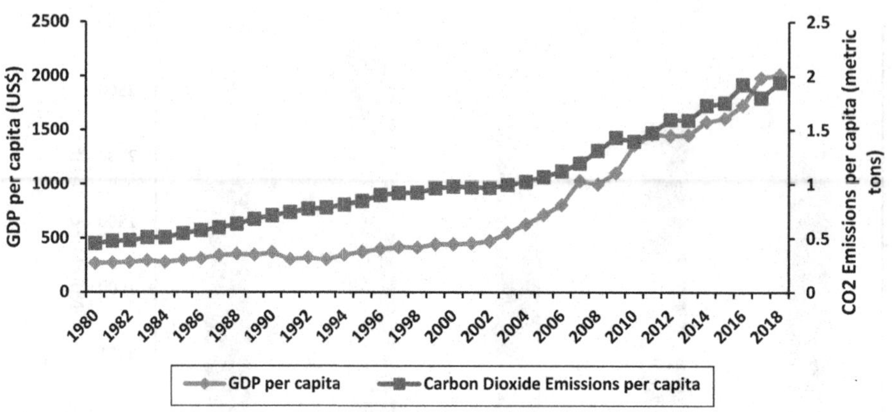

Figure 5.16 Trends in GDP per capita and CO_2 emissions from 1980 to 2018. *Source:* World Bank data.

Table 5.3 Grouping of states based on their levels of sustainability

ESI groups	*States in ESI 2011*	*States in ESI 2009*
Most sustainable states (80 – 100 percentile)	Mizoram	Mizoram
	Arunachal Pradesh	Arunachal Pradesh
	Sikkim	Sikkim
	Nagaland	Nagaland
	Manipur	Manipur
	Himachal Pradesh	Uttarakhand
More sustainable states (60 –80 percentile)	Meghalaya	Meghalaya
	Tripura	Tripura
	Uttarakhand	Himachal Pradesh
	Assam	Kerala
	Odisha	West Bengal
Moderately sustainable states (between 40 and 60 percentile)	Kerala	Assam
	Tamil Nadu	Chattisgarh
	Goa	Goa
	Karnataka	Karnataka
	Andhra Pradesh	Odisha
	Maharashtra	Tamil Nadu
Less sustainable states (between 20 and 40 percentile)	Chattisgarh	Andhra Pradesh
	Jammu and Kashmir	Jammu and Kashmir
	West Bengal	Jharkhand
	Madhya Pradesh	Madhya Pradesh
	Rajasthan	Maharashtra
Least sustainable states (between 0 and 20 percentile)	Bihar	Bihar
	Gujarat	Gujarat
	Haryana	Haryana
	Punjab	Punjab
	Uttar Pradesh	Uttar Pradesh
	Jharkhand	Rajasthan

Source: IFMR (2011).

forms of capital for the period 2001–2011 using comprehensive wealth as an indicator. The study looked at how the rankings of different states change if renewable (forests) and non-renewable (minerals) resources were considered along with human capital and produced capital as a measure of wealth (see Table 5.4). However, the study included data for the period 2001–2011.

Environmental reforms

From the previous sections it can be concluded that the reforms initially had a positive impact on economic growth. On the other hand, due to increased consumption levels, extraction of resources and increased vehicular use, pollution levels and environmental degradation have increased. How is India dealing with these current threats? Equity and Development have been at the centre of India's development policy since the first five-year plan and the importance of environmental resources has been recognized. However, since the second five-year plan natural resources have been viewed more as extractive resources (Chopra 2017). During the fourth plan period (1969–74) the need to introduce environmental aspects into planning and development was considered, following the 1972 United Nations Conference on the Human Environment in Stockholm. India made attempts to protect its wildlife through the 1972 Indian Wildlife (Protection) Act (amended 1993, 2002 and 2006). Following this, systematic efforts were made to establish an environmental regulatory system. In 1973, India enacted the Water (Prevention and Control of Pollution) Act which was amended in 1988. This was followed by the Water (Prevention and Control of Pollution) Cess Act (amended in 1992 and 2003) showing that India has been committed towards the prevention and control of pollution. Subsequently in 1980, the Forest (Conservation) Act (amended in 1988), the Air (Prevention and Control of Pollution Act) amended in 1987, the Environment (Protection) Act (amended in 1992 and 2006) were enacted. Subsequently, to the Environment (Protection) Act a series of environmental laws (on all the major environmental sectors), regulations, standards and measures were initiated (see Figure 5.17). India produced the National Environment Policy document in 2006 where the environmental policy was clearly documented.

At a national level, India has instituted several Acts (and amendments), rules and national level policies on the environment. India has brought different notifications such as environmental impact assessment, Taj Trapezium zone Pollution (prevention and control) authority on fly ash management. India has been part of several international treaties/conventions/declarations on environment and has enacted stringent environmental legislation, and created institutions to monitor and enforce legislation. India has established, a Green Tribunal to exclusively handle environmental litigation. In 2008, India adopted the National Action Plan on Climate Change and its eight-core national missions. India has linked energy security and development together with climate change mitigation and adaptation as co-benefits (Chopra 2017) and has committed to the Intended Nationally Determined Contributions (INDC), showing that India wants to be part of the global solution.

A regulatory body has been established through a two-tier management system, i.e. centre and state levels. The enactment of the various environmental laws, instruments and regulations has also given higher power to various regulatory agencies. India set up a Green Tribunal and authorized it to penalize polluters. The Supreme Court of India has, in many instances taken the role of a regulator.

Despite these efforts, environmental improvement is not apparent. Most of the indicator pollutants like particulate matter, NO_x (see Figure 5.10), seems to have been rising in major Indian cities since 1991 and is worse in the present decade. CO_2 emissions are on the rise compared to the 1990s and a direct relation between growth and CO_2 emissions can be noted in

Table 5.4 Ranking of states based on HDI, per capita GSDP and investments in comprehensive wealth

HDI	*Per capita NSDP*	*GSDP*	*Comprehensive wealth*	*Natural capital*	*Cumulative gross capital formation*	*Human capital*	*Mineral wealth*
Kerala	Goa	Maharashtra	Gujarat	Himachal Pradesh	Gujarat	Uttar Pradesh	Bihar
Goa	Sikkim	Tamil Nadu	Maharashtra	Mizoram	Maharashtra	Maharashtra	Madhya Pradesh
Himachal Pradesh	Haryana	Uttar Pradesh	Tamil Nadu	Tripura	Tamil Nadu	Andhra Pradesh	Karnataka
Tamil Nadu	Maharashtra	Gujarat	Karnataka	West Bengal	Karnataka	West Bengal	Rajasthan
Maharashtra	Tamil Nadu	West Bengal	Uttar Pradesh (incl. Uttarakhand)	Tamil Nadu	Andhra Pradesh	Bihar	Andhra Pradesh
Punjab	Gujarat	Karnataka	Andhra Pradesh	Kerala	Orissa	Tamil Nadu	Orissa
Haryana	Karnataka	Rajasthan	Odisha	Karnataka	Uttar Pradesh	Madhya Pradesh	Madhya Pradesh
West Bengal	Uttarakhand	Andhra Pradesh	Madhya Pradesh (Chhattisgarh)	Meghalaya	Jharkhand	Karnataka	
Jammu and Kashmir	Himachal Pradesh	Kerala	West Bengal	Nagaland	Haryana	Gujarat	
Gujarat	Nagaland	Madhya Pradesh	Haryana	Uttar Pradesh (incl. Uttarakhand)	West Bengal	Kerala	
Uttarakhand	Punjab	Haryana	Rajasthan	Orissa	Rajasthan	Rajasthan	
Karnataka	Jharkhand	Punjab	Punjab	Madhya Pradesh (inc. Chhattisgarh)	Chhattisgarh	Orissa	
Mizoram	Tripura	Bihar	Himachal Pradesh	Andhra Pradesh	Uttarakhand	Punjab	
Tripura	Andhra Pradesh	Orissa	Kerala	Arunachal Pradesh	Punjab	Haryana	
Sikkim	Mizoram	Jharkhand	Assam	Maharashtra	Madhya Pradesh	Assam	
Rajasthan	Arunachal Pradesh	Chhattisgarh	Bihar (Jharkhand)	Bihar (incl. Jharkhand)	Himachal Pradesh	Jammu and Kashmir	

Andhra Pradesh	Meghalaya	Assam	Goa	Rajasthan	Kerala	Himachal Pradesh
Orissa	West Bengal	Uttarakhand	Jammu and Kashmir	Jammu and Kashmir	Assam	Tripura
Nagaland	Rajasthan	Himachal Pradesh	Meghalaya	Assam	Goa	Nagaland
Meghalaya	Jammu and Kashmir	Jammu and Kashmir	Tripura	Gujarat	Bihar	Manipur
Jharkhand	Madhya Pradesh	Goa	Sikkim	Manipur	Jammu and Kashmir	Goa
Manipur	Chhattisgarh	Tripura	Manipur	Sikkim	Meghalaya	Meghalaya
Madhya Pradesh	Orissa	Meghalaya	Nagaland	Goa	Sikkim	Arunachal Pradesh
Chhattisgarh	Kerala	Nagaland	Mizoram	Punjab	Tripura	Mizoram
Bihar	Manipur	Manipur	Arunachal Pradesh	Haryana	Manipur	Sikkim
Assam	Assam	Arunachal Pradesh	Gujarat	Himachal Pradesh	Nagaland	Uttar Pradesh
Arunachal Pradesh	Uttar Pradesh	Sikkim	Maharashtra	Mizoram		Maharashtra
Uttar Pradesh	Bihar	Mizoram				Orissa

Source: Gundimeda (2018).

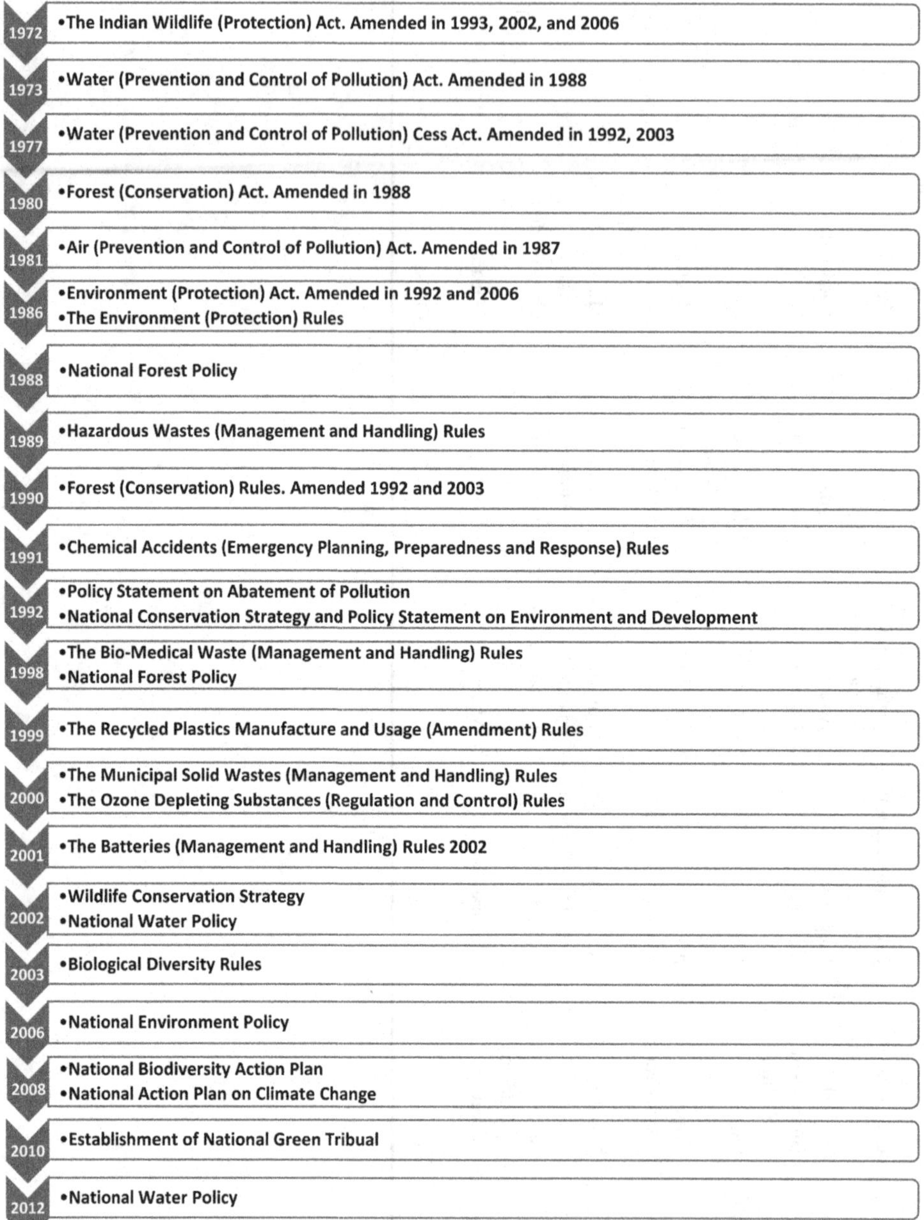

Figure 5.17 Major environmental laws, rules and policies in India. *Source*: Graphic created by authors.

Figure 5.16. According to the Environmental Performance Index, India is among the bottom five countries on the Environmental Performance Index 2018, plummeting 36 points from 141 in 2016, according to a biennial report by Yale and Columbia Universities along with the World Economic Forum.[3] The index is constructed based on Environmental Health and Ecosystem Vitality.

Conclusions

At the time India liberalized, the pulse of the economy was different, with more emphasis on economic development. Obviously, the significant positive impacts generated by economic reforms should not distract us from the fact that India remains heavily polluted. India is more urbanized and so are the environmental disasters and problems. Most of the cities are suffering from air and water pollution resulting in new challenges. The increase in corporations, changes in consumption patterns with higher environmental footprints, and the extraction of resources with little regard for the sustainability of the resources have put India's environmental and social sustainability at stake.

Environmental degradation and climate change were not major issues before the reforms and thus, the reforms did not emphasize on conservation of natural resources and the environment. However, there has been a change in the international environmental agenda since the Earth Summit adopted sustainable development as its prime goal. Since then, the countries have accepted Agenda 21 and committed themselves to achieving the millennium development goals, the sustainable development goals, and actions to tackle climate change. The structural adjustment policies that India has undertaken, such as deregulation, privatization, removing fuel subsidies, are good for growth but have impacted the environment and human health. Since the initiation of the reforms, the economy initially became more carbon intensive, but of late, the government has been emphasizing renewable sources of energy and thus could see the reduction of carbon emissions in the near future. Similarly, the government is slowly phasing out the subsidies on pesticides and fertilizers, which is expected to positively impact the environment. There is some relative improvement identified, but environmental quality seems to be a concern.

India being a centrally planned economy, did not signal the prices correctly, leading to the over-extraction of resources resulting in increased pollution and over-use of natural resources. Though India has shifted to a market-oriented model through economic reforms, the reforms in the environmental sector seem to be slower, as the environmental quality deteriorated impacting human health and thus, the productivity of the nation. Along with the economic reforms, we need reforms in our accounting system. We need measures like Green GDP which would signal the interactions between economic growth and the environment more accurately. India needs to synergize various international protocols, conventions and agreements with the acts, rules or laws that can lead to the development of joint programmes that can be implemented cost-effectively. Merely creating global or national awareness and actions is insufficient as it requires a grassroots level revolution to manage the resources. This is because most of the environmental problems are local and impact locals. Thus, locals know the best practices to manage the resources – land, forests, wildlife or biodiversity – and thus need to be empowered to act on environmental degradation, depletion or misuse. It has also been increasingly apparent that most of the environmental issues have emerged due to an unequal level playing field between the delivery agencies such as the governments, the beneficiaries and the institutions. Though competitive forces and the agents of development would ensure a level playing field, the environmental problems that are arising show that these are fallacious assumptions. Thus, the crux of the problem seems to be isolating the agents responsible for the environmental issues rather than understanding that the world has moved from a community- to an individual-based decision and action platform. India needs to move to a new phase of environmentally inclusive reforms – focusing on augmenting human capabilities, minimizing the impact on the environment and focusing on sustainable use of natural resources, waste management and prevention of environmental pollution. Emphasizing human capital development can influence the way people use natural resources. Thus, sustaining the gains from reforms requires balancing equity of present versus future generations, which requires planners to consider the environment at the centre of the reform process.

Notes

1 The Amendments can be found at Legislative Department (Ministry of Law and Justice, Government of India) at http://legislative.gov.in/amendment-acts.

2 Pratyaksh (Direct) Hastantrit (Transfer) Labh (Benefit) in Hindi. See http://pib.nic.in/newsite/PrintRelease.aspx?relid=114245.

3 https://epi.envirocenter.yale.edu/epi-topline.

References

Arrow, K. J., Dasgupta, P., Goulder, L. H., Mumford, K. J., & Oleson, K. (2012). Sustainability and the measurement of wealth. *Environment and Development Economics*, *17*(3), 317–353.

Awasthi, K. (2015). Loosing ground. Retrieved from Down To Earth: https://www.downtoearth.org.in/news/losing-ground-10579

Barro, R. J., & Sala-i-Martin, X. (1995). *Technological diffusion, convergence, and growth*. NBER Working Papers 5151. New Haven: National Bureau of Economic Research, Inc.

Barua, A., & Hubacek, K. (2008). Water pollution and economic growth: An environmental Kuznets curve analysis at the watershed and state level. *International Journal of Ecological Economics and Statistics*, *10*, 63–78.

Baumol, W. J. (1996). Entrepreneurship, productive, unproductive, and destructive. *Journal of Business Venturing*, *11*(1), 3–22.

Brundtland, G. H. (1987). Our common future—Call for action. *Environmental Conservation*, *14*(4), 291–294.

Chopra, K. (2017). Climate change policy in India. In *Development and environmental policy in India* (pp. 27–35). Springer Briefs in Economics, Singapore: Springer.

Compendium of Environment Statistics. (2016). Chapter 5 – Land use. Retrieved from MOSPI Publications: http://www.mospi.gov.in/sites/default/files/reports_and_publication/statistical_publication/social_statistics/CHAPTER_five_comp2016.pdf

Compendium of Environment Statistics. (2016). Chapter 7 – Human settlements. Retrieved from http://www.mospi.gov.in/sites/default/files/reports_and_publication/statistical_publication/social_statistics/CHAPTER_seven_comp2016.pdf

Connor, M. P. (1997). John Stuart Mill's utilitiarianism and the social ethics of sustainable development. *European Journal of the History of Economic Thought*, *4*(3), 478–506.

Dang, H., & Lanjouw, P. (2018). Inequality in India on the rise. Retrieved from UNU Wider: https://www.wider.unu.edu/sites/default/files/Publications/Policy-brief/PDF/PB-2018-6-Inequality-in-India-on-the-rise.pdf

Dasgupta, P. (2001). *Human well-being and the natural environment*. Oxford: Oxford University Press.

Dhawan, V. (2017). Water and agriculture in India. Retrieved from Background paper for the South Asia expert panel: https://www.oav.de/fileadmin/user_upload/5_Publikationen/5_Studien/170118_Study_Water_Agriculture_India.pdf

Dixit, A. (1980). The role of investment in entry-deterrence. *The Economic Journal, Royal Economic Society*, *90*(357), 95–106.

Domar, E. D. (1946). Capital expansion, rate of growth, and employment. *Econometrica, Journal of the Econometric Society*, *14*(2), 137–147.

Dreze, J., & Sen, A. (1999). *Economic development and social opportunities*. New Delhi: Oxford University Press.

Earth Observatory. (2019). Water shortages in India. Retrieved from https://earthobservatory.nasa.gov/images/145242/water-shortages-in-india

Grossman, G. M., & Krueger, A. B. (1991). *Environmental impacts of a North American free trade agreement* (No. w3914). Cambridge, Massachusetts: National Bureau of Economic Research.

Gundimeda, H. (2018). *Is economic growth linked with comprehensive wealth? Link to state-level analysis in India*. Inclusive Wealth Report 2018, 194–208. London and New York: Routledge.

Gupta, S. (2019). New data may show big cut in number of poor. Retrieved from The Times of India: https://timesofindia.indiatimes.com/india/new-data-may-show-big-cut-in-number-of-poor/articleshow/67705787.cms

Harrod, R. F. (1939). An essay in dynamic theory. *The Economic Journal*, *49*(193), 14–33.

Hartwick, J. M. (1977). Intergenerational equity and the investing of rents from exhaustible resources. *The American Economic Review*, *67*(5), 972–974.

Hartwick, J. M. (1995). Constant consumption paths in open economies with exhaustible resources. *Review of International Economics*, *3*(3), 275–283.

Institute for Financial Management and Research (IFMR). (2011). Environmental sustainability index for Indian States 2011. Retrieved from IFMRlead.org: http://www.ifmrlead.org/wp-content/uploads/2015/OWC/Environmental-Sustainability-Index-2011-for-Indian-States.pdf

Koshy, J. (2018). More river stretches are critically polluted: Central Pollution Control Board. Retrieved from The Hindu: https://www.thehindu.com/news/national/more-river-stretches-critically-polluted-cpcb/article24962440.ece

Lokhande, N., & Gundimeda, H. (2018, February 22–23). "India's MGNREGA success boils down to few States, fewer districts and fewest blocks." In *Conference Presentation*. New Delhi: South Asian University.

Managi, S., & Jena, P. R. (2008). Environmental productivity and Kuznets curve in India. *Ecological Economics*, *65*(2), 432–440.

Meadows, D. H., Meadows, D. L., Randers, J., & Behrens, W. W. (1972). *The limits to growth*. New York: Universe, *102*, 27.

Ministry of Rural Development. (2013). *Mahatma Gandhi NREGA operational guidelines*. 4th Edition, *MoRD Government of India*. Retrieved from https://nrega.nic.in/Circular_Archive/archive/Operational_guidelines_4thEdition_eng_2013.pdf

Ministry of Water Resources. (2015). Per capita availability of water. Retrieved from https://pib.gov.in/newsite/printrelease.aspx?relid=119797

Mythili, G., & Mukherjee, S. (2011). Examining environmental Kuznets curve for river effluents in India. *Environment, Development and Sustainability*, *13*(3), 627–640.

Romer, P. M. (1990). Endogenous technological change. *Journal of Political Economy*, *98*(5, Part 2), S71–S102.

Salvi, S., Kumar, G. A., Dhaliwal, R. S., Paulson, K., Agrawal, A., Koul, P. A., & Christopher, D. J. (2018). The burden of chronic respiratory diseases and their heterogeneity across the states of India: The global burden of disease study 1990–2016. *The Lancet Global Health*, *6*(12), e1363e1374.

Samuel, V. J. (2019). What is inequality? Retrieved from OxFam India: https://www.oxfamindia.org/blog/what-inequality

Solow, R. M. (1974). Intergenerational equity and exhaustible resources. *The Review of Economic Studies*, *41*, 29–45.

Solow, R. M. (1986). On the intergenerational allocation of natural resources. *The Scandinavian Journal of Economics*, *88*(1), 141–149.

Space Application Centre (SAC). (2016). Desertification and land degradation atlas of India. Retrieved from Government of India: https://www.sac.gov.in/SACSITE/Desertification_Atlas_2016_SAC_ISRO.pdf

Stiglitz, J. (1974). Growth with exhaustible natural resources: Efficient and optimal growth paths. *The Review of Economic Studies*, *41*, 123–137.

Tisdell, C. (2001). Globalisation and sustainability: Environmental Kuznets curve and the WTO. *Ecological Economics*, *39*(2), 185–196.

UNU-IHDP, & UNEP. (2012). Inclusive wealth report 2012. *Measuring progress toward sustainability*. Cambridge: Cambridge University Press.

UNU-IHDP, & UNEP. (2014). Inclusive wealth report 2014. *Measuring progress toward sustainability*. Cambridge: Cambridge University Press.

Urban Institute, & UNEP. (2018). Inclusive wealth report 2018. *Measuring progress toward sustainability*. Cambridge: Urban Institute and UNEP.

World Economic Forum. (2018). The global gender gap report 2018. Retrieved from http://www3.weforum.org/docs/WEF_GGGR_2018.pdf

World Health Organization (WHO). (2016). Ambient air pollution: A global assessment of exposure and burden of disease. Retrieved from https://apps.who.int/iris/bitstream/handle/10665/250141/9789241511353-eng.pdf?sequence=1

PART II

Trade and manufacturing

6

ECONOMIC REFORMS AND MANUFACTURING SECTOR GROWTH

Need to reconfigure the industrialisation model?*

R. Nagaraj

Introduction

Over a quarter-century of market-oriented (or liberal, or free market) reforms (1991–2016), the manufacturing (or, industrial) sector has grown annually between 7 and 8 per cent on a trend basis (depending upon the data series chosen) (Figure 6.1).[1] The growth rate after the reforms is higher than in the preceding quarter-century, but is roughly the same as in the 1980s when the reforms were initiated. India's share in global merchandise trade has moved up from nearly one-half a per cent in 2000 to one and a half per cent by 2015; and, the services exports share rose from 1 per cent to 3 per cent during the same period (Figure 6.2).

Industrial production has diversified with perceptible improvements in quality and variety of goods produced with growing domestic competition. Yet, the manufacturing (or industrial) sector's share has stagnated at about 14–15 (26–27) per cent of GDP since the reforms (Figure 6.3). Though India has avoided de-industrialisation – defined as a decline in the manufacturing (industrial) sector's share in GDP, or share in the workforce – it is staring at a quarter-century of stagnation, in contrast to many Asian economies which have moved up the technology ladder with a rising manufacturing share in domestic output and global trade (Rodrik, 2015).

However, over a longer period, Indian industry has regressed. The telling evidence of this is a comparison with China. Around 1950, both the large Asian giants were roughly at the same level of industrialisation (or lack of it); if anything India had an edge (Raj, 2006; Dharma Kumar, 1988). By 2010, however, China had become the world's second largest manufacturing nation, whilst India ranked tenth, producing one-third or one-quarter of China's industrial output (at current market exchange rate) (Figure 6.4).

* This chapter was originally published in *Economic and Political Weekly*, Volume 52, No. 2, 2017. It is reproduced with the author's permission.

 DOI: 10.4324/9780367855741-6

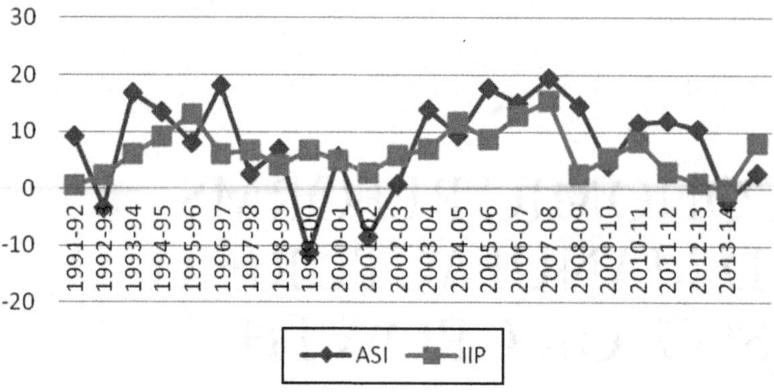

Figure 6.1 Manufacturing sector growth rate – by ASI and IIP. *Source*: CSO and RBI's *Handbook of Statistics on Indian Economy*.

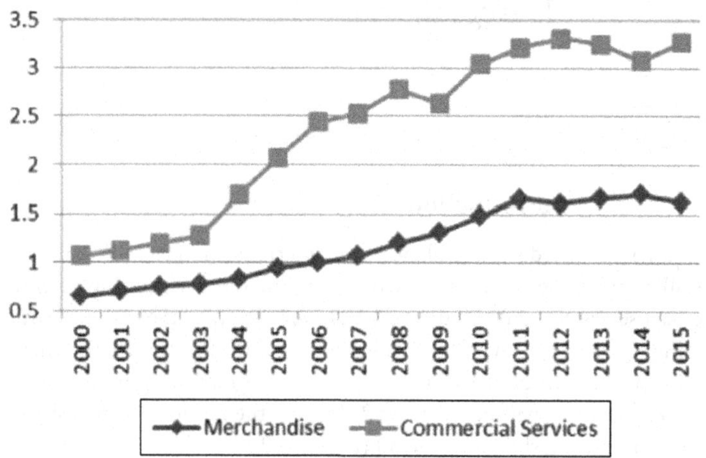

Figure 6.2 India's share in global trade. *Source*: Author's estimation using data from COMTRADE-WITS.

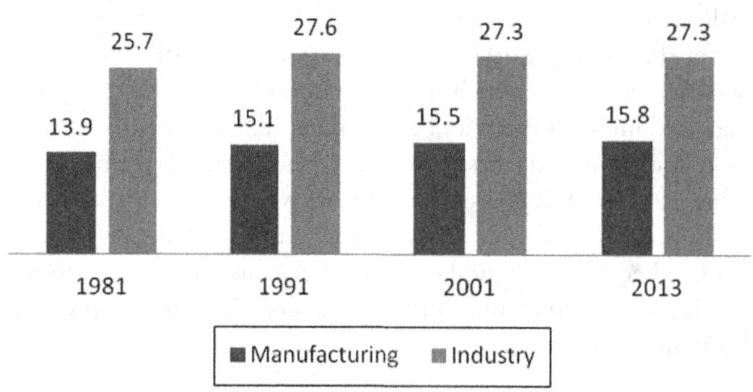

Figure 6.3 Share of manufacturing and industry in GDP. *Source*: *National Accounts Statistics*, various issues.

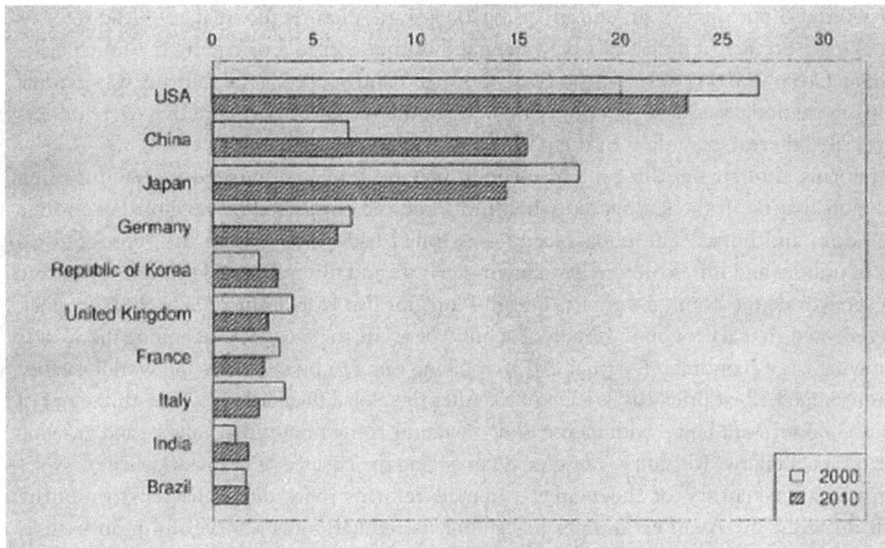

Figure 6.4 World's top 10 manufacturing nations in 2000 and 2010. *Source*: UNIDO's *International Year-Book of Industrial Statistics, 2012*.

The reforms were built on the initial success in de-licensing and import liberalisation (that is, a switch from quotas to tariffs) in the 1980s. However, deepening of the reforms since the 1990s – as part of the broader stabilisation and structural adjustment programme – meant a clear departure from the state-led domestic-oriented, capital goods focused, "heavy" industrialisation strategy – and, towards a market-friendly regime, as advocated by most mainstream economists and development agencies such as the World Bank (as evident in its official publication, *East Asian Miracle* story (WB, 1993)). The reforms were initially underwritten by structural adjustment loans from the Bretton Woods Institutions, conditional upon implementing the policy changes (as against the World Bank's predominant interest in project finance). Though perhaps modest, these loans signalled to global capital markets, and international business, Bretton Woods Institutions' endorsement of the shift in India's economic policy.

Jagdish Bhagwati, the most ardent and long-standing critique of India's planning, succinctly summarised what the reform really meant, when he said:

> The main elements of India's policy framework that stifled efficiency and growth until the 1970s, and somewhat less so during the 1980s as limited reforms began to be attempted, and whose surgical removal is, for the most part, the objective of the substantial reforms begun in the mid-1991, are easily defined. I would divide them into three major groups:
>
> 1. Extensive bureaucratic controls over production, investment and trade;
> 2. Inward-looking trade and foreign investment policies;
> 3. A substantial public sector, going well beyond the conventional confines of public utilities and infrastructure.
>
> (*Bhagwati, 1993: 46*)

In other words, to put more it graphically using Bhagwati's picturesque imagery – the reforms meant making a bonfire of industrial investment and output controls, or ending the much criticised *Permit Licence Raj*. However, in practice, the speed and scope of the reforms was gradual – slow by international standards but pretty rapid by domestic yardsticks – and they were undertaken by trial and error, regardless of the political dispensation at the helm.

The reforms, though initially centred on industry and trade, culminated in encompassing financial globalisation in the last decade when India became enmeshed in the global economic cycle of boom and burst.[2] The public sector was rolled back even within the "conventional confines of utilities and infrastructure" by allowing private and foreign capital in these industries.

India surely rode the boom during its "Dream Run" for five years from 2003 to 2008 to clock an unprecedented annual economic growth of about 9 per cent, to be counted as among the world's fastest growing large economies (Nagaraj, 2013). If China came to be known as the world's factory, India was reckoned, albeit briefly, as its back office. After the global financial crisis, as with the rest of world, India's boom went bust – with industrial deceleration, rising import dependence and growing short-term capital inflows (or, simply hot money) financing the balance of payment deficit.

After a quarter-century of the market-oriented reforms, why did India fail to emulate (or catch up with) the Asian economies to cement its reputation as a successful industrialisation nation with rising manufactured exports? Perhaps, with booming services exports India dreamt of skipping the industrialisation stage to be counted as the world's back office, leveraging its large educated (*sic*) English speaking workforce – ignoring outsourcing services' narrow employment base domestically, and even the slender market segment it was tied to in the US financial services.

We are now back to the drawing board, trying to configure out how to re-industrialise, given India's persistent economic backwardness (with half its workforce still engaged in low productive agriculture and over two-thirds of its population as yet living in villages) with bleak export prospects and fickle capital inflows financing its external deficit.

This is not a new question, however. The *Make in India* campaign seeking to raise the manufacturing sector's share in domestic output to 25 per cent (www.makeinindia.com/policies, accessed on December 2, 2016), or, the previous regime's *National Manufacturing Policy*, 2011, aiming to raise the manufacturing sector's share in GDP to 25 per cent by 2022 (http://dipp.nic.in/english/policies/national_manufacturing_policy_25october2011.pdf, accessed on December 2, 2016) are the official efforts to grapple with the question. But the real challenge apparently is to translate these lofty goals into actionable policies with suitable instruments. While working out the specifics of such a strategy is beyond the scope of the study, it hopes to lay out a broad framework of analysis for such an initiative.

This short chapter critically reviews industrial performance and policy after the reforms in 1991, and seeks to address the question of how to get over the stagnation. The first section describes the main quantitative trends in industrial performance after the reforms, the second section reviews the analytical and policy discourse on the performance, the third section discusses the need to reconfigure the development state in the present context, and the fourth section concludes with a brief discussion on policy options.

Industrial trends

Over the entire period of reforms (1991–2014), the manufacturing sector grew at an annual trend growth rate of 7.7 per cent, or 7.2 per cent as per ASI and IIP, respectively (Figure 6.1). Evidently, ASI records much wider yearly fluctuations than IIP, which would show up wide differences in the growth rates over shorter periods.[3]

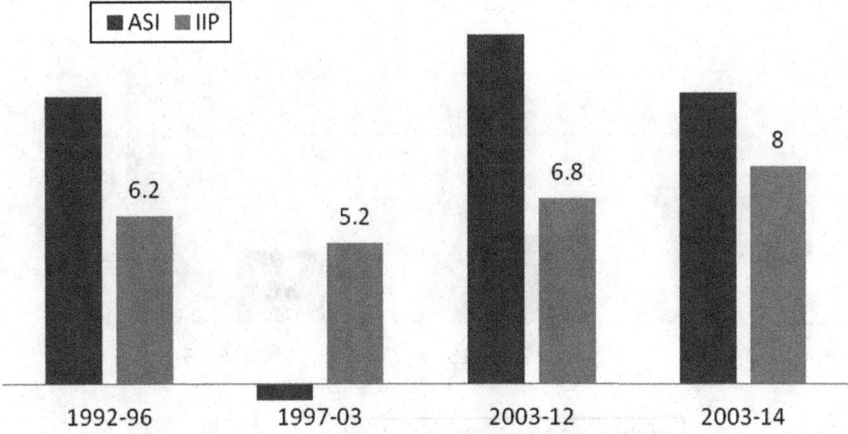

Figure 6.5 Manufacturing sector growth as per ASI and IIP. *Source*: CSO and RBI's *Handbook of Statistics on Indian Economy*.

From the foregoing graph (Figure 6.1), evidently, the 25-year period can be subdivided into three distinct phases: 1992–96, 1997–2003 and 2003–2014 (Figure 6.5). The first phase represents the initial euphoria of reforms, with booming output and investment in the anticipation of a virtuous cycle of faster growth and exports. However, with the expectations of a boost in demand not being realised, industrial growth decelerated. It coincided with the Asian financial crisis, bust of the dot.com bubble and freezing of credit markets in the US in the early 2000s.[4]

The period from 2003 to 2014 represents, as mentioned earlier, the recent debt-led cycle of boom and bust, perhaps best illustrated by the trends in India's and global exports (Figure 6.6) (Nagaraj 2013). After the global financial crash in 2008–09, capital inflows on account of quantitative easing (QE) in the advanced economies sustained economic growth until 2011–12 (as

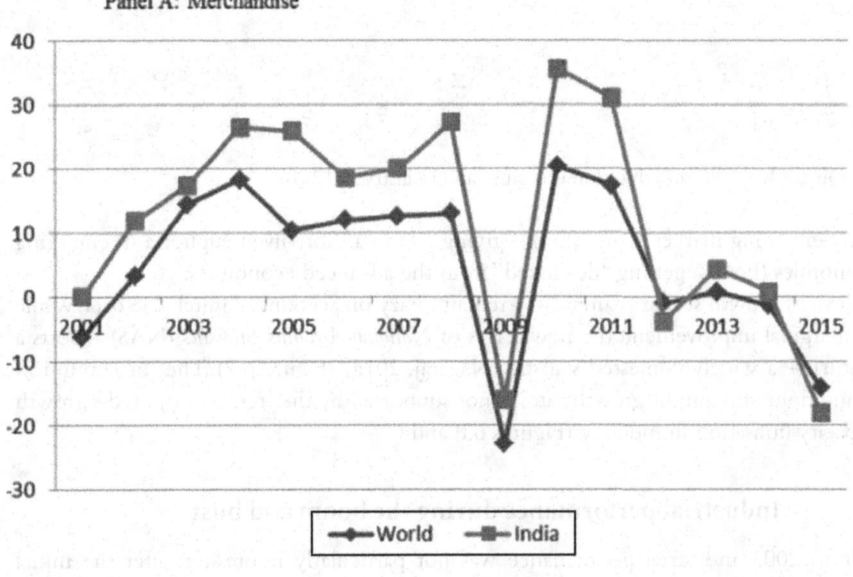

Figure 6.6 Annual merchandise export growth rate for India and the world. *Source*: Veeramani (2016).

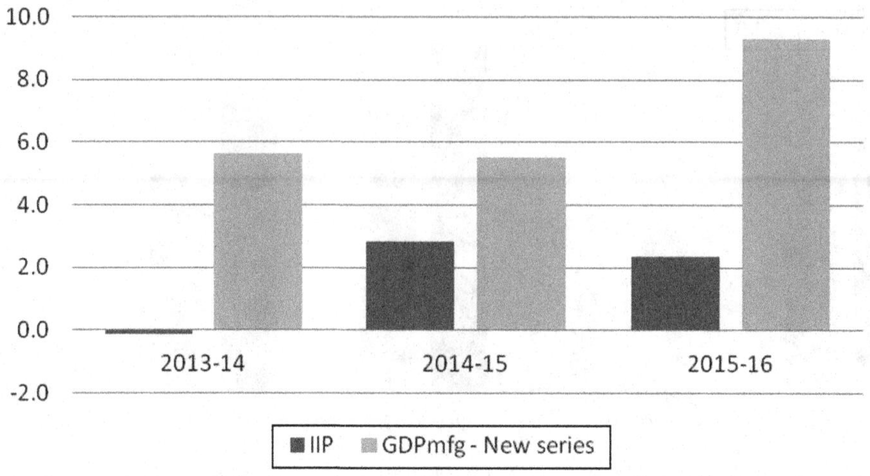

Figure 6.7 Manufacturing growth rate as per IIP and New GDP Series. *Source*: National Accounts Statistics, various issues, and RBI's *Handbook of Statistics on Indian Economy*.

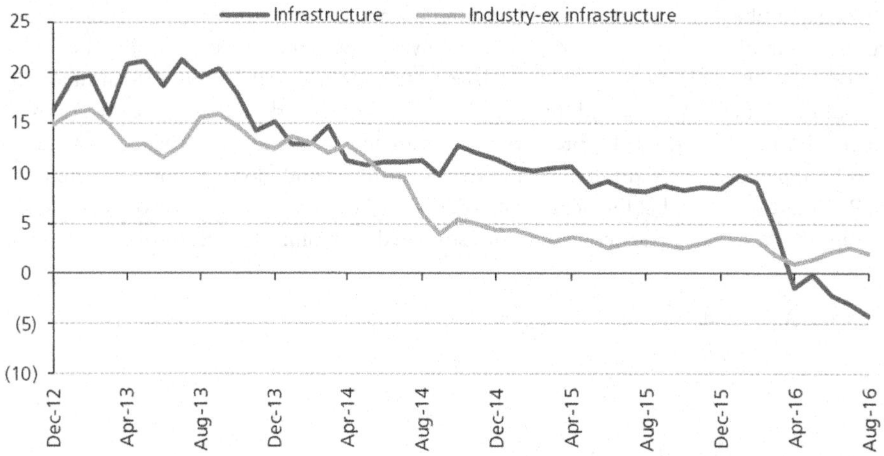

Figure 6.8 Quarterly credit growth to infrastructure and industry, 2012–16

also in many emerging market economies) – giving rise to a short-lived euphoria of emerging market economies (EMEs) getting "de-linked" from the advanced economies.

The industrial growth scenario after 2014 remains hazy on account of unreliable data. While IIP shows marginal improvement, the new series of *National Accounts Statistics* (NAS) reports a distinct upturn – a widely contested statistic (Nagaraj, 2015) (Figure 6.7). The turnaround in industrial and domestic output growth rates is not supported by the trends in (i) credit growth and (ii) capacity utilisation in industry (Figures 6.8 and 6.9).[5]

Industrial performance during the boom and bust

From 1991 to 2003, industrial performance was not particularly impressive: after the initial boom until 1996, there was a 9-year period of deceleration, when the output growth was buf-

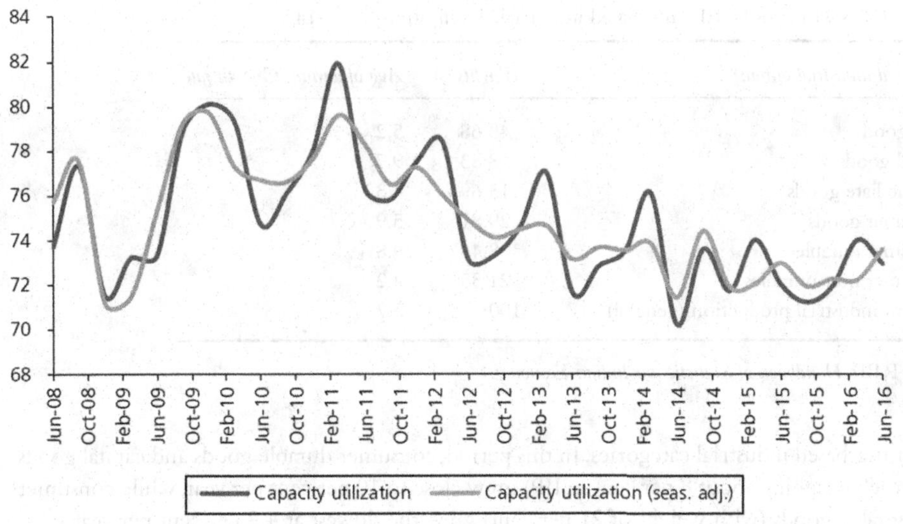

Figure 6.9 Capacity utilisation in industry, 2008–16

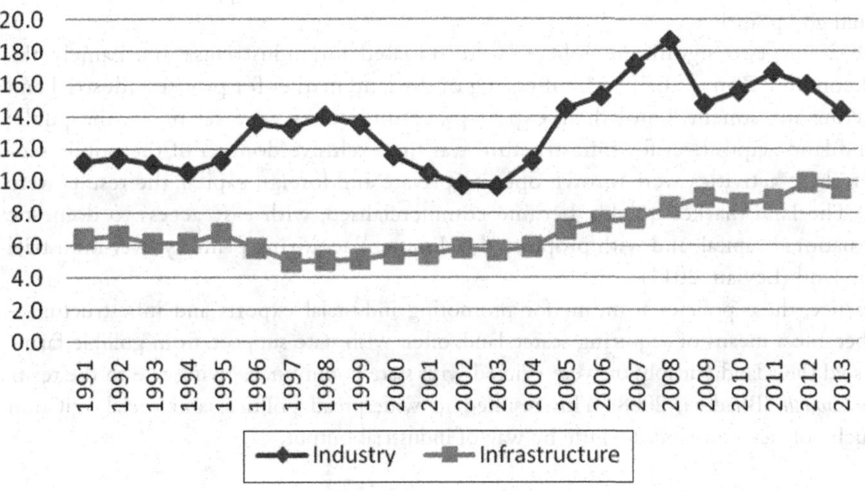

Figure 6.10 Fixed investment as percentage of GDP. *Source*: *National Accounts Statistics*, various issues.

feted by many shocks such as the Asian financial crisis. However, the following cycle of boom and bust (2003–2014) was significant in many respects. Five years of India's dream run (2003–04 to 2007–08) was surely led by outsourcing services exports, but manufacturing growth matched the boom with 10 per cent annual growth rate. This was made possible by a steep rise in domestic saving, investment and capital inflows, boosting the capital formation rate to close to 40 per cent of GDP at the peak of the boom in 2008 (Figure 6.10).

The growth rate recovered though after the financial crisis in 2008–09, albeit at a slower rate of 7.3 per cent per year in the following four years until 2011–12, but decelerated rapidly thereafter. Table 6.1 provides the average annual growth rates from 2004–05 to 2013–14, as per

Table 6.1 Growth rates by IIP's use-based industrial classification, 2005–14

Use-based industrial output	*Weights*	*Avg of annual Growth rates*
Basic goods	45.68	5.2
Capital goods	8.83	9.7
Intermediate goods	15.69	4.3
Consumer goods	29.81	5.9
Consumer durables	8.46	9.8
Consumer non-durables	21.35	4.2
Index of industrial production (general)	100	5.7

Source: RBI's *Handbook of Statistics on Indian Economy*.

IIP, for use-based industrial categories. In this period, consumer durable goods and capital goods (with each weighing about 8 per cent in IIP) grew close to 10 per cent per year, while consumer non-durable goods (with weight of 21 per cent) grew the slowest at 4.2 per cent per year.

This is also the time when foreign firms and brand names came to dominate many markets, especially consumer durables and capital goods. Import to domestic output ratio went up quite sharply in most industries (Chaudhuri, 2013). However, if indirect imports are included, the ratio would go up further.[6]

In the 2000s, two significant policies were initiated for industrialisation, namely the Special Economic Zone (SEZ) and unfreezing of the land market for private industrial and infrastructure investment. Until then, export processing zones were set up by the public sector, and land acquisition for infrastructure was the exclusive domain of the public sector. When these activities were thrown open to private and foreign capital, the results were dramatic. The land market quickly became commercialised, with easy access to domestic and international capital, and with property development acquiring primacy over industrial use of the land (Levian, 2011).

In practice, these policies – meant for promoting industrial exports and infrastructure – quickly became a means of acquiring scarce land, often with state support, from gullible farmers who sold their land cheaply, or were evicted with state connivance, giving rise to the term, *Predatory Growth* (Bhaduri, 2008). This resulted in widespread political and social agitation against such policies, contributing little by way of industrial output.

Competing explanations for the trends

How does one understand the foregoing account of industrial performance? Many would agree that industry underperformed, but the reasons proffered for it could vary considerably.[7] By no stretch of the imagination could state policy constrain industrial decision making any longer. With India's tariff being reduced comparable to the Asian levels, and with numerous bilateral trade and investment treaties, India's openness has become mostly comparable to its Asian peers. Crucially, if the much derided *Permit Licence Raj* had held up industrial growth during the planning era, then why didn't industrial output and exports fail to zoom after the reforms?

Protagonists of reforms, however, would contend that the reforms have not gone far enough or the agenda remains incomplete – with the remaining restrictions on FDI (especially in retail), labour market regulation (inability to hire and fire at will), full convertibility of capital and so on. These arguments seem questionable. There is no clear theoretically valid and empirically sound

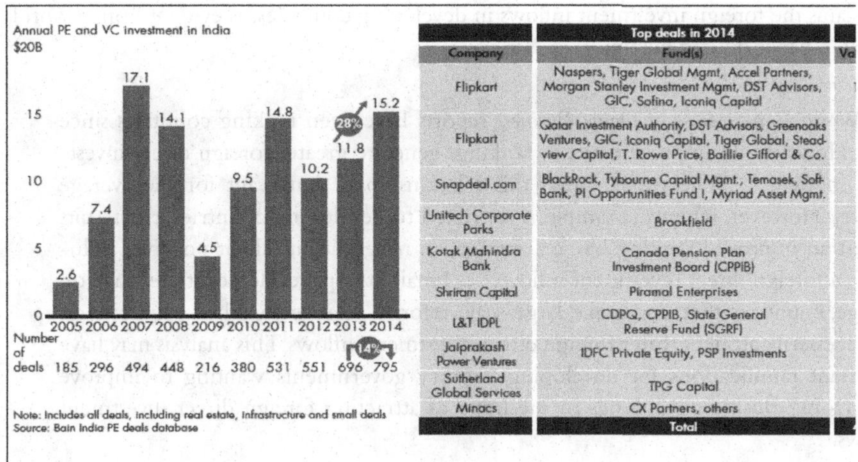

Figure 6.11 PE inflow since 2005 and illustrative list of their investment in 2015. *Source*: India Private Equity Report, 2015, Bain & Company.

association between pro-market reforms and growth (Rodrik, 2011). There is perhaps room for critically examining what has been the outcome of the liberalisation carried out thus far.

What has India's open door policy for FDI led to? In the last decade, the most significant variety of FDI inflow is private equity (PE), venture capital (VC) and hedge funds (HF) which are, by definition, loosely regulated alternative investment funds that are part of shadow banking. They are not even considered FDI by the UNCTAD definition since they are not long term. Quantitatively, the most important of these sources is PE funds, which, by definition, acquire existing assets and sell them after 3–5 years in the stock market after restructuring. These are hardly the kind of foreign capital that India needs for getting technology and acquiring industrial capability.[8] Figure 6.11 provides information on PE and VC inflows into India since 2005 and an illustrative list of projects they invested in during 2015. Economic implications of PE investment are that it is financing domestic consumption using foreign debt, not productive investment.[9]

The labour market rigidity hypothesis is seriously contested; careful reviews of the literature find little support for the widely held proposition (Kannan and Ravindran, 2009; Teitlebaum, 2013; and Sood, Nath and Ghosh, 2014). That the labour market rigidity argument holds little water now can be gauged by the recent news report that L&T, India's largest machinery and construction firm (turnover $16 billion), reportedly laid off 14,000 workers (11.2 per cent of its workforce, 1.22 lakh workers) during July–September this year.[10] It amply demonstrates that the hire and fire policy effectively rules the organised labour market today.

Arguably, the retrenched workers are temporary or contract workers who are not protected by labour laws, which are the bone of contention. But the fact that such a large enterprise employs non-permanent workers in such large numbers only goes to show how the seemingly rigid laws do not apply to a growing segment of organised workers and the laws really have no teeth, hence the contention that labour laws are holding up flexible and hence efficient use of labour simply does not hold water.

Currently, policy makers are using the World Bank's *Ease of Doing Business* (EDB) as a measure of hurdles faced by entrepreneurs, and are busy trying to improve India's global ranking to attract more foreign investment. This dubious measure, both conceptually and empirically, hardly explains the foreign investment inflows in developing countries, as evident from a World Bank research paper quoted below:

> The World Bank's *Ease of Doing Business* reports have been ranking countries since 2006. However, do improvements in rankings generate greater foreign direct investment inflows? ... The paper shows this relationship is significant for the average country. However, when the sample is restricted to developing countries, the results suggest an improved ranking has, on average, an insignificant (albeit positive) influence on foreign direct investment inflows. ... Finally, the paper demonstrates that, on average, countries that undertake large-scale reforms relative to other countries do not necessarily attract greater foreign direct investment inflows. This analysis may have important ramifications for developing country governments wanting to improve their Doing Business Rankings in the hope of attracting foreign direct investment inflows.
>
> *(Jayasuriya, 2011: Abstract)*

If the foregoing arguments are reasonable and the evidence credible, then we should look elsewhere for the reasons for the industrial stagnation. The answer perhaps lies with the structuralist economic arguments of the long-term constraints such as less than satisfactory poor agriculture performance after the reforms (Figure 6.12). Moreover, despite gradual improvements, land productivity in agriculture continues to be a modest fraction of the global average (Figure 6.13). Further, the lack of adequate public infrastructure investment (as proxied by capacity creation for power generation) seems to be holding back industrial growth (Figure 6.14).

At the moment, in the aftermath of the global financial crisis, the Indian industry is suffering from excess capacity in major industries like steel, coal and machinery as the investment rate and exports have fallen. Fixed capital formation ratio, for instance, has fallen by almost 10 percentage points, from close to 40 per cent of GDP in 2008. As the private corporate sector is mired in

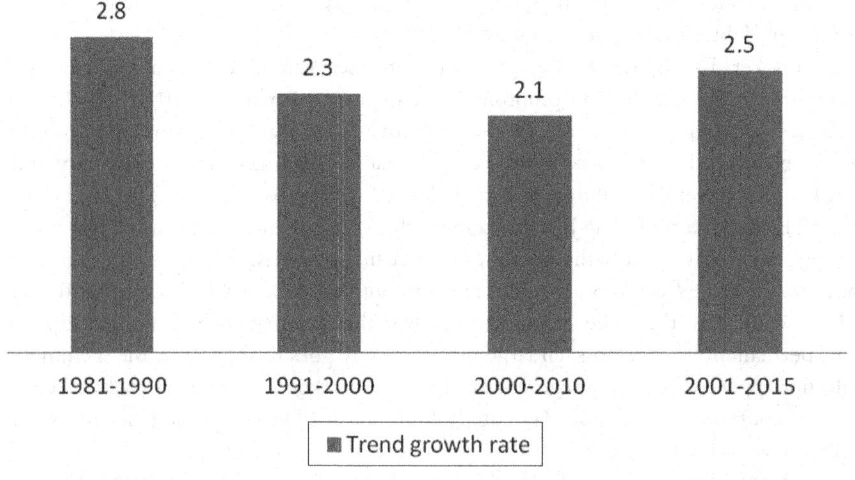

Figure 6.12 Agriculture growth rates, 1981–2015. *Source*: EPW Research Foundation, Fits times series data.

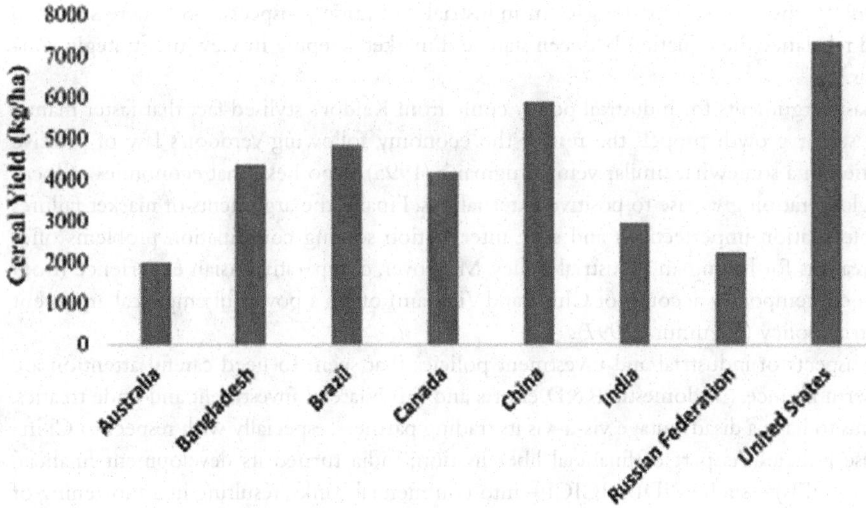

Figure 6.13 Average cereal yields in selected countries, 2013

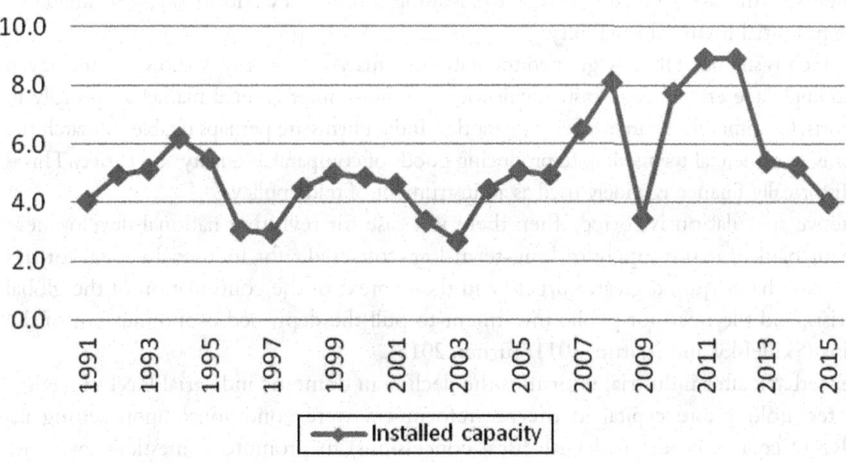

Figure 6.14 Installed capacity, annual growth. *Source*: Economic Survey, various issues.

debt, and the banking sector is left holding the non-performing assets, there is little option but to revive public investment to boost investment and domestic output (Nagaraj, 2014).

Need for reconfiguring development state

While the foregoing arguments for removing the structural constraints on industrial growth still hold, it is perhaps an opportune moment to revisit the role of state support for industrialisation. Admittedly, state intervention during the planning era (1950–1980) had many shortcomings (too widely acknowledged to bear repetition), and many aspects of it may have outlived their utility. Yet, perhaps, the rush to open up markets after 1991 (under stressed macroeconomic conditions), seems to have hurt long-term industrial and trade prospects.[11] So, there seems to be a need rebalance the equation between state and market, keeping in view the strategic considerations.[12]

The basic arguments for industrial policy come from Kaldor's stylised fact that faster manufacturing sector growth propels the rest of the economy, following Verdoon's law of positive externalities. In a somewhat similar vein, Krugman's (1995) hypothesis that economies of locational agglomeration give rise to positive externalities. Finally, the arguments of market failures due to information imperfections and state intervention solving coordination problems offer credible reasons for having an industrial policy. Moreover, comparative Asian experience (from Japan to a contemporary account of China and Vietnam) offers a powerful empirical argument for industrial policy (Suzumura, 1997).

Three aspects of industrial and investment policies that seem to need careful attention are (i) long-term finance, (ii) domestic R&D efforts and (iii) bilateral investment and trade treaties. India seems to have a disadvantage vis-à-vis its trading partners, especially with respect to China in all these policies. As part of financial liberalisation, India turned its development financial institutions (DFIs) – such as IDBI, ICICI – into commercial banks, resulting in a shortening of loan maturity, thus constraining capital intensive manufacturing and infrastructure financing. The domestic debt market was expected to fill the vacuum that has not happened (as in most industrialising countries). In response, large firms were allowed to borrow internationally even for investments in the non-traded goods sector, leading to currency and maturity mismatches, thus raising potential financial instability.

China, which is still not officially granted the status of a market economy, is known to use cheap credit (including trade credit) as an instrument for penetrating international markets, especially in project exports. Commercial sources often suggest that Indian firms are perhaps unable to match the Chinese firms' commercial terms, despite producing goods of comparable quality and variety. This is not new. Historically, finance is widely used as an instrument of trade policy.

If the above speculation is correct, then there is a case for revisiting national development or investment banks for the supply of long-term low-cost credit for industrial capital formation. Such a case has acquired greater urgency in the context of the continuation of the global financial crisis, and the need for public investment to pull the depressed economies out of the present crisis (Skidelsky and Martin, 2011; Turner, 2015).

Another setback after industrial reforms is the decline in domestic industrial R&D. Licences to import technology and capital in the pre-reform era were conditional upon setting up domestic R&D centres (sweetened with fiscal concessions) to promote domestic know-how. Post-reforms, as firms no longer needed to make such efforts, and foreign firms had no reason to invest in R&D in India that could potentially compete with their parent firms' global interests. Net result: stagnation in R&D efforts, best illustrated again with a Chinese comparison. In 1996 both China and India spend the same share of their GDP on R&D, at 0.6 per cent. However, by 2011, the ratio for China had tripled to 1.8 per cent of GDP, whereas for India the ratio had marginally moved up to 0.8 per cent (Figure 6.15). Interestingly, despite its liberal FDI policy, China did not take its eye off the strategic significance of R&D, whereas India perhaps lost its focus in the free market rhetoric (Sunil Mani, 2016a, 2016b).

At the height of financial opening up in the last decade, India signed a large number of bilateral free trade investment agreements, whose outcome for industry appears questionable (Dhar, Joseph and James, 2012). In particular, the treaty with Thailand, a large base for the Japanese automotive industry, seems to have hurt Indian automotive firms, enabling duty-free entry of goods.[13] If the observation is correct, then there is perhaps merit in reviewing such agreements.

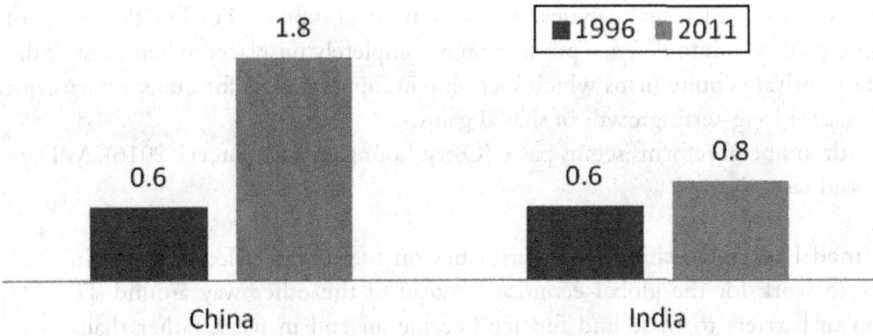

Figure 6.15 R&D expenditure as percentage of GDP in China and India. *Source*: World Bank's World Development Indicators, http://databank.worldbank.org/data/reports.aspx?source=world-development-indicators.

This is not to argue for unconditional protectionism or unalloyed faith in states' capacity to promote industrialisation but to seek for a more reasoned, rule-based support for industry. This should not be seen as a plea for putting the clock back – such a view would be ahistorical. What is needed is perhaps redefining and reconfiguring the boundaries of state and market in view of changed ground realities, comparative experience and the renewed analytical arguments for suitable state intervention.

Conclusion

Liberal economic reforms or market-friendly policy framework constructed over the last quarter-century have not served the manufacturing sector well, despite faster economic growth and output diversification. The goal of rapid industrialising to catch up with Asian peers in an open trade and capital regime employing abundant labour for labour-intensive exports did not materialise. There has been an undeniable improvement in domestic competition with a rise in the quality and variety of goods produced and exported. Yet, the manufacturing share in GDP stagnated, and, its share in merchandise exports declined and import content in domestic consumption shot up.

The eroding industrial base has found a political expression in the current political dispensation's slogan, *Make in India*, or in the previous regime's *National Manufacturing Policy, 2011*, although these ideas are yet to be translated into workable policies and suitable instruments for implementation. The easy starting point would be to try producing domestically what is being imported. The sharp rise in imports during recent years clearly shows the potential to indigenise production quickly.

Ruling dispensations regardless of their political colour and candour have argued for "finishing" or "completing" the liberal economic reforms agenda, including institutional reforms, to reap their virtuous outcomes. However, after a quarter-century of persuasion, such an advocacy rings hallow as it does not have support either in theory or in comparative experience. Worldwide rethinking on the virtues of unbridled globalisation of trade and investment after the global financial crisis is a testament to the limits of such arguments, in the current stage of political democracy.

The policy makers' single-minded focus on improving India's ranking in World Bank's *Doing Business Index* (by mainly whittling down protective measures for the working poor) seems seriously misplaced as the index has no analytical basis or empirical support. Further, the easing of entry of foreign capital even into defence production is completely misplaced when most of the FDI inflow is from private equity firms which specialise in flipping assets for quick returns, not digging their heels for long-term growth of shared gains.

Unalloyed faith in liberal reforms seems passé (Ostry, Loungani and Furceri, 2016). As Dani Rodrik (2011) said recently,

> The new model of globalization stood priorities on their head, effectively putting democracy to work for the global economy, instead of the other way around. The elimination of barriers to trade and finance became an end in itself, rather than a means toward more fundamental economic and social goals. Societies were asked to subject domestic economies to the whims of global financial markets; sign investment treaties that created special rights for foreign companies; and reduce corporate and top income taxes to attract footloose corporations.
>
> *(www.nytimes.com/2016/09/18/opinion/sunday/put-globalization-to-work-for-democracies.html).*

With global economic recession continuing eight years after the financial crisis, its political fallout in terms of Brexit, or ultra-nationalism in the US and proposed scrapping of TPP by the US seem clear signals of the limits to globalism. Considering the current global political and economic uncertainties, it would be prudent to pause and reflect on the liberal model. There is perhaps a need to revitalise the idea of a development state for retaking the initiatives for industrialisation.

Such a vision should not be misconstrued as a plea for a reversal to uncritical infant industry protection or complete de-linking from international trade and capital flows. Surely, with rising agriculture productivity, and structural transformation, industrial growth will have to increasingly turn to exports for sustaining domestic growth. Yet, for a large economy like India's – to paraphrase Arthur Lewis – exports will have to be the efficient lubricant for the large domestic economy, especially to meet the energy import needs. It calls for strategic integration with the global economy and reinventing industrial policy, keeping in view the long-term national goals.

The structuralist economic view of India's long-term constraints such as low agriculture productivity (compared to the global average), poor public infrastructure and extreme energy import dependence seems to hold considerable value to this date. So, at a macroeconomic level, such a view would call for substantial state intervention to step up domestic savings and public investment, and insulate the domestic economy from short-term volatility emanating from the global economy.

We probably need to identify industries and products in which imports are succeeding on account of easy credit, and those which require productivity improvement. There is apparently a need to reconfigure a strategy for capital goods development (in items like ICT hardware or in solar energy), in which India has become seriously import-dependent, undermining the strategic national interests. This is not, however, a plea for blanket import substitution, and export pessimism but to infuse technological dynamism to re-capture the domestic market and dynamic comparative advantage in trade. Capital and technology imports should be accompanied by commitments for R&D investment.

There is a need to reimagine the role of domestic financial institutions to provide long-term credit for capital intensive industries, infrastructure and exports – on the line advocated separately by Robert Skidlesky and Adair Turner in the current global context. These measures necessarily have a fiscal counterpart, which needs to be addressed by revisiting fiscal rules.

Similarly, domestic R&D expenditure which has barely inched up during the reforms as a share of GDP – compared to China which tripled the ratio – needs to be seriously viewed and corrected if the current political dispensation is serious of realising their dream of techno-nationalism.

Notes

1 Unless otherwise mentioned, all figures are at constant prices.
2 This is different from the earlier experience of the 1980s when India's annual economic growth (as also China's) accelerated to around 5.5 per cent, while much of the global economy got mired in debt crisis – known as the lost decade of development – after Mexico defaulted on its international payments.
3 IIP is a leading indicator of physical output with minimum lag, whereas ASI is largely based on the annual census of production accounts of large factories, data available with a 2-year lag. Usually ASI output growth estimates are higher than the IIP based estimates. The gap between the two output-series tends to diverge after about 5 years from the base year of IIP.
4 For a detailed analytical account of this phase, refer to Nagaraj (2003).
5 Considering the uncertain data quality, we would restrict the analysis up to 2014.
6 For a detailed economic analysis of this period, see Nagaraj (2013).
7 For details of the arguments reported in this section see Nagaraj (2011) for a critical review of industrial performance until the boom of 2008.
8 The surge in IPO in 2016 seems to be a case in point. Indian companies mobilised close to $3 billion (Rs. 19,379 crore) during January–September 2016, highest since 2007. Yet, it does not seem to be for augmenting fixed capital formation but for enabling PEs, which invested during the boom of the last decade to cash out their profits, or dilute promoters' equity holding to pay off PE investors; see Aarati Krishnan, "Why this time isn't different", *Business Line*, 26 October 2016.
9 As official data on FDI inflows are not available by type of institution, we have relied on non-official sources.
10 In one of India's biggest-ever layoffs, L&T sheds 14,000 employees from its workforce, by Rachita Prasad, ET Bureau, November 23, 2016.
11 For a careful account of how the changes in the policy affected industrial growth and capability see Chaudhuri (2013, 2015).
12 China's entry into the WTO seems instructive. It carefully negotiated its terms of entry, timed the entry well to take advantage of the global market for its labour-intensive goods at an undervalued exchange rate and defended the rate for well over a decade to flood the world with its cheap manufacturing. In the process, China, strategically, was able to convert its surplus labour into a trade surplus, to gain an immense advantage in global financial markets.
13 "Industry has been ruined by FTAs" says Baba Kalyani, Chairman of Bharat Forge, and Kalyani group of companies with a turnover of $2.5 billion, specialising in automotive forging, supplying to major OE manufacturers worldwide. He said recently in an interview, "Industry has been ruined by FTAs … because of the FTA, due to which companies come and set up plants here, they don't manufacture anything, they just assemble" (*The Hindu Business Line*, 10 February 2014).

References

Bhaduri, Amit (2008): "Predatory Growth", *Economic and Political Weekly*, Vol. 43, No. 16, pp. 10–14, April 19.
Bhagwati, Jagdish (1993): *India in Transition: Freeing the Economy*, Oxford: Clarendon Press.
Chaudhuri, Sudip (2013): "Manufacturing Trade Deficit and Industrial Policy in India", *Economic and Political Weekly*, Vol. 48, No. 8, pp. 60–69, February 23.
__________ (2015): "Import Liberalisation and Premature Deindustrialisation in India", *Economic and Political Weekly*, Vol. 50, No. 43, October 24.
Dhar, Biswajit, Reji Joseph, and T. C. James (2012): "India's Bilateral Investment Agreements: Time to Review", *Economic & Political Weekly*, Vol. 47, No. 52, pp. 113–122, 29 December
Jayasuriya, Dinuk (2011): *Improvements in the World Bank's Ease of Doing Business Rankings: Do They Translate into Greater Foreign Direct Investment Inflows?* World Bank, WPS5787, September 2011, Abstract.

Kannan, K. P., and G. Ravindran (2009): "Growth Sans Employment: A Quarter Century of Jobless Growth in India's Organised Manufacturing", *Economic and Political Weekly*, Vol. 44, No. 10, pp. 80–91.

Krugman, Paul (1995): *Development, Geography and Economic Theory*, Cambridge: MIT Press.

Kumar, Dharma (1988): "The Chinese and Indian Economies, 1914–1949", in Dharma Kumar, ed., *Colonialism, Property and the State*, New Delhi: Oxford University Press.

Levian, Michael (2011): "The Land Question: Special Economic Zones and the Political Economy of Dispossession in India", *Journal of Peasant Studies*, Vol. 39, No. 3–4, pp. 933–969.

Mani, Sunil (2016a): "Is the Government Justified in Reducing R&D Tax Incentives?", *Economic and Political Weekly*, Vol. 51, No. 30, pp. 22–25, July 23.

_________ (2016b): "New IPR Policy 2016: Not Based on Evidence", *Economic and Political Weekly*, Vol. 51, No. 38, pp. 28–32, September 17.

Ostry, Jonathan D., Prakash Loungani, and Davide Furceri (2016): "Neo-Liberalism: Oversold?", *Finance and Development*, International Monetary Fund, June. https://www.imf.org/external/pubs/ft/fandd/2016/06/pdf/ostry.pdf.

Nagaraj, R. (2003): "Industrial Policy and Performance: Which Way Now?", *Economic and Political Weekly*, August 30–September 5, 2003, Vol. 38, No. 35.

________ (2011): "Industrial Performance, 1991–2008: A Review", in D. M. Nachane, ed., *India Development Report*, Delhi: Oxford University Press.

________ (2013): "India's Dream Run, 2003–08: Understanding the Boom and Its Aftermath", *Economic and Political Weekly*, Vol. 48, No. 20, 2013.

________ (2014): "Economic Challenges to the New Government: A Policy Proposal", *Economic and Political Weekly*, Vol. 49, No. 21, pp. 35–41, May 24.

________ (2015): "Seeds of Doubts on New GDP Numbers: Private Corporate Sector Overestimated?", *Economic and Political Weekly*, Vol. 50, No. 13, March 28, 2015.

Raj, K. N. (2006): "The Indian and Chinese Plans: Similarities and Differences", in Ashoka Mody, ed., *Inclusive Growth – K N Raj on Economic Development*, Hyderabad: Orient Longman (first published in *Economic Weekly* on 23 June1956).

Rodrik, Dani (2011): *The Globalization Paradox: Democracy and the Future of the World Economy*, W.W. Norton & Company.

__________ (2015): *Premature Deindustrialisation*, IAS School of Social Science, Economics Working papers, Paper no. 107.

__________ (2016): "Put Globalization to Work for Democracies", *The New York Times*, September 17. http://www.nytimes.com/2016/09/18/opinion/sunday/put-globalization-to-work-for-democracies.html.

Skidelsky, Robert, and Felix Martin (2011): "For a National Investment Bank", *The New York Review of Books*, April 28.

Sood, Atul, Paaritosh Nath, and Sangeeta Ghosh (2014): "Deregulating Capital, Regulating Labour, The Dynamics in the Manufacturing Sector in India", *Economic and Political Weekly*, Vol. 49, Nos. 26–27, June 28.

Suzumura, Kotaro (1997): "Industrial Policy in Developing Market Economies", in Edmond Malinvaud, et al., eds, *Development Strategy and Management of the Market Economy*, Volume 1, Oxford: Clarendon Press for the United Nations.

Teitlelbaum, Emmanuel (2013): "Labour Regulation, Trade Unions and Unemployment", in Atul Kohli and Prerna Singh, eds, *Routledge Handbook of Indian Politics*, Abingdon: Routledge.

Turner, Adair (2015): *Between Debt and the Devil: Money, Credit, and Fixing Global Finance*, Princeton: Princeton University Press.

Veeramani, C. (2016): *Inter-Linkages between Exports and Employment in India*, Occasional Paper no. 179, Bombay: Export-Import Bank of India, November.

World Bank (1993): *The East Asian Miracle: Economic Growth and Public Policy*, New York: Oxford University Press.

7

IMPACT OF TRADE REFORMS ON LABOUR INCOME SHARE IN INDIAN MANUFACTURING

Bishwanath Goldar

Introduction

A downward trend in the share of labour in national income since the early 1990s has been observed widely across countries. This has led to the emergence of a fairly massive literature dealing with trends in labour income share prevailing globally or in different regions of the world, or in different countries or groups of countries. In many of these studies, the factors responsible for the observed, widely prevalent downward trend in labour income share across countries have been investigated. Dao et al. (2017), for instance, note that there was a downward trend in labour share in global income since the early 1990s, observed for both advanced economies (prevailed also in the 1980s) and emerging market and developing economies (EMDEs). Based on their analysis, they conclude that technological progress with varying exposure to routine occupations explains about half of the overall decline in labour income share in advanced economies, and the downward trend in labour income share in EMDEs is attributable predominantly to integration with the global economies particularly the expansion of global value chains that has contributed to raising the overall capital intensity in production.

Other studies that have reported a widely prevailing downward trend in labour income share across countries include Rodriguez and Jayadev (2010) and Karabarbounis and Neiman (2014). These two studies considered both developed and developing countries. Van Treeck (2017) and Trapp (2015) have focused exclusively on developing countries and these studies have found that, in general, there has been a downward trend in labour income share.

This chapter contributes to the growing literature on labour income share in emerging market economies by analysing the trends in labour income share in India's organized manufacturing[1] and investigating the factors that explain the observed trends. Several earlier studies on labour income share in Indian manufacturing have noted that there has been a downward trend, which is in harmony with the findings of the international research on this subject. What caused the fall in labour income share in Indian manufacturing is obviously a moot question.[2] The chapter is particularly concerned with the impact of India's trade reforms on labour income share in organized manufacturing.

It may be mentioned here that between 1990–91 and 2009–10, the income share of labour in India's organized manufacturing fell by about 10 percentage points, from 32 per cent to 22 per cent. This period also saw a virtual elimination of quantitative restrictions (QRs) on

 DOI: 10.4324/9780367855741-7

manufactured imports and a huge reduction in the tariff rates on imports of manufactured products. According to Das (2016), the *frequency ratio* capturing the extent of non-tariff barriers on imports of manufactured products declined from about 80 per cent in 1990–91 to about 5 per cent in 2009–10 and the average rate of tariff protection to Indian manufacturing fell from 121 per cent in 1990–91 to 18 per cent in 2009–10. According to Banga and Das (2012), the average tariff rate on imports of industrial products in India fell from about 82 per cent in 1990 to about 9.4 per cent in 2009.[3] These reforms directed at liberalizing manufactured imports resulted in increased import penetration of the domestic market of manufactured products and created conditions conducive to the expansion of manufactured exports from India by removing anti-export bias caused by import restrictions and by providing improved access to imported inputs, thereby leading to increased export intensity of Indian manufacturing.[4]

Given that several studies have found globalization to be an important factor explaining the fall in labour income share in EMDEs (discussed later in this chapter) and the fact that between 1990–91 to 2009–10 substantial trade liberalization took place in India which coincided with a marked fall in labour income share in organized manufacturing, it is pertinent to investigate whether trade reforms undertaken in India since 1991 were an important factor responsible for the decline in labour income share in India's organized manufacturing. The chapter makes an attempt in this direction.[5] Econometric analyses are undertaken for this purpose using industry- and plant-level panel data.

The period considered for the analysis is 1990–91 to 2017–18, a period encompassing approximately a quarter-century of economic reforms in India. The analysis of trends based on aggregate-level time series data makes use of data for this period. However, the industry-level and plant-level econometric analyses cover shorter periods (due to difficulties in obtaining the required data). The industry-level analysis is based on data for the period 1995–96 to 2014–15 and the plant-level analysis is based on data for the period 1998–99 to 2007–08.

The chapter is organized as follows. The next section presents a brief review of literature including a sub-section on previous studies undertaken on labour income share in Indian manufacturing. The third section is devoted to an analysis of trends in the income share of labour in organized manufacturing and trends in wage rate and labour productivity. The following two sections present the results of econometric analysis, respectively, at industry-level and plant-level. The data sources used and the model specification adopted are discussed and the estimates of the econometric models are presented and discussed in these two sections. Finally, the last section summarizes and concludes.

Literature review

International literature

As mentioned earlier, there is a fairly massive literature dealing with trends in labour income share globally, and in different regions, different countries and groups of countries. In many of the studies constituting this literature, the factors responsible for the observed, widely prevalent downward trend in labour income share across countries have been investigated. It is evident from this literature that a downward trend in labour income share has prevailed both among advanced economies and among EMDEs (see, e.g., Dao, et al. 2017 and OECD 2012).

Some of the studies on labour income share have examined not only the trends in labour income share at the aggregate economy level but also the trends at the sectoral level, thus looking into the trends in labour income share in manufacturing (which is an issue of greater importance and interest for the present study). These studies have found that generally there has been a downward trend in labour income share in manufacturing. Alvarez-Cuadrado et al. (2018), for example, report that the decline in labour income share in manufacturing has been more pronounced than that in services in the US and a broad set of other industrialized countries. Dao et al. (2017) find that labour income share in manufacturing has gone down over time in a majority of countries – both among advanced economies and among EMDEs.

As regards labour income share in manufacturing among EMDEs, a downward trend has been observed in several studies undertaken. As stated above, Dao et al. (2017) report that, among EMDEs, there has been a downward trend in labour income share in manufacturing in a majority of cases. This is corroborated by the findings of Rodriguez and Jayadev (2010). To mention here one more study that has come up with similar findings, Van Treeck (2017) finds that in general there has been a downward trend in labour income share in manufacturing among developing countries in the period since 2000.

A downward trend in labour income share in manufacturing has been reported in several country-specific studies. A downward trend in the income share of labour in Indian manufacturing (organized sector) has been noted by Shastry and Ramana Murthy (2003), Goldar (2004a, 2004b, 2013), Goldar and Aggarwal (2005) and Abraham and Sasikumar (2017). To give a few examples for other EMDEs, for Chinese manufacturing, a downward trend in labour income share in manufacturing has been reported by Qian and Zhu (2013) and Berkowitz et al. (2015), and similarly, Ibarra and Ros (2017) have found a downward trend in labour income share in manufacturing for Mexico (during 2002–2015). However, in some studies an upward trend in the labour income share in manufacturing, instead of a downward trend, has been observed, e.g., the study undertaken by Ng et al. (2018) for Malaysia.

What caused the labour income share to fall over time has been investigated in a large number of studies. Two important factors that have been identified are: (a) capital–labour substitution and technological advance and (b) globalization. The effect of globalization on labour income share is of particular interest in this study since its focus is on the effect of trade reforms.

To take up the technology issue first, Karabarbounis and Neiman (2014) have argued that the global decline of the labour share is connected with the global decline in the relative price of investment goods which is attributable to advances in information technology and the computer age.[6] Carbonero et al. (2017) in their study of eight European countries and the USA draw attention to the fall in the price of ICT (information communication technology) assets and present empirical evidence to argue that increased ratio of ICT capital stock to labour, i.e. ICT-labour substitution, can be potentially one of the factors that explain the fall in labour income share.

Other studies that have examined the impact of ICT capital stock on the income share of labour in advanced economies include Jaumotte and Tytell (2007) who have covered 18 advanced OECD economies in their study. They have found a significant effect of ICT capital on labour income share. They conclude that globalization and technological change have been two important factors behind the fall in labour income share. Also mentionable here is the study undertaken by Guschanski and Onaran (2016) covering the USA and several developed countries of Europe. For the USA, France, Italy and Spain, a negative effect of ICT capital on labour income share is indicated by their econometric results. But, for the UK and Germany, they do not find a significant negative effect of ICT capital on labour income share.

Turning now to globalization, there is divergence in the empirical findings on the impact of globalization on labour income share reported in various studies. Harrison (2005) used data for more than 100 countries covering about four decades and found that an increase in trade openness tends to reduce labour income share. Other studies which have found that trade openness negatively impacts labour income share include Jayadev (2007) who used data for up to 80 countries covering the time period 1972–1995.

Guerriero and Sen (2012) have analysed data for 89 countries for the period 1970–2009, covering both developed and developing countries, and have come to the conclusion that trade openness and technological innovations have a positive and significant effect on the labour income share, contradicting the findings of several other studies such as Harrison (2005). Their finding of a positive effect of technological innovations on labour income share is out of sync with a commonly held view emerging from the literature that technological change provides a major part of the explanation for the observed downward trend in labour income share among advanced economies (see, for instance, Jaumotte and Tytell 2007 and Dao et al. 2017).

The findings of some more studies on the impact of globalization on labour income share may be mentioned here to bring out the diversity in findings. Dao et al. (2017) find that overall imports and overall exports of goods and services do not matter much for labour income share, but it is the participation in global value chains that has a negative effect on labour income share for both advanced economies and EMDEs. Doan and Wan (2017) have used country-level panel data for 87 countries for 1980–2010 to study the impact of globalization on labour income share and have come to the conclusion that, in general, increases in exports have a detrimental impact and increases in imports have a positive impact on labour income share. Their finding of a positive effect of imports on labour income contradicts the findings of Harrison (2005) and Jayadev (2007). It is in some ways also in conflict with the findings of Dao et al. (2017). It, however, matches the findings of Guerriero and Sen (2012). On the other hand, the finding of a negative effect of exports on labour income share goes against the findings of Guerriero and Sen (2012).

Guschanski and Onaran (2017) have carried out an analysis of factors influencing labour income share in emerging market economies by using data for seven such economies (including India). They find that exports made by emerging economies to high wage economies tend to reduce their labour income share, but there is no such adverse effect when exports are made to other countries. This finding is in conformity with the findings of Doan and Wan (2017) inasmuch as both studies find that increases in exports tend to lower labour income share. However, the analysis carried out by Guschanski and Onaran (2017) reveals that the effect of exports on labour income share depends on the destination of exports.

Another aspect that deserves attention is the effect of foreign direct investment (FDI) on labour income share. Guerriero and Sen (2012) in their study mentioned above find that FDI inflows have a negative effect on labour income share. Decreuse and Maarek (2015) have estimated the impact of FDI on labour income share using data from 98 developing countries for the period 1980–2000 and have found that inward FDI has a negative effect on labour income share which is in agreement with the finding of Guerriero and Sen (2012). By contrast, Doan and Wan (2017) in their study mentioned earlier do not find any clear significant effect of FDI on labour income share.

Before concluding this section, the key findings of some of the studies on the impact of trade liberalization and FDI on labour income share in China may be briefly stated. Kamal et al. (2014) find a positive effect of trade liberalization on labour income share in value added in China. They have used firm-level data for the period 1998 to 2007 and considered the impact of tariff cuts. According to their estimates, the labour share in value added in 2007 was 11 per cent higher than what it would have been in the absence of trade reform. Luo and Zhang (2010) find a negative effect of FDI on labour income share which according to the authors arises from regional competition for FDI which weakens workers bargaining power. Bai and Qian (2009) have used provincial data for China for the period 1997 to 2003 to study the effects of FDI, imports and exports on labour income share and have found that neither FDI nor trade dependence had a significant impact on labour income share. Zhou (2016) has used provincial data for China to study the determinants of labour income share covering the period 1978 to 2007 and has found a positive effect of exports and a negative effect of imports on labour income share, the latter finding indicating that import competition tends to reduce labour income share. For FDI, Zhou finds a negative effect on labour income share which is in line with the finding of Luo and Zhang (2010). It is evident that empirical evidence on the impact of trade liberalization on labour income share in China is mixed – some studies have found a negative effect while some others have found a positive effect. As regards FDI, the empirical evidence is on balance indicative of a negative effect of FDI on labour income share in China.

Earlier studies on labour income share in Indian manufacturing

Several researchers have noted a downward trend in labour income share in India's organized manufacturing in the post-reform period and have tried to provide some explanation for the observed trend. Virmani and Hashim (2009), for instance, have attributed the decline in labour income share to labour-saving technical change. Shastry and Ramana Murthy (2003) have attributed the downward trend in labour income share in manufacturing to an increase in the mark-up coupled with an increase in the ratio of materials to wages. In some earlier studies undertaken by the present author (Goldar 2004a, 2004b, 2013; Goldar and Aggarwal 2005), it has been argued that a reduction in the bargaining power of trade unions in the post-reform period and increases in capital intensity of production that have taken place in Indian manufacturing in this period are among the important factors responsible for the decline in labour income share in manufacturing.

The determinants of labour income share in manufacturing have been investigated econometrically by Abraham and Sasikumar (2017). They have considered the period 2000–01 to 2011–12. They have estimated an econometric model using panel data for organized manufacturing. The observations are for different two-digit industries further disaggregated by state. The variables are taken as difference (or rate of change between 2000–01 and 2011–12). The results of the econometric analysis indicate that increases in capital–labour ratio (i.e. capital deepening) tend to reduce the income share of labour. This is in line with the findings of other studies (e.g. Goldar 2013). Increased use of ICT capital is found to have a negative effect on labour income share which is consistent with the international literature on the issue. Three other findings of the study are: (a) increased use of contract workers lowers the income share of labour, (b) increased share of women among workers employed reduces labour income share and (c) after controlling for other factors, the rate of decrease in labour income share over time is relatively lower in states which have flexible or neutral labour regulations than the states which have rigid labour regulations.

Goldar (2013) has examined econometrically the role played by trade liberalization in causing a fall in labour income share in Indian manufacturing. This has been investigated more recently by Ahsan and Mitra (2014) and Gupta and Helble (2018). In terms of the nature of the study, Goldar (2013) and Abraham and Sasikumar (2017) are similar as these are based on industry-level data of ASI (*Annual Survey of Industries*, Central Statistics Office, Ministry of Statistics and Programme Implementation, Government of India). The studies undertaken by Ahsan and Mitra (2014) and Gupta and Helble (2018) are similar since both use micro-level panel data. Ahsan and Mitra use firm (company) level data taken from the Prowess database of CMIE (Centre for Monitoring Indian Economy), whereas Gupta and Helble use plant-level data of ASI.

Goldar (2013) has used industry-level data at the level for two-digit industries. The rate of change in wage share between 1993–94 and 2007–08 is regressed on the rates of change in import intensity, import–availability ratio (i.e. import penetration ratio) and export intensity. The main finding of the study is that an increase in export intensity tends to reduce wage share. A negative effect of increased import competition on wage share is also found.

Ahsan and Mitra (2014) have used tariff data to assess the impact of trade reforms on wage share. They consider the share of wages and salaries in total sales. The tariff data relate to the period 1988 to 2003. They make a distinction between small and large firms and between high-labour-intensity industries and low-labour-intensity industries. From their analysis, they find that trade liberalization in India has led to an increase in the wage share in revenue for small, labour-intensive firms but a reduction in this share in the case of larger, less labour-intensive firms. Another interesting finding of the study is that trade liberalization, on average, led to a decline in the bargaining power of workers.

Gupta and Helble (2018) have used plant (factory) level data for the period 1998–99 to 2007–08 for their analysis. They analyse how changes in output tariff, input tariff and effective rate of protection accorded by tariff to different industries have impacted labour income share. They find that a fall in output tariff raises the income share of labour while a fall in input tariff lowers the income share of labour. However, the results change when industries are segregated according to factor intensity and technology. It is found that reductions in output tariff and input tariff tend to reduce labour income share among industrial plants in technology-intensive and human capital–intensive industries. On the other hand, reductions in output tariff and input tariff tend to raise labour income share in industrial plants belonging to labour-intensive and low-technology industries. Evidently, the key message emerging from the paper by Gupta and Helble (2018) is that the impact of import liberalization on labour income share in manufacturing plants is not uniform across industries – it depends on the nature of technology and factor intensity.

Trend analysis

Labour income share

Figure 7.1 depicts the trends in the income share of labour (i.e. the ratio of total emoluments to gross value added) in India's organized manufacturing at the aggregate level during the period 1980–81 to 2017–18. This is based on ASI data. The ASI dataset at two-digit industry level prepared by the EPWRF (Economic and Political Weekly Research Foundation) has been used. It is evident that there was a downward trend in the income share of labour in the 1980s, which continued in the post-reform period till about 2007–08. After 2007–08, there has been, interestingly, an upward trend in the income share of labour. Because of the increase that took place in labour income share after 2007–08, the level reached by 2017–18 was lower than that prevailing in 1990–91 by only about three percentage points.

The downward trend in labour income share in organized manufacturing during 1990–91 to 2007–08 and the post-2007 trend reversal in labour income share in organized manufacturing are seen not only at the aggregate level but also among two-digit industries. Analysis of trends in labour income share at two-digit industry level for the period 1990–91 to 2017–18, presented in Table 7A.1 in the Annex, brings out that there was a fall in the income share of labour in nearly all two-digit industries (19 out of 22) between 1990–91 and 2007–08, which was followed by an increase in the income share of labour between 2007–08 and 2017–18 in almost all two-digit industries (21 out of 22).

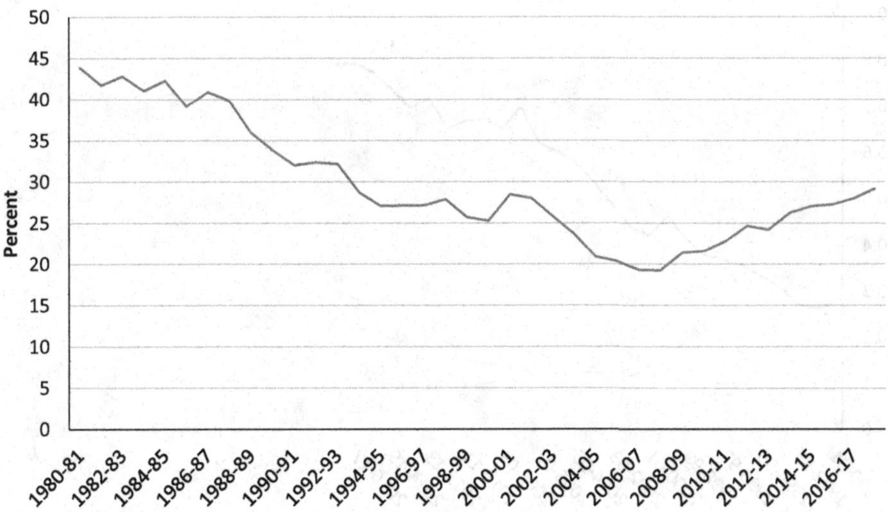

Figure 7.1 Labour income share (%), India's organized manufacturing, 1980–81 to 2017–18. Source: Author's computations based on ASI data. The ASI dataset at two-digit industry level prepared by the EPWRF (Economic and Political Weekly Research Foundation) has been used.

Labour productivity and real wages

The downward trend in labour income share during 1990–91 to 2007–08 implies that the gap between labour productivity and real product wage rate (wage rate deflated by output price index) widened over time. The fact that there has been an increase in the income share of labour in Indian manufacturing in the period after 2007–08 is a manifestation of the fact that there was a reduction in the gap between labour productivity and real product wage rate in the period after 2007–08. This may be seen from Figure 7.2 which shows, for the years 1990–91 to 2017–18, labour productivity and real product wage rate in organized manufacturing at the aggregate level.[7] The trend growth rate in labour productivity in organized manufacturing at the aggregate level was about 5.6 per cent per annum during 1990–91 to 2007–08, which was much higher than the trend growth rate in real product wage rate, at about 2.8 per cent per annum. By contrast, in the period 2007–08 to 2017–18, the trend growth rate in labour productivity decelerated to 1.9 per cent per annum and the trend growth in real product wage accelerated to 5.8 per cent per annum. It is evident that there was a marked acceleration in the growth rate in real product wage rate after 2007–08, and it significantly exceeded the growth rate in labour productivity, causing the labour income share to rise.

The acceleration in the growth rate in real product wage and the associated increase in the labour income share in Indian manufacturing in the period after 2007–08 seems to have some connection with the rate of increase in real wages in agriculture (borne out by the econometric analysis presented in the next section).[8]

Figure 7.3 depicts the real wage rate in agriculture in the period 1990–91 to 2017–18. The basic data source of agricultural wages is *Agricultural Wages in India* brought out by the Directorate of Economics and Statistics, Ministry of Agriculture and Farmers Welfare, Government of India. The wage rates of male agricultural workers have been taken. This has been deflated by the consumer price index of agricultural labourers.

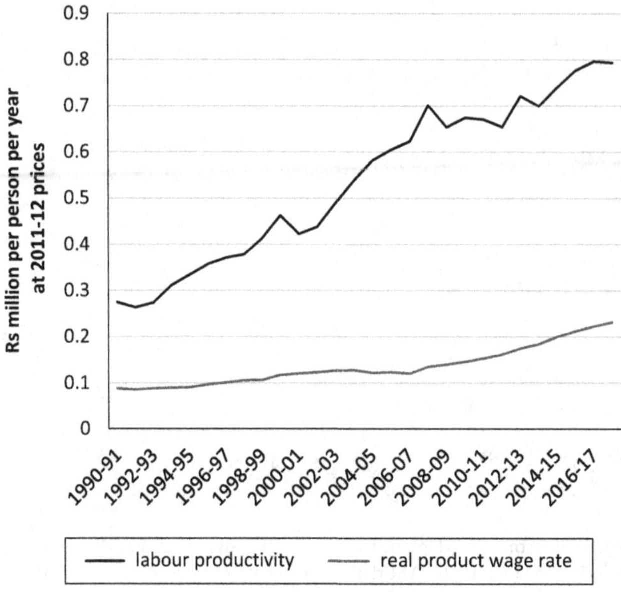

Figure 7.2 Labour productivity and real product wage rate, organized manufacturing, 1990–91 to 2017–18. *Source*: Author's computations based on ASI data. The ASI dataset at two-digit industry level prepared by the EPWRF has been used.

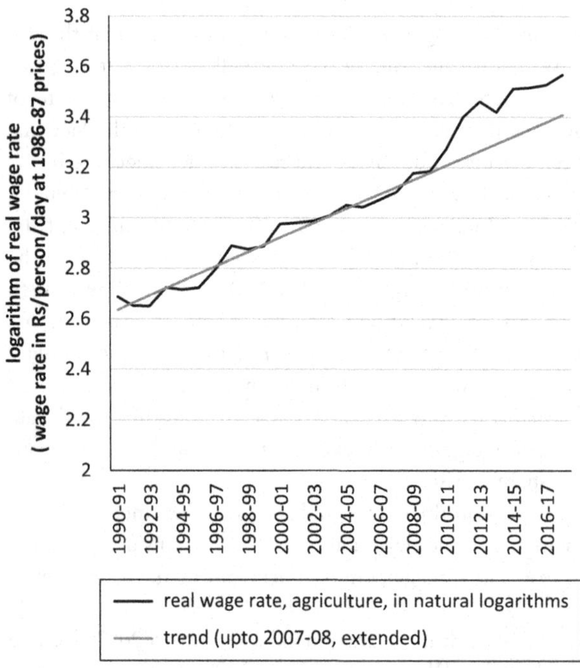

Figure 7.3 Real wage rate in agriculture, 1990–91 to 2017–18, comparison with trend in the period till 2007–08. *Note*: Logarithm of daily wage rate at constant prices is shown to facilitate comparison of growth rates. *Source*: Author's computations.

The trend line shown in the figure is based on the data for the period 1990–91 to 2007–08, i.e. the trend observed till 2007–08 has been extended for the subsequent period. It is evident from the figure that the rate of increase in real wage rate in agriculture in the post-2007 period has been much faster than the trend growth rate prevailing during 1990–91 to 2007–08. Arguably, it is this hike in the growth rate in agricultural real wage after 2007–08 which raised the reservation wage in manufacturing and thus became a contributory factor to an accelerated growth in real product wage rate in manufacturing. The acceleration in the growth rate in real product wage rate in organized manufacturing in the face of a deceleration in labour productivity growth led to an increase in the wage share in value added.

Determinants of labour income share: industry-level analysis

Data, variables and econometric methodology

This section presents an econometric analysis of determinants of labour income share in Indian manufacturing (organized) based on industry-level panel data (for 22 two-digit industries, list given in Table 7A.1 in Annex). The explanatory variables considered for the analysis are: import penetration ratio, export intensity, capital–labour ratio, level of total factor productivity given by an index (TFP)[9] and real wage rate of agricultural workers. The period covered for the analysis is 1995–96 to 2014–15.[10]

Data on the income share of labour in various two-digit manufacturing industries have been taken from ASI. The two-digit level dataset based on ASI prepared by the EPWRF has been used. Income share is computed as total emoluments divided by gross value added, both at current prices.

Capital–labour ratio is obtained as the ratio of fixed capital stock at constant prices divided by total employment. Fixed capital stock series has been constructed at two-digit industry level by the perpetual inventory method using the ASI two-digit level dataset of the EPWRF (see Goldar 2015, 2017 for details). This is divided by employment (i.e. total persons engaged) in each two-digit industry using the EPWRF dataset.

For computing import penetration ratio and export intensity for various two-digit manufacturing industries, data on value of output of various manufacturing industries and the corresponding data on imports and exports of those manufactured products have been taken from input–output tables. The data have been drawn from World Input–Output Database (WIOD) (September 2012 and November 2016 releases). The advantage of using this source is that input–output tables are available for each year. One series of input–output tables for India is available from 1995 to 2011 and the other series, taken from the November 2016 release of WIOD, is from 2000 to 2014. In the more recent series on input–output tables available from WIOD (November 2016 release), the data on production, exports and imports are available for 18 manufacturing industries. These have been mapped into the 22 two-digit industries for which data on labour income and capital–labour ratio were obtained from the EPWRF dataset. Data on production, exports and imports have been used to compute export intensity and import penetration ratio, as explained earlier (see note 4). Having computed these ratios for the period 2000 to 2014, these have been extrapolated backwards to 1995 using the series on input–output tables in WIOD September 2012 release, which cover the period 1995 to 2011.

The source of data on agricultural wages and the computation of real wages have been explained in the previous section. This does not require further discussion here. It should be pointed out, however, that this variable is common across industries and varies over time.

The model used for the analysis is given in equation (7.1) below. It explains variation in the income share of labour across industries and over time. In this equation, there are five explanatory variables: capital intensity or capital–labour ratio (KI), import penetration ratio (MPR), export intensity (XI), level of total factor productivity (TFP) and real wages in agriculture (RWA). The variables KI, TFP and RWA have been taken in logarithms.

$$SL_{it} = \alpha_i + \beta_K \ln KI_{it} + \beta_M MPR_{it} + \beta_X XI_{it} + \beta_R \ln RWA_t + \beta_T \ln TFP_{it} + u_{it} \ldots \quad (7.1)$$

In the above equation, subscript *i* denotes industry and subscript *t* denotes time (year). The error term is denoted by u_{it}. The equation has been estimated by applying the fixed effects model.

It should be pointed out that the model described above is similar to the model specification used in many previous econometric studies on the determinants of labour income share. The theoretical basis for such models is provided by the framework developed by Bentolila and Saint-Paul (2003).

The framework of Bentolila and Saint-Paul (2003) is based on a CES (constant elasticity of substitution) production function allowing for labour and capital augmenting technical change. In the estimable equation derived from the framework, there are three components: (a) capital deepening (capital–output ratio), (b) technical change and (c) effect of market imperfections (see Zhou 2016, Chapter 2, among others). Representing the relationship between the income share of labour and the capital–output ratio by a curve, a change in capital–output ratio involves a movement along the curve. Whether labour income share increases or decreases with increased capital deepening depends on the elasticity of substitution. Technological change involves a shift of the curve. Market imperfections give rise to rents and this leads to a deviation from the true curve. The impact of trade reforms or other such measures on labour income share depends on how they impact the deviation component which is dependent on the bargaining power of workers vis-à-vis firm owners. If economic reforms, particularly globalization (competition from imports, entry into export markets, entry of foreign firms, increased scope for relocating plants including relocating the plant abroad, etc.) cause the bargaining power of labour to go down, then trade reforms cause the income share of labour to go down too. How globalization and foreign direct investment (FDI) is connected with the bargaining power of workers has been discussed in the literature.

One change that has been made in the analysis presented in this chapter in comparison to the model specification commonly adopted is that capital–labour ratio has been taken as the explanatory variable rather than capital–output ratio. There are other studies which have done the same. Capital–labour ratio has been used as an explanatory variable in Doan and Wan (2017). Harrison (2005) has used labour–capital ratio as an explanatory variable instead of capital–output ratio. Hutchinson and Persyn (2012) have applied a model in which capital–output ratio as well as capital–labour ratio are included in the model. Among studies on labour income share in Indian manufacturing, Gupta and Helble (2018) have used capital–output ratio as a measure of capital intensity; but, Abraham and Sasikumar (2017) have used capital–labour ratio, as in this study.

Empirical results

The model estimates are presented in Table 7.1. The model has been estimated first by pooling data on all 22 two-digit manufacturing industries, and then it has been estimated separately for low-technology industries (food products, beverages, tobacco products, textiles and garments, leather and leather products and misc. manufacturing) and medium- and high-technology industries (e.g., basic metals, machinery, and chemicals and chemical products). The classifica-

Table 7.1 Model estimates, industry-level analysis

(Dependent Variable: Labour Income Share)

Time period: 1995–96 to 2014–15 Method: Fixed Effects Model

Explanatory variables	*All industries*	*Low-technology industries*	*Medium- and high-technology industries*
log (capital–labour ratio)	−8.63 (−6.20)***	−22.54 (−7.93)***	−4.50 (−2.65)***
log (TFP)	−1.58 (−0.85)	−9.49 (2.58)**	−1.73 (−0.68)
log (real wage rate in agriculture)	15.14 (7.40)***	32.87 (8.43)***	10.17 (3.71)***
Import penetration ratio	−20.35 (−3.39)***	13.37 (1.16)	−33.94 (−4.79)***
Export intensity	−9.72 (−1.51)	17.98 (1.43)	−7.06 (−0.83)
Constant	13.19 (1.60)	5.48 (0.35)	23.90** (2.32)
No. of observations	440	180	260
R-squared: within	0.1831	0.3617	0.2069
– between	0.2363	0.0197	0.0000
– overall	0.1938	0.0014	0.0128
F-value and prob.	18.51(0.0000)	18.81 (0.0000)	12.62(0.0000)

Source: Author's computations.

, * statistically significant at 5 and 1 per cent level, respectively.

tion of two-digit industries into low-technology and medium- and high-technology has been done following the OECD classification.[11]

The model results indicate a negative effect of capital deepening on labour income share. Also, a positive effect of agricultural real wages on the income share of labour in manufacturing is clearly indicated.

A significant negative coefficient is found for import penetration ratio when data for all industries are pooled. When the model is estimated separately for low-technology and medium- and high-technology industries, the coefficient for import penetration ratio is found to be negative and statistically significant for the latter groups of industries, but not for the former group. Rather, the coefficient of import penetration ratio in the case of low-technology industries is found to be positive. Thus, it may be inferred that increased import competition in the post-reform period had a negative effect on labour income share in medium- and high-technology industries. But, such an effect was not there on low-technology industries. Rather, import competition might have caused an increase in labour income share in value added in such industries.

The results for export intensity are similar to that for import penetration, except that the coefficients are not statistically significant. The effect of increased export intensity appears to be negative for medium- and high-technology industries and positive for low-technology industries.

The coefficient of TFP is found to be negative when all industries are pooled for model estimation. However, the coefficient is not statistically significant. When the estimation of the model is done separately for low-technology and medium- and high-technology industries, the coefficient of TFP is found to be negative and statistically significant for low-technology industries. For the medium- and high-technology industries, the coefficient is negative, but it is not statistically significant. It should be noted further that the numerical value of the coefficient is bigger for the low-technology industries than that for medium- and high-technology industries. It appears therefore that in low-technology industries, gains from TFP increases were not proportionately shared between capital and labour. The increase in labour income arising from TFP gains was relatively lower than the increases in capital income arising from TFP gains.

In a bid to verify the findings emerging from the econometric analysis based on industry-level panel data in respect of import penetration ratio, real agricultural wage rate and capital intensity, a model similar to equation (7.1) has been estimated from aggregate-level time series data for organized manufacturing for the period 1990–91 to 2014–15. Labour income share is taken as the dependent variable. Three explanatory variables are used, namely import penetration ratio,[12] real agricultural wage rate and capital intensity (capital–labour ratio). Model estimation has been done by applying the Auto-Regressive Distributed Lag (ARDL) model. The estimated long-run coefficients are found to be positive and statistically significant for real agricultural wage rate and negative and statistically significant for capital–labour ratio and import penetration ratio. This is consistent with the results for all-industry sample reported in Table 7.1. Thus, the regression results based on aggregate-level time series data are found to be similar and lend support to the results obtained from industry-wise panel data.

Determinants of labour income share: plant-level analysis

Model, data and variables

Plant-level analysis of determinants of labour income share has been carried out with the help of unit-level data of ASI. The period covered is 1998–99 to 2007–08, as in the study of Gupta and Helble (2018). The model used for the analysis is shown below:

$$SL_{ijt} = \alpha_{ij} + \beta_K \ln KI_{ijt} + \beta_M NPR_{it} + \beta_R REER_t + \beta_T \ln TFP_{ijt} + \sum \beta_X X_{ijt} + \phi t + u_{ijt} \ldots \quad (7.2)$$

In this equation, *ij* denotes *i*'th plant in *j*'th industry and *t* denotes time (year). SL is the income share of labour in gross value added (i.e. total emoluments divided by gross value added, in per cent). The explanatory variables used are capital intensity (KI), nominal protection rate i.e. tariff rate on output (NPR), real effective exchange rate (REER), level of total factor productivity (TFP), a set of other firm-level controls denoted by X (with corresponding coefficients denoted by β_X), and the time trend variable denoted by *t*. The variables are discussed further below.

Capital intensity variable has been formed by taking the ratio of deflated fixed capital stock to the number of persons employed. The net fixed capital stock figures for different manufacturing plants for different years have been taken from ASI unit-level data and deflation has been done by the implicit deflator for gross fixed capital formation taken from *National Accounts Statistics*.[13] The value of the net fixed capital stock at constant prices obtained in this manner has been divided by the number of persons employed to get the measure of capital intensity.

In the analysis presented earlier in the section on the industry-level analysis of the determinants of labour income share, import penetration ratio was used as an explanatory variable to capture the effect of import liberalization. For plant-level analysis, a different variable is used. The level of protection indicated by tariff rates is taken as the explanatory variable, as done by Ahsan and Mitra (2014) and Gupta and Helble (2018). The data on tariff rates used for the study are the same as used by

Das (2016) in his study undertaken for the RBI.[14] These tariff rates are available at 3 digit level NIC (National Industrial Classification) of 1987. This has been mapped into 4-digit NIC of 2004/1998 for use in this study. For each year, the average tariff rate for each 4-digit NIC has been applied to all plants belonging to that 4-digit industry.

For assessing properly the impact of tariff cuts on labour income share, it would be useful to control for changes in the exchange rate. This is so because the effect of tariff cuts may partly be neutralized by exchange rate depreciation. Accordingly, the real effective exchange rate (REER) (36-currency, bilateral weights, trade-based weights, data source is RBI) has been included as an explanatory variable.

Estimation of TFP at plant level has been done by applying the Levinsohn-Petrin (2003) methodology. For this purpose, a two-input Cobb-Douglas production function has been estimated, taking deflated gross value added as output,[15] and labour (number of persons employed) and capital (deflated value of the net fixed capital stock) as two inputs. The deflated value of energy used has been taken as a proxy variable to capture the productivity shocks, which is needed for applying the Levinsohn-Petrin (L-P) methodology. To make the application of L-P methodology justifiable, estimation of production function has been done by using observations of only those plants which have been covered in ASI survey at least three times during the period 1998–99 to 2007–08.[16] Derivation of the TFP index has been done by taking (a) the estimated production function parameters obtained by the L-P method, and (b) the average (Geometric mean) of value added, labour and capital inputs across plants for 1998–99 as the values for the reference plant for which the index is taken as one.

Four plant-level control variables are there in the econometric model. There are: (a) share of ICT capital stock (computers and software) in total fixed capital stock, (b) share of contract workers out of total workers employed, (c) share of imported materials in the value of total materials used and (d) manufacturing services purchased (i.e. value of work done by others on materials supplied by the industrial unit) divided by the total value of materials and fuel used. Of these four, the first two have been used by Abraham and Sasikumar (2017) in their study on determinants of labour income share in Indian manufacturing. The third control variable is connected with trade reforms since it reflects access to imported intermediate input. The fourth variable captures the extent of outsourcing done by manufacturing plants in India which is expected to have an impact.

Empirical results

The estimates of equation (7.2) are presented in Table 7.2. The estimation of parameters has been done by applying the fixed effects model.

Model estimation has been done first by pooling data for plants belonging to all 22 two-digit manufacturing industries. Then, separate estimates have been made for low-technology industries and medium- and high-technology industry, as done in the previous section. This has been followed by separate estimates of the model for labour-intensive industries[17] (hereafter called high-labour-intensity industries) and other industries (hereafter called low-labour-intensity industries).[18]

From the results presented in Table 7.2, it is seen that the coefficients of capital intensity and TFP are negative and statistically significant in all five regressions. This is similar to the findings of the analysis presented previously. It may be inferred accordingly that increases in capital intensity and gains in TFP in India's organized manufacturing in the post-reform period had a significant negative effect on labour income share. This effect was present in both low-technology industries and medium- and high-technology industries. Similarly, it was there in both high-labour-intensity industries and low-labour-intensity industries.

Table 7.2 Model estimates, plant-level analysis

Dependent variable: labour income share — Time period: 1998–99 to 2007–08 — Method: Fixed effects model

Explanatory Variables	*All industries*	*Industries grouped into:*		*Industries grouped into:*	
		Low-technology industries	*Medium- and high-technology industries*	*High-labour-intensity industries*	*Relatively low labour intensity industries*
log (capital–labour ratio)	–0.063	–0.065	–0.062	–0.075	–0.059
	(–126.6)***	(–97.7)***	(–79.6)***	(–78.1)***	(–97.9)***
log (TFP)	–0.23	–0.23	–0.23	–0.24	–0.23
	(–434.9) ***	(–299.7)***	(–313.4)***	(–200.9)***	(–385.8)***
Tariff rate	0.00002	–0.0002	0.0006	–0.004	0.0001
	(0.49)	(4.46)***	(4.46)***	(–4.63)***	(2.23)**
Ratio of ICT capital stock to total fixed capital stock	0.014	0.012	0.015	–0.004	0.018
	(3.65)***	(1.81)*	(3.15)***	(–0.41)	(4.16)***
Imported materials divided by total materials used	–0.0008	–0.009	0.005	–0.017	0.005
	(–0.24)	(–1.63)	(1.08)	(–2.44)**	(1.38)
Work done by others on materials supplied to them divided by the value of materials and fuel used in the plant	–0.017	–0.014	–0.020	–0.009	–0.018
	(–5.98)***	(–3.77)***	(–4.56)***	(–2.10)**	(–4.59)***
Share of contract workers in total workers employed	–0.042	–0.032	–0.050	–0.030	–0.045
	(–20.05)***	(–10.33)***	(–17.09)***	(–7.23)***	(–18.41)***
Real effective exchange rate	0.002	0.002	0.0007	0.002	0.001
	(10.06)***	(10.83)***	(3.63)***	(5.98)***	(8.31)***
Time trend	0.007	0.007	0.008	0.007	0.007
	(33.9)***	(26.5)***	(16.58)***	(18.3)***	(28.34)***
Constant	3.07	2.97	3.15	3.16	3.05
No. of observations	163,929	78,341	85,588	38,327	125,602
No. of plants	37,654	17,833	20,492	9297	28,397
R-squared	0.51	0.53	0.50	0.54	0.49
F-value and prob.	21994.3	10599.7	11308.0	4954.7	17100.7
	(0.0000)	(0.0000)	(0.0000)	(0.0000)	(0.0000)

Source: Author's computations.
*, **, *** statistically significant at 10, 5 and 1 per cent level, respectively.

The coefficient of the variable representing contract labour use is negative and statistically significant in all five regressions. This indicates that increased use of contract workers tends to reduce the income share of labour in Indian manufacturing. This finding is expected as relatively lower wages are paid to contract workers (see Goldar 2018). In the study undertaken by Abraham and Sasikumar (2017), a negative effect of contract labour use on labour income share in Indian manufacturing was found. Thus, in this respect, the findings of the two studies are in agreement. It may be mentioned here that in the post-reform period there has been a significant increase in the share of contract workers in total workers employed in India's organized manufacturing. Between 1995–96 and 2005–06, the share of contract workers in total workers employed in India's organized manufacturing increased by about 15 percentage points. Going by the results reported in Table 7.2 and the findings of Abraham and Sasikumar (2017), it seems that a significant part of the decline in labour income share in India's organized manufacturing between 1990–91 and 2007–08 is attributable to the growing use of contract workers.[19]

The coefficient of manufacturing services purchase intensity variable is negative and statistically significant. Such a relationship is expected. It may be inferred that as Indian industrial firms have increasingly resorted to outsourcing, this has had a negative effect on labour income share.

The coefficient of ICT capital stock share is found to be positive and statistically significant when data on all plants are pooled together. The relationship holds for relatively low labour-intensive industries but not for high-labour-intensity industries. Also, while the coefficient is statistically significant at 1 per cent level for medium- and high-technology industries, it is statistically significant only at 10 per cent level for low-technology industries. From the results obtained, it appears that increased investment in ICT capital assets does not reduce labour income share, but tends to raise it, especially in capital intensive, medium- and high-technology industries.

The finding of a positive coefficient of the ICT capital stock variable is at variance with the findings of Abraham and Sasikumar (2017) who found a negative effect using industry-level data of ASI. Why plant-level data and industry-level data show different results is unclear. This matter needs further investigation.

When plant-level data for all industries are pooled together, the coefficient of tariff rate is found to be positive and statistically insignificant. When industries are divided into groups, it is found that the coefficient is positive and statistically significant for medium- and high-technology industries, but negative and statistically significant in low-technology industries. The implication is that lowering of tariff causes a fall in labour income share in medium- and high-technology industries whereas it leads to an increase in labour income share in low-technology industries. Similarly, it is found that the coefficient of tariff rate is positive and statistically significant in low-labour-intensity industries and it is negative and statistically significant in high-labour-intensity industries such as textiles and leather products.[20] The implication of these findings is that lowering of tariff rates leads to a reduction in labour income share in low-labour-intensity industries and it raises labour income share in high-labour-intensity industries. These findings match those of Gupta and Helble (2018). This is also in line with the findings of Ahsan and Mitra (2014).

One econometric estimation issue that may be raised about the model estimates for labour-intensive and low-technology industries in Table 7.2 is that a substantial portion of the products of these industries (mostly consumer goods) was subject to quantitative restrictions till the end of the 1990s. A large number of consumer goods were freed from QRs on imports in 2000 and 2001.[21] Since the model does not include a variable to represent quantitative restrictions on imports, the inter-temporal variations in quantitative restrictions are not captured in the model, and this may have affected the results. To address this issue, the models for labour-intensive and low-technology industries have been re-estimated by using data for the period 2002–03 to 2007–08 (results not reported here). It is found that the results do not change qualitatively. The coefficient of tariff rate remains negative. The t-value goes up. Thus, the relationship is found to be stronger than that indicated by the results reported in Table 7.2. This provides a basis to argue that lowering of tariff had a positive effect on the labour income share in labour-intensive, low-technology industries. This finding matches the findings of Ahsan and Mitra (2014) and Gupta and Helble (2018).

Conclusion

There has been a downward trend in labour income share in India's organized manufacturing in the 1980s which continued in the post-reform period (since 1991) till about 2007–08. After 2007–08, there was a reversal of trend. There was an upward trend in labour income share in India's organized manufacturing after 2007–08.

This chapter investigated whether trade reforms were an important factor responsible for the decline in labour income share in India's organized manufacturing in the period 1990–91 to 2007–08. Also, it examined econometrically the impact of agricultural wages on labour income share in organized manufacturing in order to ascertain whether the acceleration in the growth rate in real agricultural wages after 2007–08 could be one of the possible causes of the trend reversal in labour income share in India's organized manufacturing after 2007–08.

The findings of econometric analysis presented in the study clearly indicate that import liberalization contributed in a significant measure to the fall in labour income share in India's organized manufacturing in the period 1990–91 to 2007–08 which coincided with a widening of the gap between labour productivity and real wages in organized manufacturing. Two other factors that caused a fall in labour income share are increases in capital intensity and increases in TFP which reflect in the main technological change. Since economic reforms in India particularly trade reforms have induced technological advance and use of more capital intensive methods of production in Indian manufacturing so as to enter export markets and meet competition from imports in the domestic market, the findings of the study in regard to the effect of capital deepening and technological advance on the income share of labour can also be traced to some extent to economic reforms.

One interesting finding of the study is that trade reforms had a detrimental effect on labour income share in medium- and high-technology, less labour-intensive industries, whereas the low-technology, labour-intensive industries were not impacted or perhaps positively impacted in regard to the income share of labour. This finding is corroborated by such findings of two earlier studies undertaken on the labour income share in Indian manufacturing, namely Ahsan and Mitra (2014) and Gupta and Helble (2018). Further research on this question will be useful. Another issue that needs further investigation is the effect of investment in ICT capital stock on labour income share in manufacturing. The econometric results obtained in this study indicate that investment in ICT capital stock has a positive impact on labour income share whereas a previous study for Indian manufacturing has found a negative impact (Abraham and Sasikumar 2017).

The increasing use of contract workers in manufacturing was found to be a major cause of the decline in labour income share. This is, however, connected with trade reforms, arguably. Thus, trade reforms may have adversely impacted labour income share by inducing an increase in contract labour use in manufacturing firms through a more competitive environment.

As regards trend reversal in labour income share in organized manufacturing, i.e. an increase in labour income share after 2007–08, the analysis indicates that an important explanation probably lies in a significant rise in the growth rate in real wages in agriculture. It appears that it is the accelerated growth in real wages in agriculture after 2007–08 that drove the wages in organized manufacturing and thus caused an increase in labour income share. The upward tendency in labour income share received further support from the fact that while there was an upward trend in the overall level of import penetration of domestic markets of manufactured products in India in the period 1990–91 to 2008–09, there was no such upward trend after 2008–09.

Annex

Table 7A.1 Labour income share, two-digit industries, 1990–91 to 2017–18

NIC code	*Description*	*Labour income share (%)*				
		1990–01	*2007–08*	*2017–18*	*Change 1990–01 to 2007–08*	*Change 2007–08 to 2014–15*
15	Manufacture of food products and beverages	33.4	24.2	29.4	−9.3	5.2
16	Manufacture of tobacco products	33.3	17.4	17.2	−15.9	−0.2
17	Manufacture of textiles	43.4	34.1	45.6	−9.3	11.5
18	Manufacture of wearing apparel, dressing and dyeing of fur	24.5	47.2	61.1	22.7	13.9
19	Tanning and dressing of leather, manufacture of luggage, hand bags, saddlery, harness and footwear	25.7	40.0	56.0	14.2	16.0
20	Manufacture of wood and products of wood and cork, except furniture, manufacture of articles of straw and plating materials	32.1	32.9	38.1	0.8	5.3
21	Manufacture of paper and paper products	25.9	24.4	31.5	−1.5	7.0
22	Publishing, printing and reproduction of recorded media	55.6	29.8	40.7	−25.8	11.0
23	Manufacture of coke, refined petroleum products and nuclear fuel	9.8	3.4	6.2	−6.4	2.9
24	Manufacture of chemicals and products	25.0	17.7	23.7	−7.3	6.1
25	Manufacture of rubber and plastic products	26.3	23.5	33.5	−2.8	10.1
26	Manufacture of other non–metallic mineral products	24.3	13.4	26.1	−10.9	12.7
27	Manufacture of basic metals	27.7	13.3	25.4	−14.4	12.0

(*Continued*)

Table 7A.1 (Continued)

NIC code	*Description*	*Labour income share (%)*				
		1990–01	*2007–08*	*2017–18*	*Change 1990–01 to 2007–08*	*Change 2007–08 to 2014–15*
28	Manufacture of fabricated metal products, except machinery and equipment	39.6	27.7	42.8	−11.9	15.1
29	Manufacture of machinery and equipment N.E.C.	38.9	27.2	35.4	−11.7	8.2
30	Manufacture of office, accounting and computing machinery	31.8	24.3	51.7	−7.5	27.4
31	Manufacture of electrical machinery and apparatus N.E.C.	32.5	21.8	37.5	−10.7	15.7
32	Manufacture of radio, television and communication equipment and apparatus	32.8	27.4	34.2	−5.4	6.7
33	Manufacture of medical, precision and optical instruments, watches and clocks	41.5	30.5	37.1	−11.0	6.6
34	Manufacture of motor vehicles, trailers and semi–trailers	34.1	25.0	35.7	−9.1	10.8
35	Manufacture of other transport equipment	51.9	24.8	29.2	−27.1	4.4
36	Manufacture of furniture; manufacturing N.E.C.	48.0	30.2	43.1	−17.7	12.9
	All	32.0	19.2	29.1	−12.8	9.9

Source: Author's computations based on ASI data. The ASI dataset at two-digit industry level prepared by the EPWRF has been used.

Notes

1 Organized or formal manufacturing is defined (in India) as encompassing industrial units which employ ten or more workers with the use of power, or 20 or more workers without the use of power.
2 The decline in labour income share is a matter of concern because it signifies a widening gap between labour productivity and real wages in organized manufacturing and has implications for income inequality.
3 In the period after 2009, there have been no major reductions in tariff rates. According to World Tariff Profile (published by the WTO, ITC and UNCTAD), the simple average rate of MFN applied tariff rate on non-agricultural products in India was 10.1 per cent in 2009, and it was at the same level in

2015. Clearly, after 2009, there has been very little reduction in MFN tariff rates, if any. However, with India entering into free trade and preferential trade agreements, the level of tariff protection of India's domestically produced manufactured products might have gone down to some extent.

4 It would be useful to discuss here briefly the trends in import penetration ratio and export intensity in Indian manufacturing at the aggregate level. The analysis of trends is based on trade data taken from *Handbook of Statistics on Indian Economy*, published by the RBI (Reserve Bank of India) and data on the gross output of Indian manufacturing (organized and unorganized segments combined) taken from the India KLEMS dataset available at the RBI website. Analysing trends in import penetration ratio (defined as imports divided by availability where availability is equal to domestic production plus imports minus exports) which is a measure of import competition being faced by the domestic manufacturing industry, it is found that there was an upward trend in import penetration ratio in Indian manufacturing during 1990–91 to 2008–09. In the period after 2008–09, there was no clear upward or downward trend in the import penetration ratio. Import penetration ratio in 2017–18 was slightly lower than that in 2008–09. As regards export intensity (defined as exports divided by output), an analysis of trends in export intensity reveals that there was an upward trend in export intensity of the manufacturing sector during 1990–91 to 2013–14. The export intensity in 2017–18 was slightly lower than that in 2013–14. But, considering the entire period 1990–91 to 2017–18, the overall trend in export intensity in Indian manufacturing was an upward one.

5 Studies on this issue and other related issues undertaken by the present author in the past include Goldar (2004a, 2004b, 2009, 2013, 2016) and Goldar and Aggarwal (2005).

6 Underlying this argument, there is an assumption that the elasticity of substitution between capital and labour is more than one. This assumption finds empirical support in the study of Piketty and Zucman (2014) who have presented empirical evidence to argue that the elasticity of substitution is more than one. There are several other studies taking by and large the same stand and in which it has been argued that the observed decline in labour income share is due to the fact that the elasticity of substitution is more than one and there has been capital deepening, i.e. increase in capital–labour ratio. But, this assertion that the elasticity of substitution between capital and labour is more than one is contested by Lawrence (2015).

7 To compute labour productivity and real product wage rate, gross value added per person engaged and total emoluments per person engaged have been taken and these series have been deflated. Data on gross value added in manufacturing at current and 2011–12 prices for the years 1990–91 to 2017–18 have been taken from *National Accounts Statistics* and the implicit deflator has been computed, which has then been used for deflation.

8 That there has been a significant increase in the growth rate of rural real wages (since July 2007) has been reported by Nadhanael (2012) who point out that MGNREGA may have played a role in the rise of real wages in rural areas.

9 For measuring TFP growth, the Tornqvist index is used. The basic data source is the ASI dataset at two-digit industry level prepared by the EPWRF. The real value of gross output is taken as the measure of output. Capital, labour, materials, energy and services are taken as five inputs. Further details of TFP growth measurement including deflators used for materials, energy and services are provided in Goldar (2017). The methodology adopted is similar to that in Goldar (2015). After computing TFP growth rates, an index of TFP has been constructed for each industry taking 1980–81 as the base (=100).

10 At the time the TFP computations were made, ASI data were available only till 2014–15. The TFP estimates for two-digit industries were accordingly made till 2014–15. Although ASI data for later years have now become available (and have been used for the trend analysis), it has not been possible for the author to extend the TFP series beyond 2014–15. This is the reason why the period covered in the industry-level econometric analysis could not be extended beyond 2014–15.

11 Gupta and Helble (2018) have divided two-digit industries into four classes: high technology, medium-high technology, medium-low-technology and low-technology. They have followed the OECD's ISEC-3 based technology intensity classification. In this study, the same approach is taken. However, only two groups have been formed instead of four. A distinction is made between low-technology, and medium- and high-technology. One point that should be noted in this connection is that Gupta and Helble have left out the manufacturing n.e.c. industry group while classifying the industries. In this study, this group has been included within the class of low-technology industries.

12 The series on import penetration ratio in Indian manufacturing described earlier in note 4 has been used for this analysis based on aggregate-level time series data.

13 For unit-level data of ASI, it is difficult to apply the perpetual inventory method for estimating capital stock. Therefore, the blanket deflation procedure is used.
14 The present author is grateful to Dr Deb Kusum Das for providing the data on tariff rates.
15 For each two-digit industry, an appropriate price index has been formed by taking data from the official series on wholesale price indices. The price index for a two-digit industry has been applied to all plants belonging to that two-digit industry.
16 Accordingly, the analysis presented in the chapter is confined to such plants.
17 Lists of labour-intensive industries have been taken from Das and Kalita (2009) and Goldar and Sadhukhan (2015). A common list has been prepared based on the two lists. This has been used for diving industries into the two groups.
18 In the studies undertaken by Ahsan and Mitra (2014) and Gupta and Helble (2018), it was found that the impact of import liberalization on labour income share in Indian manufacturing differed between labour-intensive industries and other industries. This is the rationale for adopting such a distinction in this study.
19 At the same time, it needs to be recognized that the use of contract labour may have been induced in part by import competition. Thus, trade reforms may have adversely impacted labour income share through pressure on firms to cut down cost by employing contract workers in place of directly employed workers.
20 This has been checked further by taking data on textiles and leather industry plants. The coefficient of tariff rate is found to be negative and statistically significant.
21 In July 1991, a major relaxation in QRs was made in India, with the removal of import licensing requirements in respect of intermediate and capital goods barring a handful of items. In 1999–2000, 2134 items (at 8-digit or 10-digit ITC-HS classification or sub-groups) were subject to QRs. These were mostly consumer goods. In the next two years, 2000 and 2001, about 1500 items were freed from QRs. Thus, by 2002, the fraction of manufactured items subject to QRs got reduced to a low level.

References

Abraham, Vinoj and S. K. Sasikumar (2017): "Declining Wage Share in India's Organized Manufacturing Sector: Trends, Patterns and Determinants," *ILO Asia-Pacific Working Paper* Series, International Labour Organization. Available at: https://www.ilo.org/wcmsp5/groups/public/---asia/---ro-bangkok/---sro-new:delhi/documents/publication/wcms_614777.pdf (accessed on 31 January 2019).

Ahsan, Reshad N. and Devashish Mitra (2014): "Trade Liberalization and Labor's Slice of the Pie: Evidence from Indian Firms," *Journal of Development Economics*, Vol. 108, No. C, pp. 1–16.

Alvarez-Cuadrado, Francisco, Ngo Van Long and Markus Poschke (2018): "Capital-Labor Substitution, Structural Change and the Labor Income Share," *Journal of Economic Dynamics and Control*, Vol. 87, No. C, pp. 206–31. doi:10.1016/j.jedc.2017.12.010.

Bai, Chong-en and Zen-jie Qian (2009): "On the Increase in the Chinese Aggregate Capital Income Share: An Investigation from Provincial Perspective," *Journal of Tsinghua University (Philosophy and Social Sciences)*, Vol. 24, No. 4, pp. 137–47.

Banga, Rashmi and Abhijit Das (2012): "Role of Trade Policies in Growth of Indian Manufacturing Sector," in Rashmi Banga and Abhijit Das (eds), *Twenty Years of India's Liberalization: Experiences and Lessons*, pp. 5–26, United Nations Conference on Trade and Development (UNCTAD), United Nations and Centre for WTO Studies, IIFT. Available at: http://unctad.org/en/PublicationsLibrary/osg2012d1_en.pdf (accessed on 22 September 2018).

Bentolila, Samuel and Gilles Saint-Paul (2003): "Explaining Movements in the Labor Share," *Contributions in Macroeconomics*, Vol. 3, No. 1, pp. 1–33.

Berkowitz, Daniel, Hong Ma and Shuichiro Nishioka (2015): "Declining Labor Shares and Heterogeneous Firms," *Working Paper* No. 552, Stanford, CA: Stanford Centre for International Development. Available at: https://pdfs.semanticscholar.org/a4b6/fe01c75c07e6d592685ce22573ae1414e8bc.pdf (accessed on 31 January 2019).

Carbonero, Francesco, Christian J. Offermanns and Enzo Weber (2017): "The Fall of the Labour Income Share: The Role of Technological Change and Imperfect Labour Markets," *IAB-Discussion Paper* No. 28/2017, Nuremberg: Institute for Employment Research of the Federal Employment Agency.

Dao, Mai Chi, Mitali Das, Zsoka Koczan and Weicheng Lian (2017): "Why Is Labor Receiving a Smaller Share of Global Income? Theory and Empirical Evidence," *IMF Working Paper* No. WP/17/169, Washington DC: International Monetary Fund.

Das, Deb Kusum (2016): "Trade Policy and Manufacturing Performance: Exploring the Level of Trade Openness in India's Organised Manufacturing in the Period 1990–2010," *DRG Study* No. 41, Mumbai: Reserve Bank of India.

Das, Deb Kusum and Gunajit Kalita (2009): "Do Labor Intensive Industries Generate Employment? Evidence from Firm Level Survey in India," *Working Paper* No. 237, New Delhi: Indian Council for Research on International Economic Relations.

Decreuse, Bruno and Paul Maarek (2015): "FDI and the Labor Share in Developing Countries: A Theory and Some Evidences," *Annals of Economics and Statistics*, Vol. 119/120, pp. 289–319.

Doan, Ha Thi Thanh and Guanghua Wan (2017): "Globalization and the Labor Share in National Income," *ADBI Working Paper* No. 639, Tokyo: Asian Development Bank Institute.

Goldar, Bishwanath (2004a): "Trade Liberalisation and Real Wages in Organised Manufacturing Industries in India," in A. Karnik and L.G. Burange (eds), *Economic Policies and the Emerging Scenario: Challenges to Government and Industry*, Mumbai: Himalaya.

—— (2004b): "Indian Manufacturing: Productivity Trends in Pre- and Post-Reform Periods," *Economic and Political Weekly*, Vol. 29, No. 46/47, pp. 5033–43.

—— (2009): "Trade Liberalisation and Labour Demand Elasticity in Indian Manufacturing," *Economic and Political Weekly*, Vol. 44, No. 34, pp. 51–57.

—— (2013): "Wages and Wage Share in India during the Post-Reform Period," *Indian Journal of Labour Economics*, Vol. 56, No. 1, pp. 75–94.

—— (2015): "Productivity in Indian Manufacturing (1999–2011), Accounting for Imported Materials Input," *Economic and Political Weekly*, Vol. 50, No. 35, pp. 104–11.

—— (2016): "Impact of Trade Reforms on Price-Cost Margins in Indian Manufacturing Firms," *Indian Journal of Economics*, Special Centennial Issue, Vol. 97, No. 384, pp. 87–103.

—— (2017): "Growth, Productivity and Job Creation in Indian Manufacturing," in Uma Kapila (ed), *India's Economy, Pre-liberalisation to GST: Essays in honour of Raj Kapila*, pp. 619–52, New Delhi: Academic Foundation.

—— (2018): "Use of Contract Labour in India's Organized Manufacturing: Role of Import Competition and Labour Regulations," in Niti Mehta and Anita Arya (eds), *Role of Public Policy in Development Process: Emerging Socioeconomic Scenario in the Indian Economy*, pp. 251–82, New Delhi: Academic Foundation.

Goldar, Bishwanath and Suresh Chand Aggarwal (2005): "Trade Liberalization and Price-Cost Margin in Indian Industries," *Developing Economies*, Vol. 43, No. 3, pp. 346–73.

Goldar, Bishwanath and Amit Sadhukhan (2015): "Employment and Wages in Indian Manufacturing: Post-reform Performance," *Employment Working Paper* No. 185, Geneva: Employment and Labour Market Policies Branch, Employment Policy Department, International Labour Office (ILO).

Guerriero, Marta and Kunal Sen (2012): "What Determines the Share of Labour in National Income? A Cross-Country Analysis," IZA Discussion Paper Series, *Discussion Paper* No. 6643, Bonn: Institute for the Study of Labor (IZA).

Gupta, Prachi and Matthias Helble (2018): "Adjustment to Trade Opening: The Case of Labor Share in India's Manufacturing Industry," *ADBI Working Paper* No. 845, Tokyo: Asian Development Bank Institute.

Guschanski, Alexander and Özlem Onaran (2016): "Determinants of the Wage Share: A Cross-Country Comparison Using Sectoral Data," *Greenwich Papers in Political Economy*, no. GPERC41, Greenwich, London: Greenwich Political Economy Research Centre, University of Greenwich.

—— (2017): "Why Is the Wage Share Falling in Emerging Economies? Industry Level Evidence," *Greenwich Papers in Political Economy*, no. GPERC52, Greenwich, London: Greenwich Political Economy Research Centre, University of Greenwich.

Harrison, Ann (2005): "Has Globalization Eroded Labor's Share? Some Cross-Country Evidence," *MPRA Paper* No. 39649. Available at: https://mpra.ub.uni-muenchen.de/39649/ (accessed on 18 September 2018).

Hutchinson, John and Damiaan Persyn (2012): "Globalisation, Concentration and Footloose Firms: In Search of the Main Cause of the Declining Labour Share," *Review of World Economics*, Vol. 148, No. 1, pp. 17–43.

Ibarra, Carlos A. and Jaime Ros (2017): "The Decline of the Labour Share in Mexico: 1990–2015," *WIDER Working Paper* No. 2017/183, Helsinki: World Institute for Development Economics Research, United Nations University (UNU-WIDER).

Jaumotte, Florence and Irina Tytell (2007): "How Has the Globalization of Labor Affected the Labor Income Share in Advanced Countries?," *IMF Working Paper* No. WP/07/298, Washington DC: International Monetary Fund.

Jayadev, Arjun (2007): "Capital Account Openness and the Labour Share of Income," *Cambridge Journal of Economics*, Vol. 31, No. 3, pp. 423–43.

Kamal, Fariha, Mary E. Lovely and Debashish Mitra (2014): "Trade Liberalization and Labour Shares in China," *CES Working Paper* No. 14–24, Washington DC: Centre for Economic Studies, US Census Bureau.

Karabarbounis, Loukas and Brent Neiman (2014): "The Global Decline of the Labor Share," *Quarterly Journal of Economics*, Vol. 129, No. 1, pp. 61–103.

Lawrence, Robert Z. (2015): "Recent Declines in Labor's Share in US Income: A Preliminary Neoclassical Account," *NBER Working Paper* No. 21296, Cambridge, MA: National Bureau of Economic Research.

Levinsohn, James and Amil Petrin (2003): "Estimating Production Functions Using Inputs to Control for Unobservables," *Review of Economic Studies*, Vol. 70, No. 2, pp. 317–41.

Luo, Changyuan and Jun Zhang (2010): "Declining Labor Share: Is China's Case Different?," *China and World Economy*. Vol. 18, No. 6, pp. 1–18. doi:10.1111/j.1749-124X.2010.01217.x.

Nadhanael, G.V. (2012): "Recent Trends in Rural Wages: An Analysis of Inflationary Implications," *Reserve Bank of India Occasional Papers*, Vol. 33, No. 1/2, pp. 89–112.

Ng, Allen, Tan Theng Theng and Tan Zhai Gen (2018), "What Explains the Increase in the Labor Income Share in Malaysia?", *ADBI Working Paper* No. 894, Tokyo: Asian Development Bank Institute.

OECD (2012): *OECD Employment Outlook 2012*, Paris: OECD.

Piketty, Thomas and Gabriel Zucman (2014): "Capital Is Back: Wealth-Income Ratios in Rich Countries 1700–2010," *Quarterly Journal of Economics*, Vol. 129, No. 3, pp. 1255–310.

Qian, Zhenjie and Xiaodong Zhu (2013): "Misallocation or Mismeasurement? Factor Income Shares and Factor Market Distortions in China's Manufacturing Industries," Presentation Slides, Presented at *American Economic Association 2013 Annual Conference*. Available at: https://www.aeaweb.org/conference/2013/retrieve.php?pdfid=45 (accessed on 31 January 2019).

Rodriguez, Francisco and Arjun Jayadev (2010): "The Declining Labor Share of Income," *Human Development Research Paper* No. 2010/36, New York: United Nations Development Programme.

Shastry, Rahul A. and R. V. Ramana Murthy (2003): "Declining Share of Wages in Organised Indian Industry (1973–97): A Kaleckian Perspective," *Journal of Indian School of Political Economy*, Vol. 15, No. 3, pp. 663–77.

Trapp, Katharina (2015): "Measuring the Labour Income Share of Developing Countries: Learning from Social Accounting Matrices," *WIDER Working Paper* No. 2015/041, Helsinki: World Institute for Development Economics Research, United Nations University (UNU-WIDER).

Van Treeck, Katharina (2017): "The Labor Income Share in Developing Countries: A Review and Analysis of International Panel Data", Paper prepared for presentation at the *5th Conference of the Regulating for Decent Work Network at the International Labour Office,* Geneva, Switzerland, 3–5 July 2017. Available at: http://www.rdw2015.org/uploads/submission/full_paper/657/vanTreeck_RDW2017.pdf (accessed on 18 September 2018).

Virmani, Arvind and Danish A. Hashim (2009): "Factor Employment, Sources and Sustainability of Output Growth: Analysis of Indian Manufacturing," *Working Paper* No. 3/2009-DEA, Ministry of Finance, Government of India.

Zhou, Minghai (2016): *Labor's Share of Income: Another Key to Understand China's Income Inequality*, Singapore: Springer.

8

TRADE LIBERALISATION AND EXPORT COMPETITIVENESS OF INDIAN MANUFACTURING SECTOR

An empirical study

R. Rijesh

Introduction

A major feature of the global economy in the recent decade is the increasing integration of economies through a much greater flow of goods and capital across borders. The higher economic integration through goods and services is the result of the widespread reduction in trade protective measures adopted by various economies, especially by the emerging developing economies in Asia and Africa. The reduction in trade-restrictive instruments is part of the liberalisation policy regime that aims to achieve better and sustained economic growth through an outward-oriented industrialisation strategy. The successful catch-up and industrial development experiences of the East Asian Economies in the early 1960s and the emergence of China in the recent past have reinstated the belief that an open trade regime has static as well as dynamic productivity gains to the participating economic agents. As countries' participation increases on the global stage, the role of the manufacturing sector in structural transformation and growth become crucial in the long run (Szirmai, 2013; UNCTAD, 2016).

Policies that liberalise trade and industries enable firms to integrate with the rest of the world. The increased economic integration provides opportunities for international specialisation and knowledge assimilation in the host economies. As per standard trade theories, a move from autarky to free trade through trade liberalisation induces static welfare gains in terms of inter-sectoral specialisation according to comparative advantage and dynamic productivity gains from a combination of availability of knowledge inputs, economies of scale and expansion of product varieties available to the consumers (Bernard et al., 2007). The recent theoretical literature argues substantial dynamic gains from reducing trade barriers through reallocation of resources from less productive import-competing firms to more productive and competitive export-oriented sectors that eventually enhance aggregate production efficiency (Melitz and Redding, 2014). Productivity also improves as trade liberalisation enables firms to access productive inputs such as capital goods and intermediate goods embodying superior R&D technol-

 DOI: 10.4324/9780367855741-8

ogy from abroad (Grossman and Helpman, 1991). This wider choice of technology can enable domestic producers to substantially improve their production efficiency and competitiveness in the global market.

In the era of increased economic integration, it is essential that countries improve their production efficiency to catch up with and maintain global market share. Market competition forces domestic manufacturing to invest in technology and other cost-effective methods so that the export products become competitive in the world market. As such, it can be argued that trade liberalisation creates an incentive structure that enables economies to be competitive and productive in the world market. It is in this context the present study attempts to provide empirical evidence for the impact of trade liberalisation on the export competitiveness of manufacturing products by India. We know that the Indian economy has witnessed considerable policy shifts in recent decades. Considered to be one of the major protective economies in the world, the Indian economy has witnessed a dramatic shift from the heavy state-led import substitution policy that has prevailed since the 1950s to a gradual market-oriented outward-looking policy regime since the early 1990s. One of the major elements of the outward-oriented policy regime is the systematic integration of the domestic market with the rest of the world through trade liberalisation policies by expanding the production and exports of manufacturing, thereby increasing the long-run economic growth rate of the economy.

As the shift from inward-oriented policy to outward-orientated strategy envisages heavy incidence of international trade and improved economic growth over time, the study seeks to examine the trends and nature of India's growth over a long period. This historical perspective is essential for providing the basic reference point of the discussion regarding the export performance of manufacturing since liberalisation. As such, we aim to provide a detailed description of the performance of manufacturing exports using disaggregate trade statistics at the 6-digit level. For analytical purposes, the discussion is based on four *use-based classifications*, namely, basic goods, intermediate goods, capital goods and consumer goods-producing sectors. The analysis of trade pattern, composition, direction and competitive performance is evaluated in terms of these important dimensions of industrial production. Since the competitiveness of manufacturing products is intricately related to the pattern of international trade specialisation, the study employs the Revealed Comparative Advantage (RCA) index, originally developed by Balassa in 1965, to gauge the dynamics of export competitiveness at the product level.

The rest of the chapter is organised as follows. The second section presents a descriptive account of India's economic growth from a historical perspective. The third section provides an overview of trade policy reform in India in the recent past. The fourth section details the trade performance of the Indian manufacturing sector at the aggregate and use-based classification levels. The fifth section provides empirical evidence of export competitiveness of the organised manufacturing sector of India at 6-digit levels of disaggregation, summarised at the use-based level. The final section concludes the entire discussion.

India's economic growth performance: historical evidence (1960–2018)

The Indian economy witnessed an impressive growth rate immediately after independence.[1] However, from the mid-sixties, the growth rate virtually stagnated around 3 per cent per annum.[2] Some scholars termed this slow-paced economic growth of around 3.5 per cent per annum as the 'Hindu-rate of growth.[3] The economic growth revived in the 1980s. Some scholars like Virmani (1997), Rodrik and Subramanian (2005) and Kohli (2006) among others argue that the break in growth rate during the 1980s was fuelled by 'pro-business' policies introduced in the early part of the decade. Using the multiple structural break test approach, Balakrishnan

(2010) examined the structural breaks in sectoral growth rates since 1950 and found that the shift in GDP growth rate occurred in 1978–79. In terms of various GDP components, a permanent increase in agricultural growth took place in the 1960s followed by a take-off of the service sector in the mid-1970s. The turning point in manufacturing output growth occurred only in 1982–83. They argued that the service sector growth has been the major catalyst of economic growth in India.

In Figure 8.1 we plot the average annual growth rate of GDP and per capita GDP from 1960 to 2018. We can see that the growth of GDP is cyclical during this period. The polynomial trend line suggests that the growth rate of GDP is fluctuating at a decreasing rate until the 1980s. Since the mid-1980s, an upward trend is clearly noticeable. The decadal growth performance of GDP and its major components are given in Table 8.1. It is evident that the rate of growth

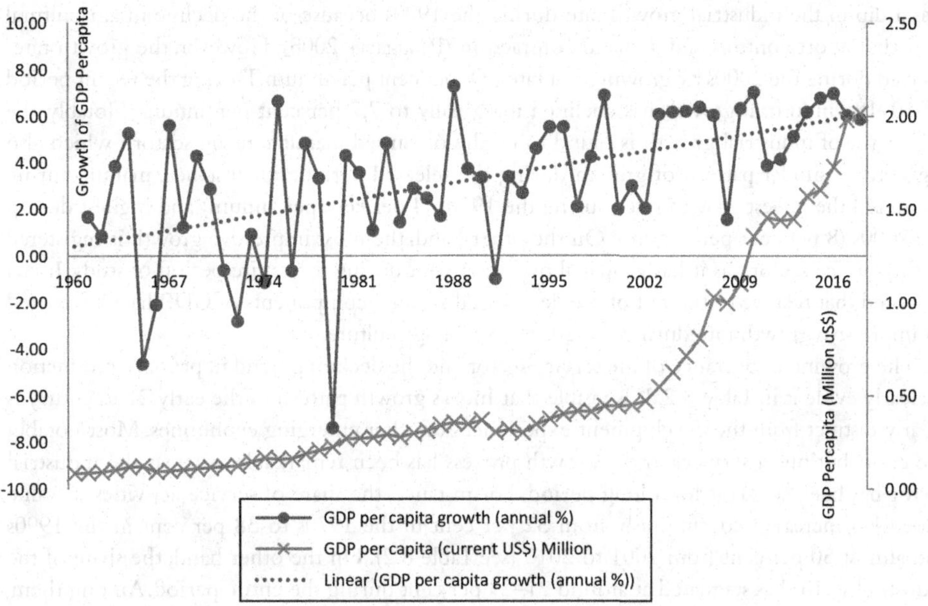

Figure 8.1 Growth of India's GDP (% per annum): 1960-2018. *Source*: Author's calculation on World Development Indicators (WDI) World Bank.

Table 8.1 India's economic growth performance (annual growth rates in %), 1960–2018

Indicators	*1960–69*	*1970–79*	*1980–89*	*1990–99*	*2000–09*	*2010–18*
GDP	3.9	2.9	5.7	5.8	6.3	7.0
GDP per capita	1.8	0.6	3.3	3.7	4.6	5.8
Agriculture	2.0	1.3	4.4	3.2	2.1	4.1
Industry	5.9	3.5	6.0	5.7	7.7	6.3
Manufacturing	5.6	4.3	5.8	5.8	8.0	7.1
Services	5.2	5.4	6.8	8.1	7.6	8.1

Source: Author's calculation based on data from the Central Statistical Office (CSO) and WDI.
Note: Sectoral components are in real value added.

of GDP is largely poor during the 1960s and 1970s (3–4 per cent per annum substantiating the 'Hindu growth rate' argument). However, there appears to be a significant revival in growth performance since the 1980s. Compared to the earlier decades, the GDP growth rate is relatively higher during the 1980s, 1990s and 2000s as GDP rose to 5.7, 5.8 and 6.3 per cent per annum, respectively. During the period from 2010 to 2018, the GDP growth rate registered an impressive rate of 7.0 per cent per annum, making India one of the fastest emerging economies in the developing world.[4] This increased GDP growth rate is accompanied by an improvement in per capita GDP, especially since the post-2000 period.

In terms of sectoral composition, Table 8.1 reveals that since the initiation of economic liberalisation growth rates in the non-agricultural sectors are consistently higher than the period of an inward-oriented policy regime.[5] Relatively, the agricultural growth rate is distinctively poor for most of the decades. Comparing the industrial growth across decades revealed that the growth rate has been consistently above 6 per cent per annum, except during the 1970s. There was a dip in the industrial growth rate during the 1990s because of the decline in agricultural growth, import controls and demand contraction (Panagaria, 2008). However, the growth rates revived during the 2000s by growing at a rate of 8 per cent per annum. During the recent period (2010–18), industrial growth has declined marginally to 7.7 per cent per annum. Notably, the key driver of industrial growth is found to be the organised manufacturing sector,[6] which also registered a similar pattern of growth during the selected period. For instance, manufacturing registered the lowest growth rates during the 1970s (4 per cent per annum) and highest during the 2000s (8 per cent per annum). On the other hand, the most impressive growth is registered in the service sector,[7] as it has grown above 6 per cent during the entire period of study. It can be noted that relative to the rest of the decades, all sectoral components of GDP have registered an impressive growth rate during the 2000s, except agriculture.

The growing importance of the service sector and the declining trend in primary production is clearly evident in Table 8.2. It is visible that India's growth pattern in the early 21st century is clearly distinct from the development experiences of other emerging economies. Most notably, the contribution of services in the growth process has been remarkable whereas the industrial sector has been stagnant for a long period. For instance, the share of service activities in value added has increased continuously from 32 per cent in the 1970s to 38 per cent in the 1990s and almost 50 per cent from 2001 to 2010 (see Table 8.2). On the other hand, the share of the industrial sector has stagnated at around 21–29 per cent during the entire period. Among them, the share of manufacturing has been virtually stagnant around 14–17 per cent. This is in sharp contrast to the pattern of structural change witnessed by the East Asian economies and China in the recent past.

Table 8.2 Sectoral contribution to GDP (percentage share) 1960–2018

Periods	*Agriculture*	*Industry*	*Manufacturing*	*Services*
1960–69	40.5	21.3	14.7	31.6
1970–79	36.4	23.4	15.9	31.9
1980–89	29.5	26.5	16.5	34.5
1990–99	25.6	27.3	16.4	38.2
2000–09	18.5	29.2	16.3	44.4
2010–18	16.4	28.2	15.5	47.2

Source: World Development Indicators (WDI), World Bank.

However, there are apprehensions regarding the sustainability of economic growth driven by the service sector.[8] Since the employment prospects in the service sector are largely concentrated in the informal sector, personal services and public administration, there is very little productivity improvement and spillover effects on other sectors. In terms of employment generation, the service sector represents only a small share of India's overall employment level (see Bosworth et al., 2007). Since the Indian economy is largely labour abundant, a growing manufacturing sector is a necessary condition to achieve faster and sustainable rates of growth over time. Manufacturing activities, having the largest employment potential, have deeper linkages with the rest of the economic activities and offer significant productivity improvements.[9] Therefore, it is expected that the future prospect of economic growth rests on developing a dynamic manufacturing sector for the absorption of the productive labour force.

Trade and industry policy regime in India since the 1980s: an overview

During the past few decades, India has been witnessing significant shifts in trade and industrialisation policy strategies. This was in sharp contrast to the earlier regime where the government actively participated in the economic decision-making. The basic premises of the earlier regime were self-sufficiency, minimal dependence and commanding heights of the public sector. Two basic policy instruments for the implementation of the industrial strategy were: the reservation of a number of industries for state-owned companies and the requirement of government permission before setting up industrial units by private firms (Bhaumik and Kumbhakar, 2010). Domestic industry, heavily insulated from international competition, was under strict regulation. Industrial policy was characterised by multiple controls over private investment that limited the areas in which private investors were allowed to operate. This includes the scale of operations, the location of new investment and the technology to be used in the production process (Ahluwalia, 2002). The continued pursuit of inward-looking policies created a large and diversified industrial sector in the country. Although initially successful, empirical analyses on the performance of the industry have highlighted several weaknesses of such blanket protection.[10]

The trade policy regime was highly protectionist and regulated through high tariff/non-tariff controls on imports. The import substitution regime was characterised by high protective tariff and pervasive import restrictive measures. Most of the imports were subjected to discretionary import licensing or 'canalised' by the monopoly of government trade organisations with some flexibility in the form of the Open General Licensing (OGL[11]) list. In this situation, non-tariff barriers acted as the major policy instrument for regulation. In order to expand and remove the bias in the export sector resulting from the overvalued exchange rates, the Indian government introduced various export promotion policies and instruments. Broad banding was introduced in 1984, which enabled the manufacturers to produce new models within their existing licensed capacity with no requirement of an additional industrial licence. This period witnessed some changes in the import regime like the decline in canalised imports.[12]

The initial steps towards the liberalisation of India's trade regime were taken during the latter half of the 1980s. This was further carried out in the 1990s with the initiation of internal as well as external liberalisation measures where an explicit recognition of outward-oriented policies was seen as a rational strategy for achieving better economic growth. In 1991, several changes were introduced in India's industrial and trade policy regime. These policy changes were part of economic reform measures implemented in the aftermath of a severe balance of payment and fiscal crisis.[13] The main objective of this phase of liberalisation was to make the Indian Industry competitive and cost-effective. As part of the reform, most of the central government control in industrial activities was dismantled. The list of industries reserved solely for the public sector was reduced to three industries: defence/aircraft and warships, atomic energy generation and railway transport.[14] The requirement that investments by large industrial houses needed a separate clearance under the Monopolies and Restrictive Trade Practices (MRTP) Act to discourage the concentration of economic power was abolished, and a new competition law for regulating anticompetitive behaviour was set up (Ahluwalia, 2002).

The economic liberalisation policies endeavoured to phase out import licensing and reduce import duties. Import licensing was abolished relatively early for capital goods and intermediates, which became freely importable in 1993, simultaneously with the switch to a flexible exchange rate regime (Ahluwalia, 2002). The protective regime gradually shifted from tariff to quantitative restrictions and there was some expansion in the OGL list. The import liberalisation was introduced so that firms could modernise their product structure by importing embodied and disembodied technology from abroad.[15] The liberal imports of capital goods and technology were viewed as a means to enable exporters to undertake technological up-gradation to compete effectively in the international market. The policy dismantled almost all entry barriers, and gradually brought down tariffs and non-tariff barriers making the economy more outward-oriented.[16] Tariffs were progressively brought down and all quantitative restrictions were removed.[17] All export subsidies were abolished and exporters were allowed tradable entitlement called Exim-Scrips for importing even restricted items needed to keep up the export performance.

As part of the macroeconomic liberalisation policy initiatives, the government undertook various measures to correct the distortion in the exchange rate regime. The exchange rate regime in India evolved from the par-value system to the basket peg system to the managed float exchange rate system. The Liberalised Exchange Rate Management System (LERMS) was put in place in 1992, which employed the dual exchange rate system,[18] and was later replaced by a more market-oriented Unified Exchange Rate System (UERS) in 1993 (Dua et al., 2010). This was accompanied by full convertibility on the current account in 1994. Since the introduction of these policies, the Indian rupee has witnessed depreciation against the dollar and other major international currencies. On the positive side, the exchange rate has been stable despite volatility in capital inflows and trade flows (Dua et al., 2010).

Another major feature of the outward-oriented strategy was liberalising foreign investment in order to increase the volume of investment and technological inflow in the economy (see Bhaumik and Kumbhakar, 2010 and Ahluwalia, 2002). Foreign Direct Investment (FDI) up to 51 per cent was allowed in some sectors, and over the years significant relaxations on the rules governing FDI across the board were initiated. Automatic approval is granted for foreign investment up to certain equity in selected sectors; 100 per cent equity ownership is allowed in a large number of industries. The procedure for obtaining permission for investment under the automatic approval limit was simplified by way of single window registration through the Reserve Bank of India (RBI). For investing in other industries or higher share equities, applications were considered through the foreign investment promotion board (FIPB). Procedures for the procurement of technology from abroad were also simplified, largely by way of the facilitation of ways for payment of patent-related royalties. The high priority industries were allowed to have automatic permission for technology transfer (Bhaumik and Kumbhakar, 2010).

These policy changes during the past few decades suggest that the Indian economy has transformed gradually and systematically from a complex inward-oriented protective regime to a more market-friendly trade regime. Moreover, post-WTO, India has witnessed some notable changes in its trade regime. This was more visible in protective instruments like tariff and non-tariff barriers, which is discussed in the next section.

Incidence of trade protection in the Indian manufacturing sector

In Table 8.3, we show two major indicators of protection, namely effective rate of protection (ERP) and import coverage ratio (ICR) for the Indian manufacturing sector from 1980 to 2000.[19] We can see that during the 1980s, protection through tariffs (measured by ERP) increased in all the sectors. On the other hand, protection through quantitative restrictions (based on import coverage ratio) such as Non-Tariff Barriers (NTBs) declined marginally for most industrial sectors.

Compared to the 1980s, trade protection declined unambiguously and markedly in the early 1990s for aggregate as well as use-based industries in general. In terms of use-based classification, the highly protected industrial sectors (in terms of both ERP and IC) are intermediate goods industries and the least protected segments are capital goods industries. By the end of the 1990s, the consumer goods sector became the major protected industry and the capital goods the least protected. This shows that, since the beginning of the trade liberalisation programme, the protective regime has significantly liberalised and industries operate in a less protective regime than before. Moreover, there is unambiguous evidence of change in preference for quantitative restrictions rather than tariff protection. During the early 1990s, the peak tariffs on manufactures were almost 400 per cent on average. This has reduced to less than 10 per cent in the recent period (World Bank, 2011).

For the analytical purpose, we collected the MFN average tariff profile of the Indian manufacturing sector from the UNCTAD TRAINS[20] database according to the 6-digit Harmonized Commodity Description and Coding System or HS and grouped them according to the four *use-based* classifications[21] scheme. Table 8.4 reports the weighted average tariffs[22] for aggregate manufacturing as well as for the four use-based product grouping, namely, raw materials, intermediate goods, capital goods and consumer goods for the period 1990 to 2018. In the case of aggregate manufacturing, the tariff rate has continuously declined over the years. For example, from 50 per cent in 1990 the tariff had declined to 26 per cent by 2000 and thereafter declined drastically and reached 8 per cent in 2018. During the 1990s, the rate of tariff protection was severely higher for production inputs such as intermediate and capital goods (above 70 per cent). Post-1990s, these segments witnessed dramatic reduction, especially in the capital goods-producing sectors. At present, the weighted average tariff for capital goods is 6 per cent which is relatively lower than other use-based products except for basic raw materials. However, all cat-

Table 8.3 India: measures of trade protection: by use-based classification, 1980–2000 (in %)

Trade protection indicators	*1980–85*	*1986–90*	*1991–95*	*1996–2000*
Intermediate goods industries				
Average effective rate of protection	147.0	149.2	87.6	40.1
Import coverage ratio	98.3	98.3	41.8	27.6
Capital goods industries				
Average effective rate of protection	62.8	78.5	54.2	33.3
Import coverage ratio	95.1	77.2	20.5	8.2
Consumer goods industries				
Average effective rate of protection	101.5	111.6	80.6	48.3
Import coverage ratio	98.7	87.9	45.7	33.4
All industries				
Average effective rate of protection	115.1	125.9	80.2	40.4
Import coverage ratio	97.6	91.6	38.0	24.8

Source: Das (2003).

Table 8.4 Tariff structure in Indian manufacturing sector: by use-based category (1990–2018)

Use-based classification	*1990*	*2000*	*2010*	*2018*
Raw materials	28.5	16.6	4.6	4.4
Intermediate goods	74.9	32.7	10.1	9.4
Capital goods	72.7	21.7	5.3	5.6
Consumer goods	25.3	31.2	10.9	11.1
Manufacturing Sector	50.3	25.6	7.7	7.6

Source: Author's calculation based on UNCTAD-TRAINS database.
Note: Reported tariffs are weighted (import) Average Tariff (MFN).

egories of the manufacturing sector have undergone a substantial reduction in protection which further reflects the growing commitment of the government to integrate the economy with the rest of the world and compete successfully in the global market. As external competition intensifies, it is imperative to examine the nature of trade performance since the post-liberalisation period. This is attempted in the next section.

Trade performance of Indian manufacturing: an empirical analysis

Since 1991, India has transformed from a relatively closed economy to one of the largest open economies in Asia (OECD, 2009). At present India is more open than the earlier regime as the measure of openness (trade share in GDP) reached 56 per cent in 2012 (see Figure 8.2).

This is significantly higher than the earlier regime of inward orientation. For instance, from 1960 to 1990, trade openness was only around 11 to 15 per cent of GDP. On average, openness increased to 22 per cent from 1990 to 2000 and around 44 per cent from 2001 to 2018. This indicates the growing significance of international trade in the economy. Evidently, one of the major components of total trade is merchandise trade, which also follows a similar pattern to aggregate trade (see Figure 8.2). Since the mid-1980s, the share of merchandise trade increased continuously up to 2012, thereafter showed a declining trend until 2016 and thereafter indicates a sign of revival. For instance, the share of merchandise trade in GDP increased from 14 per cent in 1991 to 20 per cent in 2000 and further shot up to 43 per cent in 2012. However, due to the post-global slowdown in demand, exports decelerated and reached around 27 per cent in 2016. By 2018, the trade share had improved to 32 per cent. On the other hand, the service trade in GDP increased from 4 per cent to 8 per cent and further up to 12 per cent during the same period (see Figure 8.2). Among the merchandise trade, manufacturing goods comprise the largest component and the share of exports is significantly higher than imports in all periods, except the 1960s (see Table 8.5).

In terms of growth performance, the post-liberalisation period witnessed significant improvement in goods trade (see Table 8.6). We can observe that since the second wave of reforms in the 2000s, both exports and imports have registered double-digit growth rates. Moreover, since the mid-2000s, the share of exports in GDP has been around 20 per cent. In the early 1980s, the share was below 6 per cent for most of the period. The growth of imports was relatively higher than exports as it has risen by 22 per cent per annum since 2000 (see Table 8.6). In the recent period, the share of imports in GDP has been around 25 per cent.

This significant trend is reflected in the commodity composition of India's trade baskets since the onset of liberalisation. In Table 8.7, we provide the composition of exports and imports

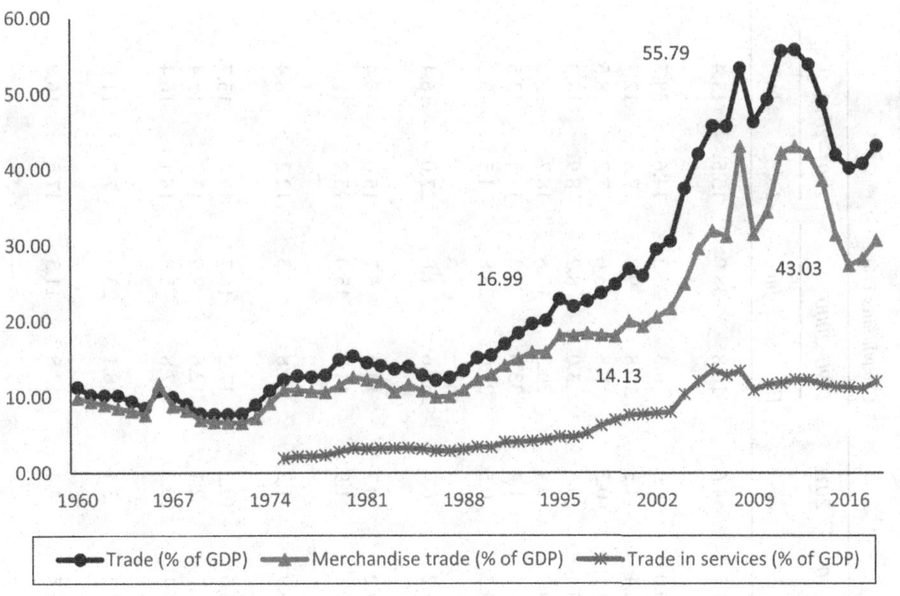

Figure 8.2 India's trade share in GDP (%): 1960–2018. *Source*: Author's calculation based on World Development Indicators (WDI) World Bank.

Table 8.5 Composition of manufacturing goods in merchandise trade of India (%) 1960–2018

Periods	*Manufacturing exports*	*Manufacturing imports*
1960–69	47.5	54.4
1970–79	53.6	49.7
1980–89	60.1	51.8
1990–99	74.2	51.9
2000–09	71.0	50.6
2010–18	67.6	49.1

Source: Author's calculation based on World Development Indicators (WDI) World Bank.

Table 8.6 Annual average growth rate of trade: 1975–2018

Periods	*Goods exports*	*Goods imports*
1975–89	9.5	12.2
1990–99	8.9	8.0
2000–09	17.2	21.5
2010–18	9.1	8.4

Source: Author's calculation based on World Development Indicators (WDI) World Bank.

Table 8.7 Distribution of manufacturing trade: by 2-digit industry classification (1990–2018) %

ISIC rev3	Description	Share of exports (%)				Share of imports (%)				Growth rates (%)			
		1990	2000	2010	2018	1990	2000	2010	2018	1990–2000		2001–2018	
										Ex	Im	Ex	Im
15	Food & beverages	12.6	11.8	7.2	9.5	2.9	6.2	4.5	4.6	10.8	38.0	13.5	15.4
16	Tobacco	0.3	0.1	0.1	0.1	0.0	0.0	0.0	0.0	6.3	23.3	14.6	38.7
17	Textiles	19.6	20.2	8.8	7.8	1.7	2.1	1.4	1.5	10.8	9.8	7.8	12.7
18	Wearing apparel	20.1	17.4	5.6	5.1	0.0	0.1	0.1	0.3	8.8	45.0	7.2	28.5
19	Leather	9.8	4.8	2.0	2.0	0.6	0.6	0.4	0.6	3.0	8.2	8.9	15.3
20	Wood	0.1	0.1	0.1	0.2	0.1	0.1	0.2	0.4	20.3	17.8	18.7	23.5
21	Paper	0.1	0.5	0.4	0.6	3.0	2.2	1.3	1.4	33.6	6.3	14.5	13.5
22	Publishing & printing	0.3	1.3	0.3	0.2	0.5	1.9	0.3	0.5	28.0	28.8	4.5	3.0
23	Refined Petroleum	4.4	4.6	22.7	18.1	19.1	8.3	5.2	6.0	254.6	1.8	27.0	16.4
24	Chemicals	11.4	14.6	15.0	19.2	23.8	21.2	19.2	20.7	13.4	6.7	15.0	15.4
25	Rubber & plastics	1.8	2.1	2.0	2.4	0.9	1.3	1.4	1.9	14.8	15.0	15.2	17.6
26	Non-metallic minerals	0.8	2.0	1.2	1.7	0.8	0.8	0.9	1.2	21.8	7.3	12.2	18.4
27	Basic metals	3.8	5.7	11.7	7.4	12.7	21.9	28.0	19.2	17.2	16.7	19.6	15.7
28	Fabricated metal	3.3	4.0	2.7	3.0	1.2	1.5	1.7	2.1	12.6	9.9	13.0	18.4
29	Machinery & equipment	4.0	3.2	4.4	5.9	13.5	10.0	11.4	10.3	7.8	5.9	18.1	16.4
30	Office machinery	0.9	0.7	0.4	0.2	1.7	5.2	2.3	3.1	18.1	23.6	7.7	11.6
31	Electrical machinery	1.5	1.8	2.7	3.1	3.1	3.3	3.7	4.4	12.8	11.3	17.5	16.8

32	TV & equipment	0.8	0.7	2.4	1.2	3.5	4.9	8.4	12.4	16.5	13.6	26.7	23.1
33	Medical & optical	0.6	0.9	0.9	1.3	4.1	3.6	2.9	3.4	17.3	8.2	15.3	14.5
34	Motor vehicles	2.4	2.2	5.1	6.1	2.2	2.0	2.5	2.5	10.4	9.7	22.6	18.8
35	Other Transport equipment	1.4	1.2	4.3	4.8	4.6	2.7	4.1	3.7	9.5	22.7	27.2	28.2

Source: Author's calculation based on UN Comtrade database (WITS).
Note: Share denotes each products relative position in total manufacturing (ISIC rev3, 15–35) trade (%).

based on ISIC rev3 for selected years, namely, 1990, 2000, 2010 and 2018. In 1990, the largest export items were mostly less technology-intensive products such as wearing apparel (20 per cent), textiles (20 per cent) and food & beverages (13 per cent). The highly technology-intensive products such as machinery (6 per cent), motor vehicles (2 per cent) and communication equipment (1 per cent) had a very low presence. The situation did not change much by 2000 as textiles, food and related products still dominated the export baskets. However, since then, there have been some notable changes. For instance, it is evident that technology-intensive commodities like chemicals (18 per cent) and refined petroleum (13 per cent) have emerged as the largest exportable items. Similarly, some of the non-traditional export items having a significant presence in the recent period are transport equipment (11 per cent) and the machinery sector (9 per cent). In terms of growth rates, most of the skills- and knowledge-intensive products exhibited double-digit growth rates during the 1990s and from 2001 to 2018 (see the last columns of Table 8.7).

The import product composition clearly shows the heavy dependence on high technology products and petroleum over the years (see Table 8.7). For instance, chemicals, machinery, petroleum and metal products dominated the top four imported items during all the selected periods. Machinery items, including both electrical and non-electrical components occupied around 20 per cent share for the entire period. Being a labour abundant country, the trade composition of India reflects its relative advantage in less skill-intensive and labour-absorbing products. However, it has to be noted that there have been some notable shifts visible in the recent period in the export basket.

To understand the dynamics of trade composition in detail, we grouped them according to four use-based classifications of commodities (see Table 8.8). During the 1990s, the export basket consisted mainly of final consumer goods (40 per cent), like food, meat, coffee & tea, plastic, leather, garment products etc., followed by intermediate goods (37 per cent). In contrast, the lowest share is found among the capital goods-producing sectors (7 per cent) such as machinery & tools and transport equipment. Since then the consumer goods exports share has remained at a higher level while the intermediate goods sectors have witnessed a marginal decline. In contrast, capital goods exports have improved and reached around a 15 per cent share by 2018. By the end of 2018, the broad structure of the Indian export basket had not changed much as the consumer goods (45 per cent) followed by the intermediate product groups (33 per cent) remained the largest product groups in the export basket.

On the other hand, the import basket of Indian manufacturing largely consisted of raw materials (35 per cent), such as copper and aluminium, animal fats, vegetable oil, silk and textile products etc., in 1990 (see Table 8.9). This was followed by intermediate (28 per cent) and capital

Table 8.8 Trade composition: by use-based categories (1990–2018) (%)

Use-based classification	*1990*		*2000*		*2010*		*2018*	
	Ex	*Im*	*Ex*	*Im*	*Ex*	*Im*	*Ex*	*Im*
Raw materials	16.0	35.3	9.8	47.1	9.9	36.4	7.5	36.4
Intermediate goods	37.1	28.4	43.2	26.6	35.7	36.7	32.6	31.0
Capital goods	6.8	19.3	6.4	15.5	11.9	18.5	15.0	21.5
Consumer goods	40.1	17.0	40.6	10.8	42.5	8.4	44.9	11.1

Source: Author's calculation based on HS standard product groups, UN Comtrade (WITS).

Table 8.9 Region/country-wise direction of India's exports and imports (% share) 1990–2018

Year	*Trade flow*	*OECD*	*Developing countries*	*LDC*	*Africa*	*Asia*	*China*	*USA*
1990	Exports	46.6	5.4	3.2	3.1	20.6	0.1	14.5
	Imports	41.3	8.3	1.9	3.7	22.1	0.1	10.8
2000	Exports	55.8	11.2	4.1	6.0	21.8	1.8	21.6
	Imports	39.5	14.4	2.3	7.3	22.5	2.8	5.3
2010	Exports	37.3	22.0	4.3	8.5	31.3	7.9	10.7
	Imports	34.9	26.0	2.4	9.4	35.6	11.8	5.5
2018	Exports	43.3	20.5	8.0	8.2	30.7	5.1	16.0
	Imports	31.5	30.4	2.5	8.7	39.8	14.4	6.3

Source: Author's calculation based on UN Comtrade (WITS).

goods (19 per cent). The consumer goods (17 per cent) are the items with the lowest share in the import basket during this period. By the end of 2018, the share of consumer goods came down to 11 per cent while the intermediate and raw materials accounted for 31 per cent and 36 per cent share, respectively. It is evident that the sourcing of productive inputs such as capital goods and intermediate goods has witnessed a significant increase since liberalisation. For instance, the share of capital goods import increased from 19 per cent in 1990 to 22 per cent by 2018. This suggests the growing participation of Indian producers in the global value chains (GVC) as intermediate inputs and raw materials, which are the major inputs to the production process, are being sourced from abroad. Recently, Topalova and Khandelwal (2011) and Rijesh (2019) find that import liberalisation has helped Indian firms to improve their productivity.

The direction of manufacturing trade from 1990 to 2018 is given in Table 8.9. We selected some major regions (OECD, LDC, developing countries, Asia, Africa) and countries (China and USA) for the analysis. Table 8.9 reveals that the OECD has been the largest partner in the trade basket. However, post-2000 we see a declining trend and rise of developing countries, especially China. For instance, in 1990, 47 per cent of Indian exports were directed towards the OECD region, but by the end of 2010 this had declined to 37 per cent. In 1990, India exported only 5 per cent to developing countries, but by 2010, the share had increased to 22 per cent. In the recent period, there has been a revival of exports towards the OECD as it registered 43 per cent share in 2018. India's presence in LDC and Africa has been relatively modest for the last two decades. However, during these two decades, Asia has emerged as the largest market for Indian products. For instance, in 1990, 21 per cent of exported items were directed towards the Asian market which rose to 31 per cent by 2018. Among the OECD countries, exports to the USA have been highly volatile. The exports increased during the 1990s (15 per cent to 22 per cent) but declined to 11 per cent in 2010. Since then there has been a revival with a registered 16 per cent share in 2018. From 1990 to 2018, the Chinese share remained largely modest.

A similar diversification of directions for India's imports is noticeable in Table 8.10. It is clear that OECD is the largest supplier of products to the Indian market. However, the share has declined over the years. In 1990, imports from the OECD comprised 41 per cent, which declined to 35 per cent in 2000, and by 2018 stood at 32 per cent. Similar to exports, the import basket has also diversified towards the developing regions as the share increased dramatically from 8 per cent in 1990 to 30 per cent in 2018. This was largely due to the significant presence of the Asian region especially China. Chinese imports increased from less than 1 per cent in

Table 8.10 List of export competitiveness products based on RSCA: by use-based classification (1990–2018)

Use-based category	*1990*	*2000*	*2010*	*2018*
Raw materials	96 (15.2)	123 (9.4)	98 (9.4)	105 (6.8)
Intermediate goods	401 (34.4)	632 (39.9)	578 (32.4)	707 (28.3)
Capital goods	86 (2.9)	92 (1.8)	123 (5.2)	176 (8.0)
Consumer goods	400 (37.6)	464 (37.6)	362 (37.0)	445 (40.4)
Manufacturing sector	983 (90.1)	1311 (88.7)	1161 (84.0)	1433 (83.4)
Number of competitive products in total exports (%)	26.8	29.1	26.0	32.2

Source: Authors calculation based on 6-digit HS data collected from UN Comtrade (WITS).
Note: figure in brackets represent the share of selected competitive products in the total value of manufacturing exports. Figures adjacent to parenthesis are the number of competitive products.

1990 to 3 per cent in 2000. Since then this has shot up and reached around 14 per cent in 2018. In contrast, the USA share declined from 11 per cent in 1990 to 6 per cent in 2018.

The detailed analysis of products traded with these regions is given in Table 8A.1 in the appendix. The products were selected at the 6-digit level and categorised according to HS standard product groups.[23] For each region and country, the trade pattern of India's use-based groups of commodities is based on India's export of four use-based products to the region/country relative to the export of India to the world. This is given in figures in per cent adjacent to the parenthesis in Table 8A.1. The figures in brackets represent the composition of India's use-based products in a particular region/country.

Analysis of the trade pattern with selected regions/countries clearly reflects the changing nature of India's commodity trade pattern since liberalisation. For instance, the preference for the OECD as the destination for India's export of raw materials and intermediate goods has shown a declining trend. This is much sharper in terms of the import basket as the share of all use-based products declined from 1990 to 2018, except for consumer goods. In contrast, India's exports and imports of all use-based categories of products increased considerably towards developing countries during this period. The largest segments traded with these regions are not final commodities but intermediate and capital goods, which are essential for manufacturing production. The low-income regions and countries have a small presence in India's overall trade. In the case of Africa, the pattern of trade clearly reflects India's comparative advantage as the exports consist of capital and consumer goods while the imports are largely raw materials and intermediate goods.

The importance of the Asian region in India's trade is clearly evident in Table 8A.1. In the case of exports, there was a noticeable rise in raw materials, capital goods and consumer goods from the 1990s. For imports, the share of all use-based products has witnessed a dramatic increase since the 2000 period, except for raw materials. This is most reflected in the case of capital goods import, which increased from 26 per cent in 1990 to 57 per cent in 2018. This changing trade pattern is attributed to the dramatic rise of China in the recent past. During the initial period of trade liberalisation, the Chinese market had virtually no presence in India as the share of use-based products, both exports and imports were less than unity. However, in the recent past, India has been successful in increasing the share of exports of only raw materials, which has increased from 0.4 per cent to 42 per cent from 1990 to 2010. The rest of the use-based exports have not been successful in penetrating the market in China. In contrast, the Chinese exports of intermediate goods, capital goods and consumer goods to India, which was virtually non-existent in the

1990s, increased considerably during the 2000s period. For instance, the share of capital goods imported from China relative to the world, which was only 4 per cent in 2000, had shot up to 36 per cent by 2018. This clearly demonstrates the significant rise of China in the Indian trade basket. On the other hand, the importance of the USA, a major trading partner in the earlier regime, has witnessed a noticeable fall since liberalisation.

The discussion so far shows some significant changes in India's export performance since liberalisation. Earlier empirical studies have noted a significant expansion of manufacturing exports since trade liberalisation (see Lall, 1999; Tendulkar, 2000; Srinivasan, 2003, Rijesh 2020), but highlights stagnation of product structure (Lall, 1999), coupled with uncompetitive performance in the world market, especially with respect to other Asian economies (Lall, 1999; Tendulkar, 2000; Srinivasan, 2003). However, most of these studies were confined largely to the initial period of liberalisation and cover broad product groups at the highest levels of disaggregation. For exploring the dynamics of export competitiveness, what is required is a detailed analysis at the finest levels of disaggregation encompassing a large time frame. In the following section, an attempt is made to explore the link between trade liberalisation and the export competitiveness of Indian manufacturing.

Trade liberalisation and export competitiveness of Indian manufacturing: an empirical analysis

In this section, an attempt is made to assess the export competitiveness of Indian manufacturing products since the initiation of a comprehensive trade liberalisation program in the 1990s. The next section introduces the link between trade liberalisation and export competitiveness in brief. This is followed by an assessment of the export competitiveness based on the Revealed Comparative Advantage (RCA) index. The empirical analysis is based on disaggregate level trade data collected at the 6-digit HS level. For the analytical purpose, we have classified the entire manufacturing activities into four use-based categories of manufacturing for the period 1990–2018.

Link between trade liberalisation and export competitiveness

According to Krueger (1980), trade liberalisation involves making the trade regime less restrictive and not biasing the incentive structure in favour of import-competing industries but rather, providing relatively uniform across the board incentives for exports. The major elements of trade liberalisation involve the removal of quotas, import licenses and other quantitative restrictions, reduction of the level and dispersion of import tariffs, devaluation of national currencies to compensate for the removal of protection and removal of export taxes and subsidies.[24] The rationale for liberalising trade results from the theoretical prediction of trade theories that international exchange of goods and services is mutually beneficial as it allows specialisation according to comparative advantage. As per the standard trade theories, free trade enlarges the production and consumption frontiers relative to autarky. The static efficiency results from the reallocation of resources from less efficient production activities to a more efficient range of products in line with international opportunity costs and prices (Bhagwati, 1988). One of the positive benefits attributed to trade liberalisation is export-oriented development (Weiss, 2002). To quote Kruger (1980: 92) 'the commitment to an export-oriented development strategy implies a fairly liberal and efficient trade regime'.

In an open trade regime, maintaining a consistent market presence in the export market requires significant improvement in product competitiveness. By competitiveness, we refer to the relative efficiency and capacity to transform production inputs for international production and sustain the market share in the long run. The ability to compete successfully in the international market requires doing better than the rival firms in terms of sales, market share and profitability. As such, the concept of competitiveness is closely related to improving productivity (see Krugman, 1996) at the firm or industry level. We argue that trade liberalisation is one of the instruments through which competitiveness can be injected into the economy.

Trade liberalisation provides access to a wide range of products, including raw materials and intermediate products, which are essential inputs in production. The use of imported low-cost and high-quality inputs helps firms to produce better quality goods at a lower cost, which enhances competitiveness. As low-cost manufacture expands output well beyond the domestic market, price advantages can be reaped through scale economies. The increased imports provide producers with new knowledge and ideas (externality) as exporters acquire more knowledge by their interaction with foreign buyers than do producers for the home market. Trade liberalisation provides an opportunity for learning-by-doing through exporting that stimulates knowledge spillover among both exporters and other producers, resulting in dynamic benefits to the economy.

An important dimension of trade liberalisation is the potential dynamic productivity benefits from technology spillover through adaptation and imitation. The country that imports capital goods or machinery tries to imitate the same technology. This technological spillover will lead to cost reduction and thus raise the export competitiveness. In addition, with import liberalisation, firms are under pressure to sell quality products at a cheaper price (forcing them to be more competitive). This competitive pressure will ultimately result in innovation by the domestic firm that can lead to a higher export performance in the world market.

The discussion so far has pointed out several important channels through which trade liberalisation can enhance competitiveness in the international market. Therefore, in the following subsection, we describe the methods and data sources of the study followed by an assessment of the competitive performance of Indian manufacturing exports since the trade liberalisation regime.

Methods and data

The export competitiveness of Indian manufacturing is examined with the help of the Revealed Comparative Advantage (RCA) index, originally developed by Balassa (also known as the *Balassa Index*) in 1965. The RCA index identifies the 'revealed' comparative advantage of the sectors using the observed trade pattern of economies.[25] The RCA is defined as a ratio of the share of a particular product in a country's total exports to the share of all countries' product exports in the world's total exports.[26] Defined as such, RCA is given by the formula (8.1)

$$RCA = \frac{\sum x_{sj} \Big/ \sum X_s}{\sum x_{wj} \Big/ \sum X_w} \tag{8.1}$$

Here, s and w represent India and the World, j is the commodity of interest (HS 6-digit product), x is the commodity export flow and X is the total export flow. The numerator is the share of good j in the exports of India (s), while the denominator is the share of good j in the exports of the world (w). If the RCA of a given product equals 1, the percentage share of that sector is the same as the world average (Laursen, 2015). If the RCA is above 1 the country is said to be specialised in that sector and if the RCA is below 1 it is said not to be specialised (or 'under-specialised'). Defined as such, manufacturing exports reveals competitiveness only in those products for which its market share is above its average share of the world exports, i.e., RCA is greater than one. Since the index is not comparable on both sides of unity,[27] we propose making the index symmetric following Lapadre (2006) and Laursen (2015). The Revealed Symmetric Comparative Advantage (RSCA) Index is derived as follows

$$\boldsymbol{RSCA} = {(RCA-1)}/{(RCA+1)} \quad (8.2)$$

This measure ranges from –1 to +1 and is positive if the RCA is higher than one (competitive advantage) and negative if it is lower than one (competitive disadvantage). The empirical findings are given in Tables 8.10 and 8.11, and Figure 8.3 and 8A.1 in the appendix.

The trade statistics are collected from UN Comtrade of the United Nations Statistical Division (UNSD) accessed through the World Integrated Trade Solution (WITS)[28] online portal. The UN Comtrade contains annual imports and exports statistics (value and quantity) for more than 160 reporting countries for each commodity broken down by the trading partner. The trade statistics of India, which is originally compiled by the Directorate General of Commercial Intelligence and Statistics (DGCI&S), Kolkata, under the Ministry of Commerce, Government of India, is available from the UN Comtrade based on the Harmonized Commodity Description and Coding System (Harmonized System, or HS) nomenclature. Based on HS standard product group classification,[29] we categorised the entire 6-digit HS product groups into four categories of manufacturing based on their Stages of Processing (SoP) and use,[30] namely raw materials (UNCTAD-SoP1), Intermediate goods (UNCTAD-SoP2), Consumer goods (UNCTAD-SoP3) and Capital goods (UNCTAD-SoP4). India's export of use-based products at the 6-digit HS classification level is collected for the years 1990, 2000, 2010 and 2018.

Export competitiveness of Indian manufacturing: RCA analysis

In this sub-section, we provide the empirical findings of export competitiveness based on the RCA index. In 1990, the number of competitive products (i.e., RSCA>1) for the entire manu-

Table 8.11 Dynamics of export competitiveness: use-based categories (1990-2018)

Use-based categories	*Competitive for the entire period*	*Increased competitiveness*	*Declined competitiveness*
Raw materials	41	10	13
Intermediate goods	181	145	56
Capital goods	12	23	36
Consumer goods	181	47	59
Manufacturing sector	415	225	164

Source: Authors calculation based on 6-digit HS data c2 collected from UN Comtrade (WITS).
Note: The competitive performance is assessed in terms of the product position in the 1990s.

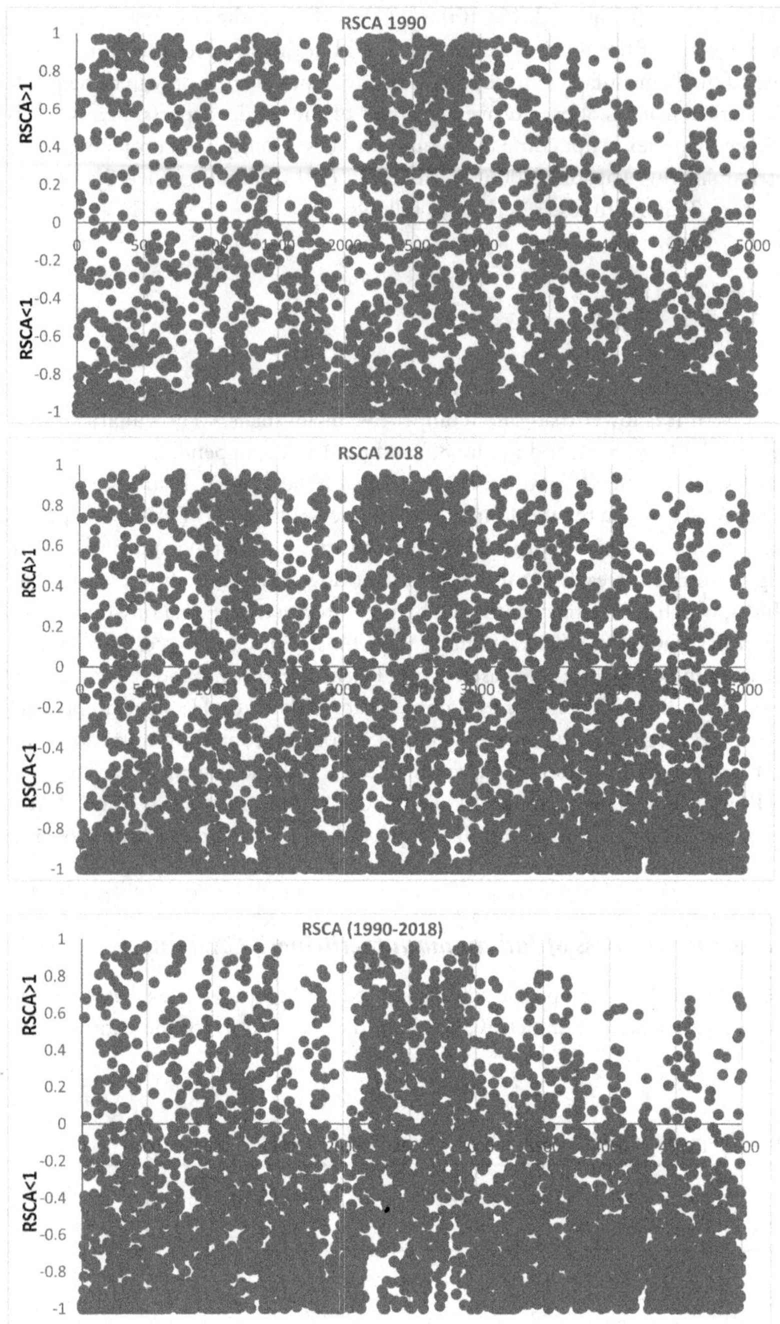

Figure 8.3 Export competitiveness in Indian manufacturing: RSCA analysis (1990–2018). *Source:* Authors calculation based on 6-digit HS data collected from UN Comtrade (WITS).

facturing sector at the 6-digit level was 983, which covers around 90 per cent of exports in value terms (see Table 8.10). Since liberalisation, the number of competitive products has increased, albeit gradually. By the end of 2018, the number of competitive products had increased to 1433, representing 83 per cent of export value. However, in terms of the overall export product distribution, the number of competitive products in the total export basket did not change much and remained in the range of 27 to 32 per cent during the period of 1990–2018 (see the last row in Table 8.10). For example, India exported around 4449 HS 6-digit products in 2018, out of which only 1433 were competitive in the world market. Another important feature from the RSCA analysis is the shift in competitive performance over time. As highlighted in Table 8.11, during the entire period of study only 415 products remained consistently competitive in the world market. However, in comparison to the early 1990s, 225 products have increased their export competitiveness while 164 products have lost their competitive edge in the world market.

Figure 8.3 depicts the distribution of competitive and uncompetitive products during 1990, 2018 and 1990–2018. For the entire period, we have calculated the average RSCA for all manufacturing products. Although a number of products have achieved a value greater than unity, there is a higher concentration of products close to −1, indicating the absence of India's export at the 6-digit level during any of the reference periods. However, comparing the upper two graphs shows that there has been an improvement in export competitiveness since liberalisation. Compared to the 1990s situation, the number of competitive products increased in 2018. However, the concentration of products in the lower range of RSCA reflects the inadequacy of Indian exports to penetrate successfully in the world market.

Analysis based on the use-based category indicates that the largest number of competitive products belongs to the intermediate product producing sectors, followed by the consumer goods segment (see Table 8.10). This remained unchanged for the entire period. Both of them occupy more than 50 per cent of trade value during the study period. Among the rest of the categories, capital goods-producing sectors have increased their competitive position. However, the total number of competitive capital goods exports continues to have a lower presence in the total value of export products from India. Since India has a relatively abundant supply of labour, the relatively lower competitive performance of capital-intensive products such as machinery and tools is not surprising.

In terms of the dynamics of competitive performance, the intermediate products have registered the largest number for the entire period (see Table 8.11). These products have been able to improve their competitive position significantly relative to other use-based products. On the other hand, the number of products that became uncompetitive in the later period is higher for capital goods and consumer goods sectors. The detailed list of competitive and uncompetitive products during 1990, 2000, 2010 and 2018 is given in Figure 8A.1 in the appendix. This clearly shows improved performance of intermediate goods and stability in the rest of the sectors.

Concluding remarks

The purpose of this chapter is to examine the nature of the export competitiveness of Indian manufacturing since the initiation of systematic trade liberalisation policy reforms in the 1990s. Since the onset of liberalisation, the economy is found to have experienced considerable economic growth. This is in sharp contrast to the experience of the 1960s and 1970s which were characterised by the 'Hindu-rate of growth'. Although the contribution of the service sector in overall growth is significant, long-run sustainability requires the development of a dynamic manufacturing industrial sector. Manufacturing is considered essential for a labour abundant country such as India as it involves higher employment potential with deep sectoral linkages and productivity potential.

The review of the policy changes reveals that the economy has moved gradually from a heavy inward-oriented, control-based industry/trade regime to a more liberalised/open trade regime since the early 1990s. In terms of levels of protection, the study noted a considerable reduction in tariff and other quantitative measures, especially among the intermediate and capital goods-producing sectors. As a result, the level of openness in terms of trade share in GDP reached 56 per cent in 2012. The increased trade performance is largely attributed to the strong growth performance in manufacturing exports and imports, which registered double-digit growth rates in the recent period. We find that the traditional labour-intensive items such as food, meat and textile products still accounted for the largest share in India's export basket. However, there is a noticeable shift in trade composition towards technology-intensive products like machinery and chemical sectors in the recent period. Using the use-based classification (BEC), we find that there is a large increase in the import of intermediate and capital goods, while the export basket is concentrated on intermediate and consumer goods. In the case of trade direction, the importance of Asia – in particular, China and other developing countries – has increased since 2000. Although the OECD is the largest trading partner, its importance declined in the recent period.

It is argued that trade liberalisation policies provide opportunities to develop a competitive export sector through static as well as dynamic benefits. The open trade regime is expected to create a favourable incentive structure for resource efficiency, reallocation and specialisation according to comparative advantage, scale economies and technology spillovers that expand manufacturing productivity and export competitiveness. Based on this line of argument, the present study examined the competitive performance disaggregate manufacturing exports for the period 1990, 2000, 2010 and 2018. The empirical analysis is carried out by constructing a Revealed Symmetric Comparative Advantage (RSCA) index at the 6-digit level of HS classification categorised into four use-based groups of commodities. The RSCA analysis reveals an improvement in export competitiveness at the aggregate as well as use-based categories of manufactured goods since reforms. However, the composition of products belonging to the competitive categories is found to be relatively small compared to the total number of exported products. Since only a few competitive products occupy a major share in the export basket, a large number of uncompetitive products have low export value. At the disaggregated level, the competitive performance of intermediate and consumer goods is notable. Even though there is a large growth in the export of machinery and equipment, the competitive performance is not satisfactory.

The empirics clearly point out that trade liberalisation policy *per se* is not sufficient to achieve higher export competitiveness in the international market. The divergent performance across product groups indicates the nature of heterogeneity and product-specific characteristics relevant to export competitiveness in the global market. In order to compete successfully, it is essential that the manufacturing sector invests more in technology and knowledge-based assets to reduce production costs and improve the quality of the exported products. The high incidence of uncompetitive products reflects a huge opportunity for Indian producers to gain an untapped global market in future. In order to realise this, the policy framework needs to reorient towards creating a well-functioning institutional apparatus, improved physical infrastructure and an environment for the development of innovative production capabilities.

Appendix

Table 8A.1 Region/country-wise composition of use-based traded goods of India (%) Selected years

BEC/Region/Countries	*Exports*				*Imports*			
	1990	*2000*	*2010*	*2018*	*1990*	*2000*	*2010*	*2018*
OECD	41.9 (100.0)	55.4 (100.0)	37.8 (100.0)	43.3 (100.0)	38.4 (100.0)	42.0 (100.0)	34.6 (100.0)	31.5 (100.0)
Raw materials	55.6 (19.1)	60.4 (10.6)	22.5 (5.9)	33.8 (5.8)	25.4 (21.7)	22.8 (27.2)	16.8 (17.7)	20.8 (24.1)
Intermediate goods	49.5 (39.5)	52.1 (40.3)	34.0 (32.1)	42.4 (32.0)	54.0 (37.1)	55.3 (37.2)	42.8 (45.3)	40.0 (39.4)
Capital goods	17.3 (2.5)	49.6 (5.7)	38.4 (12.1)	44.9 (15.5)	70.4 (32.9)	67.9 (26.6)	53.9 (28.8)	38.7 (26.4)
Consumer goods	45.2 (38.9)	59.6 (43.4)	44.4 (50.0)	44.9 (46.7)	3.6 (8.3)	21.9 (8.9)	32.7 (8.2)	28.6 (10.1)
DEVELOPING COUNTRIES	7.0 (100.0)	14.1 (100.0)	22.4 (100.0)	20.5 (100.0)	6.4 (100.0)	12.1 (100.0)	25.6 (100.0)	30.4 (100.0)
Raw materials	7.9 (23.5)	19.4 (17.0)	55.0 (24.3)	26.3 (9.5)	8.9 (37.8)	6.9 (22.7)	19.8 (28.0)	21.8 (26.1)
Intermediate goods	6.6 (45.6)	13.3 (51.3)	24.1 (38.3)	26.5 (42.0)	15.4 (52.6)	24.3 (45.1)	25.1 (35.8)	32.8 (33.4)
Capital goods	11.1 (13.9)	17.8 (10.2)	23.4 (12.4)	22.5 (16.4)	0.9 (2.1)	14.5 (15.7)	37.3 (26.9)	43.0 (30.3)
Consumer goods	2.3 (17.0)	5.9 (21.5)	13.1 (24.9)	14.6 (32.0)	0.2 (7.5)	2.6 (16.5)	27.3 (9.2)	28.0 (10.2)
LDC	4.4 (100.0)	4.8 (100.0)	4.3 (100.0)	8.0 (100.0)	1.6 (100)	1.5 (100.0)	2.4 (100.0)	2.5 (100.0)
Raw materials	2.0 (9.8)	3.4 (8.2)	5.6 (12.7)	7.9 (7.4)	1.9 (34.5)	3.1 (63.5)	5.2 (78.2)	3.9 (56.6)
Intermediate goods	3.3 (37.9)	4.6 (48.7)	4.2 (34.9)	7.9 (32.3)	4.3 (64)	1.9 (22.0)	1.1 (17.2)	2.5 (31.2)
Capital goods	9.9 (20.9)	8.1 (12.7)	4.7 (12.8)	9.6 (18.0)	0.0 (0.0)	0.3 (2.1)	0.0 (0.2)	0.1 (0.5)
Consumer goods	2.5 (31.4)	3.1 (30.4)	4.0 (39.5)	7.6 (42.3)	0.2 (1.5)	0.8 (12.4)	1.2 (4.5)	2.7 (11.7)
AFRICA	4.4 (100.0)	6.6 (100.0)	8.6 (100.0)	8.2 (100.0)	5.7 (100.0)	14.1 (100.0)	9.6 (100.0)	8.7 (100.0)
Raw materials	0.8 (4.0)	3.3 (5.4)	3.9 (4.5)	3.5 (3.2)	3.3 (31.4)	7.2 (46.4)	19.2 (72.5)	15.9 (66.4)
Intermediate goods	2.4 (29.0)	5.9 (42.1)	5.7 (23.5)	6.3 (25.1)	8.3 (63.7)	12.4 (45.2)	6.4 (24.4)	6.8 (24.2)
Capital goods	11.2 (24.7)	10.9 (11.6)	14.7 (20.3)	9.7 (17.8)	0.7 (3.9)	3.4 (7.3)	0.9 (1.8)	0.6 (1.5)
Consumer goods	3.2 (42.3)	6.1 (40.9)	10.5 (51.8)	9.8 (53.9)	10.5 (1.0)	33.4 (1.1)	1.5 (1.3)	6.2 (8.0)
ASIA	24.9 (100.0)	27.1 (100.0)	31.5 (100.0)	30.7 (100.0)	18.4 (100.0)	19.5 (100.0)	35.5 (100.0)	39.8 (100.0)
Raw materials	41.7 (32.5)	42.3 (19.0)	67.9 (21.3)	55.4 (13.5)	26.8 (42.8)	13.8 (28.9)	32.7 (33.5)	27.0 (24.7)

(*Continued*)

Table 8A.1 (Continued)

BEC/Region/Countries	*Exports*				*Imports*			
	1990	*2000*	*2010*	*2018*	*1990*	*2000*	*2010*	*2018*
Intermediate goods	22.1 (39.9)	23.9 (47.4)	31.7 (36.0)	33.1 (35.2)	20.3 (26.1)	25.5 (30.1)	26.1 (26.9)	37.5 (29.2)
Capital goods	26.1 (8.6)	28.7 (8.4)	31.1 (11.7)	32.9 (16.1)	26.3 (23.0)	36.3 (25.0)	48.4 (25.2)	56.5 (30.5)
Consumer goods	9.7 (19.0)	13.5 (25.2)	22.9 (31.0)	24.0 (35.2)	0.0 (8.1)	2.4 (16.0)	59.2 (14.5)	56.1 (15.6)
CHINA	0.1 (100.0)	2.8 (100.0)	8.1 (100.0)	5.1 (100.0)	1.8 (100.0)	4.6 (100.0)	11.2 (100.0)	14.4 (100.0)
Raw materials	0.4 (60.8)	7.7 (43.0)	41.5 (50.9)	11.4 (16.8)	0.2 (43.6)	1.2 (20.6)	0.5 (1.7)	0.3 (0.8)
Intermediate goods	0.1 (35.3)	1.9 (45.5)	9.5 (41.9)	7.9 (50.5)	0.3 (50.5)	5.0 (47.5)	10.9 (35.7)	15.4 (33.0)
Capital goods	0.0 (1.7)	1.1 (4.1)	2.2 (3.2)	3.3 (9.7)	0.0 (4.0)	4.0 (22.4)	30.3 (50.2)	35.5 (52.7)
Consumer goods	0.0 (2.2)	0.3 (7.4)	0.7 (3.9)	2.6 (23.1)	6.7 (1.9)	8.3 (9.5)	15.9 (12.3)	17.5 (13.4)
USA	11.9 (100.0)	19.5 (100.0)	10.8 (100.0)	16.0 (100.0)	10.4 (100.0)	10.9 (100.0)	5.0 (100.0)	6.3 (100.0)
Raw materials	6.5 (7.2)	16.2 (7.4)	5.0 (4.5)	12.9 (6.0)	6.1 (20.0)	1.1 (9.5)	1.3 (9.2)	4.2 (24.4)
Intermediate goods	18.2 (46.4)	20.9 (41.9)	10.6 (34.7)	14.8 (30.2)	14.9 (39.2)	6.4 (32.1)	6.3 (45.5)	8.5 (41.7)
Capital goods	7.0 (3.2)	16.5 (4.7)	12.3 (13.5)	15.6 (14.6)	16.8 (30.2)	14.2 (41.5)	9.7 (35.6)	6.8 (23.2)
Consumer goods	15.7 (43.2)	24.5 (46.0)	12.1 (47.3)	17.5 (49.2)	3.6 (10.6)	21.9 (16.9)	5.7 (9.7)	6.1 (10.7)

Source: Author's calculation based on HS standard product groups, UN Comtrade (WITS).

Note: Figure adjacent to parenthesis represent the share of India's trade of use-based industrial products (BEC) towards particular region/country relative to India's trade of use-based products to the world. Figures in parenthesis represent the share of India's trade of use-based products (BEC) in a particular region/country relative to India's total trade of use-based products with that particular region/country.

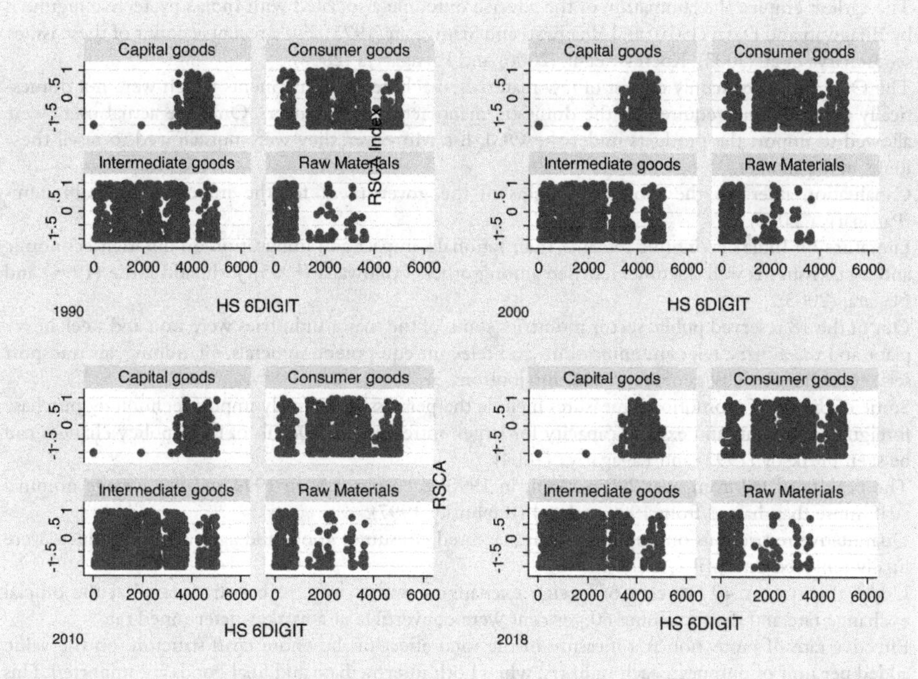

Figure 8A.1 Distribution of export competitiveness based on RSCA Index: by use-based classification (1990, 2000, 2010 & 2018). *Source*: Author's calculation based on HS standard product groups, UN Comtrade (WITS).

Notes

1 The average annual growth rate of India during 1951–1966 was 3.4 per cent per annum. This was much higher than the negligible growth rate of 0.8 per cent per annum during 1930–46 (See Krishna, 2012).

2 The issue of stagnation/deceleration in Indian growth since independence has been the subject of much debate and analysis. See, for instance, Bhagwati and Srinivasan (1984), Chakravarty (1984), Raj (1984), Dhar (1988), and Nagaraj (1990). For a recent exposition on these issues, see Balakrishnan (2010).

3 Prof Raj Krishna popularized this phrase in the seventies.

4 See OECD (2009) for an extensive discussion of emerging economies including India.

5 According to the Central Statistical Organisation (CSO), agriculture includes forestry and fishing while industry encompasses manufacturing, electricity, gas and water, mining and quarrying and construction.

6 Manufacturing is defined as the industry net of mining and quarrying, electricity, gas, water and construction.

7 Services refer to the economic output of intangible commodities that may be produced, transferred and consumed at the same time. Services correspond to ISIC divisions 50-99.

8 See, for instance, Acharya et al. (2003), Bosworth et al. (2007) and Panagariya (2008).

9 Eichengreen and Gupta (2011) argues that sustaining economic growth and raising the living standards in India requires shifting of labour out of agriculture into both manufacturing and services and not just into one or the other sector.

10 The import substitution strategy was criticized for resulting in low sectoral growth (Ahluwalia, 1985), high cost industrial structure (Pillai, 1979), technological stagnation and dependence (Chudnovsky et al., 1983, and UNCTAD, 1983), inefficiency, low productivity and lack of innovativeness (Lall, 1999).

The earliest empirical examination of the adverse outcome associated with India's protective regime is by Bhagwati and Desai (1970) and Bhagwati and Srinivasan (1975). For a recent account of these issues, see Acharya et al. (2003), Kochhar et al. (2006) and Panagariya (2008).

11 The OGL products mainly consist of raw materials, machines or components which were not domestically produced but required by the domestic manufacturing producers. Only the actual users were allowed to import the products under the OGL list. Moreover, they were not allowed to resell these items in the market.

12 Canalisation refers to the monopoly rights of the government for the imports of certain items (Panagariya, 2008).

13 Literature on India's economic reforms, their rationale, impact and implication on different economic and social issues is well documented. See among others, Ahluwalia (1995), Joshi and Little (1996) and Nagaraj (2003).

14 Out of the 18 reserved public sector industries some of the major industries were iron and steel, heavy plant and machinery, telecommunications and telecom equipment, minerals, oil, mining, air transport services and electricity generation and distribution.

15 Some of the other promotional measures include the permission to freely import technology, purchase foreign components and expand capacity for larger entrepreneurs. Details of these policy changes can be seen in Aksoy (1992) and Panagariya (2004).

16 The peak tariff fell from over 200 per cent in 1990 to 65 per cent in 1994 and the average nominal tariff more than halved from 1990 to 1994 (Kaplinsky, 1997).

17 Quantitative restrictions on imports of manufactured consumer goods and agricultural products were finally removed on April 1, 2001.

18 Under this system, 40 per cent of foreign exchange earnings were to be surrendered at the official exchange rate and the remaining 60 per cent were convertible at a market-determined rate.

19 Effective rate of protection is a measure of the total effect of the entire tariff structure on the value added per unit of output in each industry, when both intermediate and final goods are imported. This statistic is used to measure the real amount of protection afforded to a particular industry by import duties, tariffs or other trade restrictions. The import coverage ratio is the share of a country's own imports that is subjected to non-tariff barriers (OECD, 2012).

20 UNCTAD-TRAINS (Trade Analysis and Information System) is a trade and market access information system combining the database containing data drawn from UN TARMAC, a joint primary data collection with the International Trade Centre (WTO, ITC) and the WITS software.

21 This grouping is based on the Broad Economic Classification (BEC) scheme of the UN that classifies products according to their main end use. The BEC system is defined in terms of the Standard International Trade Classification system (SITC). For the analysis purpose, we adopted the standard HS classification scheme.

22 Tariffs can be either simple or weighted. Simple averages are calculated by adding the tariffs on all product lines and dividing by the number of those tariff lines. Weighted mean applied tariff is the average of effectively applied rates weighted by the product import shares corresponding to each partner country. Simple averages give the same weight to products that are not imported and to products that are imported in large amounts. The import-weighted averages under-weigh high tariffs and give zero weight to prohibitive tariffs (WTO, 2012). We prefer to use the latter.

23 WTO classifies HS groups into the following use-based categories. (1) WTO-SoP1: Raw materials, (2) WTO-SoP2: Intermediate goods, (3) WTO-SoP3: Consumer goods and (4) WTO-SoP4: Capital goods. We access India's trade data from UN COMTRADE (WITS).

24 In a narrow sense, trade liberalisation is identified as the removal of trade-restricting practices like tariff and non-tariff barriers. In a broader context, this also includes the reduction of all forms of controls and restrictions that affect economic transactions among countries, including relaxation in capital controls, exchange rate rationalization and minimal government intervention.

25 Although this index is originally used to measure comparative advantage, there has been apprehension regarding whether the index identifies comparative advantage or competitiveness. According to Siggel (2006), RCA reflects competitiveness rather than comparative advantage because export success is often due to government intervention like subsidies or other incentives providing like exchange rate misalignment.

26 For a detailed overview and application of the RCA approach, see for example Balassa (1965), Lee (1995) and Laursen (2015).

27 The index ranges from one to infinity for products with which countries have a competitive advantage but only from zero to one competitive disadvantage.

28 WITS is a data consultation and extraction software with simulation capabilities. The database was developed by the World Bank with the collaboration and consultation with the United Nations Conference on Trade and Development (UNCTAD), International Trade Center (ITC), United Nations Statistical Division (UNSD) and World Trade Organization (WTO).

29 See https://wits.worldbank.org/referencedata.html for further details.

30 Raw materials and resources such as starch, coal, basic chemicals, fertilizers etc. are used in the first stages of the production process. Intermediate products covering a wide range of semi-finished products like textile yarns, jute, tanned leathers, wood materials, refined petroleum products etc. are used in the production of other products. Consumer products, which include both durable and non-durable goods, are intended for final consumption. Capital goods are manufactured goods such as machinery and equipment used in all stages of the production of other goods.

References

Acharya, S., I.J. Ahluwalia, K.L. Krishna, and I. Patnaik, (2003), *India: Economic Growth: 1950–2000*, Global Research Project on Growth, Indian Council for Research on International Economic Relations. New Delhi: Mimeo.

Ahluwalia, I.J., (1985), *Industrial Growth in India: Stagnation since Mid Sixties*, Delhi: Oxford University Press.

Ahluwalia, M.S., (1995), 'India's Economic Reforms,' *India, The Future of Economic Reform*, Oxford, UK: Oxford University Press.

Ahluwalia, M.S., (2002), 'Economic Reforms in India since 1991: Has Gradualism Worked?', *Journal of Economic Perspectives*, 16(3), 67–88.

Aksoy, M.A., (1992), 'The Indian Trade Regime', *World Bank Working Paper*, No. 989, Washington, DC: World Bank, 1–82.

Balakrishnan, P., (2010), *Economic Growth in India: History and Prospect*. New Delhi: Oxford University Press.

Balassa, B., (1965), 'Trade Liberalisation and Revealed Comparative Advantage', *The Manchester School*, 33(2), 327–345.

Bernard, A.B., J.B. Jensen, S.J. Redding, and P.K. Schott, (2007), 'Firms in International Trade', *Journal of Economic Perspectives*, 21(3), 105–130.

Bhagwati, J.N., (1988), 'Export-Promoting Trade Strategy: Issues and Evidence', *World Bank Research Observer*, 3(1), 27–58.

Bhagwati, J., and P. Desai, (1970), *India: Planning for Industrialization*, London: Oxford University Press.

Bhagwati, J., and T.N. Srinivasan, (1975), *Foreign Trade Regimes and Economic Development*, New York: Columbia University Press.

Bhagwati, J., and T.N. Srinivasan, (1984), 'Indian Development Strategy: Some Comments', *Economic and Political Weekly*, 19(47), 2006–2008.

Bhaumik, S.K., and S.C. Kumbhakar, (2010), 'Is the Post-Reform Growth of the Indian Manufacturing Sector Efficiency Driven? Empirical Evidence from Plant-Level Data', *Journal of Asian Economics*, 21, 219–232.

Bosworth, B., S.M. Collins, and A. Virmani, (2007), 'Sources of Growth in the Indian Economy', *NBER Working Paper* No. W12901, Cambridge: National Bureau of Economic Research.

Chakravarty, S., (1984), 'Aspects of India's Development Strategy for the 1980s', *Economic and Political Weekly*, 19(20/21), 845-847+849-852.

Chudnovsky, D., N. Masafumi, and S. Jacobson, (1983), *Capital Good Production in the Third World: An Economic Study of Technology Acquisition*, London: Frances Printer.

Das, D.K., (2003), 'Quantifying Trade Barriers: Has Protection Declined Substantially in Indian Manufacturing?', *Working Paper* No. 105, New Delhi: ICRIER.

Dhar, P. N., (1988), 'The Indian Economy: Past Performance and Current Issues', in *The Indian Economy: Recent Development and Future Prospects*, edited by Robert EB Lucas and Gustav F. Papanek, New Delhi: Oxford University Press, 3–22.

Dua, P., and R. Ranjan, (2010), *Exchange Rate Policy and Modelling in India*, Development Research Group, Study No. 33, Mumbai: Department of Economic Analysis and Policy, Reserve Bank of India.

Eichengreen, B., and P. Gupta, (2011), 'The Service Sector as India's Road to Economic Growth', NBER Working Paper Series, *Working Paper* 16757, Cambridge: National Bureau of Economic Research.

Grossman, G.M., and E. Helpman, (1991), *Innovation and Growth in the Global Economy*, Cambridge, MA: MIT Press.

Joshi, V., and I.M.D. Little, (1996), *India's Economic Reforms: 1991–2001*, Oxford and New York: Oxford Clarendon Press.

Kaplinsky, R., (1997), 'India's Industrial Development: An Interpretative Survey', *World Development*, 25(5), 681–694.

Kochhar, K., U. Kumar, R. Rajan, A. Subramanian, and I. Tokatlidis, (2006), 'India's Pattern of Development: What Happened, What Follows?', *Journal of Monetary Economics*, 53(5), 981–1019.

Kohli, A., (2006), 'Politics of Economic Growth in India: 1980–2005', *Economic and Political Weekly*, 41(14), 1361–1370.

Krishna, K.L., (2012), 'Idiosyncratic Industrial Development in India: Employment Implications', *Journal of Social and Economic Studies*, 22(1), 5–22.

Krueger, A.O., (1980), 'Trade Policy as an Input to Development', American Economic Review Paper and Proceedings, 70, 288–292.

Krugman, P.R., (1996), 'Making Sense of the Competitiveness Debate', *Oxford Review of Economic Policy*, 12(3), 17–25.

Lall, S., (1999), 'India's Manufactured Exports: Comparative Structure and Prospects', *World Development*, 27(10), 1769–1786.

Laparde, L.P., (2006), 'Measuring International Specialization', *International Applied Economic Review*, 7, 173–183.

Laursen, K., (2015), 'Revealed Comparative Advantage and the Alternatives as Measures of International Specialization', *Eurasian Business Review*, 5(1), 99–115.

Lee, J., (1995), 'Comparative Advantage in Manufacturing as Determinant of Industrialisation: The Korean Case', *World Development*, 23(7), 1195–1214.

Melitz, M.J., and S.J. Redding, (2014), 'Heterogeneous Firms and Trade', in *Handbook of International Economics*, edited by G. Gopinath, E. Helpman, and K. Rogoff. Vol. 4, Elsevier, Amsterdam, 1–54.

Nagaraj, R., (1990), 'Industrial Growth: Further Evidence and towards an Explanation and Issues', *Economic and Political Weekly*, 25(41), 2313–2332.

Nagaraj, R., (2003), 'Industrial Policy and Performance: Which Way Now?', *Economic and Political Weekly*, 38(35), 3707–3715.

OECD, (2009), *Globalisation and Emerging Economies: Brazil, Russia, India, Indonesia, China and South Africa*, Paris: OECD Publication.

OECD, (2012), *The OECD Economic Outlook: Sources and Methods*, Paris: OECD Publication.

Panagariya, A., (2004), 'Growth and Reforms during 1980s and 1990s', *Economic and Political Weekly*, 39(25), 2581–2594.

Panagariya, A., (2008), *India: The Emerging Giant*, Oxford and New York: Oxford University Press.

Pillai, M.P., (1979), 'Technology Transfer, Adaptation and Assimilation', *Economic and Political Weekly*, 14(47), M121–M126.

Raj, K.N., (1984), 'Some Observations on Economic Growth in India over the Period 1952–53 to 1982–83', *Economic and Political Weekly*, 19(41), 1801–1804.

Rijesh, R., (2019), 'International Trade and Productivity Growth in Indian Industry: Evidence from the Organized Manufacturing Sector', *Journal of South Asian Development*, 14(1), 1–39.

Rijesh, R., (2020), 'Trade Liberalisation, Technology Import, and Indian Manufacturing Exports', *Global Economic Review: Perspectives on East Asian Economies and Industries*, 49(4), 369–395.

Rodrik, D., and A. Subramanian, (2005), 'From Hindu Growth to Productivity Surge: the Mystery of the Indian Growth Transition', *IMF Staff Papers*, 52(2), 193–228.

Siggel, E., (2006), 'International Competitiveness and Comparative Advantage: A Survey and a Proposal for Measurement', *Journal of Industry, Competition and Trade*, 6(2), 137–159.

Srinivasan, T.N., (2003), *Indian Economy: Current Problems and Future Prospects*, Stanford, CA: REDPR Working Paper 173, July 2003.

Szirmai, A., (2013), 'Manufacturing and Economic Development', in *Pathways to Industrialisation in the 21st Century, New Challenges and Emerging Paradigms*, edited by Szirmai, A., W. Naudé and L. Alcorta, Oxford: Oxford University Press, 53–75.

Tendulkar, S.D., (2000), 'Indian Export and Economic Performance in Asian Perspective', *ICRIER Working Paper* No. 54, Indian Council for Research on International Economic Relations, New Delhi.

Topalova, P., and A. Khandelwal, (2011), 'Trade Liberalization and Firm Productivity: The Case of India', *The Review of Economics and Statistics*, 93(3), 995–1009.

UNCTAD, (2016), 'Trade and Development Report, 2016: Structural Transformation for Inclusive and Sustained Growth', United Nations Conference on Trade and Development, United Nations, New York, Geneva.

Virmani, A., (1997), 'India: Crises, Reform and Growth', *Economic and Political Weekly*, 32(32), 2064–2068.

Weiss, J., (2002), *Industrialisation and Globalization: Theory and Evidence from Developing Countries*, London and New York: Routledge.

World Bank, (2011), *World Development Indicators*, Washington, DC: World Bank.

WTO, (2012), *A Practical Guide to Trade Policy Analysis*, Geneva: United Nation and World Trade Organisation, WTO Publication.

9

SERVICE-TRADE LIBERALIZATION AND MANUFACTURING LABOUR PRODUCTIVITY

Post-reform state-level evidence from India

Mausumi Kar

Introduction

India implemented significant liberalization in both goods and services trade between 1991 and 2005. Being one of the first signatories of the General Agreement on Trade in Services (GATS),[1] and following suitable reforms, India has become successful in making its trade in services grow more prominently than its trade in goods. The elimination of barriers to entry in services, in India, provoked a dramatic response from foreign and domestic providers. FDI inflows into services following liberalization exceeded those into other sectors. The reforms produced striking improvements in the performance of service providers. The contribution of the service sector to India's GDP increased by leaps and bounds over the last decade, reaching 53.66 per cent in 2016, and is expected to reach 62 per cent in 2020.[2] In fact, the country has experienced a boom in service trade in the last decade and its service trade to GDP ratio rose to 11.4 per cent of GDP in 2016.[3] India has emerged as the fastest growing nation in global services trade with an annual growth rate of above 9 per cent since 2001.

Notwithstanding the fact, it is claimed that India is creating a new trajectory of economic growth and catch-up that is different from that of other developing countries, which are led by manufacturing sectors. Conventional hypotheses on "de-industrialization" or "tertiarization," such as the demand-bias hypothesis (Fisher 1939;Clark 1940; Schettkat and Yocarini 2006), the productivity-bias hypothesis (Baumol 1967; Summers 1985) and the demand-for-services-as-intermediate-goods hypothesis (Francois and Reinert, 1996; Pilat and Wölfl 2005; ten RAA and Wolff 2001) might not be satisfactory explanations for the Indian experience. These hypotheses were based on the experiences of advanced industrialized countries that shared a common pattern in which manufacturing growth preceded that of the service sector. By contrast, in the Indian economy, the service sector became quite large without undergoing a historical stage where the manufacturing sector was dominant.

DOI: 10.4324/9780367855741-9

Several researchers attribute this service-led success of India to the comparative advantage of the economy. The implementation of the New Economic Policy during the 1990s and the following economic and structural reforms have played a crucial role (Arora et al. 2001) in it. Nevertheless, this view does not explain the failure in achieving similar accomplishments by other developing countries in their service sectors despite having cheap labour and the disappointing growth of other sectors in India that could benefit from cheap labour as well.

Unlike existing studies, Ok, Lee and Kim (2014) attempt to explain the service-led economic growth of India using the leapfrogging argument proposed by Neo-Schumpeterians. They argue that a late-comer country that adopts a new technological paradigm during the transition period has a possibility of shortening the time necessary for catch-up or even to create a new path for catch-up, instead of simply following the paths that were taken by the firms in leader countries (Lee and Lim 2001). This leapfrogging argument has been applied more to explain firm- or industry-level technological catch-up happening in India and might provide a useful explanation to the country-level catch-up.

Nonetheless, output in the manufacturing sector in India grew by 5.7 per cent per year in the period 1993–2005, while exports grew at almost twice that rate (Reserve Bank of India 2008). Moreover, this sector grew at a compound annual growth rate of 7.32 per cent between 2011–12 and 2016–17 and at 7.7 per cent in 2016–17.[4] The conventional explanations for the revival of Indian manufacturing point to policy reforms in manufacturing industries, such as tariff liberalization and the dismantling of the "license raj" (Aghion et al., 2008), and limited labour market reforms (Besley and Burgess 2004). On the other hand, some studies (e.g. Krishna and Mitra 1998; Khandelwal and Topalova 2011; Goldberg et al. 2009; 2010) find that pro-competitive forces, resulting from lower tariffs on final goods, as well as access to better inputs, due to lower input tariffs, liberalization of both trade and FDI regime in manufacturing increased firm-level productivity.

But these explanations miss an essential element of the story. Recent evidence suggests that a key factor for the Indian manufacturing success may actually lie outside of manufacturing itself, in the services sector. The facts reveal that the manufacturing performance depends critically on the state of service inputs, notably finance, transport and telecommunications. Moreover, reforms in the 1990s, along with a change in the international scenario following GATS, have visibly transformed these services sectors, allowing greater foreign and domestic competition with greatly improved regulation. Indian firms are no longer at the mercy of inefficient public monopolies but can now source from a wide range of domestic and foreign private-sector providers operating in an increasingly competitive environment. These improvements have enhanced firms' ability to invest in new business opportunities and better production technology, to exploit economies of scale by concentrating production in fewer locations, to efficiently manage inventories and to make coordinated decisions with their suppliers and consumers. Our chapter deals with examining the impact of this kind of spillover of services sector growth, via expansion in service trade, on the state-level manufacturing productivity of India and thereby inquiring about its role in creating a comprehensive, all-inclusive growth for the country as the manufacturing sector stands to be the driver of an economy.

Review of literature

Downstream spillovers arising from policy reform and foreign participation in the services sectors are qualitatively different from those arising from foreign direct investment in manufacturing industries. Mattoo et al. (2006) meticulously explain how the impact of liberalization of service sectors on output growth differs from that of liberalization of trade in goods. Finally, it provides some econometric evidence that openness in services influences long-run growth performance.

There has not, however, been much empirical analysis of the downstream effects of services reform, and the few existing studies have focused on specific services sectors, usually banking (Rajan and Zingales 1998; Bertrand, Scholar and Thesmar 2004). It is noteworthy to mention here that Arnold et al. (2012 and 2016), by examining the link between those reforms and the productivity of manufacturing firms using panel data for about 4,000 Indian firms from 1993 to 2005, found that banking, telecommunications, insurance and transport reforms had significant, positive effects on the productivity of manufacturing firms. Services reforms benefited both foreign and locally owned manufacturing firms, but the effects on foreign firms tended to be stronger. In a very recent study, Beverelli et al. (2017) show that decreasing services trade restrictiveness has a positive impact on the manufacturing sectors that use services as intermediate inputs in production. They identify a critical role of institutions in importing countries in shaping this effect. Countries with high institutional quality benefit the most from lower services trade restrictions in terms of increased productivity in downstream industries.

Similar important studies, but for other countries, are also worthy of mention in this respect. Arnold, Javorcik and Mattoo (2011) use firm-level data to show that increased foreign participation in services provision led to improvement in manufacturing productivity in the Czech Republic in the period 1998–2003. Zhang et al. (2010) investigate the impact of service trade liberalization on manufacturing performance in China through the channel of service outsourcing. They estimate the productivity effects of services trade liberalization by using a panel dataset of Chinese manufacturing firms over the period from 1998 to 2007 to find the positive productivity effects for firms located in east China, firms with heavy service usage, foreign invested firms and exporters. Stiroh (2002) examines the link between information technology (IT) and the US productivity revival in the late 1990s. The industry-level data shows a broad productivity resurgence that reflects both the production and use of IT. The econometric tests show that the most IT-intensive industries experienced significantly larger productivity gains than other industries. However, Ok, Lee and Kim (2014) identify that there is a very weak correlation between the growth rate of the manufacturing and services sectors of India and that distinguishes India from other newly industrializing economies of East Asia. Although China, Indonesia, the Philippines and Thailand started industrialization relatively later, the correlation between the growth rates of two sectors remained high throughout their industrialization. In the cases of South Korea and Singapore, where the tertiarization process already began during industrial maturation, the correlation was weaker and was similar to that of developed countries. The rapid growth of the service sector in India is driven by its strong productivity performance, which in turn prompted a massive inflow of workers into the sector because of higher wages. This pattern differs from other developing countries, where the expansion of the service sector did not accompany significant improvements in productivity. In the case of India, the labour productivity level is higher in the service sector than in manufacturing. So the Indian manufacturing sector experienced a growth upsurge along with a remarkable enhancement of its service sector growth in the last decade although productivity in the service sector was exquisitely high almost right from the beginning, which was attributed to some exclusive sector-specific factors leading to revealing its comparative advantage vis-à-vis others.

In fact, it is a common expectation that this phenomenal improvement in service sector productivity, more specifically the boom in service trade of the country, may influence labour productivity in the manufacturing sector by enabling access to the state of service inputs, notably finance, transport and telecommunications with enormous service sector reforms. However, a state-wise analysis of the downstream spillover effects of the service trade boom of India on labour productivity in its manufacturing counterpart is almost missing in the literature.

We intend to do that with some state control variables and try to explore the possible channels through which the relation can be advocated. Exploring whether there is a systematic link between the enhancement of services trade and the performance of firms in downstream manufacturing activities is the primary research question of our study. Subsequently, the next section elaborates the data and methodology used in the empirical exercise with the application of the Panel Data Fixed Effect Regression Model, and the fourth section presents the results of this exercise by illustrating the responsiveness of labour productivity in the manufacturing sectors of the major Indian states through the change in net exports of all services from India to the rest of the world at different time periods. Finally, the fifth section concludes.

The empirical exercise

Data and methodology

We constructed a panel of 17 states for all years from 2008–09 to 2014–15. The states chosen are major Indian states accommodating about 90 per cent of the Indian population. In alphabetical order, the states can be listed as Andhra Pradesh, Assam, Bihar, Delhi, Gujarat, Haryana, Himachal Pradesh, Karnataka, Kerala, Madhya Pradesh, Maharashtra, Orissa, Punjab, Rajasthan, Tamil Nadu, Uttar Pradesh and West Bengal.

Our main point of interest, i.e., the relationship between improved service trade of the country as a whole and the productivity of the workers in the manufacturing sector of the country at a more disaggregated level, namely state level, is controlled by a number of state-specific variables that are discussed shortly. In estimating that impact, we have also taken the technology parameter in the manufacturing sector and the average wage of the manufacturing sector of the corresponding state as independent variables. In order to overcome the problem of state-specific heterogeneity, we apply the panel data fixed effects regression model to control for all the time-invariant factors. Notably, heterogeneity in terms of the state characteristics is captured by some control variables like high school enrolment in states (proxy measure for skill formation), percentage shares of agriculture, industries (manufacturing) and services sector in the State Domestic Products (SDP from now onwards) of the corresponding states etc. But in order to avoid the collinearity problem, we intend to drop the share of the industrial (manufacturing) sectors in SDPs for the econometric exercise. The data is obtained from different distinct and comprehensive databases. Firstly, we collected trade-related data from UN Trade Statistics. The data for the manufacturing sector is extracted from the database of the Annual Survey of Industries (ASI) while other state-level statistics are assembled from Indiastat.com. Our intention is to observe the impact of the service trade boom on manufacturing labour productivity, and the boom occurred in India during 2005–06,[5] so the time period that we have chosen is quite appropriate to capture the major effect.

Variables

We chose a number of variables for the state-level panel to explain the movements in the *average labour productivity in the manufacturing sector* of the *jth* state $(Y/L)_{jt}$ measured by the ratio of total value of output and total number of workers employed in the manufacturing sector of a particular state in a particular year. The explanatory variables include *value of net export*,[6] i.e. *difference between values of Exports and Imports* ($NETEXPRTS_t$: net exports of all services from India to world) of that period along with a one-year lag and a two-year lag of the same ($NETEXPRTS_{t-1}$ and $NETEXPRTS_{t-2}$), respectively; *Average capital labour ratio* in *jth* state at time *t*, $(K/L)_{jt}$, defined as a ratio of total value of fixed capital in the manufacturing sector and total number of workers employed there; W_{jt}, average wage of the workers in the manufacturing sector in *jth* state in year *t*. Our control variables are *High school enrolment in jth state in year t*, HSE_{jt} (assuming that workers in the manufacturing sector are productive if they have at least high school education); *Percentage share of Agricultural sector's output in the SDP of the jth state in year t*, $AGRS_{jt}$; *Percentage share of Industrial sector's output in SDP of the jth state in year t*, $INDS_{jt}$; and *Percentage share of Service sector's output in SDP of the jth state in year t*, $SERS_{jt}$. We incorporate two additional terms, one interaction term ($NETEXPRTS_{t-1}\_K/L$: interaction term between Net Exports of *t–1th* period and Capital Labour ratio) to measure the marginal impact, and one square term, (*NETEXPRTS*:[2] Squared values of Net Exports) to measure the quadratic effect.

The main hypothesis – whether the service trade expansion of the country has a positive spillover effect on average labour productivity in the manufacturing sectors of the Indian states – is tested with the help of the above variables. One could include other variables like institutional arrangements at state levels[7] to get a more elaborate idea. However, on account of proper data unavailability in the appropriate form for the stipulated period we have ignored those at least for the present purpose.

Econometric specifications of the model

The detailed econometric specifications for *jth* state over *t* time periods defining the panel (with time-invariant state fixed effects captured by μ_j; ϵ_{jt} standing for the error term), are given by three equations. The basic econometric specification of the model is given by equation (9.1):

$$\begin{aligned}(Y/L)_{jt} &= \alpha_{jt} + \beta_1 NETEXPRTS_t + \beta_2 (K/L)_{jt} + \beta_3 W_{jt} + \gamma_1 HSE_{jt} \\ &\quad + \gamma_2 AGRS_{jt} + \gamma_3 INDS_{jt} + \gamma_4 SERS_{jt} + \mu_j + \epsilon_{jt}\end{aligned} \tag{9.1}$$

The actual specification for the appropriate econometric exercise is slightly modified, given by equation (9.2) that excludes the variable representing industry's share, $INDS_{jt}$:

$$\begin{aligned}(Y/L)_{jt} &= \alpha_{jt} + \beta_1 NETEXPRTS_t + \beta_2 (K/L)_{jt} + \beta_3 W_{jt} + \gamma_1 HSE_{jt} \\ &\quad + \gamma_2 AGRS_{jt} + \gamma_4 SERS_{jt} + \mu_j + \epsilon_{jt}\end{aligned} \tag{9.2}$$

Adding two variables for the one-year lagged values and two-year lagged values of net exports, equation (9.2) is modified as equation (9.3):

$$\begin{aligned}(Y/L)_{jt} &= \alpha_{jt} + \beta_1 NETEXPRTS_t + \beta_2 NETEXPRTS_{t-1} \\ &\quad + \beta_3 NETEXPRTS_{t-2} + \beta_4 (K/L)_{jt} + \beta_5 W_{jt} \\ &\quad + \gamma_1 HSE_{jt} + \gamma_2 AGRS_{jt} + \gamma_4 SERS_{jt} + \mu_j + \epsilon_{jt}\end{aligned} \tag{9.3}$$

Further adding the interaction term between Net exports of *t–1th* period and *K/L* and the squared term of net exports to this specification (9.3), the final equation for Panel data regression is represented by equation (9.4):

$$\begin{aligned}(Y/L)_{jt} &= \alpha_{jt} + \beta_1 NETEXPRTS_t + \beta_2 NETEXPRTS_{t-1} \\ &+ \beta_3 NETEXPRTS_{t-2} + \beta_4 (K/L)_{jt} + \beta_5 W_{jt} \\ &+ \gamma_1 HSE_{jt} + \gamma_2 AGRS_{jt} + \gamma_4 SERS_{jt} \\ &+ \beta_6 (NETEXPRTS_{t-1} \star k/L) + \beta_7 NETEXPRTS^2 + \mu_j + \epsilon_{jt}\end{aligned} \tag{9.4}$$

where $(Y/L)_{jt}$ denotes the average labour productivity in the manufacturing sector, μ_j captures the state fixed effect, ϵ_{jt} is the error term and α is a constant. The remaining variables are defined as above. β_6 is the coefficient of the interaction term used in our model.

Descriptive statistics for the variables under consideration and the Correlation Matrix are presented in Table 9A.1 and Table 9A.2,[8] respectively. These tables display that the panel under treatment is a strongly balanced panel with no sign of collinearity among the independent variables. Then Granger–Causality tests were performed for defining the direction of the causality between the variables of the regression equation, which established that the variable net exports of services (*NETEXPRTS*) Granger caused industrial labour productivity (*Y/L*) and the opposite is not true.[9]

In order to capture the marginal impact of a rise in capital–labour ratio on average labour productivity in the manufacturing sector of the *jth* state, when net exports of services of the previous period interact with capital–labour ratio of the *jth* state, expression (9.5) becomes useful.

$$\frac{\delta\left(\frac{Y}{L}\right)_{jt}}{\delta\left(\frac{K}{L}\right)_{jt}} = \beta_4 + \beta_6 NETEXPRTS_{t-1} \tag{9.5}$$

Results

We have reported the results of panel regression[10] in three different tables (Table 9.1, Table 9.2 and Table 9.3), following three specifications of the model given by equation (9.2), (9.3) and (9.4), respectively. Each table then contains a distinct set of results according to the inclusion and exclusion of different variables within each specification.

Firstly, three sets of regressions are reported in Table 9.1, following the specification in equation (9.2). The results with all the independent variables in equation (9.2) are presented in column 1 of Table 9.1. Column 2 drops percentage share of service sector output in SDP of the states, and shows that the value of net export has a stronger (positive and significant) impact on *Y/L* while the results obtained by ignoring the percentage share of agricultural output in SDP, presented in column 3 of Table 9.1, do not alter the results of column 1 substantially, implying a very insignificant role of $AGRS_{jt}$ in explaining the productivity impact in the manufacturing sector. Notwithstanding, wages in the manufacturing sector always positively and significantly explain the labour productivity there and percentage share of service sector output in SDP of the state negatively explains labour productivity in the manufacturing sector with a high level of significance.

Table 9.1 Results of panel regression with net exports

Dependent Variable: $(Y/L)jt$

Variable	*1*	*2*	*3*
netexprts	1.64E-07	3.32E-07**	1.26E-07
	(1.58E-07)	(1.56E-07)	(1.45E-07)
k/ljt	0.001	0.001*	0.001
	(0.0007)	(0.0008)	(0.0007)
wjt	0.121***	0.122***	0.124***
	(0.027)	(0.028)	(0.026)
hsejt	–0.002	-0.081	–0.002
	(0.151)	(0.156)	(0.151)
agrsjt	0.246	0.464	
	(0.409)	(0.421)	
sersjt	–0.453***		–0.462***
	(0.151)		(0.148)
constant	48.591**	5.687	58.289***
	(24.195)	(20.908)	(17.971)

Source: own calculations based on panel data.
Note: SE are in parentheses. *** = 1% level of sig.; ** = 5% level of sig.; * =10% level of sig.

Table 9.2 Results of panel regression with lagged values of net exports

Dependent Variable: $(Y/L)jt$

Variable	*1*	*2*	*3*	*4*	*5*
netexprts			3.08E-07**		
			(1.51E-07)		
netexprtslag1	–8.86E-07***	–9.50E-07***	–9.07E-07***	–1.11E-06***	
	(3.37E-07)	(3.58E-07)	(3.53E-07)	(3.85E-07)	
netexprtslag2				4.02E-07	1.71E-08
				(3.61E-07)	(3.47E-07)
k/ljt	0.0008	0.0013*	0.0011	0.0014*	0.0016**
	(0.0007)	(0.0007)	(0.0007)	(0.0007)	(0.0008)
wjt	0.141***	0.175***	0.128***	0.171***	0.162***
	(0.018)	(0.018)	(0.028)	(0.018)	(0.018)
hsejt	0.071	0.073	–0.075	0.094	0.080
	(0.127)	(0.135)	(0.152)	(0.136)	(0.141)
agrsjt	0.065	0.12	0.424	0.148	0.139
	(0.365)	(0.388)	(0.410)	(0.389)	(0.403)
sersjt	–0.508***				
	(0.138)				
constant	88.321***	53.388**	36.756	48.280**	21.610
	(23.215)	(22.543)	(23.639)	(22.975)	(21.821)

Source: own calculations based on panel data.
Note: SE are in the parentheses. *** = 1% level of sig.; ** = 5% level of sig.; * =10% level of sig.

Secondly, we depict five sets of regression results in Table 9.2, following specifications given by equation (9.3), containing the lagged variables of net exports. Here, we see similar implications for W_{jt} and $SERS_{jt}$ (only in column 1 of Table 9.2) as that of Table 9.1. The common

Table 9.3 Results of panel regression with interaction term (lagged net exports and *K/L*)

Dependent Variable: $(Y/L)jt$

Variable	1 (*with SE*)	2 (*with Robust SE*)	3 (*with squared NE*)	4 (*Arellano Bond*)
netexprts	4.91E-08	4.91E-08	7.61E-07*	6.78E-07*
	(1.57E-07)	(2.34E-07)	(4.00E-07)	(3.93E-07)
netexprtslag1	–6.66E-07*	–6.66E-07	–7.56E-07**	–1.72E-06***
	(3.69E-07)	(4.02E-07)	(3.66E-07)	(4.59E-07)
netexprtslag2	5.77E-07	5.77E-07	6.11E-07*	9.28E-07***
	(3.62E-07)	(3.45E-07)	(3.57E-07)	(3.88E-07)
k/ljt	0.0112***	0.0112**	0.107***	0.007**
	(0.0036)	(0.005)	(0.0035)	(0.005)
wjt	0.129***	0.129***	0.138***	0.113***
	(0.026)	(0.037)	(0.026)	(0.036)
hsejt	0.083	0.083	0.053	–0.185
	(0.149)	(0.161)	(0.147)	(0.144)
agrsjt	0.108	0.108	0.223	–0.332
	(0.385)	(0.239)	(0.383)	(0.394)
sersjt	–0.439***	–0.437***	–0.376***	–0.282**
	(0.141)	(0.154)	(0.143)	(0.151)
*netexprtslag1*k/l*	–3.16E-10***	–3.16E-10**	–3.03E-10***	–2.99E-10**
	(1.04E-10)	(1.49E-10)	(1.03E-10)	(1.38E-10)
netexprts_sq			–1.06E-14**	–4.32E-15
			(5.52E-15)	(6.24E-15)
L1				–0.141
				(0.179)
constant	62.666***	62.666**	47.183*	92.866***
	(25.427)	(24.718)	(26.315)	(25.904)

Source: own calculations based on panel data.
Note: SE are in the parentheses. *** = 1% level of sig.; ** = 5% level of sig.; * =10% level of sig.

feature of all the columns in Table 9.2 is that the values of net exports of services with one-year lag have a significant negative spillover effect on current manufacturing labour productivity although the magnitude of such effect is negligibly small.

Hence, we see the impact of an increase in one-year lagged values of net exports, leading to a very small decline in Y/L though other changes are quite similar to Table 9.1(Table 9.2, column 3). This column also indicates an important phenomenon, that if we exclude state's percentage share of SDP in services and, at the same time, include the values of current year net exports of services of the country then definitely a favourable and significant relation is established between net exports of services and manufacturing labour productivity. However, net exports of a two-year lag have no impact at all, at least in Table 9.2; nevertheless, it makes the technology variable (*K/L*) more significant. Similarly, improvement in technology significantly increases labour productivity in manufacturing if the state's share of the service sector in SDP is exempted from the calculation. Another common observation from Tables 9.1 and 9.2 helps us to infer that a higher share of the state's service sector definitely lowers Y/L in the manufacturing sector of that state, no matter whether we take net export of services of the country of the present year or the previous year.

The final sets of regression results are presented in Table 9.3, following the specifications described by equation (9.4), having four different columns where we add an interaction term and a squared term of our main explanatory variable and slight modifications in the results are observed. We have refined our results by carrying out the regression with Robust SE (presented in column 2, Table 9.3) and Arellano Bond GMM estimator techniques (presented in column 4, Table 9.3).

Here, in Table 9.3, we find that in addition to the wage variable, which consistently explains Y/L very prominently with positive significance, K/L also becomes a consistently good explaining factor and the interaction term becomes a negatively significant factor for all different sets. Column 2 of Table 9.3 shows that net exports of one period lag becomes insignificant if we consider robust standard error but otherwise it is significant and negative in its effect of spillover on labour productivity in the manufacturing sector. All the results are confirmed by taking the squared values of net exports of services. However, these results may be biased due to the presence of endogeneity in the model specification. We tested for the issue of endogeneity with the help of Generalized Methods of Moments of Arellano Bond (robust standard error), with instruments chosen by the model in the form of first-difference and lagged first-difference of the explanatory variables. The results are reported in column 4 of Table 9.3. The diagnostic test for Arellano Bond GMM estimate with GMM standard errors also shows similar results. Overall, the endogeneity test confirms that the state-level responses as obtained in the panel regression above hold sufficiently. The most important observation of this table is that, if we include the squared term of net exports then current value of net exports seems to have positive and significant repercussions on labour productivity (see column 3 and 4; Table 9.3). The constant terms are also significant throughout but educational attainment has no impact at all.

In order to capture the marginal impact of a rise in K/L on average labour productivity in the manufacturing sector of the *jth* state, when net exports of services of the previous period interact with capital–labour ratio of the *jth* state, we have estimated equation (9.5).

Here, $\beta_4 > 0$ and $\beta_6 < 0$ in all different cases; equating (9.5) with zero, we get the critical value of net exports of $t-1th$ period, below which any marginal increase in K/L will bring forth increase in Y/L in the manufacturing sector. Taking Arellano Bond estimates of β_4 and β_6, we get $NETEXPRTS^{*}_{t-1}$ as 30,100,334.45 (Rs. in lakhs).

It implies that if and only if the value of net exports of all services from India in a particular year exceeds this critical value, then marginal increase in K/L in a state will dampen the manufacturing labour productivity in that state in the year to follow. In other words, an increase in capital–labour ratio, in the form of improved service sector inputs or technology, will have a positive spillover effect in the manufacturing sector of the following year, provided the value of net exports is less than Rs. 30,100,334.45 lakhs which is quite a substantial volume.[11] So we can infer from our empirical exercise that all-round expansion of service trade may not necessarily augment the productivity of other capital intensive sectors and therefore inclusive growth may come to a stall affecting employment and income of the people there.

Concluding remarks

In our state-level evidences of empirical exercise, we find that the average labour productivity of the manufacturing sector in a particular state is definitely affected by the average wage of the sector for all the stipulated years. Higher wages certainly bring about higher levels of labour productivity. It can also be inferred that the higher the states' service sector shares of SDP, the lower will be the labour productivity in the manufacturing sector of the state, though the country's net exports of services have no significant impact on manufacturing labour productivity so long as the service sector's share of the state is included in the regression exercise. But if we exclude it, then increased net exports of the country increases Y/L of the manufacturing of the corresponding state, though with a very minuscule percentage, and when this happens, *K/L* (proxy for technology) has a significant positive impact on *Y/L*. This means that if the service share of a state's SDP is not taken into consideration then only an enhancement of service trade can have some downstream spillover effect in increasing *Y/L* through a positive repercussion in *K/L*. This is a very important observation because it signifies the role played by the state service sector. As the service trade of the country expands in the post-reform era, the service sector of the individual state becomes more efficient in drawing more capital or technology from other sectors, especially the industrial sector which is necessarily more capital intensive, thereby lessening its (industrial or manufacturing sector) labour productivity. The actual spillover effect is more prominently noticed from Table 9.2, where one-year lagged values of net exports has a significant negative impact on current labour productivity in the manufacturing sector although the values of net exports of the two-year lag have no such impact at all. Nevertheless, when net exports of the two-year lag is taken into account, we notice another unique happening, the capital–labour ratio or technological parameter becomes a significant explanatory factor of enhancement of labour productivity. We can interpret this result more interestingly in the following manner; if the expansion of net exports of services of the country in the recent past can improve the state of technology through improvement in the state of the service sector inputs used in the manufacturing sector (spillover effect), then there is a possibility of productivity improvement there. However, expansion of service trade in the previous year discourages capital to flow out of the state's service sector and therefore decreases labour productivity in the manufacturing sector of the state if the state has a significant share of service sector output in state domestic product (column 1, Table 9.2). If only we ignore the latter variable, then state *Y/L* can be improved through an improvement in *K/L*,[12] on account of more service trade of the country in the previous year. At the same time higher share of the service sector definitely lowers *Y/L* in the manufacturing sector[13] no matter whether we take net export of services of the present year or the previous year. Then in Table 9.3, when we add an interaction term and a squared term of our main explanatory variable, then slight modifications in the results are observed. We have refined our results by carrying out the regression with Robust SE and Arellano Bond GMM estimator techniques. Here, in addition to the wage variable, which consistently explains *Y/L* very prominently with positive significance, *K/L* also becomes a consistently good explaining factor and the interaction term becomes a negatively significant factor. The crucial role of the negatively significant interaction term motivates us to find the critical level of service trade (measured here by net exports of the previous year) for which marginal increase in capital–labour ratio will bring about greater productivity of labour in the manufacturing sector. All the results are confirmed by the other two exercises taking the squared form of the variable of net exports which itself has a significant negative impact, though Arellano Bond does not endorse the latter. Our study has also found that basic high school education does not flow into the enrichment of labour and thereby improvement of productivity in the manufacturing sector. As we have already mentioned (in the methodology section), the time period we have chosen is quite appropriate to capture the major effect as India's service trade boom occurred during 2005–06. Nevertheless, due to unavailability of suitable and appropriate data, the analysis has been restricted up to 2014–15, and as a matter of fact the impact of policy changes introduced thereafter could not be captured.

In a nutshell, our study concludes, in a very novel way, that expansion of trade in services does not necessarily permeate into the structural transformation of the secondary sector that is responsible for driving the economy on a higher growth trajectory after two and half decades of economic reforms. On the contrary, at a disaggregated level, the manufacturing sector may actually experience lower labour productivity and income if there is too large an expansion of the service trade. So, limitless growth of the service trade as a development strategy may not be very promising for a developing country like India that puts up inclusive growth as its long-run development goal.

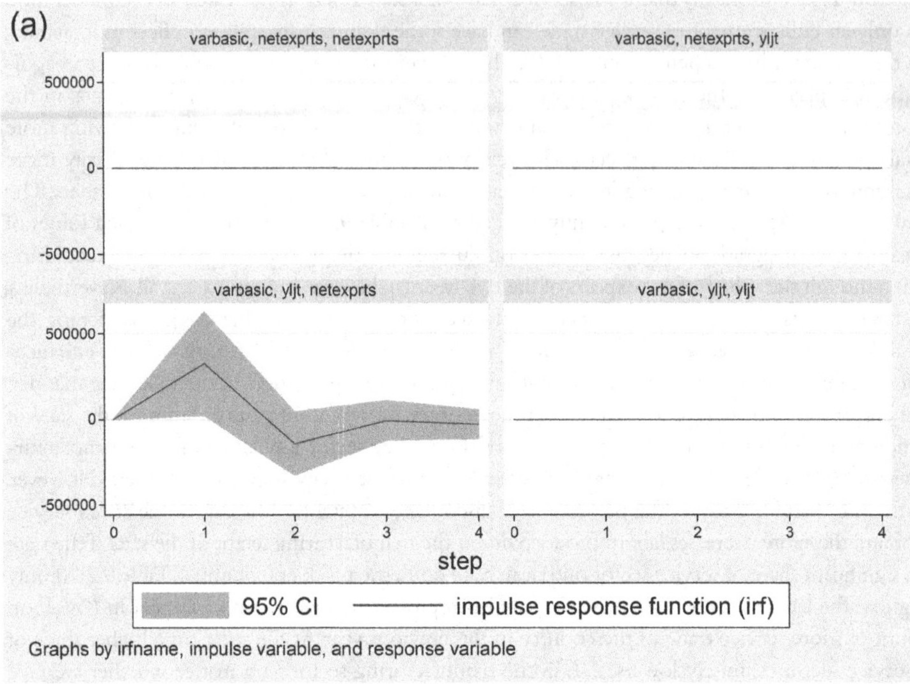

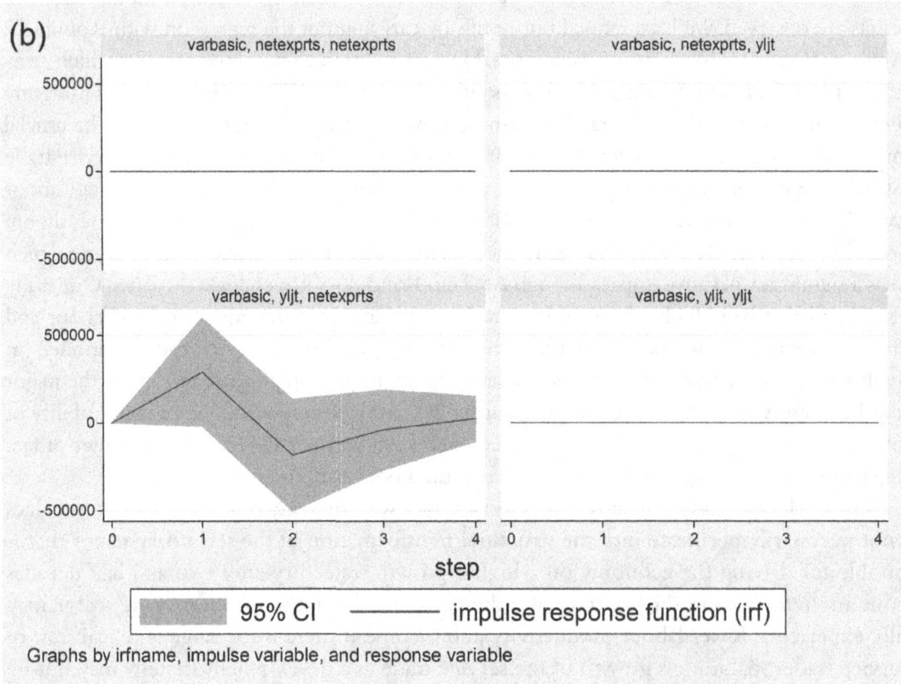

Figure 9.1 Graphs for impulse response functions associated with Granger–Causality test

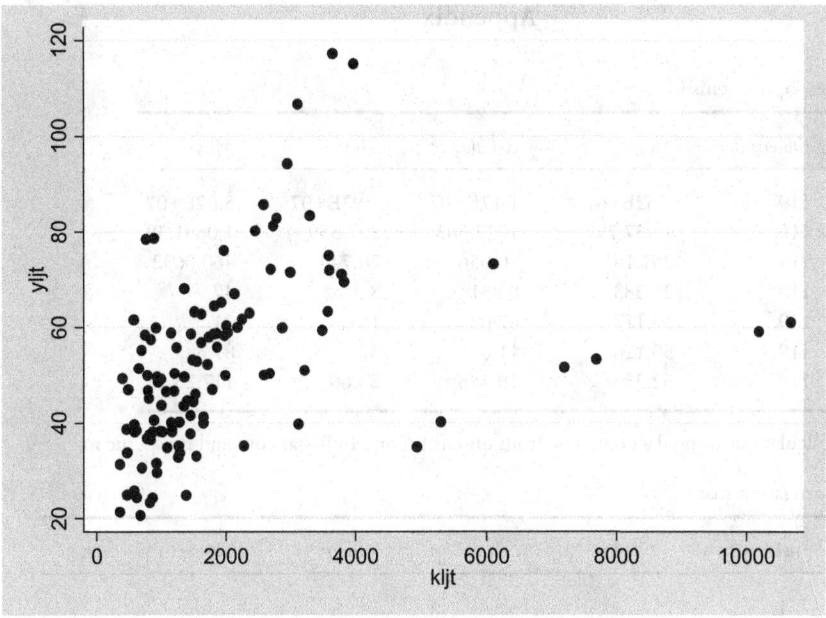

Figure 9.2 Scatter plot of labour productivity and capital–labour ratio at the state level. *Source*: ASI data obtained from www.mospi.nic.in

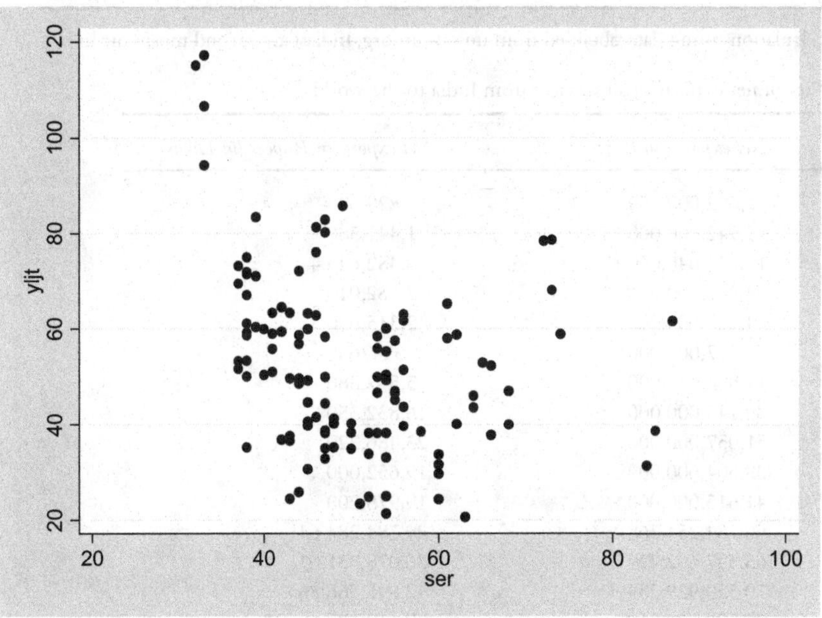

Figure 9.3 Scatter plot of labour productivity and service sector share of SDP at the state level. *Source*: ASI data obtained from www.mospi.nic.in.

Appendix

Table 9A.1 Descriptive statistics

Variable	*Observations*	*Mean*	*Std. dev*	*Min.*	*Max*
netexprts	119	3.52E+07	1.17E+07	1.97E+07	5.02E+07
k/ljt	119	1,937.797	1727.383	357.359	1,0681.38
wjt	119	201.161	80.056	70.743	460.0632
hsejt	119	21.383	8.851	8.3	47.9
agrsjt	119	17.117	6.902	1	31
sersjt	119	50.126	11.076	32	87
yljt	119	52.333	18.398	20.66	117.23

Sources: own calculations using data obtained from unstats.un.org, Indiastat.com and mospi.nic.in.

Table 9A.2 Correlation matrix

Variables	*netexprts*	*k/ljt*	*wjt*	*hsejt*	*agrsjt*	*sersjt*
netexprts	1					
k/ljt	0.2769	1				
wjt	0.5868	0.4316	1			
hsejt	0.4417	−0.0505	0.5298	1		
agrsjt	−0.0735	0.0764	−0.4234	−0.6306	1	
sersjt	−0.2763	−0.4646	−0.0927	0.2902	−0.523	1

Sources: own calculations using data obtained from unstats.un.org, Indiastat.com and mospi.nic.in.

Table 9A.3 Values of net exports of all services from India to the world

Years	*Net exports (in Us$)*	*Net exports in Rupees (in Lakhs)*
2000	1,692,000,000	829,080
2001	2,942,000,000	1,441,580
2002	16,632,640,000	8,482,646.4
2003	4,249,000,000	2,082,010
2004	4,927,000,000	2,315,690
2005	7,217,000,000	3247650
2006	11,804,000,000	5,547,880
2007	39,145,000,000	16,832,350
2008	51,057,000,000	23,486,220
2009	39,304,000,000	19,652,000
2010	41,615,000,000	19,975,200
2011	60,784,254,368	29,784,284.64
2012	65,597,692,779	36,078,731.03
2013	70,320,929,284	42,895,766.86
2014	75,575,680,319	47,612,678.6
2015	76,105,916,440	50,229,904.85

Source: UN Trade Statistics (https://unstats.un.org).

The values of net exports from India to the world are given in Table 9A.3 in the Appendix Section

Notes

1 GATS is the first set of international rules for the international trade in services. India has been a signatory to this Agreement since its inception in 1995.
2 According to the estimates of the Economic Survey, 2016–17.
3 According to World Bank estimates.
4 According to the estimates made by MOSPI(Ministry of Statistics and Programme Implementation, India).
5 According to World Bank estimates, the ratio of India's service trade to GDP reached its peak of 13.9 per cent in 2006.
6 We have taken values of net exports instead of only exports of services from India to take into account the increasing value of imports of services by India as well. Nevertheless, we found that India's services exports are much higher than its imports over the years and hence India is a net exporter in the world service trade scenario.
7 As far as institutions are concerned, in light of the categorization of Indian states as "labour friendly" or "capital friendly" (viz. Besley and Burgess, 2004), the overall situation in the state can have a serious impact on average productivity determination. However, India is still a labour surplus country with high participation in the informal sector. Apart from that, free mobility of workers across states should ideally equalize wage rates if there is a significant difference.
8 Presented in the Appendix Section.
9 Granger–Causality Test is used as a diagnostic test to check the direction of causality between net exports of the service sector and labour productivity (and therefore capital–labour ratio) of the manufacturing sector. The graphs of Impulse Response Function (IRF) are shown in Figure 9.1 in the Appendix.
10 Hausman test for the panel regression, establishes state fixed effects. The null hypothesis of the Hausman test, indicating the consistency of the random effect estimator, is soundly rejected by the chi-square test.
11 The values of net exports from India to the world are given in Table 9A.3 in the Appendix Section.
12 The scatter plot in Figure 9.2 substantiates this outcome.
13 The scatter plot in Figure 9.3 supports this outcome.

References

Aghion, Philippe, Robin Burgess, Stephen Redding, and Fabrizio Zilibotti (2008). "The Unequal Effects of Liberalization: Evidence from Dismantling the License Raj in India." *American Economic Review* 98(4): 1397–1412.

Arnold, Jens, Beata Javorcik, Molly Lipscomb, and Aaditya Mattoo (2012). "Services Reform and Manufacturing Performance: Evidence from India." *World Bank Policy Research Working Paper*, WPS 5948, World Bank, Washington, DC.

Arnold, Jens, Beata Javorcik, Molly Lipscomb, and Aaditya Mattoo (2016). "Services Reform and Manufacturing Performance: Evidence from India." *The Economic Journal*, 126(590): 1–39.

Arnold, Jens, Beata Javorcik, and Aaditya Mattoo (2011). "The Productivity Effects of Services Liberalization: Evidence from the Czech Republic." *Journal of International Economics* 85(1): 136–146.

Arora, Ashish, Vallampadugai S. Arunachalam, Jai Asundi, and Ronald Fernandes (2001). "The Indian Software Services Industry." *Research Policy* 30(8): 1267–1287.

Baumol, William J. (1967). "Macro-Economics of Unbalanced Growth: The Anatomy of Urban Crisis." *American Economic Review* VII: 415–426.

Bertrand, Marianne, Antoinette Scholar, and David Thesmar (2007). "Banking Deregulation and Industry Structure: Evidence from the French Banking Reforms of 1985." *Journal of Finance* 62(2): 597–628.

Besley, Timothy, and Robin Burgess (2004). "Can Labor Regulations Hinder Economic Performance? Evidence from India." *Quarterly Journal of Economics* 119(1): 91–134.

Beverelli, Cosimo, Matteo Fiorini, and Bernard Hoekman (2017). "Services Trade Policy and Manufacturing Productivity: The Role of Institutions." Journal of International Economics 104: 166–182.

Clark, Colin (1940). *The Conditions of Economic Progress*. London: Macmillan.

Fisher, Aallan G. B. (1939). "Primary, Secondary, Tertiary Production." *Economic Record* 15(1): 24–38.

Francois, Joseph F., and Kenneth A. Reinert (1996). "The Role of Services in the Structure of Production and Trade: Stylized Facts from Cross-Country Analysis." *Asia-Pacific Economic Review* 2(1): 1–9.

Goldberg, Penny, Amit Khandelwal, Nina Pavcnik, and Petia Topalova (2009). "Trade Liberalization and New Imported Inputs." *American Economic Review* 99(2): 494–500.

Goldberg, Penny, Amit Khandelwal, Nina Pavcnik, and Petia Topalova (2010). "Imported Intermediate Inputs and Domestic Product Growth: Evidence from India." *Quarterly Journal of Economics* 125(4): 1727–1767.

Khandelwal, Amit, and Petia Topalova (2011). "Trade Liberalization and Firm Productivity: The Case of India." *Review of Economics and Statistics* 93(3): 995–1009.

Krishna, Pravin, and Devashish Mitra (1998). "Trade Liberalization, Market Discipline and Productivity Growth: New Evidence from India." *Journal of Development Economics* 56: 447–462.

Lee, Keun, and Chaisung Lim (2001). "Technological Regimes, Catching-Up and Leapfrogging: Findings from the Korean Industries." *Research Policy* 30(3): 459–483.

Mattoo, Aaditya, Randeep Rathindran, and Arvind Subramanian (2006). "Measuring Services Trade Liberalization and Its Impact on Economic Growth: An Illustration." *Journal of Economic Integration* 21: 64–98.

Ok Wooseok, Keun Lee, and Hyoseok Kim (2014). "Service-Led Catch-Up in the Indian Economy: Alternative Hypotheses on Tertiarization and the Leapfrogging Thesis." *Seoul Journal of Economics* 27(1): 1–40.

Pilat, Dirk, and Anita Wölfl (2005). "Measuring the Interaction between Manufacturing and Services." *OECD STI Working Paper* 2005/5.

Rajan, Raghuram G., and Luigi Zingales (1998). "Financial Dependence and Growth." *American Economic Review* 88: 559–586.

Reserve Bank of India (2008). "Index Numbers of Industrial Production." Database. http://www.rbi.org.in/scripts/statistics.aspx.

Schettkat, Ronald, and Lara Yocarini (2006). "The Shift to Services Employment: A Review of the Literature." *Structural Change and Economic Dynamics* 17(2): 127–147.

Stiroh, Kevin J. (2002). "Information Technology and the U.S. Productivity Revival: What Do the Industry Data Say?" *American Economic Review* 92(5): 1559–1576.

Summers, Robert (1985). "Services in the International Economy." In Inman, R. P. (ed.), *Managing the Service Economy: Prospects and Problems*. Cambridge: CUP, 27–48.

Zhang, Yan, Yihong Tang, and Christopher Findlay (2010). *Productivity Effects of Services Trade Liberalization: Evidence from Chinese Firm-level Data*. Mimeo, University of International Business and Economics, University of Adelaide, Adelaide, Australia

10

TECHNOLOGICAL HETEROGENEITY, FDI SPILLOVERS AND EXPORT PERFORMANCE

A study of Indian manufacturing firms

Sanghita Mondal

Introduction

Since liberalisation, India's most important policy focus has been the promotion of exports. As has been pointed out by Prasanna (2010), most developing countries possess a comparative advantage in low technology, labour-intensive products. However, with the increasing competition among developing countries, the comparative advantages change and eventually disappear. Here comes the importance of technology and the knowledge base which helps in product diversity which in turn helps countries remain in the world trading market. Countries can attain this technology either by improving local technological capabilities or by importing technology or by encouraging foreign direct investment (FDI hereafter) in the domestic export sector. Innovation is a costly process and needs a proper blend of human and physical capital. Thus, most developing countries lag behind the developed countries in terms of innovation. Similarly, the import of technology needs to be decoded and hence needs a threshold level of technological capability in terms of physical and human capital.[1] On the other hand, FDI brings assets not only in terms of capital but also with superior technology and knowledge, distribution networks, product diversification and credit advantages (Hymer 1976). Therefore, FDI was seen not only as a source of non-debt financial resource but also as a source of technology, capital, market access, skills, management techniques and, most importantly, competition. In the context of recent liberalisation and globalisation, the role of FDI in the export performance of host country firms has become an important consideration. A cross-country study by UNCTAD (1999) on 52 countries has shown that there is a strong relationship between FDI and manufacturing exports, especially in developing countries. Dunning (1998) and Sun (2001) have pointed out the importance of FDI in the relocation of global resources and the international division of labour which eventually alters the productive capacity of the countries and in turn their comparative advantages.

The 1991 Industrial Policy of India clearly mentioned that:

 DOI: 10.4324/9780367855741-10

> Foreign investment would bring attendant advantages of technology transfer, marketing expertise, introduction of modern managerial techniques and new possibilities for promotion of exports. ... The government will therefore welcome foreign investment which is in the interest of the country's industrial development.
>
> *(Rao and Dhar 2011)*

The advantages mentioned in the previous section are mainly referred to as spillover benefits from foreign firms which promote exports. The export spillover channels are vividly discussed in the literature and are mentioned as information spillover (spillovers through information diffusion), imitation spillover (spillovers through the diffusion of technology), competition spillovers (spillovers through increased competition) and labour turnover. Labour turnover, competition and imitation spillovers have induced effects on the export performance of domestic firms through the enhancement of firm productivity. On the other hand, domestic firms learn from the exporting activities of foreign firms.

In the present study, we focus on the channels of FDI spillover which influence the export performance of Indian manufacturing firms. However, in this context, we disaggregate the firms according to the technology intensity sectors (by OECD definition) to ascertain whether the FDI spillover effects on export performance vary across the technology category sectors over the study period 1994–2010. It is the first attempt to investigate the spillover channels across technology sectors, therefore, the study brings out a few interesting facts about the Indian manufacturing firms' export spillovers from FDI. We use the Heckman selection method to estimate the two-stage effects of export performance of domestic firms: in the first step the firms decide whether to export and in the second step the self-selected firms decide how much to export. Our study covers more than 6000 Indian manufacturing firms over 17 years (1994–2010).

The present chapter is organised in six sections. The next section provides a brief review of the previous theoretical and empirical research on export spillovers and FDI, especially focusing on India, followed by a brief discussion of FDI and the trade activity of India since liberalisation. The fourth section is dedicated to the methodological issues. Econometric results are explained in the fifth section and the final section concludes the paper.

Review of literature

According to the literature, there are four intra-industry spillover channels from foreign investment, namely, imitation spillover, competition spillovers, skill spillovers and information spillovers which influence export activities of the host country firms. The first three channels are considered as the induced channels of export spillovers as the induced effects on exports come through the productivity enhancement of domestic firms and the last channels influence export performance by providing additional information regarding international markets to domestic firms.

As suggested by studies (see Ruane and Sutherland 2005; Greenaway et al. 2004, Anwar and Nguyen 2011; Franco and Sasidharan 2010), imitation of foreign R&D activities and technology enhance the technological capability of domestic firms. Moreover, this reduces the cost of import and implementation, in turn reducing overall production cost. An increase in technological capability and reduction in production costs boost productivity as well as export competitiveness of the local firms. Similarly, it is believed that labour turnover from foreign to local firms enhances the productivity and efficiency of the local labour by transmitting their organisational and managerial skills along with their knowledge of technology. Diffusion of skills improves the export performance of domestic firms by improving the product quality and production competence.

Many studies (Aitken and Harrison 1999) have argued that competition from foreign firms is the main source of productivity spillovers. In fear of losing the market share to their foreign counterpart, local firms tend to upgrade their production technology base or find ways to use their available resources more efficiently. It is also argued that competition from foreign firms forces the least efficient firms to leave the market, thus relocating the resources toward the firms with comparative production advantage. Therefore, in the process of winning the competition with foreign firms, productive capability and product quality both increase, which are considered the major factors of export competitiveness of domestic firms (Greenaway et al. 2004; Franco 2013).

These effects are generally considered as induced effects of FDI on export performance through the improvement of productive capacity. On the contrary, information gets assimilated from foreign to local firms through the export activities of foreign firms (Kaparty and Kneller 2011); for example, foreign firms' connection with the overseas distributors and networks, their servicing facilities, the products they export also provide an idea about the taste and demand of the consumers and so on. This effect is known as the "learning by seeing" or information spillovers which reduce the cost of attaining information and advertising, leaving productivity unchanged (Aitken et al. 1997; Sun 2001; Franco and Sasidharan 2010).

There are a number of studies which have tried to look into the FDI spillover effects on export propensity or export performance of domestic firms. Most of the studies have shown that there are positive spillover effects of FDI on the domestic export performance. For example, Sun (2001), Wang et al. (2007), Xuan and Xing (2008), Sun (2012), Chen (2013) have found that FDI has positive spillover effects on the export activity of Chinese manufacturing firms. Similarly, Johnson (2006) has shown a significant positive effect of FDI on the export activities of East Asian countries. However, none of the above studies disentangled the spillover channels. The studies which have segregated the export spillover channels from FDI have found contradicting results. Whilst Greenaway et al. (2004) found positive effects on export performance from competition, information and imitation spillovers from FDI for the UK, Ruane and Sutherland (2005) found negative effects of foreign export activities (negative information spillovers) on the export performance of Irish firms. According to Ruane and Sutherland (2005), foreign firms used Ireland as the export platform, reducing domestic firms' foreign market share.

Export spillover studies are relatively less explored in India. Earlier studies by Kumar and Siddharthan (1994) could not find any significant difference in export performance between foreign affiliates and domestic firms in restrictive policy regime. However, a number of studies for the post-liberalisation period suggest that foreign firms have shown significantly higher export performance as compared to domestic firms (Aggarwal 2002; Kumar and Pradhan 2003). Using the Tobit model, Aggarwal (2002) showed that Multinational Enterprises' (MNEs) export performance was better than domestic firms during the late 1990s. However, she did not find any evidence of a positive relationship between foreign equity share and export performance in high technology domestic firms. She argued that India was not able to attract efficiency-seeking outward-oriented FDI in the high tech sector. On the contrary, Prasanna (2010) found that between 1991–92 and 2006–07, India's export performance, especially exports of high tech products, was highly influenced by the presence of FDI. Interestingly, Banga (2003) found a significant impact of FDI only on the export intensity of non-traditional export industries in India. Similar to the previous studies, these studies also did not mention the channels of export spillovers; however, a few of these studies brought out the importance of the technology intensity of domestic firms in generating export spillovers from FDI.

In recent studies, Joseph and Reddy (2010) and Franco and Sasidhran (2010) formally investigated FDI spillover on the export performance of Indian manufacturing firms. Joseph and Reddy (2009) showed that horizontal and vertical spillovers in terms of the export intensity of foreign firms in industries did not have any spillover effect on domestic firms' export activity. They argued that economic liberalisation did not attract much export-oriented FDI to India. Contrary to foreign firms' export activity, foreign firms' domestic activity (sales in the domestic market) was found to be a significant factor in raising the export activity of domestic firms in the same industry groups except for between 1997 and 2000. This result indicates that competition from foreign firms forces domestic firms to look for markets abroad. There was no evidence of vertical spillovers on the export performance of domestic firms. Franco and Sasidharan (2010) considered various horizontal spillover channels (mentioned above) to measure the effect of foreign presence on the export performance of Indian firms. Not only the export activity of foreign firms but also, according to them, the R&D activity and human skills present in foreign firms influence the export decision and export propensity of domestic firms. While the results showed a significant positive impact of foreign R&D activities and skill on Indian firms' decision to export, there was no evidence of information spillover. However, the results are different when firms' internal R&D activity interacts with all these spillover variables; interaction between firms' internal R&D and spillover variables shows that with internal R&D activity domestic firms can absorb the positive effects of FDI presence. The effect of FDI on export decision remains similar to the export activities when indigenous firms' R&D activity is taken into consideration. The results show that for an exporting domestic firm, information or demonstration spillover is more important for the future export activity of domestic firms with the presence of internal R&D activities. The result reinforces the fact that domestic R&D activity is highly relevant in capturing any benefit from foreign presence in any form.

As can be seen from the above studies, apart from the study by Aggarwal (2002) and Prasanna (2010), there has been no study which has focused on the technology intensity sectors. However, these studies did not specify any FDI spillover channels. Thus this paper tries to bridge the gap between the two sets of studies by focusing on the effects of FDI spillover channels on export performance of the Indian firms in various technology category sectors over the time period 1994–2010.

FDI and export activity of India

FDI in India

Since liberalisation, India has been experiencing an inflow of FDI. The policy change in the post-reform period brought a major alteration in terms of the inflow of actual FDI. The total FDI inflow went up to 39 billion in 2017–18 from 34 billion in 2010 which increased from a mere 1.2 million in 1991–92. As we see from the graph in Figure 10.1, India experienced moderate FDI inflow almost till 2004–05. The policy to allow FDI up to 100% foreign equity under the automatic route in townships, housing, built-up infrastructure and construction-development projects can be observed from the FDI inflow. However, the economic slowdown of 2007–08 has shown an adverse impact on FDI inflow in India and since then the trend has remained a little volatile.

Export activity of India

In Figure 10.2 we present the major exported items of India from 1987–88 to 2019–2020. There were some noticeable changes in the commodity composition of India's exports. As seen

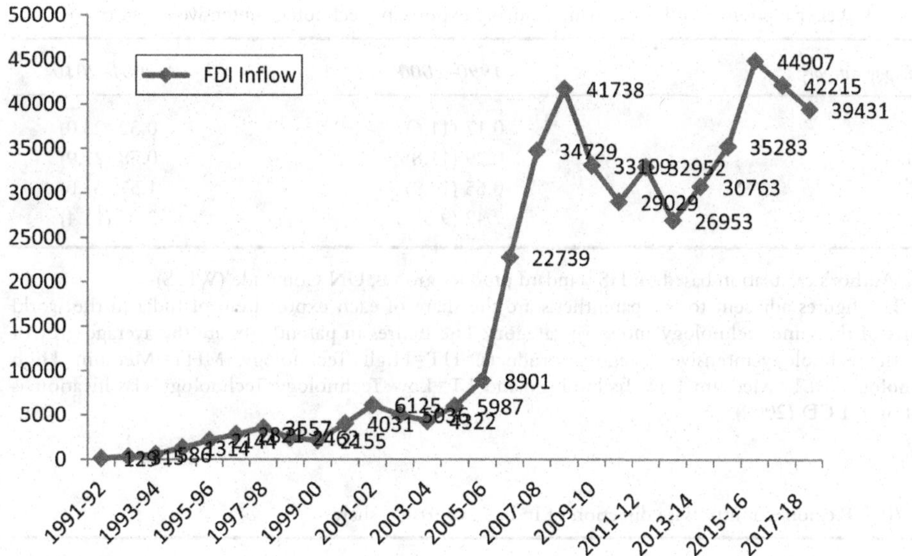

Figure 10.1 FDI inflow since 1991–92 ($ million). *Source*: *Handbook of Statistics on Indian Economy*, Reserve Bank of India.

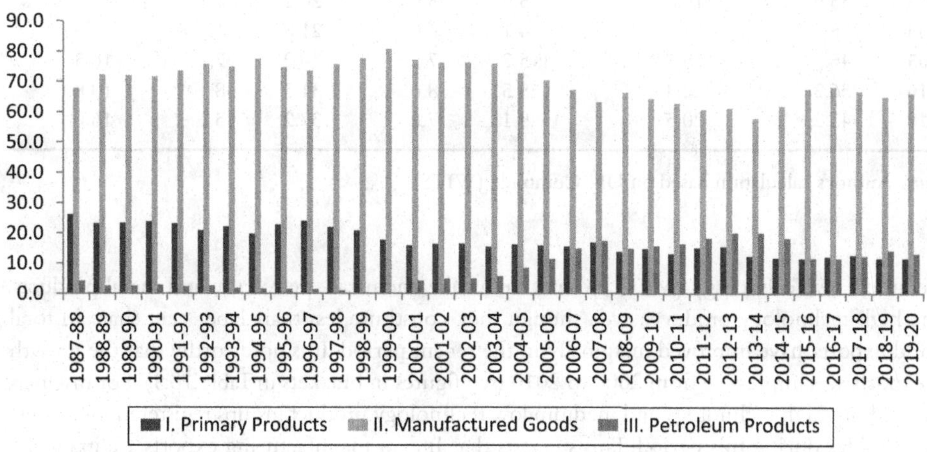

Figure 10.2 Major export basket of India: 1987–88 to 2019–2020 (% share). *Source*: Author's calculation from *Handbook of Statistics on Indian Economy*, Reserve Bank of India.

from the figure, the importance of agricultural/primary products in the export basket declined from 23 per cent in 1995 to 14 per cent by 2010 to 11 per cent in 2019–20. In contrast, the manufacturing sector has been a major constituent of merchandise exports in recent decades (around 66 per cent). The manufacturing sector recorded the fastest growth of 9.6 per cent per annum from 1995 whereas agricultural export commodities grew at a much lower rate of 6.2 per cent.

Another useful categorisation of manufacturing exports is to group them according to technology intensity (based on OECD classification). There has been a notable improvement in

Table 10.1 Relative position of Indian manufacturing exports: by technology-intensive category (%)

Technology category	*1990–2000*	*2001–2010*
HT	0.17 (11.6)	0.32 (23.0)
MHT	0.29 (11.8)	0.58 (21.9)
MLT	0.65 (14.9)	1.57 (31.0)
LT	2.42 (9.5)	2.67 (11.4)

Source: Author's calculation based on HS standard product groups, UN Comtrade (WITS)
Note: The figures adjacent to the parenthesis are the share of each export item of India in the world exports of the same technology-intensive category. The figures in parentheses are the average growth rates of technology-intensive category products. HT=High Technology, MHT=Medium High Technology, MLT=Medium Low Technology and LT=Low Technology. Technology classification is based on OECD (2009).

Table 10.2 Region/country wise direction of India's exports (% share)

Year	*OECD*	Developing *countries*	*LDC*	*Africa*	*Asia*	*China*	*USA*
1990	46.6	5.4	3.2	3.1	20.6	0.1	14.5
1995	53.9	10.8	5.9	5.6	26.2	1.1	17.0
2000	55.8	11.2	4.1	6.0	21.8	1.8	21.6
2005	46.7	18.7	5.2	7.2	30.2	7.2	16.5
2010	36.2	22.4	5.5	8.6	31.5	8.1	10.8
2018	43.2	20.5	9.1	7.3	37.2	5.1	16.0

Source: Author's calculation based on UN Comtrade (WITS).

Medium Low Technology (MLT) product items like chemicals, petroleum and metal products. The high technology products, even though they constitute less than 1 per cent share in total world exports, have improved marginally in the recent period. It is noteworthy that the growth of exports was impressive from 2000 to 2010 (see figures in brackets in Table 10.1). For instance, the medium high technology and medium low technology product groups registered impressive growth rates during this period. This suggests that Indian manufacturing exports are gradually becoming more technology oriented.

We further examined the direction of India's exports from 1990 to 2010. Table 10.2 shows that the OECD is the largest market for Indian exports. However, since the mid-2000s, there has been a gradual decline and the share had come down to 36 per cent by 2010. Notably, the importance of Asian markets increased during the same period. For instance, from 21 per cent in 1990, the market share of the Asian region had gone up to 32 per cent by 2010 which further increased to around 37 per cent in 2018. Further, there was a significant increase in exports of Indian manufacturing products to developing nations during this period. In terms of countries, the importance of the USA declined in between early to mid-2000s; however, more recently, the USA has regained its importance as India's export destination. The "boycott China" slogan seems to have worked pretty well. As we have seen recently, the preference for the Chinese market decreased from 2005/2010 to 2018.

Methods, data and variables

Data source and composition of firms

The data for the study were collected from PROWESS database provided by the Centre for Monitoring Indian Economy (CMIE). Although the database provides financial activities from 1989–90, the study has considered the data since 1994 due to the availability of observation for most of the firms. The present study covers the study period of 1994–2010. The key indicators are sales revenue of goods, import of capital goods, import of raw material and finished goods, R&D expenditure, foreign promoters' share, export of goods, profit after tax etc. However, in the process of cleaning, around 3000 firms were dropped from the dataset. First, we dropped firms that do not have sales figure for at least five year continually. We further excluded firms with no data on wages and salaries, gross fixed assets and raw materials from the sample.

To mention, the study defines foreign firms as those firms with greater than or equal to 10 per cent[2] foreign equity share for at least three years during the study period. Moving away from previous studies, to accommodate firm heterogeneity, the study decided to classify the firms according to their technological capability following the classification provided by the OECD (2011). Following the definition by the OECD (2011), Indian firms are classified into four categories, namely: High Technology (HT), Medium High Technology (MHT), Medium Low Technology (MLT) and Low Technology (LT). Interestingly, the data show that foreign firms as well as domestic firms are mostly concentrated in the MHT sector (Table 10.3).[3]

Definition of the variables

Sector-specific variables

Spillover variables (SP)

The export performance of domestic firms is influenced by various foreign activities in the economy. Apart from information spillover from foreign exporting activities, other export spillover effects on domestic firms are generated through the productivity enhancement of domestic firms. The induced channels of export spillovers occur through competition from foreign firms within industry, through the imitation of foreign technological activities and through labour turnover from foreign to domestic firms. The competition spillover (*CompSill*) variable captures the importance of foreign firms in the domestic market. As already mentioned, competition from foreign firms encourages domestic firms to improve their technology base, in turn increasing the productive efficiency. Therefore, we

Table 10.3 Type of firms, export and output share by technology sectors in the Indian manufacturing sector

Technological intensity	*DF*	*FF*	*Total*	*Export share (%)*	*Output share (%)*
HT	626	33	659	10.24	6.13
MHT	1453	113	1566	17.58	24.90
MLT	1850	75	1925	48.04	54.24
LT	2033	53	2083	24.19	14.72
Total number of firms	**5962**	**274**	**6233**		

Source: Author's calculation based on PROWESS, CMIE.

Note: HT: High technology-intensive sector, MHT: Medium high technology-intensive sector, MLT: Medium low technology intensive, LT: Low technology-intensive sector; DF: Domestic firms, FF: Foreign Firms.

expect this variable to have a positive impact on domestic firms' export performance. We define *competition spillovers* as the share of foreign firms' sales in total domestic sales of the industry.

Similarly, the cost of acquiring technologies and implementing them into the production process reduces when domestic firms imitate technologies from foreign firms. Using superior technologies in the production process enhances product quality and helps in diversifying products according to the demand of the international market. Thus, we expect both the spillover variables *RDSpill (measured in terms of foreign R&D activities)* and *TechSpill (measured in terms of technology import by foreign firms)* to have a positive effect on the export performance of domestic firms. We take the share of foreign firms' R&D expenses in sectoral R&D expenditure (*RDSpill*) and the share of royalty payment of foreign firms in sectoral royalty payment (*TechSpill*) as the measures of imitation spillovers.

The third spillover variable, skill spillover takes into consideration the level of skill embodied in the human capital in foreign firms. Following Franco and Sasidharan (2010), the study measures the variable (*SkillSpill*) by the share of foreign firms' expenditure on wages and salaries to total wages and salaries of the industry. To capture the *information spillover* (*ExpSpill*), we use foreign firms' export share in total industrial exports. As we expect domestic firms to gain from the established network and marketing knowledge of the exporting foreign firms, we hypothesise that domestic firms' export performance would be positively associated with foreign firms' export activity.

Other sectoral variables

Apart from these spillover variables, we have included two sectoral variables in the model to accommodate the importance of the sectoral export (*Sei*) and domestic activity (*Ssect*) on the export performance of domestic firms. The *Sei* variable controls the factors that affect the overall export performance of the industry (Greenaway et al., 2004). We expect a positive impact for the variable because firms located in an export-oriented industry would have a positive impact on the export performance through information assimilation from other exporting domestic firms. The *Ssect* variable accounts for the possible general spillover effects not associated with the export activities (Greenaway, 2004; Franco and Sasidharan, 2010). It also captures the fact that firms serving the larger domestic market would have lower export activity and thus we expect a negative association between export activity and *Ssect* variable.

Firm-specific variables

In our model, capital–labour ratio (*K/L*) and wage intensity (*WAGE*) represent the technological accumulation and the skill accrued in the production process, respectively. Technology and higher skill enhance productivity and in turn quality of the products, improving export competitiveness in the international market (Roberts and Tybout, 1997). The recent shift of the export concentration from the LT sector to other sectors indicates that India is slowly growing in the export of skill-intensive products. Thus, we add this variable to investigate whether capital and labour skill has positively influenced the export activity of domestic firms. Another important fact which is generally ignored in the studies is the import induced export activities of Indian firms (Pant, 1995). We have incorporated the intensity of the import of raw material and intermediate inputs (*RAWIMP*) by firms to determine the impact of imported materials on the export performance of domestic firms. According to Pant (1995), the use of high quality imported products in the production enhances the product quality and thus a positive effect is expected from the import of raw and intermediate inputs.

To compete and to achieve a competitive advantage in the international market, firms need to innovate and diversify their products constantly along with quality improvement. Internal R&D activities (*RD*) which is considered as a proxy for the innovative capacity of the firms, is expected to influence export performance positively. Along with R&D activity, firms in a developing country like India also import technology to improve their technological capability.

It is seen that India spends more on the import of technology than R&D activities. As productivity and competitiveness improve due to the incorporation of advanced technology, we expect technology imports (*TECH*) to have a positive impact on the export activities of domestic firms. Among other variables, we have added age (*AGE*) and size (*SIZE*) as control variables. The square of these variables is also added in the model to capture the non-linearity of these variables. Size can be seen as the indicator of the efficiency of the firm (Willmore, 1992) or economies of scale achieved by the firm (Pant, 1995). Thus after a certain threshold level, the firm gains the efficiency to cover the sunk cost and export more.[4] Similarly, older firms are more knowledgeable and more efficient at competing in the international market. Thus, we expect AGE to have a positive impact on export activity. However, Power (1998) found an inverted U-shaped relationship between age and export activity. Our model tries to capture that by including the square term of the variable.

Econometric methodology: Heckman selection model

To investigate the impact of FDI on export spillover the study examines the two aspects of export performance of the domestic firm: (i) firm's decision to export or not and (ii) if the firm exports, the amount it is willing to export. Underlying this behaviour is the issue of sunk cost associated with exporting activity. For capturing these two activities of domestic firms, we use the Heckman selection model (Heckman, 1979). This model treats the selection problem as the omitted variable problem. As the model takes into account a firm's decision to enter the export market or not, it alleviates the problem associated with the selectivity bias that occurs when we consider only the exporting firms. Due to the problem of self-selection, the ordinary least square (OLS) estimation can provide biased estimates. Therefore, we consider the Heckman selection model to examine the FDI spillover effects on the export performance of Indian manufacturing firms.

The Heckman selection model involves two steps. In the first step, the firms self-select to the exporting activity and in the second step, the model explores the outcome of these self-selected firms. The selection equation is given in equation (10.1)

$$\begin{aligned} DEXP_{ijt} = \alpha &+ \beta_1 DEXP_{ijt-1} + \beta_2 PROFIT_{ijt} \\ &+ \beta_3 K/L_{ijt} + \beta_4 RD_{ijt-1} + \beta_5 TECH_{ijt-1} \\ &+ \beta_6 RAWIMP_{ijt-1} + \beta_7 WAGE_{ijt} + \beta_8 Sei_{jt} + \beta_9 Ssect_{jt} \\ &+ \beta_{10} AGE_{ijt} + \beta_{11} AGE^2_{ijt} + \beta_{12} SIZE_{ijt} \\ &+ \beta_{13} SIZE^2_{ijt} + \beta_{14} SP_{jt-1} + v_i \end{aligned} \tag{10.1}$$

The outcome equation of the model is given in equation (10.2)

$$\begin{aligned} EXPINT_{ijt} = \alpha &+ \beta_1 K/L_{ijt} + \beta_2 RD_{ijt-1} \\ &+ \beta_3 TECH_{ijt-1} + \beta_4 RAWIMP_{ijt-1} + \beta_5 WAGE_{ijt} \\ &+ \beta_6 Sei_{jt} + \beta_7 Ssect_{jt} + \beta_8 AGE_{ijt} + \beta_9 AGE^2_{ijt} \\ &+ \beta_{10} SIZE_{ijt} + \beta_{11} SIZE^2_{ijt} + + \beta_{12} SP_{jt-1} + v_i \end{aligned} \tag{10.2}$$

Subscript i refers to firm, j to sectors and t to time; u_i and v_i represent the random errors in the outcome and selection equations, respectively. SP_{jt-1} represents the lag of FDI spillover variables which are competition spillover (*CompSpill*), information spillover (*ExpSpill*), imitation spillover (*RDSpill* and *TechSpill*) and skill spillover (*SkillSpill*). Notations of other variables follow as before.

There are two methods to estimate the Heckman selection model: the two-step method and the Maximum Likelihood method. As we are following the MLE model,[5] we assume that $v_i \sim N(0,1)$, $u_i \sim N(0,\sigma^2)$. The dependent variable ($DEXP_{ijt}$) of the first equation is a binary variable which takes the value 1 if the firm reports positive exports and 0 otherwise. In the next equation (equation 10.2) the dependent variable is measured as the export intensity ($EXPINT_{ijt}$) of domestic firms. The distribution of the error terms of the equations is assumed to be bivariate normal with correlation $\rho \neq 0$. Since we analyse the export behaviour of all firms including non-exporters, estimating only export intensity would lead to a sample selection bias. If $\rho = 0$ then the OLS estimates would provide consistent and unbiased estimates of the outcome variable.[6]

As we see from the above two equations, both equations include the same regressors except two variables in the selection equation in order to identify the complete model as required by the selection models (Heckman, 1979). One of the two is the lagged export status ($DEXP_{ijt-1}$) to take into account the fact that the decision to export depends on the previous export status of the firms. This means that if a firm exports at time t it would export at time $t+1$ as well. The second regressor is lagged profitability ($PROFIT_{ijt-1}$) of the firm, which is the proxy for the capacity of the firm to meet the start-up cost associated with the exporting activity (Franco and Sasidharan, 2010). Moreover, lagged values of the spillover variables and technology variables have been added considering the fact that time lag is needed to influence the export performance of domestic firms. It would deal with the endogeneity problem as well. We measured all variables on an annual basis (t).

Econometric results

The section provides a complete analysis of technology-intensive categories to get a comprehensive account of the export performance of domestic firms. The complete results are provided in Table A10.1 in the appendix.

Export decision

Spillover variables

It is interesting to see that the *CompSpill* variable is found have a significantly positive impact on the export decision of the firms in the MHT sector. In our earlier discussion, we found that FDI is largely concentrated in the MHT sector. Therefore, domestic firms are accustomed to the foreign production process and technological competency, which facilitate their production of goods of international quality. Thus, with competitive pressure from foreign firms, domestic firms decide to enter the export market. The *CompSpill* variable is insignificant but negative for other technology category sectors. In the MHT sector, the *RDSpill* variable is also positive and significant, implying that the spillover effect from foreign R&D activity has been beneficial for domestic firms in the MHT sector. The reason may be the concentration of foreign firms in the sector which motivates them to undertake R&D activities and makes it less difficult for domestic firms to imitate and implement them in the production process. For MLT, LT and HT sectors, *RDSpill* variable is also positive but insignificant.

The significantly negative coefficient of the *ExpSpill* variable indicates that the Indian HT sector is merely an export platform for foreign investors who want to serve other countries and use Indian resources for export production. Aggarwal (2002) also found that foreign equity participation adversely affects the export activity of the HT sector. For the rest of the technology-intensive sectors, the *ExpSpill* is negative but insignificant. We do not find any evidence of skill spillover (*SkillSpill*) or imitation spillover through foreign technology import (*TechSpill*) on the export decisions of domestic firms in any of the sectors.

Sectoral and firm-specific variables

It is clearly seen that apart from domestic firms within the MHT sector, the probability of domestic non-exporter firms turning into exporting firms increases with the export orientation of the industry (*Sei*) in all other technology-intensive sectors. On the other hand, the decision to export is not influenced by the domestic market activity of the industry (*Sscet*) in any of the technology categories.

Profit of the firms (*PROFIT*) is a deciding factor for firm-level export in the MHT and LT sectors while in the other two sectors this variable is insignificant. The *K/L* ratio is negative and significant for all technology category sectors, except the LT sector where it is insignificant due to low content of capital in the production. The inefficient use of capital where firms lack productive advantage in capital intensive products reduces the possibility of becoming exporters. We find that the smaller the size (*SIZE*), the higher is the probability that the firm would become an exporter in every technology-intensive sector except the firms within the MLT sector. The size variable shows a non-linear relationship with the export decision in the LT, MHT and HT sectors. In contrast, based on age (*AGE*), it is evident that older firms in the MLT sector have a higher probability of starting an export activity. We do not find any significant impact of *RD* (R&D intensity), *WAGE* (labour skill) and *TECH* (import of technology) variables on the export decision of domestic firms in the HT sector. R&D activity (*RD*) of the firms shows a positive impact on the decision to export for firms in all other technology category sectors (LT, MLT and MHT). Import of technology (*TECH*) adversely affects the export decision of the firms in the MLT sector while this variable is positive but insignificant for the MHT and LT sectors. This result again shows the lack of comparative advantage in technology-intensive products. Another possible reason may be the low availability of human capital to reap the benefits from R&D activities. In addition, import of inputs (*RAWIMP*) has a significant positive impact on export decisions of firms in technology category sectors LT, MLT and MHT; however, it is insignificant for the HT sector. The results clearly show that the Indian HT sector is not developed according to international standards and also can't utilise technology factors efficiently in the export production process to enhance their comparative advantage in technology-intensive products.

Export intensity

Spillover variables

Similar to our earlier findings, the *CompSpill* variable influences the export propensity of domestic firms positively in the MHT sectors. However, for the MLT and LT sectors, *CompSpill* is negative and significant. This implies that the firms with relatively less technology intensity are not able to compete with foreign firms within the domestic market and thus the loss adversely affects their export activities. There is no evidence of information spillover (*ExpSpill*) in any of the technology sectors either. In all technology categories – MHT, MLT and LT – except HT, this variable has a negative and significant coefficient which re-emphasises the fact that the Indian market is being used mainly as an export platform and therefore, there is no information diffusion from foreign to domestic firms. Another reason may be the difficulty of domestic firms to compete with their foreign counterparts in the international market due to their dynamic competitiveness and diversified products. This results in a loss of market share in the export market, leading to an adverse impact on foreign export activities. Though insignificant, *RDSpill* and *TechSpill* variables also have positive coefficients for the HT sector. Interesting to see that the *TechSpill* variable possesses a significant negative coefficient for the MHT sector, where foreign firms own the highest stock of imported technology. By contrast, the other imitation spillover variable, *RDSpill* shows a positive coefficient for the MHT sector, although insignificant. Skill spillover variable (*SkillSpill*) has different effects on the export activity of different sectors. While the export activity of domestic firms in the MHT sector is positively influenced by the spillover of skills from foreign firms, the HT and LT sectors are adversely affected. We do not find any evidence of skill spillover (*SkillSpill*) or imitation spillover through foreign technology import (*TechSpill*) on the export activity of domestic firms in the MLT sector.

Sectoral and firm-specific variables

Confirming our previous results on the export decision, the domestic market activity of the industry (*Ssect*) has a significant negative influence on the export activity of domestic firms in all technology category sectors. Similarly, firms within a bigger export sector (*Sei*) are always benefitted from the exporting firms within the industry. Import of inputs (*RAWIMP*) has a significant positive impact on the export intensity of domestic firms in all the technology sectors. While *K/L* ratio is insignificant in the MHT and LT sectors, adverse effects can be seen for the MLT and HT sectors. Domestic firms within the LT and MHT industries are adversely affected by the import of technology (*TECH*). The R&D intensity (*RD*) of domestic firms shows a positive impact on the export propensity of domestic firms in the HT sector although the effect is significantly negative for other sectors. This result is not surprising as most of the R&D stock belongs to the HT sector. Skill variable (*WAGE*) has no impact on the export activity of domestic firms in the HT and MHT sectors. However, this variable positively influences the export activity of domestic firms in the MLT sector and negatively the domestic firms in the LT sector. We find that the age (*AGE*) of the firms is not important in the HT and MHT sectors, while younger firms promote more export activity in the LT and MLT sectors. Contrary to the *AGE* variable, we find that size (*SIZE*) has a positive impact on the export intensity of domestic firms in all technology sectors. However, as before the non-linearity of this variable is confirmed.

From the above analysis, it is clearly evident that domestic firms are highly heterogeneous among the technology-intensive categories. The technology-intensive categorisation reveals that the FDI spillovers on export performance largely operate through competition and R&D induced channels in the MHT sector. Notably, this is the largest recipient of FDI in the recent period. Since 2000, there has been a significant expansion of medium high technology sectors like chemicals, machinery, electrical and transport equipment. The higher FDI in these sectors in the recent period has resulted in some positive effects on domestic export performance, which can be inferred from our analysis. On the other hand, information spillover, imitation spillover through the import of technology and skill spillovers are largely negative or insignificant in most of the sectors. Since India does not have a significant presence of HT industries, the insignificant results are not surprising.

Conclusion

Using econometric tools, the study examined the spillover effects from FDI on the export performance of Indian manufacturing firms from 1994 to 2010. Compared to the previous studies, our empirical estimation focuses on different aspects of the export performance of Indian manufacturing sectors. For the empirical analysis, we examined the FDI spillover effects on the export performance of Indian manufacturing firms in the technology-intensive sectors, namely, LT, MLT, MHT and HT to capture the heterogeneity of domestic firms within the technology sectors.

Based on the theoretical literature, we incorporated four different forms of FDI induced spillover channels, i.e., information spillover, competition spillover, imitation spillover and skill spillover. For the empirical estimation, we employed the Heckman selection (maximum likelihood) model, which segregates export behaviour into two stages. In the first stage, the model examines the export decision of firms and in the second stage the export intensity of the self-selected firms is estimated. Apart from these spillover variables, we also incorporated various sectoral and firm-specific control variables, which are often considered as some of the major determinant factors of export performance at the firm level.

The study did not show any evidence of competition spillover in Indian manufacturing firms except in the MHT sector. The Indian MHT sector is a relatively strong sector in the domestic and foreign markets. Therefore, firms are capable of absorbing competition from foreign firms and developing their technology base to meet the demands from abroad and domestic markets. In other sectors, firms are generally small (LT and MLT) who produce less technology-intensive products or not very developed (HT) in accordance with international standards. Therefore, domestic firms are not capable of facing the competition from technologically advanced foreign firms and lose their internal market share due to a rise in production costs. The high sunk cost associated with exporting and loss of competitive advantage due to high production cost disallows the firms from entering the foreign market.

Similarly, skill spillovers from foreign labour and imitation spillovers through technology import by foreign firms are also found to have adverse effects on the export decision and intensity of domestic firms. Globerman (1979) argued that foreign firms generally employ the most skilled workers of the investing economy, leaving few to be employed in domestic firms. Therefore, a gap is created in the skill of the domestically available workers and the workers in foreign firms. Moreover, foreign firms pay higher wages to reduce labour turnover. Higher average wages in the domestic market increase the cost of production. These two factors together cause negative skill spillover effects on the export performance of domestic firms. Similarly, due to a lack of in-firm R&D activity and human capital (absorptive capacity), domestic firms cannot imitate the technology used in foreign production. Thus, mostly we found negative effects of these two spillover variables on the export performance of domestic firms. Lastly, imitation spillover through the R&D activity of foreign firms has shown some positive impact on the export performance of domestic firms, though it is sector specific (HT sector). Information spillovers confirm the theory of India being considered as an export platform for foreign exports from India. Especially, the Indian HT sector shows significant adverse effects of foreign firms' export activities from India.

We summarise the study as follows: Indian firms do not possess a competitive advantage in technology or capital intensive products in the world market and thus we did not find much influence of technology factors on export performance. The MHT and MLT sectors are relatively important sectors in view of export promotion. Only those firms in the MHT sector benefit from foreign economic activities. The LT sector, on the other hand, being a technologically backward sector, cannot gather much benefit from foreign activities. Therefore, it is important for the Government to focus on the sectors where firms possess export competitiveness by encouraging more in-house R&D activities and skill enhancement through proper training. The import of technology or imitation of technology from foreign firms would not be beneficial unless Indian firms are equipped with the proper skills and technology. Most importantly, finding out the motive of FDI is also very important, as it seems, in the case of India, that FDI has either focused on the domestic market or has used the market as an export platform. However, in the end the study has limitations. First, this study takes into account only 6000 firms from organised manufacturing industries. There are many firms which are not listed but participate in exporting activities. Second, this study does not cover those firms; however, it should also be mentioned that the data of these firms are difficult to get. Moreover, the study covers data till 2010. The change in Government has had a beneficial impact on India's export which could not be accommodated in the study. A further study needs to be done to see the impact of the change.

Table 10A.1 FDI and export spillovers across technology-intensive sectors (1994–2010): Results from Heckman selection model (MLE)

Technology category	*Variables*	*Model 1*		*Model 2*		*Model 3*		*Model 4*		*Model 5*	
		Export decision	*Export intensity*	*Export decision*	*Export intensity*	*Export decision*	*Export intensity*	*Export decision*	*Export intensity*	*Export decision*	*Export intensity*
HT	PROFIT	–0.00285		–0.00277		–0.00267		–0.00285		–0.00290	
		(–0.97)		(–0.96)		(–0.94)		(–0.97)		(–0.98)	
	DEXP	2.593		2.593		2.593		2.594		2.598	
		(53.64)***		(53.64)***		(53.62)***		(53.65)***		(53.60)***	
	K/L	–0.00005	–0.00001	–0.00005	–0.00001	–0.00005	–0.00001	–0.00005	–0.00001	–0.00005	–0.00001
		(–2.68)***	(–2.05)**	(–2.68)***	(–2.04)**	(–2.71)***	(–2.04)**	(–2.68)***	(–2.02)**	(–2.69)***	(–2.03)**
	RD	0.2197	0.2396	0.2209	0.2388	0.2228	0.2389	0.2168	0.2327	0.2184	0.2380
		(1.01)	(2.23)**	(1.02)	(2.22)**	(1.02)	(2.22)**	(1.01)	(2.17)**	(1.01)	(2.22)**
	TECH	–0.2912	–0.4681	–0.2933	–0.7923	–0.2914	–0.7629	–0.2817	–0.8085	–0.2186	0.7567
		(–1.21)	(–0.89)	(–1.21)	(–0.91)	(–1.20)	(–0.88)	(–1.21)	(–0.93)	(–1.23)	(–0.87)
	RAWIMP	0.0359	0.4233	0.0364	0.4235	0.0384	0.4227	0.0364	0.4251	0.0356	0.4164
		(1.39)	(16.62)***	(1.40)	(16.62)***	(1.48)	(16.59)***	(1.40)	(16.69)***	(1.37)	(16.34)***
	WAGE	–0.0521	–0.0132	–0.0516	–0.0131	–0.0517	–0.0133	–0.0518	–0.0135	–0.0520	–0.0134
		(–1.23)	(–0.94)	(–1.21)	(–0.93)	(–1.22)	(–0.95)	(–1.21)	(–0.96)	(–1.22)	(–0.95)
	SEI	0.8222	0.9995	0.9202	1.0371	0.9194	0.9893	0.8372	0.9959	0.8993	1.0274
		(1.05)	(2.79)***	(1.03)	(2.99)***	(1.08)	(2.76)***	(1.01)	(2.81)**	(1.08)	(2.94)***
	SSECT	–0.705	–4.488	–0.782	–4.593	–0.934	–4.125	0.939	–2.796	–0.836	–4.600
		(–1.27)	(–3.23)***	(–1.45)	(–3.20)***	(–1.94)	(–2.71)***	(1.10)	(–1.71)*	(–1.29)	(–3.25)***
	AGE	0.0034	–0.0003	0.0034	–0.0003	0.0035	–0.0003	0.0034	–0.0003	0.0031	–0.0004
		(0.95)	(–1.32)	(1.05)	(–1.31)	(1.06)	(–1.32)	(0.93)	(–1.34)	(1.00)	(–1.35)
	SQAGE	0.00002	–0.00003	0.00002	–0.00003	0.00002	–0.00003	0.00002	–0.00003	0.00002	–0.00003
		(1.19)	(–2.22)**	(1.19)	(–2.23)**	(1.18)	(–2.22)**	(0.19)	(–2.20)**	(0.24)	(–2.20)**
	SIZE	–0.0269	0.0157	–0.0270	0.0157	–0.0271	0.0157	–0.0269	0.0155	–0.0268	0.0158
		(–4.25)***	(5.24)***	(–4.26)***	(5.24)***	(–4.28)***	(5.26)***	(–4.26)***	(5.20)***	(–4.24)***	(5.28)***
	SQSIZE	0.00002	–0.00015	0.00002	–0.00015	0.00002	–0.00015	0.00002	–0.00015	0.00002	–0.00015
		(3.58)***	(–2.35)**	(3.59)***	(–2.35)**	(3.61)***	(–2.34)**	(3.58)***	(–2.33)**	(3.56)***	(–2.37)**

	CompSpill	−0.0566	−0.0478								
		(−1.08)	(−1.38)								
	RDSPill			0.8765	0.0958						
				(1.06)	(0.92)						
	ExpSpill					−1.3874	0.0661				
						(−1.77)*	(0.87)				
	SkillSpill							−1.2550	−0.5160		
								(−1.06)	(−1.86)*		
	TechSpill									0.2937	0.0231
										(1.06)	(0.93)
	Constant	−1.298	0.368	−1.393	0.343	−1.277	0.334	−1.284	0.454	−1.476	0.350
		(−2.26)**	(4.07)***	(−2.70)**	(4.12)***	(−2.80)**	(3.74)***	(2.56)**	(4.66)***	(−2.87)***	(4.28)***
	Log likelihood	−1728.043		−1727.768		−1726.498		−1725.976		−1716.994	
	Rho	−0.20329		−0.203766		−0.2045265		−0.2058023		−0.2021173	
	Wald Chisq (29)	654.48		654.57		654.64		658.47		645.13	
	LR test	60.77***		63.81***		63.83***		63.49***		60.49***	
	Observation	6664		6664		6664		6664		6664	
MHT	*PROFIT*	0.0035		0.0034		0.0035		0.0035		0.0035	
		(1.93)*		(1.91)*		(1.93)*		(1.93)*		(1.92)*	
	DEXP	2.548		2.548		2.547		2.548		2.547	
		(82.84)***		(82.83)***		(82.86)***		(82.86)***		(82.86)***	
	K/L	−0.0001	0.0000	−0.0001	0.0000	−0.0001	0.0000	−0.0001	0.0000	−0.0001	0.0000
		(−6.24)***	(−0.72)	(−6.45)***	(−0.90)	(−6.22)***	(−0.84)	(−6.25)***	(−0.84)	(−6.23)***	(−0.95)
	RD	1.872	−0.910	1.930	−0.905	1.882	−0.922	1.887	−0.914	1.883	−0.909
		(3.34)***	(−3.98)***	(3.39)***	(−3.96)***	(3.35)***	(−4.04)***	(3.35)***	(−4.00)***	(3.35)***	(−3.98)***
	TECH	0.884	−1.329	0.872	−1.327	0.846	−1.344	0.848	−1.343	0.842	−1.348
		(1.15)	(−5.74)***	(1.14)	(−5.73)***	(1.10)	(−5.81)***	(1.10)	(−5.80)***	(1.09)	(5.82)***

(Continued)

Table A10.1 (Continued)

Technology category	Variables	Model 1		Model 2		Model 3		Model 4		Model 5	
		Export decision	Export intensity	Export decision	Export intensity	Export decision	Export intensity	Export decision	Export intensity	Export decision	Export intensity
	RAWIMP	0.916	0.382	0.915	0.382	0.909	0.382	0.909	0.381	0.908	0.382
		(7.57)***	(19.82)***	(7.56)***	(19.82)***	(7.53)***	(19.85)***	(7.53)***	(19.76)***	(7.53)***	(19.81)***
	WAGE	−0.634	−0.020	−0.635	−0.020	−0.633	−0.020	−0.635	−0.019	−0.634	−0.020
		(−7.04)***	(−0.97)	(−7.06)***	(−0.97)	(−7.04)***	(−0.96)	(−7.05)***	(−0.93)	(−7.04)***	(−0.97)
	SEI	−0.772	1.143	−0.935	1.126	−0.804	1.146	−0.938	1.155	−2.913	1.078
		(−1.06)	(2.99)**	(−1.13)	(2.94)***	(−1.08)	(3.00)***	(−1.13)	(3.02)***	(−1.12)	(2.81)***
	SSECT	0.117	−1.413	0.114	−1.397	0.159	−1.195	0.132	−1.375	0.133	−1.657
		(0.87)	(−4.06)***	(0.86)	(−4.91)***	(0.86)	(−4.04)***	(0.77)	(−4.83)***	(0.73)	(−5.45)***
	AGE	0.0026	−0.0007	0.0028	−0.0007	0.0026	−0.0007	0.0026	−0.0007	0.0026	−0.0007
		(0.70)	(−1.37)	(0.76)	(−1.37)	(0.70)	(−1.40)	(0.70)	(−1.35)	(0.71)	(−1.35)
	SQAGE	0.00002	−0.00001	0.00002	−0.00001	0.00002	−0.00001	0.00002	−0.00001	0.00002	−0.00001
		(0.43)	(−1.75)*	(0.37)	(−1.75)*	(0.42)	(−1.72)*	(0.41)	(−1.76)*	(0.41)	(−1.78)*
	SIZE	−0.0064	0.0129	−0.0062	0.0129	−0.0065	0.0129	−0.0065	0.0129	−0.0064	0.0129
		(−2.15)**	(8.48)***	(−2.08)**	(8.50)***	(−2.15)**	(8.51)***	(−2.15)**	(8.49)***	(−2.15)**	(8.51)***
	SQSIZE	0.000000	−0.000048	0.000000	−0.000048	0.000000	−0.000048	0.000000	−0.000048	0.000000	−0.000048
		(3.72)***	(−6.41)***	(3.65)***	(−6.42)***	(3.71)***	(−6.46)***	(3.71)***	(−6.41)***	(3.71)***	(−6.41)***
	CompSpill	0.6430	0.0187								
		(2.37)**	(0.81)								
	RDSPill			0.5598	0.0246						
				(3.02)***	(0.87)						
	ExpSpill					−0.4555	−0.2141				
						(−1.07)	(−2.45)**				
	SkillSpill							−0.5543	0.4333		
								(−1.06)	(2.94)**		
	TechSpill									0.0010	−0.0632
										(1.01)	(−2.47)**

	Constant	−1.6860	0.2001	−1.2066	0.2000	−1.0398	0.2385	−0.9866	0.1084	−1.1100	0.2498
		(−6.38)***	(5.17)***	(−11.24)***	(12.73)***	(−7.59)***	(11.65)***	(−4.06)***	(3.02)***	(−6.94)***	(10.53)***
	Log likelihood	−2646.496		−2644.103		−2645.861		−2645.009		−2646.273	
	Rho	−0.245925		−0.2463482		−0.2459754		−0.2459129		−0.2464958	
	Wald Chisq (31)	933.79		934.86		940.66		943.4		940.64	
	LR test	120.05***		120.39***		120.04***		120.13***		120.66***	
	Observation	16105		16105		16105		16105		16105	
MLT	*PROFIT*	0.0010		0.0010		0.0010		0.0010		0.0010	
		(0.91)		(0.91)		(0.91)		(0.91)		(0.92)	
	DEXP	2.6154		2.6159		2.6149		2.6154		2.6157	
		(95.18)***		(95.16)***		(95.15)***		(95.18)***		(95.19)***	
	K/L	−0.00006	−0.00001	−0.00006	−0.00001	−0.00006	−0.00001	−0.00006	−0.00001	−0.00006	−0.00001
		(−7.06)***	(−3.01)***	(−7.07)***	(−3.00)***	(−7.06)***	(−2.99)***	(−7.06)***	(−3.02)***	(−7.07)***	(−3.01)***
	RD	1.163	−0.172	1.169	−0.173	1.171	−0.171	1.170	−0.172	1.193	−0.172
		(3.82)***	(−3.93)***	(3.83)***	(−3.95)***	(3.82)***	(−3.92)***	(3.82)***	(−3.93)***	(3.83)***	(−3.93)***
	TECH	−2.356	−0.653	−2.355	−0.659	−2.359	−0.626	−2.358	−0.675	−2.351	−0.614
		(−5.63)***	(−1.09)	(−5.63)***	(−1.09)	(−5.64)***	(−1.07)	(−5.63)***	(−1.10)	(−5.62)***	(−1.08)
	RAWIMP	0.3081	0.7034	0.3080	0.7026	0.3084	0.7044	0.3083	0.7050	0.3074	0.7025
		(6.13)***	(27.38)***	(6.13)***	(27.34)***	(6.13)***	(27.41)***	(6.13)***	(27.39)***	(6.11)***	(27.34)***
	WAGE	−0.3710	0.4573	−0.3704	0.4584	−0.3712	0.4576	−0.3706	0.4581	−0.3710	0.4578
		(−6.26)***	(17.18)***	(−6.25)***	(17.21)***	(−6.26)***	(17.19)***	(−6.25)***	(17.20)***	(−6.26)***	(17.19)***
	SEI	0.7780	0.2220	0.7154	0.1173	0.8979	0.2750	0.7258	0.1641	0.5183	0.1414
		(1.10)	(1.01)	(1.05)	(0.54)	(1.15)	(1.23)	(1.06)	(1.05)	(1.67)	(1.01)
	SSECT	0.4466	−0.5603	0.3162	−0.5925	0.4339	−0.5622	0.3767	−0.7118	0.9172	−0.4069
		(1.25)	(−1.68)*	(1.12)	(−1.75)*	(1.24)	(−1.68)*	(1.18)	(−2.12)**	(1.52)	(−1.10)
	AGE	0.0066	−0.0020	0.0067	−0.0019	0.0065	−0.0020	0.0067	−0.0020	0.0067	−0.0018
		(1.98)**	(−2.11)**	(2.01)**	(−2.00)**	(1.96)**	(−2.12)**	(1.99)**	(−2.09)**	(1.99)**	(−1.97)**
	SQAGE	−0.00004	−0.00001	−0.00004	−0.00001	−0.00004	−0.00001	−0.00004	−0.00001	−0.00004	−0.00001
		(−0.85)	(−0.62)	(−0.88)	(−0.72)	(−0.83)	(−0.62)	(−0.86)	(−0.63)	(−0.87)	(−0.76)
	SIZE	−0.0007	0.0146	−0.0007	0.0146	−0.0007	0.0145	−0.0007	0.0146	−0.0006	0.0146
		(−0.60)	(11.10)***	(−0.60)	(11.10)***	(−0.60)	(11.08)***	−0.60)	(11.08)***	(−0.59)	(11.12)***

(Continued)

Table A10.1 (Continued)

Technology category	Variables	Model 1		Model 2		Model 3		Model 4		Model 5	
		Export decision	Export intensity	Export decision	Export intensity	Export decision	Export intensity	Export decision	Export intensity	Export decision	Export intensity
	SQSIZE	0.000000	−0.000017	0.000000	−0.000017	0.000000	−0.000017	0.000000	−0.000017	0.000000	−0.000017
		(1.33)	(−7.98)***	(1.33)	(−8.00)***	(1.33)	(−7.96)***	(1.33)	(−7.98)***	(1.32)	(−8.01)***
	CompSpill	−0.4391	−0.5855								
		(−0.97)	(−2.73)***								
	RDSPill			0.0875	−0.0371						
				(0.58)	(−0.89)						
	ExpSpill					−0.3199	−0.2568				
						(−1.03)	(−3.03)***				
	SkillSpill							−0.1591	−0.3002		
								(−1.23)	(−1.58)		
	TechSpill									0.1427	0.0561
										(1.04)	(1.50)
	Constant	−1.521	0.326	−1.656	0.179	−1.558	0.228	−1.599	0.243	−1.721	0.136
		(−5.57)***	(3.99)***	(−8.95)***	(2.99)***	(−7.88)***	(3.67)***	(−6.56)***	(3.27)***	(−8.63)***	(2.12)**
	Log likelihood	−8553.258		−8556.664		−8551.997		−8555.924		−8555.486	
	Rho	−0.0908884		−0.0911766		−0.0905595		−0.0909251		−0.0912606	
	Wald Chisq (33)	2651.9		2643.09		2654.21		2645.38		2645.01	
	LR test	33.18***		33.44***		32.92***		33.23***		33.53***	
	Observation			20114		20114		20114		20114	
LT	PROFIT	0.0049		0.0046		0.0047		0.0047		0.0047	
		(1.86)*		(1.85)*		(1.88)*		(1.85)*		(1.88)*	
	DEXP	2.6989		2.6795		2.6811		2.6811		2.6804	
		(97.42)***		(94.62)***		(95.03)***		(95.04)***		(94.58)***	
	K/L	−0.000004	−0.000001	−0.000003	−0.000001	−0.000003	−0.000001	−0.000003	−0.000001	−0.000003	−0.000001
		(−1.30)	(−0.68)	(−1.15)	(−0.71)	(−1.10)	(−0.65)	(−1.13)	(−0.70)	(−1.08)	(−0.70)

RD	0.4244	−1.5423	0.4950	−1.3250	0.4913	−1.3224	0.4190	−1.3331	0.2658	−1.1282
	(3.87)***	(−3.38)**	(3.54)***	(−3.99)**	(3.54)***	(−3.99)**	(3.53)***	(−3.01)**	(3.10)***	(−3.69)*
TECH	1.008	−1.797	1.002	−1.414	1.001	−1.586	1.002	−1.571	1.008	−1.583
	(1.13)	(−3.77)***	(1.13)	(−2.82)***	(1.18)	(−3.20)***	(1.08)	(−3.17)***	(1.07)	(−3.22)***
RAWIMP	1.339	0.711	1.675	0.706	1.656	0.706	1.657	0.710	1.630	0.674
	(11.81)***	(22.81)***	(10.07)***	(21.59)***	(10.02)***	(21.80)***	(10.03)***	(21.91)***	(9.69)***	(20.31)***
WAGE	−0.615	−0.125	−0.565	−0.117	−0.566	−0.122	−0.564	−0.121	−0.562	−0.127
	(10.35)***	(−4.66)***	(−8.89)***	(−4.15)***	(−8.94)***	(−4.40)***	(−8.91)***	(−4.36)***	(−8.86)***	(−4.61)***
SEI	0.109	5.187	0.476	5.648	0.274	5.591	0.426	5.687	0.436	5.627
	(1.08)	(13.85)***	(1.32)	(14.60)***	(1.19)	(14.51)***	(1.29)	(14.78)***	(1.29)	(14.59)***
SSECT	0.487	−1.908	0.310	−1.363	0.549	−1.279	0.849	−1.538	0.278	−1.394
	(1.43)	(14.07)***	(1.36)	(−13.72)***	(1.22)	(−13.78)***	(1.28)	(−13.95)***	(0.97)	(−13.85)***
AGE	0.0046	−0.0023	0.0038	−0.0027	0.0039	−0.0026	0.0040	−0.0028	0.0044	−0.0025
	(1.44)	(−2.34)**	(1.16)	(−2.53)**	(1.20)	(−2.48)**	(1.21)	(−2.64)***	(1.33)	(−2.43)**
SQAGE	−0.00003	0.00000	−0.00002	0.00001	−0.00002	0.00001	−0.00002	0.00001	−0.00003	0.00001
	(−0.60)	(0.22)	(−0.47)	(0.71)	(−0.47)	(0.62)	(−0.48)	(0.78)	(−0.63)	(0.62)
SIZE	−0.0063	0.0056	−0.0058	0.0054	−0.0059	0.0055	−0.0059	0.0055	−0.0059	0.0056
	(−4.08)***	(4.10)***	(−3.82)***	(3.78)***	(−3.88)***	(3.91)***	(−3.86)***	(3.92)***	(−3.87)***	(4.03)***
SQSIZE	0.00000	−0.00001	0.00000	−0.00001	0.00000	−0.00001	0.00000	−0.00001	0.00000	−0.00001
	(4.47)***	(−3.00)***	(4.14)***	(−2.74)***	(4.20)***	(−2.84)***	(4.19)***	(−2.87)***	(4.18)***	(−2.94)***
CompSpill	−0.3689	−0.4857								
	(−1.25)	(−7.20)***								
RDSPill			0.0215	−0.0340						
			(0.85)	(−0.87)						
ExpSpill					−0.4255	−0.2376				
					(−1.16)	(−2.14)**				
SkillSpill							0.0395	−0.4841		
							(1.07)	(−3.22)***		
TechSpill									−0.1046	−0.0250
									(−1.39)	(−1.09)
Constant	−1.389	0.474	−1.399	0.476	−1.377	0.484	−1.398	0.501	−1.371	0.498
	(−11.64)***	(15.29)***	(−11.47)***	(14.55)***	(−11.19)***	(14.79)***	(−11.18)***	(14.99)***	(−10.99)***	(15.21)***

(Continued)

Table A10.1 (Continued)

Technology category	*Variables*	*Model 1*		*Model 2*		*Model 3*		*Model 4*		*Model 5*	
		Export decision	*Export intensity*	*Export decision*	*Export intensity*	*Export decision*	*Export intensity*	*Export decision*	*Export intensity*	*Export decision*	*Export intensity*
	Log likelihood	–9677.838		–9340.307		–9399.212		–9397.15		–9228.581	
	Rho	–0.1506315		–0.144525		–0.1446061		–0.1446288		–0.1437032	
	Wald Chisq (35)	3591.17		3099.58		3164.2		3172.48		2994.93	
	LR test	79.29***		74.11***		74.86***		74.94***		74.76***	
	Observation	21625		21625		21625		21625		21625	

Note: *,**,*** represent the 10%, 5% and 1% level of significance. The values in parentheses are z-values.

Appendix

Notes

1 Studies have shown that developing countries were importing mainly obsolete technologies from developed countries. Pant (2015) mentioned that in the 1980s India was importing technologies which were mostly obsolete in the world market. His study also shows that, during the 1970s and 1980s, Indian firms relied on the import of technology and had restrictive policies toward technical collaborations with TNCs which raised the payments for royalty and technical knowhow to 50% of total remittances. Moreover, according to the study a very small portion of the total payment went to the actual import of drawings and designs for production while most of the payment went for the royalty and payment for technicians which means that the actual transfer of technology was very little.

2 This is the standard definition of IMF. The same definition has been used in various empirical studies on India, see, for instance, Sasidharan and Ramanathan (2007).

3 It is interesting to indicate that around 38 per cent of the total R&D stock of the manufacturing sector and about 50 per cent of the imported technology belongs to the MHT sector during the study period. However, only 18 per cent of overall manufacturing exports belongs to the MHT sector. Data shows that most of the foreign export, foreign R&D stock and foreign skilled labour (in terms of real wages) belongs to the MHT sector.

4 However, the positive influence may hold till the coordination costs are less than the profitability of the firm (Franco and Sasidharan, 2010).

5 In the Heckman two-step procedure, the inverse mills ratio is included as the independent variable in the second step of the regression analysis. Often, the inclusion of inverse mills ratio results in multicollinearity, which can have an adverse effect on the model estimates. Therefore, we prefer the Heckman maximum likelihood method.

6 Generally, Rho (ρ) takes negative values. Any component of the error that makes selection more likely makes y (dependent variable) less.

References

Aggarwal, A. (2002). Liberalisation, multinational enterprises and export performance: Evidence from Indian manufacturing. *Journal of Development Studies*, *38*(3), 119–137.

Aitken, B., Hanson, G. H., & Harrison, A. E. (1997). Spillovers, foreign investment, and export behavior. *Journal of International Economics*, *43*(1), 103–132.

Aitken, B. J., & Harrison, A. E. (1999). Do domestic firms benefit from direct foreign investment? Evidence from Venezuela. *American Economic Review*, *89*(3), 605–618.

Anwar, S., & Nguyen, L. P. (2011). Foreign direct investment and export spillovers: Evidence from Vietnam. *International Business Review*, *20*(2), 177–193.

Banga, R. (2003). The differential impact of Japanese and US foreign investments on Export of Indian Manufacturing, *ICRIER Eorking Paper* No. 106.

Chen, C., Sheng, Y., & Findlay, C. (2013). Export spillovers of FDI on China's domestic firms. *Review of International Economics*, *21*(5), 841–856.

Dunning, J. H. (1998). Location and the multinational enterprise: A neglected factor? *Journal of International Business Studies*, *29*(1), 45–66.

Franco, C. (2013). Exports and FDI motivations: Empirical evidence from US foreign subsidiaries. *International Business Review*, *22*(1), 47–62.

Franco, C., & Sasidharan, S. (2010). MNEs, technological efforts and channels of export spillover: An analysis of Indian manufacturing industries. *Economic Systems*, *34*(3), 270–288.

Globerman, S. (1979). Foreign direct investment and spillover efficiency benefits in Canadian manufacturing industries. *Canadian Journal of Economics*, 42–56.

Greenaway, D., Sousa, N., & Wakelin, K. (2004). Do domestic firms learn to export from multinationals? *European Journal of Political Economy*, *20*(4), 1027–1043.

Heckman, James J. (1979). Sample selection bias as a specification error. *Econometrica*, 47, 153–161.

Hymer, S. H. (1976). *International operations of national firms*. Cambridge, MA: MIT Press.

Johnson, A. (2006). FDI and exports: The case of the high performing East Asian Economies. The Royal Institute of Technology Centre of Excellence for Studies in Science and Innovation Working Paper, No. 57.

Joseph, T. J., & Reddy, V. N. (2010). FDI spillovers and export performance of Indian manufacturing firms after liberalisation. *Economic and Political Weekly*, *44*(52), 97–105.

Karpaty, P., & Kneller, R. (2011). Demonstration or congestion? Export spillovers in Sweden. *Review of World Economics*, *147*(1), 109–130.

Kumar, N., & Pradhan, J. P. (2003). *Export competitiveness in the knowledge-based industries: A firm-level analysis of Indian manufacturing*. New Delhi: Research and Information System for Developing Countries (RIS).

Kumar, N., & Siddharthan, N. S. (1994). Technology, firm size and export behaviour in developing countries: The case of Indian enterprises. *The Journal of Development Studies*, *31*(2), 289–309.

Pant, M. (1995). *FDI in India: The issues involved*. New Delhi: Lancer Books.

Power, L. (1998). The missing link: Technology, investment, and productivity. *Review of Economics and Statistics*, *80*(2), 300–313.

Prasanna, N. (2010). Impact of foreign direct investment on export performance in India. *Journal of Social Science*, *24*(1), 65–71.

Rao, K. S., & Dhar, B. (2011). India's FDI inflows: Trends and concepts. *Biswajit, India's FDI Inflows: Trends and Concepts (February 24, 2011)*. Available at SSRN 1770222.

Roberts, M. J., & Tybout, J. R. (1997). The decision to export in Colombia: An empirical model of entry with sunk costs. *The American Economic Review*, *87*(4), 545–564.

Ruane, F., & Sutherland, J. (2005). Foreign direct investment and export spillovers: How do export platforms fare?. *Institute for International Integration Studies Working Paper*, *58*, 21–34.

Sasidharan, S., & Ramanathan, A. (2007). Foreign direct investment and spillovers: Evidence from Indian manufacturing. *International Journal of Trade and Global Markets*, *1*(1), 5–22.

Sun, H. (2001). Foreign direct investment and regional export performance in China. *Journal of Regional Science*, *41*(2), 317–336.

Sun, S. (2012). The role of FDI in domestic exporting: Evidence from China. *Journal of Asian Economics*, *23*(4), 434–441.

UNCTAD. (1999). *World investment report 1999: Foreign direct investment and the challenges of development* . New York and Geneva: United Nations Publications.

Wang, C., Buckley, P. J., Clegg, J., & Kafouros, M. (2007). The impact of inward foreign direct investment on the nature and intensity of Chinese manufacturing exports. *Transnational Corporations*, *16*(2), 123.

Willmore, L. (1992). Tansnationals and foreign trade: Evidence from Brazil. *The Journal of Development Studies*, *28*(2), 314–335.

Xuan, N. T., & Xing, Y. (2008). Foreign direct investment and exports The experiences of Vietnam 1. *Economics of Transition*, *16*(2), 183–197.

11

NON-TARIFF MEASURES ON INDIA'S AGRI-FOOD EXPORTS

Is ease of doing business reform distractive?[1]

C. Nalin Kumar

Introduction

The issues of standards and regulations and the problems of compliance that agri-food exports face are not typically covered in the debate of agrarian challenges in the Indian context. India, unlike most of its competitors, is a country where agricultural export commodities face a high degree of competition from the domestic market. Competitiveness would arise from price and quality. The aspects of quality and certifications historically have been given lower priority owing to a number of reasons. As economies and systems evolve, quality and many other associated parameters prove to influence the price of commodities. As the price of commodities starts to depend more on quality and safety aspects and their certifications, a gradual erosion of competitiveness is witnessed. At a time when the Government of India has set a target to (1) double the income of farmers by 2022, (2) achieve a level of exports to the tune of US $900 billion through Foreign Trade Policy 2015–20 and (3) be in the club of the top 50 ranked in the Ease of Doing Business, the major imperatives are institutional reforms. This paper looks into some of these institutional aspects related to India's exports of agri-food products to major markets and builds upon instances of rejection of India's major category of exports to the European Union (EU) and the United States (US). Then a sectoral level study is carried out on a range of issues within trade facilitation of agricultural products to examine how macro level trade policy measures trickle down to micro entity levels.

Under the World Trade Organization (WTO), the Agreement on Sanitary and Phytosanitary (SPS) places broad rules on food safety and animal and plant health. There have been issues that some of these agreements are also misused for protectionist purposes. In the context of the WTO, Non-tariff Measures (NTMs) and Non-tariff Barriers (NTBs) assume importance. NTBs are basically restrictions that result from prohibitions, conditions or specific market requirements that make import or export of products difficult or costly. NTBs however also include NTMs which are policy measures other than custom tariffs that have the potential to affect the price or quantity or both of internationally traded goods. NTBs arise from different measures taken by governments in the form of laws, regulations, policies, conditions, restrictions or specific requirements, and private sector business practices or prohibitions that protect the domestic industries from foreign competition. Though NTMs are in compliance with

 DOI: 10.4324/9780367855741-11

WTO provisions, they can be invoked for protectionist purposes resulting in NTBs which go beyond meeting the non-trade objective. Thus, a measure becomes a barrier if used in a way to impede trade rather than achieving the legitimate and specific objective. Testing and certification facilities and institutional capacities thus take extreme importance for developing countries.

There are reasons to believe that for some major importing countries or groups of countries the regulatory systems could be stringent but at the same time transparent. For instance, the EU and the US have systems in place which alert the exporting country of non-compliance with a particular regulation or a consequent rejection of the exported consignment. Countries also differ in terms of the perceived risk of food-borne illnesses and that would explain the divergences in standards and regulations across the world with respect to cleanliness, quality and food safety. Many countries wake up to these issues relatively slowly. The slower progress in awareness also leads to slower evolution of the standards ecosystem within a country. When importing countries reject the consignments on the grounds of food safety, the affected countries often label the incidents as discriminatory, arbitrary and non-transparent. This chapter elaborates on these issues, and attempts to give a numerical perspective with the help of the incidents of rejection of Indian exports from the European Union (EU) and the United States (US) markets and the initiatives by Indian government agencies and private sectors. This also raises the question of trade reforms and facilitation that are reflected in the micro field levels where the exporters and related stakeholders can feel a tangible change in terms of access to regulatory information and a possible reduction in the count of export rejections. These include major initiatives at trade facilitation by the Ministry of Commerce, standardization initiatives at the level of the sectors by the respective commodity agencies and exporters' associations.

While India's Foreign Trade Policy (FTP 2015–20) gives incentives and stimulus to exports by way of schemes, it remains to be seen how sustainable and compatible the schemes are in the context of the World Trade Organization (WTO). This chapter also discusses the effect of such reform measures, specifically the reduction in the number of mandatory documents to accompany an export consignment and single window interface on India's select agri-food trade sector by attempting to link macro level policy changes to micro field level effects. The chapter is organized as follows. The next section deals with the aspects of trade policy reforms and trade facilitation as practised in India during recent years. The third section outlines some of the sensitive issues of food safety, regulatory measures and certifications in India and the non-tariff barriers India has been facing from some prominent export markets. The fourth section carries an examination of the distractive effects of reforms induced by the ease of doing business and the fifth section concludes.

India's FTP, trade reform measures and trade facilitation: sectoral percolation

Of late, the Government of India has realized the need to address issues pertaining to the time and transaction costs associated with transport, documentation and clearance in order to have sustained growth in the trade sector of the country. These sets of reforms are broadly classified as Trade Facilitation (TF). Based on this, actions have been seen from both the Ministry of Commerce and the Ministry of Finance. The Customs Department adopted the use of an information technology platform, commonly known as the Electronic Data Interchange (EDI) for faster clearance of exports and imports. Later, a portal for sharing information with other related departments known as the Indian Customs and Excise Gateway (ICEGATE) was introduced. This reduces the interface as information is easily shared among departments which otherwise would involve duplication and multiple physical visits to offices. The two Foreign Trade Policies

(2004–09 and 2009–14) also reemphasized the need to undertake TF specific initiatives and boost the trade sector.

A more aggressive and coherent initiative followed with the constitution of a Task Force on Transaction Costs by the Ministry of Commerce and Industry in October 2009. The purpose of this task force was to look into various issues affecting the competitiveness of Indian exports, provide recommendations to the government and initiate a set of executable remedial measures towards reducing delays and costs associated with trading across borders. The task force identified 44 issues across seven line Ministries/Departments for action and the government successfully addressed 23 issues resulting in a larger benefit to the stakeholders' community. Agricultural specific measures were also implemented during this first task force, such as the issue of sanitary certifications 24/7 at major airports. Subsequently, the Ministry announced the formation of the Second Task Force in 2013 under the Chairmanship of Directorate General of Foreign Trade (DGFT) to identify reasons for higher transaction cost in exports and to identify areas where Indian exporters face administrative impediments that lead to an increase in transaction cost. It is also intended to compare procedural complexities in exports between India and its major competitors.

Thus, a significant change in the approach to India's trade policy could be noticed towards the end of the last decade, with the Ministry of Commerce leading a Task Force on Transaction Cost in Exports in order to bring down both the procedural as well as physical barriers in the process involving the country's exports and imports. This also signalled an era of declining levels of incentives available for various sectors and exporters had to be competitive on their own. These initiatives were broadly classified as trade facilitation measures. What the government would expect is that trade facilitation measures would compensate the exporters for the withdrawal of incentives by introducing simple, faster and streamlined documentation and a better logistic support system. But the export community felt that incentives always constituted a significant amount that would get them a level playing field with other major producing countries in the world, especially those in the South East Asian countries. Thus, trade facilitation measures cannot, in the current state of affairs, compensate for the loss of incentives. However, both the withdrawal of incentives and trade facilitation have become India's obligation at the WTO. As part of enhancing the business environment and 'ease of doing business', the government reduced the number of mandatory documents for export from seven to three in 2015. This was also included in India's FTP 2015–20. The seven documents were (1) Bill of Lading, (2) Commercial Invoice, (3) Foreign Currency Exchange Form, (4) Packing List, (5) Shipping Bill, (6) Technical Standards Certificate and (7) Terminal Handling Receipt. The current mandatory documents required are (1) Bill of Lading, (2) Commercial Invoice cum Packing List and (3) Shipping Bill. However, this does not hold good in a practical scenario where there are half a dozen documents that the importing country insists upon. The real easing of business would only happen when those certifications were obtained with a lower number of official interfaces. To put things in perspective, a comparison of rank and a reflection on best practices in procedural time and cost (Distance to Frontier) is drawn among India and its major competing countries in the plantation and marine product sectors (Table 11.1).

1. *Ranking in the 'Trading across border' (TaB) parameter, reflecting the ease of exports, Ranked 1 (best) to 190 (worst).*
2. *Distance to Frontier (DtF) – An absolute score to measure the progress in the area – a higher score represents proximity to the best practices in the world and change in DtF indicates the progress countries achieved over one year.*

Table 11.1 Indicative ease of trading across border of India vs some of the competing producers

	Country	*2018 Rank*[1]	*2018 DtF*[2]	*2017 DtF*	*2019 Rank*	*2019 DtF*	*2020 Rank*	*2020 DtF*
1	Thailand	57	84.1	84.1	59	84.65	62	84.6
2	Malaysia	61	82.75	82.38	48	88.47	49	88.5
3	Sri Lanka	86	73.29	70.7	93	73.29	96	73.3
4	Vietnam	94	70.83	69.92	100	70.83	104	70.8
5	The Philippines	99	69.39	69.39	104	69.90	113	68.4
6	Cambodia	108	67.28	67.28	115	67.28	118	67.3
7	Indonesia	112	66.59	65.87	116	67.27	116	67.5
8	Lao PDR	124	62.98	62.98	76	78.12	78	78.1
9	**INDIA**	**146**	**58.56**	**57.61**	**80**	**77.46**	**68**	**82.5**
10	Myanmar	163	47.67	47.4	168	47.67	168	47.7
11	Bangladesh	173	34.86	34.86	176	31.76	176	31.8

Source: World Bank Ease of Doing Business Database (2018, 2019 and 2020).

It is evident from Table 11.1 that India made considerable progress in the area of TaB in recent years compared to other closely competing countries in the South and South East Asian regions. However, the assumptions of DB methodology would apply in these ranks and most of the attributes of TaB ranks and DtF are based on Mumbai's Jawaharlal Nehru Port Trust (JNPT), so this cannot be generalized across major ports in India. The latest Ease of Doing Business (DB) 2020 report has ranked India at 66th position on overall DB ranks and a major contribution to this jump is attributed to reforms in the 'construction permits' and 'trading across borders' by moving 129 and 66 positions, respectively.

The Government of India has started initiating a variety of trade facilitation measures especially to reduce the transaction costs of exports and at the same time has planned for a reduction and gradual phasing out of many incentives available in the export sector. At the WTO front, India has been going through immense pressure on the issue of the procurement of food grain to ensure food security to the poor, and finalization of the Trade Facilitation Agreement (TFA) which were part of the Bali Ministerial of the WTO in 2013. This was also the time India began to feel the effects of the Free Trade Agreements (FTAs) it signed with the Association of South East Asian Nations (ASEAN) and the consequent tariff reductions in the farm sector. Some of the ASEAN member countries have high cost competitiveness in the export of agricultural products. India has also been contemplating FTAs or similar agreements with Australia, the EU and Canada. At the domestic front, there was the First Task Force on Transaction Costs in Exports set up in 2010 which submitted its report in February 2011, with a host of recommendations which altogether brought relief to the export community. The introduction of a 24/7 issuance of certificates, especially phytosanitary certificates, at important locations was one of the major measures of the task force. The Second Task Force set up in 2013 invited views and suggestions from the stakeholders and the team also visited key trading points such as ports and airports. Reduction in trade transaction costs and simplifying procedures continue to be a long-term endeavour of the government, and the Ministry of Commerce and Industry in particular, and a substantial set of measures made it into the New Foreign Trade Policy 2015–20 announced in April 2015. Additional impetus for these measures comes from the larger objective of improving India's rank in the *Doing Business* indicators. The Ministry of Finance and the Ministry of Commerce have already adopted a number of trade facilitating measures (SWIFT,

Table 11.2 Summary of important trade facilitation measures in recent years

Sl No	*Specific reform measure*	*Details/Tangible benefits*
1	E-Bank Realization Statement (e-BRC) – Directorate General of Foreign Trade	e-BRC has enabled DGFT to capture details of realization of export proceeds directly from the banks through a secured electronic mode, enabling the implementation of various export promotion incentives without any physical interface between the banks and exporters or customs house agents. Exporters need not wait for the physical copy from the bank to be presented to DGFT and this has resulted in a significant reduction in time required for processing various incentives under the Foreign Trade Policy.
2	Reduction in the number of mandatory documents for exports (from seven to three) – Government (Finance and Commerce Ministry)	After issue of DGFT's Notification only three documents each would be mandatory for export and import as two documents (Packing List and Commercial Invoice) required by Customs have been merged into one document, whereas one document required by RBI (Foreign Exchange Control Forms – SDF for exports and A-1 for imports) and one document required by Ministry of Shipping (Terminal Handling Receipt) earlier, have now been dispensed with. 'Cargo Release Order' is not a mandatory document required by any regulatory agency, but is a commercial document issued by the Shipping line to the concerned importer. As regards, 'Technical Standard Certificate'/'Certified Engineer's Report', 'Product manual' and 'Inspection report', these documents are required in specific cases/products/tariff lines only and are not mandatory for all products. (DGFT Notification as per Press Information Bureau 12th March 2015).
3	Single Window Interface For Trade (SWIFT)	The Customs' SWIFT enables importers/exporters to file a common electronic 'Integrated Declaration' on the Indian Customs Electronic Commerce/Electronic Data Interchange (EC/EDI) Gateway i.e. ICEGATE portal. The Integrated Declaration compiles the information requirements of Customs, FSSAI, Plant Quarantine, Animal Quarantine, Drug Controller, Wild Life Control Bureau and Textile Committee. It replaces nine separate forms required by these 6 different agencies and Customs (Press Information Bureau, Govt of India, August 2016).

Source: Press Information Bureau, Government of India.

e-BRC, etc.) through the institutional arms of Customs and DGFT. Some of the key measures are summarized in Table 11.2.

Ideally, these reform measures are to facilitate the reduction in transaction costs and time, faster clearances for certification and reduction in the incidents of consignment rejections.

For exporters, the decision to export instead of selling in the domestic market comes at a significantly higher risk in the case of agricultural and marine products due to fluctuating prices, competing suppliers, burden of documentation and regulatory compliance. The export incentives are designed to compensate the exporters for infrastructural difficulties and other associated costs and provide them a level playing field with exporters from competing countries. As per the latest FTP, the exporter is eligible to get around 3.5 per cent (depending on the product) of the Free on Board (FoB) under the Merchandize Exports from India Scheme (MEIS) and 1 per cent as drawback. Providing a static percentage amount of the FoB price as export incentive (especially the post export incentive system as part of the new FTP) does not sound very prudent in the same context of fluctuating prices. Whether it is a container full of cheap rice or a container full of high value items such as shrimp or black pepper (as per current export value one container can cost up to INR 100,000), around 5 per cent of the value gets returned to the exporter in terms of tradable incentive scrips which can be sold to or utilized by other exporters. With such a static incentive, an exporter can offer the product at a lower price and undercut suppliers from a competing country as well. In such a case, the incentive amount, in effect, simply moves to the importing country. Some of these incentives are being objected to by the WTO. So, it was necessary to bring them down and phase them out in the course of time and this necessitates making the exporters competitive on their own, which was the rationale for the constitution of the task forces in reducing transaction costs in exports. These are important points to be considered before designing an incentive system and many exporters are of the opinion that they would prefer the provision of both hard and soft infrastructure instead of this sort of unsustainable and unpredictable incentive (Kumar, 2016). Eventually, the withdrawal of export incentives is to be matched with the improvements in trade-related procedures and enhanced logistics and this was one of the major impetuses for the country to embark on trade facilitation. But how much of trade facilitation measures is focused on improving the ground realities in the context of agricultural products? Or were the reforms mostly focused on attaining a higher rank in the DB? We turn towards the agricultural export sector and focus on a limited set of dimensions to see how many of the issues get addressed by way of trade facilitation.

There could be a significant reduction in export transaction costs if the exports are through some select ports and some of these could be attributed to reforms aimed at a higher rank in DB. As India has moved up significantly in DB rankings, especially during some years, one major contributor to the higher rank has been 'trading across the border'. But how did these reform measures reduce the information asymmetry existing in the sector? One possible indicator for this could be the quantum of rejection of India's exports by overseas regulators as those consignments did not meet the specific requirements of imports.

India's agri-food trade facilitation, regulatory certifications and issues of non-tariff barriers

In contrast with non-agricultural trade, agricultural products face significantly higher barriers due to seasonality, perishability and other reasons of vulnerability in the supply chain. An agri-food product has to undergo various regulatory and certification processes, involving multiple interfaces, adding to the overall costs. Of late, the physical, chemical and microbiological properties of exported products assumed greater importance subjecting them to closer scrutiny and leaving many countries deprived of the capacity to tackle newer challenges. Agricultural trade also has disadvantages in terms of quality and quantity good enough to be traded. Especially in India, agriculture is predominantly a small grower phenomenon which may require differing levels of support through government interventions to survive in the market and move forward in the value chain. Considerable processing also takes place in the unorganized sectors (Indian marine and dairy sectors are cases in point). This further adds to the challenges of trade facilitation and maintaining the safety of food within the prescribed regulatory parameters. It is clear that the conventional approaches to food safety policy that have been in place since the turn of the last century are not adequate to meet these new food safety–related challenges. Here, we adopt a broader version to include measures to comply with regulations and the requisite institutional set up to pave the way for smoother conduct of trade, with an implicit understanding that there are no separate trade facilitation measures for agricultural products but such measures would be far more useful in the context of perishable commodities.

This paper looks into two prominent sectors in India's agri-food landscape: spices and marine products. The selection of these two sectors was based on a few considerations. First, India's key position in these commodities in the international marketplace. Second, higher prevalence of non-tariff measures. Spices have been traded historically from India and India is still one of the largest producers and exporters. India also occupies a key position in marine products exports. There are specific institutions set up in India to cope with the issues of food safety and product certifications for these specific markets or country groups. Most importantly, India has been occupying some of the key quality conscious markets in the world for these products such as the EU, North America, etc. which provide a premium for India's products. A higher unit value realization from these markets for India's exports is also evident from Tables 11.1 and 11.2. However, the imposition of more stringent regulations on food safety has also meant a gradual erosion of India's stronghold across a range of products and markets. The number of notifications and rejections of exported products originating in India due to non-compliance is one of the key aspects debated in the context of NTBs.

Figures 11.1 and 11.2 illustrate the trends in India's exports of spices and marine products, respectively, to these key markets over recent years.

As observed from Figure 11.1, EU markets have been stagnant post 2011–12, though there have been enhanced exports of spices to destinations within Asia, specifically ASEAN countries. As evident from Figure 11.2, India's exports of marine products to the markets of the EU have been consistent but the exports to other major markets such as the US and ASEAN have been fluctuating.

Table 11.3 and 11.4 indicate the unit value realizations of spices and marine products from India's key export markets over the years.

As can be observed from Tables 11.3 and 11.4, there are enhanced unit value realizations from the EU and the US compared to the closer ASEAN countries. While this would also be the result of higher quality and safety compliance with reference to the markets of the EU and the US, the process of complying with stringent regulations has many implications on India's domestic trade facilitating and certifying institutions. A typical export process

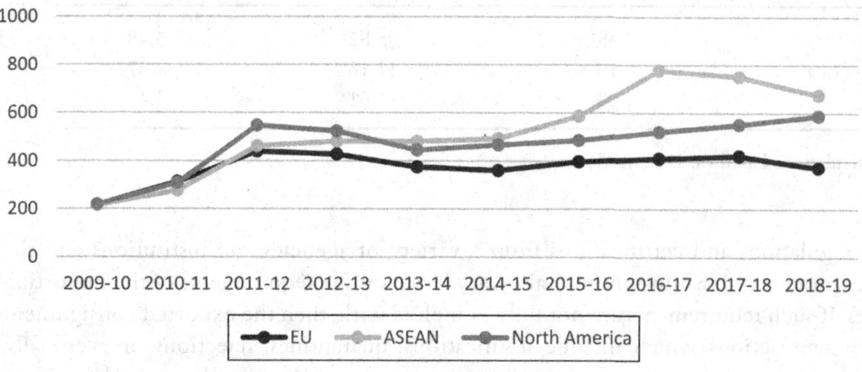

Figure 11.1 Trends in India's spice exports to major destinations – 2009–2018 (US$ millions). *Source:* DGCIS data.

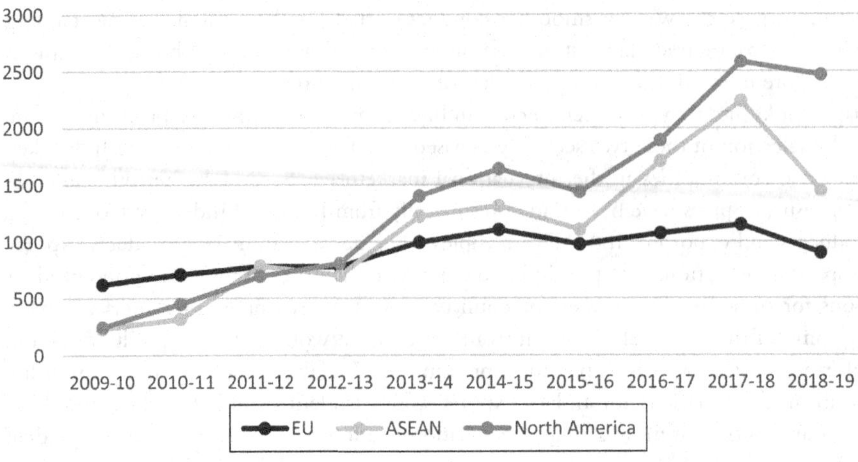

Figure 11.2 Trends in India's marine exports to major destinations – 2009–2018 (US$ millions). *Source*: DGCIS data.

Table 11.3 Unit value of India's spice exports to major destinations (US$/kilogram)

Spices	*2009–10*	*2014–15*	*2018–19*
EU	3.44	4	5.24
North America	3.1	5.48	6.24
ASEAN	1.55	1.91	2.11

Source: Calculations based on DGCIS data.

Table 11.4 Unit value of India's marine products exports to major destinations (US$/kilogram)

Marine Products	*2009–10*	*2014–15*	*2018–19*
EU	3.65	5.82	5.48
North America	6.1	11.16	8.37
ASEAN	2.04	3.61	3.47

Source: Calculations based on DGCIS data.

involves regulations and certifications from a variety of agencies and institutions and the certifying process and institutions may also vary based on the requirements of the importing countries. If such requirements are not fully complied with, then the exported consignment faces stringent actions which include notifications, quarantines, rejections or eventually, destruction of the products. Figure 11.3 illustrates a representative regulatory and certification apparatus of agri-food product exports.

As illustrated, the exported agri-food product undergoes a variety of regulatory checks and certifications within India and the institutional set ups are linked to some extent to contribute

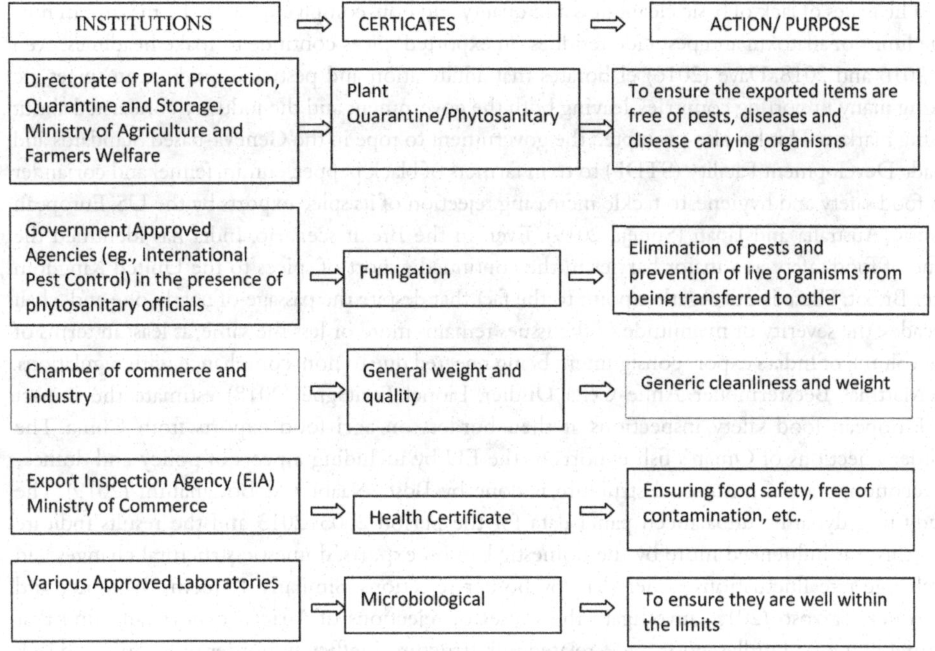

Figure 11.3 An illustrative regulatory and certification apparatus of India's agri-food exports. *Source*: Author's work based on a trade facilitation survey (2016).

to the trade facilitation objectives of the country. The spice and marine products export sectors have been experiencing barriers to entry in some of the key markets such as the EU and the US for a long time. One of the pioneering studies on the regulations on food safety and standards affecting the sectors was done by the World Bank during the early 2000s. Among them, Jaffee (2004) explored the comprehensive set of issues the Indian spice export sector was facing at that point in time. Similarly, Henson, Saqib and Rajasenan (2004) covered the fishery export sector, indicating the prevalence of these issues one and a half decades ago. Recent reports of rejection or potential tightening of regulations or sampling procedure on Indian originated exports also point to the fact that though food safety–related concerns were old, the institutions and exporters have not woken up to curtail these perennial issues. In 2018, an EU official expressed that Indian shrimp farms' compliance on antibiotics was 'insufficient', although EU buyers downplayed the threat to humans from antibiotic residues. It is also mentioned that though EU regulations are highly stringent they are highly transparent (Harkell, 2018). Behera (2019) describes that EU traders flag the falling number of Indian shrimp exporters after strict tests indicating that the stringent norms of the EU and higher chances of rejection force many exporters to divert the exports to other markets where regulations are less stringent. Sen (2020) describes the latest set of possible responses of the Trade Promotion Council of India (TCPI) by holding the certifying laboratories accountable if the consignments are rejected as well as the five-pronged strategy to boost agricultural exports to the tune of US $100 million per annum. Sen (2019) reports that India wants the EU to relax sampling norms for fish exports. The EU being the third largest market for Indian fish exports, the increased sampling frequency of 50 per cent from the earlier 10 per cent as a follow-up of the EU audit of Indian exporting firms in 2016 raised additional concerns such as increased testing costs and reduced competitiveness and delisting. Around 15 exporting firms were delisted post the EU audit.

The issues of lack of basic cleanliness and quality and non-compliance with the maximum residue limits of aflatoxin and pesticide residues on exported spices continue to make headlines, even in 2016 and 2018. Dave (2016) elaborates that adulteration and pesticide residues on spices are irking many importing countries, leaving both the government and the industry concerned about losing markets. This has also prompted the government to rope in the Geneva-based Standards and Trade Development Facility (STDF) to train farmers of black pepper, cumin, fennel and coriander on food safety and hygiene, to tackle increasing rejection of its spice exports by the US, European Union, Australia and Japan (Suneja 2019). Even in the Brexit scenario, India has identified the issue of food safety as a major barrier in the continued export of spices to the United Kingdom after Brexit. These issues together point to the fact that despite the passage of nearly one and a half decades, the severity or magnitude of the issues remains more or less the same, at least in terms of the volume of India's export consignment being rejected due to non-compliance with regulations.

Matthias Beestermöller, Anne-Célia Disdier, Lionel Fontagné (2018) estimate the impact of European food safety inspections at their borders on agri-food exports from China. The border rejections of Oman's fish exports to the EU by including aspects of policy and domestic economic and institutional structure is done by Bose, Naabi and Boughanmi (2019). The study uses dynamic unbalanced panel data for the period 2003–2013 and the results indicate that this was influenced more by the domestic ban on exports, domestic structural changes and exchange rate fluctuations rather than by border rejections. Similarly, Kareem, Brummer and Martinez-Zarzoso (2015) investigate the causes of rejections of African exports and find that natural domestic hurdles, poor trade-related infrastructure, inefficient border procedure and lack of trade facilitation increased the incidence of border rejection of Africa's exports confirming much of the literature that the strengthening of institutions and trade facilitation are the key for a sustained penetration of key export markets.

The European Union and the United States have a system of notifying the exporter and exporting country of the condition of the product on arrival. This section focuses on some of these issues by taking the case of India's exports to the European Union and the United States and draws certain preliminary inferences from the instances of notifications and rejections by them on consignments from India. Broadly, a notification implies that the said product has not met all the physical, chemical and microbiological regulations at the port of import and the Rapid Alert system sends the details to all member countries in the EU and issues a warning. The affected exports have to undergo complete scrutiny until many subsequent consignments are cleared in order to get the alert lifted. India is one of the few countries in the world where export demand for agricultural products competes with domestic demand of a very high order. At the same time, the export market sustainability involves a series of compliance measures, most of which have evolved in recent years, throughout the supply chain.

The notifications can be broadly classified into two types for the alerts issued by the EU on a consignment from India. These are:

(i) **Notifications due to a genuine food safety concern**: these include all notifications for which the basic concern is of public health such as the presence of mycotoxins, pesticide residues, normal decay, pathogens, other residues, adulteration, etc.

Two illustrations from the Rapid Alert would appear like this: (1) *Aflatoxins (B1=9.0 µg/kg-ppb) in crushed chillies from India. (2) Cadmium (1.4 mg/kg – ppm) in frozen squid (Loligo spp) from India.*

(ii) **Notifications due to information asymmetry or lack of sufficient documentation**: these include notifications arising not due to the presence of a public health risk,

> but shortcomings in the documentation accompanying the consignment or unapproved processing of the product. This is also due to the lack of updated knowledge on the part of the exporter such as processing was done in an unauthorized facility, the consignment was not accompanied by a requisite health certificate, etc. The product may be free from any genuine food safety or plant quarantine concern, however, since the documentation and other associated requirements were not met, the products are put on alert or rejected.

Two illustrations from the Rapid Alert would appear like this: *Absence of Health Certificate(s) for curry leaves from India. (2) Unlabelled irradiation or irradiation in an unauthorized facility.*

Figure 11.4 presents the magnitude of various issues faced by exports from India at the EU border over recent years.

While these are the absolute numbers or incidences of notifications, there are also specific measures such as border rejection and destruction of the consignment included in the figure. Another area highlighted is the prevalence of information asymmetry wherein cases are reported as lacking documentation, such as the absence of a health certificate. Evidently, cases of information asymmetry have been on the rise over recent years and so too the incidence of border rejections as a proportion of total notifications, though there are year-on-year variations.

By looking at the major classified product categories affected during 2014–18 as listed in Figure 11.5, it could be observed that four broad product categories constitute 84 per cent of all notifications. These classifications are as per the EU's registry. Nuts and nut products have been the hardest hit followed by fruits and vegetables and herbs and spices, indicating a requirement for product-specific interventions.

Achieving a particular food safety or plant health level may not be difficult for a small producer, but the specific and timely information on how to demonstrate compliance with the regulation is where the issue could be. Regulations need not be necessarily stringent but one would require more awareness through institutions so that compliance could be demonstrated. This is the broad conclusion one would arrive at after examining the rejections of Indian spice exports to the EU, where the reasons are, apart from genuine food safety or plant health issues, lack of sufficient documentation such as the absence of health certificates or processing in an unauthorized facility etc., though the product might have complied with the stipulated residue levels. The second issue is that of competitiveness. Figure 11.4 points to the magnitude of this

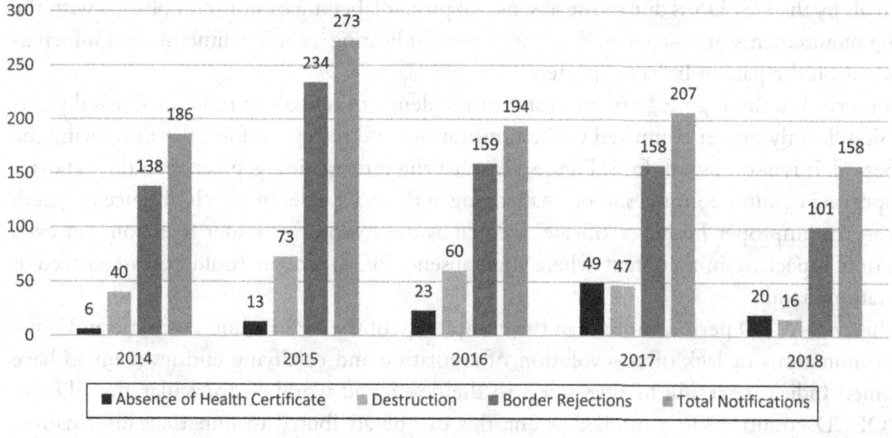

Figure 11.4 Intensity of border rejections of India's exports by EU from 2014 to 2018. *Source*: Compilation based on European Commission's Rapid Alerts data.

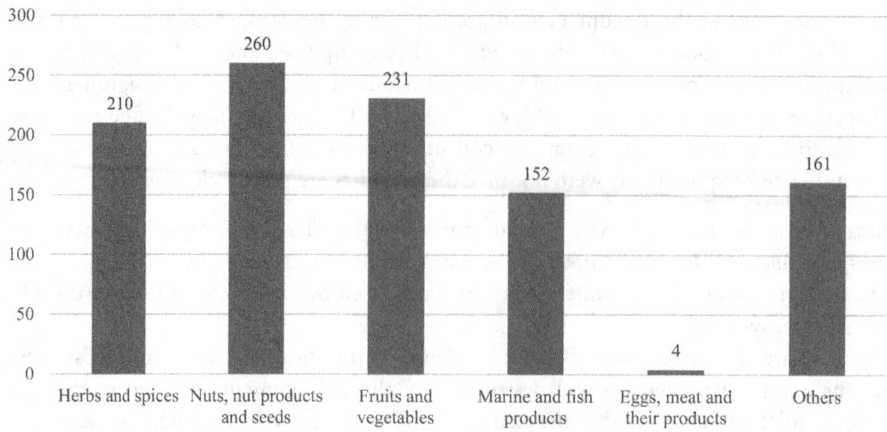

Figure 11.5 Number of EU border alerts by product categories from 2014 to 2018. *Source*: Compilation based on European Commission's Rapid Alerts data.

issue where the products have been rejected owing to a lack of sufficient documentation. A typical issue would be listed as 'absence of health certificate' or 'improper health certificate(s) for okra from India'. For instance, during 2017 there were 225 total notifications on Indian originated products out of which 158 were classified as border rejections and 47 consignments were destroyed as the final action taken. The reasons for destruction include rupture of cold chains, spoilage, changes in organoleptic characteristics, etc. Importantly, consignments were also subjected to destruction due to 'absence of health certificate' and this was categorized as 'adulteration/fraud' (RASFF portal, 2018).

This study also looks at the incidence of import refusals of India's products by the US over the same period. The US Food and Drug Administration (USFDA) database provides an explanation of the differences at the sectoral-product category level (43 FDA pre-defined categories). While the total USFDA refusals have remained high, there has been a particularly negative impact on the agricultural and allied sectors products which have seen the highest refusals (Figure 11.6). An examination of the reasons for refusal indicates that a significant portion of the refusals by the USFDA is due to the absence of proper labelling or non-compliance with the labelling requirements or absence of documentation, indicating a similar dimension of information deficit on the part of India's exporters.

As observed in the Figure 11.6, the count or incidence of refusals of India-originated products is significantly higher compared to the notifications and rejections from the EU during the same period. It is also obvious from Figure 11.6 that the information gap between the exporter and importing country continues to be challenging as there are cases in which 'absence of health certificate' or 'improper health certificate' is listed as the reason for border rejection and even destruction, especially in a context where such absence of document could be categorized as 'adulteration/fraud'.

In this post-WTO period, more than the complexity of the SPS regime, domestic and institutional limitations or lack of co-evolution of regulating and certifying entities seem to have constrained India's successful market access to the developed world, in particular, the EU and a few OECD countries. To a modest extent, this can be attributed to imperfect information. The particular sampling techniques for testing, and the practice of frequently changing the sensitivity levels for testing results, the resort to emergency notification clauses and suggesting

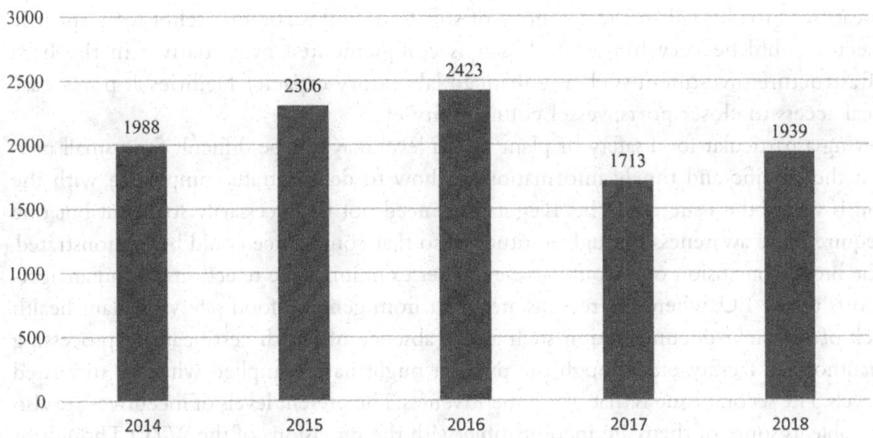

Figure 11.6 USFDA refusals of exports from India in recent years. *Source*: US Food and Drug Administration OASIS Database.

a testing procedure or equipment which does not exist in the exporting country are indeed trade distorting. The continuing number of rejections and notifications definitely implies more concerted efforts are still required within India's regulatory and certifying institutions. Thus, it would be easy to conclude that progress in DB ranks and specifically trading across borders may not facilitate these sectors by any significant measure as the sector level priorities that have to be initiated by the respective boards and regulatory bodies are different.

Summary, conclusion and policy recommendations

There are several imperatives that would make for a successful trade in agricultural products and trade facilitation is an important one. How important and proactive are institutions in this context? This chapter has furnished some of the important insights into two sectors to understand the relevance and efficiency of measures in making business easier and more sustainable. It is easy to conclude that many of the macro or aggregate level measures do not trickle successfully to specific sectors or the sectors simply lack sufficient capacity to assimilate them. Another important aspect in the context of regulatory compliance is that regulations as such are not stringent, but complying with them is an issue because of many other factors as illustrated, such as lack of access to the latest information, logistic related vulnerability beyond the control of exporters and so on. These issues throw light on the major impediments for those new and potential exporters aspiring to get into the export business and those who aspire to move forward in the value chain. This should have been a major consideration in the trade policy making itself especially when the targets for exports are as high as US$900 billion during the FTP 2015–20.

The chapter had a very specific objective of examining whether the issue is about the difficulty in meeting the stated regulations of the importing country or has something to do with access to information on the complex and changing regulations. These are two aspects of the same issue in the agrarian context; however, they require different types of facilitation. This takes us to the issue of how trade facilitation measures are carried out at the sectoral levels. The last few years have witnessed a slew of measures by the Ministry of Commerce and related departments in easing the procedural obstacles to trade and reducing transaction costs. But a coherent policy approach is something still to wait for. As most of the measures broadly fall in the category of soft trade infrastructure, relief for a specific export sector could be very limited unless it is complemented by initiatives in the hard trade infrastructure investment such as enhanced laboratory capacity, facilities at ports, ease of physical access to closer ports, vessel connectivity, etc.

Achieving a particular food safety or plant health level may not be difficult for a small producer, but the specific and timely information on how to demonstrate compliance with the regulation is where the issue could be. Regulations need not be necessarily stringent but one would require more awareness through institutions so that compliance could be demonstrated. This is the broad conclusion one would arrive at after examining the rejections of Indian agri-food exports to the EU, where the reasons are, apart from genuine food safety or plant health issues, lack of sufficient documentation such as the absence of health certificate or processing in an unauthorized facility, etc., though the product might have complied with the stipulated residue levels. The second issue is that of competitiveness. The present levels of incentives are also not sustainable as some of them are incompatible with the provisions of the WTO. Though, at present, most of the exporters perceive them essential to get a level playing field with competing countries, they also feel that a static set of incentives does not have much role in the context of price fluctuations. Any support is always welcomed by the trade community but support is essential when competitiveness is really affected. This could be in the context of either a higher price in the domestic market or lower priced supply from competing countries. This is where trade facilitation matters the most. The Doing Business and Trading across Borders measures of the World Bank are grossly inadequate for capturing the real world export process in India. This is because any approach to improving exports can be seen only as a necessary condition to boost the country's trade performance, whereas, a sufficient condition would be the build-up of trade infrastructure to reduce the turnaround time required for transactions and also to lower trade transaction costs, i.e., to focus on trade facilitation measures. This, however, demands a continued commitment at the policy level to identify factors hindering progress on the business front, and simplify and harmonize the rules and regulations to address the structural rigidities.

The contribution of this chapter lies in providing an institutional perspective on the regulatory export process, delineating the reasons for the notifications and rejections of Indian exports based on the available information on the counts of notifications, and examining the trickling of larger central level trade facilitation initiatives at the sectoral level. This could also be because of a lack of sufficient or proactive participation of representatives from sectors in the trade policy making process. It is thus easy to conclude with what matters more to India's trade policy reforms in the near future – export incentives or sector-specific trade facilitation?

Note

1 The author thanks the Indian Council of Social Science Research (ICSSR) for the research grant under which a part of this study was carried out. Thanks are also due to the stakeholders in the sector for providing various insights.

Bibliography

Anderson, J. E., and E. van Wincoop (2004), "Trade costs", *Journal of Economic Literature*, Vol. 42 (3), 691–751.

Beestermöller, M., A.-C. Disdier, and L. Fontagné (2018), "Impact of European food safety border inspections on agri-food exports: Evidence from Chinese firms", *China Economic Review*, Vol. 48, 66–82.

Behera, N. (2019), "EU traders flag falling no. of Indian shrimp exporters after strict tests", *Economic Times*, July 19, 2019.

Bose, S., A. M. R. Al Naabi, H. Boughanmi, and J. B. Yousuf (2019), "Domestic ban versus border rejections: A case of Oman's fish exports to the EU", *SAGE Open*, Vol. 9 (1): 1–12.

Dave, V. (2016), "Cleanliness problem in spice export: Adulteration, pesticide residues irking various importing countries; industry alarmed", *Business Standard*, June 15, 2016.

Directorate General of Commercial Intelligence and Statistics (DGCIS) (2010, 2015, 2019), *Database*, Government of India, New Delhi.

European Commission (2014–2018), *Rapid alert system for food and feed (RASFF Portal)*. Available at RASFF - food and feed safety alerts (europa.eu).

Harkell, L. (2018), "EU official: India shrimp farm compliance on antibiotics 'insufficient'", *The Undercurrent News*, January 29, 2018.

Henson S., M. Saquib, and Rajasenan, (2004). "Impact of sanitary measures on exports of fishery products from India, *the case of Kerala*', Agriculture and Rural Development Discussion Paper 17, The World Bank, Washington DC.

Jaffee, S. (2004). "Delivering and taking the heat: *Indian spices and evolving product and process standards*", Agriculture and Rural Development Discussion Paper 19, The World Bank, Washington DC.

Kareem, F. O., B. Brümmer, and I. Martinez-Zarzoso (2015), "Food safety standards, compliance and European Union's rejection of African exports: The role of domestic factors", *Global Food Discussion Papers*, No. 74, Georg-August-Universität Göttingen, Research Training Group (RTG) 1666 – GlobalFood, Göttingen. doi: 10.22004/ag.econ.211042

Kumar, C. Nalin (2016), "Sensitivity of India's Agri-food exports to the European Union: An institutional perspective", Working Paper No 366, Institute for Social and Economic Change, Bangalore.

Ministry of Commerce, *Foreign trade policy (2009–14 and 2015–20)*, Government of India, New Delhi.

Ministry of Commerce (2011), *Report of the task force on transaction cost in exports*. Ministry of Commerce, New Delhi.

Ministry of Commerce (2014), *Report of the second task force on transaction cost in exports, directorate general of foreign trade* (DGFT), Ministry of Commerce, New Delhi.

Press Information Bureau (2015), *DGFT notification dated 12th March 2015*, Government of India, New Delhi.

Press Information Bureau (2016), *Notification on SWIFT dated 19th August 2016*. Government of India, New Delhi.

Sen, A. (2019), "India wants EU to relax sampling norms for fish exports, reduce clearance time", *The Hindu Business Line*, March 29, 2019.

Sen, A. (2020), "TCPI: Make labs accountable for rejection of food exports by US, EU", *The Hindu Business Line*, January 04, 2020.

Sengupta, N. (2007), *The economics of trade facilitation*, Oxford University Press, New Delhi.

Suneja, K. (2019), "India ropes in global institution to curb contamination in spice shipments", *Economic Times*, May 18, 2019.

United States Food and Drug Administration (FDA) (2014–2018), *OASIS database*. Available at Import Refusal Report (fda.gov).

Wilson, J., and T. Otsuki (2003), "Balancing risk reduction and benefits from trade in setting standards", In: Unnevehr, L. J. (Ed.) *Food safety in food security and food trade*. A 2020 Vision for Food, Agriculture, and the Environment, IFPRI, Washington, DC.

Wilson, J. S., C. L. Mann, and T. Otsuki (2003), "Trade facilitation and economic development: A new approach to quantifying the impact", *World Bank Economic Review*, Vol. 17 (3), 367–389.

World Bank (2018–2020), *Ease of doing business report*, World Bank and International Finance Corporation, Washington, DC.

PART III

Financial sector developments

12

TERMS OF REFERENCE OF THE FIFTEENTH FINANCE COMMISSION

Use of 2011 population and horizontal inequality

Pinaki Chakraborty and Manish Gupta

Public services which are at the core of a more equitable social order and human resource development are population centric. The shift to latest demographics is necessary since public expenditures by states and therefore their needs are related to current population.

Introduction

Fifteenth Finance Commission's terms of reference (ToR) have evoked a sharp response from the southern states. The ToR[1] mandates the Commission to use the 2011 population for tax sharing and devolution of resources instead of the 1971 population as was the practice in the past. Between 1971 and 2011, with the exception of Telangana, the population shares of the four southern states Andhra Pradesh, Karnataka, Kerala and Tamil Nadu have declined from 22.01 to 18.147 per cent. It has been pointed out that, other things remaining the same, the use of the 2011 population for sharing of tax revenues by the Commission would result in a decline in the flow of resources to these states. However, there is a need to widen this debate beyond the southern states. Between 1971 and 2011, the population shares of ten states have declined, including the four southern states. The other six states are Assam, Goa, Himachal Pradesh, Odisha, Punjab and West Bengal.[2] Thus, the use of the 2011 population would also adversely affect these states and some among them, for example, Assam, Odisha and West Bengal are economically less prosperous.

In the context of the use of the 2011 population, what the Fourteenth FC did was significant. In addition to assigning a weight of 17.5 per cent to the 1971 population in the tax sharing formula, the Commission gave 10 per cent weightage to the 2011 population to reflect a demographic change. This did not result in a decline in tax shares of the ten states that had experienced a decline in population share between 1971 and 2011. Thus, it is too early to make a judgement about the outcome of the use of the 2011 population on resource sharing by the Fifteenth FC.

It is in this context, the chapter examines the likely implications of the use of the 2011 population by the Fifteenth FC. It seeks to address the following question: will the use of the

 DOI: 10.4324/9780367855741-12

2011 population result in a decline in the inter se shares of states that experienced a decline in population shares between 1971 and 2011? Hypothetical scenarios are developed to examine the likely implication of the use of current/latest population numbers on the shares of states.

The rest of the chapter is organised as follows: the next section examines the use of population as a criterion by the FCs in India for the distribution of shared taxes with the states. Until the mid-1970s (i.e., till the Sixth FC), FCs in India had used the latest population numbers in determining states' share in shareable taxes. In many federal countries, population (latest population) has been used as one of the criteria for sharing of revenues between federal and provincial governments. The third section presents the cross country experience in the use of population criteria. The fourth section presents the views of different states in India on the use of population criteria – whether to use the 1971 population or the latest 2011 population. The fifth section examines in detail the reasons for the decline in the share of southern states in the shareable taxes since the Eleventh FC.[3,4] To what extent is the population criterion responsible for this decline? The sixth section presents hypothetical scenarios using the latest and current population to examine the likely impact on the inter se shares of states. The final section provides concluding observations.

Population criteria and Finance Commissions

The FCs in India have been using a number of criteria for inter se determination of shares of taxes to state governments. Population being a neutral indicator of need has been used by all 14 FCs. The use of population in determining states' share in shareable taxes only ensures equal per capita transfers to all states and does not take into account the fiscal and cost disabilities arising due to asymmetries in the fiscal capacity of states.

There was a convention to use the latest census figures for distributing the shareable proceeds of taxes to the states until the mid-1970s. The Seventh FC was the first Commission which had a ToR mandating it to use the 1971 population while recommending the distribution of Union tax proceeds to states. This was the consequence of the Forty-Second Constitutional Amendment Act, 1976, which froze the seats in the National Parliament and the state Legislative Assemblies on the basis of the 1971 population until 2000 through amendment of the Articles 82 and 170(3) of the Constitution of India. The 42nd Amendment of the Constitution of India also placed the subjects of population control and family planning in the concurrent list. The National Family Welfare Policy of 1977, in order to give a fillip to the family welfare programme, stipulated the use of the 1971 population where population was a factor in the transfer of resources to states. This provision was to continue until 2001. In 2000, this clause was reviewed and through the enactment of the Constitution (84th Amendment) Act, 2001 it was extended up to 2026. The basic argument given in favour of using the 1971 population was that it would boost the family planning programme in the country. Hence, all FCs since the Seventh FC were bound by their ToR to use the 1971 population. The Fifteenth FC was constituted by a presidential order on 27 November 2018. The ToR of the Fifteenth FC states that 'the Commission shall use the population data of 2011 while making its recommendations'. This marks an important departure from the terms of reference of the earlier FCs.

The first seven FCs assigned weights ranging between 75 and 100 per cent to population (Figure 12.1).[5] From the Eighth FC onwards the emphasis of the FCs shifted more towards equity considerations and population was assigned a relatively lower weight. The weights assigned to population since the Eighth FC ranged between 20 and 27.5 per cent with the exception of the Eleventh FC, which assigned a weight of 10 per cent to population. The criteria and weights used by the fourteen FCs is presented in annexure Table 12A.2.[6]

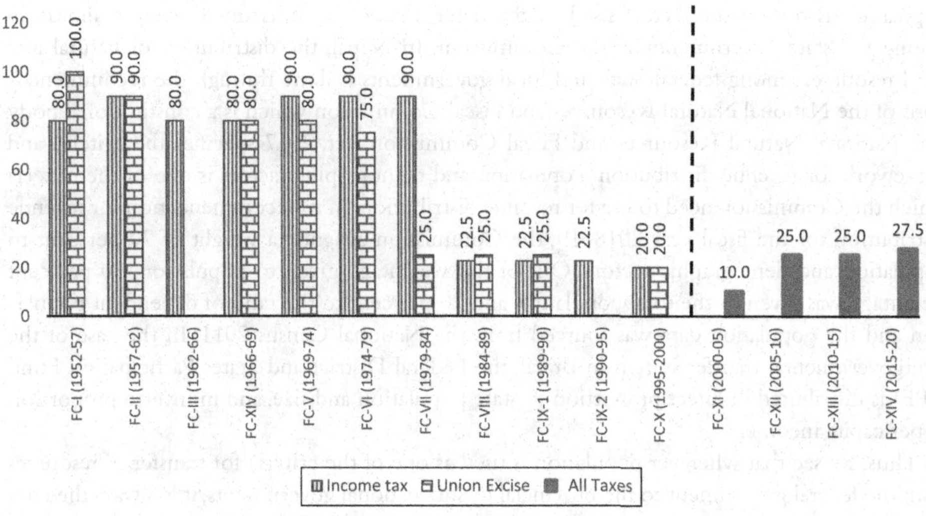

Figure 12.1 Weights (in %) Assigned to Population by the Finance Commissions in determining inter se shares of states. *Note*: 1) Prior to the Eleventh FC, only two taxes Income Tax and Union Excise Duties were shared with the states. However, from Eleventh FC onwards all central taxes became part of the divisible pool to be shared with the states; 2) Population share of 27.5 per cent in case of Fourteenth FC includes both 1971 population (17.5 per cent weight) and demographic change (10 per cent weight). *Source*: Reports of the various Finance Commissions.

Population criterion: cross country experience

Population has been used as one of the criteria for sharing of revenues between federal and provincial governments in many federations. In the case of Kenya, the Commission on Revenue Allocation,[7] which is an independent Commission set up under Article 215 of the Constitution of Kenya 2010, has in its second revenue sharing formula for the period 2016–17 to 2018–19 used six parameters including population. Population was assigned a weight of 45 per cent. In its first revenue sharing formula (for the financial year 2012–13 to 2015–16) population was assigned a weight of 45 per cent. Similarly, in the case of South Africa, the sharing of revenues between federal and provincial governments is done through the recommendations of the Financial and Fiscal Commission[8] which is a permanent statutory body established in terms of section 220 of Constitution, 1996 and the Financial and Fiscal Commission Act, 1997. For horizontal distribution of national revenues, the Commission uses a number of criteria including population share of provinces (called the Basic share) and assigned it a weight of 16 per cent (in 2014). In the case of Pakistan, the 7th National Finance Commission (NFC), which is the latest Commission whose award is in operation, have used population as one of the criteria of horizontal distribution of revenues between federal and provincial governments and assigned it a weight of 82 per cent.[9] In Indonesia, the *Dana Alokasi Umum* (DAU) or the general allocation funds is the biggest component of the fiscal equalisation fund.[10] The horizontal distribution of DAU among the provinces is based on fiscal need which comprises a number of parameters including population which is assigned a weight of 30 per cent. In the case of Nigeria, the Revenue Mobilization Allocation and Fiscal Commission, a federal government agency was established in 1989 by Decree No. 49 to administer fiscal transfers across levels of government and to provide advice on mobilising revenue at the state and local levels. Current population is one of the factors used in the determination of horizontal revenue allocation among the state governments by the Commission. In Nepal, the distribution of natural and fiscal resources among federal, state and local governments is done through the recommendations of the National Natural Resources and Fiscal Commission which is a constitutional body. The National Natural Resources and Fiscal Commission Act, 2017 specifies the criteria and framework for revenue distribution. Population and demographic factors is one of the criteria which the Commission need to use for revenue distribution. In its recommendation for revenue distribution for the fiscal year 2018–19, the Commission assigned a weight of 70 per cent to population and demographic factors. Out of the weightage given to population, 80 per cent weightage was given to the total population and 20 per cent to the ratio of dependent population and the population data was sourced from the National Census 2011. In the case of the intergovernmental transfer system in Brazil, the Federal District and States Participation Fund (FPE) is distributed in direct proportion to state population and size, and in inverse proportion to per capita income.

Thus, we see that wherever population is used as one of the criteria for transfer of resources from the federal government to the provincial or sub-national governments, it is always the current or latest available population. In that context, the use of dated population is unique to the Indian transfer system.

States' views on population: 2011 or 1971

The use of the 2011 population as mandated by the ToR of the Fifteenth FC has created a divide among states. We review the formal views of states on the use of population as submitted by them to the Thirteenth and Fourteenth FCs. In their memorandum submitted to the Fourteenth FC, many states have suggested using population numbers based on the latest census as public goods and services have to be provided to the entire population while others have suggested continuation of the use of the 1971 population. The latter group argued that the use of the latest population figures would penalise those states that have taken effective population control measures. One of the states, in its memorandum to the Fourteenth FC suggested that as growing urbanisation imposed additional challenges in terms of providing services to its population, additional weight should be assigned to states where population has grown rapidly and which are also urbanising at a fast pace. Since short-term migration was not captured in the Census estimates, the state had argued that a proxy parameter like growth in urban population could be used as an indicator for inter se distribution, thereby implying using the latest census population (i.e., the 2011 census). Within the population criteria, there have been suggestions by states for assigning additional weights to the scheduled caste/scheduled tribe population in order to introduce an element of equity. The views of the state governments with respect to the population criteria and its variants as submitted by them to the Fourteenth FC are presented in Table 12.1.

From Table 12.1 one can see that 13 states were in favour of using the 1971 population while nine states had suggested using the 2011 census population numbers; seven states did not suggest which population numbers to use in their memoranda to the Commission. The prominent ones in this category are Kerala and Odisha. While Odisha was in favour of using a composite of SC/ST population, Kerala suggested that there was a need to redefine population criterion by incorporating cost disabilities imposed by the share of aged population in the total population, level of urbanisation, forest area and effective population density.

The report of the Thirteenth FC mentioned that some of the states in their memoranda submitted to the Commission were in favour of using the latest census population (i.e., 2001

Table 12.1 Population criteria and weights (in %) suggested by states in their memoranda to the Fourteenth Finance Commission

States	*Population 1971*	*Population 2011*	*Composite urban population*	*Composite SC/ST population*	*Dispersal of population within the state*	*Population growth between 1971 and 2011*
(1)	*(2)*	*(3)*	*(4)*	*(5)*	*(6)*	*(7)*
Andhra Pradesh	30					
Arunachal Pradesh						
Assam	10			5	5	
Bihar		20				
Chhattisgarh		15				
Goa	25					
Gujarat		25				
Haryana		40				
Himachal Pradesh	20					
Jammu & Kashmir	10					
Jharkhand	10			5		5
Karnataka	20		10			
Kerala						
Madhya Pradesh		10				
Maharashtra	35					
Manipur						
Meghalaya		10				
Mizoram						
Nagaland						
Odisha				20		
Punjab	35			15		
Rajasthan	25					
Sikkim		20				
Tamil Nadu	33.3					

(*Continued*)

Table 12.1 (Continued)

States	*Population 1971*	*Population 2011*	*Composite urban population*	*Composite SC/ST population*	*Dispersal of population within the state*	*Population growth between 1971 and 2011*
(1)	*(2)*	*(3)*	*(4)*	*(5)*	*(6)*	*(7)*
Telangana		25				
Tripura	15					
Uttar Pradesh		25				
Uttarakhand						
West Bengal	30					
No. of states	**13**	**9**	**1**	**4**	**1**	**1**

Source: Report of the Fourteenth Finance Commission.

population) while others had urged the Commission to use the 1971 population. The report, however, did not provide the names of states that were in favour of the 1971 or 2001 population. Our examination of the memorandum submitted by individual states to the Commission revealed that four states (Andhra Pradesh, Karnataka, Kerala and Tamil Nadu – the southern states) suggested using the 1971 population while Gujarat, Haryana, Jammu and Kashmir and Sikkim (four states) suggested using the 2001 population. Uttarakhand was averse to the use of the 1971 population while Maharashtra had no issues with the 1971 population but both the states did not explicitly mention their preferences in their respective memoranda. Assam, Odisha and Chhattisgarh were not in favour of the use of population criteria per se. Thus, from the examination of memoranda of the states to the Thirteenth and Fourteenth FCs, we observed that there was no uniformity among the states with respect to the use of population criteria. However, the southern states had expressed their preference for the use of the 1971 population.

Interpreting southern states' opposition

It has been pointed out that the shares of the southern states have been declining since the Eleventh FC and the use of the 2011 population would further reduce their shares in tax devolution. The shares of southern states in the inter se distribution of tax revenues have declined from 21.073 per cent in case of the Eleventh FC to 19.785 per cent under the Twelfth FC. It further declined to 18.575 per cent under the Thirteenth FC and was 17.978 per cent under the Fourteenth FC. It is important to understand the reasons for the decline in their shares.

FCs have used a number of criteria for inter se distribution of tax revenues among states (see annexure Table 12A.2 for the criteria used by the FCs starting from the First FC). We have grouped the criteria adopted by the last four FCs (i.e., Eleventh to the Fourteenth FC) into four broad categories, namely: (a) need (consisting of population, area and demographic change); (b) equity (which includes income distance, fiscal capacity distance and index of infrastructure); (c) performance/efficiency (comprising tax effort and fiscal discipline) and (d) others (forest cover). These criteria along with the weights used by FCs from the Eleventh to the Fourteenth FC are presented in Figure 12.2. One can see that since the Eleventh FC, while the share of equity-based criteria in the distribution of tax revenues has declined, there was an increase in the share

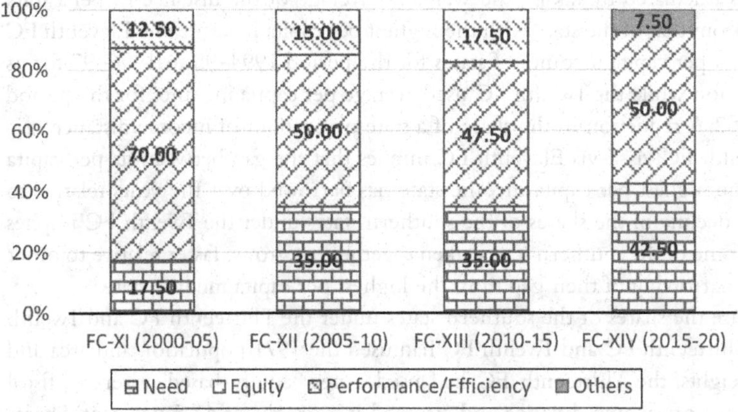

Figure 12.2 Criteria and weights for devolution of funds to states – FC-XI to FC-XIV. *Source*: Reports of the various Finance Commissions.

of need-based criteria like population, area etc. Efficiency/performance criterion which was used by the earlier three Commissions (i.e., Eleventh, Twelfth and Thirteenth FCs) was discontinued by the Fourteenth FC and a new criterion, forest cover, representing fiscal disabilities of states was introduced by the Commission.

The choice of criteria and their weights by the FCs have impacted the inter se shares of states. In order to examine the reasons for the decline in the shares of southern states we decompose their aggregate shares into shares under individual criteria used by FCs from the Eleventh to the Fourteenth. For this we have used the data provided in the reports of the respective FCs to derive the share of states under each of the criteria. Examination of the different criteria used by the Commissions reveals that need and equity are the two most important criteria being used by the Commissions, together accounting for 80 per cent or more weights being assigned to them. We, therefore, focus on these two sets of criteria while the remaining criteria (i.e., efficiency/performance-related criteria and others) are clubbed together as 'Others'. The shares of the southern states under different criteria used by FCs are presented in Table 12.2.

Let us examine the reasons for the decline in the shares of southern states from 21.073 per cent under the Eleventh FC to 19.785 per cent under the Twelfth FC. Although, a number of criteria used by the two Commissions were the same, namely, population (1971), area, income distance, fiscal discipline and tax effort, the weights assigned to these criteria by them were different. The Twelfth FC had assigned a relatively higher weight to the need-based criteria (population and area) while the Eleventh FC assigned more importance to the income distance (i.e., equity) criteria. Population, area and income distance together accounted for 80 per cent of the weight assigned by the Eleventh FC and 85 per cent by the Twelfth FC. Let us examine what would have happened to the shares of the southern states if Twelfth FC had assigned the same weights as the Eleventh FC to population, income distance, area and others criteria. Under this scenario the shares of the southern states at 18.899 per cent would have been lower than under the Eleventh FC mainly due to the decline in their shares under the income distance criteria (shares of southern states under the income distance criterion declined from 12.396 per cent under Eleventh FC to 9.683 per cent). Although the share of the southern states is higher under the other criteria, this increase is more than outweighed by the decline in their shares under income distance (see Table 12.2). Thus, the fall in southern states' share under the Twelfth FC vis-à-vis Eleventh FC can be attributed to the reduction in their shares under the income distance criterion.

Income distance is calculated by taking the weighted average of the distance of per capita income of each state from that of the state with the highest per capita income. The Eleventh FC had used the average of per capita incomes of states for the period 1994–95 to 1996–97 for its income distance criterion while the Twelfth FC used average per capita incomes for the period 1999–2000 to 2001–02. A reduction in the share of a state on account of income distance criterion under the Twelfth FC vis-à-vis Eleventh FC implies that the gap between its per capita income and that of the highest per capita income state has narrowed over the years relative to other states. Thus the decline in the shares of the southern states under the Twelfth FC implies that the per capita income of the southern states taken together has grown faster relative to other states resulting in the narrowing of their gap from the highest per capita income state.

Let us now compare the shares of the southern states under the Thirteenth FC and Twelfth FC. While both the Thirteenth FC and Twelfth FC had used the 1971 population and area and assigned the same weights, the Thirteenth FC had used a new equity-based criterion, fiscal capacity distance instead of income distance and assigned it a weight of 47.5 per cent. Shares of the southern states under the Thirteenth FC at 18.575 per cent were lower than their shares under the Twelfth FC.[11] If we assume that the Thirteenth FC had assigned the same weights as

Table 12.2 Shares of southern states (in %)

	Criteria	*1971 population*	*Income distance*	*Area*		*Others*	*Total*
Eleventh FC	**Weights**	**10.0**	**62.5**	**7.5**		**20.0**	**100.0**
	Southern states' share	2.492	12.396	1.331		4.854	21.073
Twelfth FC	**Weights**	**25.0**	**50.0**	**10.0**		**15.0**	**100.0**
	Southern states' share	6.231	7.746	1.748		4.060	19.785
Twelfth FC with Eleventh FC weights	**Weights**	**10.0**	**62.5**	**7.5**		**20.0**	**100.0**
	Southern states' share	2.492	9.683	1.311		5.413	18.899
	Criteria	*1971 population*	*Fiscal capacity distance*	*Area*		*Others*	*Total*
	Weights	**25**	**47.5**	**10**		**17.5**	**100.0**
Thirteenth FC	Southern states' share	6.231	6.317	1.748		4.279	18.575
Thirteenth FC with Twelfth FC weights	**Weights**	**25.0**	**50.0**	**10.0**		**15.0**	**100.0**
	Southern states' share	6.231	6.649	1.748		3.668	18.296
	Criteria	*1971 population*	*Income distance*	*Area*	*Demographic change*	*Others*	*Total*
	Weights	**17.5**	**50.0**	**15.0**	**10.0**	**7.5**	**100.0**
Fourteenth FC	Southern states' share	4.362	7.501	2.622	2.110	1.383	17.978
Fourteenth FC with Twelfth FC weights (Scenario a)	**Weights**	**15.0**	**50.0**	**10.0**	**10.0**	**15.0**	**100.0**
	Southern States' share	3.739	7.501	1.748	2.110	2.766	17.864
Fourteenth FC with Twelfth FC weights (Scenario b)	**Weights**	**25.0**	**50.0**	**10.0**		**15.0**	**100.0**
	Southern states' share	6.231	7.501	1.748		2.766	18.246

Source: Authors' calculation using data from the reports of various Finance Commissions.
Note: Although index of infrastructure used by Eleventh FC is an indicator of equity, we have included it in the 'Others' category.

the Twelfth FC to the need and equity criteria, in such case the shares of the southern states at 18.296 would also have been lower than under the Twelfth FC. Thus we see that in the case of the Thirteenth FC, the decline in the shares of southern states as compared to the Twelfth FC was due to the use of a different equity criterion, fiscal capacity distance. In other words, the decline in the shares of southern states was on account of the equity criterion.

The Fourteenth FC, in addition to using the 1971 population (17.5 per cent), income distance (50 per cent) and area (15 per cent) had introduced a new criterion, demographic change, where for the first time the 2011 population was used for inter se distribution of national tax revenues. The Commission assigned a weight of 10 per cent to demographic change. The Fourteenth FC had used another criterion, forest cover, to reflect fiscal disabilities of states and assigned it a weight of 7.5 per cent. The share of the southern states in the inter se distribution was 17.978 per cent which was lower than their shares under the previous three FCs (Table 12.2). Let us consider a scenario where we assume that the Fourteenth FC had assigned weights to population, area and income distance criteria similar to those assigned by the Twelfth FC. Here we consider two sub-scenarios, namely, (a) we assign 15 per cent weight to the 1971 population, 10 per cent to the 2011 population (i.e., to demographic change), 10 per cent of area and 50 per cent to income distance and (b) we assign 25 per cent weight to the 1971 population and no weight to demographic change, 10 per cent of area and 50 per cent to income distance. These are presented in Table 12.2. In the first scenario the shares of the southern states would be 17.864 per cent while in the other scenario their shares would be 17.846 per cent. In both cases the shares of southern states would have been lower vis-à-vis the Twelfth FC and the difference is on account of equity (i.e., income distance) and 'others' criteria. In the case of the Twelfth FC, the criterion 'Others' comprised of tax effort and fiscal discipline (i.e., efficiency/performance criteria) while in the case of the Fourteenth FC, it included forest cover.

Thus, it is evident from the above discussion that the reduction in the inter se shares of the southern states since the Eleventh FC is mainly on account of equity criteria used by successive FCs. This means that the gap between the per capita income of the southern states and the state with the highest per capita income in the country has narrowed down over the years relative to the other states. In other words, during this period the southern states have grown at a faster rate relative to the rest of the states.

Some hypothetical scenarios

In the last four decades since 1971, the demographic composition of states has undergone considerable change. While some states have achieved replacement level fertility, others still have a very high total fertility rate. Migration is also an important factor that affects the population of states apart from natural factors like fertility and mortality. It imposes a burden on the destination state. Migration can happen due to both pull factors and push factors. Use of the 1971 population ignores all these factors affecting the demographic composition of states and therefore does not reflect the true fiscal needs of a state. Public services which are at the core of a more equitable social order and human resource development are population centric. The shift to the latest demographics is necessary since public expenditures by states and therefore their needs are related to the current population. It is important to factor in the changing demographic realities while deciding on the allocation of resources across states. This was for the first time explicitly recognised by the ToR of the Fourteenth FC which stated that 'the Commission may also take into account the demographic changes that have taken place subsequent to 1971'.

FCs have to make an assessment of the needs of states for their award period which in the case of the Fourteenth FC is the period from 2020–21 to 2024–25. The Commission should ideally use the (projected) population of states for each of the years of its award period to assess the needs of states. Or it can use the average of the (projected) population of states during its award period. Another option is to use the population of the mid-year of the award period of the Commission. We generate three hypothetical scenarios to examine the likely impact on the inter se shares of states.

Scenario-1 (using 2011 population)

Population is a neutral indicator of the quantum of public services that are needed. Use of latest population figures makes an assessment of expenditure needs more realistic. In case the current population is not available, then the next best alternative is to use the latest available population figures which in our case is the 2011 census population. In this scenario we use the 2011 population.

Using the data provided by the Fourteenth FC in its report we construct a scenario where we use the same set of criteria and weights that was used by the Commission but instead of using the 1971 population we use the 2011 population. In other words, wherever directly or indirectly the Commission had used the 1971 population we replace it with the 2011 population and derive the shares of states. We call this scenario-1. The 1971 population was used by the Commission in the following criteria: population (direct use) and income distance (indirect use[12]). We compare the state-specific shares thus obtained with those recommended by the Fourteenth FC and Thirteenth FC. The results are presented in Table 12.3. Column 4 gives the inter se shares of states under our hypothetical scenario-1 while columns 5 and 6 show the differences in states' shares under scenario-1 and those recommended by the Fourteenth FC and Thirteenth FC, respectively.

From Table 12.3 one can see that the share of southern states as a group has declined while that of NE&H states has increased under scenario-1 when compared with those under Thirteenth FC and Fourteenth FC. However, the change in the shares of individual southern states is not in the same direction when we compare scenario-1 with the Thirteenth FC and Fourteenth FC. For example, with the use of the 2011 population under scenario-1, the share of Karnataka is higher than that recommended by the Thirteenth FC which had used the 1971 population but was lower than that under the Fourteenth FC which had used a combination of 1971 and 2011 population numbers. Similarly, we find that the change in the shares of some states like Uttar Pradesh, Bihar, Chhattisgarh, which are some of the poorer states, is not in the same direction when we compare scenario-1 with the Thirteenth FC and Fourteenth FC. In other words, use of the 2011 population may not necessarily result in a decrease in the shares of each of the southern states. The final outcome, however, would depend on the choice of criteria and weights used by the Commission and is not necessarily dependent on the use of population numbers only.

Scenarios-2 and 3 (using mid-FC award period population)

For a more realistic assessment of the expenditures needs of states it is important to use current population numbers. This means using population numbers for states pertaining to each year of the award period of the Commission. Alternatively, one can use the population of the mid-year of the award period of the Commission. In the case of Fourteenth FC, the mid-year of its award period was 2017–18 and in the case of the Fifteenth FC it is 2022–23. We construct a

Table 12.3 Change in inter se shares of states

States	*Thirteenth FC shares (%)*	*Fourteenth FC shares (%)*	*Scenario-1 shares (%)*	*Difference in Shares*	
				(Scenario-1) – (Fourteenth FC)	*(Scenario-1) – (Thirteenth FC)*
(1)	*(2)*	*(3)*	*(4)*	*(5)*	*(6)*
Andhra Pradesh	6.937	4.305	3.685	**–0.620**	**–0.821**
Arunachal Pradesh	0.328	1.370	1.384	0.014	1.056
Assam	3.628	3.311	3.180	**–0.131**	**–0.448**
Bihar	10.917	9.665	10.472	0.807	**–0.445**
Chhattisgarh	2.470	3.080	3.042	**–0.038**	0.572
Goa	0.266	0.378	0.370	**–0.008**	0.104
Gujarat	3.041	3.084	3.112	0.028	0.071
Haryana	1.048	1.084	1.160	0.077	0.112
Himachal Pradesh	0.781	0.713	0.712	**–0.001**	**–0.069**
Jammu & Kashmir	1.551	1.854	1.988	0.133	0.437
Jharkhand	2.802	3.139	3.209	0.070	0.407
Karnataka	4.328	4.713	4.500	**–0.213**	0.172
Kerala	2.341	2.500	1.986	**–0.514**	**–0.355**
Madhya Pradesh	7.120	7.548	7.918	0.371	0.798
Maharashtra	5.199	5.521	5.529	0.008	0.330
Manipur	0.451	0.617	0.628	0.011	0.177
Meghalaya	0.408	0.642	0.680	0.038	0.272
Mizoram	0.269	0.460	0.477	0.017	0.208
Nagaland	0.314	0.498	0.545	0.047	0.231
Odisha	4.779	4.642	4.172	**–0.470**	**–0.607**
Punjab	1.389	1.577	1.491	**–0.086**	0.102
Rajasthan	5.853	5.495	6.138	0.643	0.285
Sikkim	0.239	0.367	0.371	0.004	0.132
Tamil Nadu	4.969	4.023	3.453	**–0.570**	**–1.516**
Telangana	–	2.437	2.430	**–0.007**	–
Tripura	0.511	0.642	0.653	0.011	0.142
Uttar Pradesh	19.677	17.959	18.843	0.884	**–0.834**
Uttarakhand	1.120	1.052	1.054	0.002	**–0.066**
West Bengal	7.264	7.324	6.816	**–0.509**	**–0.448**
All states	**100.000**	**100.000**	**100.000**	–	–
Southern states	18.575	17.978	16.055	**–1.923**	**–2.520**
NE&H states	9.600	11.527	11.673	0.146	2.073

Source: Author's calculation based on the Reports of the Thirteenth and Fourteenth FCs.

Note: (1) Negative value in columns 5 and 6 indicate a decline in state's share under the hypothetical scenario as compared to Fourteenth FC and Thirteenth FC recommended shares, respectively. (2) In column 6, the change in Andhra Pradesh's in computed by taking the combined share of Andhra Pradesh and Telangana under the hypothetical scenario.

scenario to examine what would happen to states' inter se shares if the Fourteenth FC had used 2017–18 population numbers. We call this scenario-2. We also examine what would happen if the Fifteenth FC were to use similar criteria and weights that were used by the FC-XIV but with some modifications. We use the 2022–23 population wherever the Fourteenth FC had used the 1971 and 2011 populations, update the income distance criteria by taking 2015–16 per capita income of states and also, for forest cover criteria, use the latest forest cover data published by Forest Survey of India. This is our scenario-3.

The results of the two hypothetical scenarios, scenario-2 and scenario-3 are presented in Table 12.4. We compare the outcome of the two hypothetical scenarios with the inter se shares recommended by the Eleventh, Twelfth, Thirteenth and Fourteenth FC.

Our results show that while the shares of the southern states declined in scenario-2 and scenario-3, the use of mid-award year population would not necessarily result in the redistribution of resources in favour of poorer states. The share of Bihar (undivided Bihar) at 14.597 per cent under the Eleventh FC was higher vis-à-vis that under scenario-2 (13.877 per cent) but marginally lower than that under scenario-3 (14.826 per cent). The Eleventh FC had assigned a weight of 62.5 per cent to the income distance criteria and 10 per cent to population. Similarly, the shares of UP (undivided UP) under the Twelfth FC and Thirteenth FC were higher than that under scenario-2 but marginally lower than that in scenario-3. The Twelfth FC had assigned a weight of 50 per cent to income distance and 25 per cent to the 1971 population while the Thirteenth FC had used a new indicator, fiscal capacity distance instead of income distance and assigned it a weight of 47.5 per cent and 25 per cent weight was assigned to the 1971 population. Although the shares of the southern states have declined, the benefits of this redistribution have accrued to other states and were not necessarily confined to the northern states or the poorer states only. Although the use of the current or 2011 census population can be seen to be adversely affecting the transfer of resources to states that have reduced the population growth, the inter se shares of states would eventually depend on the choice of criteria and weights that the Fifteenth FC decides to use.

Moreover, a balancing provision in the ToR of the Fifteenth FC is that the Commission is also mandated to propose measurable performance-based incentives in the progress made by a state towards replacement rate of population growth, which refers to the total fertility rate that will result in a stable population without increasing or decreasing it. While several states have achieved the replacement rate of population growth, there would be many states that still have to make efforts towards achieving this. Given that performance is measured ex-post, the Commission can devise ways to reward states that have already achieved replacement rate of population growth more as compared to those that have not. The Commission can suggest an appropriate grants mechanism to reward these states or use it as one of the criteria for determining inter se shares of states. Finally, it is the Commission that will have to decide on taking a comprehensive view of the commonalities and special characteristics of individual states while making an assessment of the need and at the same time adhering to its ToR and make recommendations that are in the interest of both the Union and the state governments.

Concluding observation

Thus to conclude, it is premature to assume that states where population share has declined will receive lower transfers. It would depend on how the Fifteenth FC views this component of the ToR and suggests mechanisms to ensure fairness, stability and predictability in the transfers recommended by it. The fundamental question here is not about state-specific

Table 12.4 Inter se shares of states under scenarios-2 and 3

States	*Eleventh FC shares*	*Twelfth FC shares*	*Thirteenth FC shares*	*Fourteenth FC shares*	*Scenario-2*	*Scenario-3*
(1)	*(2)*	*(3)*	*(4)*	*(5)*	*(6)*	*(7)*
Andhra Pradesh	7.701	7.356	6.937	4.305	3.539	3.403
Arunachal Pradesh	0.244	0.288	0.328	1.370	1.387	1.366
Assam	3.285	3.235	3.628	3.311	3.169	3.144
Bihar	14.597	11.028	10.917	9.665	10.618	11.372
Chhattisgarh	–	2.654	2.470	3.080	3.073	3.086
Goa	0.206	0.259	0.266	0.378	0.368	0.360
Gujarat	2.821	3.569	3.041	3.084	3.112	2.917
Haryana	0.944	1.075	1.048	1.084	1.166	1.052
Himachal Pradesh	0.683	0.522	0.781	0.713	0.706	0.712
Jammu & Kashmir	1.290	1.297	1.551	1.854	1.998	2.031
Jharkhand	–	3.361	2.802	3.139	3.259	3.454
Karnataka	4.930	4.459	4.328	4.713	4.445	3.292
Kerala	3.057	2.665	2.341	2.500	1.907	1.475
Madhya Pradesh	8.838	6.711	7.120	7.548	7.962	8.132
Maharashtra	4.632	4.997	5.199	5.521	5.498	4.960
Manipur	0.366	0.362	0.451	0.617	0.662	0.715
Meghalaya	0.342	0.371	0.408	0.642	0.690	0.737
Mizoram	0.198	0.239	0.269	0.460	0.479	0.471
Nagaland	0.220	0.263	0.314	0.498	0.543	0.542
Orissa	5.056	5.161	4.779	4.642	4.106	4.366
Punjab	1.147	1.299	1.389	1.577	1.489	1.656
Rajasthan	5.473	5.609	5.853	5.495	6.167	6.268
Sikkim	0.184	0.227	0.239	0.367	0.371	0.367
Tamil Nadu	5.385	5.305	4.969	4.023	3.384	3.316
Telangana	–	–	–	2.437	2.404	1.926
Tripura	0.487	0.428	0.511	0.642	0.651	0.673
Uttar Pradesh	19.798	19.264	19.677	17.959	19.044	19.918
Uttarakhand	–	0.939	1.120	1.052	1.055	0.954
West Bengal	8.116	7.057	7.264	7.324	6.749	7.336
All states	**100.000**	**100.000**	**100.000**	**100.000**	**100.000**	**100.000**
Southern states	21.073	19.785	18.575	17.978	15.678	13.412
NE&H states	7.299	8.171	9.600	11.527	11.711	11.713
Other states	92.701	91.829	90.400	88.473	88.289	88.287
Bihar + Jharkhand	14.597	14.389	13.719	12.804	13.877	14.826
MP + Chhattisgarh	8.838	9.365	9.590	10.628	11.035	11.218
UP + Uttarakhand	19.798	20.203	20.797	19.011	20.099	20.872

Source: Author's calculation.

gain or loss due to the use of the 2011 population but the approach of the FC in dealing with the changes arising due to the ToR. The tax sharing formula used by some of the recent FCs was a combination of factors reflecting equity, need and efficiency. The ultimate outcome would, however, depend on how Commissions treat each of these factors in arriving at the horizontal allocation of resources.

The Fifteenth FC has been asked to propose measurable performance-based incentives for efforts and progress made by states in moving towards the replacement rate of population growth. To address this, the Commission may need to make a distinction between incentive and reward. Analytically, incentive is something in the absence of which things would not have happened the way they have actually happened. In this context, establishing the link between the use of the 1971 population as an incentive for the success of the family planning programme in states is hard to establish. The issue of fertility transition is complex and depends on a host of factors. Attributing the success of the family planning programme to the incentive design emanated due to the use of the 1971 population for resource sharing is incorrect. Secondly, when it comes to reward, it should always be ex-post performance. Since the decline in population in ten states and its adverse impact on resource transfers is real, designing an appropriate grant mechanism to reward these states should be done by the Union government. Is there a need to wait for an FC recommended incentive structure for that?

However, there is a fundamental question about the use of population for resource sharing purposes. For any FC which is required to assess the fiscal needs of states for the purpose of tax sharing and grants, one needs to ask whether such an assessment requires the use of population. If the answer is yes, then should the Commission be asked to use a particular reference population? Binding Commission's work to a particular reference population is arbitrary and unfair to all the stakeholders including the Commission. In that context, although the use of the 2011 population is important, the most fair criterion to assess need will be the current population.

Annexure

Table 12A.1 Change in population shares between 1971 and 2011

States	*Population 2011*		*Population 1971*		*Difference in shares (2011–1971)*
	In crore	*shares (%)*	*In crore*	*shares (%)*	
(1)	*(2)*	*(3)*	*(4)*	*(5)*	*(6)*
Andhra Pradesh	4.939	4.149	2.769	5.098	-0.949
Arunachal Pradesh	0.138	0.116	0.047	0.086	0.030
Assam	3.121	2.621	1.463	2.693	-0.072
Bihar	10.410	8.745	4.213	7.757	0.988
Chhattisgarh	2.555	2.146	1.164	2.143	0.003
Goa	0.146	0.123	0.080	0.146	-0.024
Gujarat	6.044	5.077	2.670	4.916	0.161
Haryana	2.535	2.130	1.004	1.848	0.282
Himachal Pradesh	0.686	0.577	0.346	0.637	–0.061
Jammu & Kashmir	1.254	1.053	0.462	0.850	0.203
Jharkhand	3.299	2.771	1.423	2.620	0.151
Karnataka	6.110	5.132	2.930	5.395	–0.263
Kerala	3.341	2.806	2.135	3.931	–1.125
Madhya Pradesh	7.263	6.101	3.002	5.527	0.574
Maharashtra	11.237	9.440	5.041	9.283	0.157
Manipur	0.257	0.216	0.107	0.198	0.018

Table 12A.1 (Continued)

States	*Population 2011*		*Population 1971*		*Difference in shares (2011–1971)*
	In crore	*shares (%)*	*In crore*	*shares (%)*	
(1)	*(2)*	*(3)*	*(4)*	*(5)*	*(6)*
Meghalaya	0.297	0.249	0.101	0.186	0.063
Mizoram	0.110	0.092	0.033	0.061	0.031
Nagaland	0.198	0.166	0.052	0.095	0.071
Odisha	4.197	3.526	2.194	4.041	–0.515
Punjab	2.774	2.330	1.355	2.495	–0.165
Rajasthan	6.855	5.758	2.577	4.744	1.014
Sikkim	0.061	0.051	0.021	0.039	0.013
Tamil Nadu	7.215	6.061	4.120	7.586	–1.526
Telangana	3.519	2.956	1.582	2.913	0.044
Tripura	0.367	0.309	0.156	0.287	0.022
Uttar Pradesh	19.981	16.785	8.385	15.439	1.345
Uttarakhand	1.009	0.847	0.449	0.827	0.020
West Bengal	9.128	7.667	4.431	8.159	–0.492
All states	**119.045**	**100.000**	**54.308**	**100.000**	
a) 4 Southern states (AP, Kar, Ker & TN)		18.147		22.010	–3.862
b) 6 states where 2011 population shares declined		16.844		18.172	–1.328
c) Remaining 19 states		65.008		59.818	5.190

Source: Population numbers are taken from the Report of the Fourteenth Finance Commission.
Note: Negative values in column 6 indicates a decline in population share of state in 2011 lower vis-à-vis 1971.

Table 12A.2 Criteria and weights (in %) used for tax devolution by Finance Commissions (FC-I to FC-XIV)

Finance Commission		*Population*	*Contribution*	*Unspecified*	*Backwardness*	*Income Distance*	*Inverse per capita income*	*Poverty*	*Revenue Equalisation*	*Non-plan Revenue deficit*	*Area adjusted*	*Infrastructure distance*	*Fiscal Discipline*	*Tax effort*	*Fiscal capacity Distance*	*Demographic Change*	*Forest cover*
First (1979–84)	Income Tax: 55%	80	20														
	Union Excise: 40%	100															
Second (1979–84)	Income Tax: 60%	90	10														
	Union Excise: 25%	90		10													
Third (1979–84)	Income Tax: 66.66%	80	20														
	Union Excise: 20%			100													
Fourth (1979–84)	Income Tax: 75%	80	20														
	Union Excise: 20%	80			20												
Fifth (1979–84)	Income Tax: 75%	90	10														
	Union Excise: 20%	80			6.66	13.34											
Sixth (1979–84)	Income Tax: 80%	90	10														
	Union Excise: 20%	75				25											
Seventh (1979–84)	Income Tax: 85%	90	10														
	Union Excise: 40%	25					25	25	25								

(*Continued*)

Table 12A.2 (Continued)

Finance Commission		*Population*	*Contribution*	*Unspecified*	*Backwardness*	*Income Distance*	*Inverse per capita income*	*Poverty*	*Revenue Equalisation*	*Non-plan Revenue deficit*	*Area adjusted*	*Infrastructure distance*	*Fiscal Discipline*	*Tax effort*	*Fiscal capacity Distance*	*Demographic Change*	*Forest cover*
Eighth (1984–89)	Income Tax: 85%	22.5	10			45	22.5										
	Union Excise: 45%	25				50	25										
Ninth (1989–90)	Income Tax: 85%	22.5	10			45	11.25	11.25									
	Union Excise: 40%	25				50	12.5	12.5									
Ninth (1990–95)	Income Tax: 85%	22.5	10		11.25	45	11.25										
	Union Excise: 45%									16.5							
Tenth (1995–2000)	Income Tax: 77.5%	20				60					5	5		10			
	Union Excise: 47.5%	20				60					5	5		10			
Eleventh (2000–05)	All Union Taxes: 29.5%	10				62.50					7.5	7.5	7.5	5			
Twelfth (2005–10)	All Union Taxes: 30.5%	25				50					10		7.5	7.5			
Thirteenth (2010–15)	All Union Taxes: 32%	25									10		17.5		47.5		
Fourteenth (2015–20)	All Union Taxes: 42%	17.5				50					15					10	7.5

Source: Reports of Finance Commissions (FC-I to FC-XIV).

Notes

1 The Presidential Order constituting the Finance Commission (FC) lists out the functions of the Commission. This constitutes the Terms of reference (ToR) of an FC. The Commission's ToR are specified in the Constitution under Article 280(3) of the Constitution of India. These are (a) the distribution between the Union and the states of the net proceeds of shareable taxes (prior to the 80th Constitutional Amendment in 2000, only Personal Income tax compulsorily and Union Excise duties, if needed and all taxes thereafter) and the allocation to each state its respective share; (b) principles which should govern the grants-in-aid of the revenues of the states out of the Consolidated Fund of India. Later two sub-clauses were added following the 73rd and 74th amendments of the Constitution in 1992 which required the Finance Commission to recommend measures needed to augment the Consolidated Fund of a state to supplement the resources of Panchayats and Municipalities in the state on the basis of the recommendations of the State Finance Commission. Finally, the President can refer any other matter to the Commission in the interest of sound finance.

2 Their shares in total population declined from 18.172 per cent to 16.844 per cent during this period. Annexure Table 12A.1 presents the change in population shares between 1971 and 2011.

3 Prior to the Eleventh FC, only two taxes – Income tax and Union Excise duties were shareable with the states. Calculating the share of each state in total devolution recommended by the Commissions prior to the Eleventh FC is not easy.

4 India initiated the process of economic reforms in 1991. One of the components of the reforms process was the restructuring of the tax system in the country which involved simplification of procedures and reduction in rates of income and corporation tax, selective reduction in excise duties and a substantial reduction in customs duties. The premise was that the tax reforms and better compliance would provide stimulus to growth which would more than offset the loss in revenues on account of rate cut. The Tenth FC recommended an alternative scheme of devolution where they designed a system of vertical resource sharing in which all central taxes are pooled and a proportion of it is devolved to the states. The Commission pointed out 'in the context of the current economic reforms, this new arrangement is likely to have distinct advantages over the present system' of sharing only two taxes.

In pursuit of the recommendation of the Tenth FC to the effect that the proceeds of all taxes to be shared, the 80th Amendment to the Constitution was carried out in 2000 which made a fundamental change in the pattern of sharing tax revenues. Article 270 of the Constitution was amended to include net proceeds of all taxes levied by the Union to be shared with states, with the exception of duties and taxes referred to in Articles 268, 269 and 269-A, surcharges, and any cess levied for a specific purpose under an Act of Parliament, and Article 272 was omitted. The Eleventh FC was the first Commission to recommended sharing a proportion of net proceeds of all central taxes with the states.

5 Though the Seventh FC assigned a weight of 90 per cent to population in determining the inter se shares for Income tax, the weight assigned by it to population in the sharing of Union Excise Duties was 25 per cent.

6 Prior to the Seventh FC, the distribution was largely based on population and jurisdictional contribution. Hence, these are not presented. For details see reports of FCs.

7 The core mandate of CRA is to recommend the basis for equitable sharing of revenues raised nationally between the national and the county governments, and among the county governments.

8 For more details see www.ffc.co.za/

9 Prior to 7th NFC, horizontal distribution of revenues was done on the basis of provincial populations shares only.

10 Funds transferred from the central government to regional governments are referred to collectively as fiscal equalisation funds.

11 The share of the southern states were 19.785 per cent under FC-XII.

12 The 1971 population was used to scale the income distance criterion. This we refer to as indirect use of population criterion.

Bibliography

Bhaskar, V. (2018), "Challenges before the Fifteenth Finance Commission", *Economic and Political Weekly*, Vol. 53, No. 10, pp. 39–46.

Chakraborty, Pinaki (2018), "15th Finance Commission: Is it just a South India vs North India debate?" *Mint*, 10 April. (URL: www.livemint.com/Opinion/HwPfh9cGN3BtWX2EJaUzcJ/15th-Finance-Commission-Is-it-just-a-South-India-vs-North-I.html)

Commission on Revenue Allocation (2016), *CRA Recommendation on the Criteria for Sharing Revenue among Counties for Financial Years 2016/2017, 2017/2018 and 2018/19*, Nairobi, Kenya, March.

Fadliya, and Ross H. McLeod (2010), "Fiscal transfers to regional governments in Indonesia", Working Papers in Trade and Development, WP No. 2010/14, Crawford School of Economics and Government, The Australian National University, Canberra, December.

Finance Commission (2000), *Report of the Eleventh Finance Commission (for 2000–2005)*, New Delhi.

Finance Commission (2004), *Report of the Twelfth Finance Commission 2005–2010*, New Delhi.

Finance Commission (2009), *Report of the Thirteenth Finance Commission 2010–2015*, New Delhi.

Finance Commission (2014), *Report of the Fourteenth Finance Commission*, New Delhi.

Forum of Federations, http://www.forumfed.org/

Ministry of Finance (2002), *Tax System and Administration in Brazil – An Overview*, Tax Study 08, Federal Revenue Service, Brasilia, August.

National Natural Resources and Fiscal Commission (2018), *Recommendations on the Revenue Distribution from Federal Government to the Provincial and Local Governments for the Fiscal Year 2018/19*, Kathmandu, June.

Reddy, G.R. (2018), "Upholding fiscal federalism: Terms of reference of the Fifteenth Finance Commission", *Economic and Political Weekly*, Vol. 53, No. 10, pp. 19–21.

Revenue Mobilization Allocation and Fiscal Commission, http://www.rmafc.gov.ng/, Nigeria.

Shah, A., R. Qibthiyyah, and A. Dita (2012), "General purpose central-provincial-local transfers (DAU) in Indonesia: From gap filling to ensuring fair access to essential public services for all", *Policy Research Working Paper* 6075, The World Bank, Jakarta, June.

Social Policy and Development Centre (2018), *A Study of Intergovernmental Fiscal Transfers in India and Pakistan*, SPDC, Karachi, January.

13

DYNAMICS OF GLOBALIZATION AND INFLATION IN POST-REFORM INDIA[1]

Madhabendra Sinha, Rishab Das, Sudhansu Sekhar Mahapatra, Abhijit Dutta and Partha Pratim Sengupta

Introduction

Stabilization of prices is one of the foremost goals of macroeconomic policies along with the achievement of a better rate of growth of output and full employment. Central banks of their respective nations partially judge their performances according to their abilities to keep inflation at a low level. Therefore, one question arises – why has managing inflation at a lower level been given such priority? When inflation occurs at a remarkably high rate, prices and wages are not increasing proportionately; the resultant inflation distorts the distribution of income. Moreover, variations in relative prices lead to uncertainty, which can make it more difficult for firms to make decisions for the future. The interaction between the inflationary price rising situation and the tax system distorts the decisions made by people. Taxes are imposed on the nominal values of commodities. As a result, a high rate of inflation leads to a very large tax burden on buyers. A high rate of inflation can affect the decision making of the people by confusing them to a larger extent. Under stable price conditions, it is easy to plan and invest in the long term, while volatility through a high rate of inflation makes people more short-sighted.

The last quarter of the twentieth century experienced wider assimilation of product and financial markets across the globe. The share of international trade in the gross domestic product (GDP) across the globe has been rising since the early 1970s, and there was an acceleration of this trend from the early 1990s. At the same time, the economies of Eastern Europe have integrated to a greater extent, and the South East Asian market economies (ASEAN) have appeared as important participants in the system of global trading. While the biggest impact in this phenomenon has been due to the opening up of their economies by China and India.

The economic openings of China and India have led to an enormous enhancement in the supply of labour around the globe at low cost. Thus many firms from the USA have moved their production units to these developing economies to bring down production costs. Not only the United States, but companies from countries such as Singapore, South Korea, Mexico and Taiwan, which were themselves low-cost producers at one point are shifting their bases to reap the benefits of low production costs elsewhere. It can also be observed that during the last two decades trade surpluses in China and other East Asian countries have grown significantly,

 DOI: 10.4324/9780367855741-13

and the ratio of the volume of imports to the volume of domestic production has increased evidently in the USA. Based upon these events there has been a decline in global inflation. Besides, the growing volume of trade through globalization has also reduced the unit costs of labour due to the increase in the productivity of labour, since for the rise in the production of goods and services resources are usually concentrated in the efficient sectors of production.

According to the database provided by the World Bank, inflation came down during the period starting from 1990 to early 2000, and the average rate of inflation in most industrialized countries has been moderately low since the early 1990s, reflecting the achievement of attaining price stabilization from the late 1970s and early 1980s. Specifically, the rates of inflation have been around 2 to 3 per cent, with very modest dispersion across the nations. On the contrary, the average in early 1989 was about 9 per cent with a wider dispersion. Inflation rates in industrial economies have also become less volatile. The average rates of inflation across the emerging economies have come down radically since the early 1990s, in many cases the rate of inflation has fallen from double- or triple-digit level to around 5 per cent. Import prices of non-oil commodities have come down by around 0.25 per cent a year in the advanced countries (International Monetary Fund (IMF), 2006).

The counter-narrative is that the same forces which steered the rate of inflation in this aforementioned period can potentially lead to a rise in prices. With greater integration of emerging countries in the global market, it can be observed that individuals in these countries have been raising their investments in the domestic economy and consuming a significant part of their wealth, and their real wages have improved through productivity gains in the earlier period. This leads to an improvement in domestic demand and that will come into better placement with their production capacity and declining cost advantages, and the countries will become less influential at exerting downward pressure on inflation globally (Kohn, 2006). For example, the massive consumer class in China and, to a lesser extent in India, makes gas more expensive for both countries. Inflation is highly influenced by energy prices. When energy costs remain elevated in the long run, their spillover effects on other sectors start to show up in the form of higher prices.

Monetary policy is another instrument that can be used to control inflation. Usually, the central bank raises the interest rate on borrowings for commercial banks. Owing to that, commercial banks have to increase the rate of interest on credit for people, resulting in the shifting of the preference of individuals from investment in new ventures to saving money. This would reduce the supply of money in the market and control inflation. Besides, the central bank may reduce the capacity of credit creation by commercial banks to manage inflation. Additionally, policy actions can manipulate the expectations regarding the future performance of the economy, with the expectation for wages and prices, and those expectations can influence current inflation directly.

Studies conducted by Buiter (2000), Ball and Moffitt (2001) and Kamin et al. (2004) have explained the recent performance of inflation quite differently, i.e., in terms of the improved credibility of the monetary policy and the broad efficiency gains of uncertain duration or cyclical situations. But Rogoff (2015) argued that globalization has amplified the incentive for central banks to maintain the rate of inflation at a low level. Additionally, fiscal policy is cited too as a tool for inflation control. The government can control inflation either by reducing private spending or by decreasing government expenditure under the fiscal policy, while some experts pin most of the credit of low inflation on greater productivity gains.

Inflation has remained outstandingly subdued despite a significant increase in commodity prices, a high rate of economic growth and also externally accommodating monetary policies in developing countries like India. The low and stable rate of inflation reflects global competition more intensively, which inhibits the producers from raising prices and putting pressure on wages to fall. Therefore, producers in developing countries with low production costs do continue to integrate the local economy into the global trading circulation, ensuring a low rate of inflation. As the reasons behind the recent movement of prices, another group of economists emphasizes the influence of the monetary policy, gains from the rise in productivity and other factors.

So, it can be argued that, in the existing literature on inflation, the complicated association between globalization and inflation is rather unexplored. In this regard, the case of the Indian economy has been a growing concern, where the globalization policy has brought a ground-breaking transformation from the inner-looking and import-substituting conventional policies to a more competitive and external oriented approach to integrate the nation with the globe. In this connection, the inflationary effect of economic liberalization in India is expected to be an imperative part of pieces of evidence to be included in the empirical documents on the macroeconomic returns of globalization. Therefore, researchers and policymakers should give prior attention to both external and internal market stabilization policies together for overall economic benefits. However, existing evidence does not highlight these issues properly, particularly in the Indian context. Against this backdrop, the present study empirically examines the impact of globalization on inflation in India by using the time series data collected from the Reserve Bank of India (RBI) over the period from 1991–92 to 2018–19 in a suitable causality framework.

The remainder of the chapter is structured as follows. The review of existing related literature on the topic is discussed in the next section and a brief description of inflation trends in India is given in the third section. Econometric methodologies used in the study are described carefully with the documentation of the data source. The final section summarizes and concludes the paper after the elaborate analysis of the empirical results in the earlier section.

Survey of literature

The literature examining the dynamic relationship between globalization and inflation is sparse. The study of Triffin and Grubel (1962) was the first endeavour to examine the relationship between trade openness and inflation based upon information on five advanced countries from the European Economic Community.[2] According to the finding of this study, a high degree of economic integration is likely to reduce inflationary price rising forces. Romer (1993) explained the reasons for the inverse relationship between trade openness and inflation. The study argued that 'when an economy is not open enough, then the incentive for expansion is greater and the equilibrium rate of inflation is higher'. Thus, the models predict an inverse relationship between inflation and openness.

Lane (1997) tried to relate the rate of time-consistent inflation with the extent of trade openness of a country and observed that the mechanism which links the developmental impacts of monetary policies (and therefore the inducements to inflate) to trade openness is not influenced by the terms of trade effect of large country but is somewhat due to the imperfectly competitive scenario and price rigidity of nominal type in the non-traded sector, and this prediction was also supported by the empirical evidence.

Ashra (2002) carried out a study based upon 15 developing countries from Latin America, South and East Asia, for three years using a panel data model. In this study international trade, i.e., the total value of exports and imports as a percentage of GDP, has been used as an indicator of the openness for all the countries in the panel. The findings of this study expose that international trade of goods and services had a considerable influence on the rate of inflation. Furthermore, it can be observed from the findings that there was a direct influence of the rise in exports on the inflationary price rising situation, but the association between imports and the rate of inflation is negative.

The key findings of the study of Kim and Beladi (2005) revealed an inverse relationship between trade openness and price levels, but it is only for developing countries, not for the developed countries. Therefore, the findings of the present study do not corroborate the findings of the study done by Triffin and Grubel (1962). Countries such as the USA, Belgium and Ireland have exhibited a direct impact of trade openness on price levels.

The International Monetary Fund (IMF, 2006) furnished a comprehensive data set on the global inflationary price rising trends since the 1970s. The empirical pieces of evidence found from these furnished data sets confirm the proposition that the moderating effects of globalization on domestic prices help in suppressing unit labour costs and labour compensation. Besides, the decline in the relative unit intermediate costs plays an important role in explaining the faster decline in relative prices of the manufacturing products.

Ciccarelli and Mojon (2010) argued that inflation across the industrial nations is mostly global and the rate of inflation within a particular country usually converges to this global rate of inflation. This finding deviates from the argument of general economic theory, i.e., monetary policy can control inflation. However, the argument in the study done by Woodford (2009) did not corroborate the findings of the previous study, as according to this argument globalization has not reduced the ability of the central banks to control domestic inflation of the respective country.

By using the multivariate cointegration technique and the model of vector error correction, Mukhtar (2012) found Romer's hypothesis, i.e., long-run inverse relationship between openness and inflationary price rising situation, on the Pakistan economy during the period 1960 to 2007. However, Zakaria (2011) used annual time series data from 1947 to 2007 and the generalized method of moments (GMM) in this study, where the results reveal a direct relationship between trade openness and inflation in Pakistan. However, according to the finding of this study, each of the other control variables, such as money supply, fiscal deficit, exchange rate depreciation, overseas inflation, terms of trade, foreign debt has an inverse relation with the rate of inflation in Pakistan. Therefore, the findings of these two studies provide us with contradictory outcomes if we only focus on the relationship between trade openness and inflation.

Neely and Rapach (2011) distinguished the global, regional and domestic components of inflation. Their findings illustrate that around half (49 per cent) of domestic inflation can be attributed to national factors, and the rest of domestic inflation is due to external reasons. This appears to be consistent with the general hypothesis for emerging economies where afflation is the most detrimental factor to price stability. Raj and Misra (2011) worked on core inflation in India. Results showed global supply-side shocks such as oil prices are reflected in domestic prices, leading to a belief that in the short run the central bank cannot manage the headline inflation entirely. Anand (2014) studied the effects of liberalization on macroeconomic indicators in India, showing that two factors that stood out in causing spillover of inflation into other sectors were oil prices and food inflation.

The major concerns associated with the available literature as discussed above are that no such empirical work is observed in India's context examining the long-run dynamic relationship between globalization and inflation. Moreover, methodologies applied and data period covered in existing pieces of evidence need to be revised and updated as per the present circumstances. In addition to that, a further study has to be conducted using the consumer price index (CPI) as the measure of inflation in place of the wholesale price index (WPI). Finally, along with the trade openness (trade to GDP ratio), FDI should also be taken into consideration while measuring the extent of globalization. This background encourages carrying out the present empirical study for accomplishing the earlier mentioned research gaps in the existing literature.

Trends of inflation in India

In India, inflation rates are usually cited in terms of the WPI for all commodities. The WPI is computed from 676 listed commodities, where these commodities are categorized into three groups, all of which have a different weight in inflation. Out of 676 commodities, 102 belonged to the category of 'Primary articles' (having weight 20.12 per cent), 19 belonged to the group of 'Fuel and power' (having weight 14.91 per cent). The remaining 555 items belonged to the group of 'Manufactured items' (bearing the weight 64.97 per cent). India used WPI as the measure for inflation but the CPI has been declared as the new benchmark to compute inflation (April 2014). CPI is usually assessed based on the monthly price fluctuations and based on a significant lag, which makes them unsuitable for policy use.

The economic strategies deployed by policymakers in India have been very unique since independence. It started with an inward-looking orientation based on state interventionism and import substitution as protectionist policies and then gradually moving towards greater integration with the world economy. In the years before the economic reforms introduced in 1991, inflation would show tumultuous variations. On some occasions crossing 25 per cent, several times higher than the average 4–5 per cent that has been the story since the turn of the millennium. Several reasons caused such problems at different periods, such as food shortage, the printing of excess money to support deficit financing and pay debts, wars, the influx of refugees in huge numbers, hoarding, black marketing, smuggling, increase in oil prices. Out of the earlier mentioned price-influencing factors, hike in foods and oil prices were significantly noticeable, since these two factors have spillover effects on other sectors of the economy. Studies have shown that over half of inflation in India has been contributed by food prices. What makes food inflation even more dangerous is the fear of facing food inflation which leads to activities such as hoarding. Often monetary and fiscal policies did not prove to be fruitful and the government had to resort to cracking down on hoarders.

It can be observed that during the 1970s in India, there were two oil price hikes, and the second case which happened in 1979–80 had a relatively larger influence on prices; even though the wholesale price index-based assessment of inflation reveals just the opposite fact, i.e., the first oil price hike had a greater impact on the general price level than that of the second oil price hike. The relatively lower inflationary price rising situation that followed the second oil shock was a consequence of the substantial and readily available food stocks, which enabled the nation to cope with the scarcity (RBI, 1980).

The 1980s was a period of continued high rates of inflation in India. The main reason behind this was the decision of the RBI to pay off the debts through the creation of money. The money supply grew at a higher rate to meet the fiscal deficit through the creation of money by the RBI,[3] resulting in the rate of inflation staying at a higher level during this decade. At the end of this decade, India was facing a severe crisis in its balance of payment (BOP), due to high inflation, high fiscal deficit and current account deficits and a tremendous increase in oil prices due to the Gulf war. Exports had slumped and foreign exchange reserves had fallen to alarmingly low levels. The IMF in return for the loan to free India from this crisis forced the government to bring about a slew of reforms in the economy. In 1991, the Indian government introduced the following reforms, such as liberalization of imports, acceptance of the flexible exchange rate system, convertibility of its currency, deregulation of interest rates, de-reservation of the public sector, abolition of the industrial licensing and the restrictive provision of the Monopolies and Restrictive Trade Practices (MRTP) Act, noticeable reduction in fiscal and revenue deficit, rejection of the practice of automatic monetization of the fiscal deficit, etc.

The commencement of the process of economic reforms did not pull down the inflationary price rising trends immediately. It remained high in the first half of the 1990s, and the rise in prices was attributable to the remarkable rise in fuel prices and administered prices of other items, and exchange rate adjustment in July 1991, which pushed up the price of imports. The scenario changed in the second half of the 1990s. Several factors brought about the change. RBI's policy of sterilizing the capital inflows through the open market sales of government securities, judicious use of the liquidity adjustment facility (LAF) and greater stress on the process market borrowing reduces the degree of monetization of fiscal deficit. Food inflation had come down, global inflation was low and depreciation of the Indian Rupee had jumped. The subsequent years saw a lengthened period of subdued inflation despite a significant increase in commodity prices and the high rate of economic growth. Inflation was no more as volatile as it used to be.

Inflation again started to move up towards the end of 2008; by 2012 it had crossed 12 per cent from a satisfactory 6.39 per cent in 2007. The reason for this rise in prices was again the usual suspects – food inflation and an increase in the price of crude oil. RBI took major steps to arrest this growing inflation. These included suppressing the easy flow of money to farmers by maintaining high interest rates. The curbing of such agricultural loans was seen as necessary because it was felt that they were resulting in an increase in rural wages. The RBI also raised the repo rate by 0.25 per cent to reach 8 per cent in January 2014. Instead of reducing the repo rate, the RBI reduced the statutory liquidity ratio (SLR) multiple times. Apart from these monetary measures other steps were taken such as dis-incentivizing the exports of agricultural products and introducing curbs on the grain stock. The slowdown in global inflation also helped the cause. These measures meant RBI met its inflation target well before its estimated dates.

As mentioned earlier, there is a consensus in the context of India that inflation is usually driven mostly through a rise in the price of primary goods or food articles. This view has been approved by scholars, researchers and common people over the years. This has created the possibility of the development of a completely new theory, i.e., the theory of structural inflation. The price rising situation in developing nations is quite different from developed ones, which cannot be explained either by the theory of demand–pull inflation or by the theory of cost–push inflation. Therefore, the structural theory of inflation has developed a separate theory to explain the inflationary price rising situation for developing nations. In the Indian context like other developing nations, a rise in the price of food grains raises wages in the industrial sector. Consequently, the cost of production in the industrial sector will rise, and the price of industrial products will rise. In the government sector of developing nations like India, the increase in prices and wages creates some additional non-developmental public expenditure. If the growth of public expenditure outpaces the growth of public revenues, then this will lead to an increase in budget deficits, and financing these deficits through the central bank's credit to the government affects inflation adversely.

Methods and data

There are different views about the effect of globalization on inflation. It is, therefore, necessary to investigate the dynamic relationship between these two variables in India as a developing country where inflation is the issue of concern for policymakers. So to explore the effect of globalization on inflation in India, the basic null hypothesis, to be tested empirically in this study, is: globalization does not have any dynamic impact on inflation in India.

We collect the quarterly data on consumer price index (CPI), trade openness (TRO), FDI inflow (FDI) and money supply (MSP) from the *Handbook of Statistics on Indian Economy* published by the RBI (2019) over the period of globalized India starting from 1991–92:Q1 to 2018–19:Q4. Data on GDP at factor cost at constant prices and per capita GDP (PCI) are also obtained from the RBI (2019) over the period from 1996–97:Q1 to 2018–19:Q4. For the earlier period from 1991–92:Q1 to 1995–96:Q4, the data on GDP and PCI are calculated by utilizing the data on the index of industrial production (IIP) collected from the same source. One thing that should be pointed out here is that the foreign exchange rate has been an important indicator of globalization; however, the current study does not use it as an independent regressor due to its strong possible linkage with trade openness, particularly in the case of the Indian economy. So, in order to explore the long-run dynamic linkage between globalization and inflation, empirical exercises of the study employ data on variables of CPI, TRO, FDI, MSP and PCI, collected from RBI (2019) over the period from 1991–92 to 2018–19. The study period is relevant from the aspects of globalization and econometric methodological points of view, as it looks at the long-term causal relationship. Table 13.1 summarizes all variables used in the study along with their definitions and data source.

The existence of a correlation among the successive observations is a common characteristic of the macro or time series variable/s. This correlation normally disappears in cross-section data and its analysis. For instance, there is a strong association between the current period's national income and the previous periods' national income of a country. As a result, a time series variable is likely to have the trend behaviours over times. However, there are two types of trends in the time series data. One is the stochastic trend and the other is the deterministic trend. Time series data contains the former trend if it has a unit root. If there is a stochastic trend, i.e., there is a unit root in the time series, then the straightforward estimation of the time series regression will provide misleading results. For this reason, first, we should be taking care of the problem of unit root in the time series variable, and test its existence in the time series by invoking the Augmented Dickey-Fuller (ADF) and Phillips-Perron (PP) unit root tests. In this study, we carry out the earlier mentioned unit root tests by incorporating the intercept parameter and the trend component in the ADF estimated relation for the time series variables. After incorporating both intercept and trend components in the ADF, the estimated relation for all time series variables used in our study can be presented as follows:

$$\Delta CPI_t = \varphi_{01} + \beta_1 t + \rho_1 CPI_{t-1} + \sum_{i=1}^{P} \gamma_i \Delta CPI_{t-1} + \varepsilon_{1t} \tag{13.1}$$

Table 13.1 Definitions and data source of variables

Variables	*Definitions*	*Source*
CPI	Consumer price index	*Handbook of Statistics on Indian Economy*, Reserve Bank of India (2019)
TRO	Trade openness [(Export + Import) ÷ GDP]	
FDI	Net inflows of foreign direct investment (FDI)	
MSP	Money Supply [Broad Money (M_2)]	
PCI	Per Capita GDP at factor cost at constant prices	

Source: Authors' presentation from RBI (2019) database

$$\Delta TRO_t = \varphi_{02} + \beta_2 t + \rho_2 TRO_{t-1} + \sum_{i=1}^{P} \gamma_i \Delta TRO_{t-1} + \varepsilon_{2t} \tag{13.2}$$

$$\Delta FDI_t = \varphi_{03} + \beta_3 t + \rho_3 FDI_{t-1} + \sum_{i=1}^{P} \gamma_i \Delta FDI_{t-1} + \varepsilon_{3t} \tag{13.3}$$

$$\Delta MSP_t = \varphi_{04} + \beta_4 t + \rho_4 MSP_{t-1} + \sum_{i=1}^{P} \gamma_i \Delta MSP_{t-1} + \varepsilon_{4t} \tag{13.4}$$

$$\Delta PCI_t = \varphi_{05} + \beta_5 t + \rho_5 PCI_{t-1} + \sum_{i=1}^{P} \gamma_i \Delta PCI_{t-1} + \varepsilon_{5t} \tag{13.5}$$

Equations (13.1) to (13.5) illustrate the equation required for the ADF unit root test, for the variables CPI, TRO, FDI, MSP and PCI, respectively. The ADF test statistic is the t-value of the estimated coefficient of ρ. The PP test is almost similar to the Dickey-Fuller (DF) unit root test; however, it is used in the non-parametric analysis. The test statistic in the PP test is also developed through the addition of a correction factor to the t statistic used in the DF test. The tests will be performed on their first-difference forms. It is noteworthy to state here that the choice of lag length is important for conducting the ADF unit root test.[4] We invoke the Engle and Granger (1987) theory of cointegration by utilizing the methodology developed by Johansen and Juselius (1990). The concept of cointegration was developed by Granger (1981), which is applied to recognize the long-term equilibrium relationships between the variables, in the sense that as the variables move together over time the short-term disturbances will be corrected from the long-term trend. Engle and Granger (1987) have shown that if two-time series are cointegrated, then there must be a causal link between the variables at least in one direction.

$$\begin{aligned} CPI_t = \theta + \sum_{i=1}^{p} \beta_i CPI_{t-i} + \sum_{j=1}^{r} \varphi_j TRO_{t-j} + \sum_{j=1}^{r} \pi_j FDI_{t-j} \\ + \sum_{j=1}^{r} \gamma_j MSP_{t-j} + \sum_{j=1}^{r} \eta_j PCI_{t-j} + \nu_t \end{aligned} \tag{13.6}$$

or,

$$\begin{aligned} \Delta CPI_t = \theta + \sum_{i=1}^{p} \beta_i \Delta CPI_{t-i} + \sum_{j=1}^{r} \varphi_j \Delta TRO_{t-j} + \sum_{j=1}^{r} \pi_j \Delta FDI_{t-j} \\ + \sum_{j=1}^{r} \gamma_j \Delta MSP_{t-j} + \sum_{j=1}^{r} \eta_j \Delta PCI_{t-j} + \delta ECM_{t-1} + \nu_t \end{aligned} \tag{13.6a}$$

Based on the null hypothesis to be tested in this study, we represent the model of cointegration and cointegration with error correction mechanism in equations (13.6) and (13.6a), respectively, where ν_t is the random disturbance with zero mean and serially uncorrelated. ECM denotes the error correction mechanism and the coefficient of that (δ) would represent the long-run equilibrium relationship among the variables on correcting the errors in short runs. We are supposed to apply Zivot and Andrews (2002) test to find the structural breaks as the study uses time series data.

Empirical results

The estimated values of the statistics derived from the ADF and PP unit root tests are reported in Table 13.2. It is revealed from these estimated values that the null hypothesis of the presence of unit roots is accepted for the original series, which indicates that all of the series of the variables of interest are non-stationary at level, and all of these series are integrated of order one, i.e. I(1), as their first differences are found to be stationary. It should be mentioned here that results of the structural break adjusted Zivot and Andrews (2002) test for all variables are almost the same as the results of the ADF and PP tests, and that is why the analysis can be carried out based on ADF and PP tests outcomes.

For examining the dynamic relationship between inflation and globalization along with other variables as mentioned in the previous section/s, we have invoked the theory of cointegration developed in Engle and Granger (1987). All of the variables of interest are having the same order of integration. Therefore, all of these variables are likely to have a common trend, and we can examine the possible cointegrating relation among these variables. For this reason, we apply a test for examining the cointegrating relationship. It can also be argued here that inflation, globalization and related variables in India follow the time trend.

The results of Johansen's cointegration test are reported in Table 13.3. Both trace or LR test statistics and eigenvalues are combined for checking the hypothesis on the presence of cointegrating relations. These findings recommend the existence of only one cointegrating equation, as trace and maximum eigenvalue report at 5 per cent level. Therefore, it can be concluded that there exists a long-run dynamic relationship between globalization and inflation in India.

Table 13.4 reports the results of the estimations of vector error correction models (VECM) containing the ECM terms in each equation. It is observed that the equation ofVECM, having CPI as the dependent variable and up to two-period lags values of TRO, FDI, MSP and PCI as explanatory regressors in their first-differenced forms, is statistically significant. So, findings depict that CPI is influenced by TRO and FDI with both one and two-period lags. PCI and MSP with one period lag also have a direct and significant effect on CPI. Results of another

Table 13.2 Estimated results of ADF and PP unit root tests

Series	*ADF test statistics*		*PP test statistics*	
	Level	*First difference*	*Level*	*First difference*
CPI	0.12	–4.32**	–0.52	–4.89***
TRO	0.39	–5.89***	0.38	–5.07**
FDI	–0.16	–4.99***	–0.22	–4.71**
MSP	0.99	–5.81***	0.42	–5.16**
PCI	–0.18	–4.53**	–0.11	–4.72***

Source: Estimation of authors using RBI (2019) database.
Note: ** and *** indicate significance at 5% and 1% levels, respectively.

Table 13.3 Estimated results of Johansen cointegration test

Unrestricted cointegration rank test

Tests	*Hypothesized no. of CE(s)*	*Eigenvalue*	*Statistic*	*5% Critical value*	*Probability***
Trace	None*	0.58	32.21	29.00	0.03
	At most 1*	0.30	12.90	10.01	0.02
	At most 2	0.02	0.25	4.91	0.19
	At most 3	0.03	0.28	4.88	0.22
	At most 4	0.02	2.51	4.22	0.19
Maximum eigenvalue	None*	0.56	21.98	20.66	0.03
	At most 1*	0.28	9.01	8.22	0.01
	At most 2	0.03	0.33	3.09	0.46
	At most 3	0.06	0.27	4.52	0.23
	At most 4	0.02	1.61	4.24	0.26

Trace and max-eigenvalue tests indicate 1 cointegrating equation(s) at 5% level.
* indicates the rejection of the null hypothesis at 5% level.
** indicates the MacKinnon-Haug-Michelis (1999) p-values.

Source: Estimation of authors using RBI (2019) database.
Now we test the long-run dynamic relationship among the variables with their directions of causalities through the utilization of the structure of error correction mechanism (ECM) by incorporating a two-period lag according to the minimum AIC (Akaike Information Criterion) rule. The estimation results indicate that globalization and per capita GDP have a long-run equilibrium relationship with inflation in India.

VECM equation imply that both one- and two-period lags of FDI positively promote TRO. It is also revealed from the results of VECM that, with their two-period lag values, both FDI and MSP positively influence PCI even though some of these influences are significant and others are insignificant.

So, in general, empirical outcomes of the study indicate that both trade openness and FDI inflow positively and significantly influence the level of inflation measured by CPI in India, which means globalization is a major responsible cause of price inflation in India. As usual, the money supply is also found to be a significant factor in the price rising situation in India. Furthermore, it is essential to note that the aggregate domestic demand of the economy measured by per capita GDP significantly influences the inflation level to increase in India. The study also observes some related findings including positive associations between trade openness and FDI inflows, the direct impact of FDI inflows and money supply on per capita GDP, etc. It should be mentioned here that all of the findings can be explained and justified by existing open economy macroeconomic theories.

Summary and conclusion

Results of the econometric estimation of this study reveal that in the Indian context, trade openness and FDI inflow have positively and significantly influenced the rate of inflation measured by CPI. However, inflation has been influenced by per capita GDP and money supply significantly only in the case of one period lag. Therefore, in India trade openness has raised

Table 13.4 Estimated results of vector error correction models

Error correction:	*D(CPI)*	*D(TRO)*	*D(FDI)*	*D(MSP)*	*D(PCI)*
D(CPI(-1))	0.24**	–0.01	0.21	0.17	–0.01
	[2.67]	[–1.36]	[1.74]	[1.46]	[–0.42]
D(CPI(-2))	0.19**	0.00	0.14	0.15	0.05
	[2.83]	[0.47]	[1.17]	[1.36]	[2.73]
D(TRO(-1))	0.11**	0.11*	0.08**	14.83	2.48
	[3.59]	[1.99]	[2.61]	[1.96]	[2.05]
D(TRO(-2))	0.09*	0.06*	0.02**	12.76	4.25
	[2.09]	[2.08]	[2.38]	[1.80]	[3.73]
D(FDI(-1))	0.09**	0.02*	0.45	0.91	–0.01
	[3.09]	[2.03]	[0.93]	[2.01]	[–0.19]
D(FDI(-2))	0.03**	0.03**	0.36	0.52	0.02**
	[2.60]	[2.89]	[0.70]	[1.07]	[2.78]
D(MSP(-1))	0.02*	0.03	–1.20	–1.40	–0.02
	[2.01]	[0.61]	[–1.94]	[–2.40]	[–0.24]
D(MSP(-2))	–0.11	0.00	–0.20	0.05	0.02**
	[–0.09]	[–0.01]	[–0.31]	[0.07]	[2.35]
D(PCI(-1))	0.08**	0.11	1.00	0.95	0.19
	[2.61]	[0.84]	[0.52]	[0.50]	[0.63]
D(PCI(-2))	–12.74	–0.07	–4.76	–5.80	–1.24
	[–1.09]	[–0.58]	[–2.67]	[–3.43]	[–4.57]
C	206**	182**	141	110	109*
	[2.11]	[1.96]	[–1.06]	[–2.08]	[1.83]
R^2	0.61	0.22	0.41	0.19	0.24
Adj. R^2	0.56	0.20	0.31	0.12	0.21
F-statistic	5.41	3.88	3.95	1.47	3.58
Prob. (F-statistic)	0.00	0.01	0.03	0.19	0.02

Source: Estimation of authors using RBI (2019) database.
Note: *, ** and *** indicate significance at 10%, 5% and 1% levels, respectively.

the rate of growth of price level instead of reduced it. Data from different sources expose that in India during the post-globalization period there has been a noteworthy enhancement in the FDI inflow. Hence, during the phases of high rate of inflation, the demand-side effect of FDI inflow is stronger than the supply-side effect. This is also corroborated by the coefficient of per capita GDP in the VECM at lag one.

Moreover, the estimated coefficient of the money supply is significant and positive at one lag. This reveals that an increase in the money supply affects prices adversely. Therefore, if the monetary policy instrument is used to raise the money supply then this increase in the money supply will raise the price level, and vice-versa. Therefore, the findings of this study corroborate the underlying theories on the influences of FDI inflow, money supply or monetary policy instruments and per capita income on the inflationary price rising situation. However, the theoretical view of the influence of trade openness on the inflationary price rising situation has not been empirically proved.

Globalization means a greater degree of trade openness, which raises imports and exports and increases the flow of capital across globalized nations. There are many arguments on the impacts of globalization on the rising trend of prices within the nations open to the world economy.

According to the view of some researchers and policymakers, globalization leads to a rise in global competition which stabilizes the rate of price increase and keeps prices at a low level. The producers in developing countries with low production costs continue to integrate the local economy into the global trading circulation, and these forces ensure a low rate of inflation. Besides, an increase in international trade through globalization usually raises the productivity of labour through the efficient allocation of resources, which will bring down the unit costs of labour and costs of other inputs, and thus reduce prices.

Moreover, while the economy of developing nations is globalized, the investors of the advanced economies shift their production units to the former economies to bring down production costs. However, a rise in FDI flow has a positive impact on GDP growth in the hosting nations (Nair and Winhold, 2001; Makki and Somwaru, 2004; Nosheen, 2013; Iamsiraroj and Ulubasoglu, 2015). If the growth of national income increases per capita income (PCI), then the aggregate demand will rise significantly. This rise in aggregate demand influences the price rising situation adversely. Thus, the final impact of globalization on inflation through the rise in FDI flow is indeterminate and depends on the relative strength of the demand- and supply-side influences.

Another group of economists has argued in favour of the efficient application of the monetary policy instrument for controlling price rising trends within the economy of a nation. The central bank of the respective country usually uses this policy instrument through an increase in the interest rate on borrowings. As a result, commercial banks of the respective nations raise the rate of interest on credit, which leads to an increase in savings and a decline in the rate of investment. This rise in savings and decline in investment will bring down the money supply and reduce consumer demand, and finally, inflation will be managed.

In connection with the empirical outcomes of the study, two major issues should be explicitly articulated. The first is related to highlighting a substantial distinction between the core and headline inflation in a developing economy like India. It is a fact that the interpretations of the short-run interrelationships among the headline inflation, commodity price and foreign exchange rate fluctuations might be different from the observations indicating the long-run impact of FDI and allied inflows on core inflation through the changes in productivity over time. This particular issue points out the fundamental limitation of the present study, as no prominent answer could be provided on the basis of current econometric exercises. Secondly, the issue related to the inflation targeting practice adopted by the Reserve Bank of India since 2016 should also be incorporated into the subsequent associated studies. However, no such significant influence of the inflation targeting practice could be found in the current study dealing with the data over the period from 1991–92 to 2018–19. Over a long period, that kind of practice might be responsible for a structural break in the long-term inflation in India.

India during the period of post-globalization has experienced several phases of rising prices. There was very little impact of globalization and economic policy reform in 1991 on the price rising trend in India. After a few years the rate in price increase was controlled to some extent; however, since 2008 in India, a relatively steeper rising trend in prices has been observed. According to the scholars and researchers who have conducted their research on the inflation happening in India, irrespective of phases, one of the common and major reasons behind the high rate of inflation is the increase in the price of primary goods or food articles.

Notes

1 Authors are grateful to anonymous referees for kind and helpful comments. They are also thankful to Dr Komol Singha (coordinator) and other organizers of *National Seminar on India after a Quarter Century of Economic Reforms – the Benefits and Costs*, Department of Economics, Sikkim University, 5–6 October

2018 where an earlier version of the paper was presented. Important comments made by Prof Pinaki Chakraborty of National Institute of Public Finance and Policy, New Delhi; Prof Saikat Sinha Roy of Jadavpur University and Dr Pradyut Guha of Sikkim University are gratefully acknowledged. Useful disclaimers apply.

2 Actually in Triffin and Grubel (1962), the impacts of trade openness and integration on the deficit in the balance of payments and inflationary price rising trend have been examined.

3 During that period fiscal deficit was automatically monetized through RBI's credit to the central government.

4 Akaike (1969) Information Criterion (AIC) is used for choosing the number of lags used in the ADF test for the existence of the unit root.

References

Akaike, Hirotugu (1969): "Fitting autoregressive models for prediction," *Annals of the Institute of Statistical Mathematics*, Vol 21, No 1, pp 243–247.

Anand, Namrata (2014): "An overview of Indian economy (1991–2013)," *IOSR Journal of Economics and Finance*, Vol 3, No 3, pp 19–24.

Ashra, Sunil (2002): *Inflation and openness: A study of selected developing economies*, Indian Council for Research on International Economic Relations, Working Paper No. 84, New Delhi, India.

Ball, Laurence, and Robert Moffitt (2001): *Productivity growth and the Phillips curve*, National Bureau of Economic Research, Working Paper No. 8421, Massachusetts, USA.

Buiter, Willem H. (2000): "Optimal currency areas Scottish Economic Society/Royal Bank of Scotland annual lecture, 1999," *Scottish Journal of Political Economy*, Vol 47, No 3, pp 213–250.

Ciccarelli, Matteo, and Benoit Mojon (2010): "Global inflation," *The Review of Economics and Statistics*, Vol 92, No 3, pp 524–535.

Engle, Robert F., and Clive W. J. Granger (1987): "Co-integration and error correction: Representation, estimation, and testing," *Econometrica*, Vol 55, No 2, pp 251–276.

Granger, Clive W.. J. (1981): "Some properties of time series data and their use in econometric model specification," *Journal of Econometrics*, Vol 16, No 1, pp 121–130.

Iamsiraroj, Sasi, and Mehmet Ali Ulubaşoğlu (2015): "Foreign direct investment and economic growth: A real relationship or wishful thinking?" *Economic Modelling*, Vol 51, pp 200–213.

International Monetary Fund (IMF) (2006): "How has globalization affected inflation?" *World Economic Outlook*, Vol 3, pp 97–134.

Johansen, Søren, and Katarina Juselius (1990): "Maximum likelihood estimation and inference on cointegration – with applications to the demand for money," *Oxford Bulletin of Economics and statistics*, Vol 52, No 2, pp 169–210.

Kamin, Steven B., Mario Marazzi, and John W. Schindler (2004): *Is China exporting deflation?* Board of Governors of the Federal Reserve System, Working Paper No. 791, Washington, D.C., USA.

Kim, MinKyoung, and Hamid Beladi (2005): "Is free trade deflationary?" *Economics Letters*, Vol 89, No 3, pp 343–349.

Kohn, Donald L. (2006): "The effects of globalization on inflation and their implications for monetary policy," Federal Reserve Bank of Boston, Appropriate Adjustment Considerations and Policies, Conference Series (Proceedings), Vol 51, pp 341–349.

Lane, Philip R. (1997): "Inflation in open economies," *Journal of International Economics*, Vol 42, No 3–4, pp 327–347.

MacKinnon, J. G., Haug, A. A., and Michelis, L. (1999): "Numerical distribution functions of likelihood ratio tests for cointegration", *Journal of applied Econometrics*, Vol 14, No 5, pp. 563–577.

Makki, Shiva S., and Agapi Somwaru (2004): "Impact of foreign direct investment and trade on economic growth: Evidence from developing countries," *American Journal of Agricultural Economics*, Vol 86, No 3, pp 795–801.

Mukhtar, Tahir (2012): "Does trade openness reduce inflation? Empirical evidence from Pakistan," *Journal of Economic Cooperation and Development*, Vol 33, No 2, pp 33–52.

Nair-Reichert, Usha, and Diana Weinhold (2001): "Causality tests for cross-country panels: A new look at FDI and economic growth in developing countries," *Oxford bulletin of Economics and Statistics*, Vol 63, No 2, pp 153–171.

Neely, Christopher J., and David E. Rapach (2011): "International comovements in inflation rates and country characteristics," *Journal of International Money and Finance*, Vol 30, No 7, pp 1471–1490.

Nosheen, Misbah (2013): "Impact of foreign direct investment on gross domestic product," *World Applied Sciences Journal*, Vol 24, No 10, pp 1358–1361.

Raj, Janak, and Sangita Misra (2011): *Measures of core inflation in India–an empirical evaluation*, Reserve Bank of India, Department of Economic and Policy Research, Working Paper No. 16, Mumbai, India.

Reserve Bank of India (RBI) (1980): *Reserve Bank of India bulletin*, Mumbai, India.

Reserve Bank of India (RBI) (2019): *Handbook of statistics on Indian economy 2018–19*, Mumbai, India.

Rogoff, Kenneth (2015): "Costs and benefits to phasing out paper currency," *NBER Macroeconomics Annual*, Vol 29, No 1, pp 445–456.

Romer, David (1993): "Openness and inflation: Theory and evidence," *The Quarterly Journal of Economics*, Vol 108, No 4, pp 869–903.

Triffin, Robert, and Herbert Grubel (1962): "The adjustment mechanism to differential rates of monetary expansion among the countries of the European economic community," *The Review of Economics and Statistics*, Vol 44, No 4, pp 486–491.

Woodford, Michael (2009): "How important is money in the conduct of monetary policy?" *Journal of Money, Credit and Banking*, Vol 40, No 8, pp 1561–1598.

Zakaria, Muhammad (2011): "Openness and inflation: Evidence from time series data," *Doğuş Üniversitesi Dergisi*, Vol 11, No 2, pp 313–322.

Zivot, Eric, and Donald W. K. Andrews (2002): "Further evidence on the great crash, the oil-price shock, and the unit-root hypothesis," *Journal of Business & Economic Statistics*, Vol 20, No 1, pp 25–44.

14

FINANCIALISATION OF NON-FINANCIAL CORPORATIONS IN INDIA

An empirical investigation in the post-reform period[1]

Sushant Kumar Singh

Introduction

The globalisation of finance capital has become a burning topic since the financial crisis of 2008. Earlier, financial services were confined to banks, which used to mobilise savings and allocate them to different projects after evaluation. However, since the expansion of the financial sector under the neo-liberal and financial deregulation policies, financial services have become the core business of economic activities in an economy. Many studies conducted in the recent past, especially since the 2008 financial crisis, have displayed that the financial sector is adopting an increasingly dominant posture in a global economy and there has been a parallel slide of fortunes in the real economy, causing a contraction of real investment. The analysis of the globalisation of financialisation has recently emanated as one of the most ground-breaking ideas from the radical political economy to analyse the financial crisis starting in 2007–09, and provides insight into the structural transformation of the capitalist mode of surplus generation. Financialisation is a process with increasing importance of financial markets, financial motives, financial institutions and financial elites in the operation of the economy and its governing institutions, both at the national and international level in economic policy making and free market operation (Epstein 2001). According to Krippner (2005), financialisation can be defined as the accumulation of profit through financial means, such as interest, dividend and capital gains as opposed to through trade and commodity. The term financialisation also denotes the growing size and importance of financial transaction as part of overall economic activity (Orghanzi, 2008).

Many studies done in the recent past, in the context of advanced countries, have put forward the undesirable impact of the overwhelming encroachment of the financial sector on the real sector and the changing investment pattern of non-financial corporations (NFCs). According to these, financialisation has negatively impacted the real accumulation process in the US by changing NFCs' investment behaviour (Costa Lapavitsas 2009; Crotty 2005; Orhangazi 2008; Epstein 2005; Stockhammer 2004; Krippner 2005; Palley 2007). While Crotty (2005) pointed

 DOI: 10.4324/9780367855741-14

out that, under the financialisation process, the NFCs' objectives have changed from the 'management's view of the firm' to the 'portfolio view of the firm' which has led to 'short-termism' (short-term investments or quick gain) taking the significant position in the decision making process of firms instead of 'long-termism' (capital investment), and argues there has been a shift in the financialisation era from 'patient' financial markets to 'impatient' financial markets.

The same phenomena are also seen in India since massive neo-liberal reform and financial liberalisation after 1991. The process of financial liberalisation was marked by "gradualisation" which involves liberalisation of regulatory control over markets, institutions and instruments. Attempts were made to enhance the commercial decision and free market operation. The first generation of reform was characterised by creating an environment of operating flexibility and functional autonomy for financial service industries. And a most interesting feature was to adopt the international best practice in financial systems like that of the US and UK's monetary policy, banking supervision, corporate governance, etc.; diversification of ownership of public banks has been done by allowing private investment up to 49% in a government bank. Another important development was the opening up of a mutual fund to the private sector in 1992 and also allowing offshore investment in equity abroad. The Indian capital market was opened up for foreign institution investors (FIIs). All these lead to NFCs' focus to shift to the financial sector to earn quick profits to raise share price in the stock market and de-prioritise production activities. The liberalisation of the financial sector leads to an increase in the speculative income in India and the development of a massive equity market which affects the function of the banking system. According to Nayyar (2016), financial deregulation and reform norms have induced the downsizing of the development of finance institutions, which were the essential providers of finance for long-term industrial investment and have created a space for public and private commercial banks. Since the reforms in India, financialisation has manifested the complex relation between non-financial corporations and the financial sector. A change in a non-financial firm's behaviours is reflected in an increase in the share of financial assets in the firm portfolio and increasing indebtedness and growing buy back of shares among large corporations. Mr Vyas, CEO and MD of CMIE has indicated that net fixed assets of the non-financial corporation are shrinking. Only 20% of NFCs have a growth rate of assets that is above average. We can observe how the power of financialisation is slowly strengthening its position in the Indian economy. In 2013, the Companies Act 1956 was amended regarding the matter of dividend reserve. The earlier Companies Act 1956 restricted companies from transferring more than 10% of the profit after tax to the dividend reserve. In the amendment of 2013, this cap was removed. Companies are now free to either not transfer or transfer any amount they like to the reserve fund for dividend payment. Dividend payment was earlier constrained to a certain percentage of the volume of profit but now rests on managerial decisions that factor in differing alignments towards shareholders and direct stakeholders in the company.

Growing financialisation of corporate activities is because of a high cash discount rate, a liberal import regime and the risk–return matrix which tempts corporates into involving more in trading/marking or financial activities over investment in the manufacturing sector. And the interest arbitrage opportunities arising from low External Commercial Borrowing (ECB) and sub-BPLR (i.e., below Benchmark Prime Lending Rates) interest rates for high-end corporates, mean that when creditors/investors' confidence is low they become more short-term/cash focused and safety/security-oriented. The result is higher liquidity-holdback, accelerated investment, and less capital expenditure. High CD rates incentivise cash transactions which increase the need for higher cash holding. Cash-constrained firms offer high discounts in exchange for an accelerated payment that gives significantly better returns on cash than fixed investment (Deputy General Manager, SIDBI, Lucknow, 31st March 2012, Hindu Business Line).

It has become important to provide a measurement of the financialisation of the economy when the phase of capitalist development under which the profit-making process is occurring is primarily through financial channels rather than through trade and commodity production. This study seeks to outline the changing behaviour of NFCs from indicators visible in their annual financial statements and articulate the interrelations between financialisation and corporate decisions in India. Many questions arise when we see the increase in financialisation in an economy. What are the dynamics of the finance capital? What are the adverse impacts of financialisation on income distribution and economic growth? What are its various dimensions and what kind of policies can be implemented to reduce the negative impact of financialisation and make it a more effective and efficient system for real growth in an economy? There is a broad consensus among economists that the development of financial systems is crucial for real economic growth. At the same time, however, the question as to which kind of financial structure and institution, from the perspective of the political economy, is favourable for the steady and sustainable real growth of an economy, has always been a topic of debate among scholars. A full analysis of financialisation clearly incorporates a large set of issues. This paper specifically attempts to consider one aspect of financialisation in the Indian context – to examine whether there has been an increase in the financial income as a share of profits and financial payment in the non-financial sector. Has the investment in financial assets risen and investment in physical assets declined in the balance sheet of the NFCs since the 1990s? This paper will closely scrutinise sector-wise consolidated annual financial statements of firms by analysing the pattern of assets holding, sources of earning and expenses, to identify the investment behaviour of Indian firms. This paper is divided into five sections. The next section discusses the data used in this study. The third section discusses the available literature regarding the financialisation process in India, while the fourth section shows the changing sources of income of NFCs. In the fifth section we try to establish the changing portfolio of assets. The final section investigates the trends in financial incomes and financial payments of firms.

Data and methods

Data used in this study was sourced from the CMIE Prowess Database. It gave time series data of firms' annual financial statements for the period from 1990 to 2014. The data obtained is appropriate for the study owing to the period in question – the post-reform period. This time period accounts for the series of measures taken in accordance with the financial liberalisation policy in India. The CMIE prowess data base provides a consolidated financial statement of the Indian firms as well as a sector-wise financial statement. This chapter will closely scrutinise the firm-wise and sector-wise consolidated annual financial statements of NFCs by analysing the pattern of assets holding, source of earning, cash flow and expenses to identify the investment behaviour of the NFCs. All the data in the graph, shown as a percentage of some variable, are taken at a nominal value (no need of inflation adjustment), while other data which are shown in several graphs in absolute value are inflation adjusted through the GDP deflator method. The limitation of the empirical investigation of this paper is, while taking the consolidated balance sheet of the NFCs, I have not strictly considered the heterogeneity of the NFCs in terms of size, turnover and the different nature and characteristics of the firms.

Financialisation of non-financial corporations in India

This chapter attempts to demonstrate empirically the financialisation of Indian non-financial corporations (NFCs) in the post-reform period. Has the investment portfolio of non-financial corporations changed in favour of financial assets and activities? We also seek to identify real investment and financial investment of NFCs and their changing impact over time on the net profits of NFCs.

The Investment Commission of India (2004) recommend many policy changes to induce industrial growth such as labour reforms, the removal of sectoral caps and permission for an 'automatic route' for all investments, promotion of special economic zones (SEZs) through eased policy for land acquisition. The Commission found delays in land acquisitions, allotment of mining leases and environment clearances to be the main factors contributing to the slow growth rate in the manufacturing sector. They also sought liberalisation of the banking sector, allowance of FIIs to invest up to 49% in the Indian banking sector and, allowance of FDI in PSUs. The long and short of it is that the government is keen to liberalise real and financial markets and open the domestic economy to the world market and link its financial structure with the global financial system to meet its investment requirement.

RBI Financial Stability Report, June 2014, stated that the NFCs' asset composition in balance sheets is changing in favour of financial assets. NFC is aiming to use their enormous cash balance to improve their return on assets, by aggressively engaging in financial activities. Income from financial activities of NFCs shows a 150% increase from 100 billion rupees in 2004 to around 250 billion rupees in 2013. The sharp rise in the share of cash and bank balance in total assets of the firm reported by the RBI could be due to various reasons ranging from an uncertain economic environment to industry-specific business cycles, but they emphatically show that firms are shifting their portfolio towards financial assets.

> Financial income (with a predominant share of 'interest income') of the top 10 NFCs (in terms of income from financial operations as against their core activities) in FY2013–14 has consistently surpassed the comparable income items of their counterparts (top 10 banks in terms of treasury income)[2] in the banking sector, makes them important players in the 'financial' sector too. While the NFCs in the Indian system may not be directly engaged in credit intermediation at this stage, information regarding the non-core 'financial' activities of large NFCs may need to be captured as part of macro-prudential surveillance.
>
> *(RBI financial stability report, June 2014)*

Figures 14.1 and 14.2, part of the RBI report, depict the increasing share of cash and bank balance in total assets of the firms and increasing income from financial activities of NFCs. Income from financial activities of large NFCs increased at a rate higher than the treasury income of banks. The trend of large amounts of cash accumulation (in various liquid forms) by non-financial companies (NFCs), resulting from various reasons ranging from an uncertain economic environment to industry-specific business cycles, has been commonly associated with advanced economies and other fast growing big economies. The previous FSR mentioned a similar phenomenon of changing asset composition in favour of financial investments of Indian corporate entities. Further, the aggregate share of cash and bank balances in total assets of large NFCs has broadly seen an increasing trend since 2004.

In an economic report published by the RBI on June 30, 2014, the Governor of RBI ascribes the recent slow growth rate of the manufacturing sector to the 'poor risk-appetite' of the Indian Corporate than the financial sector. According to this report, complex legal and regulatory frameworks in key areas, such as for mining activity, land acquisition process and environmental clearance has dipped the business class 'animal spirit' and has negatively impacted investment in the manufacturing sector. Apart from inflexible labour laws and lack of FDI

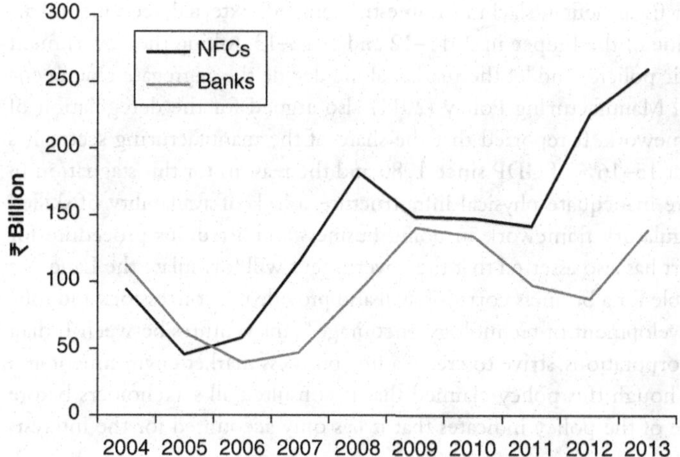

Figure 14.1 Income from financial activities of non-financial companies and treasury income of banks
Source: RBI Financial Stability Report, June 2014.

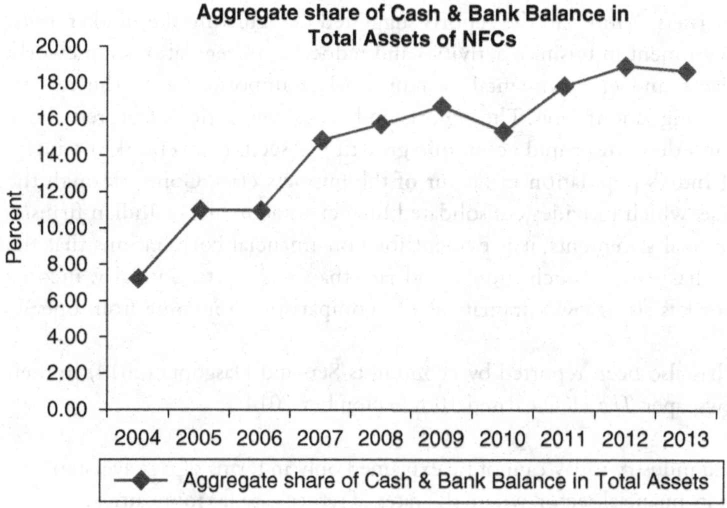

Figure 14.2 Aggregate share of cash and bank balances in total assets of large NFCs Source: RBI Financial Stability Report, June 2014.

inflow, the Investment Commission of India, 2007–08 has reported other reasons behind slackness in investment in the real sector such as bureaucratic practices, divergence between the Centre and the States on investment-related policies, poor infrastructure and unclear identification/specification of priority sectors and restrictions in several sectors of significant investment potential. On the sluggish growth rate of industrial sector in India onwards 2010, the Economic Survey, 2013–14 suggested that the key reason for the deceleration of the industrial sector since 2010 has been contraction in the mining sector which in its turn has been caused by the slowing down of production in coal, lignite, crude oil, iron ore and natural gas. The Economic Survey of India, 2014–15 reported that the economic slowdown in India was a consequence of persistent inflation, elevated fiscal deficit, slacking domestic demand, external account imbalances, and the oscillating value of the Rupee in 2011–12 and 2012–13. Asking the government not to intervene in economic policies and let the market alone decide the aggregate macroeconomic picture, the National Manufacturing Policy (2011) also argued for the deregulation of the complex regulatory framework. It reported that the share of the manufacturing sector has remained stagnant in India at 15–16% of GDP since 1980 and the reasons for this stagnation in the manufacturing sector are inadequate physical infrastructure, a lack of availability of skilled workforce and complex regulatory framework in doing business and a tedious procedure for starting a business. The report has also asserted that the government will formulate the Land Act for making land easily available for a business corridor, will also provide tax concessions and subsidies for the indigenous development of technology, encourage joint ventures between Indian business firms and foreign corporations, strive to create a free business market environment and refrain from intervention. Though this policy claimed that it consulted all stakeholders before formulation, the very nature of the policy indicates that it has only accounted for the interests of the business class.

The reports and recommendations mentioned above have overlooked the behaviour of NFCs in the era of the neo-liberal environment and massive financial liberalisation. They have disregarded the changing portfolio in the balance sheet of the firms, how the process of financial liberalisation has made an investment in financial assets appear more attractive than investment in real assets. Almost all the reports suggested deregulating the market, non-intervention of the government in business activities and reduction of regulatory frameworks regarding land acquisition and environmental clearance. Most importantly, all the reports strongly advocate reforming labour laws. The reports and recommendations featured above indicate the government's desire for rapid economic growth but seem to overlook the interests of the majority of India's population in favour of the business class. Going through the CMIE Prowess Database, which provides consolidated financial statements of Indian firms as well as sector-wise financial statements, it is evident for non-financial corporations that the share of financial assets has seen a much more rapid rise than real assets. Similarly, income from the financial sector has also grown dramatically in comparison to income from operating activities.

The same concern has also been reported by economists Sen and Dasgupta (2014) in their recent article in the newspaper *The Hindu*, dated 10th September 2014:

> Stagnation in Indian industry today cannot be explained only in terms of risk aversion unless one looks at its financial sector, where the rates of returns are far more attractive. The share of industrial securities as a proportion of investment in NFCs dropped from around 40 percent in 2002–03 to around 15 percent or even less by 2011–12 and the following years. As opposed to this, the share of financial securities rose from less than 60 percent to 70 percent. The current strategy of corporate India to get embroiled in the high profit, high-risk world of finance may eventually turn out to be a dangerous game for the economy as a whole.

The high propensity of Indian corporates to invest in the financial sector makes an important case to examine the assets composition of firms' balance sheets as well as their cash flow statements. The financialisation of the productive economic activities marked a significant influence in India in the course of several financial reforms that took place under the new economic policy of 1991. This financial deregulation has changed corporate behaviour regarding investment decisions and portfolio management. Financial assets have become more attractive to

Indian corporates as they facilitate short-term gains that ensure the stability of shareholders' faith in firms (Sen and Vaidya 1999; Chandrasekhar 2006; 2011).

> Asset growth rates for corporates have sharply fallen, from 32.8 percent in 2008 to zero percent in 2012, and falling further to (–)6 percent in 2013. The profitability of assets has followed a similar path and, except for 2010, the profit rate saw a steady decline from 5.7 percent in 2008 to 2.4 percent in 2013. The performance of the corporate sector has unmistakably been dwindling, not only in terms of its contribution to real investment but also in terms of the growth of overall assets and their profitability.
>
> *(Sen and Dasgupta, 2015)*

Dilution of the MRTP Act encouraged big firms and big business groups to diversify their business activities, thereby removing any special control over large firms by the government. Now, no new approval is needed for big firms to take decisions regarding the form and value of the financial investment. Financial liberalisation has facilitated enough space for speculative activities by firms in the capital market and allowed free entry in the financial sector. Many industrial groups such as Reliance, Tata, Birla, etc. have started diversifying their business in the financial sector by establishing non-banking financial corporations as either their subsidiary companies or other financial institutions engaged in financial activities like providing loans, credit cards or mutual fund investment. Non-financial companies are utilising their resources to establish such non-banking financial firms and are also investing huge amounts in equity to raise initial capital for these firms in the stock market to mobilise resources and engage in speculative activity to earn quick profits.

> The tendency of corporates under financialisation to prefer short-term financial assets (as opposed to long-term physical investments) is at the core of an explanation of the industrial stagnation that prevails in the majority of countries in the world economy at present. Indian corporates seem to follow a path of short-termism in the face of uncertainty in deregulated financial markets. At the same time, the search for quick returns in high-risk, short-term assets deters investments in physical assets. The result, however, has been that corporates have seen low growth rates in their gross assets.
>
> *(Sen and Dasgupta, 2015)*

Figure 14.3 depicts the rising share of finance, insurance and real estate (FIRE) as a percentage of the total GDP of India. Non-financial sectors clearly show either a constant or stagnant trend as the percentage of GDP compared to the FIRE sector. This indicates financial sector incomes are growing faster than other productive sectors. The share of FIRE sectors in GDP increased by around 83%. Since 1991, the growth rate of the FIRE sector (shown in Figure 14.4) is consistently higher than the growth rate of the GDP, rising rapidly after 2003–04 and remaining consistently above the growth rate of the GDP (except in 2010–11). This is a clear indicator of the expansion of the financial sector and the lagging behind of the industrial sector in the Indian economy. Figure 14.5 above depicts the declining growth rate in the industrial sector as well as in the manufacturing sector from the year 2010, displaying the recent slump in productive activities in the Indian economy. Only the service and FIRE sectors have a positive growth rate, which clearly indicates that the stagnancy in the real sector is stirring NFCs to become involved in financial activities to maintain their overall profitability.

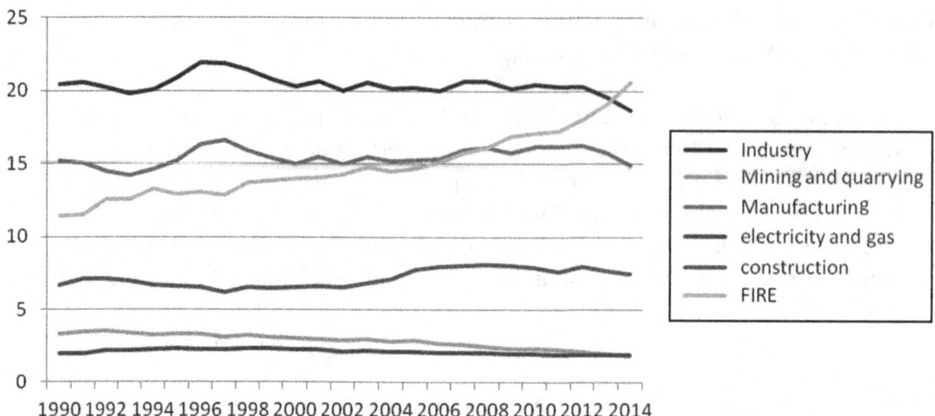

Figure 14.3 Sectoral compositions in GDP (base price 2004–05) Source: RBI Database (Author's calculation)

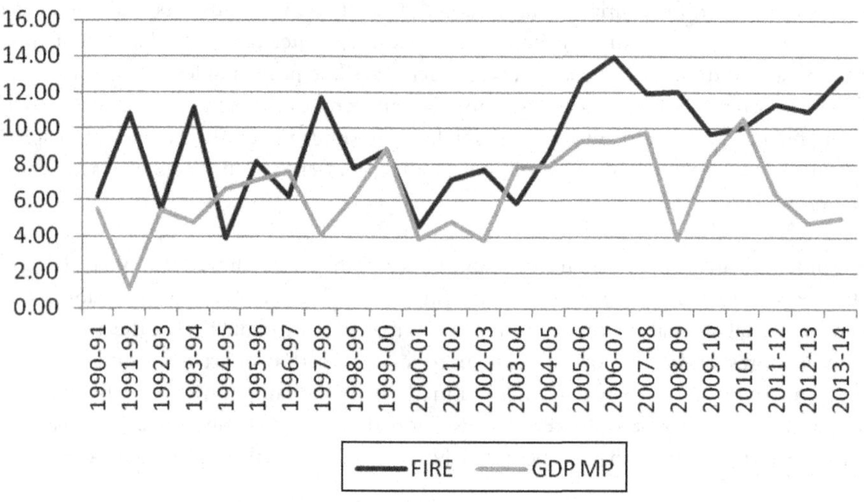

Figure 14.4 GDP at MP and FIRE sector growth rate (base price 2004–05) Source: CMIE Prowess Database (Author's calculation).

Changing pattern of non-financial firms' sources of income

In this section, I will attempt to analyse the changing pattern of earnings of NFCs since the reforms. Changing sources of income (increasing share of financial income in the total income of NFCs) of the non-financial sector from non-financial activity to financial activity is one of the indicators, which shows a shift in activity from the production of goods and services to lending, borrowing and investment in financial assets (speculative activities). Below are the figures which will explain the trend in the share of a different source of income of NFCs in their total income.

Under the era of neo-liberalisation and globalised financial structure, the volume of sales as a percentage of the total income of all non-financial corporations of India has shown a declining

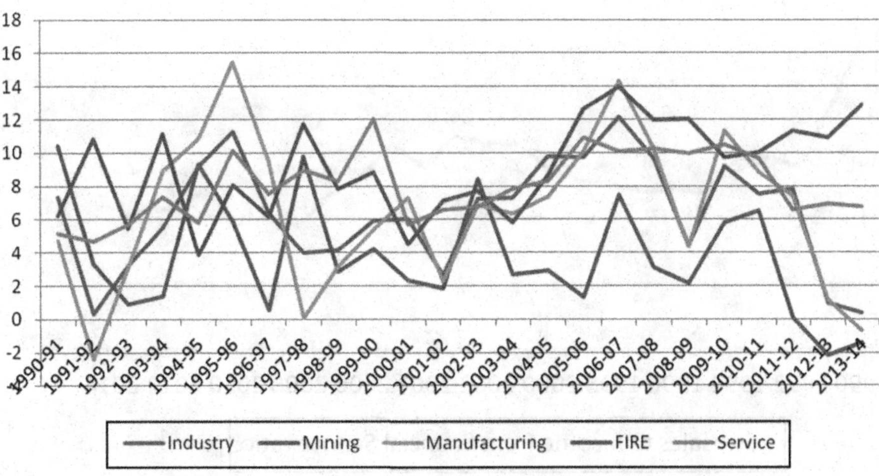

Figure 14.5 Sector-wise growth rate at factor cost (base price 2004–05) Source: RBI *Handbook of statistics on Indian Economy*.

trend. As the income from sales declines, the firms' income from the financial sector shows an upward trend. Figures 14.6, 14.7 and 14.8 clearly show that the earnings of NFCs depict a shifting trend towards the financial sector. Here, income from financial activities of firms includes income from investment in financial assets (equity shares, preference shares, purchase of bonds and debentures) in the form of dividends, interest and other commissions from financial activities. Falling sales volume may affect the capacity utilisation of the firms which in turn could affect investment decisions as can be seen in Figures 14.6 and 14.7. Figure 14.8 depicts the share of income from financial activities in the total income of NFCs increased by 150% from 1% in 1990 to 2.5% in 2014. Figure 14.6 depicts the ratio of sales to income from financial activities declined by 57% from 92.9 in 1990 to 39.2 in 2014. Figure 14.9 explains the trend in the total financial income of NFCs relative to its non-financial income. It also depicts that during the financial crisis and afterwards, the ratio of financial income to non-financial income increased

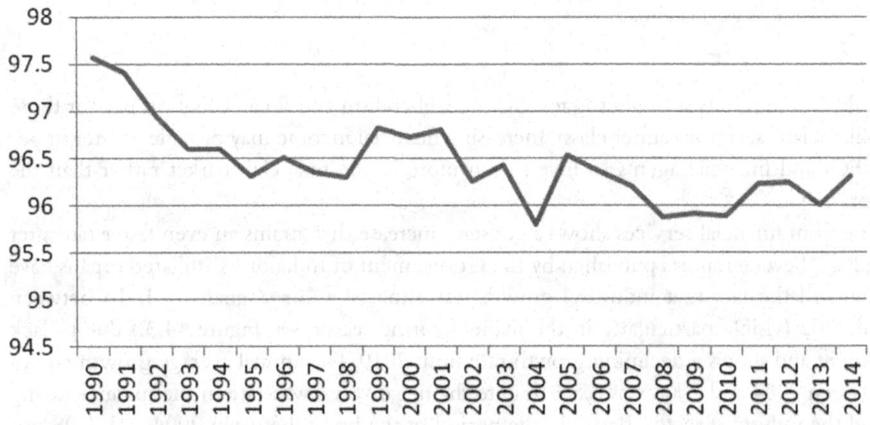

Figure 14.6 NFCs sales as a percentage of total income. *Source*: CMIE Prowess database (Author's calculation).

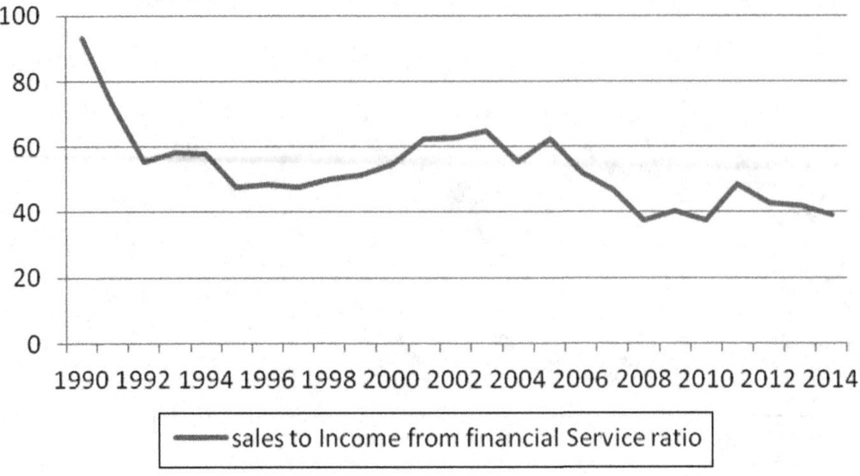

Figure 14.7 Ratios of sales to income from financial activities for the NFCs. *Source*: CMIE Prowess Database (Author calculation).

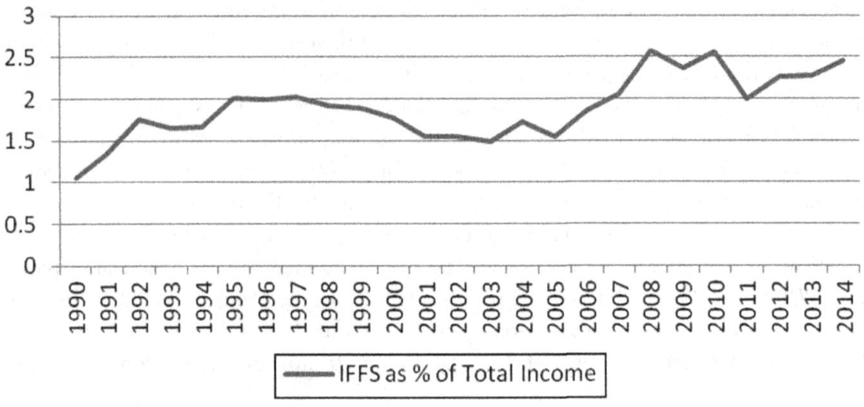

Figure 14.8 NFCs income from financial activities as % of total income. *Source*: CMIE Prowess Database (Author's calculation).

dramatically. These results strongly suggest that neo-liberalism and financialisation pay for those owning financial assets (the rentier class). Increasing financial income may provide greater impetus to NFCs and financial agents to invest even more in the financial market rather than the real sector.

Income from financial services shows a constant increase that attains an even faster rate after the year 2002. Several reports published by the Government of India or its affiliated organs have also recognised the fact that industrial growth was either slow or stagnant in India between 1995 and 2002 (visible particularly in the manufacturing sector; see Figure 14.3.) due to lack of investment and shows a declining growth rate from 2010. The annual average growth rate of GDP between 2004 and 2008 was 8.5% despite the negative growth rate in the manufacturing sector and the industrial sector. Basically, the period of the boom between 2004 and 2008 was due to two factors. One of the factors that characterised this period was the service-led growth

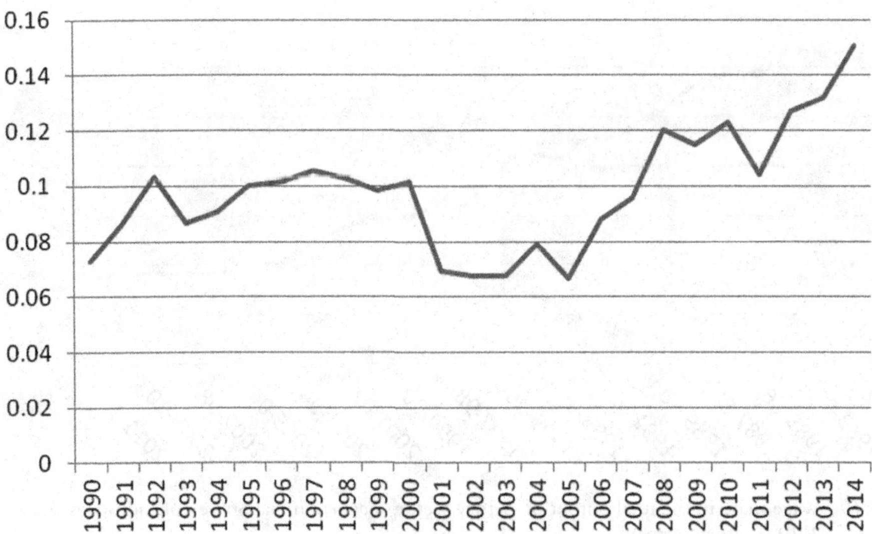

Figure 14.9 Ratio of financial income to non-financial income of NFCs. *Source*: CMIE Prowess Database (Author's calculation).

of the Indian economy since 1990. The second factor was the high growth rate in the FIRE sector. In this period, service shows a high average growth rate of 9.88% since 1990 while the FIRE sector witnessed 11.8% compared to the 8.5% growth rate of GDP. Because of such stagnancy in growth in NFCs, many such firms have started investing in the financial sector to compensate for their losses in the real sector. My central claim is that accumulation is now increasingly occurring through financial networks.

The steadily declining sales volume of non-financial corporations, especially in the manufacturing sector, is simply due to a lack of demand in the market. It indicates that the purchasing power of the consumer has declined in the era of financial globalisation as the financial sector is increasing its share of surplus in the economy continuously. Financialisation has negatively impacted wage share in the US economy (Lazonick and O' Sullivan 2002; Hein 2012; Dunhaupt 2013). In the Indian context, Banerjee and Piketty (2005) reported that average income growth among the top 1% of the tax units was 71% in real terms between 1987–88 and 1999–2000 whereas their share in total consumption was 8%. The growth in income among the top 0.01 per cent is 285% even though per-capita consumption increased by just 19% and per capita, household consumption increased by only 40%. Wage share in the private corporate sector has been declining in India since the mid-1980s. This is evidence of the pace of increasing income inequality in India.

As is evident from Figure 14.10, there is a decline in the wage share in total output that contributes to a decline in total consumption based on the assumption that the major share of consumption comes from wages and workers' propensity to consume is relatively higher than the rentiers and capitalists (under-consumption). A decline in the share of consumption is a strong indicator of falling sales volume. With a pessimistic picture in the real sector and increased international competition from transnational giants, domestic firms attempt to reduce the wage costs to increase their market share by reducing the prices. The only way in which they could gain over their competitors is if the wage share falls. There is, however, a paradox here. A fall in the wage share may seem beneficial for an individual firm, but it is not good for the economy as a whole due to the resultant demand effects of such a fall – the famous 'paradox of cost'. So,

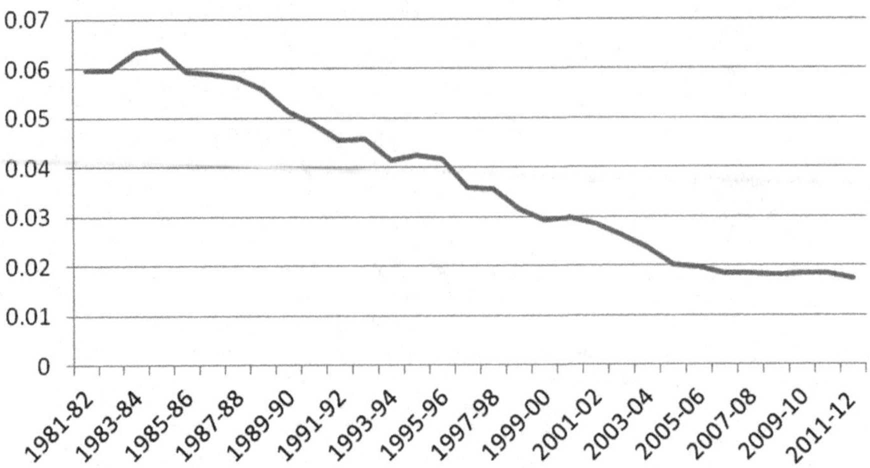

Figure 14.10 Wage share in the total output of factory sector. *Source*: Annual Survey of Industries 2011–2012 (Factory sector).

while the profit margins could rise, the rate of profit from real activities might actually fall unless the investment rises to a higher proportion than the extent of under-consumption. But there is no reason why investment should rise while the demand is falling. All this, therefore, results in a rise in the profit margin but a fall in the rate of profit arising out of real sector activities. With dwindling returns from the real sector, NFCs are indulging in financial investments to maintain their overall rate of profit. Increasing share value orientation of firms under NFCs puts pressure on them to maintain stock prices and shareholder value through paying higher rates of the dividend. The financial income occupies the space for the operating income of a firm.

The declining trend in the sales of NFCs along with the rapid increase in income from financial services in proportion to total income has also been observed across different sub-sectors of NFCs. Figures 14.11 and 14.12 show that sales as a percentage of total income are declining while income from financial activities in proportion to the total income of NFCs shows a continuous increasing trend across all sectors. Electricity, real estate and construction and mining sectors show a greater fall in sales income as a percentage of total income. At the same time in these sectors, income from financial activities has shown the greatest jump in the composition of sales and financial income in total income. We observe the same trend in earnings across different sub-sectors of non-financial sectors like manufacturing, mining, electricity and gas, service sector and real estate and construction. Figures 14.11 and 14.12 clearly explain that the prime source of income as a percentage of the total income of different sub-sectors of the non-financial sector show a declining trend after reforms. Mining and electricity sectors show more fluctuation during these years while other sectors like manufacturing, service and real estate show a declining trend or remain stagnant. The manufacturing sector, the most important constituent of the non-financial sector, shows either declining or stagnancy in income from sales which indicates contraction in manufacturing output. FICCI's report (2013) on the Indian mining industry stated that while this sector was contributing 3.4% to GDP in 1992–93, this share had come down to 2% of GDP in 2012–13. It shows a negative rate of growth in its production. First, it declined to 3% of GDP in 1999–2000 and again, plummeted to 2.3% of GDP in 2009–10. The mining sector has witnessed negative growth of −0.6% for two consecutive years (2011–12 and 2012–13). This dismal trend is very discernible in Figure 14.11 which has the highest fluctuation in sales volume of the mining sector. At the same time, the income from financial activities shows a

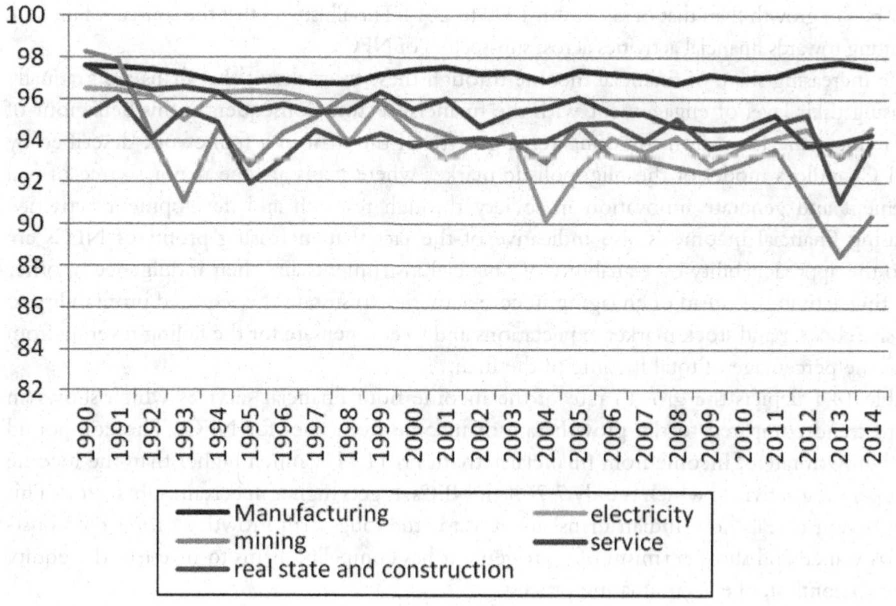

Figure 14.11 Sales as a percentage of total income. *Source*: CMIE Prowess Database (Author's calculation).

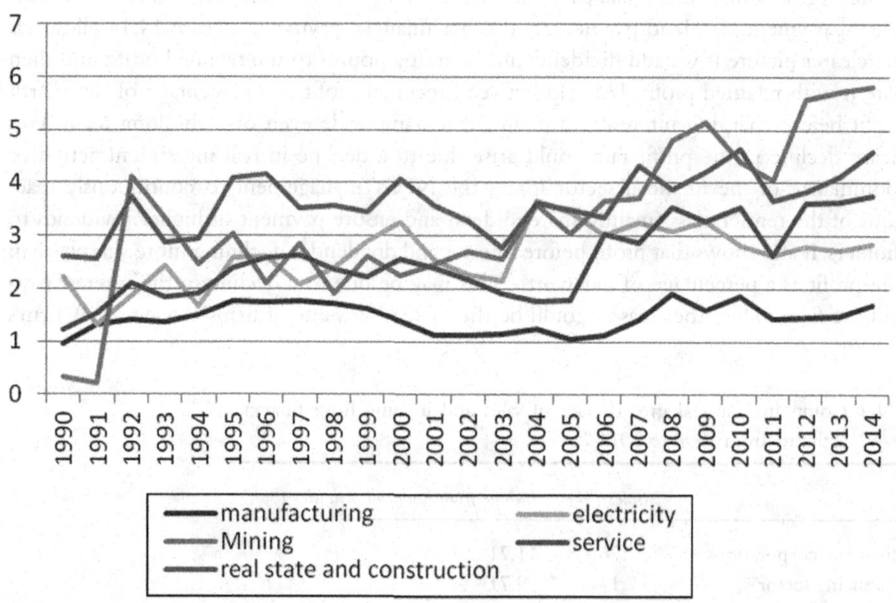

Figure 14.12 Income from financial activities as percentage of total income. *Source*: CMIE Prowess Database (Author's calculation).

higher rate of growth than that of sales from 1990 to 2014. This illustrates that the sources of income are shifting towards financial activities across sub-sectors of NFCs.

The increasing share of financial income through these years shows that firms are gradually increasing their level of engagement with the financial sector. Consequently, this behaviour of firms reduces the focus from the long-term growth of the firm in a framework described by Alfred Chandler's model of the oligopolistic market where firms are the major source of real investment and generate innovation in society through research and development activities. Increasing financial income is also indicative of the fact that increasing profits of NFCs are due to the approachability or availability of financial instruments and their indulgence in other marketing activities, instead of engaging in core activities, to sustain the required profitability to meet shareholder and stock market expectations and to compensate for the falling revenue from sales as the percentage of total income of the firm.

Table 14.1 depicts the growth rate of the income from financial services which shows an upward trend compared to the growth rate of income from sales for NFCs. The compound annual growth rate of income from financial activities is 11.71%; much higher than the income from operating activities which is only 7.76% in NFCs. It gets higher in certain sub-sectors. This phenomenon reveals how Indian firms' appetite for the long-term growth of their core business has waned and short-termism of management has compelled firms to invest in the equity market to continue the accumulating process.

Figure 14.13 is descriptive of the continuously declining rate of profit of NFCs; how a major portion of their earnings flows into the financial sector. First, it shows the trend of decline in their profit rates due to the lack of real investment activities. Second, it shows the large gap between profit before depreciation interest and taxes and retained profit. This wide gap persists due to the large amount of financial payments made out by NFCs to the financial sector regarding interest payment, dividend payment, and other financial payments. Figure 14.14 allows us to get a clearer picture if we add dividend and interest amounts to the retained profit and then compare it with retained profit. The gap between retained profit as a percentage of net worth and profit before charging interest and dividend remains wide even over the long term. This significant decline in the profit rate could arise due to a decline in real investment activities. The dominance of the financial sector forces the NFCs' management to continuously react in favour of the rentier class (mainly shareholders) and ensure payment of higher dividends to shareholders. It also shows that profit before interest and dividend is declining more sharply than retained profit as a percentage of net worth. This may be due to a decline in the interest payment of the firms. The other reason could be the increasing value of firms' net worth. A firm's

Table 14.1 Compound annual growth rate of sales and income from financial activities from 1990 to 2014

	Sales (%)	*Income from financial activities (%)*
Non-financial corporations	7.76	11.71
Manufacturing sector	7.14	9.71
Electricity sector	10.43	11.65
Mining sector	7.69	21.71
Real estate and construction	10.36	13.03
Service sector	9.46	14.86

Source: CMIE Database (Author's calculation).

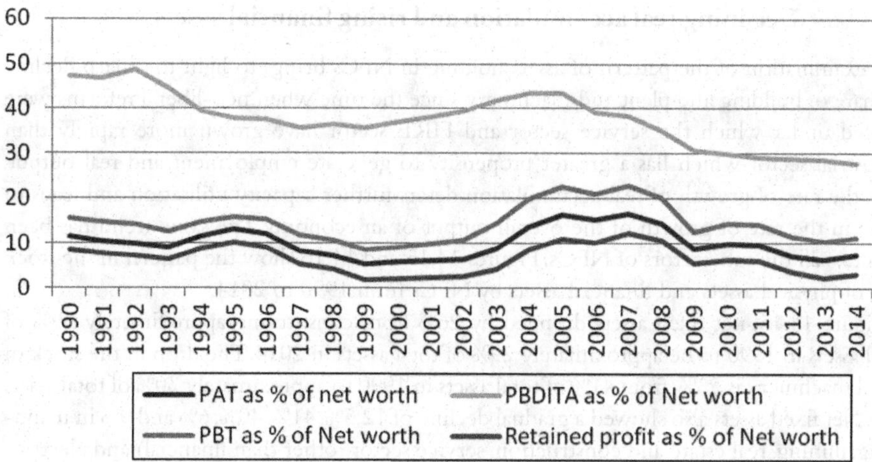

Figure 14.13 Profit after and before interest, tax and depreciation as percentage of net worth. *Source*: CMIE Prowess Database (Author's calculation)/

net worth comprises share capital and reserve and surplus. An increase in share capital implies a new issue of equity to either reduce the debt level of firms or to finance real investment. An increase in reserve and surplus means the transfer of a proportion of profit for specific reserves such as capital redemption account, general reserve, share premium account. These reserves are maintained to safeguard the interests of, primarily, preference shareholders, and then, creditors of the firm. Capital redemption account is used by firms exclusively for stock buyback and to redeem preference shares.

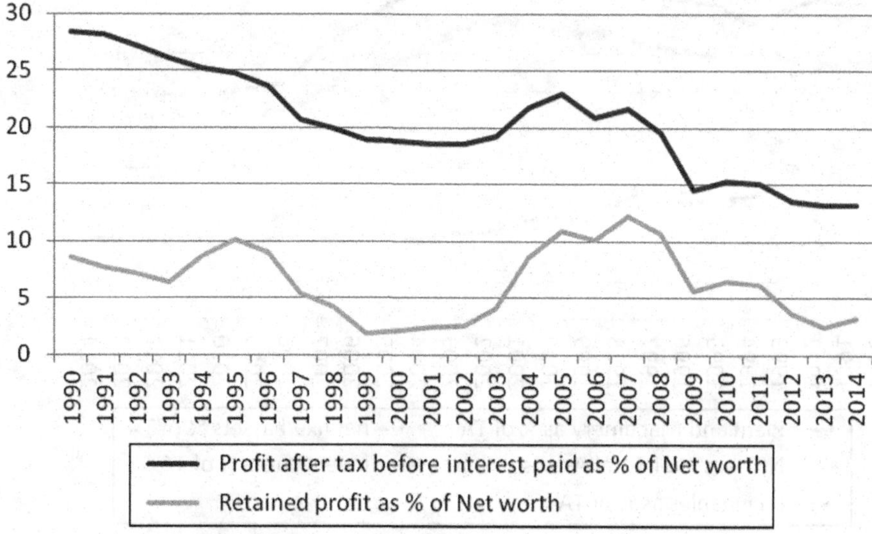

Figure 14.14 NFCs' trend in profit before interest and dividend and, retained profit as % of net worth. *Source*: CMIE Prowess Database (Author's calculation).

Declining real accumulation and rising financial assets

A close examination of the pattern of assets holding in NFCs brings to light the sharp decline in the share of building and plant and machinery since the time when neo-liberal reforms were introduced under which the service sector and FIRE sector have grown more rapidly than the industrial sector which has a greater propensity to generate employment and real output. A fall in the rate of growth of real accumulation deters further capacity utilisation and leads to a decline in the rate of growth of the overall output of an economy. The same trend has been found across all the sub-sectors of NFCs. Figures 14.15 and 14.16 show the pattern in the stock holding of physical assets and financial assets by NFCs from 1990 to 2014.

In Figure 14.15, net fixed assets dropped by 26% from constituting approximately 39% of the total assets in 1990 to be approximately 29% of total assets in 2014. The drop in the stock of plant and machinery is 23%, from 41% of total assets in 1990 to approximately 30% of total assets in 2014. Net fixed assets also showed a gradual decline of 12.5%, 41%, 40%, 6% and 9% in manufacturing, mining, real estate and construction, service sector (other than financial) and electricity, respectively, from 1990 to 2014. Inventories and receivables of firms show the dynamics of trading activities and are considered as the firm's current assets. The stock of inventories and receivables shows the potential demand in the market for the non-financial goods and services. These components also show the declining trend in the consolidated balance sheets of NFCs highlighting the slump in their trading activities. However, when it comes to financial assets, NFCs' balance sheets demonstrate some interesting facts. The pattern in the holding of financial assets by NFCs in Figure 14.16 demonstrates a rising trend during the entire period of 1990–2014. Of all financial assets held by NFCs, loans and advances show the most brisk growth in their share of total assets. Ranking second regarding growth rate among financial assets, investment in equity and preference shares and debts shows a continuously increasing trend. Both the

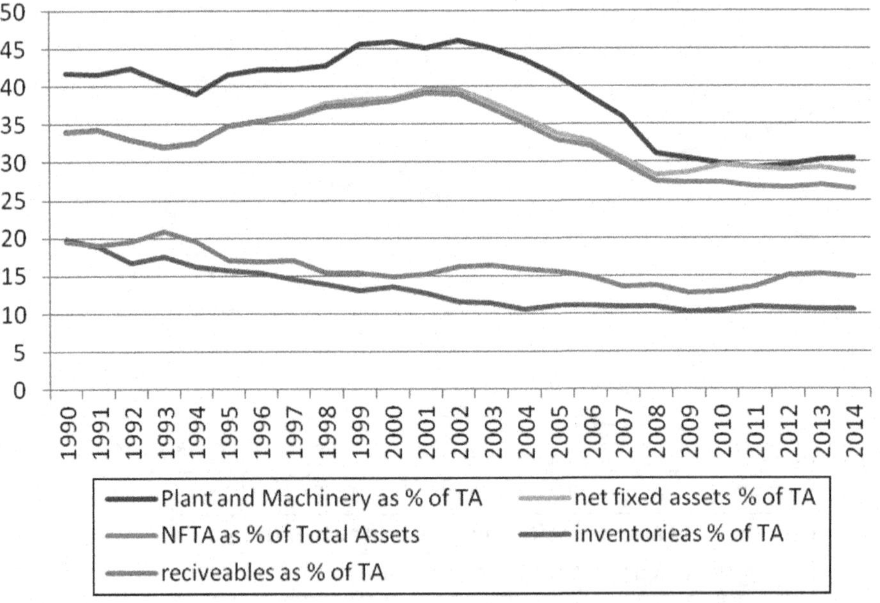

Figure 14.15 Trend in fixed assets as a portion of total assets of NFCs. *Source*: CMIE Prowess Database (Author's calculation).

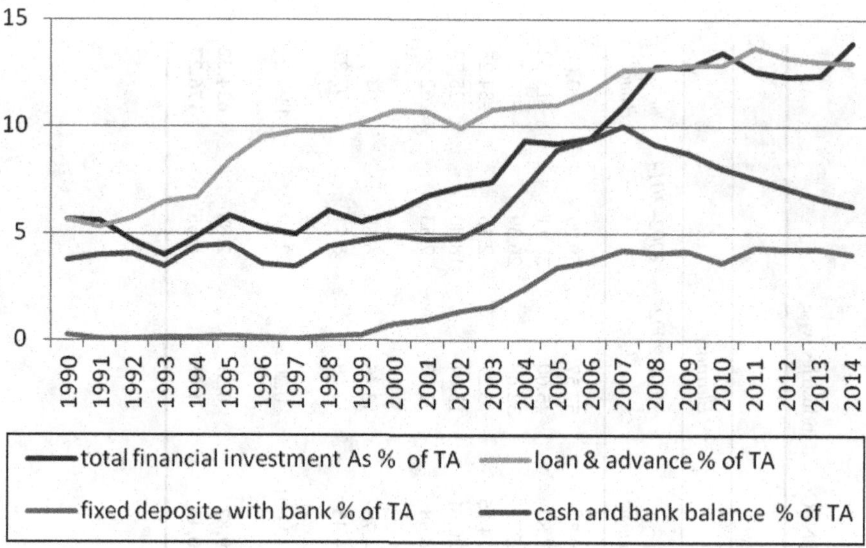

Figure 14.16 Trend of financial assets as percentage of total assets in balance sheet of NFCs. *Source*: CMIE Prowess Database (Author's calculation).

phenomena point to the fact that NFCs have started behaving increasingly like lenders of funds and stock market players. Loans and advances and financial investments increased by 140% and 160%, respectively, from 1990 to 2014. Other financial assets like fixed deposits with bank and cash and bank balance also show an increasing trend. Here, financial investments include the total investment made by firms in equity shares, preference shares and debentures. Tables 14.2 to 14.4 show the trend in the structure of firm-level balance sheet summarising changes in NFC real investment and financial investment behaviour over the post-1990 period. I will attempt to analyse the changing share of financial assets and physical assets in the consolidated balance sheet of NFCs and across all sub-sectors of the NFCs in two periods from 1990–2002 to 2003–14. This analysis will depict the pattern in the acquisition of the kind of assets by firms. It shows the investment portfolio shift away from fixed capital and towards financial assets for NFCs and in all sub-sectors of NFCs.

Tables 14.2 to 14.4 attempt to compare the average share of physical assets and financial assets in total assets of NFCs in two time periods (1990–2002 and 2002–2014) and across all sub-sectors. It emerges that the share of financial assets increased in the second phase (2002–2014) and the share of physical assets declined over the past two decades in the consolidated annual financial statements. All real assets (gross fixed assets, net fixed assets and plant and machinery) declined by 4.59%, 11.40% and 17.10%, respectively. Whereas the average share of financial assets such as loan and advance, investment in financial assets, cash and bank balance and fixed deposits with banks increased by 45%, 98.68%, 82% and 91.7%, respectively. This increase in the average percentage of total financial assets in two decades includes investment in both group companies as well as non-group companies and is an unprecedented phenomenon. This is again evidence that Indian corporates are investing in financial assets to earn short-term profit rather than investing in core operating activities such as setting up new plants, carrying out research and development or providing incentives to direct stakeholders of firms for the long-term growth of the industry. This behavioural change is the result of financial liberalisation under which the Indian economy opened up for global capital and FIIs were given access to invest

Table 14.2 Share of physical assets and financial assets in total assets of the consolidated balance sheet of NFCs and industries wise

Average % of total assets									
Assets	*Non-financial corporations*			*Manufacturing*			*Electricity*		
	1990–2002	*2002–2014*	*% change*	*1990–2002*	*2002–2014*	*% change*	*1990–2002*	*2002–2014*	*% change*
Gross fixed assets	54.23	51.75	−4.59	53.34	53.18	−0.30	57.57	59.29	3.00
Net fixed assets	35.88	31.79	−11.40	35.38	32.59	−7.89	45.00	38.11	−15.32
Plant & machinery	42.88	35.54	−17.10	22.89	23.64	3.27	32.68	26.39	−19.24
Inventories	15.36	10.86	−29.35	18.08	15.52	−14.15	3.27	2.15	−34.25
Sundry debtors	17.41	14.64	−15.96	17.56	13.94	−20.61	15.04	18.90	25.73
Financial investment	5.56	11.05	98.68	6.31	10.01	58.68	2.07	7.53	262.90
Loans & advances	8.36	12.16	45.43	7.96	10.73	34.78	3.43	6.65	94.18
Cash & Bank balance	4.19	7.64	82.20	3.76	6.55	74.45	2.59	5.11	97.27
Fixed deposits with bank	0.34	3.48	917.61	0.23	3.48	1434.01	0.20	2.50	1168.58
IGC	**2.08**	**6.57**	**215.64**	**17.94**	**35.86**	**99.87**	**0.39**	**2.88**	**634.52**
IOTGC	**3.48**	**4.48**	**28.64**	**11.11**	**15.60**	**40.43**	**1.68**	**4.65**	**176.27**

Source: CMIE Database (Author's calculation).

Table 14.3 Share of mining, real estate and service sector in total assets of the consolidated balance sheet of NFCs and industries-wise

Average % of total assets									
Assets	*Mining*			*Real sector and construction*			*Service*		
	1990–2002	*2002–2014*	*% change*	*1990–2002*	*2002–2014*	*% change*	*1990–2002*	*2002–2014*	*% change*
Gross fixed assets	88.29	62.59	–29.11	29.49	16.28	–44.79	47.77	50.54	5.81
Net fixed assets	42.99	26.82	–37.62	20.02	11.44	–42.86	31.61	32.30	2.16
Plant & machinery	30.46	17.60	–42.22	11.17	6.17	–44.73	12.06	13.66	13.28
Inventories	8.63	3.74	–56.71	28.04	25.13	–10.38	15.10	6.23	–58.72
Sundry debtors	13.95	6.63	–52.44	22.16	17.68	–20.20	19.50	14.40	–26.14
Financial investment	4.30	12.09	181.06	5.85	12.85	119.67	5.53	12.42	124.8
Loans & advances	10.26	24.49	138.62	12.84	21.60	68.26	12.84	12.79	–0.43
Cash & bank balance	3.26	16.11	394.33	5.96	6.40	7.37	7.40	9.60	29.63
Fixed deposits with bank	0.19	8.46	4396.11	1.12	2.78	146.70	0.83	3.16	283.11
I G C	**0.33**	**8.83**	**2555.14**	**2.88**	**8.08**	**180.20**	**2.37**	**8.43**	**255.56**
I O T G C	**3.97**	**3.27**	**–17.74**	**2.97**	**4.77**	**60.81**	**3.16**	**4.00**	**26.60**

Source: CMIE Database (Author's calculation).
*IGC – Investment in group company; IOTGC – Investment in other than group company.

Table 14.4 Compound annual growth rate of physical and financial assets of the consolidated balance sheet of NFCs

Assets	*Compound annual growth rate (1990–2014)*					
	Non-financial corporations	*Manufacturing*	*Electricity*	*Mining*	*Real estate and construction*	*Service*
Gross fixed assets	8.46	6.98	9.62	8.48	8.30	12.92
Net fixed assets	8.16	6.92	8.77	7.36	8.80	12.32
Plant & machinery	7.52	11.74	27.04	10.61	15.38	15.94
Inventories	6.15	5.48	6.45	3.61	12.12	6.83
Sundry debtors	7.71	6.11	10.54	4.79	11.71	10.94
Investment	13.08	8.33	16.88	27.29	19.83	19.15
Loans & advances	12.76	11.25	24.52	26.74	16.41	11.99
Cash and bank balance	11.33	9.53	11.54	19.14	9.38	12.13
Fixed deposits with bank	22.84	31.49	73.56	67.40	16.78	16.12
Investment in group company	23.22	32.12	43.81	50.49	29.55	28.22
Investment in non-group co.	8.07	6.57	9.79	20.90	11.90	12.89
Sales	7.76	7.14	10.43	7.69	10.36	9.46
Income from financial services	11.71	9.71	11.65	21.71	13.03	14.86

Source: CMIE Prowess database (Author's calculation).

in the domestic stock market in any type of equity. Ghosh (2005) argues that the reduction in controls over the investments that can be undertaken by financial agents and specifically, breaking down the "Chinese wall" between banking and non-banking activities is a hallmark of liberalisation; as is the easing of conditions for the participation of both firms and investors in the stock market by diluting or doing away with listing conditions, by providing freedom in pricing of new issues, by permitting greater freedoms to intermediaries, such as brokers and by relaxing conditions with regard to borrowing against shares and investing borrowed funds in the market.

An article published in the *Hindu Business Line* (19 March 2012), 'Corporate finance – less CapEx, more financialisation', reported that the annual studies of RBI of non-financial non-government public limited companies found an alarming investment pattern.The ratio of the total capital formation to total use of funds contracted from 67% to 52% in the second decade (2000–10) compared to the first decade (1990–2000). Meanwhile, for the second decade (2000–10), investment in financial assets, loans and advances and fixed deposits with banks increased by 91%, 17% and 269%, respectively. Conversely, the manufacturing sector, the major component of NFCs, shows a very gloomy trend in respect of real investment. Net fixed assets declined by approximately 8%, and plant and machinery showed an insignificant increase of just 3%. However, financial assets such as loans and advances, investment and fixed deposits with the bank had an increase of 345%, 58% and 1400% (an increase of 3.25 percentage points), respectively. In the same article, Managing Director of CMIE states that half of the non-finance companies' net fixed assets were shrinking, and only about 20% of the companies have above average growth in their assets; 41% of the money raised by 47 companies through IPOs during the 2008–10 period was placed in liquid assets, and about 35% of it was used for capital expenditure. The total investment in preference shares and equities and loans and advances has increased its share in total assets tremendously.

> The period of rapid growth during the 2000s, the large corporate sector was flush with funds with which to expand its productive capacity – indeed, it was able to fund its capital expenditure from its savings. However, instead of using these funds to expand its productive capacity, it diverted a large and growing share of these funds to the financial sphere – as a lender and an investor (or, more bluntly, a rentier and a speculator). The share of funds devoted to fixed assets, plant and machinery declined; the share of funds devoted to financial investments spurted. A much larger share of the funds raised from the share market was placed in 'liquid assets' – such as shares and bonds – than in capital expenditure.
>
> *(Deputy General manager, SIDBI, Lucknow;* Hindu Business Line, *31 March)*

Figure 14.17 demonstrates that financial assets held outside the company, including financial investment in non-group companies and other financial assets held in the form of deposits in banks and loan and advances, have ascended rapidly in proportion to total assets. Financial investment in group companies has been found peculiarly higher than financial investment in the non-group companies. That is, more NFCs are investing in the shares of a group company than in the shares of some other company in the stock market. This pattern shows two things.

- First, firms are diversifying their business by investing in subsidiaries or indulging in acquisitions and mergers to appreciate their stock market value and monopolise the market. The character of the diversification of business is unclear. Either big business groups want to

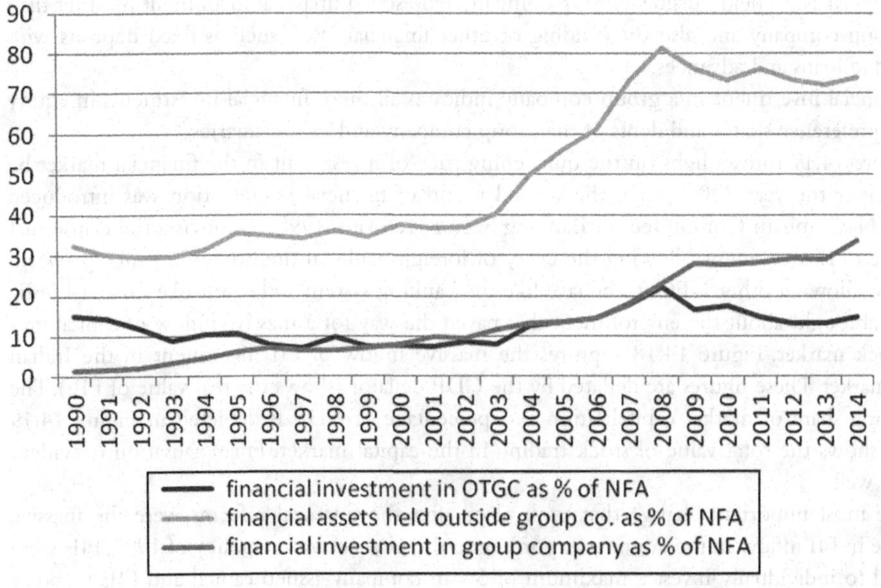

Figure 14.17 NFCs' financial assets held outside company and in group company as percentage of net fixed assets. *Source*: CMIE Prowess Database (Author's calculation).

jump into businesses of all kinds rather than invest in research and development in their core business for long-term growth or they are investing in group company to keep the group company's share prices artificially high in the stock market.

- Second, they might be investing in the group company to provide the capital base for expanding business diversification or specifically in those group companies that are involved in the financial market business (such as dealing in mutual funds, insurance, hedge funds), and through it, they are interested in investing in the financial market.

Majumdar (2008) refers to this multi-company character of Indian NFCs as 'Group Company'. He argues that a group company can include either those companies whom the group itself has promoted or those companies that the central authority of a group company has promoted or acquired. He also recognises that in the group company framework, group assets can also be redistributed among its companies from time to time, and businesses and companies may be transferred to other firms. Funds raised through one company may be routed to other companies. All such events in the history of Indian business group companies are generally consequences of the unilateral strategic choice of the central authority of the business groups not a product of mutual negotiation between the management of different companies. The increasing event of financial investment in other than a group company features more prominently after 1998. In the year 1998, Narasimham Committee on Banking Sector Reforms suggested strong liberalisation of the financial sector. It recommended a reduction in CRR (Cash Reserve Ratio) and SLR (Statutory Liquidity Ratio), granting free entry and exit of firms in the banking sector and also allowed foreign banks to enter the Indian banking sector. It also recommended the deregulation of the stock market and granted greater independence to FIIs to invest in the Indian market.

Financial investment in other than a group company means financial investment done in equity shares, preference shares and bonds of other companies in the stock market and also in government bonds.

Financial assets held outside a group company represent a financial investment in other than the group company and also the holding of other financial assets such as fixed deposits with banks and loans and advances.

Financial investment in a group company indicates all those financial investments in equity shares, preference shares and debts of the group company and its subsidiaries.

Figure 14.17 throws light on the quickening pace of investment in the financial market by NFCs after the year 2000, when the second round of financial liberalisation was introduced by the Narasimham Committee on Banking Sector Reforms, 1998. Removing the clause that restricted FII investment, allowing the entry of foreign banks in the domestic banking system and also allowing other NFCs to behave like the banking system and invest like financial institutions, brought about the environment that paved the way for a massive inflow of capital into the stock market. Figure 14.18 captures the massive inflow of FII investment in the Indian stock market. These figures are deflated by the GDP deflator (shows the real value of FIIs). The increasing share of market capitalisation as a percentage of GDP is depicted in Figure 14.19 which shows the total value of stock trading in the capital market. Financialisation is evident here as well.

The most important change that took place after the financial reforms were the massive increase in FII inflow in the country. According to the new economic policy of 1992, FIIs were allowed to individually invest a maximum of 5% in company-issued capital and FIIs together were allowed to invest up to 24% of the total capital issued by companies. However, in the second round of reforms that were ushered in during the year 2000, the investment limit of FIIs

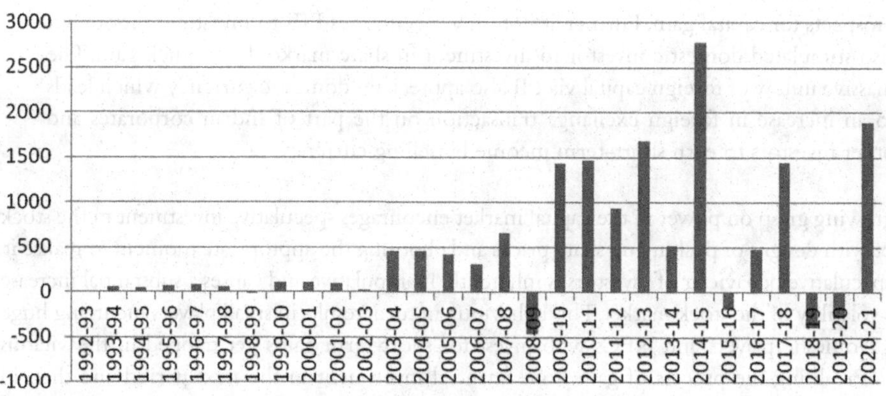

Figure 14.18 Foreign financial institution investments. *Source*: NSDL.

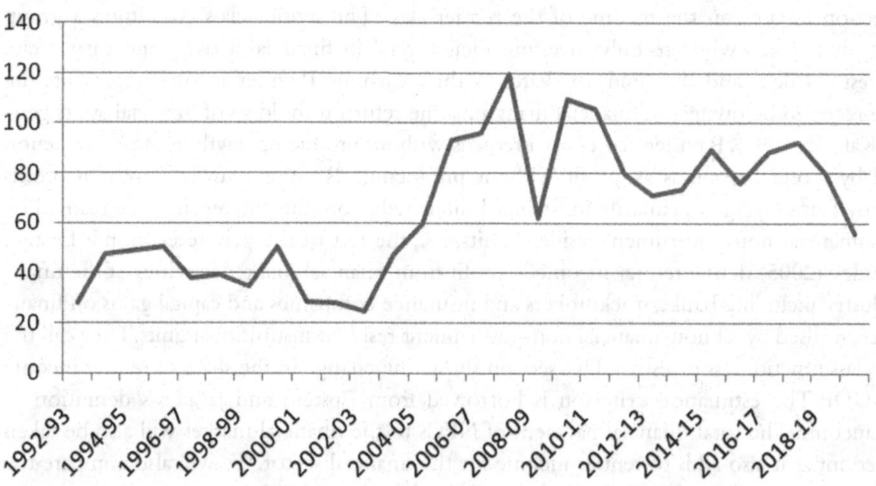

Figure 14.19 Market capitalisations at BSE as % of GDP. *Source*: RBI Database.

was increased. FIIs were now approved to individually invest up to 10% of a company's issued capital and FIIs together could invest a maximum of 40% of the capital issued in the stock market. Market capitalisation soared up to 120% of GDP in 2006–07 and remained around 80% of GDP in 2013. These changes substantially increased the presence of FIIs in the capital market, and the stability of the stock market too came to rely more on them.

According to Chandrasekhar and Pal (2006):

> This phenomenon of a surge in FII investment after reforms has made the market speculative and more volatile and also changed the Indian corporate behaviour regarding the choice of their portfolio investment. As the increase in the FII investment in share market leads to a tremendous increase in the price of shares and indicated good

prospects for capital gain. Further, it not only incentivises FIIs to investment more but also stimulated domestic investor to investment in share market for a quick gain. The massive inflow of foreign capital via FII also appreciates domestic currency which leads to an increase in foreign exchange transaction on the part of Indian corporates and other investors to earn short-term income by selling currency.

FIIs' growing grasp on power in the capital market encourages speculative investment in the stock market with designs of pushing up share prices and choosing the appropriate moment to realise it. This speculative behaviour of investors is inherently manipulative and causes a substantial increase in the volatility of the stock market. This behaviour, in turn, results in small players incurring huge losses. Domestic players and NFCs who invest for short-term gains get trapped in the vicious circle of realising the process of gain from financial investment in the next period and then in the next period eventually and sometimes permanently deterring investment in the real sector.

Increasing share of the rentier class in the cash flow of firms

This section focuses on the income of the rentier class. The rentier class constitutes a group of economic agents who are only investing their capital in financial activity and earn a rate of interest on debt and dividend on shares as their earning. Rentier income represents the income received by owners of financial firms, plus the return to holders of financial assets generally (Kalecki, 1990). Rentier classes earn returns without producing anything, a phenomenon termed by Costa Lapavitsas as 'profit without producing'. Rentier returns consist of profits earned by firms engaged primarily in financial intermediation plus interest income realised by all non-financial non-government resident units, i.e., the rest of the private economy. Epstein and Jayadev (2005) define rentier income as profit from financial market activities of the financial industry including banks, stockbrokers and insurance companies and capital gains on financial assets realised by all non-financial non-government resident institutional units. They call the rentier class functionless investors. This section shows the change in the share of rentier income in the GDP. The estimation criterion is borrowed from Epstein and Jayadev's definition of rentier income. The total financial payment of NFCs to the financial market will also be taken into account as it also adds to rentier income for the financial sector. We will also compare the profit rate and net value of financial corporations with those of NFCs.

Epstein, Power and Abrena (2003) present the estimation of rentier income share of 29 OECD countries. They state that the rise in rentier share occurred over two time periods: one when it rose rapidly in the 1960s to 1970s and then when it rose in the 1980s to 1990s. The definition of rentier income that they employ includes all the income accrued to financial institutions and holders of financial assets. Again Epstein and Power (2003) presented a renewed estimate of rentier share in OECD economy. They reported that the rentier share of income started increasing more dramatically in the 1980s, perfectly coinciding with the regime of neoliberal monetary and financial policy initiated by Margaret Thatcher and Paul Volcker. Epstein and Jayadev (2005) point out that Epstein, Power and Abrena's (2003) estimation is not corrected for inflation and might display an imprecise result. Therefore Epstein and Jayadev (2005) have attempted to correct this issue by estimating the rentier share of income after adjusting for inflation for 15 OECD countries. They reported in their research that rentier share in the UK went from 11.48% to 24.5%, in Korea from 7% to 15% and in the US it went up by 40% (from 25% to 35%) from the 1970s to the 1990s. In their fresh estimation, they found evidence of a negative correlation between rentier share of income and non-financial share of income. We will empirically investigate here how financial payments in terms of interest and dividend payment are increasingly going into the hands of the rentier class, especially the financial sector. Financial institutions are increasingly extracting huge amounts of surplus from the real sector. The increasing payments made by NFCs to the financial sector as well as decreasing investment for purchasing physical assets are depicted in Figures 14.20, 14.21 and 14.22.

Financial payment includes dividend payments, interest payments and purchase of financial investments. The real investment includes the purchase of fixed assets and employing working capital. Figure 14.21 shows the pattern of cash outflow of the company. Total cash outflow includes all the cash payments of the firm in an accounting period related to operating activities, investment activities and financial activities. Financial payment as a percentage of total cash outflow skyrocketed by from 9% of total cash outflow in 1990 to 63% of cash outflow in 2014. On the other hand, the purchase of fixed assets, as a proportion of total cash outflow increased from 48% in 1995 to 11% of total cash outflow in 2014. Figure 14.20 shows the increasing

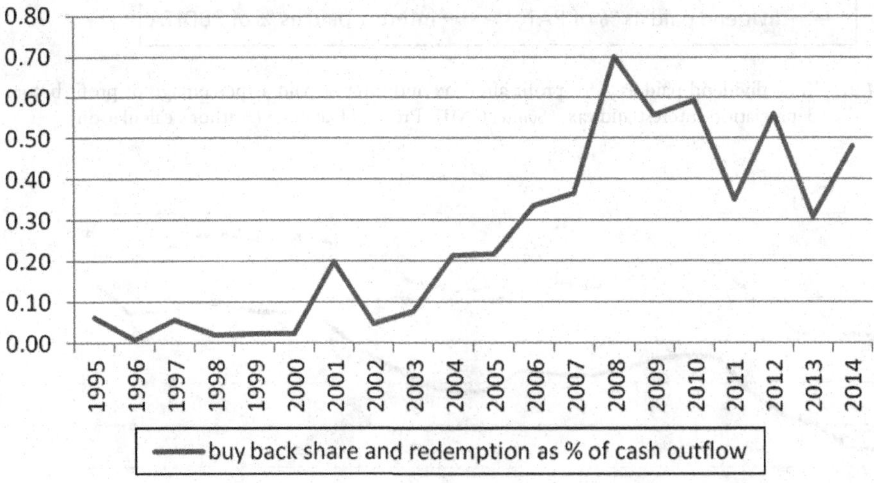

Figure 14.20 Buyback and redemption of shares as % of total cash outflow. *Source*: CMIE Prowess Database (Author's calculation).

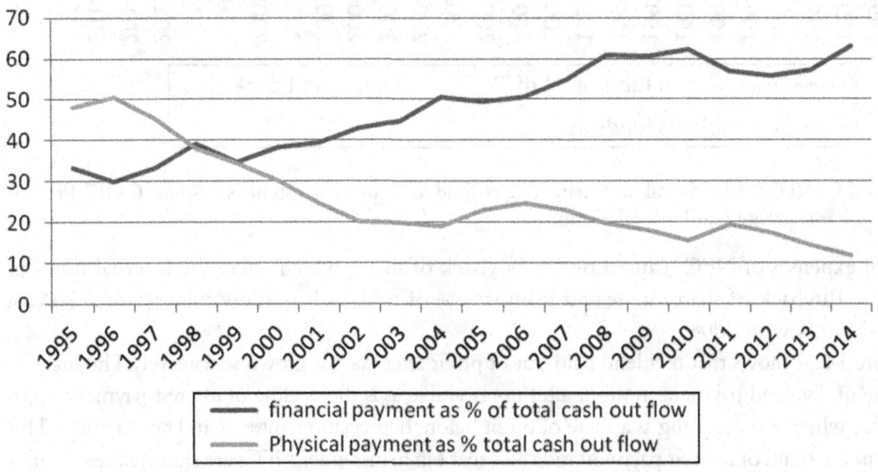

Figure 14.21 Financial payments and real payments as percentage of total cash outflow in cash flow statements. *Source*: CMIE Prowess Database (Author's calculation).

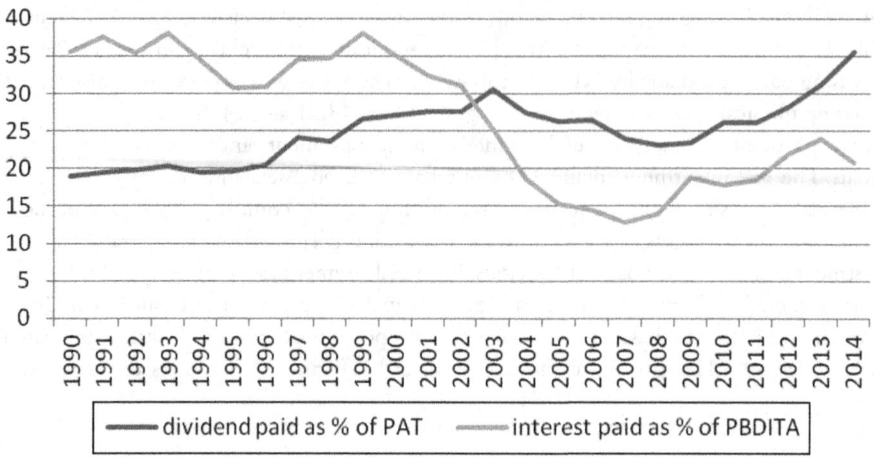

Figure 14.22 Total dividend paid as % of profit after tax and interest paid as percentage of profit before depreciation interest and tax. *Source*: CMIE Prowess Database (Author's calculation).

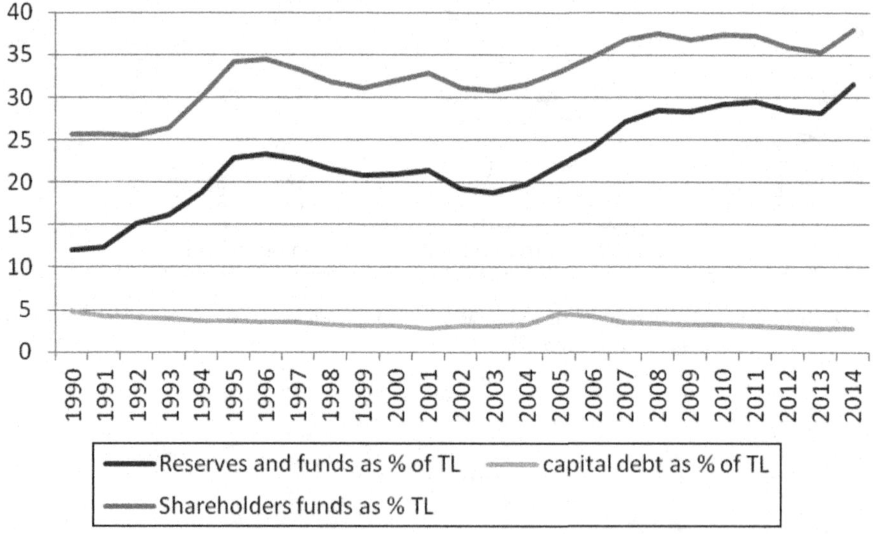

Figure 14.23 NFCs' debt capital and shareholders fund as % of total liabilities. *Source*: CMIE Prowess Database (Author's calculation).

financial expenses of NFCs caused by the buyback of shares which affect the internal funds of the firms. Buyback of shares increased from 0.06% of total cash outflow in 1995 to 0.70% of total cash outflow in 2008.

Figure 14.22 shows that dividend paid out of profit after tax has grown successively. The increasing share of dividend payment in profit after tax is visible as is the decline of interest payment up to 2008 after which it starts rising as a share of profit before depreciation, interest and tax payment. This decline in the trend of interest payment indicates that big firms under NFCs are shifting their financing pattern from debt capital to share capital which is observable in increasing dividend payment. We can also ascertain from Figure 14.23, that the debt capital of firms is gradually declining just as the percentage of total liabilities of NFCs and shareholder funds is showing a constantly increasing trend. Therefore, it specifies that firms are shifting to the stock market as a primary means to mobilise resources for real investment. Mobilising resources from shares issued is not the same as debt capital. In debt capital, the rate of return is fixed and is not subject to speculation whereas the rate of return is not fixed on shares. Dividend payment on shares is dependent on the profit earning of firms. Shareholders are not treated as the company's creditors but are formal partners of the company. Therefore, the increasing power of shareholders leaves the firms' management obliged always to keep the profit high. At the same time, firms also face competition in the market which limits them from increasing the price of commodities to earn a higher profit. In such an environment, firms under NFCs demand labour reforms and the deregulation of the market to reduce their cost of production. The other scenario involves NFCs' search for alternative earning opportunities in the financial or real estate market to keep their profits high to fulfil the interests of shareholders and compromise with not just their long-term growth strategy but also their relationship with direct stakeholders such as workers.

An interesting example that illustrates the relationship between retained profit and real long-term accumulation is that of Infosys. In 2014 the Infosys board announced they would pay 40% of post-tax profit as dividend to shareholders and in 2015 they increased it to 50%. Chief Financial Officer (CFO) said, 'We are consistent with our objective of increasing shareholders returns'. Earlier, Infosys used to give a dividend payout of less than 40%. Sanjeev Hota of Share Khan told NDTV that a higher dividend payout and bonus issue was good news for investors as it increased overall return (capital appreciation and dividend income) for the investors and that this indicated that the company is confident that it will be able to generate sufficient cash in future to meet its dividend payout requirement (NDTV& *The Economic Times*, April 24, 2015). However, some analysts also say that a higher dividend payout ratio indicates that Infosys does not have any other profitable opportunity to deploy its cash. As of March 31, 2015, Infosys had a cash balance of Rs 30,367 crore. But then it also enunciates that Infosys does not see investing in research and development and delivering incentives to its employees to maintain a high-road relationship between workers and the management as profitable in the long term or as a long-term growth opportunity for the company.

Bloomberg Business reported on May 7, 2015, that the most profitable Indian oil explorer, ONGC was looking for a fund for investment as cash had dried up. ONGC's surplus cash has been sucked out by the government either in the form subsidy or dividend payments.

Figure 14.24 shows the comparison between the total payment to the financial sector every year and income earned from the financial sector in the form of interest and dividends for NFCs and the amounts mentioned have been deflated using the GDP deflator. Here, the estimation of financial payment includes interest payment, dividend payment and buyback of shares and purchase of an investment. In calculating the financial income, we have included total interest received, dividend received and sales of investment (financial assets). Remarkably, financial payment has always been greater than financial income year after year. The logic, given by policy makers and desired by big firms, is that financial liberalisation and market deregulation will channelise the resources to the real sector. Firms think that short-term investment in the financial market will ensure adequate funds in the next period for long-term investment in the real sector. Nonetheless, this hypothesis is not getting validated under the atmosphere of financialisation because the earning from financial investment remains lower than financial payment year after year. Figure 14.25 shows the use of available funds for financial payment and real investment. In the early part of the 1990s, the share of real investment of total funds was higher than the share of financial payments. The trend reversed after 1999. This shows an upward trend in the use of funds for financial purposes in the cash flow statement of firms. We have calculated total

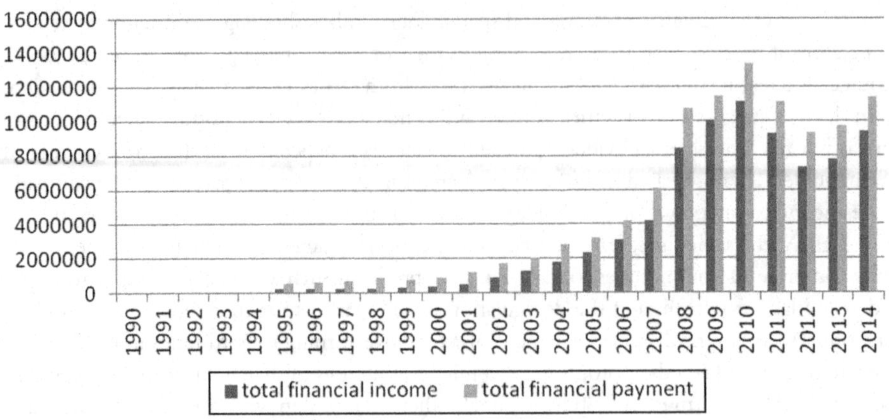

Figure 14.24 NFC total financial income received and total financial payments. *Source*: CMIE Prowess Database (Author's calculation).

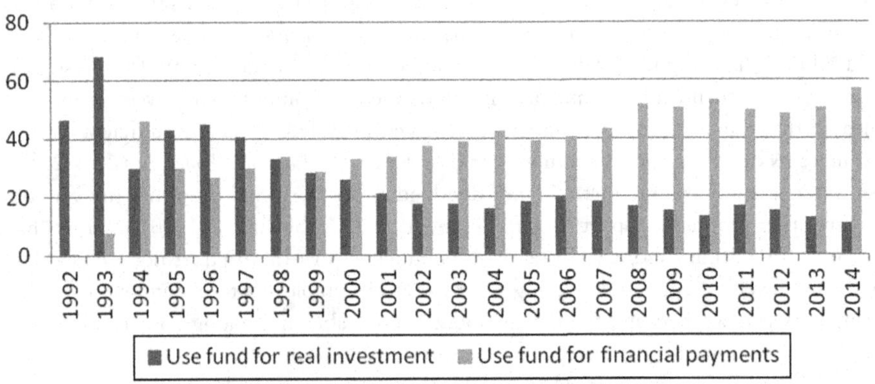

Figure 14.25 Uses of funds for financial payment and real investment as percentage of total funds. *Source*: CMIE Prowess Database (Author's calculation).

funds by aggregating all the cash inflows such as operating profit, interest received and dividend received, cash proceeds from the issue of shares, the sale of investment and assets and long-term borrowing from the market. Once again this proves how the regime's continuous engagement of NFCs in the financial sector under financial liberalisation has increased the financial liabilities of the firms. Increasing financial liability has entrapped NFCs in the vicious circle of speculative activities. The firms are playing in the capital market indefinitely to either absolve themselves from created debt or to invest in anticipation of earning huge gains in the short term. If, for once, a firm earns huge gains in the market, it anticipates again even higher than before. If, contrarily, the firm lost money in the market, it would again look to recover this money in the next period and continue investment, perhaps with an even more diverse and large portfolio. This behaviour of firms keeps them engaging with the financial sector indeterminately and affects the real sector accumulation process unfavourably.

Figures 14.26 and 14.27 depict the increasing share of the financial sector in the economy. Figure 14.26 compares the profit before tax of financial corporations with non-financial corpo-

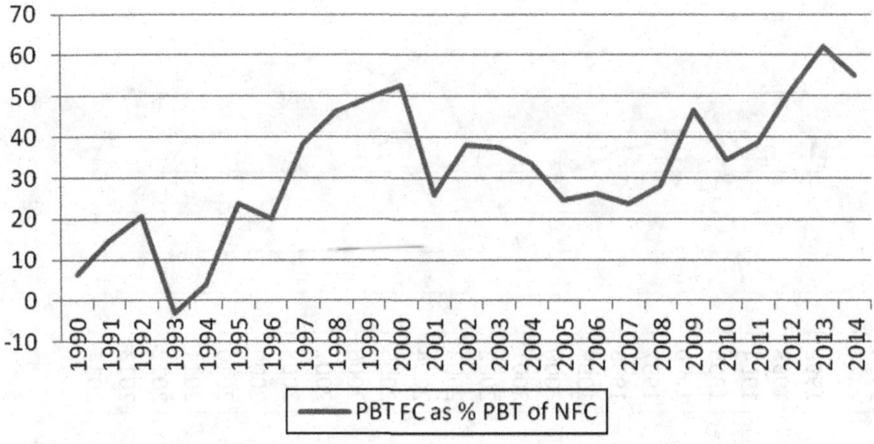

Figure 14.26 Profits before tax of financial corporations as % of profit before tax of NFCs. *Source*: CMIE Prowess Database (Author's Calculation).

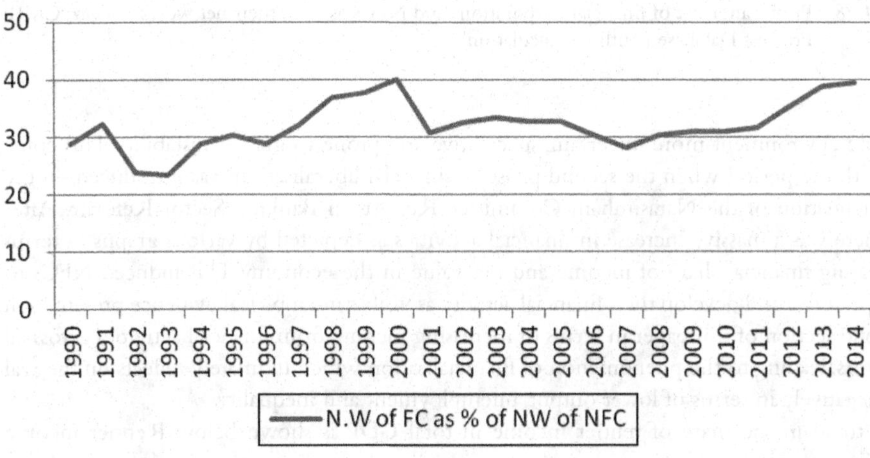

Figure 14.27 Net worth of financial sector as % of net worth of NFC. *Source*: CMIE Prowess Database (Author's calculation).

rations. The profit before tax in the financial sector, shown as a percentage of the profit before tax in the non-financial sector, saw a steep rise to 60% in 2013 from around 6% in 1990. In estimating the profit rate, I have borrowed from Dumenil and Levy (2001), calculating profit after tax as a percentage of the net worth of firms. Figure 14.27 plots the ratio of the net worth of the financial sector to the net worth of the non-financial sector. In the early 1990s, this ratio stood at 28% before swiftly soaring to 40% in 2000. Around the financial crisis of 2008, it fell to 30% but again saw an augmentation to settle at nearly 40%. In Figure 14.28, we compare the profit rate between financial corporations and non-financial corporations. It shows that after 2000 the profit rate in the financial sector shows a greater increase than the profit rate of NFCs. It makes evident that either in terms of net worth or in terms of its rate of profit, the financial sector has dramatically usurped a large share of the real sector in the national income, leading to further proliferation of new financial institutions and financial innovations and making the

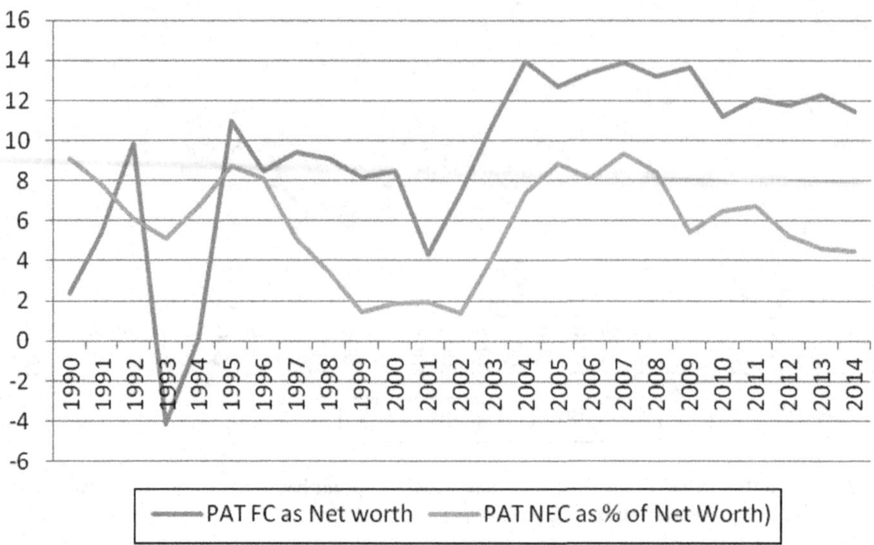

Figure 14.28 Profits after tax of financial corporations and NFCs as % of their net worth. *Source*: CMIE Prowess Database (Author's calculation).

economic environment more uncertain, speculative and prone to greater instability. This coincided with the period when the second phase of financial liberalisation was introduced on the recommendation of the Narasimham Committee Report on Banking Sector Reforms. After 2000, there was a massive increase in financial activities as depicted by various graphs in terms of increasing financial share of income and net value in the economy. This induced NFCs to indulge in it too and develop their financial activity as visible in empirical evidence presented in the second section of this paper in terms of increasing income from financial activities across all sub-sectors, leading to the phenomenon of financialisation which ultimately reflects on the real sector negatively in terms of lower output, unemployment and inequality.

The trend in the share of rentier income in total GDP is shown below. Rentier income calculation:

Rentier Income = NFCs' gross income from financial activities (Interest and dividend) + Profit after tax of financial corporation's (Banks, financial institution, NBFC, Insurance company).

The definition of rentier income has been borrowed from Epstein and Jayadev (2005), in a broad sense, according to which rentier income consists of the profit earned by firms engaged primarily in financial activities plus the interest income realised by all non-financial, non-government resident units. I have followed their definition except in regard to the dividend earned by NFCs which I have considered as an integral part of rentier income.

In Figure 14.29, rentier income shows a massive upsurge in the share of the total GDP in India between 1990 and 2014. Rentier income has been calculated after adjusting for inflation through the GDP deflator. Rentier income has shown a 360% increase in its share in GDP from 2.8% of GDP in 1990 to 12.9% of GDP in 2014. In the period of financial crisis from 2007 to 2009, it shows an even higher increase in its share of GDP. This phenomenon is leading to a dramatic increase of rentier income and strengthening rentier class political hegemony in the economy.

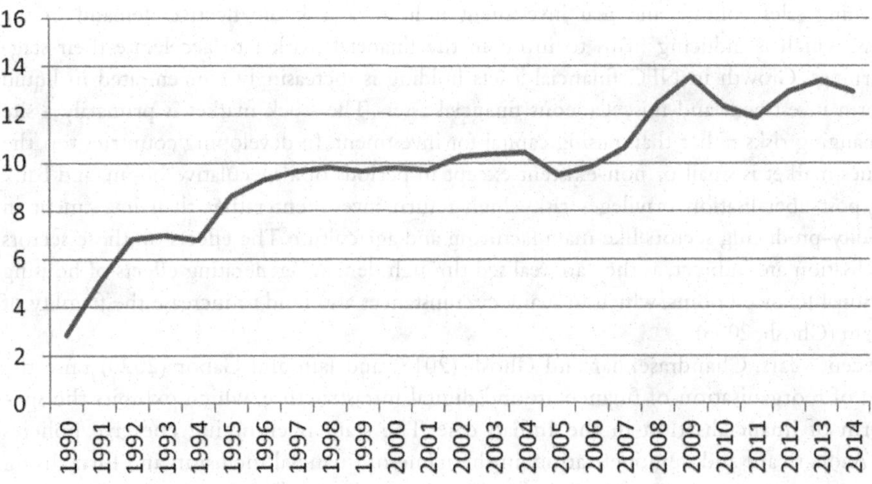

Figure 14.29 Rentier incomes as % of GDP. *Source*: CMIE Prowess Database (Author's calculation).

This environment created by the expanding role of financial activities with the idea of cushioned growth in the real economy actually affects the growth of the real sector adversely: If a speculative bubble in the financial market leads to a financial crisis, it squeezes the liquidity in the economy and increases the current cost of the transaction. This results in a lack of effective demand for real goods and negatively impacts the sales volume of NFCs and their profit rate which further leads to a decline in real investment by NFCs in the wake of lower profit rate expectation, subsequently resulting in lower employment growth and decay in living standards. Financial liberalisation is destroying the main motive of the financial sector which is to mobilise and allocate resources according to the priorities sector which can then secure maximum social returns.

Conclusion

The above discussion established the changing investment behaviour of firms in a scenario of low pace of growth rate in the real sector. The empirical trend shows that the firms are increasingly investing in financial assets and paying out huge chunks of their profits to financial agents and income from financial activities is increasing at a higher rate than income from primary activities of the firms. The study also found a sharp concentration of financial assets in the consolidated balance sheet of the NFCs and a declining trend in the creation of new physical assets, which means a fall in the growth of the real accumulation process and financial activities and financial motives taking the dominant position in economic activities. The results presented in this paper show that the concentration of financial assets and rentier income in terms of interest and dividend income went up dramatically between 2000 and 2014. The process of financialisation is taking place mainly through the expansion of the stock market and the derivatives market. Different forms of financial innovation such as mutual funds, private insurance schemes, facilitation of credit to NFCs on the basis of risk analysis and private rate of return instead of accounting for social returns from investment and increasing hedge funds in the economy are causing the proliferation of speculative behaviour in economic agents, making the economy head towards the financialisation of the real sector.

Declining sales volume and real investment indicate a lack of effective demand in the economy, which is inducing firms to invest in the financial market to accelerate their stagnant earnings. Growth in NFC financial assets holding is increasingly concentrated in liquid short-term investment and miscellaneous financial assets. The stock market is primarily a site for exchanging risks rather than raising capital for investment. In developing countries too, the new issues market is small or non-existent except in periods of a speculative boom, and bank lending post-liberalisation privileges risky high-return investment rather than investment in commodity-producing sectors like manufacturing and agriculture. The effects on those sectors of liberalisation are indirect, as they are realised through demand-generating effects of housing and personal finance booms, which in many circumstances also tend to increase the fragility of the system (Ghosh, 2005).

In recent years, Chandrasekhar and Ghosh (2018) and Jain and Gabor (2020) raise the concern of reorganisation of finance around digital infrastructure, which exhibits the specific form of financialisation in the Indian case. The state is enforcing coercive policies such as Aadhar card and demonetisation, in the name of financial inclusion and formalising e-transaction, respectively. But these kinds of policies are actually transferring income to the financial intermediaries, raising inequality and promoting state surveillances. The RBI bulletin July 2019 marked a major shift in the pattern and volume of financial transactions during the period 2012 to 2018. Household savings are shifting from physical assets to financial assets (mutual funds, insurance, pension fund etc.). Loans and advances from the banking sector are declining, whereas from NBFCs they are increasing. Private NFCs are reducing their reliance on borrowings from banks.

Financial liberalisation also facilitates space for the creation of an oligarchy of financial corporations and non-financial corporations. Financial firms who are members of this group would like to finance only those NFCs who are a part of this conglomerate. Over the long term, this leads to the creation of a monopoly in the market and kills the smaller financial and non-financial firms. The surge in capital inflow makes the trend in the exchange rate rather volatile. It has been observed in many developing countries that an appreciation in the exchange rate leads to increased investment in non-tradable goods instead of the real sector having huge, short-term gains. This phenomenon in the economy heavily contributes to a boom in real estate and the stock market instead of the manufacturing sector which is considered to be the main driver of potential economic growth and employment. This process of financialisation in an economy is leading to a decline in real economic activities and even deindustrialisation in developing countries.

Due to inaccessibility to the CMIE Prowess Database, the analysis after the year 2014 could not be incorporated. We need more research in this area to accurately explore the link between poverty, unemployment and income inequality in the Indian economy due to financialisation. We need to investigate the dynamics of rentier income and its impact on the functional distribution of income between wages and profit in this new era of intense liberalisation and globalisation of the Indian economy.

Notes

1 This paper is a part of the contributor's MPhil dissertation submitted to the Centre for Economic Studies and Planning, Jawaharlal Nehru University. The contributor is thankful to his MPhil supervisor Dr Rohit for his comments and valuable suggestions.

2 According to RBI, the treasury income for banks includes net profit (loss) on sale of investments, on revaluation of investments and on exchange transactions.

Bibliography

Azad, R. (2011): "A Steindlian Model of Concentration, Debt, and Growth", *Metroeconomica*, 63(2), 295–334.

Azad, R. (2012): *It's not Over: Structural Drivers of the Global Economic Crisis*. Oxford University Press, New Delhi.

Banerjee, A. and T. Piketty. (2005): "Top Indian Incomes, 1922-2000", *World Bank Economic Review*, 19, 1–20.

Bhaduri, A., and Marglin, S. (1990): "Unemployment and the Real Wage: The Economic Basis for Contesting Political Ideologies," *Cambridge Journal of Economics*, 14, 375–393.

Boyer, R. (2000): "Is a Finance-Led Growth Regime a Viable Alternative to Fordism? A Preliminary Analysis," *Economy and Society*, 29(1): 111–145.

Baran, P., and Sweezy P. (1966): *Monopoly Capital*. New York: Monthly Review Press.

Brenner, R. (2002): *The Boom and the Bubble: The US in the World Economy*. London: Verso.

Chandrasekhar, C. P., and Ghosh, J. (1999): "The Indian Economic Reform Process and the Implications of the Southeast Asian Crisis," in *Action Programme on Structural Adjustment, Employment and the Role of the Social Partners*. Geneva: Employment and Training Department International Labour Office; Employment and Training papers 55.

Chandrasekhar, C. P. and Pal, Parthapratim. (2006): Financial liberalization in India: An Assessments of its nature and outcomes, *Economic and Political Weekly*, 41(11): 975–90.

Chandrasekhar, C. P. (2008): "Global Liquidity and Financial Flow to Developing Countries: New Trends in Emerging Markets and Their Implications," *G24 Discussion Paper Series No.52*, UNCTAD.

Chandrasekhar, C.P. (2011): "Financial Liberalisation and Fragility in Developing Countries: The Indian Experience", *Journal für Entwicklungspolitik*, XXVII, 28–46.

Chandrasekhar, C.P. and J. Ghosh. (2018): "The Financialization of Finance? Demonetization and the Dubious Push to Cashlessness in India", *Development and Change*, 49 (2): 420–436.

Clark I. (2009): "Owners and Managers: Disconnecting Managerial Capitalism? Understanding the Private-Equity Business Model," *Work, Employment and Society* 23(4): 775–86

Crotty, J. (1990): "Owner-Manager Conflict and Financial Theories of Investment Instability – A Critical Assessment of Keynes, Tobin, and Minsky," *Journal of Post Keynesian Economics*, 12(4): 519–542.

Crotty, J. (2000): "Slow Growth, Destructive Competition, and Low Road Labour Relations': A Keynes-Marx-Schumpeter Analysis of Neoliberal," Available at http://www.umass.edu/peri/research.html

Crotty, J. (2005): "The Neoliberal Paradox: The Impact of Destructive Product Market Competition and 'Modern' Financial Markets on Nonfinancial Corporation Performance in the Neoliberal Era," in Epstein, G. (ed.) *Financialization and the World Economy*. Northampton, MA: Edward Elgar, pp 77–110.

Crotty, J. (2005): The Neoliberal Paradox: The Impact of Destructive Product Market Competition and Impatient financial markets on nonfinancial corporation in the neoliberal Era. *Review of Radical Political Economics*, 35(3): 271–79

Dumenil, G., and Levy, D. (2001): "Costs and Benefits of Neoliberalism: A Class Analysis," *Review of International Political Economy*, 8(4): 578–607.

Dumenil, G., and Levy, D. (2004): "The Real and Financial Components of Profitability (USA 1952–2000)," *Review of Radical Political Economics*, 36(1): 82–110.

Dünhaupt, P. (2013). 'The effect of financialization on labor's share of income'. *Institute for International Political Economy Berlin*. Working Paper 17/2013.

Economic Survey 2013–14, 2014–15.

Epstein, G. (2001). "Financialization, Rentier Interests, and Central Bank Policy," *manuscript, Department of Economics, University of Massachusetts, Amherst, MA, December.* Paper prepared for PERI Conference on "Financialization of the World Economy", December 7-8, 2001, University of Massachusetts, Amherst.

Epstein, G. (2005): "Introduction: Financialization and the World Economy," in Epstein, G. (ed.) *Financialization and the World Economy*. London: Edward Elgar, pp 3–16.

Epstein, G., and Jayadev, A. (2005): "The Rise of Rentier Incomes in OECD Countries: Financialisation, Central Bank Policy and Labour Solidarity," in Epstein, G. (ed.) *Financialisation and the World Economy*. Northampton, MA: Edward Elgar, pp 46–76

Epstein, G., and Power, D. (2003): *Rentier Incomes and Financial Crises: An Empirical Examination of Trends and Cycles in Some OECD Countries*. PERI Working Paper, No. 57, Political Economy Research Institute. Available at: http://ssrn.com/abstract=395160.

Epstein, G.A., and Jayadev, A. (2005): "The Rise of Rentier Incomes in OECD Countries: Financialisation, Central Bank Policy and Labour Solidarity," in Epstein, G.A. (ed.) *Financialisation and the World Economy*, (pp. 46–74). Cheltenham: Edward Elgar.

Ghosh, J. (2005): "The Economic and Social Effects of Financial Liberalization: A Primer for Developing Countries," DESA Working Paper No. 4, October. http://www.un.org/esa/desa/papers/2005/wp4_2005.pdf

Hein, Eckhard. 2012: *The Macroeconomics of Finance-Dominated Capitalism-and its Crisis*. Northampton, MA: Edwrd Elgar.

Investment Commission of India Recommendation (2004).

Jain, S. and Gabor, D. (2020): "The rise of digital financialisation: the case of India". *New Political Economy*, 25(5): 1–16.

Kalecki, M. (1937): "The Principle of Increasing Risk," *Economica*, 4: 440–447.

Kalecki, M. (1971): *Selected Essays in the Dynamics of the Capitalist Economy*. Cambridge: Cambridge University Press.

Kalecki, M. (1990): *Collected Works of Michal Kalecki, vol. I.* In: Capitalism: Business Cycles and Full Employment, J. Osiatynski (eds.), trans. C.A. Kisiel, Oxford: Oxford University Press.

Krippner, G. (2005): "The Financialization of the American Economy," *Socio-Economic Review*, 3(2): 173–208.

Lapavitsas, C.. (2009): "Financialised Capitalism: Crisis and Financial Expropriation,"*Historical Materialism*, 17(2): 114–148.

Lapavitsas, C. (2013): *Profiting without Producing; How Finance Exploits Us All*. London: Verso.

Lazonick, W. and O'Sullivan, M. (2002): Corporate Resource Allocation and Employment Opportunities in the United States. In: Lazonick, William and O'Sullivan, Mary (eds.). *Corporate Governance and Sustainable Prosperity*. Palgrave Macmillan: New York.

Nayyar, Deepak. (2015): "Birth, Life and Death of Development Finance Institutions in India", *Economic and Political Weekly*, 50(33): 51–60.

Nayyar, Deepak. (2017): Development Banks and Industrial Finance – The Indian Experience and its Lessons. In: Noman, Akbar and Stiglitz, Joseph (eds.). *Efficiency, Finance, and Varieties of Industrial Policy – Guiding Resources, learning, and Technology for Sustained Growth*, New York: Columbia University Press, pp 191–221.

National Manufacturing Policy (2011).

Orhangazi, Ö. (2008): "Financialisation and Capital Accumulation in the Non-financial Corporate Sector: A Theoretical and Empirical Investigation on the US Economy: 1973–2003," *Cambridge Journal of Economics*, 32, 863–886.

Palley, T. I. (2007): *Financialisation: What It Is and Why It Matters*, Economic Working Paper 525. Levy Economics Institute, Washington, DC.

Patnaik, P. (1999): "The Real Face of Financial Liberalisation," *Frontline*, 16(4), Feb. 13–26.

Patnaik, P. (2005): "The Economics of the New Phase of Imperialism," Paper presented at IDEAS Conference on The Economics of the New Imperialism. New Delhi: Jawaharlal Nehru University, January 22–24, 2004.

RBI Financial Stability Report (June 2014).

Sen, S. and Dasgupta, Z. (2014): "What Deters Investment in India Today?" *The Hindu*, 10th September 2014.

Sen, S., and Dasgupta, Z. (2015): *Financialisation and Corporate Investments: The Indian Case*, Working Paper No. 828. Levy Economics Institute of Bard College, Washington, DC.

Sen, K. and Vaidya, R. (1999): *The Process of Financial Liberalization in India*, New Delhi: Oxford University Press.

Stockhammer, E. (2004): "Financialization and the Slowdown of Accumulation," *Cambridge Journal of Economics*, 28: 719–741.

Van Treeck, T. (2009): "A Synthetic, Stock-Flow Consistent Macroeconomic Model of Financialisation," *Cambridge Journal of Economics*, 33(3): 467–493.

15

SHADOW BANKING AND EVALUATION OF SYSTEMIC RISKS IN THE POST-REFORM PERIOD

A case study of gold loan NBFC in India[1]

Dawa Sherpa

Introduction

Under the backdrop of financial liberalisation and associated deregulation in many countries, the emergence of shadow banking and its importance from the point of view of systemic stability of the financial system and consequent recessionary impact on the real economy cannot be overlooked. Shadow banking exists side by side with the traditional formal banking system performing similar kinds of banking services except that they are lightly or not at all regulated by the regulators and do not enjoy the liquidity facility of the central bank. Such unregulated non-bank credit intermediations are known as shadow banking activities. These institutions are highly leveraged, deeply interconnected and more prone to bank runs. Shadow banks have emerged as the fastest growing subsector of financial systems across the globe (both North and South) and were at the heart of the global financial crisis, 2007–08 (Lyasandrou and Nesvetailova 2015, Gorton 2010). According to the Financial Stability Board (FSB) 2017 report, the global shadow system peaked at US$ 62 trillion in 2007, declined to US$ 59 trillion during the crisis and rebounded to US$ 99 trillion at the end of 2016. The shadow banking system's share of total financial intermediation reached 30 per cent in 2016 (FSB, 2017).

Shadow banks are growing at a phenomenal rate in developing countries like India. In contrast to the shadow banks in the developed world, shadow banking in most of the developing countries consists of a broad spectrum of financial institutions and activities, which may not resemble the typical Anglo-Saxon model of financial system (Sinha 2013). The research on emerging economies has not extensively covered the unregulated area of finance (non-bank credit intermediation) which is growing in size and interconnection (Öncü 2013).

Shadow banking in the context of developed economies has been extensively studied and a vast literature on this topic has been generated within a short span of time since the onset of the global financial crisis in 2007 (Adrian and Ashcraft 2012, Pozsar et al. 2013). However, extensive and detailed research on shadow banking activities in emerging economies particularly with respect to the Indian economy is still lacking. As such, this paper attempts to fill this research gap by analysing the rise of shadow banks in the Indian financial system in the post-liberalisation

 DOI: 10.4324/9780367855741-15

period with particular emphasis on gold loan Non-Banking Finance Companies (NBFCs), which are the emerging shadow financial entities in India.

The chapter is broadly divided into three sections. The first section mainly deals with the concept of shadow banking in general, summarises its salient features and the systemic risks associated with shadow banking activities. The second section analyses the evolution of Shadow banking in India, its pattern of assets and liability structure, its interconnection with other parts of the financial system, emerging systemic risks and regulatory challenges for the policymakers. Finally, the third section examines the rise of a new kind of shadow banking activities in the form of gold loan NBFCs.

Data sources and methodology

The data used for analysis in this chapter are drawn from the Centre for Monitoring Indian Economy (CMIE) – Prowess Database, Report on Trend and Progress of Banking in India – Reserve Bank of India (RBI), Financial Stability Board Reports (FSB) – Reserve Bank of India and gold loan non-bank financial companies' annual reports.

Non-inferential statistical analysis using time series data along with suitable tables and charts (pie diagrams, line plots and bar charts) are used to study the emergence of shadow banking in India in the post-liberalisation period.

An overview of shadow banking

Shadow banking being a less researched phenomenon in India, some important aspects of shadow banks are covered here so as to provide an appropriate conceptual framework through which analysis and interpretations are done in the later sections.

Definition of shadow banking

The term "shadow banking" was first coined by McCulley (2007) in the context of the United States (US) financial system and was used later by other scholars and policymakers. McCulley defined shadow banking as "the whole alphabet soup of levered up non-bank investment conduits, vehicles, and structures". Further, he identified shadow banks as a collection of all leveraged financial intermediaries whose liabilities were perceived as safe as bank deposits. The rise of shadow banking in the US was visible with the emergence of money market funds in the 1970s. Money market funds provided financial instruments that acted like quasi-deposits but were not regulated as bank deposits.

Depending on the focus and the approach of study, shadow banking has been a wide spectrum of definitions and measurements (IMF 2014, Sherpa 2013). However, the definition used by the Financial Stability Board (FSB)[2] is most widely accepted and is defined as "a system of credit intermediation that involves entities and activities outside the regular banking system, and raises systemic risk concerns and regulatory arbitrage concerns" (FSB 2011). Therefore, shadow banking is essentially credit intermediation outside the regulated banking system, which has the potential to pose systemic risk to the financial system. The US Financial Crisis Inquiry Commission's report of 2010 also followed a similar connotation of shadow banking as non-bank credit intermediation.

Features of the shadow banking system

Notwithstanding the multiplicity of definitions of shadow banks, certain important properties of shadow banks can be briefly summarised as follows:

i. Market mediated credit intermediation: Shadow banks are money market funding for capital market lending (Mehrling 2013). They primarily rely on volatile short-term wholesale funding (Asset Backed Commercial Papers (ABCP)[3], Money Market Mutual Funds (MMMF)[4], Repo agreements) from markets to fund long-term assets which creates liquidity-risk mismatch (United Nations Conference on Trade and Development 2011). Compared to banks their assets are more risky and illiquid (Acharya et al. 2013).
ii. Reliance on non-core funding: According to Shin 2010, core funding mainly consists of bank deposits from non-financial corporate bodies and households. Non-core funding includes all other sources of financing, especially market-based funding. Shadow bank primarily relies on such non-core liabilities for financing real activities (Shin 2010, Artak Harutyunya et al., 2015).
iii. No government guarantee for funds raised: Shadow banks liability (deposits) are not insured like those of banks. In case tail risk materialises then they do not have deposit insurance schemes as typically exist for traditional banks, which makes them more resilient during stress periods (Adrian and Ashcraft, 2012, Pozsar et al 2013).
iv. No liquidity support from central bank: Shadow banks essentially lack liquidity support from the central bank. They lack the facility of emergency liquidity from the central bank which banks have access to during a time of distress (Acharya et al. 2013).
v. Highly leveraged and pro cyclical: Light regulation allows shadow banks to take high risk and leverage. Pro cyclical credit of shadow banks accentuates asset boom bust cycle (Anand Sinha 2013, FSB, 2013).
vi. Interconnected and opaque: Deeper interconnection and interdependence with other parts of the financial system makes them highly complex entities (FSB 2012). The opacity and complexity of shadow banking activities increase vulnerabilities, as investors tend to retrench and flee towards quality and transparency (Caballero and Simsek 2009).

Systemic risks of shadow banking

When shadow banking performs credit intermediation (maturity and leverage) without liquidity support from the central bank and its interconnections with regular banks are strong, shadow banking increases the financial fragility of the system. The systemic risks related to shadow banking can be broadly divided into four types:

i. **Run risk:** Shadow banks are vulnerable to bank-like risks including run risk as they perform bank-like credit intermediation in a deregulated environment. Since assets are risky, illiquid and of longer tenure than short-term liability, the risk arises of liquidity and maturity mismatches between assets and liability sides. These risks are higher for shadow banks as they do not have access to central bank liquidity facilities during distress and operate outside bank-like prudential regulation and supervision (Adrian 2014, Sinha, 2013).
ii. **Leverage and pro-cyclicality risk:** Lack of regulation of borrowing can cause shadow banks to be highly leveraged. When the asset price is rising then the margin on secured financing is low, and shadow banking increases its leverage. If a recessionary tendency develops in the economy, then the value of collateral securities falls and the margin increases, forcing these shadow banks to sudden deleveraging and margin spirals, making the financial system more fragile (Brunnermeier and Pedersen 2009, Sinha 2013).
iii. **Regulatory arbitrage:** Stringent prudential regulation and supervision can induce banks to shift their activities to less regulated zone (off balance sheet activities) of the financial system, thereby saving capital and increasing profit (FSB 2013, Gorton 2010, Sinha 2013).

iv. **Contagion risks:** Due to high interconnection with other financial entities, from both asset and liability side, any shock in the shadow banking system can easily spread across the network of the financial system. This contagion can transmit to the rest of the financial system through ownership linkages, fire sales and a flight to quality (IMF 2014). Shadow banks can also contribute to the formation of asset bubbles, as being less regulated entities; they can increase their leverage to risky sectors (Pozsar et al. 2013).

Shadow banking in the Indian context

The Indian financial system is a public bank dominated system but in the post-liberalisation era the activities of other financial institutions (OFIs) have also gained importance over time. Scheduled commercial banks, both government and private, are the major players in the field. Urban cooperative banks and regional rural banks are specialised institutions serving the needs of urban and rural regions. After the implementation of financial liberalisation in the 1990s the new players like mutual funds, insurance companies and Non-Bank Financial Companies (NBFCs) have emerged as major players in the field, in terms of size, growth and interconnections.

Non-Banking Financial Companies (NBFCs) are financial institutions, engaged in diverse financial activities. NBFCs are engaged in the business of loans and advances, acquisition of shares/stocks/bonds/debentures/securities issued by the government or local authority or other marketable securities of a like nature, leasing, hire-purchase, insurance business and chit business (RBI 2014). In India, some NBFCs' nature closely approximates the Financial Stability Board's (FSB) definition of shadow banking as "credit intermediation involving entities and activities (fully or partially) outside the regular banking system". The FSB has estimated the size of the Indian shadow banking sector to be around US$ 335 billion (see Figure 15.1) in 2013, which is the fifteenth largest in the world. It has also become the fastest growing segment in the Indian financial system. Claessens and Ratnovski (2014) defined shadow banking, in their activity-based definition as, "all financial activities except traditional banking which require a private or public backstop to operate". Since the majority of the liabilities consist of bank loans there is an implicit guarantee (public backstop) on the activities of the NBFCs. According to Sinha (2013), NBFCs constitute the core[5] shadow banks as they perform credit intermediation similar to banks, outside the purview of banking regulation. The deposits of NBFCs are not insured and also they cannot avail the liquidity facility of the RBI. However, the debate on whether

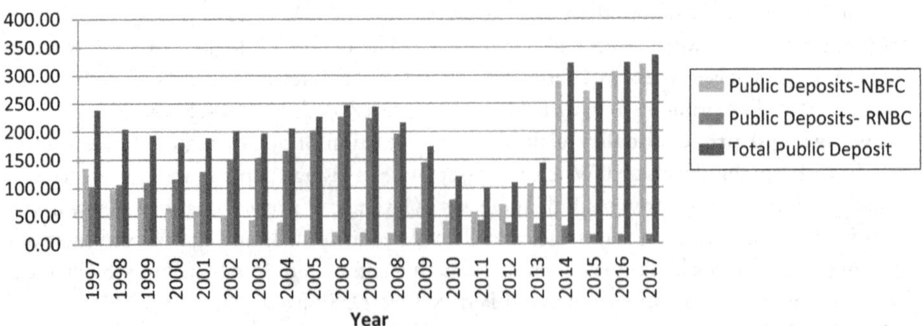

Figure 15.1 Public deposits collected by the NBFCs-D and RNBCs (in Rs billion). *Source*: Report on Trend and Progress of Banking in India, 2002–18.

the NBFCs in India can be considered shadow banks (as defined by the FSB) is not yet settled (Öncü 2013; Sherpa 2013).

Notwithstanding the debate on the consideration of the entire NBFCs sector as shadow banking, the study uses NBFCs as a rough measure of shadow banking due to the following reasons:

i. NBFCs satisfy most of the criteria of shadow banking activities used by the FSB and other authors, like non-bank credit intermediation, provision of implicit public backstop, lack of liquidity facility by RBI and deposit insurance by deposit insurance and credit guarantee corporations (DICGC).
ii. Credit intermediation will require deposit taking but it can also be done using borrowed funds from banks which most NBFCs-ND-SI[6] (Non-Banking Financial Corporations-Non-Deposit taking-Systemically Important) does.

Shadow banking in India is quite different from its developed counterparts as regulation is increasing[7] and the activities and instruments associated with the global financial crisis are not allowed or even if they are allowed then they come under tight regulation (Sinha 2013; Öncü 2014). Even though the NBFCs are engaged in credit intermediation outside the formal banking system, the increasing regulation of NBFCs by regulators has led some scholars to arrive at an ambivalent position on the status of the NBFCs being identified as shadow banks in India (Gandhi 2014). In 2011, assets of OFIs in India accounted for US$ 375 billion vis-à-vis bank assets of US$ 1518 billion and Gross Domestic Product (GDP) of US$ 1766 billion. The total assets of the NBFCs in India reached 13 per cent of its GDP in 2013. Among the BRICS countries, India has the third largest shadow banking sector (FSB 2014).

Asset size

The size of the assets of the NBFCs is gaining systemic importance in the financial system over the past years. The assets of the NBFCs sector has increased from Rs 3664 billion in 2007 to Rs 19671 billion in 2017. The growth rates of the asset of the NBFC sector have been higher than those of the banking sector, which can be seen in Table 15.1.

The assets of NBFCs accounted for 9.9 per cent of bank assets on March 31, 2007, and increased to 15.4 per cent in 2017, which denotes the significance of NBFCs in the Indian shadow banking system (Figure 15.6).

Types of NBFCs

The NBFCs are categorised according to their liability and activity status. According to the liability structure, they are categorised into two types: Category "A" companies – Deposit taking NBFCs (NBFCs-D), and Category "B" companies – NBFCs not raising public deposits (NBFCs-ND). The NBFCs-D are subject to capital adequacy norms, exposure norms (in real estate and unquoted shares), Asset Liability Management (ALM) discipline and reporting requirements, to protect depositors' money. Until 2006, Category B companies (NBFCs-ND) were subjected to lighter regulations, but due to its increasing size, enhanced risk taking capacity, wider financial market inter-linkages and complexity, the Reserve Bank of India (RBI) created a new NBFC category in 2006, called the "systemically important" non-deposit taking NBFCs (NBFC-ND-SI). Among NBFCs-ND, those whose assets were Rs 1 billion and above were further classified as systemically important' non-deposit taking NBFCs (NBFC-ND-SI)

Table 15.1 Comparison of assets of banks vis-à-vis NBFCs (Rs billion)

Year	*Bank asset (Rs. billion)*	*Growth rate of bank asset (%)*	*NBFCs asset (Rs. billion)*	*Growth rate of NBFCs asset (%)*	*NBFCs asset as percentage of bank asset (%)*
2007	36,996.7		3,664.5		9.9
2008	43,230.1	16.8	4,790.0	30.7	11.1
2009	50,709.5	17.3	5,439.5	13.6	10.7
2010	59,476.0	17.3	6,226.1	14.5	10.5
2011	68,869.5	15.8	7,384.5	18.6	10.7
2012	78,092.7	13.4	8,522.1	15.4	10.9
2013	87,641.8	12.2	12,852.4	50.8	14.7
2014	96,764.5	10.4	14,111.0	9.8	14.6
2015	105,804.0	9.3	17,288.0	22.5	16.3
2016	116,862.9	10.5	17,231.0	–0.3	14.7
2017	127,910.9	9.5	19,671.0	14.2	15.4

Source: Report on Trend and Progress of Banking in India, 2006–18.

NBFCs-ND-SI. NBFCs-ND-SI were subject to prudential regulations such as capital adequacy requirements, reporting requirements and exposure norms. Later capital market exposure and asset liability management (ALM) reporting and disclosure norms were also imposed on them. In November 2014, the RBI increased the threshold amount of asset for ND-NBFCs to be declared as NBFC-ND-SI from Rs 1 billion to Rs 5 billion.

Deposit taking non-bank financial companies (NBFCs-D)

The rising regulation on deposit taking NBFCs, especially after the implementation of the Shah Committee Report in 1997, resulted in a sharp decline in the number of deposit taking NBFCs. The number of deposit taking NBFCs declined from 1536 in 1999 to 168 in 2017. A similar decline was observed even in the case of Residuary Non-Banking Financial Companies (RNBCs). A Residuary Non-Banking Company is a special category of NBFC whose principal business is receiving deposits and investing in RBI approved securities. RNBCs have to invest 100 per cent of their deposit liability into highly liquid and secure instruments.

The total public deposits collected by the NBFCs-D showed a downward trend between 1997 to 2012 but this trend reversed afterwards as shown in Figure 15.1. The public deposit of the NBFCs decreased sharply from Rs 135.75 billion in 1998 to Rs 108 billion in 2014 and recovered to Rs 334.5 billion in 2017. The public deposits of the RNBCs declined continuously from 2008 to 2017. NBFCs flourished under minimal regulations but there was a sharp contraction of the deposit taking NBFCs after the tightening of the regulations.

Figure 15.2 shows that the deposit of the NBFCs-D as a percentage of bank deposits fell sharply from 3.9 per cent in March 1997 to 0.29 per cent in March 2017.

A large concentration of "loan and advances" category formed 88 per cent of the total assets of the NBFCs-D in the year 2017 (Figure 15.3a), which shows that concentration risk remains in the asset structure. Figure 15.3b shows that borrowing from banks and debentures forms the majority of the liability structure of the NBFCs-D. These two categories formed more than half of the liabilities of the NBFCs-D.

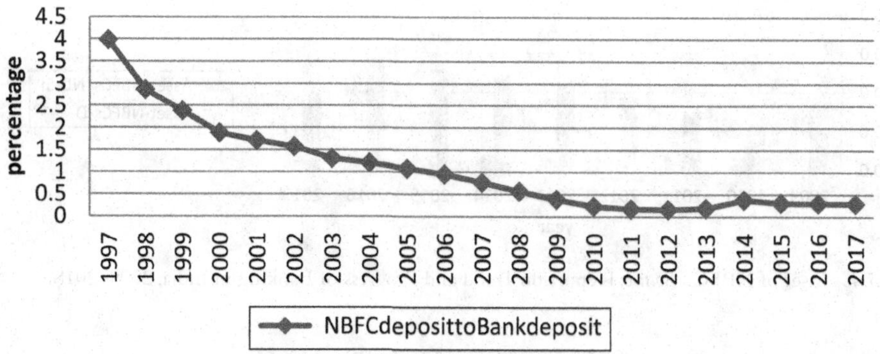

Figure 15.2 Deposit of the NBFCs-D as percentage of bank deposit. *Source*: Report on Trend and Progress of Banking in India, 2006–18.

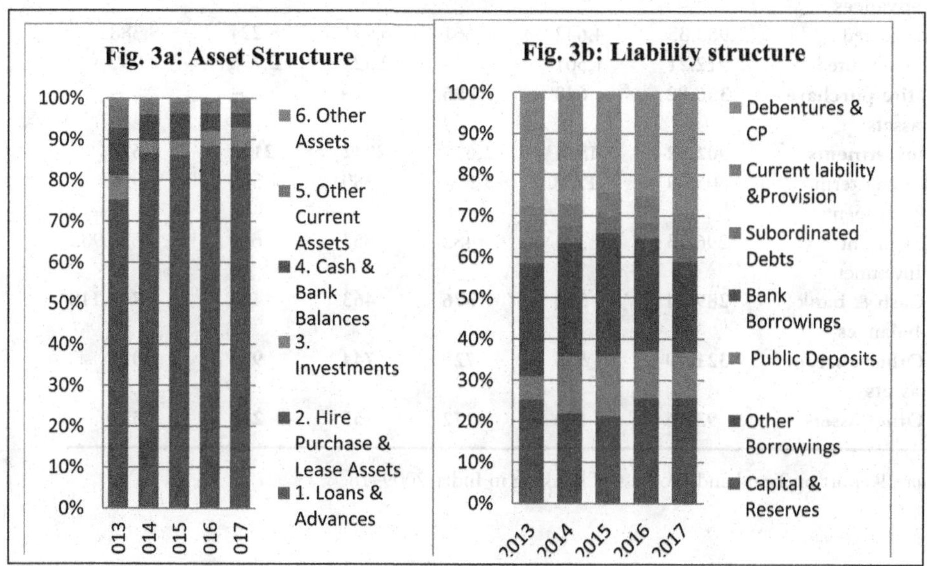

Figure 15.3 Asset and liability structure of the NBFCs-D (2013–2017). *Source*: Report on Trend and Progress of Banking in India, 2013–17.

Non-deposit taking systemically important nonbanking financial companies (NBFCs-ND-SI)

From the perspective of financial stability, the NBFC-ND-SI has emerged as an important player in the Indian financial system. Rapid asset growth and widespread inter-linkages of the NBFCs-ND-SI with the rest of the financial system have the potential to create systemic risk in the financial system. The assets of the NBFC-ND-SI consisted of 90 per cent of the total assets of the NBFCs in March 2017 (see Figure 15.4). Due to the systemic importance, Capital to Risk Weighted Assets Ratio (CRAR) norm was imposed on the NBFC-ND-SI from April 2007. They were required to maintain minimum capital (consisting of Tier I and Tier II capital) of 15 per cent of its aggregate risk weighted assets.

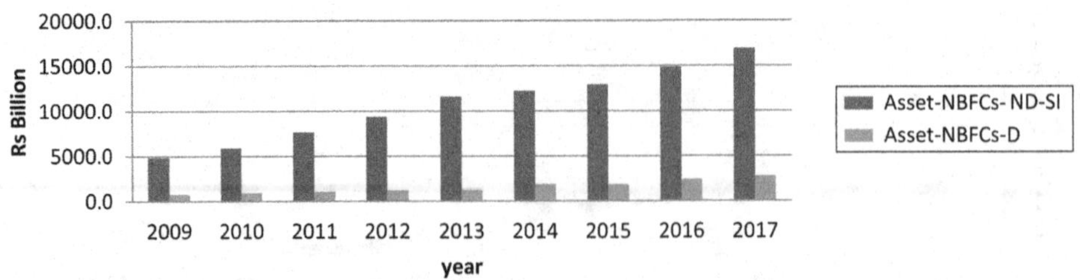

Figure 15.4 Asset of NBFC. *Source*: Report on Trend and Progress of Banking in India, 2009–2018.

Table 15.2 Asset side of the consolidated balance sheet of the NBFCs-ND-SI

Year	*2009*	*2012*	*2014*	*2015*	*2016*	*2017*
1. Loans & advances	**2,865.55**	**6,143**	**8,455**	**9,516**	**11,000**	**12,347**
1.1. Secured	1,953.35	4,642	6,661	6,991	8,224	9,388
1.2. Unsecured	912.21	1,501	1794	2,525	2,776	2,959
2. Hire purchase assets	**356.82**	**640**	**896**	–	–	–
3. Investments	**902.42**	**1544**	**2,075**	**2042**	**2172**	**2,628**
3.1. Long-term investments	605.69	1170	1,593	1,389	1,560	1,999
3.2. Current investments	296.73	374	482	653	612	628.902
4. Cash & bank balances	**289.34**	**334**	**376**	**463**	**485**	**700.118**
5. Other current assets	**321.19**	**536**	**728**	**744**	**952**	**1021**
6. Other assets	**93.76**	**156**	**172**	**155**	**223**	**321**

Source: Report on Trend and Progress of Banking in India, 2009–18.

The total assets of the NBFCs-ND-SI increased around 500 percentages points within a period of eight years. It is seen in Table 15.2 that they increased from Rs 4829 billion in 2009 to Rs 16917 billion in 2017. The asset size of the NBFCs-D is relatively smaller than the asset size of the NBFCs-ND-SI. Table 15.2 shows that "loans and advances" formed the major part of the asset structure of the NBFCs-ND-SI followed by "investment" and "hire and purchases" in all years from 2009 to 2017.

The composition of asset structure of the NBFCs-ND-SI sector is highly skewed, with "loans and advances" forming the major part. The share of loans and advances in the total asset increased from 60 per cent in 2009 to 73 per cent in 2017 (Figure 15.5). Hence, the asset concentration risk is high for NBFCs-ND-SI.

The liability structure of the NBFCs-ND-SI sector (Table 15.3) shows that the category of "total borrowing" occupies the major share followed by the category of "reserves and surplus". The total borrowing increased from Rs 3191 billion in 2009 to Rs 8902 billion in 2014.

Figure 15.6 shows the composition of secured borrowings by the NBFCs-ND-SI sector, which reveals that they mostly rely on debentures and banks loans for their secured borrowing.

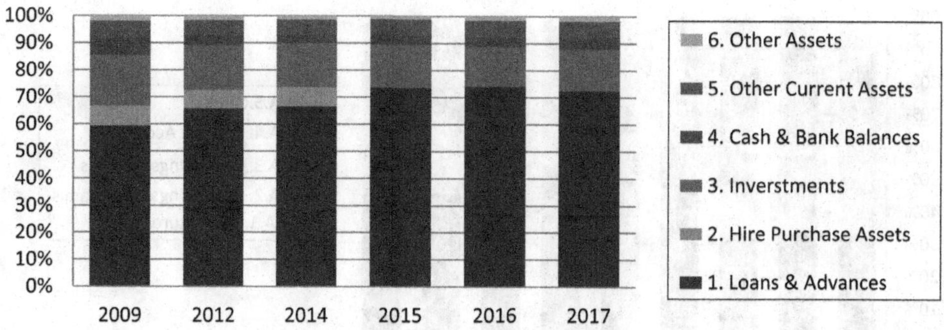

Figure 15.5 Composition of asset structure of the NBFCs-ND-SI (2009–17). *Source*: Report on Trend and Progress of Banking in India, 2009–18.

Table 15.3 Liability side of the consolidated balance sheet of NBFC-ND-SI

Year	*2009*	*2012*	*2014*	*2015*	*2016*	*2017*
1. Share capital	317.56	524	695	630	726	912
2. Reserves & surplus	990.11	1,891	2,457	2,271	2,699	3,192
3. Total borrowings	3,191.75	6,530	8,902	9,411	10,661	11,917
A. Secured borrowings	1,495.69	3,627	4,830	4,982	5,317	5,805
B. Unsecured borrowings	1,696.06	2,902	4,072	4,429	5,344	6,112
4. Current liabilities & provisions	329.66	408	647	608	746	995.7

Data source: Report on Trend and Progress of Banking in India, 2009–18.

The share of borrowing from banks in secured borrowing by the NBFCs-ND-SI has partially declined over time from 41 per cent in 2012 to 37 per cent in 2017 and borrowing through debentures has increased from 48 per cent in 2012 to 50 per cent in 2017.

The composition of unsecured[8] borrowing by the NBFCs-ND-SI sector (Figure 15.7) also shows a similar pattern, where debentures, commercial paper and bank borrowing occupy the major share in unsecured borrowing over time. The share of debentures in total unsecured borrowing also increased from 41 per cent in 2009 to 47 per cent in 2017, whereas the share of bank lending declined from 27 per cent in 2009 to only 7 per cent in 2017. Unlike the case of secured borrowings, the sharp fall in the share of bank borrowing in unsecured borrowing and simultaneously the rise in market-based wholesale borrowing (debentures and commercial papers) has been observed. This rising share of market-based wholesale borrowing in unsecured borrowing of NBFCs-ND-SI should be a cause of concern for the regulators.

The banks' exposure to the NBFCs-ND-SI is increasing as shown by rising secured borrowing from banks in Figure 15.8. The amount of total borrowing from banks increased from Rs. 786.93 billion in 2009 to Rs 2388.27 billion in 2014 and reached Rs 2527 billion in 2017.

The rising exposure of the banks to the NBFCs-ND-SI sector can be measured by the total loans provided by banks to this sector as a percentage of total liability of the NBFCs-ND-SI sec-

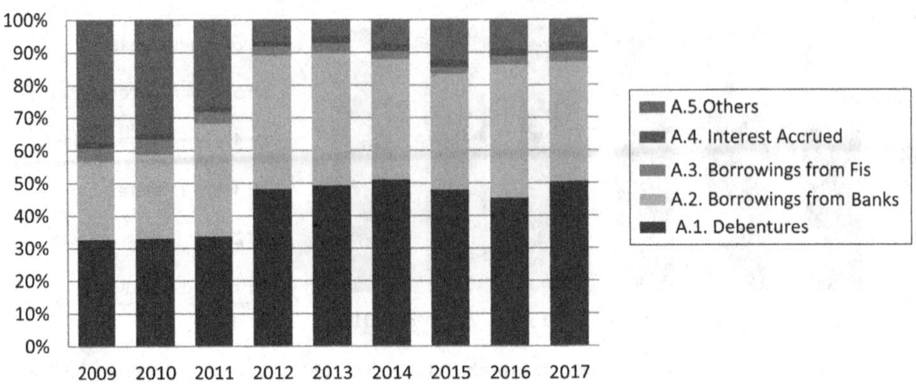

Figure 15.6 Composition of secured borrowing by the NBFCs-ND-SI. *Source*: Report on Trend and Progress of Banking in India, 2009–18.

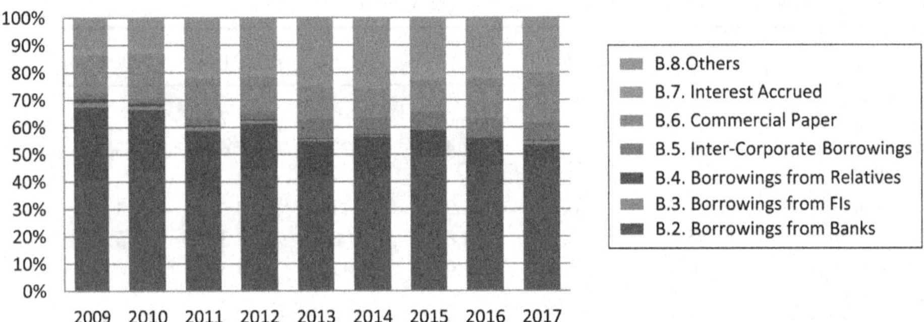

Figure 15.7 Composition of unsecured borrowing by the NBFCs-ND-SI. *Source*: Report on Trend and Progress of Banking in India, 2009–18.

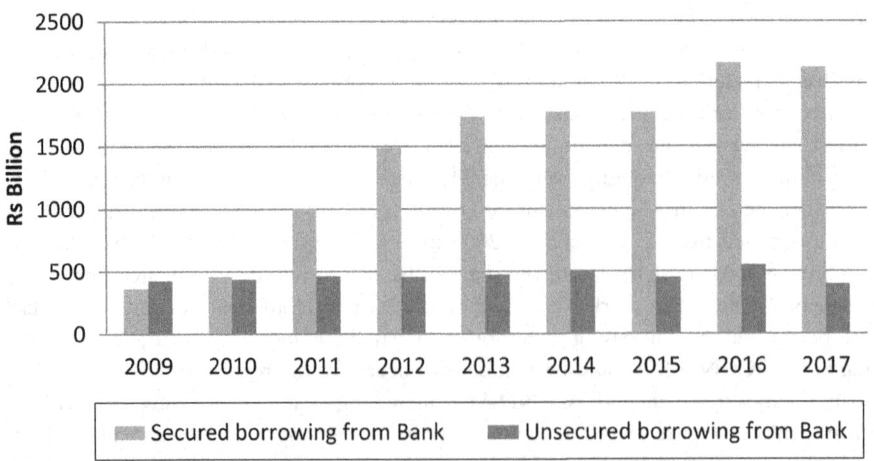

Figure 15.8 Secured and unsecured borrowing from bank by the NBFCs-ND-SI. *Source*: Report on Trend and Progress of Banking in India, 2009–18.

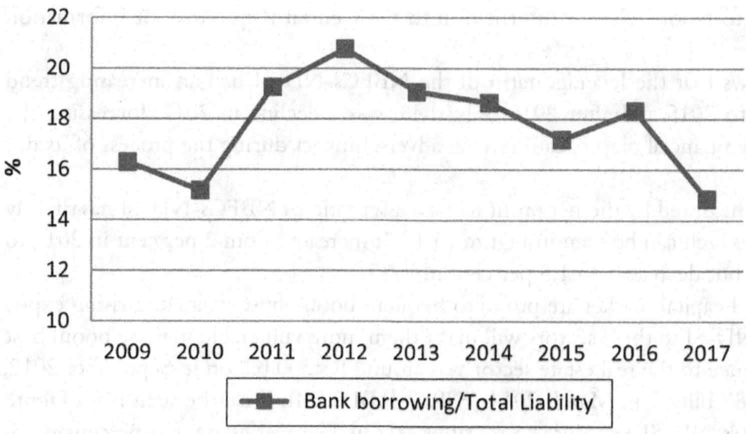

Figure 15.9 Bank borrowing as percentage of total liability of the NBFCs-ND-SI. *Source*: Report on Trend and Progress of Banking in India, 2009–18.

tor. The share of bank borrowing as a percentage of total liability of the NBFCs-ND-SI sector increased from 15.18 per cent in 2010 to 18.3 per cent in 2016, after which it declined to 14.8 per cent in 2017, which is evident from Figure 15.9.

Overall capital adequacy or the CRAR of the NBFCs-ND-SI sector is at a secured level. Figure 15.10 (a) shows that the capital adequacy ratio of NBFCs-ND-SI decreased from 28 per cent in March 2012 to 24.6 per cent in March 2017. The CRAR remained above the regulatory minimum of 15 per cent from June 2012 to March 2017.

The asset quality of the NBFCs-ND-SI has been deteriorating continuously, which is one of the major causes of concern. It can be seen from Figure 15.10 (b) that the gross NPA to total advances increased from 1.5 per cent in June 2012 to 6.1 per cent in March 2017. The rapid increase in GNPA indicates deteriorating asset quality of NBFCs-ND-SI. As such, the RBI has issued separate guidelines for banks and the NBFCs to identify and reduce the NPA. The

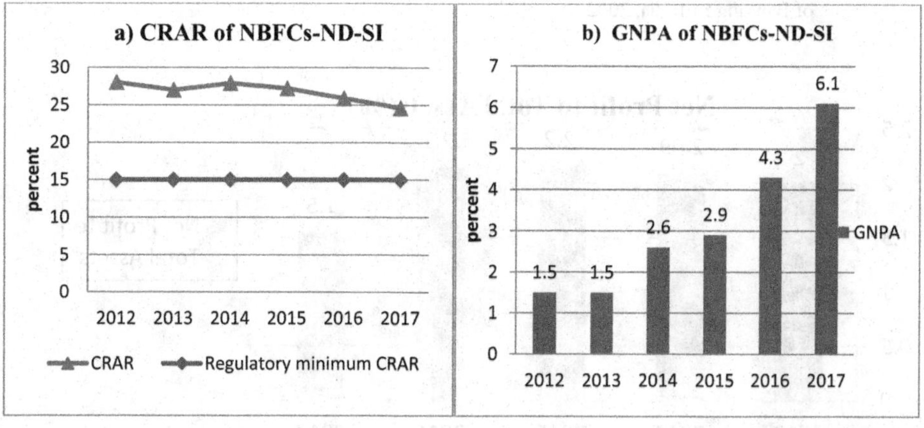

Figure 15.10 CRAR of the NBFCs-ND-SI b) NPA and GNPA ratio. *Source*: Report on Trend and Progress of Banking in India, 2016–17.

NBFCs are directed to report relevant information to the Central Repository of Information in Large Credit.

Figure 15.11 shows that the leverage ratio of the NBFCs-ND-SI had an increasing trend from the year 2010 to 2015 and after 2016 only, there was a decline in 2017. Increasing the leverage of such large financial players can have an adverse impact during the process of its de-leveraging.

The profitability measured by the net profit to total asset ratio of NBFCs-ND-SI has slightly improved over time, which can be seen in Figure 15.12. It increased from 2 per cent in 2013 to 2.1 per cent in 2015 but decreased to 1.5 per cent in 2017.

The real estate and capital market are prone to frequent boom–bust cycles and rising exposure of the NBFCs-ND-SI to these sectors will make them more vulnerable to these boom bust cycles. The total advance to the real estate sector was around Rs 300 billion in September 2012, which reached Rs 485 billion in March 2014 (FSR – RBI 2014). It can be seen from Figure 15.13 that the NBFCs-ND-SI exposure to sensitive sectors like real estate as a percentage of total assets increased from 4.8 per cent in 2016 to 6.3 per cent in 2017.

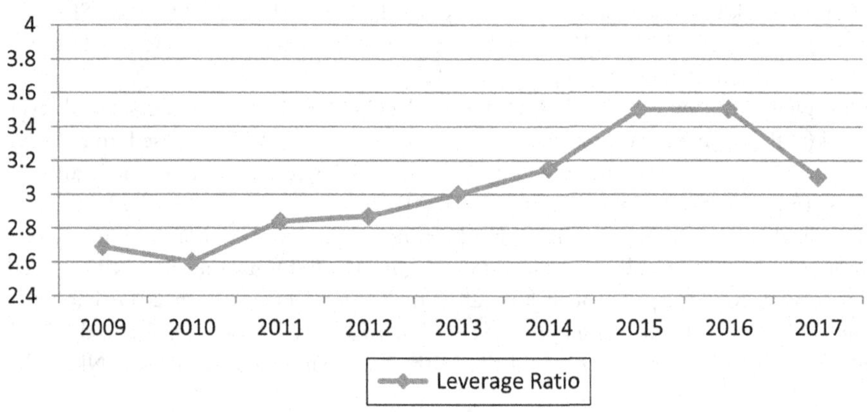

Figure 15.11 Leverage Ratio of the NBFCs-ND-SI (2009–2017). *Source*: Report on Trend and Progress of Banking in India, 2002–18.

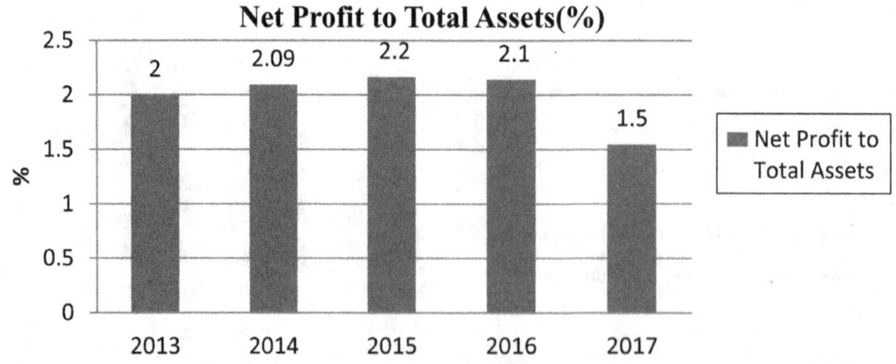

Figure 15.12 Trend in returns on assets of the NBFCs-ND-SI. *Source*: RBI-FSR, 2018.

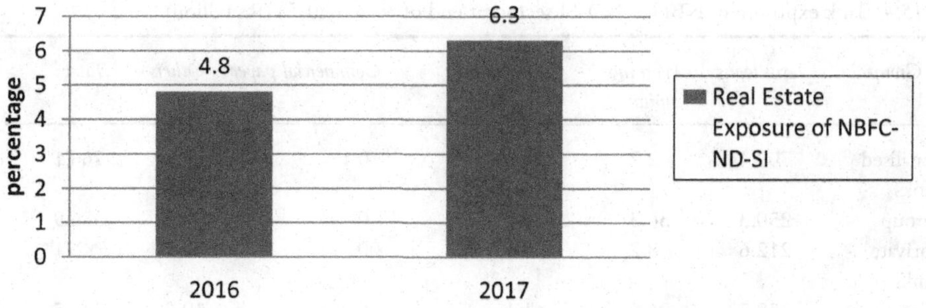

Figure 15.13 Real estate lending to total asset of NBFC-ND-SI (%). *Source*: Report on Trend and Progress of Banking in India, 2017–18.

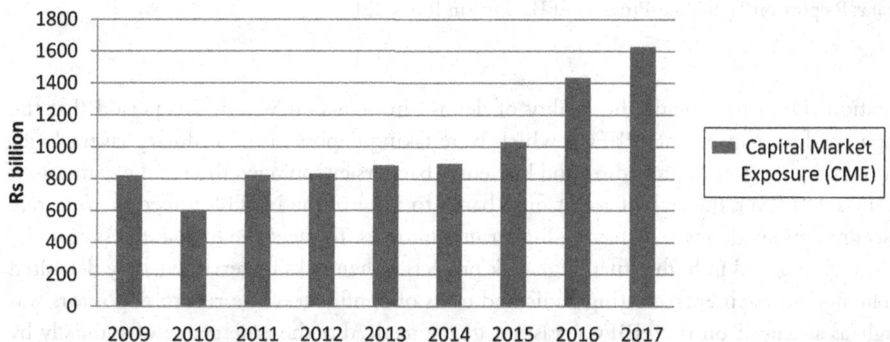

Figure 15.14 Capital market exposure (CME) of NBFC-ND-SI. *Data source*: Report on Trend and Progress of Banking in India, 2009–18.

Similarly, the advance of NBFCs-ND-SI to the capital market was 8.8 per cent of total advances in March 2014 which increased to 9.6 per cent in 2017. The exposure to capital market increased from Rs 818 billion in 2009 to Rs 1629 billion in 2017 (Figure 15.14). Such a marked increase in exposure of NBFCs-ND-SI to sensitive sectors (Real estate and capital market) can create financial stability problems.

Table 15.4 shows that the exposure of nationalised banks to the NBFCs-ND-SI was highest, followed by the new private banks and the SBI group. The majority of exposure of the nationalised banks was in the form of term loans, which accounted for Rs 709.4 billion in 2013. The SBI group had the third largest exposure to the NBFCs-ND-SI, mainly in terms of bank lending. New private banks had the second highest exposure in the form of term loans and the highest exposure in the form of debentures. Foreign banks had the least exposure of Rs 102.4 billion to the NBFCs-ND-SI in 2013. However, in terms of exposure through Commercial Paper (CP), foreign banks had the highest amount, Rs 50.2 billion in 2013. Both the SBI group and old private banks had minimum exposure through CP.

Regulation of the NBFCs

A large number of failures of several banks in the late 1950s and early 1960s led to a huge loss of ordinary depositors' money. This failure compelled the RBI to form the Deposit Insurance

Table 15.4 Bank exposure of NBFCs-ND-SI sector (at end of March 2013) (Rs billion)

Bank Group	*Term loans*	*Working capital*	*Debentures*	*Commercial paper*	*Others*	*Total*
Nationalised banks	709.4	2.7	26.6	0.1	27.3	766.1
SBI group	250.3	136.3	0.2	0	0.2	386.9
Old private banks	212.6	8.2	0.1	00	0	221
New private banks	338.5	26.9	61.1	0.3	19.8	446.5
Foreign banks	50.7	0.7	0.4	50.2	0.5	102.4
Total	1,561.4	174.6	88.4	50.6	47.8	1,922

Data source: Report on Trend and Progress of Banking in India, 2013.

Corporation (DIC) to provide the facility of deposit insurance. It was in this period that the RBI tightened its grip on the NBFCs, which were taking deposits from ordinary savers. Light regulation, simple sanction procedure and low entry barriers encouraged the rapid expansion of the NBFCs. However, the lack of credit from banks to most of the NBFCs forced them to rely on unsecured public deposits by paying higher interest rates. To meet the high-interest cost, the NBFCs were engaged in high return high-risk projects. When risks materialised, they defaulted on public deposit payments, creating panic and crisis of confidence. The risk to depositors was also high, as a deposit on the NBFCs was not guaranteed. Also, the emergence of some 'fly by night' NBFCs raised regulatory concerns, and the consequent failure of large NBFCs in 1964 compelled the RBI to increase regulation of the NBFCs sector. As such, the RBI made amendments to the RBI Act, 1934 and introduced Chapter III B in 1964 to regulate the deposit-taking companies. This amendment to the RBI Act of 1934 started the regime of new regulations for the entire NBFCs sector. The NBFCs were required to register reports and be supervised by the RBI. Deposit taking by nonregistered NBFCs was prohibited (Acharya, Öncü 2013). The Reserve Bank of India Act, 1934 was amended on 1 December 1964 by the Reserve Bank Amendment Act, 1963 to include provisions relating to nonbanking institutions receiving deposits and financial institutions. It was observed that the existing legislative and regulatory framework required further refinement and improvement because of the rising number of defaulting NBFCs and the need for an efficient and quick system for redressal of grievances of individual depositors.

NBFCs in India are regulated by different regulators. While merchant banking, venture capital funds are regulated by SEBI, insurance companies are under IRDA and chit fund companies are regulated by the state government. Still, the regulations applied to the NBFCs sector are less rigorous as compared to banks. Both NBFCs-D and NBFCs-ND-SI are not subjected to Cash Reserve Ratio (CRR). Table 15.5 shows the regulatory differences between banks and NBFCs. It shows that CRR and SLR are not applicable in the case of NBFCs-ND-SI but in the case of NBFCs-D, 15 per cent SLR is required, which is much lower than the 19.5 per cent SLR for banks. There are also no restrictions on financial activity and foreign ownership for both types of NBFCs. Deposit taking NBFCs also have to maintain a minimum investment grade credit rating to access public deposits. Any NBFCs-D whose credit rating falls below this threshold are not allowed to take deposits from the public.

Table 15.5 Regulatory differences between banks and NBFCs

Requirement		*Bank*	*NBFC-D*	*NBFCs-ND-SI*
Liquidity as % of demand and time deposits	Cash Reserve Ratio(CRR)	4%	NA	NA
	Statutory Liquidity Ratio	19.5%	15%	NA
Capital as % of risk weighted assets (CRAR)		9%	15%	15%
Nonperforming asset norms(days in delinquency)		90	90	90
Restriction of financial activity		Yes	NA	NA
Restriction of foreign ownership		Yes	NA	NA
Priority sector lending as % of total credit		40%	NA	NA

Source: Acharya et al. (2013) & DBIE-RBI, 2018.

Rising interconnection of the NBFCs

Figure 15.15 shows that the investment by Scheduled Commercial Banks (SCBs), Asset Management Companies (AMCs) and Insurance Companies in NBFCs have increased over time. The investment from SCBs comprises the largest source of funding for NBFCs. The investment of AMCs has grown substantially from a minuscule amount of Rs 425 billion in 2012 to Rs 2338 billion in 2017. Even surpassing the insurance funding, AMCs emerged as the second largest source of financing for the NBFCs sector in 2017. Similarly, investment of insurance companies has increased by 153 per cent within six years. The investment was Rs 780 billion in January 2012 and reached Rs 1200 billion in 2017.

Hence shadow banks in India in the post-liberalisation era have become more vulnerable to shocks generated outside the system and have increased systemic risk due to their interconnection with all other markets of the financial system, both domestically and globally.

Emerging shadow banking entities in India: gold loan NBFCs

Gold loan NBFCs have emerged as the fastest growing shadow financial entities of India. From 2008 to 2012, their asset has grown 1200 per cent. Around 48 per cent of liability of gold

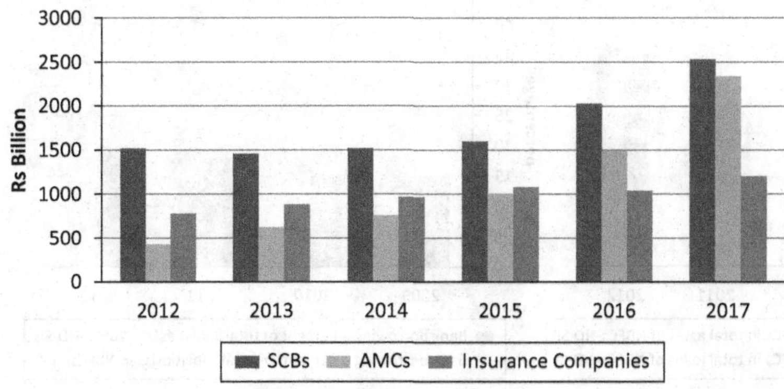

Figure 15.15 Investment by SCBs, AMCs and insurance companies in NBFCs (Rs billion). *Source:* FSR-RBI, 2017.

loan NBFCs consists of bank loans and 85 per cent of assets are concentrated in just loan and advances given from gold loans in 2012 (RBI 2013). The growth of gold loans by NBFCs was highest among its competitors. The compound annual growth rate of outstanding NBFCs gold loans was 98.5 per cent compared to 57.5 per cent CAGR of bank gold loan in the period from 2008 to 2012 (Figure 15.16).

The NBFCs are dependent on bank loans for funding their business, but it can be seen from Figure 15.17a that the share of gold loan NBFCs was much higher than all other types of NBFCs-ND-SI from 2009 to 2012. Such high reliance on banks for funding can cause problems for them, especially if the banks' willingness to lend goes down. The importance of gold loan NBFCs can be judged from the fact that among all the NBFCs-ND-SI, the share of gold loan NBFCs in the total assets of the NBFCs-ND-SI reached 4.8 per cent in 2012. Similarly, the proportion of the gold loans of the NBFCs-ND-SI reached 6.3 per cent in 2012 (see Figure 15.17b.

Figure 15.18a shows that the dominant share of liability growth was contributed by borrowing from banks. The debentures also contributed 22.9 per cent growth in its liability. The assets side Figure 15.18b shows that loans and advances contributed significantly in the growth of assets.

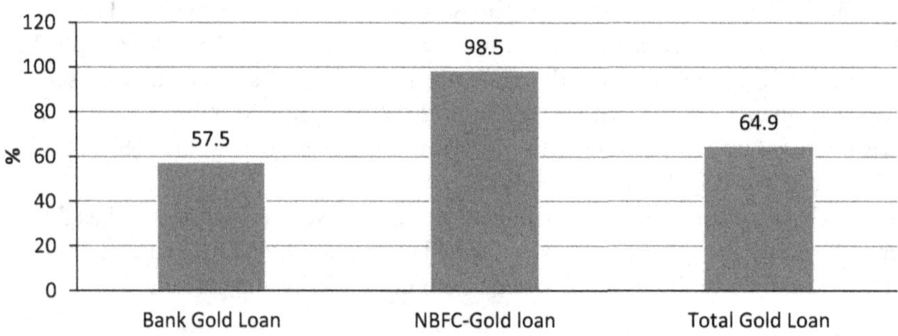

Figure 15.16 CAGR (%) of gold loans outstanding (2008–12). *Source*: RBI, 2013.

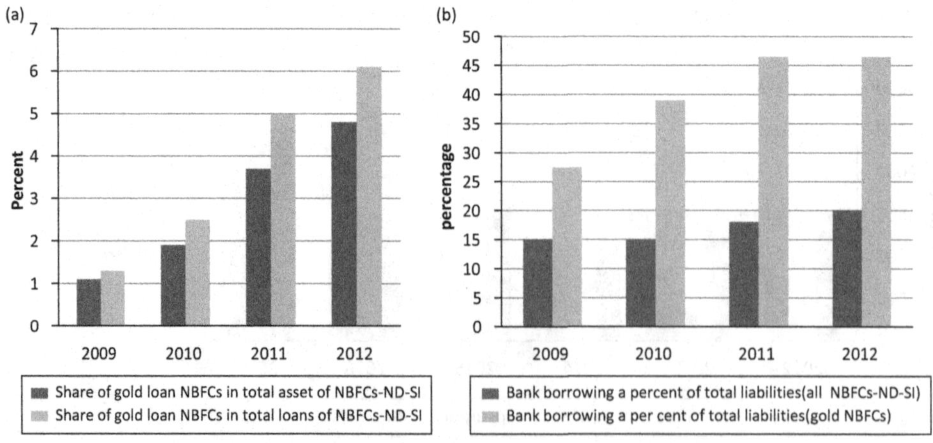

Figure 15.17 a) Dependency of NBFCs on bank borrowing b) Share of gold loan NBFCs in total asset and loans of NBFCs-ND-SI. *Source*: RBI, 2013.

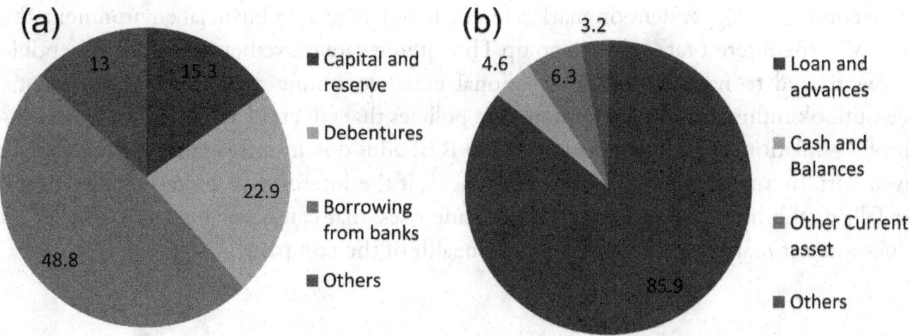

Figure 15.18 Factors contributing to balance sheet growth in 2012 over 2008. *Source*: RBI, 2013

Risks associated with gold loan NBFCs

Even though most financial firms are exposed to various risks associated with their business, gold loan NBFCs are exposed to certain additional risks. Some distinctive risks associated with gold loan NBFCs are the following:

i. **High concentration and collateral risk**

Most of the gold loan NBFCs' assets consist of gold loan portfolio and liability, bank loans and debentures. So, concentration risk is high on both sides of the balance sheet. The gold loan NBFCs give loans to their customers by taking gold jewellery as collateral. The value of the collateral of loan remains quite stable as long as the gold price is stable. However, if there is a fall in the price of gold in the international market, the price of gold in the domestic market also falls, worsening the asset quality of the gold loan portfolios of NBFCs and banks, which has been witnessed in the past years. High loan to value ratios (LTVs) (due to intense competition to gain market share), with largely bulleted repayment structures (principal and interest paid together) in the sector, leave a limited cushion for a correction in the value of the security.

ii. **Unstable income source**

Large numbers of customers of gold loan NBFCs take loans for 6 to 12 months. This short loan tenure implies that the share of the current assets will be large in the total assets. The short-term nature of loans implies that the company's prime income source, i.e. interest income, also lasts for a short period. Most customers do not obtain new loans after settling their old debt with the company. Increasing competition among gold loan NBFCs will make the matter even worse. The short-term nature of their loans and potential instability of interest income can make the financial health of gold loan NBFCs highly vulnerable.

iii. **Business cycle risk**

The majority of the customers of gold loan NBFCs are individual borrowers who are financially more vulnerable than large corporates to business shocks during the economic downturn. Moreover, most of these individuals belong to the middle-income group, making them more susceptible to economic shocks. Adverse economic conditions can severely impact the repayment capacity of the customers, increasing credit risk for gold loan NBFCs.

iv. **High interest rate risk**

The income of gold loan NBFCs depends on the level of net interest margin that they can maintain. Deregulation of the financial sector has made the determination of the interest rate completely dependent on market forces. In a deregulated financial environment, the volatility in the interest rate tends to go up. The interest rate movement is highly susceptible to news related to national and international macroeconomic conditions. The domestic price outlook influences the RBI's monetary policies that affect the interest rate. The adoption of an inflation-targeting approach by the RBI adds downward rigidity to interest rate movements. In a rising interest rate environment, if the interest rate corresponding to the asset falls or the interest rate on the liability side rises, that can have an adverse impact on the net interest margin and overall financial health of the company.

Case study of gold loan company

The big player in the formal gold loan market, Muthoot Finance Ltd, is chosen for the purpose of this case study. It falls under the category of non-deposit taking systemically important NBFCs (ND-SI-NBFCs). Data for company is extracted from the Centre for Monitoring Indian Economy (CMIE) Prowess Database, 2018 and Annual Reports of the company.

Gold loan NBFC – Muthoot Finance Ltd.

Muthoot Finance Ltd., a flagship company of the Muthoot Groups, is the largest NBFC player in the organised gold loan market in India. The company started its gold loan business from as early as 1939 and was incorporated in 1997. It was registered with RBI as an NBFC in 2001 and got the status of NBFC-ND-SI in 2005. It has a pan-Indian presence with 4370 branches in 29 states and Union Territories with a customer base of 200,000 in September 2018. The gold kept as loan security has reached 168 tonnes, and the retail loan assets under management were Rs 323,186 million in September 2018. The market capitalisation of the company was Rs 161,445 million on 30 September, 2018.

Interest rate policy

The interest rate on gold loans depends on the loan amount, loan tenure and LTV. Also minor variation in interest rates is found depending on the branch location. A fixed interest rate is

Table 15.6 Loan feature of Muthoot Finance Ltd

Loan Feature	*Muthoot Finance Ltd.*
Rate of interest (%)	12 – 24
Loan to value ratio (LTV) (%)	75
Loan tenure: minimum–maximum	One day to 36 month
Minimum loan amount (Rs)	1500
Maximum loan amount (Rs)	No limit
End use restriction	No
Processing fee	Rs 10–Rs 20
Processing time	Few minutes
Pre-payment penalty	Nil
Documentation	Document of identity proof and one document of residential proof.

Source: Company website, FAQ section, www.muthootfinance.com/services/gold-loan/.

Table 15.7 Interest rate and loan tenure

Scheme	*Slab period/s*	*Kerala*	*Other South Indian branches*	*All other branches*
Muthoot Best Value Loan (MBL)	Up to 1 month	14% p.a.	14% p.a.	14% p.a.
	>1 up to 3 months	18% p.a.	18% p.a.	18% p.a.
	>3 up to 6 months	21% p.a.	21% p.a.	21% p.a.
	>6 up to 12 months	24% p.a.	24% p.a.	24% p.a.

Data source: Company website, www.muthootfinance.com/services/gold-loan/.

charged according to a monthly compounding basis on the outstanding balance of the customer, which is given in Table 15.7. Delay in interest payment for loans outstanding for 12 months will be charged an additional 2 per cent p.a. penal interest rate besides the standard interest rate.

Business

The total asset of the company increased eight-fold within nine years. It increased from Rs 37,741 million in 2009 to Rs 323,062 million in 2018 as seen in Figure 15.19.

The assets of the company are highly concentrated. Gold loans account for 85 per cent of its total assets. Figure 15.20 shows that gold loan assets under management have steadily increased from Rs 33,000 million in 2009 to Rs 306,000 million in March 2018.

Figure 15.21 shows an upward movement of gold price in the domestic market, which coincided with the rising trends of both total assets (Figure 15.19) and gold loan (Figure 15.20) of Muthoot. As gold price got stabilised after 2012, the asset of Muthoot also got stabilised in the same period.

Profitability

Both rising net worth and profit before tax show high profitability of the gold loan business model of the company (Figure 15.22). The Muthoot gained 300 per cent rise in profit and 800 per cent rise in net worth of the company in the past eight years. Very few corporates have achieved such a high level of profitability.

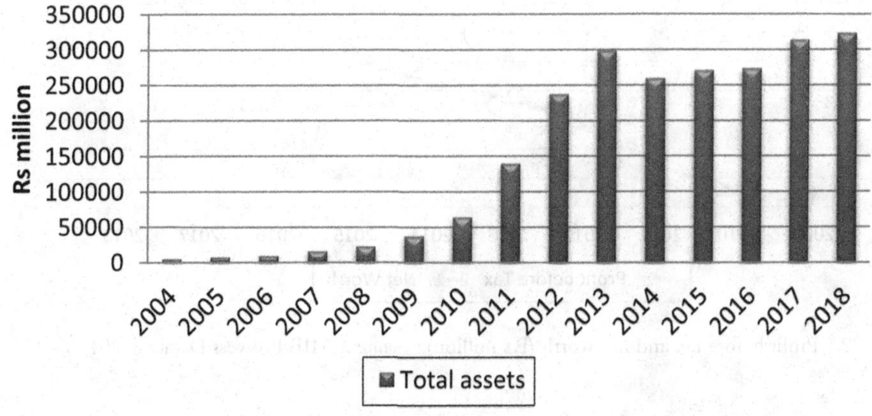

Figure 15.19 Total assets of Muthoot Finance Ltd. *Source*: CMIE Prowess Database 2018.

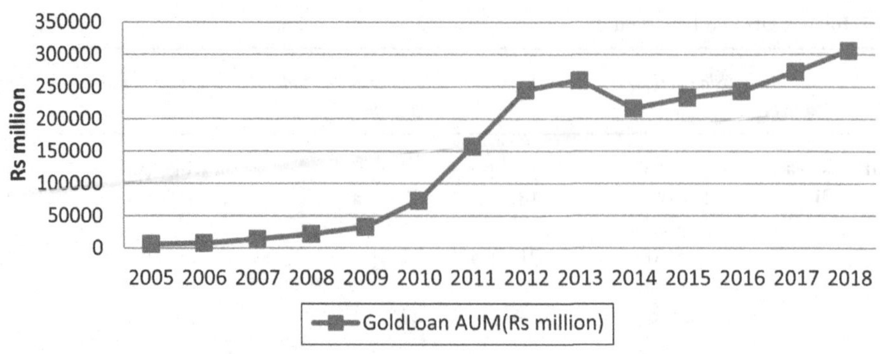

Figure 15.20 Gold loan asset under management (AUM) (Rs million). *Source*: Annual Reports, 2009–18.

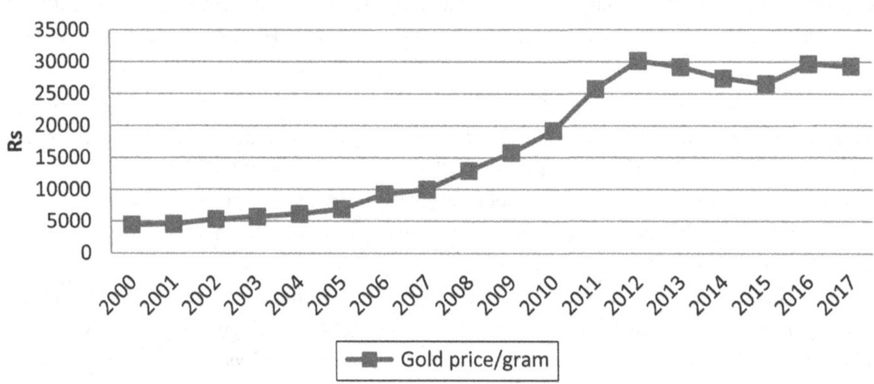

Figure 15.21 Trend in gold price/10 gram. *Source*: DBIE-RBI, 2018.

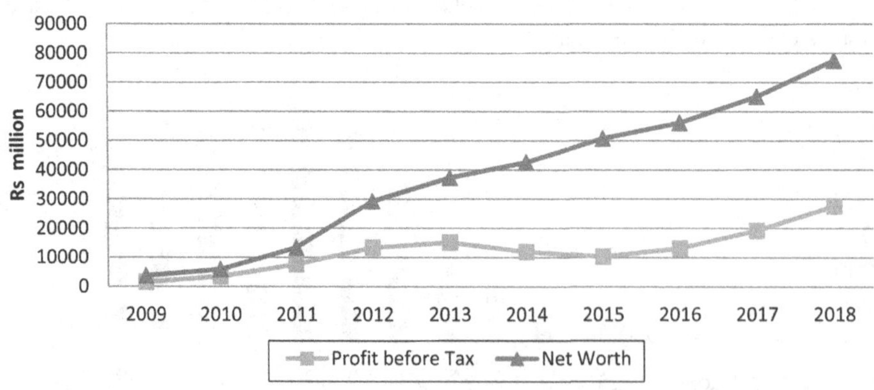

Figure 15.22 Profit before tax and net worth (Rs million). *Source*: CMIE Prowess Database 2018.

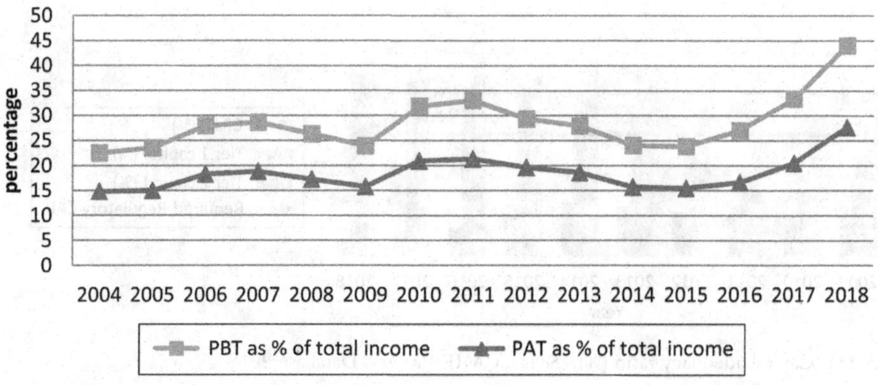

Figure 15.23 Rate of profit (PAT and PBT). *Source*: CMIE Prowess Database 2018.

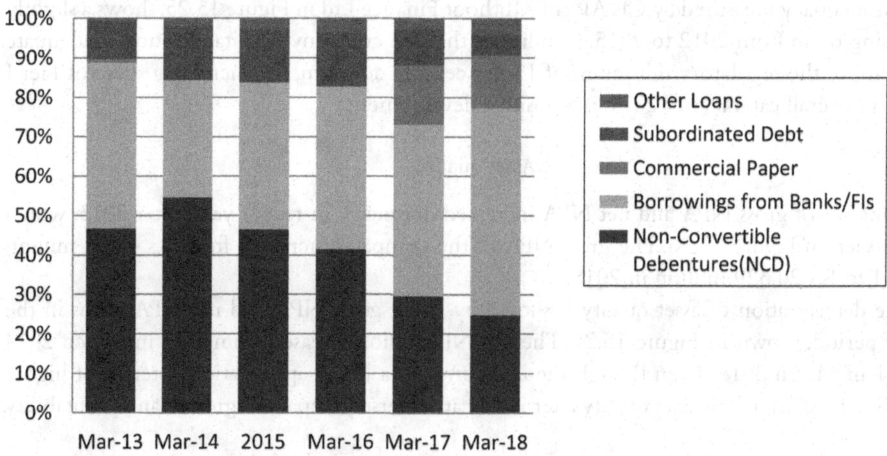

Figure 15.24 Liability structure data. *Source*: CMIE Prowess Database 2018.

The measures of profit like Profit After Tax (PAT) and Profit Before Tax (PBT) in Figure 15.23 show fluctuations before 2015; however after 2015, both show increasing profitability of the company.

Pattern of liability

Figure 15.24 shows that the major share of liabilities is occupied by debentures, which consist of 52 per cent of the total liability in 2014. The amount of funds raised through debentures and bonds has decreased over time, as in 2018 its share in the total liability structure was about 25 per cent only. The company has also raised an increasing amount of funds through secured short-term bank loans, the amount of which increased from Rs 101364 million in 2013 to Rs 111836 million in 2018.

The share of bank lending has increased over time. Despite the fluctuation in total share, bank loans are the largest source of funding for the company. Hence, the concentration of bank loans on the liability side remains.

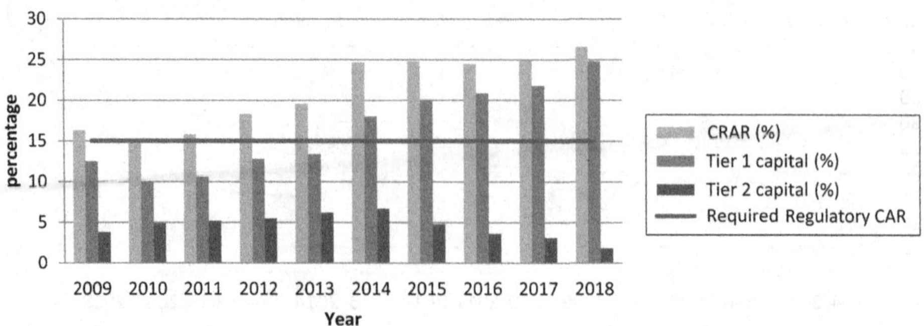

Figure 15.25 Capital adequacy ratio (%). *Source*: CMIE Prowess Database 2018.

Capital adequacy

Capital adequacy measured by CRAR, of Muthoot Finance Ltd in Figure 15.25, shows a slightly increasing trend from 2012 to 2015. It indicates that the company's capital position is adequate and is above the regulatory minimum of 15 per cent. In addition, the increasing share of Tier I capital in overall capital after 2014, is a positive development.

Asset quality

The amount of gross NPA and net NPA increased drastically in recent years after 2013, which can be seen in Figure 15.26. The gross NPA of the company increased from Rs 460.1 million in 2011 to Rs 20,329 million in 2018.

The deterioration of asset quality is shown by rising gross NPA and net NPA ratios in the recent period, shown in Figure 15.27. The net NPA ratio increased from 1.57 in March 2014 to 6.21 in March 2018. Even though the company has a high capital ratio (in terms of higher CRAR), the sharp fall in asset quality after 2017 can adversely impact its growth and profitability.

Leverage and liquidity

Figure 15.28 shows that the leverage of the company is falling as indicated by the falling debt to equity ratio. It shows the possibility of further leverage for the company. The liquidity

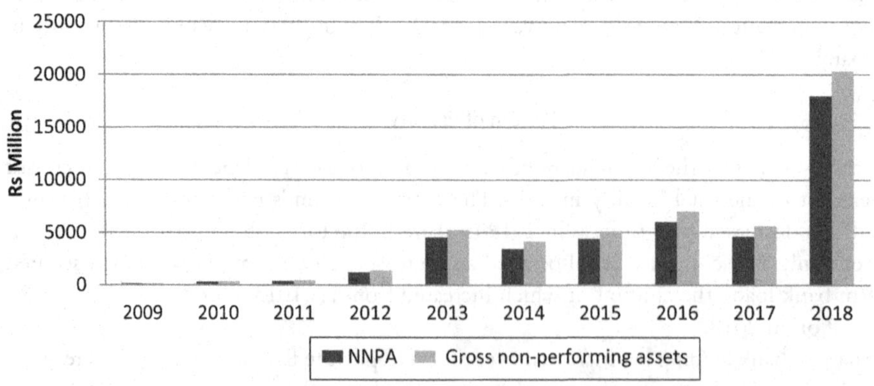

Figure 15.26 Gross NPA and net NPA. *Source*: CMIE Prowess Database 2018.

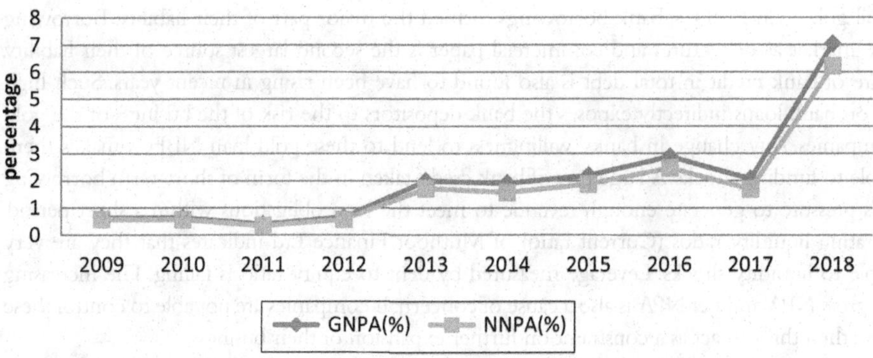

Figure 15.27 Trend in gross NPA and net NPA. *Source*: CMIE Prowess Database 2018.

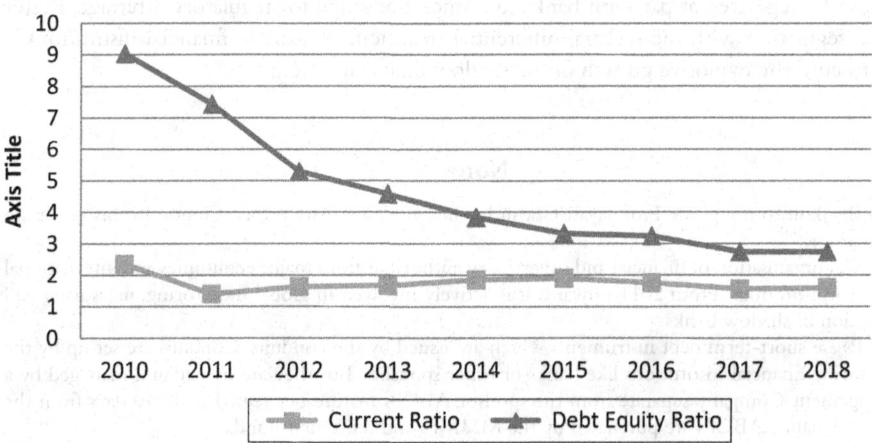

Figure 15.28 Leverage (debt to equity ratio) and liquidity (current ratio). *Source*: CMIE Prowess Database 2018.

positions of the company also show a declining trend over time which can cause an adverse impact on its business. The current ratio of the company fell sharply from 2.36 in 2010 to 1.6 in March 2018.

Conclusion

Shadow banks existed over a long time without creating any systemic concern for the financial system as a whole. It was only when the rapid process of financial deregulation started in the country that these institutions started getting more interconnected and hence became systemically more important. Shadow banking in India is quite different from its developed counterparts as regulation is increasing and the activities and instruments associated with the global financial crisis are not allowed or even if they are allowed then they come under tight regulation. In the case of India, it was the process of liberalisation that allowed these institutions to get interconnected with the formal banking system; also, the regulatory forbearance in the case of many NBFCs. In the case of India, caps on banks' lending to the NBFCs should be further brought down.

For all gold loan NBFCs, bank borrowings formed the major part of their liability. Borrowing from the market as debentures and commercial paper is the second largest source of their liability. The share of bank credit in total debt is also found to have been rising in recent years. Such high reliance on bank loans indirectly exposes the bank depositors to the risk of the business of the gold loan companies. Any change in banks' willingness to lend to these gold loan NBFCs makes them vulnerable to funding shocks. A large part of bank credit taken in the form of short-term borrowing also adds pressure to generate enough revenue to meet the loan obligations within a short period. Deteriorating liquidity ratios (Current ratio) of Muthoot Finance Ltd indicates that they are very vulnerable to liquidity shocks. Leverage measured by debt to equity ratio is falling. The increasing trend of gross NPA and net NPA is also a cause of concern. If companies are not able to control these bad assets, then this can act as a constraint on further expansion of their business.

Regulation of the gold loan NBFCs should be increased and their dependence on banks should be reduced. The reduction of bank funding going to shadow banking will automatically limit the leverage capacity of most shadow banking institutions. Shadow banking activities should also be regulated at par with banks to reduce the scope for regulatory arbitrage. Better structural regulation with the sectoral differential treatment of shadow financial institutions is needed to curb the explosive growth of the shadow financial system.

Notes

1 I am thankful to my guide Prof. Jayati Ghosh for her guidance. Any errors if found in this paper are solely mine.

2 FSB is an organisation of financial and supervisory authorities from major economies and international financial institutions. From 2011 onwards it is actively involved in global monitoring, measuring and regulation of shadow banks.

3 ABCPs are short-term debt instruments which are issued by the conduits. Conduits are set up by the sponsoring financial institutions like banks or other sponsors. But they are owned and managed by a Management Company separate from the sponsor. ABCPs mature between 1 and 270 days from the date of issuance. ABCPs are purchased by the MMMFs and retirement funds.

4 MMMFs are open-ended mutual funds which invest short-term fixed income securities like US Treasuries and Commercial papers. The returns on MMMFs are higher than that on bank deposits. But MMMFs lack deposit insurance which is provided to the banks by the government.

5 NBFCs are considered here as core shadow banks as the OFIs (which are considered as shadow banks by the FSB) accounted for 20 per cent of bank assets whereas the assets of NBFCs sector alone accounted for 13.4 per cent in 2013.

6 For details see section on types of NBFCs.

7 Recent regulatory measures: Unrated Asset finance companies will have to get themselves rated before 31 March 2016, to accept or renew public deposits. Minimum Tier I capital requirements for non-deposit taking NBFCs with asset size Rs. 500 crore and above and all deposit taking NBFCs will be 8.5 per cent by the end of March 2016 and 10 per cent by the end of March 2017. Similarly, the asset classification norm for NBFC-ND-SI and deposit taking NBFCs has been reduced to just 90 days. Previous norms were 6 to 12 months. The provision for standard assets for NBFC-ND-SI and NBFC-D has increased to 0.4 per cent. The new provision had to be 0.30 per cent at the end of March 2016, 0.35 per cent by the end of March 2017 and 0.40 per cent by the end of March 2018. The earlier provision for the standard assets was 0.25 per cent (RBI, 2014).

8 "Unsecured loans" means the loans not secured by any tangible asset.

Bibliography

Acharya, Viral V., Hemal Khandwala, and T. Sabri Öncü (2013): "The Growth of a Shadow Banking System in Emerging Markets: Evidence from India." *Journal of International Money and Finance* 39: 207–230.

Adrian, Tobias., Adam Ashcraft, Hayley Boesky, and Zoltan Pozsar (2012): "Shadow Banking." *Revue d'Economie Financiere* 105: 157–184.

Adrian, Tobias, Adam Ashcraft, and Boeskyet Hayley (2012): *Shadow Banking*. Federal Reserve Bank of New York Staff Reports No. 559.

Adrian, Tobias, Adam B. Ashcraft, and Nicola Cetorelli (2013): *Shadow Bank Monitoring*. FRBNY Staff Report 638, Federal Reserve Bank of New York, New York.

Bhaskar, P. (2014): "Non-Banking Finance Companies: Game Changers." Available at https://www.rbi.org.in/scripts/BS_SpeechesView.aspx?Id=870

Brunnermeier, Markus, and Lasse Heje Pedersen (2009): "Market Liquidity and Funding Liquidity." *Review of Financial Studies* 2(6): 2201–2238.

Caballero, Ricardo, and Alp Simsek (2009): *Complexity and Financial Panics*. NBER Working Paper 14997, National Bureau of Economic Research, Cambridge, MA.

Claessens, Stijn, and Lev Ratnovski (2014): *What Is Shadow Banking?* IMF Working Paper, WP 14/25, International Monetary Fund, Washington, DC.

Financial Crisis Inquiry Commission (2010): "Shadow Banking and the Financial Crisis." Available at http://fcic-static.law.stanford.edu/cdn_media/fcic-reports/fcic_final_report_full

Financial Stability Board (2011): "Shadow Banking: Scoping the Issues." April, Available at http://www.financialstabilityboard.org/publications/ r_110412a.pdf

Financial Stability Board (2012a): "Global Shadow Banking Monitoring Report 2012." 18 November, Available at http://www.financialstabilityboard.org/publications/r_121118c.pdf

Financial Stability Board (2012b): "Strengthening Oversight and Regulation of Shadow Banking: An Integrated Overview of Policy Recommendations." 18 November, Available at https://www.fi nancialstabilityboard.org/publications/r_121118.htm

Financial Stability Board (2013): "Strengthening Oversight and Regulation of Shadow Banking: An Overview of Policy Recommendations." August 2013 Available at http://www.financialstabilityboard.org/publications/r_130829a.pdf

Financial Stability Board (2014): "Global Shadow Banking Monitoring Report 2014." Available at http://www.financialstabilityboard.org/publications/r_141030.pdf

Financial Stability Board (2017): "Global Shadow Banking Monitoring Report 2017." Available at https://www.fsb.org/wp-content/uploads/P050318-1.pdf

Gandhi, R. (2014): "Danger Posed by Shadow Banking Systems to the Global Financial System – The Indian Case." Address at the Indian Council for Research on International Economic Relations Conference on Governance and Development: Views from G20 Countries, Mumbai. 21 August 2014 available at https://bit.ly/2ATEO8g

Gorton, Gary, Andrew Metrick, Andrei Shleifer, and Daniel K. Tarullo (2010): "Regulating the Shadow Banking System [with Comments and Discussion]." *Brookings Papers on Economic Activity*, 2010: 261–312.

Harutyunyan, Artak, Mr Alexander Massara, Giovanni Ugazio, Goran Amidzic, and Richard Walton (2015): *Shedding Light on Shadow Banking*. International Monetary Fund, Washington, DC.

IMF (2014): "Shadow Banking around the Globe: How Large and How Risky?" in *Global Financial Stability Report*, Chapter 2. International Monetary Fund, Washington, DC.

Lysandrou, Photis, and Anastasia Nesvetailova (2015): "The Role of Shadow Banking Entities in the Financial Crisis: A Disaggregated View." *Review of International Political Economy*, 22(2): 257–279.

McCulley, Paul (2007): "Teton Reflections." *PIMCO Global Central Bank Focus*, September 2007.

Mehrling, Perry, ZoltanPozsar, James Sweeney, and Daniel H. Neilson (2013): "Bagehot was a Shadow Banker: Shadow Banking, Central Banking, and the Future of Global Finance, Central Banking, and the Future of Global Finance." Accessed at http://papers.ssrn.com/sol3/papers.cfm?abstract_id=2232016.

Muthoot Finance Ltd. (2018): "Company Website, FAQ Section." http://www.muthootfinance.com/services/gold-loan/

NBFC Sector (2014, December 5): "Trends, Regulatory Framework and Way Forward." Retrieved January 6, 2015, from, http://www.careratings.com/upload/NewsFiles/SplAnalysis/NBFCSectorReport.pdf

Öncü, T. Sabri (2013): "Are Indian NBFCs Shadow Banks? Do They Pose Systemic Risks?" *Economic and Political Weekly*, 48(51): 10–11.

Pozsar, Zoltan, Adrian Tobias, Adam Ashcraft, and Hayley Boesky 2013: "Shadow Banking." *Economic Policy Review* 19(2): 1–16.

Reserve Bank of India (2006–08) (2009–10) (2010–11) (2011–12) (2012–13) (2013–14) (2014–15) (2015–16) (2016–17) (2017–18): *Report on Trend and Progress of Banking in India*, Mumbai.

Reserve Bank of India (2011): "Recommendations of the Working Group on Issues and Concerns in the NBFC Sector." Available at https://www.rbi.org.in/Scripts/PublicationReportDetails.aspx?UrlPage=&ID=647

Reserve Bank of India (2013): "Report of the Working Group to Study the Issues Related to Gold Imports and Gold Loans NBFCs in India." January, available at https://rbidocs.rbi.org.in/rdocs/PublicationReport/Pdfs/RWGS02012013.pdf

Reserve Bank of India (2014) (2015) (2016) (2017): *Financial Stability Report*, RBI, Mumbai.

Sherpa, Dawa (2013): "Shadow Banking in India and China: Causes and Consequences." *Economic and Political Weekly*, 48(43): 113–122.

Shin, Hyun Song, and Kwanho Shin (2010): *Procyclicality and Monetary Aggregates*. NBER Working Paper No. 16836, National Bureau of Economic Research, Cambridge, MA. Available at http://www.nber.org/papers/w16836

Shrestha, Min B. (2007): *Role of Non-Bank Financial Intermediation: Challenges for Central Banks in the SEACEN Countries*. SEACEN Centre, Malaysia.

Sinha, Anand (2013): "Regulation of Shadow Banking – Issues and Challenges." Address at the Indian Merchants' Chamber, Mumbai, 7 January, available at http://www.rbi.org.in/scripts/BS_SpeechesView.aspx?id=777

PART IV

FDI, R&D and innovation

16

BILATERAL INVESTMENT TREATIES AND OUTWARD FDI FROM INDIA[1]

Vinish Kathuria

Introduction

In the last two and a half decades of economic liberalization, the economic policy orientation of several developing and transition countries, including that of India, has moved towards foreign direct investment (FDI) assisted development approach from the earlier inward-looking industrialization strategies (Sirr et al., 2017). A striking aspect of this financial liberalization is the proliferation of bilateral investment treaties (BITs) between sovereign states. BITs are designed to protect the investments of foreign firms by establishing a broad set of investors' rights and, in several cases, allowing investors to take legal recourse against host governments if these rights are violated (Kerner, 2009).

Interestingly, studies that have analyzed the impact of BITs on FDI have seen the effect only on the inward FDI to developing countries (see, for example, Hallward-Driemeier, 2003; Tobin and Rose-Ackerman, 2005; Salacuse and Sullivan, 2005; Neumayer and Spess, 2005; Kerner, 2009; Sirr et al., 2017 among others). With post-economic liberalization, the world has also witnessed a surge in outward foreign direct investment (OFDI) from developing countries. This study looks into the role of BITs in spurring OFDI from a developing country's perspective.

Since FDI (be it inward or outward) is a risky venture due to huge amounts of sunk costs involved for the investing firm, two types of market imperfections arise – adverse selection and time inconsistency (Bellak, 2015). Both of these imperfections deal with the impact of the past on future investment decisions (ibid.). One reason for these market imperfections is that once committed by an investor, this may create a short-term incentive for host governments to change their policies. According to Buthe and Milner (2008), post-FDI, host governments have an incentive to change the terms to maximize benefits, which is termed as an "obsolescing bargain". The strengthening of bargaining power may appear favorable to the host country initially but has unfavorable implications (Bellak, 2015).

Information asymmetry here implies that the information about the true intentions of a government is often private (Kerner, 2009). For a foreign investor, it is extremely costly to obtain such information, especially when the investor is dealing with countries that lack credible institutions, e.g. some developing countries (Bellak, 2015). Due to the information asymmetry, investors' expectations will be based on their experience with past policies, which will determine their future investment decisions. According to Bellak (2015), this argument would hold independent of the motivation of the policy change. For instance, a host country government

 DOI: 10.4324/9780367855741-16

may have lowered its taxes in the very recent past to maximize the chances of getting re-elected or to attract FDI; or a host country government may have raised its taxes due to budget consolidation purposes.

The time-inconsistency argument in the context of foreign investment implies that the short-term incentives for host country governments are more important than the long-term incentives. This suggests that once an investment has taken place, the foreign government may change their behavior against the foreign investor (Sirr et al., 2017; Bellak, 2015). Different ways in which this is manifested include raising tax levels, raising tariff levels, changes in regulation, mandating local partner, fees, selective law enforcement, imposing new labor requirements, expropriation, etc., thereby shifting surplus from the foreign investor to the state (Guzman, 1998, p. 81).[2]

These imperfections result in a credibility deficit of the host government. As a consequence, an optimal investment may not take place or may occur in a sub-optimal way, which would be either too small or too large (Bellak, 2015). Among the policy options to remedy the credibility problem in foreign investment policies, BITs are the important ones.[3] BITs address the adverse selection problem through their signaling function, as they have *ex ante* costs and the time-inconsistency problem through their protection function thus creates *ex post* costs (commitment) (Kerner, 2009).

By first signing and then ratifying a BIT, host countries give a signal to a foreign investor that the country is trustworthy. Since many of the developing countries who are signing these treaties lack credible institutions and are small, they spend a considerable amount of time and other scarce resources to negotiate, conclude, sign and ratify treaties (Neumayer and Spess, 2005). Any investor can observe this signal once the BIT is ratified, regardless of whether investments in the past are protected or not. To the extent that *ex ante* costs effectively convey credibility, any investor should be more willing to invest in a country that signs and ratifies BITs.

BITs protect investors against some types of political risk through the inclusion of several substantive (e.g. expropriation, unfair treatment) and procedural standards (e.g. investor–state dispute settlement provisions). Post-signing BITs countries can suffer high *ex post* costs if they violate the agreement (Kerner, 2009, p. 74). In other words, a BIT is a commitment device, which makes those commitments costlier to break (Büthe and Milner, 2008, p. 744).

Thus, the *ex ante* and *ex post* costs of signing and ratifying a BIT lead to increased credibility of the country, which results in increased investment. The literature so far has focussed on the role of BITs in attracting FDI. See, for example, the works of Neumayer and Spess (2005), Desbordes and Vicard (2009), Kerner (2009), Büthe and Milner (2008) among others. This study contributes to the literature by carrying out the analysis for an emerging country, namely India, to see the role of BITs in outward foreign direct investment (OFDI). This study is different from other studies as earlier studies have looked into the impact of BITs on inward FDI to developing countries and not outward FDI from a developing country.

The rest of the chapter is organized as follows: the next section gives a brief review of the literature on the impact of BITs on FDI. The third section gives the trend of OFDI and BITs with a focus on India. The fourth section deals with model building with the role of BITs in explaining FDI. The section also formulates the hypotheses to be tested. The fifth section gives the data and variables. The sixth section provides the results, and also compares the results with that of other studies, and the final section concludes the chapter.

Literature review: impact of Bilateral Investment Treaties (BITs)

The role of policy and institutions in attracting FDI has been analyzed in several studies. Some of these studies have looked into the role of specific policies such as BITs in influencing FDI. This section reviews some of these studies.

Hallward-Driemeier (2003) is one of the pioneering studies that has looked into the FDI flow from 20 developed countries to 31 developing countries over the 31 years from 1980 to 2000. Using 537 country pairs and fixed-effect model, the study does not find a positive impact of BITs on FDI inflow to the developing countries. However, the study finds the statistical significance of the interaction of BITs with different institutional indicators. This suggests that the signing of a BIT complements the institutions but they are not a substitute for good institutions, which are *a sine qua non* for attracting FDI.

Tobin and Rose-Ackerman (2005) carried out two different analyses: one with nondyadic FDI inflows for 63 countries over 31 years from 1980 to 2000 with data averaged over a five-year period and second, a dyadic analysis of 54 countries with FDI from the USA to these countries. In the nondyadic analysis, the study finds that a higher number of BITs signed raises the FDI only at a low level of risk. With an increase in risk, more BITs reduce the FDI inflow. In the dyadic analysis, also, the study does not find any statistical impact of BITs on FDI flows from the US to the developing countries, irrespective of the political risk in these countries.

Salacuse and Sullivan (2005) is another study that carries out two kinds of analysis – a cross-sectional analysis of FDI inflows for 1998, 1999 and 2000 and a fixed-effect estimation of the bilateral flow of FDI from the US to 31 developing countries over the period 1991–2000. The study finds a positive impact of signing of BITs with the US on FDI inflow to the developing countries but an insignificant impact of BITs with other OECD countries.

Neumayer and Spess (2005) use a much longer time series (1970 to 2001) and also cover more countries (119 in total) to ascertain the impact of BITs on FDI. The study, contrary to the earlier findings, finds a positive effect of BITs on FDI inflows. The effect is positive and statistically different from zero at all levels of institutional quality, but sometimes conditional on institutional quality.

Kerner (2009), covering the years from 1982 to 2001 for FDI from 22 OECD countries to 127 developing countries, found that BITs result in FDI and they attract it through both channels – direct and indirect. Desbordes and Vicard (2009) argued that the impact of BITs on FDI may be mediated through the quality of political relations between the home and host countries. Using bilateral FDI for 30 OECD and 32 non-OECD countries for the period 1991 to 2000 and event data to measure interaction among countries, the study found that BITs result in an increase in FDI more for countries that have tense relationships than for countries having a friendly relationship.

Given the heterogeneity in results in past studies, recently one study (Ballack, 2015) carried out a meta-analysis covering 42 empirical studies. The paper concluded that the theoretical reasoning of the positive impact of BITs on FDI is not confirmed empirically. In another deviation, Sirr et al. (2017) argued that the impact may be different depending upon the nature of FDI. Using 10-year data from 1999 to 2008 for US FDI investment in 28 developing and transition countries, they found that BITs are more positively linked to vertical FDI than to horizontal FDI. The study concluded that BITs tend to act as a stronger substitute for better institutions in the case of vertical FDI rather than horizontal FDI.

As can be deduced from the review of literature, the findings are still contradictory. Besides, all these studies have looked at the impact from an inward FDI point of view to the developing countries from the US or OECD countries, but not from the outward FDI from any of these developing countries. This is a significant research gap, which the present study fills.

Outward FDI and Bilateral Investment Treaties: relevance and status for India

According to UNCTAD (2015), the stock of OFDI from developing economies reached US$ 4.8 trillion in 2014, forming 18.5 percent of global OFDI stock, up from 3.1 trillion in 2010

(15.3 percent of global OFDI stock), which increased from US$ 740 billion (10.15 percent of global outward FDI stock) in 2000. On flow basis, OFDI from developing and emerging economies grew from US$ 122 billion in 2005 to US$ 340 billion in 2010 to US$ 468 billion accounting for over one-third of total OFDI witnessed at a global level (ibid.). Similarly, of the total 5948 BITs signed up to 2014, over 75 percent were by middle income, developing and poor countries.

India is at the forefront of this phenomenon and performance. The data shows that India's OFDI flow, which averaged around US$ 22 million during 1985–95, increased substantially in the next ten years, reaching US$ 2,175 million in 2004 and peaking at US$ 21,147 million in 2008 (Figure 16.1). Post the 2008 global economic crisis, the value continuously declined to reach a nadir of 1,671 million in 2013 and picking up again to 9,848 million in 2014. In terms of OFDI stock, India with the US$ 129 billion of accumulated investment at the end of 2014 was the eleventh largest outward investing economy among all emerging markets (data source: UNCTAD, 2015).

Beginning in 1994, when India first signed two bilateral investment treaties (BITs) – one with the UK and other with the Russian Federation – it had signed 84 BITs by 2014.[4] Figure 16.1 gives the trend of BITs until 2014. The figure also gives cumulative BITs signed. Of the 84 BITs signed, over 80 percent have been ratified (Table 16.1). Interestingly of the 15 unratified BITs, ten are with African countries. From the table, we can see the spread of Indian BITs, which cover all continents except North America.

The last two columns of the table give the average time taken (in months) and region-wise range of time taken to ratify the treaty. At the minimum, it took one month (for South Korea) to bring the treaty into force, whereas it took more than ten years in the case of Turkmenistan for the treaty to become effective. Of the 14 BITs to be ratified, five were signed more than ten years ago, and seven were signed more than five years ago, and one was signed more than 15 years ago.

Figure 16.2 gives the cumulative BITs in force and cumulative OFDI from India since 1995. As can be seen from the figure, the signing and ratification of BITs was an important activity

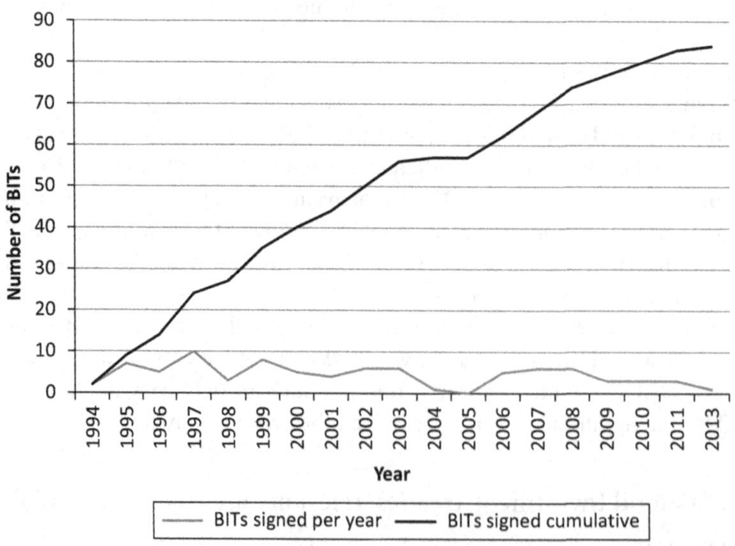

Figure 16.1 Trend in BITs signed

Table 16.1 Distribution of BITs across regions and av. time gap (in months)

Region	*BITs signed*	*BITs ratified*	*% ratified*	*Av. time gap (months)*	*Range (months)*
Africa	12	2	16.7	22.75	21.5 – 24
Central Asia	5	5	100.0	44.5	11 – 125
East Asia	9	9	100.0	17.4	1 – 49.5
South Asia	4	3	75.0	16.3	7.5 – 29
Eastern Europe	19	17	89.5	24	8 – 95
Europe	17	17	100.0	26.1	5 – 109
Middle East	11	11	100.0	23.4	7 – 47
Pacific	2	2	100.0	11	8 – 14
South America	5	4	80.0	24	7 – 44
Total	**84**	**70**	**82.4**	**24.3**	

Source: Own compilation based on data from UNCTAD.

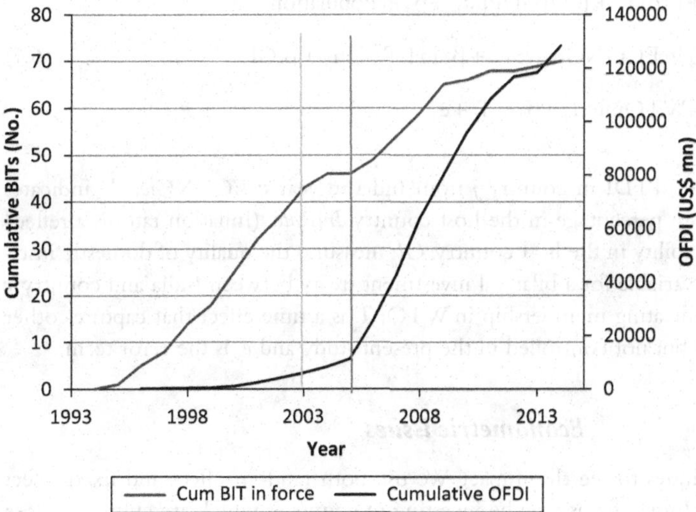

Figure 16.2 Trend in BITs signed and cumulative OFDI

until 2003 and thereafter again became important from 2005 to 2009. On the other hand, outward FDI from India took off from 2005 onwards until 2011.

Hypothesis and model

In order to fathom the impact of BITs on OFDI, we look into the determinants of OFDI with BITs as the main factor after controlling for several variables like size of the host country, quality of institutions, membership in regional agreements, macroeconomic stability among others (see for example, the works of Neumayer and Spess 2005; Tobin and Rose-Ackerman, 2005; Hallward-Driemeier, 2003 among others).

We hypothesize that if the signaling effect of BITs has worked, resulting in taking care of the market imperfections, then it should result in increased OFDI from India. Taking a cue from other studies (Neumayer and Spess, 2005; Tobin and Rose-Ackerman, 2005 among others), we use per capita GDP of the host country, its population, inflation and economic growth of the host country, membership of WTO, institutional quality, etc., as control variables. Regarding GDP per capita, a priori, it is difficult to predict its coefficient sign, since greater GDP per capita reflects both high purchasing power and more nominal wages, which exert positive and negative effects on FDI, respectively (Globerman and Shapiro, 2002). A country with a large number of people is potentially a signal for big markets and would attract more OFDI. A growing economy would attract more investment; we use the economic growth of the host country as a variable affecting OFDI. We include a measure of institution quality depicting investment risk (i.e., an indicator of the quality of domestic legal and political institutions as a proxy for the host-country-specific risk), and a dummy for the entry into the BIT (BIT). Larger risks given by the lower value of GI (governance index), reflecting high investment costs and uncertainty, should reduce OFDI by Indian firms, while a BIT is expected to increase OFDI. Lastly, we also control for macroeconomic stability using the inflation rate (IR).

$$\begin{aligned}\ln \mathrm{OFDI}_{jt} = {} & \beta_0 + \beta_1 BIT_j + \beta_2 \ln \mathrm{GDPpc}_{jt} + \beta_3 \ln \mathrm{Population}_{jt} \\ & + \beta_4 \ln \mathrm{ECONGrowth}_{jt} + \beta_5 \ln \mathrm{Inflation}_{ij} + \beta_6 \mathrm{GI}_{jt} \\ & + \beta_7 \mathrm{WTOmem}_j + \beta_{8-12} \mathrm{T}_t + \mathrm{e}_{jt}\end{aligned} \quad (16.1)$$

where $OFDI_{jt}$ is the outward FDI in country j from India in year t; $ECONGrowth_{jt}$ indicates annual economic growth in percentage in the host country, $InfRate_{jt}$ (Inflation rate) is a reflection of macroeconomic stability in the host country, GI_{jt} measures the quality of domestic institutions, BIT_j is a dummy variable for a bilateral investment treaty between India and country j; *WTOmem* is a dummy indicating membership in WTO; T_t is a time effect that captures other factors influencing OFDI but not controlled in the present study and e_{jt} is the error term.

Econometric issues

We use panel data techniques to see the impact. We use both random-effect and fixed-effect methods. We suspect that Indian firms may be investing in countries which are culturally close to India. This closeness and consequently high OFDI might be because of two sources: (a) the host country also has colonial ties with India; and/or (b) the host country speaks the same language as India. These ties, as well as other variables like legal restrictions on inward FDI in host countries or climate or geographical distance from India, are time-invariant. To see the relevance of these factors, the Hausman test, which tests the random-effects assumption that these time-invariant factors are uncorrelated with the explanatory variables, is carried out. We, however, speculate that the Hausman test would reject random effect as data shows that OFDI to countries speaking the same language (English) is four times higher than that to countries speaking other languages (Mandarin or Spanish or French). Similarly, OFDI to former colonies is 3.5 times that to countries not having a historical relationship.[5] Another issue in analyzing the role of BITs is the potential reverse causality problem. To mitigate potential reverse causality problems, we lag all explanatory variables by one period. Figure 16.2 demonstrates this causality. Ideally, one would like to tackle this problem more comprehensively with the help of instrumental variable regression. However, practically all explanatory variables (GDP per capita, inflation, good institutions, etc.) are potentially subject to reverse causality, and it would be simply impossible to find adequate and valid instruments.

Data and variables

The study used eight-year data from 2007 till 2014[6] and collected it from different sources. OFDI data was sourced from the RBI website, which gives firm-wise monthly OFDI figures. The data consists of information about the name of the Indian party, name of the joint venture (JV)/wholly-owned subsidiary (WOS), whether JV or WOS, overseas country, major activity and what kind of financial commitment – is it equity or loan or some guarantee. The data shows that in these eight years, Indian firms invested in 151 countries – five of which are non-sovereign. Apart from the year 2007, on average, Indian firms invested in 100 countries every year, over 85 percent (except in 2008) of the investment in ten countries only. Table 16A.1 in the appendix gives these top ten destinations for Indian firms starting from 2007. The Netherlands, Mauritius, Singapore, the USA and the UAE feature every year in the top 10 list in these nine years. The UK also figures as a key destination every year except in 2007. Interestingly, a non-sovereign tax haven – British Virgin Island figures in the top ten destinations every year. For the analysis, we have excluded this and other non-sovereign jurisdictions/countries – Panama, Isle of Man, Bermuda, Channel Islands consisting of Jersey and Guernsey, and Cayman Islands, which are commonly labeled as tax havens, as the purpose of investment is to evade tax.[7] These tax havens account for 8.5 percent of total OFDI in these eight years.

One problem often encountered in studies looking into the determinants of FDI (be it outward or inward) or trade is the preponderance of zero investment (or trade). This is because of two reasons – first, the investment is lumpy and is a sunk cost for the firm. Thus, if a firm invests in one year in a location, it may not reinvest or invest in other locations immediately. Second, there is a demonstration/signaling effect in investment – as a result, firms competing in an industry may prefer the same destination for outward investment too. Incidentally, of the 146 sovereign countries preferred for investment by Indian firms, only 51 have received OFDI every year. Dropping the countries which received zero FDI in a year would result in selection bias (Desbordes and Vicard, 2009). In terms of observations, this would mean eliminating 391 observations (35 percent) of the total 1120 observations.

For the analysis, we convert OFDI to different countries to constant US$ of 2005 with the help of the US GDP deflator. As used by some of the studies (see, for example, Neumayer and Spess, 2005), we also use the absolute value of outflow instead of OFDI stock or OFDI inflow as a percentage of the host country's GDP. It is possible that the OFDI increase might have happened because of the increased rate of the conclusion of the BITs and both may be moving in the same direction, thus showing a spurious relation. This is dealt with employing year dummies to account for any year-to-year variation in total FDI flows unaccounted for by our explanatory variables, which should mitigate potential spuriousness of any significant results.

Data source

For GDP, GDP growth rate and inflation, we have used World Development Indicators data from the World Bank.[8] For a few countries for which GDP growth and inflation data was not available for the year 2014, we used some other sources.[9] We extrapolated data for GDP for some of the countries to get values for 2014. For three countries – Myanmar, Syria and Liechtenstein – most of the information was missing; hence, they were excluded from the

Table 16.2 Mean comparison of BIT signed vs. non-BIT signed

	Non-BIT signed		*BIT signed*	
	Mean	*Std. dev.*	*Mean*	*Std. dev.*
FDI (US $ mn)	103.78	653.18	227.44*	1,002.0
GDPPC (US $)	16,276.71	70,037.53	16,785.43	16,507.55
GI (Governance indicator)	−0.21	0.96	0.38*	0.97
GDP growth (%)	3.89	6.51	3.23*	4.22
Inflation (%)	6.23	8.69	5.7	8.62
WTO membership (Yes = 1, No = 0)	0.75	0.43	0.88*	0.33
N	684		436	

Source: Own compilation.

analysis. Thus, for the final analysis, the study uses 1120 observations (140 firms for eight years). Of these 1120 observations, for nearly 39 percent of them, the bilateral investment treaties dummy is one.

For governance-related variables, we have used World Governance Indicators data from the World Bank.[10] The data covers six key aspects of governance: (a) control of corruption; (b) government effectiveness; (c) political stability and absence of violence; (d) regulatory quality; (e) Rule of Law; and (f) voice and accountability. These indicators can achieve a maximum of 3 and a minimum of −3. Denmark (a), Singapore (b), Luxembourg (c), Singapore (d), Finland (e) and Norway (f) are the countries which receive top spot for each of these indicators respectively; whereas Afghanistan (for a, c and e), Central African Republic (b), Libya (d) and Uzbekistan (f) figure in the bottom for these indicators. For the present analysis, we have used the "Rule of Law" as the indicator influencing OFDI and as a robustness test, we have tried with other indicators too.[11]

Before we estimate our model, Table 16.2 compares the mean of OFDI, per capita GDP, GDP growth, governance and WTO membership of the two groups – those which signed BITs against those which did not sign BITs. From the table we see that OFDI to those groups of countries which have signed BITs with India tends to be higher they have better governance, more WTO membership with differences being statistically significant at minimum 10 percent level. However, there is no statistical difference in inflation in the two groups.

Results

Table 16.3 gives the results of the random-effect (RE) and fixed-effect (FE) model for testing the effect of BITs on India's OFDI. Columns 1 and 2 report the results for FE and RE, respectively. Interestingly, contrary to our speculation, the Hausman test supports RE against FE. This implies the omitted time-invariant variables are uncorrelated with other explanatory variables. Subsequently, we explain RE results only. From the results, we see that signing and ratifying BITs has no statistically significant impact on OFDI from India. However, a country's per capita income, economic growth and potential market size as measured by its population have a positive influence on OFDI from India. Economic sta-

Table 16.3 Testing for effect of BITs – fixed effect (FE) and random effect (RE) model (log FDI outflow in 2005 US$)

	FE	*RE*	*FE*	*RE*
VARIABLES	*(1)*	*(2)*	*(3)*	*(4)*
BITs	–0.186	0.0196	–0.216	0.000946
	(0.446)	(0.286)	(0.450)	(0.289)
ln GDPpc	0.0698	0.333**	0.102	0.331**
	(0.749)	(0.137)	(0.752)	(0.137)
ln population	1.626	0.475***	1.672	0.475***
	(1.464)	(0.0957)	(1.467)	(0.0960)
Economic growth	0.0157*	0.0156*	0.0156*	0.0156*
	(0.00947)	(0.00891)	(0.00948)	(0.00891)
Inflation	–0.00854	–0.00828	-0.00851	–0.00818
	(0.00667)	(0.00656)	(0.00668)	(0.00657)
Rule of Law	–0.378	0.557**	–0.481	0.506**
	(0.503)	(0.221)	(0.540)	(0.247)
WTO membership		0.558		0.568
		(0.414)		(0.415)
BITs x Rule of Law			0.319	0.137
			(0.608)	(0.299)
Year effect	Yes	Yes	Yes	Yes
Constant	–25.17	–9.457***	–26.19	–9.467***
	(24.52)	(2.051)	(24.61)	(2.057)
Observations	980	980	980	980
R-squared	0.017		0.018	
Number of Countries	140	140	140	140
Hausman Test	9.73		9.81	
	0.136		0.1997	

Notes: Standard errors in parentheses; ***, **, * implies significance at 1, 5 and 10 percent respectively; Hausman Test is asymptotically χ^2 distributed with *p*-values in brackets.

bility, as measured by inflation, though it comes up with the right sign, is not statistically significant from zero. Regarding institutions, we find that a country with a higher regard for the Rule of Law tends to influence Indian firms' decision to invest. However, becoming a member of the WTO does not enthuse Indian investors.

The results, though, do not find the support of the positive role of BITs in OFDI, so we conjecture that it is not only BIT, it is the complementary effect of the Rule of Law and BIT together which may propel investment in the host country. There are several studies that have advocated the relevance of complementarity (see, for example, Neumayer and Spess, 2005; Desbordes and Vicard, 2009; Bellak, 2015 among others). Correspondingly, we use an interaction term between Rule of Law and BIT to see their complementary effect. Results are reported in columns 3 and 4. We do not find any evidence of this as the interaction term though is positive, and is not statistically different from zero. All other variables, including BITs, retain the same sign and significance level. Based on the results, we can say that BITs have not influenced India's OFDI; rather it is the other macro and country-specific variables that have determined the outward FDI from India.

Conclusions

In the last two and half decades, with the change in countries' development approach from import-substituting industrialization to foreign direct investment (FDI) assisted development, several developing and transition countries have aggressively signed bilateral investment treaties to safeguard foreign investors. Several studies exist that have looked into the role of BITs in spurring FDI to developing countries from the US and other OECD countries with conflicting results. This chapter tries to see the role of BITs in outward FDI (OFDI) from India. Since FDI is a risky venture due to the huge amount of sunk costs involved for the investing firm, two types of market imperfections arise – adverse selection and time inconsistency. BITs, through signaling, try to mitigate these market imperfections. The study differs from other studies as it looks at the role of BITs in outward FDI and not in inward FDI and that too for a developing country. For the analysis, the paper uses OFDI data from India for the period 2007 to 2014 for 140 countries. Of these 140 countries, India has BITs with over 50 countries. Our results show that OFDI from India is not influenced by BITs. It is the economic growth, per capita income and size of the country (in terms of population) that has induced OFDI.

The study, though, did not find that signing and ratifying BITs has positively influenced outward FDI from India, which has important implications. Since BITs favor foreign over domestic investors by treating them differently, does this mean their efficacy (as also found in the present analysis) becomes somewhat limited? From a welfare maximization point of view, investment policies with allocation bias between domestic and foreign investors have limitations. The measures, which treat all investors alike are a preferable type of investment promotion policy with few side effects on the allocation of resources (e.g. subsidies or tax breaks, provision of infrastructure) (Bellak, 2015).

Though we find that BITs are not an influential factor in spurring OFDI from India, through their FDI protection function, they may still contribute to the sustainability of OFDI. This is because BITs permit taking legal recourse against host countries in certain situations. Interestingly, this investor protection right is guaranteed even after the termination/lapse of BITs. This implies that the aggregate OFDI though may not have gone up with BITs, but investor protection may still have enhanced the effects of other types of investment policies.

Regarding future work, as discussed, the study treats all BITs identically, so one possible extension would be to look into details of treaties and then carry out the analysis. Segregating the countries based on their per capita income and then doing analysis for countries at the same level of development as India could be another extension. Also, similar to Sirr et al. (2017), we can look into whether the nature of FDI has any connection with BITs or not. Another possible extension of the present work is carrying out the analysis with the inclusion of earlier years, especially from 1995 onwards, when more BITs signing just became a fad. As mentioned, the focus of the current regime has shifted beyond BITs with the termination of 61 BITs in the last 5–6 years – it would be interesting to see how this regime shift has affected OFDI.

Appendix

Table 16A.1 Top ten OFDI destinations (and volume in US $ million) since 2007

OFDI destinations	*2007*	*2008*	*2009*	*2010*	*2011*	*2012*	*2013*	*2014*	*2015#*
Netherlands	1,178.91 (1)	993.8 (6)	1,594.88 (4)	7937.41 (3)	2,648.96 (3)	3,963.08 (3)	7,207.56 (1)	1,1786.27 (1)	732.06 (5)
Mauritius	890.01 (2)	2,489.17 (2)	2,490.14 (3)	11385.93 (2)	7,834.8 (1)	5,508.66 (1)	3,849.61 (3)	5,329.23 (3)	3,226.18 (1)
Singapore	740.31 (3)	4,547.59 (1)	4,680.29 (1)	12071.87 (1)	7,185.36 (2)	4,184.39 (2)	4,832.4 (2)	5,739.48 (2)	2,459.79 (2)
Cyprus	710.02 (4)	643.36 (8)	2526.96 (2)	444.84 (8)					210.05 (10)
United States of America (USA)	622.62 (5)	1,348.04 (4)	1,368.73 (5)	2087.47 (4)	1,783.91 (6)	2,943.26 (4)	2,387.76 (4)	1,708.407 (6)	1,681.63 (3)
Thailand	411.51 (6)								
British Virgin Islands	317.41 (7)	1,034.53 (5)	552.29 (7)	750.93 (6)	1,587.37 (8)	843.05 (8)	1,415.56 (8)	2,861.65 (5)	
Denmark	314.23 (8)								
Cayman Islands	263.14 (9)						1,526.19 (7)	508.95 (10)	
United Arab Emirates (UAE)	211.32 (10)	1,382.66 (3)	1,249.03 (6)	1808.81 (5)	1,341.35 (9)	1,463.27 (5)	1,798.15 (6)	1,392.08 (7)	950.39 (4)
United Kingdom (UK)		849.41 (7)	361.14 (10)	691.09 (7)	1,675.01 (7)	1254.16 (7)	1,900.25 (5)	519.65 (9)	634.39 (6)
Russia		545.7 (9)	470.98 (8)						
Egypt		423.8 (10)							
China			373.25 (9)						
Hong Kong				308.3 (9)					
Indonesia				257.79 (10)					
Australia					2405.24 (4)	1262.26 (6)			
Switzerland					1,077.03 (10)	651.69 (9)	769.35 (10)	781.85 (8)	492.06 (7)
Panama					1,934.63 (5)				
Luxembourg						382.01 (10)			295.59 (9)
Azerbaijan							813.52 (9)		
Mozambique								3,648.84 (4)	
Malaysia									448.122 (8)
OFDI for top 10 countries	**5,658.48**	**1,4258.06**	**1,5667.69**	**3,7744.44**	**2,9437.66**	**2,2455.83**	**2,6500.35**	**3,4276.61**	**1,1130.26**
Total OFDI	**6,599.003**	**1,7758.98**	**1,7772.53**	**4,0508.26**	**3,3937.81**	**2,5585.64**	**3,0425.53**	**3,6775.32**	**1,2517.42**
Percentage	**85.75**	**80.29**	**88.16**	**93.18**	**86.74**	**87.77**	**87.10**	**93.21**	**88.92**
No. of Countries	**70**	**95**	**104**	**101**	**108**	**109**	**112**	**109**	**91**

Note: # Till August 2015 only; Countries in shades are Tax havens.

Notes

1 The author is thankful to Ms. Himagiri Sudha for collecting the data and arranging it. The usual disclaimers apply. Our thanks to the reviewer for very useful comments. An earlier version of the chapter was presented in the National Seminar on "India after a Quarter Century of Economic Reforms – The Benefits and Costs" Organized by Sikkim University, Gangtok (Sikkim) during October 5–6, 2018. We are extremely thankful to the seminar participants for very useful comments.

2 Of all these actions, expropriation is the most extreme. There is, however, a counter-argument that government may resist the temptation to go for drastic renegade, including seizing assets today so as to maintain a reputation that would attract future investment (Guzman 1998).

3 There are three kinds of agreements which aim at protecting the investors' interests. These are International Investment Agreements (IIAs), Bilateral Investment Treaties (BITs) and Preferential Trade Agreements (PTAs) with investment provisions. IIAs are of three kinds – investment protection treaty, investment liberalization and protection treaty, and investment chapter under the Economic Partnership Agreement (EPA)/ Free Trade Agreement (FTA). To some, BITs is also one category of IIAs (Bellak, 2015).

4 After 2014, in the last five years, India has signed only one new BIT. This treaty is with Belarus signed on 24 September 2018. Interestingly, India has unilaterally terminated 61 BITs. Even though India has terminated nearly three-quarters of the BITs, the investor protection remains. This is because the rights enshrined in BITs are often guaranteed for a substantial period after expiration (Bellak, 2015).

5 The OFDI to countries speaking the same language is US$ 336 million against 85.6 to others; whereas OFDI to countries which were also British Colonies until 1947 is the US $359 against 102 to other countries. Both these differences are statistically significant at 1 percent level.

6 We could not carry out analysis beyond 2014 for the reason indicated in note 3 that in the last 5–6 years India has signed only one new BIT. There seems to be a different policy towards BITs as after 2014 with the NDA government in power, India has terminated 61 BITs.

7 The OECD identifies three key factors in considering whether a jurisdiction is a tax haven: nil or only nominal taxes, protection of personal financial information and lack of transparency (Source: www.oecd.org/ countries/monaco/listofunco-operativetaxhavens.htm accessed in December 2015).

8 Source: http://data.worldbank.org/data-catalog/world-development-indicators.

9 These other sources include www.tradingeconomics.com/; www.inflation.eu and www.stats.govt.nz/ browse_for_stats/economic_indicators/GDP.aspx.

10 Source: http://data.worldbank.org/data-catalog/worldwide-governance-indicators.

11 All six indicators are highly correlated with correlation coefficient significant at even 1 percent level.

References

Bellak, C. (2015) *Economic Impact of Investment Agreements*. Vienna: Vienna University of Economics and Business. Department of Economics Working Paper No. 200.

Büthe, T., and H.V. Milner (2008) "The Politics of Foreign Direct Investment into Developing Countries: Increasing FDI through International Trade Agreements?", *American Journal of Political Science*, 52(4), 741–762.

Desbordes, R., and V. Vincente (2009) "Foreign Direct Investment and Bilateral Investment Treaties: An International Political Perspective", *Journal of Comparative Economics*, 37(3), 372–386.

Globerman, S., and D. Shapiro (2002) "Global Foreign Direct Investment Flows: The Role of Governance Infrastructure", *World Development*, 30(11), 1899–1919.

Guzman, A.T. (1998) "Why LDCs Sign Treaties that Hurt Them: Explaining the Popularity of Bilateral Investment Treaties", *Virginia Journal of International Law*, 38, 639–688.

Hallward-Driemeier, M. (2003) *Do Bilateral Investment Treaties Attract FDI? Only a Bit… and They Could Bite*. Washington, DC: World Bank. World Bank Policy Research Paper WPS 3121.

http://www.data.worldbank.org/data-catalog/world-development-indicators. Accessed in Nov. 2015.

http://www.data.worldbank.org/data-catalog/worldwide-governance-indicators. Accessed in Nov. 2015.

http://www.oecd.org/countries/monaco/listofunco-operativetaxhavens.htm. Accessed in Dec. 2015.

http://www.tradingeconomics.com/; http://www.inflation.eu. Accessed in Nov. 2015.

http://www.stats.govt.nz/browse_for_stats/economic_indicators/GDP.aspx. Accessed in Nov. 2015.

Kerner, A. (2009) "Why Should I Believe You? The Costs and Consequences of Bilateral Investment Treaties", *International Studies Quarterly*, 53(1), 73–102.

Neumayer, E., and L. Spess (2005) "Do Bilateral Investment Treaties Increase Foreign Direct Investment to Developing Countries?", *World Development*, 33(10), 1567–1585.

Salacuse, J.W., and N.P. Sullivan (2005) "Do BITs Really Work? An Evaluation of Bilateral Investment Treaties and Their Grand Bargain", *Harvard International Law Journal*, 46, 67–130.

Sirr, G., J. Garvey, and L.A. Gallagher (2017) "Bilateral Investment Treaties and Foreign Direct Investment: Evidence of Asymmetric Effects on Vertical and Horizontal Investments", *Development Policy Review*, 35(1): 93–113.

Tobin, J., and S. Rose-Ackerman (2005) *Foreign Direct Investment and the Business Environment in Developing Countries: The Impact of Bilateral Investment Treaties*. Yale Law School Center for Law, Connecticut. Economics and Public Policy Research Paper No. 293.

UNCTAD (2015) *World Investment Report 2015*. New York and Geneva: United Nations.

17

TRADE LIBERALIZATION AND TECHNOLOGICAL SPILLOVERS IN THE INDIAN PHARMACEUTICAL INDUSTRY, 1999–2014[1]

Loitongbam Bishwanjit Singh

Introduction

The spectacular growth of the Indian pharmaceutical industry (IPI) is mainly due to various legislative reforms of the Indian government. Since India's implementation of Trade Related Aspects of Intellectual Property Rights (TRIPS), in compliance with the World Trade Organization (WTO) accession, there has been a significant change in the policy, growth and development of the IPI. For example, India had implemented TRIPS in compliance with the WTO accession in 1995. The Indian Patent Act 1970 had been amended three times; once in March 1999, again in June 2002, and the third time in April 2005. It implies that India could not produce drugs patented by foreign companies through reverse-engineering. As a result, R&D expenditures by domestic and foreign pharmaceutical companies, mergers and acquisitions (M&A) and patent activity and patent filings by Indian pharmaceutical firms have significantly increased.

R&D expenditures had increased from 3.88% growth rate in the Pre-TRIPS period to 5.07% growth rate in the Post-TRIPS (Kiran and Mishra, 2009a). The total R&D expenditure significantly increased from 2005 onwards, i.e., from $40.82 million in 1999 to $326.15 million in 2005 to $1,134.16 million in 2014 (Table 17.1). Both domestic and foreign R&D expenditures have increased significantly in absolute terms. However, in terms of percentage share, domestic R&D expenditure shares have occupied major shares of the total. The percentage share of R&D expenditure incurred by domestic firms had increased from 62.03% in 1999 to 71.59% in 2005 and to 84.27% in 2014. Foreign R&D expenditure consistently decreased from 2006 onwards. R&D expenditure incurred by foreign companies had decreased from 37.97% in 1999 to 28.41% in 2005 and to 17.22% in 2014. It indicates that after the full the implementation of product patent, pharmaceutical companies have started investing huge amounts in R&D activities and domestic companies are taking the lead.

By 2014, out of the top ten companies that had invested substantially in R&D activities, eight are Indian domestic companies (Table 17.2). Ranbaxy Laboratories Ltd. and Mylan Laboratories Ltd. are the only two foreign companies included in the list. These eight companies' shares accounted for more than 57% of the total R&D expenditure in 2014. The first top pharmaceutical companies in terms of R&D expenditure percentage share in 2014 are Dr. Reddy's

DOI: 10.4324/9780367855741-17

Table 17.1 R&D expenditures of the Indian pharmaceutical industry: 1999–2014 (in US$ million and in %)

Year	*Total R&D (in $ million)*	*Domestic R&D (in $ million)*	*Foreign R&D (in $ million)*	*Domestic R&D (% change)*	*Foreign R&D (% change)*
1999	40.82	25.32	15.50	62.03	37.97
2000	58.27	39.80	18.47	68.30	31.70
2001	71.60	54.17	17.43	75.66	24.34
2002	96.35	76.53	19.82	79.43	20.57
2003	134.37	91.68	42.69	68.23	31.77
2004	226.69	160.94	65.75	71.00	29.00
2005	326.15	233.48	92.67	71.59	28.41
2006	423.11	293.98	129.13	69.48	30.52
2007	547.22	422.65	124.57	77.24	22.76
2008	641.49	489.45	152.04	76.30	23.70
2009	613.83	474.66	139.17	77.33	22.67
2010	799.16	622.72	176.44	77.92	22.08
2011	959.84	773.66	186.18	80.60	19.40
2012	959.96	794.67	165.29	82.78	17.22
2013	1,045.23	869.25	175.98	83.16	16.84
2014	1,134.61	956.17	178.44	84.27	15.73

Source: Prowess database, CMIE.

Table 17.2 Top 10 R&D expenditure incurred by pharmaceutical companies in 2014 (in US$ million)

Sl. No.	*Companies*	*2005*	*2010*	*2011*	*2012*	*2013*	*2014*
1	Dr. Reddy's Laboratories Ltd.	57.64	88.29	121.29	123.62	127.69	170.31
2	Lupin Ltd.	17.4	78.47	107.45	103.89	130.48	152.33
3	Ranbaxy Laboratories Ltd. [Merged]	75.35	101.26	105.86	86	82.17	86.52
4	Cipla Ltd.	20.42	55.1	57.74	60.89	66.87	83.9
5	Cadila Healthcare Ltd.	16.25	38.75	56.52	71.22	81.37	71.43
6	Mylan Laboratories Ltd.	3.65	51.2	56.32	55.08	69.74	69.12
7	Sun Pharmaceutical Inds. Ltd.	16.98	31.67	34.96	36.4	50.09	61.5
8	Aurobindo Pharma Ltd.	8.22	21.38	30.99	31.66	38.33	41.8
9	Piramal Enterprises Ltd.	11.34	7.95	9.55	36.62	43.58	39.35
10	Wockhardt Ltd.	11.53	8.77	7.4	8.88	36.94	32.53

Source: Prowess database, CMIE.

Laboratories Ltd. (15.02%), Lupin Ltd. (13.43%) and Cipla Ltd. (7.39%). Thus, domestic pharmaceutical companies are spending on R&D activities much more than foreign companies.

However, after trade liberalization in 1991 and patent policy changes thereafter, the market shares of the MNCs in the domestic market increased. In the domestic formulation market, their shares increased from less than 20% in March 2008 to 28% in December 2010 with the taking over of Ranbaxy by Daiichi Sankyo in June 2008; Dabur Pharma by Fresenius Kabi Oncology in August 2008; Shantha Biotechs by Sanofi-Aventis in July 2009 and the domestic formulations business of Piramal Healthcare by Abbott in May 2010. Among the top ten pharmaceutical companies in India, the number of MNCs increased from one (i.e. GSK) in March 2008 to three (i.e. GSK, Ranbaxy and the Abbott group) in December 2010. The Abbott group, which was the thirtieth largest company with a market share of only 1.1% in March 2008 (comprising Abbott, Piramal Healthcare and Solvay Pharma) now became the largest company in India occupying 6.2% market share followed by the Cipla (5.7%). If the MNCs have taken over some remaining major Indian companies such as Cipla (5.7% market share in 2010), Sun (4.3%), Cadila Healthcare (3.9%), Mankind (3.2%), Alkem (3%), Lupin (2.9%), their share will exceed 50%, immediately paving the way to dominate the IPI. Furthermore, with the abolition of the Foreign Exchange Regulation Act (FERA), the MNCs listed on the Indian stock exchanges increased their equity stakes, accounting for more than 50%. For instance, Novartis increased foreign equity from 50.93% in 2005 to 76.42% in 2010, Pfizer from 40% to 70.75%, Abbott from 61.7% to 68.94% and Aventis from 50.1% to 60.4% (Chaudhuri, 2011). This is not welcoming news for the domestic firms.

After IPRs reform, many foreign MNCs expanded their industry activities to India. They gave attention to doing collaborative research with domestic pharmaceutical companies. They started outsourcing research activities in an effort to reduce their R&D cost. Since investment in R&D involves a high cost of money with uncertain outcomes, it is this cost consideration and the availability of a vast pool of human resources that bring foreign MNCs to India. Now the problem faced by domestic pharmaceutical firms is that they are not only lacking in investments, skills and technologies but also restricted from accessing technical innovation that comes from reverse engineering. Under such circumstances, domestic firms are struggling for survival. Thus, the importance of undertaking R&D efforts in India's knowledge industry like pharmaceutical industry has increased. With the deepening of the globalization process in which each country not only relies on others for trade but also learns from others through technology transfer, how Indian domestic pharmaceutical companies can grow their business in the changing business environment is a big question.

The present chapter tries to estimate the impact of foreign ownership and patent protection upon India's pharmaceutical firms' R&D activities and on the nature of these "R&D spillovers". The results suggest that there is a positive and highly significant level of foreign ownership effect on R&D activity and TRIPS implementation has insignificant effects on R&D innovation. We contribute to the empirical literature by providing a quantitative evaluation of the importance of foreign ownership and patent protection on R&D activities. Investment in R&D benefits both domestic and foreign firms through spillover effect. The chapter is arranged as follows. The next section gives the literature reviews. The third section shows methods, data and variables. The fourth section summarizes the empirical results and the fifth section concludes.

Literature review

A patent provides protection to a patentee from imitators and a country with a relatively higher productivity level innovates more and can easily adopt new technology (Eaton and Kortum,

1996). It stimulates innovation and contributes in economic development only in developed countries (Kim et al., 2012) and in those countries with a high level of development, education and economic freedom (Qian, 2007; Sweet and Maggio, 2015). Developing countries can also benefit from the implementation of IPRs if they can implement the same IPRs standard of the developed countries (Lai and Qiu, 2003) through technology transfer, increase in R&D activities, etc. (Dinopoulos et al., 2010) and by increasing royalty payments for technology transfers to affiliates, R&D expenditures and foreign patent filings (Branstetter et al., 2006; Vita 2013). However, Helpman (1993) argued that though there is a temporary increase in innovation, the developing countries lose from tighter IPRs.

Knowledge spillovers and their relation to economic growth are empirically well established by Griliches (1979, 1998). However, international R&D spillovers are asymmetrical across countries. For example, Griliches (1986; 1998); Griliches and Mairesse (1990); Nadiri (1993) and Wakelin (2001) found that R&D increased productivity growth through benefits from foreign technical advances and effective use of existing resources. Coe and Helpman (1995) found that returns on R&D activity were high in both output and international spillovers and a country's productivity level depends on its own and its trading partners' R&D stocks. They argued that foreign R&D stimulated domestic productivity more to those economies which were more open to foreign trade and to those firms which were engaged more in their own R&D. Confirming their findings, Aw et al. (2007) found that exports and R&D were complementary for productivity growth, with R&D activities facilitating its ability to benefit from exposure to the export market.

Conversely, some literature has pointed out that there is a negative spillover effect. For instance, Aitken and Harrison (1999) found that there were no knowledge spillovers to domestic owned firms using the panel data on Venezuela firms due to the market stealing effect. Eaton and Kortum (1996) found that there is significant heterogeneity in knowledge spillover among OECD countries. Knowledge spillovers are not beneficial to the US (Eaton and Kortum, 1996) or the UK (Girma et al., 2008). Feinberg et al. (2001) and Iyer (2012) also found that there was no R&D spillover effect from both foreign and domestic MNCs on domestic firms in India. The reasons behind these include R&D spillovers only took place among MNCs themselves. Foreign firms didn't significantly affect domestic firms' productivities.

The effect of stronger IPRs and implementation of TRIPS on innovation for the pharmaceutical industry in the developing economies is very contentious. Croix and Kawuara (1996) examined the effect of the adoption of product patents for the Korean chemical and pharmaceutical industry and found that the adoption of stronger patent laws decreased Korea's wealth. Allred and Park (2007) argued that patent strength reduced domestic patent filings and had insignificant effects on R&D and foreign patent filings for developing countries. Ala (2013) also found the negative effects of TRIPS implementation on innovation in the case of Bangladeshi pharmaceutical firms. The implementation of TRIPS did not improve R&D capabilities in Bangladesh and reduced competitiveness in LDCs (Ala, 2013).

But, in India, the implementation of TRIPS had increased the patenting activities and R&D investments of the domestic pharmaceutical companies and increased sales and export performances of the companies (Chaudhuri, 2007; Chadha, 2009; Bedi et al., 2013. India had had more success in industrial capabilities than other developing countries like Brazil due to changes in national policy after the IPRs reform (Guennif and Ramani, 2012; Pradhan, 2003). Niosi et al. (2012) for India and Jiatao (2003) for China also confirmed that diffusion patterns, shaped by national policies, were critical as the process is uneven among developing countries. Though the implementation of TRIPS resulted in some welfare loss it would not have much detrimental effect on the IPI (Chaudhuri et al., 2006). It increased domestic firms' profits in India.

Method, data and variables

Method

To analyze the evidence on the relation between globalization and innovation in the Indian pharmaceutical firms, we rely on the work of Girma et al. (2008). Foreign ownership and export are used as a proxy for the globalization process. This paper uses logistic regression to examine the relationship between innovation and foreign ownership and trade liberalization. To check multicollinearity, we use a logit fixed effects model. One of the benefits of using the logistic regression model is that it is very robust, simple and appropriate for dichotomous dependent variables. The specification of the estimate is given by:

$$Logit\left(R \,\&\, D_{it} = 1\right) = f(\text{lagged ownership, lagged export, lagged TFP, lagged TRIPS, lagged firm attributes}) \quad (17.1)$$

R&D is a dummy equal to one if it has any positive R&D expenditure in time t and zero otherwise (i = 552 companies, t = 1999–2014). Foreign ownership (indicated by lagged ownership) is the share of foreign equity participation at the firm level in the previous year, which varies between 0% and 100%. If foreign ownership in a firm increases that firm's productivity, the coefficient of ownership will be positive. Lagged export is a dummy, 1 indicates a firm's export in time, $t-1$ and 0 otherwise. It is expected that exports should have positive coefficient if exports increase firm's productivity. Lagged TFP indicates a firm's productivity in time, $t-1$. TFP refers to the total factor productivity. It is used to measure firm's productivity.

We estimate TFP using the Levinsohn-Petrin (L-P) semi-parametric. The simultaneity problem is one of the most common problems faced in the calculation of productivity. For example, inputs used in calculating productivity often correlated with productivity. This simultaneity problem cannot be completely solved by a random or fixed effects model. However, the L-P method is used to take care of this kind of productivity shock. Under this method, TFP is estimated by using output, labor input, capital and raw materials. It assumes that the intermediate input's demand function is a monotonic function of productivity. It controls the correlation between input levels and the unobserved firm-specific productivity. It uses inputs as the control. The coefficient of TFP is expected to be a positive sign, as higher productivity firms will invest more on R&D activities.

TRIPS is a dummy – 1 indicates the years after which India fully implemented the 'product patent' in 2005, and 0 indicates the year before 2005. We expect the coefficient of TRIPS will be positive on R&D activities since undertaking R&D activities is necessary to fight tough competition with many foreign competitive firms for their survival. By protecting IPRs, TRIPS allows technology transfer and diffusion, and relates to a set of administrative and market-organizing regulated rules. It enables agents to use or transfer resources among each other. It allows governments to achieve economic efficiency which is one goal observed in IPRs regulations, or product liability and safety regulations. The firm attributes include firm size. It is a control variable. We expect a positive sign of its coefficient as firm size represents market power and capabilities. Large firms have higher market access and higher capabilities than small firms. It is expected that size will increase the productivity growth of firms.

Data and variables

The paper uses annual census data of over 552 pharmaceutical firms, allowing us to measure the productivity effects of foreign ownership. We obtained our data from the Center for Monitoring Indian Economy's (CMIE) Prowess Database.[2] This database has been used in many empirical studies for the Indian economy such as Pradhan (2002), Saranga and Phani (2009), Iyer (2012), etc. The study covers the period from 1999 to 2014. The share of foreign equity participation for a firm in time *t* is a proxy for foreign ownership. Its value ranges between 0% and 100%. Output, capital, size, exports and raw materials of the firm in time *t* are taken from the CMIE's Prowess Database. Output is defined as the total sales of the firm in time *t*. Number of employees is taken as a proxy for firm's size. It represents the market size and capabilities of a firm. Since most of the companies in the CMIE database don't fully disclose their employment number, we use labor input from the Annual Survey of Industries (ASI) data. We follow the Iyer, 2012 to calculate labor inputs for each firm. It is calculated by dividing the total wage bill of a firm for a given year by the average industry wage rate for that year. However, since the ASI has not provided wage rates for the last two years, labor inputs for these particular years have been obtained from the Prowess database, i.e. labor input for 1999 to 2012 is taken from the ASI data and that of 2013 and 2014 from the CMIE database. TRIPS is a dummy variable. It refers to India's TRIPS compliance and it is taken from Kyle and Mcgahan (2012).

Empirical results

The major empirical findings are presented in this section. Table 17.3 gives the results of the empirical estimation provided by equation (17.1). In column (1) and (2), it is calculated by using the logit model. Column (2) differs from column (1) in that lagged size is added in column (2). In column (1) and (2), the coefficients of foreign ownership are positive and highly significant at 1% level, which are 0.035 and 0.026, respectively. The coefficients of export dummy are positive and highly significant. The coefficient of TFP is also positive and significant (p=0.000) in column (1) and is positive and insignificant in column (2). Surprisingly, the coefficient of TRIPS, in both columns, is negative and insignificant. The coefficient of size, in column (2), is also positive and significant (p=0.000). However, these estimated coefficients are likely to be biased due to ignoring unobserved heterogeneity.

To check biasness, we re-estimate the equation (17.1) using the logit fixed effects model in column (3) and (4). We run a Hausman test and the result indicates rejection of the null hypothesis of uncorrelated time-invariant unobserved heterogeneity with the regressors, and only the fixed effect is consistent. In column 3, we find that the latter yields a higher positive coefficient of foreign ownership which is significant at 5% level. The export coefficient is highly positive and significant, which is 1.497. The coefficient of TFP is positive and significant. In column (4), when we added firm attributes i.e., lagged size to the baseline model, the coefficients of both foreign ownership and TFP become positive but insignificant. The export coefficient has a similar pattern, positive and significant. The effect of TRIPS is still negative and insignificant. The coefficient of firms' size is positive and significant. Its effect is very small. It suggests that there is a positive relationship between firm size and innovation, indicating that larger firms have a higher possibility of undertaking R&D activities. Large firms have higher market access and can appropriate economic rent from innovative activities. Since R&D undertaking requires a large amount of investment and also involves risks, large firms can undertake such kinds of activities, given their resource base and economies of scale. Thus, the larger the firm size the higher its probability of doing R&D activities.

Table 17.3 Impact of foreign ownership and IPR protection on the innovation of firms in the Indian pharmaceutical industry

R&D Dummy						
	Logit		*Fixed Effects*		*Random Effects*	
	(1)	*(2)*	*(3)*	*(4)*	*(5)*	*(6)*
Lagged Ownership	0.035	0.026	0.048	0.038	0.073	0.054
	(0.005)***	(0.005)***	(0.023)**	(0.024)	(0.017)***	(0.018)***
Lagged Export	2.405	2.214	1.497	1.498	2.843	2.623
	(0.180)***	(0.186)***	(0.421)***	(0.426)***	(0.452)***	(0.451)***
Lagged TPF	0.000	0.000	0.000	0.000	0.000	0.000
	(2.01e-07)***	(3.01e-07)	(6.03e-07)**	(9.07e-07)	(5.86e-07)***	(8.25e-07)
Lagged TRIPS	−0.041	−0.078	−1.712	−1.922	−1.652	−2.018
	(0.541)	(0.559)	(1.116)	(1.187)	(0.969)*	(1.013)**
Lagged Size		0.000		0.000		0.000
		(2.61e-09)***		(1.15e-08)*		(8.10e-09)***
Year fixed effects	YES	YES	YES	YES	YES	YES
Constant	−2.255	−2.093			−2.993	3.026
	(0.266)***	(0.272)***			(0.595)***	(0.607)***
N	1717	1676	468	448	1717	1676
Log likelihood	−808.39	−756.93	−169.95	−159.24	−445.19	−417.48
Prob>Chi2	0.0000	0.0000	0.0003	0.0000	0.000	0.0000
	LR Chi2(15) = 742.19	LR Chi2(16) = 779.54	LR Chi2(15) = 40.96	LR Chi2(16) = 48.21	WALD Chi2(15) = 111.71	WALD Chi2(17) = 108.13
Pseudo R^2	0.3146	0.3399				

Source: Author's Calculation.
Notes: Robust standard errors are in parenthesis. *** indicates significance at 1% level, ** at 5% level and * at 10%. Standard errors in parentheses.

The positive coefficient of foreign ownership indicates that foreign-owned firms are more likely to undertake R&D activities. Foreign MNCs have been losing their market shares and profits, due to a drop in sales and expiry of patents for blockbuster drugs, rising costs and declining R&D revenues. India has now implemented product patent fully. India has the largest number of US-FDA–approved facilities outside the United States with a large pool of cheap and skilled manpower. India is becoming a global hub of offshore outsourcing for R&D activities. Chaudhuri (2007) also pointed out that by 2005, offshore outsourcing to domestic firms has started to include highly advanced R&D activities. They found that India is a profitable place to reallocate their R&D activities. Therefore, they returned to India.

Furthermore, pharmaceutical products are knowledge-based products. These products are non-excludable (Grossman and Helpman, 1991). The patentees of new products might not get full compensation from all the agents that make use of it. They only get benefits from the patents on their new products. Therefore, they want to discover more new products. Once a new drug has been developed, its marginal cost of production becomes lower. The formula of the drugs need not be improved. The same formula can be applied to produce at different locations. Given India's comparative advantages, foreign MNCs invest in R&D in order to get monopoly rents from new varieties of drugs. Such moves enable foreign MNCs to produce drugs at a lower cost. It also saves time and money. They can sell these drugs in both emerging and regulated markets. Thus, foreign firms invest and relocate their R&D activities in India.

This positive coefficient also suggests an interesting fact that there is international technology spillover in the Indian pharmaceutical industry. This finding is in contrast with some of the previous literatures on this industry. Changes in national economic policy and the global pharmaceutical scenario might play a significant role in this regard. For instance, implementation of product patent in India has provided businesses with longer-term protection and had a positive influence on R&D intensity (Sharma et al., 2017). Such strict IPR protection has increased expenditure on R&D (Zambad et al., 2014) as it provided larger incentives for R&D (Bhan and Kabiraj, 2014). After adopting trade liberalization policy and implementation of TRIPS, many of the Indian pharmaceutical companies are now restricted from accessing technical innovation that comes from reverse engineering. They are also lacking in investments, skills and technologies. Therefore, they either go for merger and acquisitions (M&A) or consolidate their business by acquiring the manufacturing facilities or brands of other firms. As an example, Indian domestic companies such as Dr. Reddy's, Aurobindo, Cadila Healthcare, Torrent, have signed supply agreements with foreign MNCs such as GSK, Astrazeneca and Abbot. Accordingly, Dr. Reddy's will supply about 100 branded formulations to GSK in different emerging markets such as Latin America, Africa, the Middle-East and Asia-Pacific (excluding India). Likewise, Aurobindo will supply more than 100 formulations to Pfizer for the regulated markets of US and EU countries, and more than 50 products for about 70 non-US/EU markets. Besides revenues sharing, Pfizer paid upfront license fees to Aurobindo (Dinar, 2005). Similar trends were also seen in other developing countries like Argentina, Brazil and Mexico after the regulatory policies change (Jha, 2007).

Another possible reason for this positive spillover may be due to globalization and competition among the developing countries. Globalization also leads to dumping. Due to dumping, some bulk drugs producing companies stopped manufacturing drugs in Andhra Pradesh, Gujarat and Karnataka (Lalitha, 2002). Bulk drugs exports don't enjoy a comparative trade advantage any longer. It is estimated that the Indian bulk drugs industry is losing its business amounting to Rs 2,500 crore a year due to cheap bulk drugs imports from China (Chaudhuri, 2011). India is shifting its pharmaceutical exports from regulated markets to unregulated markets. She faced tough competition in the regulated markets, particularly from other developing countries like

China. In order to get a bigger slice of the pie in the regulated generic markets particularly in the United States, Indian pharmaceutical companies must improve the quality of such drugs. Producing such high-quality drugs requires firms to be more innovative. Therefore, firms must invest more in R&D activities to increase their productivity levels.

The positive and significant export coefficient suggests that exporting firms are more likely to invest in R&D. This is consistent with the findings of Girma et al. (2008). They found that the previous year's exporting activities increased the innovative capacities of Irish firms through an increase in R&D activity. Likewise, Indian pharmaceutical companies increase their probability to undertake R&D activities when they enter export markets. In entering export markets they face tough competition from many MNCs. They must learn to get new skills and knowledge in order to be more competitive so that they can produce niche products. It necessitates domestic firms improving their product qualities, designs, production processes so that they can meet the demands of domestic and foreign markets. For such a task, their managerial and operational efficiencies must increase. Undertaking exports activities helps them achieve such efficiencies through interaction and collaboration with foreign agents. These activities lead to an increase in a firm's innovative capabilities. Such kind of export competitiveness is only possible when firms invest huge amounts in R&D activities (Pradhan, 2002), as investments in innovation are required to increase a firm's capabilities.

The coefficient of TFP is positive and significant. But its coefficient is very minimal. It shows that firms with a higher productivity level are more likely to perform R&D activities. Productive firms are generally large in size and have more financial flexibility. They can invest a large amount of money for innovative activities, thereby enhancing their innovative capabilities. Therefore, productivity plays an important role in undertaking innovative activities. Surprisingly, the coefficient of TRIPS is negative but insignificant. The negative coefficient suggests that TRIPS implementation does not encourage R&D activities. This is quite the opposite of our expectation.

For robustness checking, we re-estimate the equation (17.1) using the random logit model. Table 17.3 gives the results. In column (2) firm's size is added. The results are consistent with different methods. The coefficients of ownership and export are all positive and significant in both columns. The coefficient of TFP is positive and significant in column (1) but positive and insignificant in column (2) when firm size is added. The only difference is the coefficient of TRIPS. The coefficient of TRIPS, in both columns, becomes negative but significant ($p=0.088$; $p=0.46$). It suggests that trade liberalization and TRIPS implementation are not conducive to increasing R&D activities in the IPI. This confirms the finding of Allred and Park (2007) that patent protection has insignificantly affected R&D activities in developing economies. Patent systems have restricted imitation and copycat of patented technologies (Alfred and Park, 2007). Besides, patent protection also increases transaction costs for technological exchange. Stronger patent protections increase the cost of technological inputs. This reduces technology transfers among countries. Due to stricter patent protection, local agents must pay for access to technological inputs and knowledge that used to be free. Since most of the Indian pharmaceutical firms are small firms, only large firms can undertake R&D activities. It implies that the small firms could not undertake R&D activities due to financial and resource constraints.

Patent holders are suspicious of domestic pharmaceutical companies doing reverse-engineering and imitation of their patented drugs. They try to restrict them from accessing their technologies. This reduces the chances of local agents increasing innovative capabilities through imitation or learning by doing. This reduces innovation. It also hints that the monopoly power of foreign MNCs has increased with the increase in their market share in the domestic pharmaceutical industry. Stronger patent protection provides them incentives not to upgrade or develop new technologies in India. They want to exploit more opportunities from existing technologies. They gain economic rents longer with fewer introductions of new technologies, leading to a slower rate of innovation activities. McCalman (2001) confirmed that stronger patent protection resulted in significant loss to India.

Conclusion

With full implementation of TRIPS and allowance of 100% FDI through the automatic route, the Indian pharmaceutical industry has gained market confidence and changed continuously. Public health spending, patient awareness and insurance coverage have increased. For example, Ayushman Bharat Pradhan Mantri Jan Arogya (AB PM-JAY) launched in 2018 provided health insurance and uplift sub-centers and primary health centers. Under this scheme, nearly 40% of the poor have been covered and 16,085 hospitals have been empanelled and over 10 crore e-cards issued. Around 17,150 health and wellness centers have operated across the country. The government plans to set up additional 1.5 lakh health and wellness centers by 2022.

The structure of this industry has also changed. Many new entrants have taken the lead. Now the leading domestic pharmaceutical companies need to invest more in R&D spending to drive innovations and to grab new and emerging opportunities. Allowing 100% FDI in this industry increases M&A. But there is doubt whether such moves would improve domestic manufacturing as many foreign companies could use this rule for setting up their local subsidiaries in India to import and trade in products. If this turns out to be true, then it would pose a serious threat to the survival of many domestic companies. Therefore, it is necessary for domestic companies to increase their R&D spending as growth would come from innovation and owning intellectual properties.

Thus, the main purpose of this chapter was to investigate the impacts of foreign ownership and IPR protection on innovation in the IPI. What emerges is that foreign firms encourage domestic pharmaceutical firms to undertake R&D activities. They increase domestic firms' innovative activities. It will in turn make the industry more competitive in the long run through this technology spillover. Larger R&D investment enables larger innovations (Bhan and Kabiraj, 2014).

Exporting firms are more likely to invest in R&D activities. Since pharmaceuticals is a knowledge-intensive industry, entry into export markets depends on firm-specific knowledge like better qualities, innovative design and marketing. Otherwise, they cannot compete with their global peers. Such kind of export competitiveness is only possible when firms invest a huge amount in R&D activities.

It has been believed that TRIPS may have provided incentives and confidence to MNCs to take advantage of the country's strength in manufacturing and to look for locations for R&D in India. Zambad et al. (2014) pointed out that TRIPS implementation facilitated the transfer of technology from foreign firms to their Indian partners. However, to our surprise, TRIPS had a negative and insignificant effect on innovation. But using the random logit model, we showed that it had a negative and significant effect. Moving from logit model to random logit model showed that trade liberalization and TRIPS implementation are not conducive to increasing R&D activities at least for this industry. It is believed that unless patent reforms have a significant impact on a developing country's R&D, they could have largely negative impacts on domestic patenting. Our finding suggests that it is necessary for firms in developing countries to undertake R&D investment to develop similar or better technology. So, consumers may gain in spite of having monopoly distortion markets due to product patenting (Bhan and Kabiraj, 2014).

The present findings reveal that an increase in overall innovation/R&D can provide a long-term thrust to Indian pharmaceuticals. Otherwise, other global competitors like China might overtake India's position as a world leader in generic medicine production. China has made a huge investment in R&D and has created a support system to incubate new firms. These enable Chinese companies to leap from old technologies into creating biologics. Consequently, China has entered into a new phase of pharma innovation. China had contributed to over 10% of the new drug launches in the world in 2018; 7.8% of the drug innovation is in the pipeline. But India is lacking behind China in the creation of biologics though India continues to be hailed as the largest generic producer globally. Therefore, India must reinvent itself to move forward from generics producer towards end-to-end drug manufacturer.[3] It requires multidimensional efforts from both government and the industry. Recently, the Modi Government has given top priority to addressing the R&D deficit in the pharmaceutical sector. The Union Finance Ministry had given assurance to increase R&D investment in medicine, biotechnology and pharmaceuticals. The government's decision to promote domestic manufacturing of Active Pharmaceutical Ingredients (API) and Key Starting Materials (KSMs) through the setting up of bulk drug parks and production-linked incentives is a very welcome policy for the industry.

Finally, we would like to recommend adding more variables such as location, FDI, etc. in future work. Whether location and FDI play significant roles in technology spillovers will be an interesting issue. Other variables like compulsory licensing and parallel imports may have an impact on pharmaceutical exports and innovation. Since our analysis is based on only one industry i.e., the pharmaceutical industry, it is highly recommended to examine the effect of foreign ownership on more disaggregated data. Indian firms collaborating with other developing country firms are focused more on gaining market access. They should rather focus on developing linkages with MNCs in advanced markets to leverage regulatory costs. Owing to binding constraints of data availability, the data on post-reform period analysis is restricted up to 2014–15.

Notes

1 The initial draft of this paper was presented in National Seminar on "*India after a Quarter Century of Economic Reforms – The Benefits and Costs*" held at Sikkim University, Gangtok, Sikkim, India from October 5–6, 2018. We would like to thank the participants for their comments and suggestions. We would also like to thank anonymous reviewers for their suggestions that helped us in improving the manuscript.

2 Prowess database comprises public listed companies and covers most of the organized industrial activities, banking and organized financial and other services sectors in India. Though Prowess gives some information on the number of employees, this data is mostly not available for a majority of the firms in the database. Department-wise employee data is not available. Data for foreign equity in Prowess is available from March 1999 and for only 552 pharmaceutical companies. Hence due to the lack of a better alternative, for the purpose of the study, the study period starts from 1999 and the study is restricted to only 552 pharmaceutical companies.

3 *The Economics Times*, "Two Twin challenges for Indian pharma-boosting drug discovery and localising API production". Retrieved from https://health.economictimes.indiatimes.com/news/pharma/twin-challenges-for-indian-pharma-boosting-drug-discovery-and-localising-api-production/79247974.

References

Aitken, B.J. and Harrison A.E. (1999): "Do Domestic Firms Benefit from Direct Foreign Investment? Evidence from Venezuela," *The American Economic Review*, Vol. 89, No. 3, pp 605–618.

Ala, M.U. (2013): "A Firm-Level Analysis of the Vulnerability of the Bangladeshi Pharmaceutical Industry to the TRIPS Agreement: Implications for R&D Capability and Technology Transfer," *Procedia Economics and Finance*, Vol. 5, pp 30–39.

Allred, B. and Park, W. (2007): "Patent Rights and Innovative Activity: Evidence from National and Firm-Level Data," *Journal of Business International Studies*, Vol. 38, No. 6, pp 878–900.

Aw, B.Y., Roberts, M.J. and Winston, T. (2007): "Export Market Participation, Investments in R&D and Worker Training, and the Evolution of Firm Productivity," *The World Economy*, Vol. 30, No. 1, pp 83–104.

Bhan, A. and Kabiraj, T. (2014): "Incentives for Product and Process Innovations: A Case for the Drug Industry," *Indian Economic Review*, Vol. 49, No. 2, pp 193–204.

Bedi, N., Bedi P.M.S. and Sooch, B.S. (2013): "Patenting and R&D in Indian Pharmaceutical Industry: Post-TRIPS Scenario," *Journal of Intellectual Property Rights*, Vol. 18, No. 2, pp 105–110.

Branstetter, L.G., Fisman, R. and Foley, C.F. (2006): "Do Stronger Intellectual Property Rights Increase International Technology Transfer? Empirical Evidence from U. S. Firm-Level Panel Data," *The Quarterly Journal of Economics*, Vol. 121, No. 1, pp 321–349.

Chadha, A. (2009): "TRIPs and Patenting Activity: Evidence from the Indian Pharmaceutical Industry," *Economic Modelling*, Vol. 26, No. 2, pp 499–505.

Chaudhuri, S. (2007): *Is Product Patent Protection Necessary in Developing Countries for Innovation? R&D by Indian Pharmaceutical Companies after TRIPs*, Indian Institute of Management, Calcutta. Working Papers Series No. 614/ Sep. 2007.

Chaudhuri, S. (2011): *Multinationals and Monopolies Pharmaceutical Industry in India after TRIPs*, Indian Institute of Management, Calcutta. Working Papers Series No. 685/ Nov. 2011.

Chaudhuri, Sh., Goldberg, P.K. and Jia, P. (2006): "Estimating the Effects of Global Patent Protection in Pharmaceuticals: A Case Study of Quinolones in India," *The American Economic Review*, Vol. 96, No. 5, pp 1477–1514.

Coe, D.T. and Helpman, E. (1995): "International R&D Spillovers," *European Economic Review*, Vol. 39, No. 5, pp 859–887.

Dinar, K. (2005): "Learning to Innovate: The Indian Pharmaceutical Industry Response to Emerging TRIPs Regime," DRUID Academy Winter 2005 PhD Conference. January 27-29, 2005, Aalborg, Denmark. Retrieved from http://www2.druid.dk/conferences/viewpaper.php?id=2576&cf=17

Dinopoulos, E. and Segerstrom, P. (2010): "Intellectual Property Rights, Multinational Firms and Economic Growth," *Journal of Development Economics*, Vol. 92, pp 13–27.

Eaton, J. and Kortum, S. (1996): "Trade in Ideas Patenting and Productivity in the OECD," *Journal of International Economics*, Vol. 40, No. 3–4, pp 251–278.

Feinberg, S.E. and Majumdar, S.K. (2001): "Technology Spillovers from Foreign Direct Investment in the Indian Pharmaceutical Industry," *Journal of International Business Studies*, Vol. 32, No. 3, pp 421–437.

Girma, S., Görg, H. and Hanley, A. (2008): "R&D and Exporting: A Comparison of British and Irish Firms," *Review of World Economics*, Vol. 144, No. 4, pp 750–773.

Griliches, Z. (1979): "Issues in Assessing the Contribution of R&D to Productivity Growth," *The Bell Journal of Economics*, Vol. 10, pp 92–116.

Griliches, Z. (1986): *Productivity, R&D, and Basic Research at the Firm Level in the 1970s*. American Economic Review, Vol. 76, pp. 141-154.

Griliches, Z. (1998): *The Search for R&D Spillovers*. University of Chicago Press, Chicago.

Griliches, Z. and Maisesse J. (1990): "*R&D and Productivity Growth: Comparing Japanese and U.S. Manufacturing Firms*. NBER Working Paper No. 1778, Cambridge: University of Chicago Press.

Grossman, G.M. and Helpman, E. (1991): "Endogenous Innovation in the Theory of Growth," *The Journal of Economic Perspectives*, Vol. 8, No. 1, pp 23–44.

Guennif, S. and Ramani Sh.V. (2012): "Explaining Divergence in Catching-Up in Pharma Between India and Brazil using the NSI Framework," *Research Policy*, Vol. 41, No. 2, pp 430–441.

Helpman, E. (1993): "Innovation, Imitation, and Intellectual Property Rights," *Econometrica*, Vol. 61, No. 6, pp 1247–1280.

Iyer, C.G. (2012): "Foreign Firms, Indian Multinationals and Spillovers in the Indian Pharmaceutical Industry," *Indian Growth and Development Review*, Vol. 5, No. 2, pp 131–150.

Jha, R. (2007): "Options for Indian Pharmaceutical Industry in the Challenging Environment," *Economic and Political Weekly*, Vol. 42, No. 39, pp 3958–3967.

Jiatao, L. and Jing, Zh. (2003): "Explaining the Growth of International R&D Alliances in China," *Managerial and Decision Economics*, Vol. 24, No. 2–3, pp 101–115.

Kim, Y.K., Lee, K., Park, W.C. and Choo, K. (2012): "Appropriate Intellectual Property Protection and Economic Growth in Countries at Different Levels of Development," *Research Policy*, Vol. 41, pp 358–375.

Kiran, R. and Mishra, S. (2009a): "Changing Pragmatics of the Indian Pharmaceutical Industry in the Pre and Post TRIPS Period," *International Journal of Business and Management*, Vol. 4, No. 9, pp 206–220.

Kiran, R. and Mishra, S. (2009b): "Performance of the Indian Pharmaceutical Industry in Post-TRIPS Period: A Firm Level Analysis," *International Review of Business Research Papers*, Vol. 5, No. 6, pp 148–160.

Kyle, M. and McGahan, A. (2012): "Investments in Pharmaceuticals Before and After TRIPS," *The Review of Economics and Statistics*, Vol. 94, No. 4, pp 1157–1172.

La Croix, S. and Akihiko, A.. (1996): "Product Patent Reform and Its Impact on Korea's Pharmaceutical Industry," *International Economics Journal*, Vol. 10, No. 1, pp 109–124.

Lai, E.L.C. and Qiu, L.D. (2003): "The North's Intellectual Property Rights Standard for the South?," *Journal of International Economics*, Vol. 59, No. 1, pp 183–209.

Lalitha, N. (2002): "Indian Pharmaceutical Industry in WTO Regime: A SWOT Analysis," *Economic and Political Weekly*, Vol. 37, No. 34, pp 3542–3555.

McCalman, P. (2001): "Reaping What You Sow: An Empirical Analysis of International Patent Harmonization," *Journal of International Economics*, Vol. 55, No. 1, pp 161–186.

Nadiri, M.I. (1993): "Innovations and Technological Spillovers," Working Paper No. 4423, (Aug, 1993). http://www.nber.org/papers/w4423.

Niosi, J., Hanel P. and Reid, S. (2012): "The International Diffusion of Biotechnology: The Arrival of Developing Countries," *Journal of Evolutionary Economics*, Vol. 22, No. 4, pp 767–783.

Pradhan, P.J. (2002): "FDI Spillovers and Local Productivity Growth: Evidence from Indian Pharmaceutical Industry," *Artha Vijnana*, Vol. 54, No. 3–4, pp 317–332.

Pradhan, P.J. (2003): "Liberalization, Firm Size and R&D performance: A Firm Level Study of Indian Pharmaceutical Industry," *Journal of Indian School of Political Economy*, Vol. 14, No. 4, pp 647–666.

Qian, Y. (2007): "Do National Patent Laws Stimulate Domestic Innovation in a Global Patenting Environment? A Cross-Country Analysis of Pharmaceutical Patent Protection, 1978–2002," *The Review of Economics and Statistics*, Vol. 89, No. 3, pp 436–453.

Saranga, H. and Phani, B.V. (2009), "Determinants of Operational Efficiencies in the Indian Pharmaceutical Industry," *International Transactions in Operational Research*, Vol. 16, pp 109–130.

Sharma, R., Paswan, K.P., Ambrammal, S.K. and Dhanora, M. (2017): "Impact of Patent Policy Changes on R&D Expenditure By Industries in India," *The Journal of World Intellectual Property*, Vol. 30, No. 7, pp 52–69.

Sweet, C.M. and Maggio, D.S.E. (2015): "Do Stronger Intellectual Property Rights Increase Innovation?," *World Development*, Vol. 66, pp 665–677.

Vita, G. D. (2013), "The TRIPS Agreement and Technological Innovation," *Journal of Policy Modelling*, Vol. 35, pp 964–977.

Wakelin, K. (2001), "Productivity Growth and R&D Expenditure in UK Manufacturing firms," *Research Policy*, Vol. 30, No. 7, pp 1079–1090.

Zambad, S. and Londhe B.R. (2014): "To Study the Scope & Importance of Amended Patent Act on Indian Pharmaceutical Company with Respect to Innovation," *Procedia Economics and Finance*, Vol. 11, pp 819–828.

18

ECONOMIC LIBERALISATION AND THE DEVELOPMENT OF MOLECULAR DIAGNOSTICS INDUSTRY IN INDIA

An innovation system perspective[1]

Nidhi Singh

Introduction

The increased economic integration of the Indian economy through liberalization has created an environment in which it has become imperative to develop and advance technological capabilities for the purpose of catching up and remaining competitive in the market. However, the pathways adopted for catching up in the area of healthcare technological development in India is rather sub-optimal. This is apparent from the innovation making pathways chosen for the development of an innovation system in the case of matured technologies such as chemicals and pharmaceuticals where the pathways adopted were deviated from contributing towards the country's specific healthcare needs and requirements (Abrol et al., 2019). Similarly, the impact of economic liberalization for advanced emerging healthcare technologies like regenerative medicines, stem cell research and RNA interference etc. is also worrying as it is facing various constraints and challenges (Chaturvedi, 2007, 2012; Lander and Thorsteinsdottir, 2011; Tiwari and Desai, 2011). The existing studies recognize that the path dependence model of learning, lack of collaborative efforts and target-based research often hinder the innovation process. In this context, the present study contends that the innovation system pathways for the development of emerging diagnostics technologies like molecular diagnostics under the umbrella of economic liberalisation need to be context-specific to tackle the prevailing healthcare needs of society.

'Molecular diagnostics'[2] (or MDs) is a broad term describing a class of diagnostic tests that assess a person's health at a molecular level, detecting and measuring specific genetic sequences in deoxyribonucleic acid (DNA) or ribonucleic acid (RNA) or the proteins they express (Constance, 2010). It is the most dynamic and transformative area of medical diagnostics, leading to advances in research and treatment that are revolutionizing healthcare across a wide range of diseases and health conditions (Poste, 2001). At present, MDs are the emerging biomedical technology based on modern biotechnological approaches,[3] which is based on the technological capabilities in the form of transition from the imitative production stage to the

 DOI: 10.4324/9780367855741-18

innovative development stage (exploratory learning). In this context, the process of innovation system development for a technology follower country like India with immature biotechnology and biomedical healthcare innovation system in terms of the indigenous learning process and knowledge accumulation requires considerable effort on the part of the key actors participating in the development of MDs.

Being an emerging technology worldwide, the MDs industry is dominated by the presence of large multi-national companies (MNCs) from countries like the USA, Germany, Japan and China. The industry growth is mainly driven by the large increase in the number of hospitals and diagnostic centres, rise in disease burden and transition from communicable to non-communicable diseases (NCDs) and the increasing government support for healthcare, which has exposed the need to bridge gaps in India's medical diagnostics landscape. In particular, the lack of localised and competitively priced products in high-end medical devices and unsuitability of products imported from the industrialised world in the resource-constrained healthcare facilities of Indian rural and small towns continues to be a large concern for the policymaker. In this context, there is a need to study the system building activities of MDs industrial base for effective development according to the healthcare needs and challenges in the context of resource-poor conditions.

Since the beginning of the 1990s, India has embarked on a series of economic reform measures that aim to correct the market distortions and inefficiency in different sectors of the economy. The proponents of economic liberalisation argue that relaxing the protective controls and regulations would enable economic agents to function according to market incentives, which would lead to higher economic welfare in the long run. As part of the policy package, several sectors were deregulated and government control through inspection and licensing was abolished. Since the private players were given far more thrust and support, it was expected that several new industries and technologies would emerge in the new environment. Since the market forces were given a far greater role in resource allocation, the responsibility of the government was largely confined to establishing frameworks, rules, regulations and other supporting activities. Although theoretically appealing, there is a clear need to understand the dynamics of liberalisation in the development of innovation and knowledge creation in specific industrial sectors. This is especially true in the case of the healthcare system, which is known to have significant externalities and market failure. Studies have indicated that since the 1990s the public expenditure on basic services and social sector development has reduced considerably (Gupta and Sarkar, 1994; Joshi, 2006). This reflects the withering away of the government as part of the policy reforms in the 1990s.

Therefore, the purpose of the present study is to examine the development of MDs innovations in the industrial base and use in clinical practices to meet the local needs in the context of significant economic liberalisation policy changes in recent decades. From the perspective of the theory of innovation system building, the study has the following objectives: (i) to examine the structure and performance of the MDs industrial sector in India, (ii) to analyse the growth of production, investment and innovation capabilities of the MDs industry, (iii) to identify the system building challenges in the development and diffusion of MDs industrial technology in the context of ongoing economic reforms in the economy.

The chapter is divided into eight sections including this introduction. The next section provides the analytical framework, methodology and data sources. The third section provides a literature review of MDs related healthcare innovation system in India. An overview of the MDs industry in India in terms of import-dependency, market size, growth and the structures (key actors) of the industry is given in the fourth section. The fifth section empirically analyses the system building activities of the industry actors' performance in terms of production, technology and investment capabilities. The sixth section provides a comprehensive account of the challenges and system weaknesses of industrial actors based on a case study of selected key actors. The seventh section provides system challenges and failures, and the final section concludes.

Analytical framework

One of our main argument is that under the umbrella of economic liberalization, the pathways for the development of MDs innovation system need to be context-specific to deal with the prevailing healthcare needs and challenges. As such, the study undertakes an innovation system perspective for MDs in two ways. *First*, it uses the Technological Innovation System (TIS)[4] framework to identify the innovation actors and institutions and their functions involved in the development of a MDs innovation system. The major advantage of the TIS perspective is that instead of only examining the *structural* component and characteristics of the innovation system, the focus is on the dynamics of the *key processes or functions*[5] that directly influence the development, diffusion and use of *new and emerging technology* such as MDs. *Second*, it uses the system failure framework (SFF)[6] to identify the constraints and challenges faced by the innovation actors and institutions in building a MDs innovation system. Since MDs has transformative effects on existing diagnostic technology in a context-specific basis, we use the SFF developed by Weber and Rohracher (2012) to identify the system weaknesses to address the challenges of building a MDs innovation system in meeting the needs and requirement of the healthcare system of India. The major motive of combining these two frameworks of innovation system perspective is to study the context-specific steps undertaken during the liberalisation regime for tackling the identified challenges that are needed at the level of policymaking, institution building and system development.

The primary objective of our study is the identification of system building[7] activities of industrial base actors for the development of MDs innovation system in the Indian healthcare system. Therefore, we have developed an analytical tool to examine the interrelationship of key industrial actors and institutions to understand the inter-linkages and interaction in the innovation process. Based on the requirements of system building activities for the formation of MDs innovation system, we propose a *socially responsible innovation system approach* (RISA) framework for the study. The RISA as an analytical tool will help us to assess the MDs innovation system by identifying the performances of industrial actors through *TIS functions* and the mechanisms that either facilitate or hinder the innovation process through *system failure* analysis. System-building activities in RISA are measured through interactive learning, competence building for advanced MDs technologies that cater to the demand for local health care priorities and social problems. For brevity, the comprehensive analytical framework of the study is summarised in Figure 18.1.

Methods and data

In order to examine the innovation process of MDs industrial system, we study the performance of key actors and institutions using the data collected at the secondary and primary level. The secondary data analysis is expected to reveal the innovative capability, institutional apparatus and system issues concerning MDs industrial base. The structural challenges and system building problems are explored through the case study of selected industrial actors through a direct personal interview (primary survey).

The nature of trade orientation at the macro level is explored by examining the aggregate data of import of MDs products from the rest of the country (world) to India. Due to lack of data availability at the disaggregated level, MDs products are proxied by two commodities, namely, (a) reagents, which correspond to HS code 300620 and 382200 and (b) instruments and equipment, which correspond to HS code 903180 and 903190[8]. The import data is collected

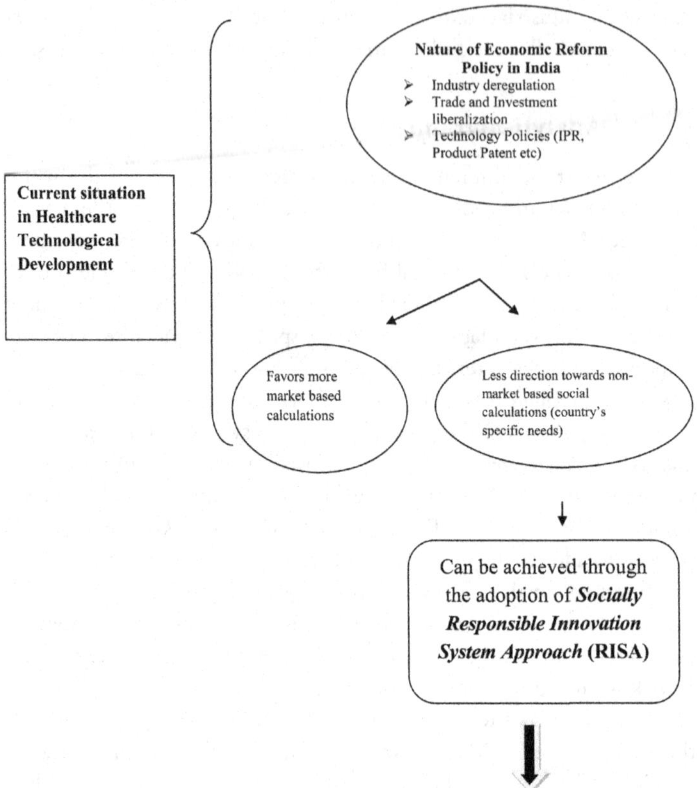

1. Performances of *TIS Functions* for the development of system building activities

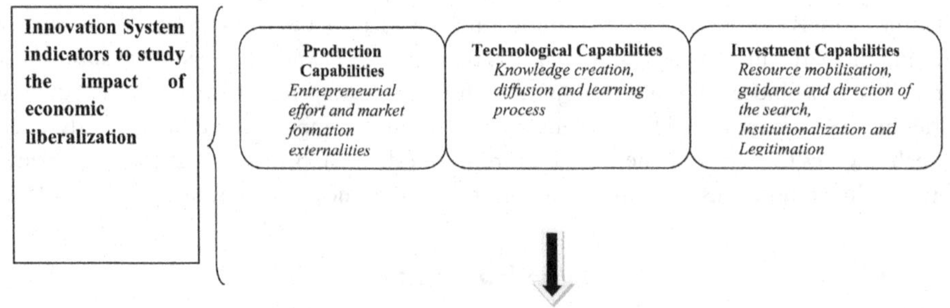

2. Challenges in the performances of system building activities for the development of Socially Responsible Innovation System: Analysis of *System Failures* (Directionality, Demand articulation, Policy coordination, reflexivity)

Figure 18.1 Analytical framework to study the system building activities by industrial base actors' in the development of MDs innovation system in India

from the UN Comtrade database, accessed from the World Integrated Trade Solution (WITS) online portal. Since trade data is available across different nomenclature, we select standardised Harmonized Commodity Description and Coding System (Harmonized System, or HS 1996) for commodity classification. To study the nature of protection, the levels of applied tariffs imposed by India on these selected products were collected from the UNCTAD TRAINS database, accessed from the WITS online portal.

We explore the dynamics of MDs manufacturing and service capability using firm-level data collected at the disaggregated level. The firm-level statistics are mainly collected from two secondary sources: (1) Bloomberg Terminal and (2) Prowess IQ Version 1.7. The former is a computer software program developed by Bloomberg L.P. The Bloomberg Terminal enables the researchers to access the financial market data of firms that are listed across various stock markets in the world. The latter is online client software with an interactive querying system maintained by the Centre for Monitoring Indian Economy (CMIE) Pvt. Ltd. Prowess database consists of the financial performance of all listed (stock market) and a large number of unlisted companies in India. The financial performance indicators are based on the audited Annual Financial Reports of companies and information submitted to the Ministry of Company Affairs, company filings with stock exchanges and prices of securities listed on the major stock exchanges. We use the Bloomberg Terminal to access the financial performance of major MDs market player in India at the *global level* and Prowess IQ[9] is used to collect data for the existing follower firms (both foreign and domestic) in the recent period. We use appropriate Wholesale Price Index (WPI) of manufacturing products, which is available from the Office of the Economic Advisor, Ministry of Commerce & Industry, Government of India, to convert the reported nominal variables into constant series (base 2004–05=100). The coverage of the firm-level analysis is from 2000 to 2018 which is mainly based on the availability of firm-level data and the emergence of MDs segments in the recent period, especially post-2000.

We use a range of indicators to examine the nature of innovation capability in MDs industry. The *production capability* is assessed by examining the composition and trend in firms sales, exports, imports and labour productivity (LP) index. The *technology capability* is explored by examining the nature of R&D intensity (ratio of R&D expenditure to sales), import of finished goods, royalty, technical fees. Finally, the *investment capability* is studied by examining the trend in the capital–output ratio (i.e., Gross Fixed Capital Asset (GFA) or investment to total sales). Apart from R&D intensity, GFA intensity and LP, the rest of the variables are derived from the cumulative sum of individual variables. Therefore, except LP, the construction of most of the indicators follows the standard statistical procedure and therefore is not elaborated here.

We use Labour Productivity (LP) as an indicator of the productivity of firms/industry. By productivity we mean the efficiency in production, i.e., how much output is obtained from a given factor input (Syverson, 2011). In this study, the measured productivity indicator is Single Factor productivity that reflects the units of sales (output) produced per unit of employees. For construction, LP is defined as the ratio between the volume measure of output (real sales) and input use (total number of persons employed). As such, LP is derived by using equation (18.1)

$$LP_{it} = \frac{Q_{it}^{SAL} / L_{it}}{Q^{SAL}{}_{2000} / L_{2000}} * 100 \tag{18.1}$$

where Q_{it}^{SAL} is the sales volume index by firm or industry i in year t, L_t is the measure of labour input proxied by the total person employed by firm or industry i in year t, $Q^{SAL}{}_{2000}$ is the sales volume indices in the base year 2000 and L_{2000} is the total employees in the base year 2000. An improvement in LP_{it} indicates that the rate of output growth is faster than the growth rate in factor input.

We use the share and growth analysis for assessing the composition and trend pattern of firms. The growth rate is measured using the Compound Annual Growth Rate (CAGR) method which measures growth rates over multiple time point where the identified variable is assumed to have a compounding rate over time. The CAGR is computed as follows.

$$CAGR = \left(\frac{X_{t1}}{X_{t0}}\right)^{\frac{1}{n}} - 1 \tag{18.2}$$

where X_{t1} denotes final year value of 2018; X_{t0} is base year value, for example 2000; n is the number of years. The advantage of CAGR is that it is based on a geometric average and the calculation requires only the initial and terminal year values. For computing growth rates, we have used the respective WPI index, base 2004–05=100 to deflate the variable to remove inflation (price) effects. For making a constant series of sales value, we use the average WPI indices for chemicals, non-electrical machinery and other manufacturing sectors. The constant GFA is derived from deflating the nominal variable by the WPI of machinery and machine tool, base 2004–05=100. The rest of the variables are at current prices.

The role of young start-ups and policy supporting instruments in developing the indigenous product for social needs is assessed through secondary data and primary survey. System building outcomes are assessed in terms of how the pursuit of the market and non-market calculations-based system activity has impacted the development of the industrial base through enterprise formation and market creation for the benefit of innovation-making for resource-poor settings in the case of MDs. Further, for an in-depth understanding of the challenges (system failures) encountered by each firm in the performance of system building activities, the study attempted an in-depth analysis of the major firms under the selected category of MDs industrial base in India. The method the study follows is a case study approach through conducting field visits and formal interviews with the CEOs of the four MDs firms, i.e., Bhat Bio-Tech (domestic firm), OmiX Research and Diagnostics Laboratories Pvt Ltd (start-up firm), Roche Diagnostics (foreign subsidiary firm) and Dr. Lal Path Labs (service provider).

Literature review

To the best of our knowledge, empirics on the development of MDs under the healthcare innovation system in India are not available. However, there are studies that have analysed the impact of economic reforms on related healthcare technologies in India. Therefore, as a background for the present study, some of these important studies are briefly reviewed in this section. The purpose of the section is to bring out the crux of such studies to track the theoretically informed stylised facts specific to the catching up issue for the development of MDs innovation system in the context of economic reform policies in India.

The Indian innovation system for healthcare lacks capabilities for modern biomedical technological developments as it is characterized by medical pluralism, low government spending, high out-of-pocket spending and a large, unregulated private sector (Chaturvedi, 2012; Engle,

2015). Healthcare providers range from highly qualified specialists to unqualified practitioners and local healers as well as large state-of-the-art laboratory chains, medium-sized facilities and small neighbourhood laboratories offering associated laboratory services. They are largely commercial players driven by profit motives (market-based calculation) and lack formal/official quality assurance or accreditation (Engle, 2015).

India remains a technology follower country in the field of the biomedical technological innovation system and innovation capabilities remain underdeveloped in spite of the efforts for building the capacities and capabilities for research infrastructure, human resources, fiscal support and R&D incentives etc. (Aggarwal, 2006). In their study, Tiwari and Desai (2011) focused on the challenges of the development of an emerging technology stem cell innovation system in India. They argued that in order to deal with the complexities of technologies it is very important to foster R&D and training collaborations. Their study emphasises the challenges of collaboration building in India for stem cell research in terms of lack of shared vision, delayed accomplishments, maintaining access to additional funding, suitable organisational structure and increased competition between groups. Chaturvedi (2007) found that India is lacking in the development of innovation capabilities for modern emerging biomedical innovations like regenerative medicines, stem cell research and RNA interference, etc.

In India, the biomedical innovation system for MDs is embedded in the capabilities of systems under development for healthcare, biotechnologies, *in-vitro* diagnostics and pharmaceuticals. The biomedical sector draws on technologies and social/human capacities already established by pharmaceutical and biotechnology sectors that are traditionally focused on a process engineering model for innovations (Lander and Thorsteinsdóttir, 2011). While process engineering has led to the successful development of the Indian generic pharmaceutical industry and, for example, in an area like vaccines, the Indian biotechnology firm Shanta Biotechnics, Hyderabad developed a novel method for producing a low cost Hepatitis B vaccine, it is apparent that the innovation policy regime needs a systematic realignment. This suggests that the path-dependent model of learning (reverse engineering) adopted by the firms using process innovations to undertake low-cost manufacturing hinders the transition. As this model may not be appropriate for new start-ups entering the area of modern biomedical technologies the implication is clear that the development of MDs based innovations faces the handicaps and limitations of the biotechnological innovation system.

In this context, Chaturvedi (2007) argued that to meet the increasing specific needs and demands there is a need to restructure innovation policies according to sectoral requirements from the perspectives of innovation chains and production systems. According to him, there is a need to encourage targeted research and generate enabling conditions at the firm and institutional levels for the promotion of the biomedical sector and to increase financial support for new start-ups entering the biomedical sector. This requires policy frameworks that take account of the growing complexities of the innovation process and strengthen innovation systems at the national and sectoral levels (Chaturvedi, 2007).

Visalakshi (1993) argued that under the current regime of innovation, the main challenges of development and diffusion of *indigenous* immunodiagnostics are the non-availability of ELISA plates and various raw materials from an indigenous source – these have to be imported which draws high import duties. Imported products remained relatively cheaper and therefore preferable to indigenous products. Companies did not want to venture into the diagnostic business because of a lack of economic incentives as there was a low revenue return in this business. Throughout the 1990s the customs duty structures remained more favourable for the bulk imports of finished kits than for local production – i.e., the duties on raw materials were higher than the duties on finished products (Ghosh et.al., 1997).

Existing evidence reveals that when India as a technology follower country adopted a reverse innovation strategy to be successful with the development of healthcare technologies like biopharmaceutical and vaccines it became difficult for the country to deal with the challenge of cheaper imports destroying the prospects of local production (Lander and Thorsteinsdottir, 2011). Ramani and Visalakshi (2001) found that commercialization of new biotechnologies was hindered in India due to lack of coordination among different innovation actors, variations in their culture, trade barriers, lack of indigenous capabilities, lack of demand articulation and creation, lack of regulatory institutions, lack of promotion of local manufacturers etc. All of these factors discouraged indigenous product development for the commercial market. As a result, diagnostic pharmaceutical companies closed their R&D operations. They preferred to continue with the trading of diagnostics.

Exploring the issue of innovation challenges of an incubation centre managing biotech innovations, Acharya (2013) identified three issues, namely longer gestation period due to nature of pure R&D, challenges of Intellectual Property Right (IPR) and the issue of commercialization. The author stresses the role of special policy intervention for biotech-based start-ups that facilitate synergistic coordination between the incubation centres to leverage each other's strength.

The studies discussed so far suggest that the impact of economic reforms policies on the development of healthcare technologies is sub-optimal. In the following sections, we examine the major barriers that have influenced the pathways of system building activities performed by various innovation actors in the development of India's MDs innovation system.

MDs industrial base in India: status and import dependency

The MDs industry, which is growing on the lap of *In-Vitro Diagnostics* (IVD) industry, is currently at an evolving stage in India. The main components of MDs are reagents, instruments/equipment and services. The domestic market segment consists of sales of reagents, instruments and kits to the clinical laboratories. The high growth of reagents is because of their increased usage in various testing that includes virology tests, cancer detection, tuberculosis testing, blood screening and HPV testing as well as identification and predisposition to several conditions such as cancer and cystic fibrosis. The largest growing segment of the instrument segment is semi-automated analysers. Since the sector is technologically evolving and emerging rapidly, the resource-poor conditions in India provide considerable challenges.

Consequently, the sector is characterised by a *heavy dependence on imported products from abroad.* At present, imports are preferred over domestic manufacturing supply, which is facilitated by the existence of inverted duty structure[10] and the lack of favourable policy and regulatory framework. Currently, the import dependency on MDs instruments/equipment is 90 per cent and on MDs reagents is 75 per cent to meet the domestic demand (see Figure 18.2). Since the industry is largely import driven, this has an implication on the prospects of building domestic industrial capability. In the following subsection, the study provides a comprehensive assessment of the trend, pattern and structure of the level of import dependency in the market, which is a direct upshot of the economic reform policy by the government.

Incidence of import dependency in MDs

For the analysis, the MDs sector is broadly classified as reagents and instruments/equipment. The import data is collected from the UN Comtrade accessed from the World Integrated Trade Solution (WITS) online portal. Since the trade data is available across different nomenclature, the study uses the Harmonized Commodity Description and Coding System (Harmonized

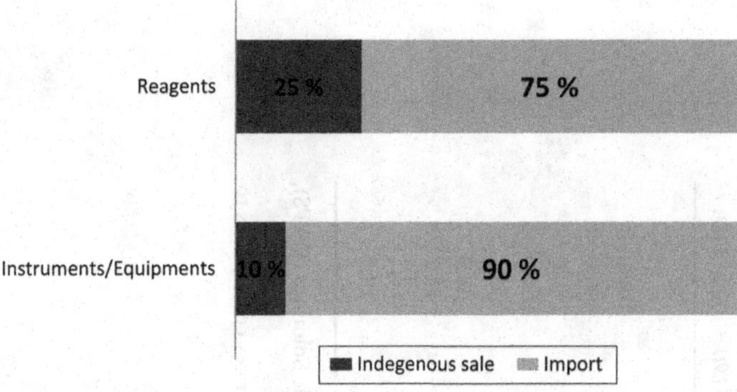

Figure 18.2 Segment-wise import proportions of MDs industry. *Source:* Adapted from the Association of Indian Medical Device Industry (AIMED).

System, or HS) for commodity classification. According to the HS 1996 classification, reagents correspond to code 300620 and 382200 and the instruments and equipment belong to code 903180 and 903190.[11] The aggregate import data (i.e., the cumulative figure of reagent and instruments/equipment) from 2000 to 2018 is depicted in Figure 18.3.

It is evident that there is a steady and sharp rise in the import of MDs product, which is especially prominent since the mid-2000s onwards. For instance, the import of MDs increased from $151 million in 2000 to $846 million in 2008. Thereafter, it reached $1320 million in 2012. Based on the simple average annual growth rates, the import has grown at the rate of 15 per cent per annum from 2000 to 2018 (See Table 18.1 for further details). In terms of the source region, the OECD has been the major supplier, although there has been a gradual shift towards Asian countries in the recent period. The break-up of MDs imports into the detailed disaggregated level (at the 6-digit HS coding) further confirms the similar pattern of heavy import dependency observed at the aggregate level (see Table 18.1).

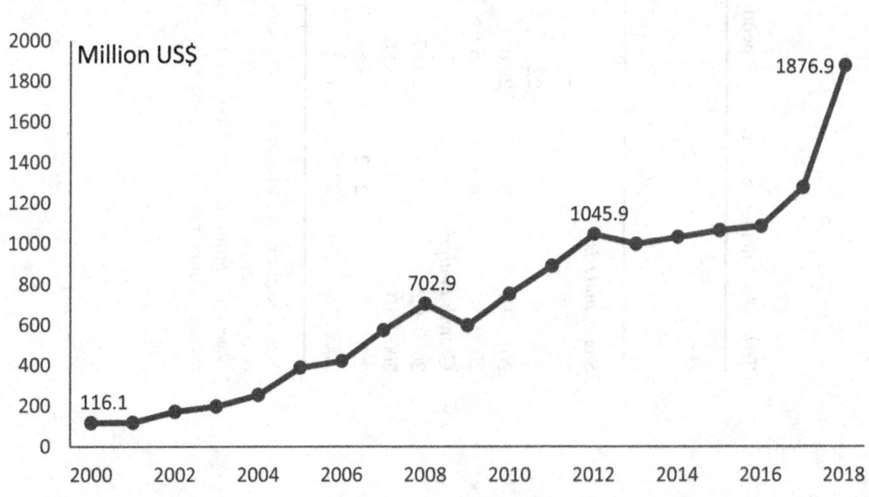

Figure 18.3 Trend in import of MDs in India (2000–18) million US$. *Source:* Author's calculations based on UN Comtrade data, accessed from WITS online portal.

Table 18.1 Incidence of import dependency at the disaggregate level, 2000–18

Periods	*Reagents*			*Instruments and equipment*			
	300620	*382200*	*300620+382200*	*903180*	*903190*	*903180+903190*	*Total MDs*
Share analysis							
2000–05	0.6	25.7	26.3	54.0	19.7	73.7	100.0
2006–10	0.1	22.3	22.4	58.0	19.6	77.6	100.0
2011–18	0.3	29.8	30.2	50.3	19.5	69.8	100.0
2000–18	0.4 (1.2)	26.5 (98.7)	26.9	53.5 (72.7)	19.6 (27.3)	73.1	100.0
Growth analysis							
2000–05	–8.5	20.87	20.2	28.4	44.6	32.2	28.7
2006–10	49.4	18.38	18.5	18.0	8.1	15.1	15.7
2011–18	26.2	14.88	14.9	11.5	17.7	12.6	13.1
2000–18	23.0	17.51	17.4	18.0	22.5	18.7	18.1

Source: Author's calculation from the data collected from UN Comtrade, accessed from World Integrated Trade Solutions (WITS), online database.

Note: (a) Figures in parenthesis are the share of individual products in each MDs segments (b) The growth rates corresponds to average annual rates in per cent.

Exploring the relative share of each product group in total MDs imports, it is evident that the instruments and equipment (74 per cent) accounted for the largest share relative to the reagents (26 per cent). Among the MDs segment, the largest share (43 per cent) is accounted for by MDs kits and sets, tools for measuring/checking instruments, automotive diagnostic tools and accessories (HS 903180), followed by prepared diagnostic or laboratory reagents with or without backing (HS 38220) with an overall share of 21 per cent. Reagents for determining blood groups or blood factors (HS 300620) have an insignificant share (0.3 per cent) relative to accessory, testing equipment, probes, assays, enzymes (HS 903190) which represented a 16 per cent share from 2000 to 2016. Further, there is a noticeable rise in the import of HS 903180 and HS 382200 during periods 2 and 3, respectively. Reagents and instruments/equipment witnessed double-digit growth rates of 17 per cent and 14 per cent, respectively. Since the products of reagents have low share and base in the overall MDs, the growth rates are found to be relatively higher than instruments and equipment.

The largest imported instruments and equipment consists of high ended technology-intensive products such as polymerase chain reaction (PCR), semi-automated analysers, micro-array microchips, instruments of biosafety lavel-3 (BSL-3), electronic equipment, etc. The prevalence of diseases, complexity and the need for quick diagnosis has created substantial demand for these advanced MDs tools in big hospitals and private nursing homes, including diagnostic and pathological laboratories. Among the reagent segments of MDs, such as enzymes, endonucleases, ligases, cloning and expression vectors, antibodies, biomarkers, etc., the majority of demand emanated from the heavy prevalence of cancers, infectious diseases (virology testing) and blood screening. Overall, we see that there is significant demand for MDs product in India which is catered for mainly through imports.

A plausible reason for increased dependency on imports is the substantial reduction in protective instruments such as tariffs as part of the ongoing liberalisation policy regime. Since 2000, there has been a drastic reduction in the level of applied tariffs on MDs products (see Figure 18.4). The simple average tariff rates applied on MDs declined drastically from 28 per cent in 2000

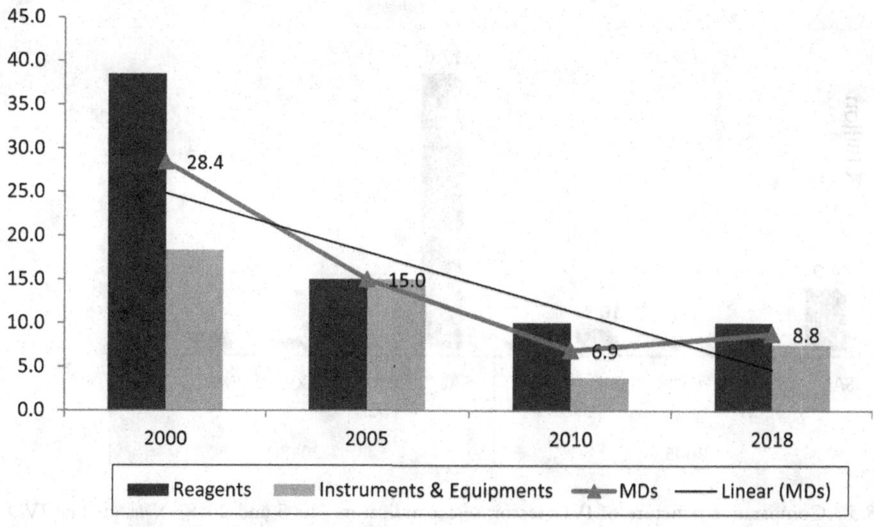

Figure 18.4 Level of protection in MDs (2000–18): average applied tariff rate (%). *Note*: Tariff data is based on simple average tariff rates applied by most favoured nation (MFN). *Source*: Author's calculations from UNCTAD TRAINS database, accessed from World Integrated Trade Solutions (WITS), online database.

to 9 per cent in 2018. This declining trend is corroborated across reagents and equipment/instruments, though the level of decline in tariff protection is relatively sharp in the former. The reduction in tariffs has made the availability of MDs product relatively easier for domestic end-users and that has induced a significant rise in demand.

Performance of system building activities by the MDs innovation actors: empirical evidence

Production, technology and investment capability of MDs industry: empirical results from firm-level data

Since the MDs industry is a sub-part of the IVD segment, we collected the financial performances of 45 IVD companies (both manufacturing and service providers) from Prowess IQ (CMIE) database. Out of the total IVD firms, five firms are involved in the MDs segment. For understanding the basic structure of the IVD sector, the study uses basic performance indicators such as firms' sales revenue, expenditure on royalties, technical fees, etc., the export of goods, import of goods and expenditure on R&D in 2005 and 2006. The comparative structure of IVD during the two periods is illustrated in Figure 18.5.

The most striking observation is the remarkable growth in firms' sales revenue over time. For instance, the cumulative production sales of IVD shot up from Rs 44 billion in 2005 to Rs 217.6 billion in 2018, growing at a rate of 12 per cent per annum based on CAGR. The higher growth rate in sales is accompanied by a significant rise in imports, reflecting the heavy dependency of IVD technology from external sources and insufficient capability to generate domestic technology from in-house R&D effort in the sector. The significant rise in imports is facilitated by the liberal trade policy that has reduced import duty considerably since economic reforms.

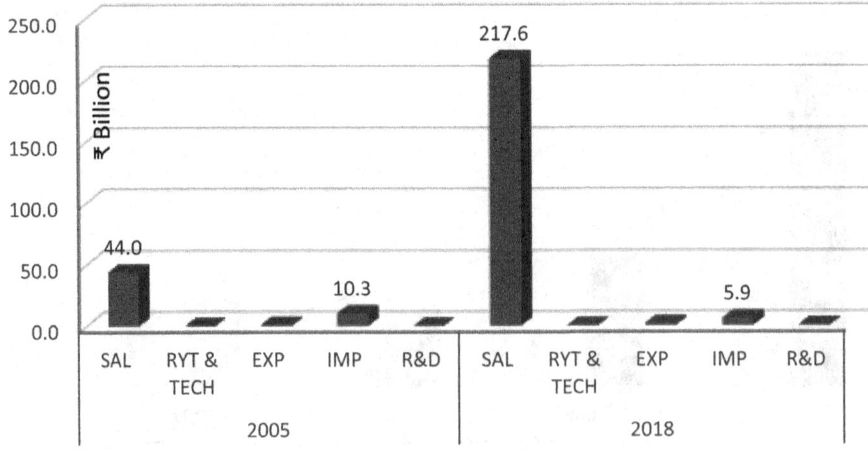

Figure 18.5 Comparative structure of IVD sector: select indicators (2005 and 2018) *Note*: (a) The IVD data consists of both manufacturing firms as well as service providing firms, (b) SAL = sales revenue, RYT & TECH = expenditure on royalties, technical fees etc., EXP = exports of goods, IMP = import of goods, R&D = expenditure on research & development. All values are in Rs. million. *Source*: Author's calculations based on PROWESS IQ, CMIE database.

Evaluation of innovation capability in MDs manufacturing sector

As noted earlier, foreign multi-national companies (MNCs) dominate the MDs market in India. This is largely due to the first-mover advantage of MNCs as they possess distinctive technical and scientific knowledge that makes possible core product specialisation and market dominance with sizeable monopoly power in the market. Since the financial performance of the major MNC companies in India is not available from the Prowess, the study collected the consolidated Annual Financial Statements of four leading MNCs from Bloomberg Terminal at the global level. The leading MNCs are Becton Dickinson and Co, Cepheid US, QGEN US and Roche Holding AG. The production and technological capabilities are assessed through the relative share and growth rates of sales revenue, R&D expenditure and LP (base 2000=100) for the selected period. The summary statistics are given in Table 18.2.

The cumulative figure of MNCs firms reveals considerable improvement in production (sales) and technological (R&D and LP) capability over the years. The study observes that MNCs are keen on increasing their technological capability as the rate of growth in R&D expenditure and R&D intensity is relatively higher than sales revenue and LP growth for all firms, except Cepheid US. This is not surprising as, for such a high knowledge and scientific field as MDs, firms tend to devote a larger portion of investment towards in-house R&D. The increase in R&D expenditure across firms reflects the *superior technological advantage of MNCs* in the global market. Among the four companies, Roche Holding AG is the leading market player as the sales revenue is substantially higher than the rest of the firms in the sample. For instance, the sales revenue of Roche went up from $17 billion to 51 billion from 2000 to 2016, with a CAGR of 7 per cent per annum. On the extreme, the sales of Cepheid US increased only moderately from $0.01 billion to $0.6 billion (CAGR of 32 per cent per annum) during the same period. Not surprisingly, Roche spends a sizeable amount on R&D (around 90 per cent of overall R&D expenditure) relative to other MNCs. This clearly explains the dominant position of Roche manufacturing in the Indian market. In addition, there is a large improvement in productive efficiency as LP has increased considerably across manufacturing, especially the post-2005 period. This indicates that MNCs are the major actors in providing *knowledge creation and learning* activities in the MDs industry. However, since many of the MNCs do not have considerable manufacturing facilities in India, the scope for *knowledge diffusion through networking and positive externalities* towards developing domestic manufacturing is rather limited.

The substantial investment in scientific and technical knowledge by the leading (dominant) MNCs firms has enabled them to have a unique comparative advantage in supplying diverse quality but relatively expensive MDs products in the global market. The emergence of MNCs players has led to the *formation of a market* that is highly concentrated with considerable knowledge barriers to entry. In this context, to compete and survive in the MDs market, it is essential for the rest of the following firms to develop and build manufacturing capability over time. As such, the performance of the *fringe* firms in the domestic market is examined using the data collected from Prowess IQ. The analysis will provide an evaluation of the effort towards building *TIS process* in terms of *knowledge creation, learning, diffusion, entrepreneurial activities, market creation, resource mobilisation and institutional rules and regulation* governing the MDs industry. The CMIE database provides the details of only a few MDs manufacturing firms in India, namely, Abbott India Ltd, Siemens Healthcare Diagnostics Ltd, Span Divergent Ltd and Bhat Bio-Tech (India) Pvt. Ltd. The first two are foreign affiliates and the rest are domestic firms. Based on the financial performance and capability indicators, the summary statistics of domestic and foreign affiliates are given in Table 18.3.

Table 18.2 Production and technological capability of leading manufacturer of MDs: selected years (million US$)

Company/indicators	*2000*	*2005*	*2010*	*2016*	*2000–16 (CAGR)*
Becton Dickinson and Co.					
Sales revenue	3618.3	5414.7	7372.3	12483.0	8.0
R&D expenses	223.8	272.0	431.0	828.0	8.5
	(6.2)	(5.0)	(5.8)	(6.6)	
Labour productivity (2000=100)	100.0	146.5	176.8	169.4	3.4
Cepheid US					
Sales revenue	7.1	85.0	212.5	596.3	31.9
R&D expenses	15.1	19.0	42.5	124.2	14.1
	(213.2)	(22.3)	(20.0)	(20.8)	
Labour productivity (2000=100)	100.0	463.3	381.7	430.1	9.5
QGEN US					
Sales revenue	216.8	398.4	1087.4	1338.0	12.0
R&D expenses	22.2	39.1	126.0	176.1	13.8
	(10.2)	(9.8)	(11.6)	(13.2)	
Labour productivity (2000=100)	100.0	157.7	128.8	173.3	3.5
Roche Holding AG					
Sales revenue	16991.0	28532.2	45672.1	51356.2	7.2
R&D expenses	2340.8	4583.8	9645.7	11709.9	10.6
	(13.8)	(16.1)	(21.1)	(22.8)	
Labour productivity (2000=100)	100.0	159.4	215.8	208.1	4.7
Cumulative Total					
Sales revenue	20833.2	34430.3	54344.3	65773.4	7.4
R&D expenses	2601.8	4913.9	10245.2	12838.2	10.5
	(60.8)	(13.3)	(14.6)	(15.9)	
Labour productivity (2000=100)	100.0	158.2	217.3	192.4	4.2

Source: Author's calculations based on the data collected from Bloomberg Professional Terminal, Bloomberg.

Note: The figures are collected from the financial statements at the global level; figures in brackets are R&D expenditure to net sales; CAGR refers to compound annual growth rates in percent; labour productivity shows the sales revenue (output) per unit of employee (labour), expressed in an index form (2000=100).

For the entire MDs manufacturing segment, the production capability, as reflected by the sales intensity, export intensity and import intensity, is impressive. The growth rate of sales revenue, which is an indicator of *entrepreneurial effort and market formation*, is 9 per cent per annum for the entire period. The production performance is relatively lower than the rate of growth of exports (11 per cent per annum) and imports (15 per cent per annum). As before, the rate of growth in manufacturing imports is relatively higher, especially among foreign firms. The

Table 18.3 Production, investment and technological capability of MDs manufacturing industry: select indicators

Type of firms	*Indicators*	*Share analysis (%)*				*CAGR (%)*
		2000	*2005*	*2010*	*2018*	*2000–18*
Domestic firms	Sales composition	4.3	7.2	7.5	0.1	−13.9
	Export composition	6.0	31.4	47.4	0.0	−100.0
	Import composition	3.8	7.9	12.2	0.1	-100.0
	GFA/Sales		42.1	40.7	41.6	−0.9
	LP index (2005=100)		100.0	189.9	204.3	6.1
	R&D intensity	0.3	0.5	2.8	0.0	−100.0
	Finished goods Import intensity	0.0	0.0	35.4	0.0	0.0
	Royalty, technical fees intensity	0.0	0.3	0.1	0.0	0.0
Foreign firms	Sales composition	95.7	92.8	92.5	99.9	9.6
	Export composition	94.0	68.6	52.6	100.0	8.6
	Import composition	96.2	92.1	87.8	100.0	13.9
	GFA/Sales	20.2	15.4	24.2	3.7	2.8
	LP index (2005=100)		100.0	130.7	178.3	4.9
	R&D intensity	0.6	0.3	0.1	0.2	−5.7
	Finished goods Import intensity	33.1	58.4	79.9	0.0	−100.0
	Royalty, technical fees intensity	0.8	0.0	0.0	0.0	13.9
Total MDs (Rs millions)	Sales composition	100.0 (4438.1)	100.0 (5623.9)	100.0 (8560.0)	100.0 (22052.5)	9.3
	Export composition	100.0 (57.9)	100.0 (58.9)	100.0 (115.3)	100.0 (239.5)	8.2
	Import composition	100.0 (375.5)	100.0 (584.9)	100.0 (1546.6)	100.0 (3634.2)	13.7
	GFA/Sales	22.0 (859.1)	17.3 (1004.3)	25.4 (2720.1)	9.8 (1010.8)	2.5
	LP index (2005=100)		100.0	96.6	147.3	3.3
	R&D intensity	0.5 (21.1)	0.3 (16.7)	0.3 (34.9)	0.1 (7.1)	−5.9
	Finished goods Import intensity	31.9 (119.6)	53.8 (314.4)	74.4 (1151.2)	0.0 (0.0)	−100.0
	Royalty, technical fees intensity	0.7 (28.8)	0.0 (1.1)	0.0 (1.2)	0.0 (0.0)	13.7

Source: Author's calculations based on PROWESS IQ, CMIE database.

Note: (a) The total Rs million for Sales and GFA is at 2004–05=100 prices. The rest of the series are in current prices (b) the share figures for Sales, Exports, Imports and Finished Goods import are based on aggregate total MDs of respective categories in % (c) GFA denotes Gross Fixed Capital Asset (i.e., Investment), (d) LP denotes Labour Productivity Index for the period 2000 to 2016, base 2005=100, (e) CAGR corresponds to compound annual growth rates in per cent, (f) Total MDs represents the aggregate values of domestic and foreign firms in the databases.

major imported items largely consist of finished goods which further confirms our observation that the creation of knowledge and learning activities is largely carried out by the large MNC companies in India.

From the analysis of firms' technological capability that reflects the *creation, diffusion and learning process*, we find that the level of R&D intensity is extremely negligible (less than 1 per cent of sales revenue) with a negligible rate of growth over time. Rather than focusing on indigenous development of technology, firms' strategy is to obtain technology from abroad. This is evident from relatively faster rates of growth in expenditure on royalties, technical fees, etc., and import of finished goods from abroad, representing the import of technology. This indicates that knowledge accumulation and development (*learning effort*) is largely confined to dependence on imported goods embodied with foreign R&D efforts. The productivity analysis in terms of LP, which reflects the *knowledge efficiency* in production, has increased at the rate of 3 per cent per annum for the aggregate sector. On the investment level, firms are found to be less capital-intensive over time and the growth rate lags behind LP across firms. This indicates that there is some evidence of improved *knowledge efficiency* at the firm level in the recent period.

The *structure* of the market among domestic manufacturers and foreign affiliates clearly indicates a sharp disparity in manufacturing capability between the two. For instance, in terms of production, foreign firms dominate the Indian market with over 95 per cent of sales revenue. A similar pattern is observed for export and import intensity across different periods. As before, most of the domestic sales are satisfied through the import of finished products from abroad by foreign affiliated companies, which witnessed a peak of 80 per cent in 2010. For the rest of the capability indicators, domestic firms are found to be moderately better in terms of technical capability (LP, R&D intensity and Royalties, technical fees) and investment capability (investment–sales ratio). However, the rates of growth of most of the variables are marginally higher among foreign-affiliated firms. This indicates that foreign companies carry out most of the critical TIS process and the rate of *diffusion of knowledge and networking channel* for *indigenous product development* is limited.

The company-wise analysis shows that the performance of Abbott India Ltd, Siemens Healthcare Diagnostics and Span Divergent Ltd is relatively superior in terms of CAGR. The emergence of MDs firms, although considerably small, indicates *emerging entrepreneurial* efforts in the domestic market. All firms are found to have improved the level of resource efficiency as the LP index has witnessed considerable growth across manufacturing. A common feature of the domestic follower firms is the apparent lack of technological dynamism (*knowledge creation and development*) investment in formal R&D. Based on the available innovation capability indicators, it is evident that Indian firms lag far behind relative to foreign firms in terms of knowledge capability. This indicates that substantial investment in MDs manufacturing capabilities is required to help them catch up in the near future.

Performance of MDs service providers

The study analysed the growth performance of major service providers of MDs using the Prowess data for the selected years. The service providers available from the database are the Apollo Hospitals Intl. Ltd, Dr. Lal Pathlabs Ltd, Fortis Healthcare Ltd, Max Healthcare Institute Ltd, Metropolis Healthcare Ltd, Reliance Life Sciences Pvt. Ltd, S R L Diagnostics Pvt. Ltd and Wockhardt Hospitals Ltd. Our empirical analysis is based on sales revenue and investment (GFA) intensity across service providers, which provides some amount of knowledge functioning in the service segment of the MDs industry (see Table 18.4).

Table 18.4 Growth of service providing firms in India: select indicators (Rs crores)

Service firms	*2000*		*2005*		*2010*		*2018*		*Growth rates (CAGR)*	
	Sales	*GFA*	*Sales*	*GFA*	*Sales*	*GFA*	*Sales*	*GFA*	*Sales*	*GFA*
Apollo Hospitals Intl. Ltd					84.4	133.9	157.7	172.2	8.1	3.2
Dr. Lal Pathlabs Ltd							1024.0	226.4	0.0	0.0
Fortis Healthcare Ltd			58.8	78.2	205.7	140.2	658.9	285.0	20.4	21.4
Max Healthcare Institute Ltd			41.6	86.8	336.8	303.5	1058.9	629.1	28.3	16.5
Metropolis Healthcare Ltd			3.9	21.5	114.4	70.7	482.7	185.5	44.9	18.0
Reliance Life Sciences Pvt. Ltd						0.0	716.3	550.1	0.0	0.0
S R L Diagnostics Pvt. Ltd	4.9	10.6	21.0	21.0			277.8	165.9	25.2	16.5
Wockhardt Hospitals Ltd			129.1	120.2	408.6	182.5	465.3	709.1	10.4	14.6
All	**4.9**	**10.6**	**254.5**	**327.7**	**1149.8**	**830.8**	**4683.9**	**2751.0**	**46.5**	**31.7**

Source: Authors calculations based on PROWESS IQ, CMIE database.
Note: GFA denotes Gross Fixed Capital Assets in Rs crores; sales data are given in Rs crores.

At the beginning of 2000, there were hardly any service providers in the domestic market. However, the sizeable demand spurt in MDs over time has provided the entry of a large number of health service providers in the market, especially since 2005. This reflects the formation of *market, entrepreneurial activities and knowledge diffusion* over time. Among the major service provides, the Max Healthcare Institute Ltd is found to have the largest market share, followed by Fortis Healthcare Ltd and Reliance Life Sciences Pvt. Ltd in 2016. These service providers also invest (*resource mobilisation*) a large amount of expenditure on machinery, equipment and other fixed assets, as the capital–sales ratio is higher and grew at double-digit rates during the period from 2000 to 2018. In terms of sales volume growth, the major service provider is Metropolis Healthcare Ltd (44 per cent), followed by Max Healthcare Institute Ltd (29 per cent per annum) and Fortis Healthcare Ltd (21 per cent per annum). The analysis reveals the *emergence of sizable entrepreneurial class* and *organisation activities* in this sector.

Thus, the empirical analysis of system building activities of industrial base for the MDs innovation system development illustrates that it is at a very nascent stage and mostly built up by the presence of large MNC (foreign) firms in terms of meeting the growing domestic demand. Foreign firms have considerable market domination as they have a comparative advantage in terms of low entry barriers for selling finished MDs product in the local market. The major TIS functional activities are largely monopolised by these firms, especially related to the generation of *knowledge, learning, diffusion, entrepreneurship and market domination*.

The existing major domestic diagnostic firms have only recently entered the market and suffer from considerable cost and other challenges in meeting domestic demand. Domestic firms are largely into packaging and selling the knocked down or semi-knocked down diagnostic products because of higher import duties on reagents and components required for the manufacturing of these products. The heavy reliance on finished imported products indicates a *lack of knowledge creation and development learning* capability for indigenous product development by the domestic firms since economic liberalisation.

On a positive note, recently a few domestic firms have started in-house development of reagents that compete with high cost imported substitute products. Another significant development is the growing number of *start-up firm* initiatives that are able to supply cost-effective products that meet core healthcare requirements in an indigenous manner.

Market entry of start-up firms and indigenous product development

One of the distinguishing features of the MDs industry is the emergence of young start-up firms which is changing the landscape of product development. Compared to foreign firms and large domestic firms, the young start-ups are playing a significant role in developing system-building activities for the development of MDs (*knowledge creation, development learning and diffusion*) that is relevant for a country's specific diagnostic needs.

The study finds that most of the young start-up firms have considerable involvement and investment desire in finding a cost-effective cure for diseases such as bloodstream infections, TB, malaria, thyroid disorders, autoimmune diseases, HIV, etc., that are known to be neglected by the industry and professional bodies. Table 18.5 shows clearly the product profiles of young start-up firms and their focused disease area specific for local needs under the resource-poor setting. This indicates that the incentives of these firms to create and develop diagnostic products are largely ruled by *social-based calculations*.

Table 18.5 Product/services and diseases/health condition focused by young start-up firms

Young start-ups	*Products/services profile*	*Diseases/Health condition focused specifically for local needs*
Xcyton Diagnostics Ltd	Molecular diagnostics and services (Syndrome Evaluation System (SES) for the detection of infectious diseases	CNS infections, bloodstream infections (sepsis, pneumonia, dengue, antibiotic resistance, pyrexia, chikungunya). Immunosuppressed infections, ophthalmic infections, HPV infections
ReaMetrix	Reagents, immunoassays	HIV/AIDS, autoimmune diseases, stem cell analysis, Leukaemia/Lymphoma, immune phenotyping.
Achira labs	Reagents, instruments and rapid diagnostic kits	Thyroid disorders, fertility, diabetes and infectious disease
BigTech Labs	Microfluidic devices, Elisa, PCR	TB and infectious diseases
Bisen Biotech	Diagnostic reagents	Infectious diseases
Revelations Biotech Pvt. Ltd	Molecular diagnostics	Infectious and non-infectious diseases, metabolic disorders and genetic horoscope
Chromous Biotech Pvt. Ltd	MDs, immunology reagents, kits and contract research services	TB & other infectious diseases

Source: Author's compilation based on information available on companies websites as on July 2017.

Indigenous MDs product development

A major positive feature of start-up firms is their involvement in developing MDs products indigenously (*knowledge development, market formation and entrepreneurial activity*). The study finds that so far the young start-up firms like Big-tech labs, ReaMetrix India, Achira labs, Xycton, BisenBiotech Revelations Biotech and Chromous Biotech have been able to develop 11 indigenous diagnostic products specially focusing on infectious diseases like TB, malaria, HIV and non-infectious diseases like cancer that are more prevalent in India (see Table 18.6 for further details).

Among the start-up players, the big-tech labs, Bhat Biotech, Revelations, Bisen and Chromous are the main *entrepreneurial actors* developing indigenous products. The big-tech labs have been playing a major role (dominant player); it is a homegrown firm that has significantly benefited from the promotional schemes of the State (*resource mobilisation function*). Various promotional schemes have been constituted by the government under the Global Strategy on Public Health, Innovation and Intellectual Property (GSPOA) programme to promote system-building activities of industrial base by encouraging Public–Private Partnerships (PPP) through financial support. The major ones include NMITLI of Council of Scientific & Industrial Research (CSIR), Biotechnology Industry Research Assistance Council (BIRAC), Biotechnology Industry Partnership Programme (BIPP) and Small Business Innovation Research Initiative (SBIRI) of the Department of Biotechnology (DBT). These schemes aim to *facilitate* and mentor the generation and translation of innovative biotech ideas into products and services and *promote* academia–industry collaboration and international linkages, and encourage techno entrepreneurship for the creation and sustainability of viable bio-enterprises.

Table 18.6 Indigenous product development and technological focus of young start-up firms

Companies	*No. of indigenous products*	*Technological focus*
Big-tech labs	4	Micro-PCR devise and reagents for low throughput, rapid, point-of-care *in-vitro* diagnosis of infectious diseases, suitable for harsh conditions. Novel MDs for eye diseases and low vision enhancement devices Point of care rapid diagnostic kit for TB point-of-care detection of infectious disease using handheld micro PCR. Truenat ® MTB is a MDs test for detection of mycobacterium tuberculosis (MTB). It is a disposable microchip with pre-loaded PCR reagents – enabling the user to just add a nucleic acid sample and start the test. It allows accurate detection of MTB in < 1 hour in near-patient settings.
ReaMetrix India	1	Dry-Tri: Cold-chain independent and easy to use CD4/CD8 assay reagent for HIV management, suitable for harsh conditions.
Achira labs	2	Microfluidic chips based point-of-care device for low-throughput rapid MDs. Point-of-care *in-vitro* diagnosis of infectious diseases
Xycton	1	Syndrome Evaluation System (SES), a technology that comprises of rapid multiplex amplification and accurate identification of the virulence-associated genes of the causative agents and organism.
BisenBiotech	1	TB screen test for diagnosis of pulmonary and extrapulmonary tuberculosis: evaluation of prototype kit at selected hospitals/peripheral health centre/research laboratories
Revelations Biotech Pvt. Ltd	1	Development of low cost rapid quantitative PCR technology for molecular diagnosis
Chromous Biotech Pvt. Ltd	1	Multiplex Fast-PCR based diagnosis and prognosis of tuberculosis.

Source: Adapted from Singh and Abrol (2017).

Analysis of the projects funded under these schemes indicates that so far these schemes have been able to support and assist various *domestic and start-up firms* in their establishments and funding the research activities for the development of MDs technologies. The promotional schemes for start-up firms supported by the government are shown in Table 18.7.

Thus it is evident that the system-building activities for indigenisation are mostly carried out by the young start-up firms (i.e., *technological knowledge production based on social welfare calculations*) as there is a lack of system building activities from the established domestic firms at the industrial level. The young firms are able to develop MDs technologies specific to local needs but are in a very nascent stage (i.e., lack of market growth and entrepreneurial development). The major factor for the success-

Table 18.7 Promotional schemes supporting system building activities of start-up MDs firms

Departments	*Promotional schemes*	*Firms which are supported*
DBT	Biotechnology Industry Partnership Program (BIPP) in 2010 under the management of Biotechnology Industry Research. BIRAC has been set up with a vision to stimulate, foster and enhance the strategic research and innovation capabilities of the Indian biotech industry particularly SME's	Supporting Big-Tech labs for the development of the point-of-care detection of infectious disease using handheld micro PCR. Supporting Revelations Biotech for the development of low cost rapid quantitative PCR technology for molecular diagnosis. Supporting Chromous Biotech Multiplex Fast-PCR based diagnosis and prognosis of tuberculosis.
	Small Business Innovation Research Initiative (SBIRI) in 2005. SBIRI is managed by the Biotechnology Industry Research Assistance Council (BIRAC). SBIRI is set up to promote Public-Private Partnership.	Supporting Bhat Bio-Tech India (P) Limited, for the development of MDs for malaria. Supporting Bisen for the development of MDs for TB. Supporting Genomix Molecular Diagnostics (P) Limited, for the development of MDs for malaria.
CSIR	CSIR launched the programme of New Millennium Indian Technology Leadership Initiative (NMITLI) in 2001. NMITLI is set up to promote public–private partnerships.	Supporting Big-Tech labs for the development of novel MDs for eye diseases and low vision enhancement devices, point-of-care rapid MDs kit for TB.

Source: Compiled on the basis of information available on websites of DBT, CSIR as on July 2017.

ful indigenous product development under the existing resource-poor setting for the young firms is the increasing support from government initiatives related to the R&D programme and funding (i.e. government support in *direction and search of knowledge creation and resource mobilisation*). This is encouraging as it will lead to further product development using indigenous technology that caters to the requirement of specific domestic needs of the country in future.

System building challenges of MDs industry: evidence from primary survey

The secondary data analysis at the firm level reveals considerable disparity in the level of performance of domestic Indian firms and foreign firms. The young start-up firms, having severe resource constraints, carry out most of the innovative efforts and activities. This clearly suggests the existence of a mismatch between the available supply and potential demand of MDs in the market. Since the MDs technology is largely emerging and the market risk is sizeable, domestic industry faces a number of innovation challenges. In order to study these aspects, the study supplements the secondary analysis with the help of a primary data survey of major industrial firms supplying MDs in the market. These four firms are Bhat Biotech, Roche Diagnostics, Omix Labs, and Dr Lal Path Lab. The objective of the case study is to understand the *major challenges, uncertainties and obstacles that firms experienced in conducting R&D, manufacturing and adopting business strategies for MDs development.*

Case study 1: Bhat Bio-Tech India (P) Ltd (domestic firm)

Bhat Biotech was started in 1994 by Dr Shama Bhat and is located at Veerasandra Industrial Area, Electronics City, Bangalore. The firm specialises in the design, development, manufacture and marketing of various *in-vitro* diagnostic products and biotechnology based products. The prominent system-building challenges of the company are the following:

a) ***Issue of market competition***

At the international level, the company faces severe price competition from Chinese products that are marketed at a very low rate as compared to the prevailing domestic prices (dumping). Mostly Chinese companies are based in the US, while the manufacturing plants/facilities are based in China. In addition, there is quality competition from Taiwanese and Korean companies that are far superior to Chinese kits. In the domestic market, the product and price competition is from four companies, namely J Mitra, the market leader for HIV kits; Span diagnostics, a leader in biochemistry; Tulip manufactures for the rapid tests and Xcyton, which has kits like HIV Elisa and HCV Elisa.

b) ***Marketing threats***

According to the company, a lack of awareness and education at the end-user level (lab technicians) for following the procedures or protocols enclosed with them while performing those tests is a major issue. In addition, the false perception of the end-users leads to difficulty in the performance of the test accurately, which undermines the reputation of the products. Even though the company follows global standards, the labs often hesitate to use Indian products.

c) ***Issues in industry–academia partnerships***

Bhat Biotech has some industry collaboration with academia for domestic manufacturing. However, they lack the development of commercial products, as the patented products are often not commercially marketable products. There is a lack of industry–academic partnership which results from the failure to provide evidence of proof for the technology developed by the academic community, which is essential for commercialisation.

d) ***Aspects of regulation***

The existing regulatory system is not well versed in diagnostic development. Since diagnostics are regulated under the drugs category, the regulatory system is rather weak with non-transparent guidelines and procedures. The company felt that the set of procedures should be equally accessible to all concerned players and the concerned targets and deadlines should also be applicable to the regulatory bodies to ensure the speed of operations.

Case study 2: OmiX Research and Diagnostics Laboratories Pvt Ltd (start-up firm)

OmiX is a start-up biotech company, founded in June 2014, and currently incubated at the Bangalore Bioincubation Centre. The company developed a platform that allows for cost-effective DNA testing for pathogens, outside of laboratory settings. The major system building hurdles are as follows.

a) ***Challenges and uncertainties concerning technological development***

The main challenge stems from the focus of product development specific to needs because the decision to have specialisation in any specific disease area requires a thought process according to the user demand. Since the initial product entry requires wider reach and impact, the company spent almost two years on deciding to focus on the development of MDs platforms for infectious diseases and another two years in the development of generic MDs platforms. According to the company, the development of MDs devices takes a longer time period and convergence of different expertise including specialised manpower. As a result, the focus has shifted towards developing reagents for MDs kits that require a shorter development period.

b) ***Issues in access to finance and other challenges***

The biggest challenge is obtaining loanable credit to invest in product development. The initial investment by BIRAC is not sufficient to cover development expenditure. The other challenge is the uncertainty concerning the required strategies for scaling up the existing products developed in the market. Access and ready availability of loanable funds is one of the major challenges. Since there is a considerable time lag in the introduction of new products/devices in the market, most of the VC investors seem reluctant to provide funding on time. Unlike software domains where things can be fixed fast, one mistake in biotechnology can take the unit back 18–24 months.

c) ***Issue of market competition***

The major competitive threat is from other start-up firms, especially in terms of the application of grants for funds from agencies like BIRAC, adoption and development of advanced technology, development of price-competitive products that are relatively cheap, affordable and user-friendly (ease of use and just in time) for the market.

d) ***Challenges in the formation of interactions with research institutes***

The firm has no collaborative research with science research institutes. However, there are service agreements or consultancy agreements with the Indian Institute of Science (IISc), National Chemical Laboratories (NCL) etc. Major bottlenecks are the existing IP clauses that demand 50 to 100 per cent of ownership that is difficult for the firm to bear.

e) ***Issue of regulation mechanism***

The lengthy period, usually 2–4 years, involved in obtaining international safety approvals (e.g., FDA) has substantial costs. Companies argue that the regulatory authorities in India are not equipped to certify products and/or medical devices. The presence of heavily funded MNCs in the domestic market further adds to the operating costs.

Case study 3: Roche Diagnostics in India (foreign subsidiary firm)

Roche Diagnostics is a foreign firm in India that focuses on the Professional and MDs portfolios. The customer base varies from large hospital chains, global laboratory chains with business in India to local laboratory chains and government-owned health centres and hospitals. The annual turnover of Roche India is around $58 million in 2016 with a steady growth rate of 18 per cent. The major innovation challenges the company faces in India are the following.

a) ***Technology adoption, technical and institutional issues***

Even though Roche is able to access technology-intensive products in India either through the direct import route or through CKD (Completely Knocked Down) kits which are then assembled within India, there are several challenges that the company faces. These include high rates of import taxation and high cost of manufacturing, low margins when competing with locally manufactured products and low rate of consumption due to higher selling price.

The lack of a structured laboratory and medical diagnostics industry in India restricts product up-gradation. This makes the placement of sophisticated instruments in the small laboratories and hospitals extremely costly. Since the company does not have production units in India, most of the products are imported from Germany, the US, Switzerland and Japan, which are relatively expensive to the end-user. The poor budget and pricing models of hospitals and labs prevent the procurement of expensive but quality instruments of Roche locally.

Case study 4: Dr Lal Path Labs (service provider)

Dr Lal Path Labs was founded by Dr (Major) S.K. Lal in 1949 with six employees. Currently, the company has a network of 150 labs and 2,000 collection centres in India. The company labs offers over 3,495 diagnostic and related healthcare tests and services and is capable of performing all of the diagnostic healthcare tests and services currently prescribed by Indian physicians. The major system-building challenges are the following.

a) ***Issue of market competition***

The company argues that the diagnostic healthcare service industry is highly competitive because of low barriers to entry. The major competition from the rival service providers is related to the ability to offer similar or superior services, the service prices, the breadth of the testing offerings, the geographical reach of the network, the ability to process samples and accurate reports of data on time, customer relationships and quality of the facilities. Moreover, the company faces intense competition from the standalone centres and hospital-based labs that offer diagnostic packages as well as home sample collection services.

b) ***Types of uncertainties and challenges***

According to the company, the major uncertainty in business is associated with the rapid and fast-changing technological advancements of MD. These advanced technologies often provide non-invasive diagnostic healthcare tests that are more convenient and cost-effective than the point-of-care testing equipment currently in operation. This can reduce the demand for laboratory testing services and income of the company. Further, increased testing by physicians in their offices and home use by patients affect the market for laboratory testing services. The business performance often suffers from the *uncertainty of the performance of business partners and franchises* that are responsible for setting up facilities, procuring equipment instruments and supplies, recruiting employees, running facilities and sourcing the samples for providing diagnostic healthcare services. Since the company does not have binding control over the standard of operation of the laboratories and patient service centre, the success and quality rest with the franchisees.

The business is facing severe *challenges from the Indian healthcare industry*, including the provision of quality patient care in a competitive environment and competitive price subject to regulation by the government. The market competition requires the company to retain new customers in accordance with the quality of testing, IT infrastructure, reputation in the medical community, the pricing of services and ability to employ qualified personnel. This is also related to the difficulty in obtaining the most recent innovative diagnostic healthcare equipment and technology for efficient service delivery. The sale volume also suffers from seasonal fluctuations associated with disease prevalence. Increased prevalence of a particular virus or pathogen in the general population often causes an increased demand for specific diagnostic healthcare testing. The company also addressed the lack of a comprehensive and stringent regulatory framework for prescribing minimum standards for facilities and services for clinical establishments. Since the implementation is a State subject, Centre-State friction creates an uncertain environment for lab growth. Further, the lack of maintenance and enforcement of IPR has an adverse impact on the reputation of the company brand.

Issues of MDs industrial development in India: analysis of system failures

The discussion so far on the system building activities for MDs innovation in the industrial sector indicates several issues and challenges. Although considerable progress has been made in the recent period, the industrial base has not been able to emerge as a significant player in the IVD market. The conceptualisation of MDs development experience as a system process and the empirical analysis through secondary data and case studies reveal a number of persisting issues that hinder the effective transformation of the technology to serve society's needs and requirements on a larger scale. Therefore, in this section, an attempt is made to evaluate the performance of MDs industrial base in terms of a *system failure* framework to identify the major shortcomings in the system. The technology innovation system is examined through three important components of innovation system failures as proposed by Weber and Rohracher (2012), namely, market failure, structure failure and transformation failure.

Based on the detailed empirical analysis of the structure and performance of industrial actors through the TIS framework, we find that the innovative activities of MDs revolve around *knowledge creation and development* (knowledge accumulation, innovation capability and creation of specific industry products), *entrepreneurial activities* (category of firms/management), *direction of search* (search for improving technical knowledge in production and the focus towards disease segments), *market formation* (structure of the market and product composition), *resource mobilization* (financial instruments) and *institutionalization* (regulatory framework). In essence, we find that the system building activities of the industrial base are largely emerging in India. However, the sector is experiencing a *number of issues* in meeting the buoyant diagnostic demand. Some of the prominent ones are as follows.

(a) ***Lack of domestic innovation capability***

The analysis reveals that the present structure of the industrial base lacks the capability to manufacture indigenous products that serve the demands of the healthcare system under the resource-poor setting. Since the domestic industry is highly dependent on imports and concentrated by the presence of large MNCs, there is very limited knowledge externality among domestic firms. Imported products from other countries, both as an original equipment manufacturer and in the finished form are still prevalent. The innovative activities through formal R&D by manufacturing firms lag far behind that of leading MNCs in the market.

(b) ***Lack of investment capability***

We find a lack of investment capability in system building activities for competence building. Although the government has made some efforts to assist young start-up firms, these are largely small, especially when considering the requirements of needs and competence building. Emphasis on indigenous research has been notably lacking amongst the local players owing to the deficiency of required skills, technical expertise and the infrastructure to support the elevated costs for conducting R&D. There is evidence of a lack of sufficient public investment in the process of learning, competence building and innovation making.

(c) ***Absence of social calculation based system building activities by large foreign firms and domestic firms***

In the context of an ongoing trade liberalizations policy regime, the production choices of large domestic and foreign firms' system-building activities have largely ignored the relevant social-based calculations; since the profit-seeking commercial market–based incentives often fail to produce products that are effective and well-targeted towards healthcare goals. Even though the entrepreneurs of start-up firms are helped through the mobilization of financial resources like EMR, promotional schemes promoting PPPs, the market formation of these firms are often weakened because of competitive pressure from imports. The indigenous products of start-ups face comparative disadvantage in the market dominated largely by foreign firms.

(d) ***Lack of strategic regulation***

The current deregulation policy regime of the government has resulted in a large import of finished MDs products that are found to be maladapted to the resource-poor settings in the country. India lacks an effective analytical and clinical validation process that involves accreditation from a clinical laboratory performing diagnostic tests to get the certificate from the regulatory body (NABL, CLIA and CAP). The regulatory measures for diagnostics are poorly developed since only less than 10 per cent of clinical laboratories are currently accredited. The burden of cost for implementation of the quality control programme and a general lack of awareness is leading to a lack of pressure for appropriate innovation.[12] Although the government has begun several steps to develop a properly defined regulatory framework for the medical devices industry, the institutionalisation and legitimation of system building functions involving regulatory apparatus are currently lacking in MDs.

It is evident that MDs market structure is characterised by market imperfections and knowledge asymmetry because of the concentration of production technology in the hands of a few large MNCs. The presence of high-level technical complexity and uncertainty has created considerable information asymmetry and under-investment in knowledge accumulation activities by private Indian firms. Since knowledge has public good externalities, private market calculations will often undermine the external social cost to the environment in which the firm operates. This further discourages additional in-house R&D investment of domestic firms and indigenous supply of products that meet the healthcare demand of the larger sections of the society. The presence of market-failures suggests that there is a need to increase public investments to become the catalyst of knowledge diffusion in the domestic market.

The small and nascent manufacturing base reflects a lack of highly developed ecosystem conducive for domestic production and indigenous product development. This relates to the failure to create well-functioning system components including sufficient infrastructure facilities, network interdependencies, supply-side capabilities and formal institutional regulatory mechanisms. Since there is a lack of collaborative and interactive functioning between industry and science base/translational base actors, there is evidence of knowledge network failure. Because of low levels of private investment in knowledge creation and credit constraints, the infrastructure failure creates a further problem at the supply-side. This, in turn, affects the domestic players' manufacturing capability, as there are considerable entry barriers in terms of MNCs' monopoly in knowledge assets and R&D. The maladapted imported products further erode the competitive position of emerging domestic players. Such capability failures are directly related to the failure of the government to create effective regulatory mechanisms. Such institutional inadequacies are reflected in terms of insufficient regulatory accreditation bodies, inadequate rules and procedures for quality checking, supply chain mismanagement, costly procedures in setting up manufacturing activities for start-up firms and non-complacent regulatory practices and uncertainty involved in clinical practices faced by service providers.

The failure to enhance the competitive landscape of developing domestic manufacturing with cost-effective indigenous industrial products is further reflected in the analysis of system building activities under the multidimensional functions. In terms of transformative change, there are failures with respect to directionality, demand articulation and policy coordination. Since the resource-poor context of India demands the development of inexpensive and effective products that are directed towards social health goals, the increased reliance on imported innovative products from abroad reflects directionality failure. This indicates a clear absence of a goal-oriented policy approach which is shared equally across public departments. Given that large sections of the population have limited economic means and suffer from a series of health hazards, the failure to anticipate correctly the effective demand of reagents and equipment suggests the problem of demand articulation by the industrial firms. Since the innovation landscape is influenced by diverse policy goals, including industrial policy, trade policy, innovation policy, IPR, standards etc., there should be coherence between different policy choices. This is clearly lacking as evident from the increased thrust for making industrial goods domestically under the 'Make-in-India' initiatives (industrial policy) while simultaneously witnessing considerable import of finished MDs products because of the steep reduction in tariff and NTBs (trade policy) on MDs products.

Conclusion

The main purpose of the study has been to examine the role of industrial base actors in the development of MDs innovation system in the context of the ongoing economic liberalisation policy regime in India. The study finds that being a technologically and scientifically complex segment of IVD, the development of MDs industrial sector depends on the interactive and interrelated web of the relationships among various actors/organisations and institutions. As such, the study proposes a *Socially Responsible Innovation System Approach* as the analytical framework to assess the MDs innovation in serving society's healthcare needs and requirements. The building blocks of *SRISA* are based on the analysis of a *Technological Innovation System* framework, which is considered appropriate for studying the functional aspects of the emerging MDs innovation system. Since the development of MDs depends on a host of country- and sector-specific characteristics, an attempt is made to assess the issues and challenges of building a responsible industrial base in the country. This helped us to use the *system failure approach* to evaluate the performance of system building activities according to social needs. We use various secondary data sources at the firm level and conducted a primary survey of selected firms to explore the system dynamics.

The study finds that the system-building activities of the industrial base in India are constituted by the formation of entrepreneurial activities by foreign firms, large domestic firms and young start-up firms. The domestic manufacturing sector is nascent but emerging with a considerable presence of MNCs. Since the domestic production capability is not well developed, the domestic health demand is largely met through MDs' imports because of the reduction in tariff and other protective instruments as part of the ongoing trade liberalisation policy regime since the 1990s. The market is largely served by the MNCs, which possess a unique competitive advantage over domestic manufactures in terms of technology, quality, standards and efficient delivery. In terms of production, technology and innovation capability, the study finds a distinctive gap between domestic and foreign market players. System building activities of the domestic firms are concentrated in low priced high volume segments.

A distinctive feature of the MDs market in India is the emergence of a large number of young start-up firms in the recent period. These firms were able to successfully utilise policy instruments and learn to develop cost-effective indigenous products catering to the local needs such as TB, malaria and HIV etc. However, in terms of the overall health demand requirement and international competitive position, the Indian industry remains far behind the efficient frontier. The study finds that there are several challenges and issues that restrict the domestic industry to develop and diffuse technical innovations in MDs. We find that the government has been an important institutional player for industrial development by initiating policy initiatives such as Make-in-India, development of medical technology clusters/parks, initiatives to foster PPPs/PDPs and promotional schemes to strengthen firms' R&D.

In terms of socially responsible criteria, the study finds several issues and challenges in the progress of MDs' industrial base in the healthcare system of the country. Because of the absence of well-functioning organisations, market imperfections, lack of interactions and dialogue among various sub-actors and institutions, the system has not been found to be developed adequately. This is further harmed through the lack of transformative initiatives resulting from the lack of well-directed, planned and coordinated policy initiatives by the government. Therefore, the future growth prospect of MDs industries depends largely on how far these structural rigidities and institutional arrangements are effectively aligned towards serving the wider healthcare problems of society. This suggests a pro-active targeted State intervention and support to rectify the negative effects of market-oriented economic reforms.

Notes

1 This work is part of my PhD Thesis and I would like to thanks my supervisors Prof. Dinesh Abrol and Prof. Pranav Desai. I would also thank Dr Rijesh, participants of Sikkim University Conference and the anonymous referee for providing valuable inputs and suggestions. However, any remaining errors are solely my responsibility.

2 Molecular diagnostics identify gene, RNA and protein variations that shed light on whether a specific person is predisposed to have a disease, whether the person actually has a disease, or whether a certain treatment option is likely to be effective for a specific disease (AdvaMedDx, 2013).

3 Modern biotechnological approaches are considered as the third generation of biotechnologies that are explicitly based on underlying scientific progress unlike the first and second generation of biotechnology that does not require solid scientific understanding (Mckelvey et al., 2004).

4 TIS is defined as a 'network of agents interacting in a specific economic/industrial area under a particular institutional infrastructure or set of infrastructures and involved in the generation, diffusion, and utilization of emerging technology' (Carlsson and Stankiewicz; 1991; Bergek et al., 2008). The focus is on the working of technological functions of particular economic systems.

5 The main *function* in system of innovation is to pursue innovation process that involves creation, diffusion and use of knowledge. The determinants factors that influence the functions of innovation systems are known as system of innovation activities (Edquist, 2005).

6 The framework was initially developed by Klein-Woolthuis et al. (2005); van Mierlo et al. (2010).

7 System building is 'the deliberate creation or modification of broader institutional or organizational structures in a technological innovation system carried out by innovative actors' (Musiolik et al., 2012).

8 The detailed description of these HS codes are as follows: (a) 300620: Reagents for determining blood groups or blood factors (b) 382200: Prepared diagnostic or laboratory reagents with or without backing (c) 903180: MDs Kits, MDs tools (measuring/checking instruments), MDs sets, electronic molecular diagnostic medical instruments/equipment, automotive diagnostic tools, MDs accessories (d) 903190: Accessory for MDs instrument, testing equipment, probes, assays, enzymes.

9 It has to be noted that Prowess IQ has certain limitations when used to assess the innovative performance of emerging firms in industries like MDs. For instance, many emerging firms in India are not listed in the Prowess IQ database. For the listed firms, there is large discontinuity in key performance variables over time. This is more severe in the case of reported R&D figures which is largely motivated

by fiscal incentives like accelerated depreciation, easy import, tax rebate etc. (see Kathuria, 2001 for further details).

10 Inverted duty structure represents a situation when the custom import duty (i.e., tariff) on finished products is lower than the intermediate inputs used to produce the finished products. Such rates discriminate against domestic manufacturing value added.

11 The detailed description of these HS codes are as follows: (a) 300620: Reagents for determining blood groups or blood factors (b) 382200: Prepared diagnostic or laboratory reagents with or without backing (c) 903180: MDs Kits, MDs tools (measuring/checking instruments), MDs sets, electronic molecular diagnostic medical instruments/equipment, automotive diagnostic tools, MDs accessories (d) 903190: Accessory for MDs instrument, testing equipment, probes, assays, enzymes.

12 Among all the laboratories participating in quality control programme, 75 per cent exist in only five states, accounting for 30 per cent of the population. Since most of these laboratories are private, the population residing in rural areas not only lacks access to private labs but also is more likely to undergo maladapted and substandard testing which is subject to inadequate safety protection.

References

Abrol, D., Guha, A., John, R., & Singh, N. (2019): "India's Domestic Pharmaceutical Firms and Their Contribution to National Innovation System-Building," Special Article, *Economic & Political Weekly*, Vol 54, No.35, August 31, 2019, pp 34–43

Achrya, M. (2013): "Challenges in Managing Incubation of Innovation in Biotechnology Sector in India," *Asia Pacific Journal of Innovation and Entrepreneurship*, Vol 7, No.3, pp 53–69.

AdvaMedDx and DxInsights (2013): "Introduction to Molecular Diagnostics: The Essentials of Diagnostics Series," https://dx.advamed.org.

Aggarwal, A. (2006): "Special Economic Zones: Revisiting the Policy Debate," *Economic and Political Weekly*, Vol 41, No 43/44, pp 4533–4536.

Bergek, A., Jacobsson, S., & Sandén, B.A. (2008): "'Legitimation' and 'Development of Positive Externalities': Two Key Processes in the Formation Phase of Technological Innovation Systems," *Technology Analysis & Strategic Management*, Vol 20, No.5, pp 575–592.

Carlsson, S. (1991): "On the Nature, Function and Composition of Technological Systems," *Journal of Evolutionary Economics*, Vol 1, No.2, pp 93–118.

Chaturvedi, S. (2007): "Exploring Interlinkages between National and Sectoral Innovation Systems for Rapid Technological Catch-Up: Case of Indian Biopharmaceutical Industry," *Technology Analysis & Strategic Management*, Vol 19, No.5, pp 643–657.

Chaturvedi, S. (2012): "India's Development Partnership: Key Policy Shifts and Institutional Evolution," *Cambridge Review of International Affairs*, Vol 25, No.4, pp 557–577.

Constance, J.A. (2010): *The Future of Molecular Diagnostics; Innovative Technologies Driving Market Opportunities in Personalized Medicine*. Business Insights Ltd., New York

Edquist, C. (2005): "Systems of Innovation – Perspectives and Challenges," in J. Fagerberg, D. C. Mowery & R. R. Nelson (Eds), *The Oxford Handbook of Innovation*. Oxford: Oxford University Press, pp 181–208.

Engel, N., Ganesh, G., Patil, M., Yellappa, V., Pai, N. P., Vadnais, C., & Pai, M. (2015): "Barriers to Point-of-Care Testing in India: Results from Qualitative Research Across Different Settings, Users and Major Diseases," *PLoS One*, Vol 10, No.8, pp e0135112.

Ghosh et al. (1997): *Business Opportunities in Medical Diagnostics in India: A Market Report*. Biotech Consortium India Ltd, New Delhi.

Gupta, S.P. & Sarkar, A. K. (1994): "Fiscal Correction and Human Resource Development: Expenditure at Central and State Levels," *Economic and Political Weekly*, Vol 29, No.13, March, 26, pp 741–751.

Joshi, S. (2006): "Impact of Economic Reforms on Social Sector Expenditure in India," *Economic and Political Weekly*, Vol 41, No.4, January, 28, pp 358–365.

Kathuria, V. (2001): "Foreign Firms, Technology Transfer and Knowledge Spillovers to Indian Manufacturing Firms: A Stochastic Frontier Analysis," *Applied Economics*, Vol 33, No.5, pp 625–642.

Lander, B., & Thorsteinsdóttir, H. (2011): "Developing Biomedical Innovation Capacity in India," *Science and Public Policy*, Vol 38, No. 10, pp 767–781.

McKelvey, M., Rickne, A., & Laage-Hellman, J. (2004): "Stylized Facts about Innovation Processes in Modern Biotechnology," in McKelvey, M. D., Rickne, A., & Laage-Hellman, J. (Eds.). *The Economic*

Dynamics of Modern Biotechnology. Edward Elgar Publishing, Cheltenham, UK and Northampton, MA, pp 20–41.

Musiolik, J., Markard, J., & Hekkert, M. (2012): "Networks and Network Resources in Technological Innovation Systems: Towards a Conceptual Framework for System Building," *Technological Forecasting and Social Change*,Vol 79, No.6, pp 1032–1048.

Poste, G. (2001): "Molecular Diagnostics: A Powerful New Component of the Healthcare Value Chain," *Expert Review of Molecular Diagnostics*,Vol 1, No.1, pp 1–5.

Ramani, S. V., & Visalakshi, S. (2001): "The Role of Resources and Incentives in the Integration of Biotechnology in Developing Countries: An Indian Case Study," *International Journal of Biotechnology* Vol 2, No.4, pp 297–312.

Singh, A. (2017): "In-Vitro Diagnostics (IVDs) Innovations for Resource-Poor Settings: The Indian Experience," *African Journal of Science, Technology, Innovation and Development*,Vol 9, No.5, pp 617–636.

Syverson, C. (2011): "What Determines Productivity?" *Journal of Economic Literature*, Vol 49, No.2, pp 326–365.

Tiwari, S., & Desai, P. N. (2011): "Stem Cell Innovation System in India: Emerging Scenario and Future Challenges," *World Journal of Science, Technology and Sustainable Development*,Vol 8, No.1, pp 1–23.

van Mierlo, B., Arkesteijn, M., & Leeuwis, C. (2010): "Enhancing the Reflexivity of System Innovation Projects with System Analyses," *American Journal of Evaluation*,Vol 31, No.2, pp 143–161.

Visalakshi, S. (1993): "Evaluation of Hybridoma Leased Diagnostic Kits for Their Commercial Prospect," in S.Visalakshi & S. Mohan (Eds), *ELISA as Diagnostic Tool—Prospect and Implications*. Wiley Eastern, New Delhi, pp 90–91.

Weber, R. (2012): "Legitimizing Research, Technology and Innovation Policies for Transformative Change: Combining Insights from Innovation Systems and Multi-Level Perspective in a Comprehensive 'Failures' Framework," *Research Policy*,Vol 41, No.6, pp 1037–1047.

Woolthuis, R. K., Lankhuizen, M., & Gilsing, V. (2005): "A System Failure Framework for Innovation Policy Design," *Technovation*,Vol 25, No.6, pp 609–619.

PART V

Social sector in India

19
AGRICULTURE NUTRITION LINKAGES IN INDIA[1]

Aviral Pandey

Introduction

In the post-reform era, market mechanism (invisible hand) has affected almost all sectors of the economy. It has a significant impact on per capita income and poverty alleviation across the states of India. Unfortunately, we do not see much significant improvement in the case of nutritional outcome in most of the states of India. Recent global reports on food security[2] and hunger[3] also point out the existing position of India in the world in terms of food insecurity and malnutrition.[4] At the disaggregate level, the situation of food insecurity is serious in states like Bihar, Jharkhand, Chhattisgarh, Odisha and Assam, where poverty is on the higher side and dependence of its residents on agriculture is also high [Pandey and Gautam, 2014]. Here, the blockage of the pathway[5] between agriculture and nutrition has been seen as a responsible factor for low improvement in nutritional outcomes in the states of India (Kadiyala et al. 2014). Recent changes, which have mainly emphasised on commercialisation of agriculture (with unequal distribution of land across households), have affected the linkage between agriculture and nutrition and, its effect can be seen in terms of an increase in the list of rare nutritious species in India. The linkage between agriculture and nutrition has become highly dependent on the profitability of crop production. In this scenario the linkage between agriculture and nutrition is hard to find at the micro level in India, where more than 80 per cent of farmers are small and marginal, and profitability in agriculture is becoming limited.

However, the government has taken initiatives to improve the nutrition status in the country: such as though Integrated Child Development Services (ICDS), the National Health Mission, the Janani Suraksha Yojana, the Matritva Sahyog Yojana, the Mid-Day Meal Scheme and the National Food Security Mission. However, concerns regarding malnutrition have persisted despite improvements over the years. Recently, Government of India (GOI) launched a **National Nutrition Mission**, similar to the National Health Mission. This is to enable integration of nutrition-related interventions cutting across sectors like women and child development, health, food and public distribution, sanitation, drinking water and rural development. Besides this, improved agriculture leading to better household food security has also been identified as a fundamental determinant of processes that lead to food security, adequate dietary intake and nutritional status and health; yet, there is limited empirical and recent evidence of the existence of linkages between agriculture, nutrition and health in a country like India at micro

 DOI: 10.4324/9780367855741-19

level or state level. Against this backdrop, the present chapter deals with the existing situation of agriculture and nutrition linkages[6] in India. The chapter is divided into five sections. The next section presents the diverse aspects of malnutrition in the world and India. The third section gives details of the analytical framework of nutrition linkages: factors affecting nutrition in India. The fourth section presents the existing relationship between nutrition, agriculture, women's empowerment and other factors in India. Finally, the conclusion and way forward are discussed in the last section.

Food insecurity and malnutrition in the world, India and states

This section presents a brief overview of food insecurity and malnutrition in the world and the states of India. The section is mainly based on information collected from three important reports: the report on the Global Hunger Index (GHI),[7] the report on Global Food Security[8] Index (GFSI) and NFHS 4 & NFHS 5 (up to reports released in the first round). The recent Global Hunger Index (2020) report speaks about the increased severity of hunger and malnutrition due to Covid-19 in countries that were already facing problems of high hunger and undernutrition (Headey 2020). According to the 2020 GHI, of the 107 countries, three suffer from levels of hunger that are alarming – Chad, Timor-Leste and Madagascar – and 31 countries have serious levels of hunger. According to the 2020 GHI, Botswana, El Salvador, Eswatini, Kenya, Lesotho, Madagascar, Malaysia, Mauritania, Mongolia, Mozambique, Oman, Rwanda, Timor-Leste and Venezuela experienced increased levels of hunger in 2020 in comparison to 2012. This report concludes that, given the current trajectory, the goal of achieving zero hunger by 2030 will not be fully achieved. At the regional level, hunger is highest in the regions of Africa south of the Sahara and South Asia, whose 2020 GHI scores are 27.8 and 26.0, respectively. Child undernutrition, as measured by child stunting[9] and child wasting, is higher in South Asia than Africa south of the Sahara.

The Global Food Security Index (2019) report shows that developed countries like Singapore, Ireland, the United States, Switzerland and Finland are the top five food-secure countries of the world. Unfortunately, India stands at 72 in the list of 113 countries and the situation of India is almost similar to countries like Guatemala, Tunisia, Algeria, etc. in terms of GFSI. Disaggregate level data also reveal the fact that the condition of India is not good in terms of quality and safety in comparison to affordability and availability. India stands at 70th in terms of affordability, at 61st in terms of availability and 85th in terms of quality and safety in the list of 113 countries. Report on global food security indicates that less than 10 per cent of agricultural land is equipped for irrigation in 79 of the 113 countries included in the study (70 per cent). Under emerging climatic risk it is expected that water stress may further affect the food security situation in the world. This report also indicates that relative spending on agriculture compared with the sector's contribution to GDP has declined globally since the early 2000s. Access to financing for farmers is highly correlated with overall performance in GFSI. Comparison of GHI across different time periods (GHI 2017) shows that the situation has improved in several countries in the last 25 years (from 2017). Relatively rapid improvement in agricultural productivity, public policy such as National Nutrition Action Plan (NNAP), complemented by investments in agriculture, disaster resilience, food fortification and other related initiatives (Shekar et al. 2017), increased household assets (a proxy for household wealth), increased maternal education levels, improved sanitation levels, and implementation and utilisation of health and nutrition programs, including antenatal and neonatal care (Headey and Hoddinott 2015) and law and order have identified as significant factors responsible for the improvement in the level of nutrition. Still, some countries and some regions are facing serious challenges in terms of hunger.

In the case of India, the child wasting rate has not substantially improved over the past 30 years. But the country has made progress in other areas. Its child stunting rate, while still relatively high at 38.4 per cent (2015–16), has decreased in each of the reference periods (1992 to 2016), down from 61.9 per cent in 1992 (see Table 19.2). Comparison of NFHS 3 and NFHS 4 reports shows a declining trend of the child malnutrition situation in India

Table 19.1 State-wise child malnutrition in India

Name of state	*Stunted*		*Wasted*		*Underweight*	
	NFHS 4	*NFHS 5*	*NFHS 4*	*NFHS 5*	*NFHS 4*	*NFHS 5*
Jharkhand	45.3	N.A.	29	N.A.	47.8	N.A.
Bihar	48.3	42.9	20.8	22.9	43.9	41
Madhya Pradesh	42	N.A.	25.8	N.A.	42.8	N.A.
Uttar Pradesh	46.3	N.A.	17.9	N.A.	39.5	N.A.
Gujarat	38.5	39	26.4	25.1	39.3	39.7
Dadar Nagar Haveli	41.7	39.4	27.6	21.6	38.9	38.7
Chhattisgarh	37.6	N.A.	23.1	N.A.	37.7	N.A.
Rajasthan	39.1	N.A.	23	N.A.	36.7	N.A.
Maharashtra	34.4	35.2	25.6	25.6	36	36.1
Karnataka	36.2	35.4	26.1	19.5	35.2	32.9
Odisha	34.1	N.A.	20.4	N.A.	34.4	N.A.
Andhra Pradesh	31.4	31.2	17.2	16.1	31.9	29.6
West Bengal	32.5	33.8	20.3	20.3	31.6	32.2
Assam	36.4	35.3	17	21.7	29.8	32.8
Haryana	34	N.A.	21.2	N.A.	29.4	N.A.
Meghalay	43.8	46.5	15.3	12.1	29	26.6
Telengana	28.1	33.1	18	21.7	28.5	31.8
NCT Delhi	32.3	N.A.	17.1	N.A.	27	N.A.
Daman & Diu	23.4	N.A.	24.1	N.A.	26.7	N.A.
Uttarakhand	33.5	N.A.	19.5	N.A.	26.6	N.A.
Chandigarh	27.6	N.A.	11.4	N.A.	25.1	N.A.
Tripura	24.3	32.3	16.8	18.2	24.1	25.6
Goa	20.1	25.8	21.9	19.1	23.8	24
Tamil Nadu	27.1	N.A.	19.7	N.A.	23.8	N.A.
Lakshadweep	27	32	13.8	17.4	23.4	25.8
Puducherry	23.7	N.A.	23.6	N.A.	22	N.A.
Andaman and Nicobar	23.3	22.5	18.9	16	21.6	23.7
Punjab	25.7	N.A.	15.6	N.A.	21.6	N.A.
Himachal Pradesh	26.3	30.8	13.7	17.4	21.2	25.5
Arunachal Pradesh	29.4	N.A.	17.3	N.A.	19.5	N.A.
Nagaland	28.6	32.7	11.2	19.1	16.8	26.9
Jammu & Kashmir	27.4	26.9*	12.1	19*	16.6	21*
Kerala	19.7	23.4	15.7	15.8	16.1	19.7
Sikkim	29.6	22.3	14.2	13.7	14.2	13.1
Manipur	28.9	23.4	6.8	9.9	13.8	13.3
Mizoram	28	28.9	6.1	9.8	11.9	12.7

Source: Author's compilation using NFHS 4 and NFHS 5. *Note*: * Excluding Ladakh.

between 2005–06 and 2015–16, but the pace of reduction in malnutrition was higher in the period of 1991–1999 in comparison to the post-1999 period (1999–2015). In 2005–06, 48 per cent of children under five years of age were stunted and 42.5 per cent were underweight; these figures fell to 38.4 per cent and 35.7 per cent, respectively, in 2015–16. The decline in the child malnutrition rate is somewhat lower (the proportion of children under five years of age stunted and underweight declined by 20 per cent and 16 per cent, respectively). But the recent NFHS (2020) report indicates a depressing situation of malnutrition. Eighteen of the 22 states and Union Territories (UTs) recorded a rise in the percentage of children under five years of age who are stunted, wasted and underweight compared with 2015–16 (see Table 19.1). According to a World Bank 2019 report, India has the second highest number of stunted children in South Asia (at 38 per cent), after Afghanistan (41%). Wasting is highest in India at 21 per cent, followed by Sri Lanka at 15 per cent and Bangladesh at 14%, the report said. Normally, one can find that poverty and food insecurity are interrelated with each other. This relationship is more visible in economies like India. Presently, India has the world's highest population of stunted children. Around 48 million children (as per NFHS 4) are stunted in India and, this is expected to increase further in 2020 (as preliminary findings of NFHS 5 show a depressing situation of malnutrition).

NFHS 4 shows spatial variation across states in terms of child malnutrition in India (see Table 19.1). In terms of the percentage of children stunted, Bihar is at the lowest rank. In terms of the percentage of children wasted and underweight, Jharkhand is at the lowest rank among all states of India. State-wise variation is higher in terms of the percentage of children underweight and wasted across states of India. Adult malnutrition is also high in India, especially among women in the 15–49 years age group. In 2015–16 (as per NFHS 4), around 23 per cent of women and around 20 per cent of men in the 15–49 years age group were facing malnutrition problems in India (value of their Body Mass Index (BMI) was below normal). Men were better off, but the proportion of thin women in the total population and the gap between men and women in terms of malnutrition have changed since 2005–06, when the value was 35.5 per cent and the gap between men and women was 1.3 per cent. In terms of adult malnutrition, except Madhya Pradesh, Uttar Pradesh, Himachal Pradesh, Manipur, NCT Delhi, Chandigarh, the percentage of women in the 15–49 years age group who were thin was higher than their counterparts in all states of India. The gap between the percentage of women and men in the 15–49 years age group who were thin was greater in Dadar Nagar Haveli (9 per cent) and Jharkhand (7.7 per cent).

Table 19.2 Indicators of undernourishment in India from 1990 to 2015

Indicators	*1990*	*1997*	*1999*	*2005*	*2015*
Percentage of children under 5 years of age who are stunted	66.2	48.5	51.0	48	38.4
Percentage of children under 5 years of age affected by wasting	21.3	19.3	20	19.8	21
Percentage of children under 5 years of age who are underweight	59.5	41.1	44.4	42.5	35.7

Source: FAOSTAT and NFHS 4.

Nutrition linkages: factors affecting nutrition in India

The analytical framework

The widely accepted framework to conceptualise factors affecting malnutrition is given by UNICEF, which identifies access to food and health services, maternal and child care practices and household amenities relating to sanitation and safe drinking water as responsible factors for determining the situation of malnutrition. This chapter broadly follows the UNICEF framework, with greater concentration on agriculture and women's empowerment related variables. Agricultural livelihood affects the nutrition of individual household members through multiple pathways and interactions. The framework given in Figure 19.1 helps us to understand how agriculture can improve access to food and health care; how they (food and health) impact and are affected by the enabling environment; and how they ultimately affect the nutrition of individual men, women and children (Herforth and Harris 2014).

The pathways may not always be linear, and there are many interactions among them. In general, they can be divided into three main routes at the household level: (1) food production, which can affect the availability of food for household consumption, as well as the price of diverse foods; (2) agricultural income for expenditure on food and non-food items; and (3) women's empowerment, which affects income, caring capacity and practices and female energy expenditure (these are highly correlated with female literacy and access to resources). Acting on all of these three routes is the enabling environment for nutrition. Here, several key components such as: natural resource environment, food market environment, health, water, and sanitation environment, nutrition/health knowledge and norms and other factors, such as policy and governance also play important roles. These components may affect the nutrition of consumers or communities, including farming households. Child nutrition outcomes ultimately feed back into national economic growth and household assets and livelihoods, including those that contribute to both agricultural and non-agricultural sources of income.

In this chapter, the focus has been given on six dimensions that may explain malnutrition in India: agriculture and livestock performance, women's empowerment (women's education, female-headed household), child care practices, basic household amenities, access to and utilisation of health services by women and children and social structure. The analysis is carried out for undernutrition among children less than five years of age, adults from 14 to 49 years of age, both combined and separately using variables related to agriculture and malnutrition across 28 major states[10] of India and using correlation and regression analysis. As recent data for the major 28 states are available for the year 2015–16, so this study is based on 2015–16 data (NFHS 4). Details of explanatory variables are given in Table 19.3.

To determine the level of malnutrition for the population of the states of India, normalised malnutrition indices have been constructed combining variables/indicators of undernutrition among children under five years of age and adults from the age group 15 to 49 years. Three indicators of child undernutrition being used here are: percentage of stunted, wasted and underweight children under five years of age. Two indicators of adult undernutrition being used here are: percentage of thin men and women (BMI less than 18.5 kg/m^2) in population. Data for these indicators were taken from NFHS-4 survey findings. Each of these indicators of malnutrition is first normalised according to the formula:

$$\text{Normalised Indicators} = \frac{\text{Actual value - Minimum value}}{\text{Maximum value - Minimum value}}$$

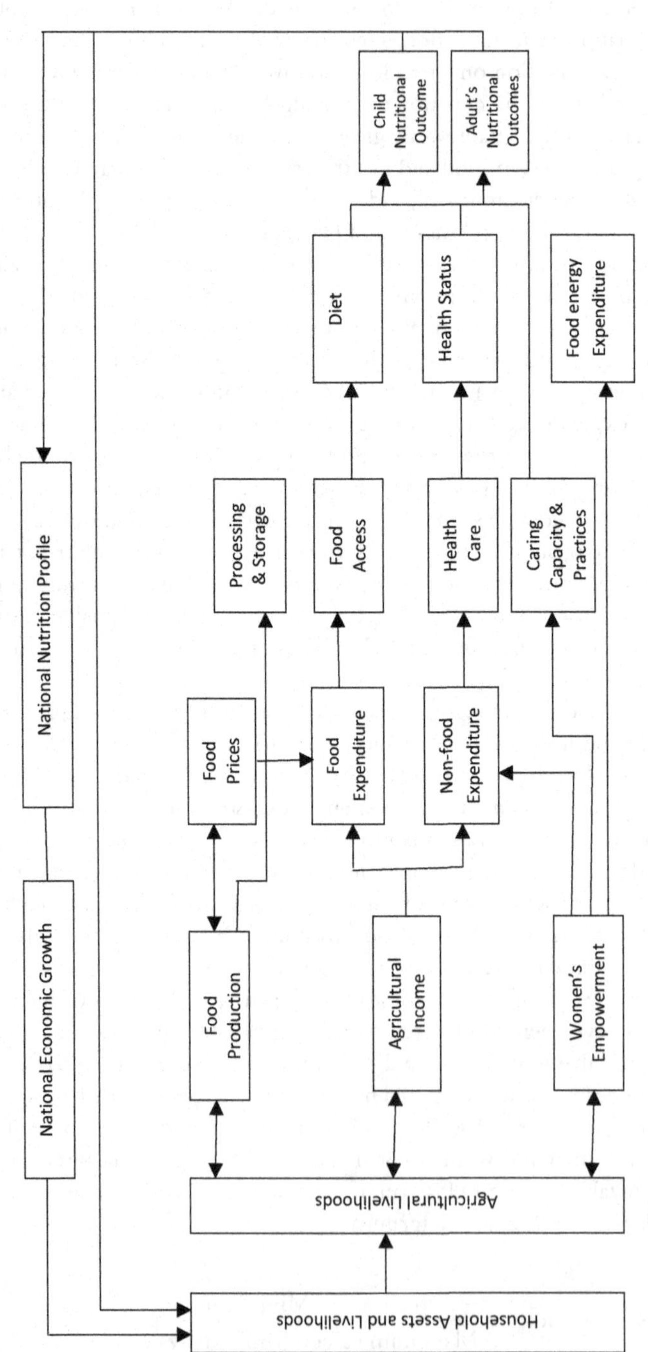

Figure 19.1 Conceptual pathways between agriculture and nutrition. *Source:* Herforth and Harris (2014).

Table 19.3 Variables and data source

Dimensions	*Variables details*	*Variables*	*Data source*
Agriculture and livestock performance	Gross value of output from agriculture per acre of land (in Rs/Ha at constant 2011–12 prices)	GVOAL	Directorate of Economics & Statistics, DAC&FW and CSO
	Gross value of output from livestock per acre of land (in Rs/Ha at constant 2011–12 prices)	GVOLL	Directorate of Economics & Statistics, DAC&FW and CSO
	Gross value of output from fisheries per acre of land (in Rs/Ha at constant 2011–12 prices)	GVOFL	Directorate of Economics & Statistics, DAC&FW and CSO
	Percentage of output from fruit and vegetables in total agriculture output (at constant 2011–12 prices)	AGDIV	Directorate of Economics & Statistics, DAC&FW and CSO
	Per capita gross state domestic product from agriculture and allied sector (in Rs/1000 rural population at constant 2011–12 prices)	PCGSDPA	CSO and Census 2011
	Cropping intensity (percentage)	CROPIN	Directorate of Economics & Statistics, DAC&FW and CSO
Women's status/ women's empowerment	Literacy rate among women aged 15 to 49 (In percentage)	LITW	NFHS 4
	Female headed households (in percentage)	FEAHEAD	Census 2011
Childcare practices	Children under age 3 years breastfed within one hour of birth (in percentage)	BERFEED	NFHS 4
	Children age 6–23 months receiving an adequate diet (in percentage)	CHIADIET	NFHS 4
Household infrastructure and amenities	Proportion of households using improved sanitation facility (in percentage)	IMPSANI	NFHS 4
	Proportion of households with an improved drinking-water source (in percentage)	IMPWATER	NFHS 4
Access to and utilisation of healthcare services	The percentage of the last live births in the 5 years preceding the survey that were assisted by health personals (in percentage)	LIBHP	NFHS 4
	The percentage of children aged 12 to 23 months who have received all basic vaccinations (BCG, measles, and three doses each of polio and DPT) (in percentage)	CRBV	NFHS 4
Social structure	Percentage of SC & ST population in total population	SCST	Census 2011

The normalised malnutrition index is then estimated as a simple average of normalised values of the indicators. Three indices of malnutrition are constructed: Adult Malnutrition Index (AMI), combining two indicators of adult undernutrition; Child Malnutrition Index (CHILDMI), combining three indictors of child malnutrition; Combined Malnutrition Index (CMI), combining three indictors of child and two indictors of adult undernutrition. It may be kindly noted that these indices do not include children between 5 and 14 years of age or those who are over 50 years of age. Value of each indicator is between 0 and 1.

Table 19.4 shows geographical distribution of malnutrition in India. Table 19.4 points out some important facts about malnutrition in India. It is expected that high income states

Table 19.4 States as per level of malnutrition in India

Category	*AMI*	*CHILDMI*	*CMI*
Low malnutrition	Sikkim, Mizoram, Arunachal Pradesh, Kerala, Manipur, Lakshadweep, Puducherry, Andaman and Nicobar, Punjab, Jammu & Kashmir, Nagaland	Mizoram, Manipur, Kerala, Jammu & Kashmir, Nagaland, Sikkim, Himachal Pradesh	Mizoram, Sikkim, Manipur, Kerala, Jammu & Kashmir, Nagaland, Lakshadweep, Arunachal Pradesh
Medium malnutrition	Daman & Diu, Goa, Tamil Nadu, Haryana, NCT Delhi, Andhra Pradesh, Himachal Pradesh, Uttarakhand, Tripura, Chandigarh, Karnataka	Chandigarh, Punjab, Lakshadweep, Andaman and Nicobar, Tripura, Goa, Arunachal Pradesh, Tamil Nadu, Puducherry, Telengana, Daman & Diu, NCT Delhi, Andhra Pradesh, Uttarakhand, Assam, West Bengal, Haryana, Meghalaya	Punjab, Andaman and Nicobar , Puducherry, Goa, Himachal Pradesh, Chandigarh, Tamil Nadu, Daman & Diu, Tripura, NCT Delhi, Haryana, Andhra Pradesh, Uttarakhand, Telengana
High malnutrition	West Bengal, Maharashtra, Meghalaya, Telengana, Odisha, Assam, Dadar Nagar Haveli, Rajasthan, Chhattisgarh, Uttar Pradesh, Gujarat, Jharkhand, Bihar, Madhya Pradesh	Odisha, Maharashtra, Chhattisgarh, Karnataka, Rajasthan, Uttar Pradesh, Gujarat, Dadar Nagar Haveli, Madhya Pradesh, Bihar, Jharkhand	West Bengal, Assam, Meghalaya, Odisha, Karnataka, Maharashtra, Rajasthan, Chhattisgarh, Uttar Pradesh, Gujarat, Dadar Nagar Haveli, Bihar, Madhya Pradesh, Jharkhand

Source: Author's calculations based on NFHS 4.

Note: For all indices (AMI, CMI and CHILDMI), low malnutrition represents that value of index is equal or lower than 1/3 (maximum value–minimum value) of the index, medium malnutrition represents that value of index is equal or lower than 2/3 (maximum value–minimum value) and greater than 1/3 (maximum value–minimum value) of the index and high malnutrition represents that value of index is higher than 2/3 (maximum value–minimum value) of index.

should have a low level of malnutrition, but the situation of malnutrition shows that malnutrition is higher in Maharashtra, Karnataka and Gujarat (higher per capita income states of India). Agriculture based states like Bihar, Uttar Pradesh, Jharkhand, Madhya Pradesh are facing high child malnutrition problems in India. Odisha, Maharashtra, Chhattisgarh, Karnataka, Rajasthan, Uttar Pradesh, Gujarat, Dadar Nagar Haveli, Madhya Pradesh, Bihar, Jharkhand are facing high child malnutrition in India. On the other hand, Sikkim, Mizoram, Kerala, Manipur, Jammu & Kashmir (J&K), Nagaland are in better positions in terms of all three malnutrition indices in India.

Agriculture–nutrition linkages in India: macro perspective

Performance of agriculture in India: an overview

Indian economy has had a more than 5 per cent growth rate since 1991. It has affected the per capita income of the country considerably. It has also resulted in low poverty in India. Yet India is home to one-third of the world's poor. The biggest failure of the 25 years of liberalisation (besides, some authors argue that the turning point of the economic growth in India was 1980–81) is that, despite such high growth, employment creation has simply not been commensurate. In fact, employment elasticity in agriculture reduced from 0.49 during 1983 to 1993–94, to –0.42 between 2004–05 and 2011–12 (Nayyar 2017; IHD 2014). Recent studies on income growth in the world and other countries show that inequality has increased in India, especially since liberalisation. Piketty and Chancel (2017) argue that the period between 1951 and 1980 witnessed a decline in the share of the super-rich in the national income pie, and a rise in the share of the bottom half of India's population. But, between 1980 and 2014, the situation reversed.

One of the important factors behind this pattern is the silent crisis in agriculture, and the situation worsened in the era of liberalisation. Compared with the immediate pre-liberalisation period (1980–83 to 1990–1993), agriculture growth in India recorded a visible deceleration during the post-liberalisation period (1990–93 to 2003–06). This was succeeded by an unambiguous turnaround in the years coinciding with the Eleventh Five-Year Plan (2007–12) (Chand & Parappurathu 2012) and again experienced both deceleration and acceleration during the Twelfth Five-Year Plan (2012–17). Figures on farmers' suicide, especially those who are dependent on the market, show how the crisis is deepening in the farm sector in India. The decline in public investment in irrigation, water management, scientific research and agriculture marketing has adversely affected the farm sector growth in India in the post-liberalisation period. On the other hand, because the process of employment diversification has been slower than the process of income generation in the agriculture economy, the ratio of per worker income in agriculture, which was already low at only 0.28 per cent in 1971, crashed to 0.15 per cent in 2011 (Nadkarni 2018). Comparison between Indian agricultural worker's relative income (ratio of per worker income in agriculture to per worker income in non-agricultural sector) with that in other countries shows that the ratio is generally lower than one in all countries except Kenya, where it is above two. Few countries have improved the level of per worker relative income in agriculture, mainly by drawing a significant portion of their agricultural workforce into other sectors (Nadkarni 2018). Unfortunately, this did not happen in India. The trend shows that under the influence of climate change, farmers' vulnerability has increased. Between 2005–06 and 2013–14, the coefficient of variation was only 0.27 in the case of overall GDP growth but it was 0.69 in the case of agricultural GDP. It seems that agriculture is becoming unviable for farmers in India. This can be seen in terms of farmer suicide and unplanned out-migration in rural India.

There is variation in agriculture performance across states in India. Certain states have done better than others (see Table 19.5). For instance, between 2004–05 and 2010–11 (Period I), agriculture and the allied sector in Mizoram and Tripura grew at around 9 per cent per annum, whereas in Jammu & Kashmir (J&K), Punjab, Himachal Pradesh, Kerala and Goa it grew at less than 2 per cent or even at negative rates. Again, between 2010–11 and 2014–15 (Period II), agriculture and the allied sector in Jharkhand grew at 11.05 per cent, in Madhya Pradesh at around 18 per cent and in Sikkim at around 12 per cent, and whereas in J&K, Punjab, Kerala, Tamil Nadu, Rajasthan, Maharashtra and Mizoram it grew at less than 2 per cent or at negative rates. Performance of various sub-sectors of agriculture and forestry given in Table 19.5 also shows the existing situation across states in India.

Besides the fact that agriculture is not performing well, agriculture remains the largest employer in several states of India. As per NITI Aayog State Statistics, in Chhattisgarh, Arunachal Pradesh, Maharashtra, Nagaland, Mizoram, Gujarat, Sikkim, Madhya Pradesh, Karnataka, Andhra Pradesh, Bihar, Meghalaya, Uttar Pradesh, Himachal Pradesh, Orissa, Assam, Uttarakhand, Rajasthan, Jharkhand more than 60 per cent of the workforce is employed in the agriculture sector in rural areas. More than 80 per cent of the total rural population lives in these states of India. This shows the importance of agriculture in India. Thus, an impact of the agriculture performance on nutrition is expected in the case of India.

Agriculture–nutrition linkages in India

Under skewed and vulnerable agriculture growth,.the performance of the agriculture–nutrition linkage is under threat in India (Hoda et al. 2017; Pandey 2016). Against this backdrop, the study seeks to analyse the existing linkage between agriculture, including livestock and nutrition in India. Since malnutrition is determined by the interplay of multiple factors over time, the relative levels of agricultural prosperity may be more relevant than the growth rate over a specified number of years (Gulati et al. 2012), so the study is based on one time period data for all states of India. To capture agriculture prosperity, including livestock and fisheries, a number of indicators have been used in this study. Besides agriculture, livestock and fisheries, variables related to women's status and education, child care practices, household's infrastructure and amenities, access to utilisation of healthcare services have also been used in this study (details are given in Table 19.3). Correlation and regression analyses have been used to analyse linkages between agriculture, other variables and nutrition in this study.

The findings of the correlation analysis given in Table 19.6 indicate that states where agriculture income and agriculture productivity are on the higher side are facing low levels of malnutrition in India. States where diversification towards fruit and vegetables is on the higher side are facing low child malnutrition problems. The relationship between agriculture diversification and adult malnutrition is negative, but it is not as significant as it is in the case of child malnutrition. The relationship between livestock performance and fisheries and malnutrition is also negative (but it is not as significant as we find in the case of agriculture). Besides the fact that the livestock sector has grown at an appreciable and sustainable rate in the last 40 years (agriculture and its allied sectors) (DFI – I, 2017), the insignificant relationship between nutrition and livestock raises serious questions.[11] The analysis also shows that states where agriculture productivity is on the higher side also have a higher level of livestock productivity. But, the insignificant correlation between livestock and malnutrition raises the question of why such a situation is emerging in the states of India. Analysis of rank-wise distribution of states shows that states like Jharkhand, Bihar, Uttar Pradesh, Gujarat and Rajasthan are facing high malnutrition problem, while these states are better in terms of livestock productivity in India. We find

Table 19.5 Performance of various sub-sectors of agriculture across states (Rs lakhs @ 2004–05 prices)

	Crops and livestock sector		*Forestry*		*Fisheries*		*Agriculture and allied total*	
	Growth in GSDP		*Growth in GSDP*		*Growth in GSDP*		*Growth in GSDP*	
	Period I★	*Period II*★	*Period I*	*Period II*	*Period I*	*Period II*	*Period I*	*Period II*
Jammu & Kashmir	2.64	−1.97	−1.49	−0.13	−3.27	1.69	1.95	−1.69
Maharashtra	5.59	−1.38	1.92	6.44	0.41	2.21	4.78	0.07
Orissa	4.07	−0.23	0.95	−0.85	4.26	8.95	3.67	0.32
Goa	−2.74	0.34	2.69	9.28	−0.8	4.7	−1.8	2.49
Tamil Nadu	4.12	1.2	1.83	3.63	5.1	2.73	4.04	1.46
Punjab	1.91	1.23	3.3	4.46	3.12	2.53	1.98	1.38
Kerala	−2.25	1.35	2.8	2.66	0.57	2.08	−1.46	1.59
Rajasthan	6.08	1.77	1.78	1.56	8.8	7.77	5.54	1.77
West Bengal	2.1	1.86	1.98	13.86	3.96	3.2	2.39	2.72
Haryana	4	2.16	2.58	3.07	14.7	7.27	4.01	2.25
Uttarakhand	2.14	2.52	2.46	6.76	6.84	1.14	2.23	3.63
Karnataka	6.07	2.97	4.49	3.31	10.54	2.06	5.97	2.98
Bihar	4.57	3.75	−2	−1.88	1.79	12.61	3.77	3.74
Uttar Pradesh	2.65	3.82	2.13	2.19	7.29	3.66	2.67	3.69
Andhra Pradesh	4.52	3.95	2.19	4.89	6.4	15.91	4.71	6.43
Chhattisgarh	6.18	5.46	1.9	2.77	9.56	8.51	5.42	5.19
Gujarat	4.92	5.83	0.63	2.75	3.53	3.15	4.35	5.47
Himachal Pradesh	0.7	6.94	5.3	5.34	2.03	7.56	1.88	6.53
Jharkhand	6.9	12.79	3.98	2.95	18.13	12.62	6.48	11.05
Madhya Pradesh	4.61	19.43	1.58	0.91	1.47	12.85	4.28	17.99
Mizoram	14.4	−1.77	−0.57	0.43	0.97	7.01	9.09	−0.91
Tripura	6.44	1.83	18.2	9.42	16.05	15.43	8.73	4.66
Assam	2.92	2.67	4.78	4.43	3.81	9.61	3.16	3.3
Nagaland	3.16	4.41	4.58	3.7	11.15	3.46	3.56	4.25
Manipur	5.22	6.14	−0.23	−0.21	1.69	8.22	4.16	5.51
Meghalaya	2.55	9.14	1.07	−0.34	−4.65	6.17	2.04	6.99
Sikkim	4.13	13.14	−2.18	0.85	3.64	35.36	3.48	12.29
All India	3.64	5.1	2.08	2.16	4.57	7.21	3.52	4.94

Source: State of India Agriculture reports of various years.
★Period I – 2004–05 and 2010–11 and Period II – between 2010–11 and 2014–15.

Table 19.6 Correlation matrix: AMI, CHMI, CMI and explanatory factors

	CHILDMI	*AMI*	*CMI*	*GVOAL*	*GVOLL*	*GVOFL*	*AGDIV*	*CROPIN*	*FEAHEAD*	*SCST*	*LITW*	*CHIADIET*	*BERFEED*	*IMPSANI*	*IMPWATER*	*LIBHP*	*CRBV*	*PCGSDPA*
CHILDMI	1.00																	
AMI	0.90*	1.00																
CMI	0.98*	0.97*	1.00															
GVOAL	−0.37*	−0.41*	−0.40*	1.00														
GVOLL	−0.17	−0.21	−0.19	0.60*	1.00													
GVOFL	−0.21	−0.15	−0.19	0.19	0.05	1.00												
AGDIV	−0.46*	−0.30	−0.40*	0.33	−0.04	0.32	1.00											
CROPIN	0.00	−0.02	−0.01	−0.08	0.06	−0.14	−0.34	1.00										
FEAHEAD	−0.45*	−0.39*	−0.43*	0.29	0.13	0.43*	0.36	−0.15	1.00									
SCST	−0.29	−0.24	−0.28	0.04	−0.29	−0.28	0.44*	−0.37*	0.07	1.00								
LITW	−0.53*	−0.56*	−0.56*	0.24	−0.07	0.23	0.06	0.11	0.40*	0.07	1.00							
CHIADIET	−0.55*	−0.55*	−0.57*	0.35	0.33	0.07	0.37	−0.11	0.34	0.25	0.08	1.00						
BERFEED	−0.48*	−0.48*	−0.50*	0.15	−0.26	0.37*	0.43*	−0.46*	0.41*	0.27	0.42*	0.48*	1.00					
IMPSANI	−0.72*	−0.79*	−0.77*	0.32	0.12	0.18	0.07	0.22	0.55*	0.13	0.72*	0.31	0.37	1.00				
IMPWATER	0.11	0.03	0.08	0.04	0.12	0.04	−0.22	0.49*	−0.02	−0.34	0.06	−0.18	−0.18	0.21	1.00			
LIBHP	−0.09	−0.17	−0.13	0.05	0.25	0.33	−0.27	0.17	0.13	−0.61*	0.29	−0.02	0.16	0.26	0.34	1.00		
CRBV	−0.19	−0.21	−0.20	0.12	0.19	0.42*	0.05	0.34	0.31	−0.42*	0.18	0.26	0.15	0.18	0.24	0.59*	1.00	
PCGSDPA	−0.38*	−0.51*	−0.45*	0.04	0.06	−0.01	−0.21	0.29	0.03	0.17	0.55*	−0.09	0.01	0.70*	0.22	0.20	0.04	1.00

Note: * shows 5 per cent level of significance,

significant negative correlation between the percentage of female-headed households and child malnutrition in the states of India. It reflects that states where women have higher access to resources are facing lower malnutrition problems in India. The linkage between women's literacy (among women aged 15 to 49) and nutrition is also in the expected direction, and shows that states where women are literate are facing low malnutrition problems in India. The findings also indicate that states where the practice of breastfeeding is on the higher side are facing low malnutrition problems in India. States where households have higher access to improved sanitation are also facing low levels of malnutrition in India. States where children aged 6–23 months are receiving an adequate diet are also facing low malnutrition problems in India. Overall, it can be seen here that the states where the presence of female headed households is on the higher side have a higher level of female literacy, have a higher percentage of children under the age of three years breastfed within one hour of birth. These states are also better in terms of nutritional outcome in India.

This study also attempts to test the linkage between agriculture and nutrition using regression analysis. Explanatory variables have been selected on the basis of coefficient analysis and theoretical logic. To identify the role of explanatory variables in explaining variation between the values of three indicators of malnutrition, three different equations have been used. The relationship between adult malnutrition and explanatory variables is given in Table 19.7. The sign of regression coefficient is along the expected line, except percentage of female-headed household. The estimated coefficients of variables other than agriculture productivity and percentage of female headed households are robust (significant at 1 per cent level of significance). On the other hand, the relationship between sanitation and AMI indicates the presence of inter linkages between cleanliness and nutrition in the states of India. The relationship between agriculture diversification and AMI indicates the presence of interlinkages between agriculture diversification and nutrition in the states of India. The relationship between child malnutrition and explanatory variables is given in Table 19.8. The relationship between sanitation and CHILDMI indicates the presence of interlinkages between cleanliness and nutrition in the states of India. The relationship between agriculture diversification and CHILDMI indicates the presence of interlinkages between agriculture diversification and nutrition in the states of India. The relationship between CHILDDIET and CHILDMI indicates the presence of interlinkages between childcare practice and nutrition in the states of India. The relationship between combined malnutrition and explanatory variables

Table 19.7 Regression result: AMI and explanatory factors

Variable	*AMI*	*AMI*	*AMI*
GVOAl	−0.00022		
AGDIV		−0.0049*	
PCGSDPA			0.016
FEAHEAD	0.005	0.014	0.012
LITW	−0.00065	0.00053	−0.00018
IMPSANI	−0.011*	−0.013	−0.014*
Constant	1.2*	1.18*	1.049*
No. of observations	28	28	28
Adjusted R^2	**0.58**	**0.67**	**0.58**
F value	**10.53**	**14.41**	**10.59**

Note: * shows 1 per cent level of significance.

Table 19.8 Regression result: CHILDMI and explanatory factors

	CHILDMI	*CHILDMI*	*CHILDMI*
GVOAl	–0.0001		
AGDIV		0.002*	
PCGSDPA			0.003
FEAHEAD	0.003	0.010	0.003
LITW	–0.002	–0.002	–0.002
CHIADIET	–0.011*	–0.009*	–0.011*
BERFEED	–0.002	0.000	–0.002
IMPSANI	–0.006*	–0.008*	–0.007*
_cons	1.21*	1.22*	1.17*
No. of observations	28	28	28
Adjusted R^2	0.55	0.68	0.55
F value	6.71	10.90	6.61

Note: * shows 1 per cent level of significance.

Table 19.9 Regression result: CMI and explanatory factors

	CMI	*CMI*	*CMI*
GVOAl	–0.0001		
AGDIV		–0.004*	
PCGSDPA PCAGDP			–0.0002
FEAHEAD	0.007	0.012	0.006
LITW	–0.002	–0.002	–0.002
CHIADIET	–0.011*	–0.010*	–0.012*
BERFEED	–0.003	–0.00004	–0.002
IMPSANI	–0.008*	–0.009*	–0.008*
_cons	1.26*	1.25*	1.22*
No. of observations	28	28	28
Adjusted R^2	0.65	0.74	0.65
F value	9.67	13.96	6.61

Note: * shows 1 per cent level of significance.

is given in Table 19.9. The estimated coefficients of variables agriculture diversification, child care practice and sanitation are robust. The relationship between sanitation and CMI indicates the presence of interlinkages between cleanliness and nutrition in the states of India. The relationship between agriculture diversification and CMI indicates the presence of interlinkages between agriculture diversification and nutrition in the states of India. The relationship between CHILDDIET and CMI indicates the presence of interlinkages between childcare practice and nutrition in the states of India. The relationship between sanitation and CMI indicates the presence of interlinkages between cleanliness and nutrition in the states of India. At the outset, the regression analyses show that household infrastructure and amenities, agriculture performance and childcare practices are playing effective roles in explaining the difference between levels of malnutrition across the states of India.

Conclusion and way forward

Improvement in agriculture and livestock performance can change the life of millions of malnourished people in India. But, it is also true that agriculture alone cannot improve the situation of malnutrition in India. The results also confirm the multidimensional nature of nutrition linkages in the case of India. In fact, the results show that in the present context other variables look more affective than agriculture in solving the malnutrition problem in India. Women's literacy and access to improved sanitation facilities are also playing an important role in the reduction of the level of malnutrition in the states of India. These findings are very important for the policy implication in the states of India. It is also true that there are certain state-specific characteristics that are also influential in deciding the level of malnutrition in India. But, there are certain policies that can be implemented at macro level in the states of India to improve the level of nutrition. Agriculture performance can improve the level of nutrition in India if resources are equally distributed, diversification in agriculture is promoted, linkage between agriculture income and livestock performance is promoted and women are empowered.

This study is based mainly on secondary data. Further studies are required to assess the emerging linkage between agriculture and nutrition at the micro level. Covid-19 has also affected the nutritional situation in different parts of world and India is highly vulnerable to the malnutrition crisis as Covid-19 has badly affected the income of rural households in states like Bihar. But the present government is trying to uplift the farming community's income through providing direct income support, technical and financial supports for adopting climate smart agriculture, and promoting community-based entrepreneurship (like FPO) among farmers. Thus, how these policies are affecting the nutrition situation in the states of India can be an important area of future research. States like Bihar, Jharkhand, etc. have been focusing on the cultivation of traditionally known nutritious crops (Marwa, etc.). Its impact on reducing malnutrition among farming households will be an interesting area of future research.

Notes

1 This is part of work done by the author on self-initiative basis on the issue of agriculture–nutrition linkage in India and its states. Data used in this paper have also been used for other study by the author.
2 At the 1996 FAO Rome World Food Summit, food security was defined as a condition that exists when "all people, at all times have physical and economic access to sufficient, safe and nutritious food that meets their dietary needs and food preferences for an active and healthy life".
3 "Hunger" refers to the index (Global Hunger Index – GHI) based on four component indicators, namely undernourishment, child wasting, child stunting and child mortality. Taken together, the component indicators reflect deficiencies in calories as well as in micronutrients.
4 Malnutrition refers to deficiencies, excesses or imbalances in a person's intake of energy and/or nutrients.
5 Presently, 30 crops provide 95 per cent of human food energy needs, four of which (rice, wheat, maize and potato) are responsible for more than 60 per cent of our energy intake.
6 There are several factors which decide the level of nutrition in human beings. In this work an analysis of the route between agriculture and nutrition has been discussed.
7 The Global Hunger Index considers the core issues of undernourishment, child stunting, child wasting and child mortality.
8 The Global Food Security Index considers the core issues of affordability, availability and quality across a set of 113 countries. The GFSI now includes an adjustment factor on natural resources and resilience.
9 Stunting refers to a child who is too short for his or her age.
10 Andhra Pradesh, Arunachal Pradesh, Assam, Bihar, Chhattisgarh, Goa, Gujarat, Haryana, Himachal Pradesh, Jammu & Kashmir, Jharkhand, Karnataka, Kerala, Madhya Pradesh, Maharashtra, Manipur, Meghalaya, Mizoram, Nagaland, Odisha, Punjab, Rajasthan, Sikkim, Tamil Nadu, Tripura, Uttar Pradesh, Uttarakhand, West Bengal.

11 Band et al. (2016) in their study also did not find any association between livestock keeping and malnutrition. However, they found that mixed farming (crop farming and keeping livestock) was associated with a significant reduction in malnutrition among children under five years old.

References

Banda, Y., Simuunza Martin, C., and Mumba, C. (2016): Relationship between Household Livestock Keeping and Nutritional Status of Under-5 Children in Rural Parts of the Eastern Province of Zambia, *SAGE Open*,Vol. 6, No. 4, pp 1–7.

Chancel, L., and Piketty, T. (2017): *Indian Income Inequality, 1922–2014: From British Raj to Billionaire Raj?* WID, World Working Paper Series No. 2017/11, July 2017, World Wealth and Income Database, The Source for Global Inequality Data, World Inequality Lab.

Chand, R., and Parappurathu, S. (2012): Temporal and Spatial Variations in Agricultural Growth and Its Determinants, *Economic & Political Weekly Supplement*,Vol. 47, No. 26 & 27, pp 55–64.

DFI–I (2017): *Report of the Committee on Doubling Farmers' Income Volume I "March of Agriculture since Independence and Growth Trends"*, Document prepared by the Committee on Doubling Farmers' Income, Department of Agriculture, Cooperation and Farmers' Welfare, Ministry of Agriculture & Farmers' Welfare, Government of India, New Delhi.

Global Food Security Index (2017): *Measuring Food Security and the Impact of Resource Risks*, The Economist Intelligence Unit Limited, London, UK.

Global Food Security Index (2019): *Strengthening Food Systems and the Environment through Innovation and Investment*, The Economist Intelligence Unit Limited, London, UK.

Global Hunger Index (2020): *Global Hunger Index: One Decade to Zero Hunger Linking Health and Sustainable Food Systems*, Chatham House, Dublin / Bonn.

Gulati, A., Ganesh, A. K., Shreedhar, G., and Nandakumar, T. (2012): Agriculture and Malnutrition in India, *Food and Nutrition Bulletin*,Vol. 33, No. 1, pp 74–86.

Headey, D. D., and Hoddinott, J. (2015): Understanding the Rapid Reduction of Undernutrition in Nepal, 2001–2011, *PLOS One*. https://doi.org/10.1371/journal.pone.0145738.

Headey, D., Heidkamp, R., Osendarp, S., Ruel, M., Scott, N., Black, R., Shekar, M., Bouis, H., Flory, A., Haddad, L., and Walker, N. (2020): Impacts of COVID-19 on Childhood Malnutrition and Nutrition-Related Mortality, *Lancet*. https://www.thelancet.com/journals/lancet/article/PIIS0140-6736(20)31647-0/fulltext.

Herforth, A., and Jody, H. (2014): *Understanding and Applying Primary Pathways and Principles. Brief 1, Improving Nutrition through Agriculture Technical Brief Series*, Arlington, VA: USAID/Strengthening Partnerships, Results, and Innovations in Nutrition Globally (SPRING) Project.

Hoda, A., Rajkhowa, P., and Gulati, A. (2017): *Unleashing Bihar's Agriculture Potential: Sources and Drivers of Agriculture Growth*, Working Paper 336, Indian Council for Research on International Economic Relations, New Delhi.

IHD (2014): *India Labour and Employment Report, Institute for Human Development*, New Delhi: Academic Press.

Kadiyala, S., Harris, J., Headey, D., Yosef S., and Gillespie, S (2014): Agriculture and Nutrition in India: Mapping Evidence to Pathways, *Annals of the New York Academy Science*,Vol. 1331, pp 43–56.

Nadkarni, M.V. (2018): Crisis in Indian Agriculture, *Economic & Political Weekly*,Vol. 53, No. 17, pp 28–34

Nayyar, Deepak. (2017). Economic Liberalisation in India Then and Now. *Economic &Political Weekly*,Vol. liI No. 2, pp 41–48.

Pandey, A. and Gautam, R. (2014): Food Security and Poverty in India: Key Challenges and Policy Option, *The Indian Economic Journal*,Vol 62, No. 2, pp 985–999.

Pandey, A. (2016): System of Rice Intensification (SRI) Methods in Bihar: A District Level Study, *Journal of Rural Development*,Vol. 35, No. 2, pp 211–237.

Piketty, T., and Chancel, L. (2017): *Indian Income Inequality, 1922–2015: From British Raj to Billionaire Raj?* WID, World Working Paper series No. 2017/11. Paris, France.

Shekar, M., Kakietek, J., Dayton, J. E., and Walters, D. (2017): *An Investment Framework for Nutrition Reaching the Global Targets for Stunting, Anemia, Breastfeeding, and Wasting, Directions in Development--Human Development*. Washington, DC: World Bank.

20
ECONOMIC REFORMS, UNDERNUTRITION AND PUBLIC PROVISIONING OF FOOD

Anjana Thampi

Introduction

In the 1990s, a puzzle was identified – the much lower incidence of child stunting and underweight in most sub-Saharan African countries as compared to certain South Asian countries including India, in spite of the higher average per capita incomes and lower infant mortality rates in India. Ramalingaswami, Jonsson and Rohde (1996) termed it 'the Asian enigma'. The puzzle continues to persist even after almost three decades of economic reforms.

'[T]he elimination of regular hunger and undernutrition is a much harder task than the eradication of famines' (Drèze and Sen 1989, p. 266), partly because of the much higher number of affected people and partly because the measures require not just preserving entitlements in the short run, but also providing greater than established entitlements over the longer term. Far from achieving this task, the news in India was filled with the starvation death of 11-year-old Santoshi in Jharkhand in September 2017, after her family was denied access to their entitled food rations in the absence of Aadhaar card seeding. Starvation deaths continue to be reported in states such as Jharkhand, Karnataka, Uttar Pradesh and Odisha (Right to Food Campaign 2018).

Santoshi's story highlights the link that underlies this article, the extent of hunger and undernutrition in the country even after 25 years of economic reforms, and the changing role of the Public Distribution System (PDS) in alleviating this situation. As of 2015–16, more than one-third of the children in India are either stunted[1] or underweight[2] or both, and more than one-fourth are wasted[3] (MHFW 2017). These children may not reach their physical or mental potential. The undernutrition figures are all the more dramatic in a country with an average annual GDP growth rate of 7.7 per cent between 2004–05 and 2013–14. The undernutrition prevalence is far higher than in most other countries of the world, many of which have lower per capita incomes or economic growth rates. Further, the latest data covering 22 states suggest an increase in child malnutrition in several states between 2015–16 and 2019–20. The COVID-19 pandemic is likely to have worsened the nutritional situation, as indicated by surveys of vulnerable communities (Right to Food Campaign 2020). In such a situation, it is imperative to understand whether food provisioning programmes have any impact on child nutritional indicators; this could determine the direction that development expenditures need to take to further progress in this regard.

 DOI: 10.4324/9780367855741-20

This chapter has two objectives. The first is to compare state-level variations in the incidence of hunger and undernutrition using the methodology used to calculate the Global Hunger Index (GHI). The second is to assess whether the PDS has had any impact on improving the nutritional indicators of children. The next section describes the data and methodology. The third section covers the broad trends in child anthropometric indicators, and the determinants of these indicators. In the fourth section, hunger indexes are calculated and analysed for each state. The fifth section links the PDS to the previous discussion, traces its evolution, and assesses its nutritional impact. The final section concludes.

Data and methodology

The data from the second (1998–99), third (2005–06) and fourth (2015–16) rounds of the National Family Health Surveys (NFHS) are used to show the trends in child anthropometric indicators in India. When comparing across all three rounds, the undernutrition prevalence for children below three years of age was calculated from the unit-level data of NFHS-3 and 4.

India ranked among the worst 17 countries in the world in terms of hunger and undernutrition as per the GHI 2018. In this chapter, the same methodology was used to calculate state hunger indexes. One of the component indicators of the GHI is the proportion of undernourished population, which is calculated using the Food and Agriculture Organisation (FAO) balance sheets of the availability of food. However, these food balance sheets are not available for individual states. Instead, the 61st (2004–05) and 68th (2011–12) rounds of the National Sample Survey consumer expenditure survey (NSS CES) data on household consumption of food were used to calculate the actual intake of calories using the conversion factors in Gopalan, Sastri and Balasubramanian (1991). The undernourished population included those with calorie intake below a cut-off. As in Menon, Deolalikar and Bhaskar (2009), the calorie cut-off that corresponds to the undernourishment prevalence in India in the GHI report was used. The calorie cut-off that corresponds to the undernourishment prevalence of 21 per cent in India for the years 2003–05 (IFPRI/Welthungerhilfe/Concern Worldwide 2009) was used to calculate the 2006 index. By the consumer expenditure survey of 2004–05, this corresponds to 1600 kilocalories per person per day. Similarly, the calorie cut-off that corresponds to the undernourishment prevalence of 14.5 per cent (IFPRI/Welthungerhilfe/Concern Worldwide 2017) was used to calculate the 2016 index. This cut-off is 1592 kilocalories per person per day by NSS CES 2011–12. This exercise is done so as to follow the GHI severity scale. The actual prevalence of undernourishment is much higher.

Another component indicator of the hunger index is the under-five mortality rate. The ranks of countries are not directly comparable before and after 2015 as the calculation of the GHI was revised in this year. For one, the indicator on the proportion of underweight children was replaced with the proportions of child stunting and wasting. Also, the formula used in calculating the index was changed. Currently, the indicators are standardised using thresholds that are slightly above the highest values of the indicator observed worldwide between 1988 and 2013.[4] The standardised undernourishment and child mortality indicators are assigned a weight of one-third each, and the two standardised child anthropometric indicators are each assigned a weight of one-sixth. The values of the four indicators are then aggregated to yield the GHI. The same procedure was followed to calculate the state hunger indexes.

Trends in nutritional indicators

Since 1975, there has been a decline in severe child undernutrition, as per the National Nutrition Monitoring Bureau surveys conducted in nine states (Deaton and Drèze 2009). However, pro-

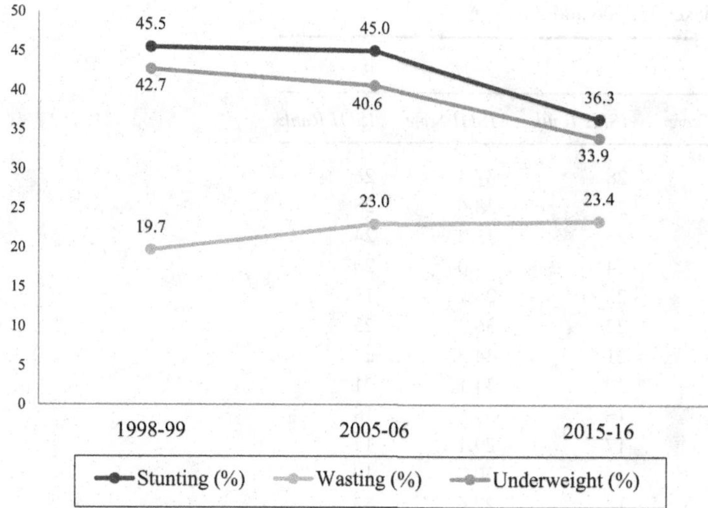

Figure 20.1 Trends in anthropometric indicators of children under three in India. *Source*: NFHS 2, 3 and 4.

gress halted soon after economic reforms were implemented – the proportions of stunted and underweight children below three years of age roughly stagnated between 1998–99 and 2005–06 (Figure 20.1). In the decade since then, there have been improvements in these indicators. This would seem to indicate that the years of high economic growth between 2003 and 2011 (excluding 2008–09) translated into nutritional improvements over this decade. However, celebrating these improvements would be premature – the levels of child undernutrition in India are still very high, starkly so when compared with other countries. In addition, the third indicator on child wasting worsened over the same decade so much so that almost a quarter of children under three years of age were wasted in 2015–16. Child wasting is higher in India than in almost all other countries in the world (WHO 2017).

Further, the key indicators of nutrition from the 2019–20 NFHS conducted in 22 states and union territories suggest a disconcerting picture. Rather than continuing the improvements achieved between 2005–06 and 2015–16, the data show a reversal of the child nutritional gains in several of the states surveyed in 2019–20 (MHFW 2020).

There is no evidence of genetics accounting for the puzzle (Coffey et al. 2013). Rather, some of the determinants of nutritional status include the disease environment (Ramalingaswami et al. 1996; Deaton 2013), the education, health and nutrition of women (Ramalingaswami et al. 1996), parental education, access to public services and household amenities (Kjelsrud and Somanathan 2017). Another factor that has recently received attention is the use of sanitation facilities (Spears 2013; Coffey and Spears 2017).

While acknowledging the importance of other factors in influencing and determining nutritional status, this chapter focuses on the intake of food through the PDS. As reports of starvation deaths affirm, adequate food intake is itself not a given for many individuals in the country.

State hunger indexes

The national-level indicators mask strong regional variations in the extent of child well-being. Since 2006, the International Food Policy Research Institute has calculated the GHI every year

Table 20.1 State Hunger Indexes in 2006 and 2016

State	*2006*		*2016*	
	ISHI Score	*ISHI Rank*	*ISHI Score*	*ISHI Rank*
Madhya Pradesh	51.1	28	37.4	26
Jharkhand	47.5	27	38.6	28
Bihar	43.8	25	35.7	24
Chhattisgarh	43.7	24	34.0	20
Odisha	39.2	23	28.1	15
Gujarat	38.3	22	36.3	25
Karnataka	37.5	21	34.3	23
Uttar Pradesh	37.3	20	34.1	21
Maharashtra	36.9	18	30.6	18
Tamil Nadu	36.4	17	29.1	17
Rajasthan	36.0	16	30.8	19
West Bengal	33.4	14	27.6	13
Haryana	33.0	13	27.7	14
Assam	32.1	12	28.6	16
Andhra Pradesh	31.4	11	24.3	10
Kerala	28.9	7	25.2	11
Himachal Pradesh	26.6	4	18.1	1
Punjab	23.3	2	21.3	7
All-India	**38.2**		**31.6**	

Source: Computed using NSS CES Rounds 61 and 68, NFHS 3 and 4.

to assess the progress in reducing hunger and undernutrition around the world. The hunger index for each state in India was calculated using the updated GHI methodology for 2006 and 2016, and the term India State Hunger Index or ISHI was used (Menon, Deolalikar and Bhaskar 2009). Ranks are assigned to all 28 states[5] according to their ISHI scores. Table 20.1 shows only 18 of the larger states, but the ranks in the table refer to the overall ranking.

Almost all of the major states, with the exception of Himachal Pradesh, have a 'serious' or 'alarming' hunger and undernutrition situation. In certain cases, this exercise shows the discrepancy between the position of a state in terms of level and growth rate of domestic product and its nutritional position. Two such states are Gujarat and Maharashtra – two of the richest and fastest growing states in the country, but with hunger indexes similar to or even higher than in some of the poorest states in 2006 and 2016.

Over the same period, the poor states of Odisha and Chhattisgarh greatly improved their ISHI ranks. The improvements in these two states can be linked to the emergence of food policy as a major issue in their regional politics. Chhattisgarh enacted its own food security act in 2012 even before the National Food Security Act (NFSA) was implemented in 2013. From 2004, the state government made efforts to reform the rationing system in the state. Following the success of these steps (Khera 2011a, 2011b; Puri 2012), Odisha also moved towards reforming the rationing system, and this was evident in greater access (Aggarwal 2011). Greater access to food through the system could improve child health either directly, or through better maternal health. Over the decade, Chhattisgarh and Odisha also improved the coverage of ICDS services to the extent that they had the highest coverage by 2015–16 (IIPS and Macro International 2007; IIPS and ICF 2017).

In Himachal Pradesh, hunger and undernutrition were the lowest in the country as per the index, and the situation had improved the most since 2006. The experiences of Himachal Pradesh, along with Kerala and Tamil Nadu, are strongly linked to the history of universal provisioning of essential services in these states, and this was achieved through public action and social and political movements (Drèze and Sen 2013).

To summarise, the national-level data shows the positive development that the prevalence of child stunting and underweight improved between 2005 and 2015, unlike in the previous decade. However, the prevalence of under-five wasting increased during the same period. Further, even with the improvements, Indian children are among the most undernourished in the world. The period of rapid economic growth between 2003 and 2011 appears to have had a limited role in improving child anthropometry (Thampi 2019). It bears noting here that it would be more difficult to attain further improvements after severe undernutrition has been reduced.

Vollmer et al. (2014) advanced three explanations for the weak relationship between economic growth and progress in nutritional indicators – unequal distribution of income, inadequate household spending on child nutrition and insufficient improvements in public services. All three explanations are plausible in the Indian context and are rooted in the structural problems in the economy and the nature of the growth process (Thampi 2019). Therefore, effective policies to tackle the structural problems are required. In the meanwhile, food provisioning programmes could be useful in providing shorter-term relief, along with interventions to improve maternal and early child health, and provision of clean drinking water and sanitation facilities. The most heavily discussed indicators of undernutrition are of children below the age of five years, while the PDS is more relevant for a later stage of child development. Nevertheless, given recent indications (Deaton 2008) and evidence (Singh, Park and Dercon 2014) of 'catch-up growth', whereby interventions can reverse nutritional insults in early childhood, understanding the anthropometric impact of this programme on children is crucial. While it is naturally desirable to deal with poor child nutrition as early as possible, the possibility that it may be handled at a later stage as well offers tremendous potential for such interventions and for the children themselves.

Public distribution system

One of the explanations advanced in the previous section was that even households which experience rising incomes may not be using the additional income in ways that improve child nutrition. In such a situation, access to subsidised food can enable members of the household to meet their nutritional requirements. Currently, there are various government programmes which provide access to cheap or free food to different sections of the population. This chapter focuses only on the PDS. The PDS provides subsidised cereals and other items to households classified as Below Poverty Line (BPL) or Antyodaya Anna Yojana (AAY). With the implementation of the NFSA, the classification of households has changed to priority and AAY households. Priority households are entitled to 5 kilograms of foodgrains per person per month, and AAY households are entitled to 35 kilograms per month.

Any assessment of the functioning of the PDS cannot ignore the recent evidence from primary and secondary data (Himanshu and Sen 2011; Khera 2011a, 2011b) of a revival of the system initially in a few states, later inspiring a similar recovery in other states (Himanshu and Sen 2013b). The revival was a result of measures by the state governments to expand coverage, reduce issue prices, shift ownership to community groups, and implement technological improvements in the system. There is evidence of an increasing impact of the PDS on the nutritional status of children aged between 7 and 19 years in some of the states where the system has been functioning well or reviving over the past decade (Thampi 2017). The study is all the more relevant with the continuing debate on cash versus in-kind transfers that gained traction over the past decade.

Phases in the evolution of PDS

The PDS was first put in place in 1939 by the British government during the Second World War as a regulatory measure against speculative trade in foodgrains. Four phases in the functioning of this system have been identified[6] (Bapna 1990; Swaminathan 2000). The first phase (1939–60) saw a restricted coverage. The Fair Price Shop scheme was introduced in Bombay, and later extended to six other cities. Rural rationing was first introduced in the Malabar region of present-day Kerala during 1942–43, in response to mass mobilisation and the food crisis (Ramachandran 1997). After being briefly withdrawn at the end of the war, the PDS was expanded to a limited extent in the 1950s.

In the second phase (1960–78), major organisational changes were introduced. The Food Corporation of India (FCI) and the Agricultural Prices Commission (currently the Commission for Agricultural Costs and Prices) were set up in 1965. With droughts and price fluctuations in the mid-1960s, imports of foodgrains were at an all-time high (Suryanarayana 1995). Thereafter, the food and agricultural policy were geared towards achieving self-sufficiency in production, stabilising prices and protecting low-income consumers. Subsequently, imports of foodgrains reduced (Suryanarayana 1995). The growth of domestic production and buffer stocks in the third phase (1978–91) led to a sustained expansion of the PDS. With an expansion in the network of ration shops and quantities distributed, the rationing system came to be viewed as a poverty alleviation measure.

The fourth phase after 1991 was the period of structural adjustment in the economy and the weakening of the rationing system. The system was criticised as having an urban bias (Dantwala 1976; George 1984; Drèze and Sen 1989; Howes and Jha 1992), high costs and a high level of leakages (Bhagwati and Srinivasan 1993). There were proposals to dismantle or minimise the role of the FCI and replace the PDS with a system of food stamps (Bapna 1990; Bhagwati and Srinivasan 1993). The solution was seen to partly lie in targeting the rationing mechanism to poor households (Dantwala 1993; Radhakrishna et al. 1997).

In 1992, the rationing system was restructured to the Revamped PDS (RPDS). The RPDS was replaced by the Targeted PDS (TPDS) in 1997, which provided subsidised items to households identified as below the official poverty line. Swaminathan (2000) identified various costs of targeting, which include diluting rights, increasing exclusion errors, raising delivery and administrative costs and reducing political support for the programme. Following the shift to the targeted system, leakages have doubled (Planning Commission 2008).

During this phase, there were increases in the issue prices, and reduction in the quantity distributed through the PDS; stocks thereby increased. In April 2001, the People's Union for Civil Liberties filed a public interest litigation, which argued that the right to food is linked to the right to life guaranteed by the Constitution. The petition brought to attention the prevalence of widespread hunger and undernutrition in the country, even while there were excess food stocks in the FCI godowns. In response, the Supreme Court issued orders to strengthen various social security programmes, including the PDS and MDM. The orders recognised the right to food, and this was further strengthened by the NFSA.

To the four stages of development of the PDS, a fifth phase can be added, beginning from the mid-2000s and characterised by a partial recovery of the system through concerted efforts in certain states. In the discussions leading up to the passage of the NFSA, the proposal to dismantle the rationing system and put in place cash transfers or food coupons was re-energised (Basu 2011). Such proposals need to be taken together with the recent evidence of a revival of the PDS in some states after 2007, which was replicated in many other states by 2011–12.

Khera (2011b, p. 106) showed that the PDS is not 'uniformly and irreparably defunct'. The revival of the system, particularly in Chhattisgarh and Odisha, was validated by field studies as well (Aggarwal 2011; Khera 2011a; Puri 2012; Chatterjee 2014). The reforms include expansion of coverage, reduction of issue prices, technological changes to improve monitoring, increasing commissions of fair price shop dealers, collective management of ration shops, in addition to the inclusion of subsidised pulses and edible oil in a few states (Khera 2011a). The revival continued on to 2011–12, by which time more states such as Bihar, Assam and West Bengal had also begun to reform their rationing system (Himanshu and Sen 2013a). These reforms are reflected in a higher effect of the system on reducing poverty in these states after 2004–05 (Drèze and Khera 2013; Himanshu and Sen 2013a). The system became more inclusive by covering more households at lower MPCE levels and from the disadvantaged social groups (Rahman 2014). Although still high, leakages also reduced by 2011–12 (Drèze and Khera 2015).

The Aadhaar (Targeted Delivery of Financial and Other Subsidies, Benefits and Services) Act was implemented in 2016, and Aadhaar-based biometric authentication (ABBA) was imposed on the delivery of social security entitlements, such as mid-day meals and the PDS. This is in clear violation of the judgement passed by the Supreme Court in March 2014, whereby no one can be excluded from accessing entitlements due to the lack of an Aadhaar card.

In Delhi, a pilot of Aadhaar-enabled transactions through Point of Sale (PoS) devices was initiated in 42 ration shops in 2015. In spite of evidence of implementation problems with the PoS devices and Aadhaar authentication (Delhi Rozi Roti Adhikar Abhiyan and Satark Nagrik Sangathan 2017), this system was expanded to the remaining shops in January 2018. However, following complaints of exclusion of eligible beneficiaries, the Delhi government put Aadhaar-enabled PoS transactions on hold on 20 February 2018, and instead announced door-to-door delivery of rations directly to the beneficiaries.

The imposition of ABBA in Rajasthan and Jharkhand has excluded many vulnerable families from accessing rations, pensions and work, without affecting pilferage by dealers (Drèze, et al. 2017). More hard-hitting evidence of exclusion are the starvation deaths of the young and old following denial of rations to their families in the absence of Aadhaar seeding with PDS (Pandey 2017; Bhatnagar 2018a, 2018b; Right to Food Campaign 2018). These reports signal the relevance of the rationing system in the lives of the food-insecure population in the country.

Earlier studies

The nutritional impact of the rationing system has mainly been studied through intermediate outcomes such as the intake of nutrients. The effect of the system on calorie intake was found to be marginal just after the shift to the targeted system for wheat-purchasing households in rural areas (Kochar 2005). In later years, the PDS had a positive effect on the calorie intake for rice-purchasing households, with the system allowing for higher calorie consumption through unsubsidised items from other food groups as well (Kaul 2014). Kaushal and Muchomba (2015) did not find any effect of the system on nutrient intake. However, their analysis uses data until 2004–05, prior to the state-level reforms. Himanshu and Sen (2013b) concluded that the contribution of the rationing mechanism to calorie intake increased after the reforms, and estimated that a shift to cash transfers would cost many times more than the current system of Minimum Support Price–PDS to maintain the same levels of calorie intake. At the state level, Krishnamurthy, Pathania and Tandon (2014) found evidence of improved consumption of rice and calories in Chhattisgarh between 1999–2000 and 2009–10. In Odisha, the reformed PDS reduced calorie insecurity among beneficiary households, particularly for the economically and socially disadvantaged groups (Kumar et al. 2017). A field survey in the severely food-insecure district of Koraput in Odisha in 2012 showed that the PDS protected beneficiaries against shortfalls in foodgrains (Chatterjee 2014). Nevertheless, Chatterjee stressed the need to expand coverage further, as many vulnerable households were still excluded in this district. Rahman (2016) also found an improvement in nutrient intake and dietary quality in the Kalahandi–Balangir–Koraput (KBK) region of this state after the PDS was made universal in this region in 2008.

There have been fewer studies of the effect of the system on child anthropometry, and the available studies show a limited or no effect. Tarozzi (2005) studied the effect of a rise in PDS issue prices of rice in Andhra Pradesh in 1992–93 and concluded that the system had a limited impact on child anthropometric indicators at the time. At the national-level, Desai and Vanneman (2015) did not find any impact of the rationing system on the anthropometric indicators of under-five children in 2011–12. Thampi (2017) studied the state-level effects of the system and found an impact on the longer-term nutritional indicator in states where the PDS has been functioning well for many years and on the shorter-term indicator in states where it has revived in recent years.

Purchase of PDS cereals

To take account of the vast variations in implementation, states are divided into three groups on the basis of the changes in functioning after 2004, and a state-level analysis is conducted. Khera (2011b) classified states into functioning, reviving and languishing on the basis of whether the average per capita purchase of rationed rice or wheat in the state was higher than one kilogram per month. In this article, her classification is modified to combine the total purchase of rationed cereals by the household, and a benchmark of two kilograms per capita per month is used (Figure 20.2). The states in which the per capita monthly purchases exceeded two kilograms in all three years are the functioning states, those in which the purchases increased to two kilograms per capita are the reviving states, and the others are the languishing states. In Figure 20.2, states are arranged in descending order of PDS cereals purchases in 2004–05 within each group. The reviving states are further sub-divided into two, according to whether the average per capita quantity exceeded the benchmark in 2009–10 or 2011–12.

By this classification, more than half of the states in the country were either functioning or reviving by 2011–12. The functioning states comprise four north-eastern states, three southern states and two northern states. The states which revived by 2009–10 are Kerala, Chhattisgarh, Meghalaya and Odisha. Uttarakhand, Goa, Assam and Bihar joined this list by 2011–12. The rationing system in the remaining states is languishing, according to this indicator.

Expansion of coverage

To link the quantities of PDS cereals purchased with the extent of coverage by state, consider Figures 20.3 and 20.4, which show the percentages of households that purchased rice or wheat from the PDS in the rural and urban areas of four states in each group.[7] The state-wise indicators of utilisation of the PDS in terms of the proportions of households and monthly purchase

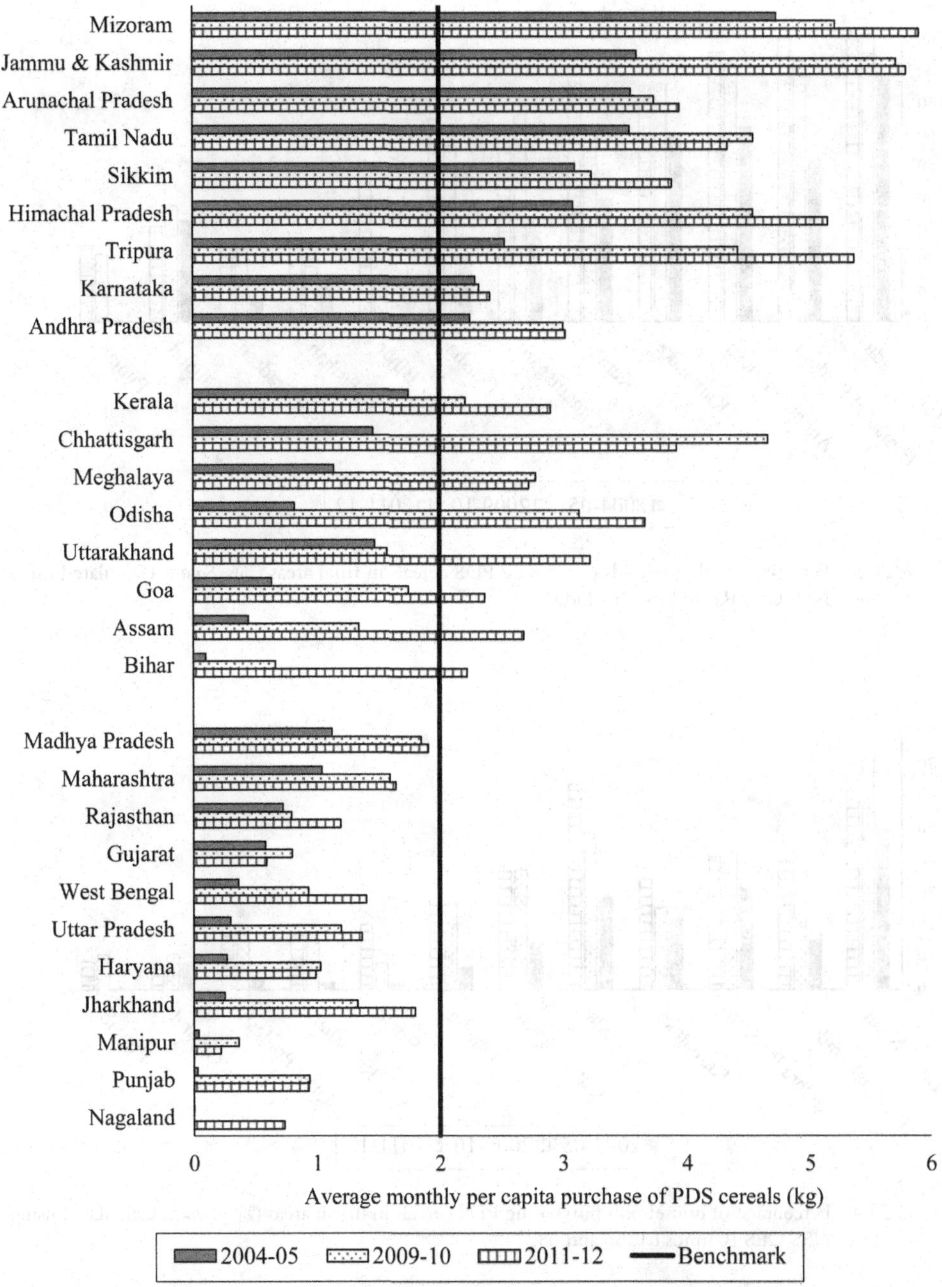

Figure 20.2 Average monthly per capita purchase of cereals from PDS (kg). *Source*: Calculated using NSS CES Rounds 61, 66 and 68.

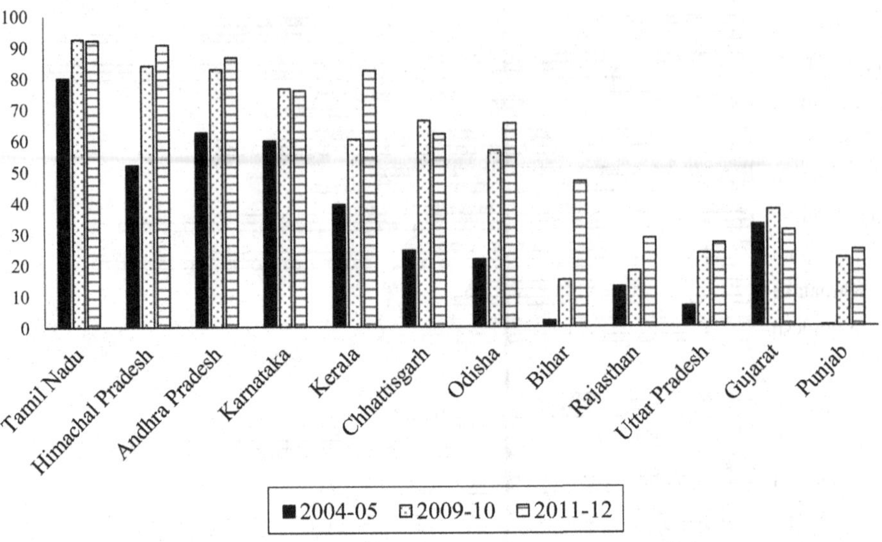

Figure 20.3 Percentage of households purchasing PDS cereals in rural areas (%). *Source*: Calculated using NSS CES Rounds 61, 66 and 68.

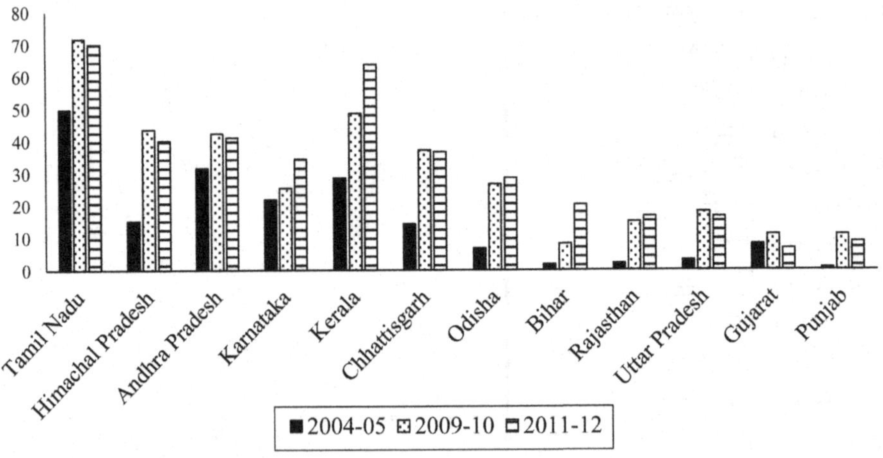

Figure 20.4 Percentage of households purchasing PDS cereals in urban areas (%). *Source*: Calculated using NSS CES Rounds 61, 66 and 68.

quantities reflect the improvements in the functioning and reach of the PDS in certain states over the past decade. These results need to be understood in the context of the targeting that was put in place in 1997. Ironically, the improvements have been noted in those states that have moved back to a more universal system along with other reforms and technological improvements. The revival of the PDS has therefore not only been sustained but has also inspired a similar revival in other states.

PDS as a counter to food budget squeeze?

The improvements in the functioning and reach of the system in terms of poverty reduction have been noted in earlier literature. However, in the context of the poverty–nutrition divergence, it is of interest to see whether there is also a divergence in the impact of the PDS on anthropometric indicators. This question arises in the context of an identified 'calorie consumption puzzle' – a long-term decline in the average intake of calories even with rising real consumption expenditures (Chandrasekhar and Ghosh 2003; Deaton and Drèze 2009).

Various explanations have been given to explain this puzzle, including declining calorie needs (Rao 2000; Deaton and Drèze 2009), falling purchasing power (Patnaik 2010), dietary diversification (Mittal 2007), under-reporting of meals eaten outside (Smith 2015), squeeze on the food budget (Basole and Basu 2015), and even voluntary choice of luxuries over food (Banerjee and Duflo 2011). It is likely that rather than one explanation for the entire economy, multiple explanations are plausible, each exerting their influence on different sections of society. Of these, the food budget squeeze hypothesis is a convincing explanation for the calorie intake decline among the poorer sections of the society. The rapid rise in non-food essentials such as health, education and, in particular, fuel absorbed the rise in total expenditure so that the real food expenditures remained stagnant over time (Basole and Basu 2015). Of the non-food essentials, the steepest increase was in real fuel expenditures. Basole and Basu (2015) use this to show the effect on calorie intake.

I therefore check to see whether the PDS could act as a counter to this food budget squeeze by using the implicit subsidy, as calculated in the previous section. I use the following equation to estimate it,

$$H = \beta_1 + \beta_2 \cdot Fuel + \beta_3 \cdot Sub + \beta_4 \cdot C + \varepsilon$$

where H refers to the anthropometric indicator of the child in the age group 7–12 years, *Fuel* refers to the share of fuel in the monthly per capita consumption expenditure of the household, *Sub* refers to the implicit subsidy through the purchase of PDS rice or wheat, and C includes the control variables, such as age and sex of the child, nutritional status and education of the mother, household income, social group, household size, literacy of the household head, household composition, rural/urban sector, state, source of drinking water and sanitation facilities. The dependent anthropometric variables are the weight-for-age, height-for-age and Body Mass Index (BMI)-for-age z-scores of the child.

The share of fuel in MPCE as a proxy for the food budget squeeze has had a negative and significant impact on all three child nutritional indicators (Table 20.2). The PDS as a source of subsidised cereals has helped in countering the effect of the food budget squeeze on nutritional status to an extent. This counter worked by reversing the worsening of the underweight parameter by half, and the BMI-for-age parameter by one-seventh. The results from this exercise could be extended to a deeper analysis at the state level in further research.

Conclusion

Following economic reforms, India has been one of the fastest growing countries in the world, but this is incongruent with the hunger and nutritional situation in the country. Indian children continue to be among the most undernourished in the world. Multiple starvation deaths have been recorded in different states over the past one year alone. Constructing hunger indexes for

Table 20.2 Impact on child anthropometry

Indicator	*Share of fuel in MPCE*	*PDS implicit subsidy*
Weight-for-age z-score	–0.10*	0.05*
	(0.06)	(0.03)
Height-for-age z-score	–0.14***	0.00
	(0.04)	(0.01)
BMI-for-age z-score	–0.26***	0.04**
	(0.04)	(0.02)

Source: Calculated using IHDS-II.
Note: *** $p<0.01$, ** $p<0.05$, * $p<0.1$.
Robust standard errors are given in parentheses.

states on the lines of the GHI shows that almost all states have a 'serious' or 'alarming' hunger and undernutrition situation. There is also a discrepancy between the income position and nutritional position of certain states. The available evidence suggests that economic growth has had a limited role in improving nutritional indicators.

One of the possible explanations identified for the weak relationship between economic growth and child nutritional indicators is that households may not be directing a sufficient share of their expenditures towards improving child nutrition. At least for the poorer sections, this could be an involuntary shift compelled by the squeeze on their food budget with rising expenditure on non-food essentials. In this context, I consider whether the PDS helps in meeting nutritional requirements through its provision of subsidised food. It is also of interest to understand the nutritional impact of the PDS in light of the recent reforms implemented in the system in certain states. A distinction was made between functioning, reviving and languishing states on the basis of their recent performance.

The analyses in this article showed that the PDS has reversed the adverse impact of the food budget squeeze on child nutritional indicators to an extent. I therefore argue that for the gains from economic growth to be fully reflected in nutritional parameters, systems such as the PDS need to be in place and their smooth functioning needs to be ensured by enforcing measures to eliminate corruption and reduce leakages. Such mechanisms would work towards improving 'access to adequate quantity of quality food at affordable prices', as ensured by the NFSA.

Notes

1 A stunted child has height-for-age at two or more standard deviations below the median of the reference population of the WHO Child Growth Standards.
2 This refers to low weight-for-age.
3 This refers to low weight-for-height.
4 The threshold for undernourishment is 80, for child wasting is 30, for child stunting is 70 and for child mortality is 35.
5 Telangana was combined with Andhra Pradesh as the NSS CES 2011–12 was conducted before the separation.
6 The descriptions of the first three phases draw mainly on Bapna (1990), and of the fourth phase on Swaminathan (2000).

7 Four states from each of the three groups of states are considered, due to their relatively larger sample sizes in the dataset used.

References

Aggarwal, Ankita. 2011. "The PDS in Rural Orissa: Against the Grain?" *Economic & Political Weekly* 46 (36): 21–23.

Banerjee, Abhijit V., and Esther Duflo. 2011. *Poor Economics: A Radical Rethinking of the Way to Fight Global Poverty*. New York: Public Affairs.

Bapna, S. L. 1990. "Food Security through the PDS: The Indian Experience." In *Increasing Access to Food: The Asian Experience*, edited by Davendra Singh Tyagi and Vijay Shankar Vyas, pp. 99–144. New Delhi: Sage Publications.

Basole, Amit, and Deepankar Basu. 2015. "Fuelling Calorie Intake Decline: Household-Level Evidence from Rural India." *World Development* 68: 82–95.

Basu, Kaushik. 2011. "India's Foodgrain Policy: An Economic Theory Perspective." *Economic & Political Weekly* 46 (5): 37–45.

Bhagwati, Jagdish, and Thirukodikaval Nilakanta Srinivasan. 1993. *India's Economic Reforms*. New Delhi: Ministry of Finance, Government of India.

Bhatnagar, Gaurav Vivek. 2018a. "Aadhaar and Hunger: Second Jharkhand Woman Starves to Death after Being Refused Rations." *The Wire*. 2 January. https://thewire.in/featured/aadhaar-hunger-jharkhand-starvation-death-rations.

—. 2018b. "Aadhaar Glitch: Another Woman Dies of Hunger in Jharkhand after Being Denied Ration, Say Activists." *The Wire*, 2 February. https://thewire.in/politics/aadhaar-glitch-another-woman-dies-hunger-jharkhand-denied-ration-say-activists.

Chandrasekhar, C. P., and Jayati Ghosh. 2003. "The Calorie Consumption Puzzle." *Business Line*, 11 February. https://www.thehindubusinessline.com/2003/02/11/stories/2003021100210900.htm.

Chatterjee, Mihika. 2014. "An Improved PDS in a 'Reviving' State: Food Security in Koraput, Odisha." *Economic & Political Weekly* 49 (45): 49–59.

Coffey, Diane, Angus Deaton, Jean Drèze, Dean Spears, and Alessandro Tarozzi. 2013. "Stunting among Children: Facts and Implications." *Economic & Political Weekly* 48 (34): 68–70.

Coffey, Diane, and Dean Spears. 2017. *Where India Goes: Abandoned Toilets, Stunted Development and the Costs of Caste*. Noida: Harper Collins.

Dantwala, M. L. 1976. "Agricultural Policy in India since Independence." *Indian Journal of Agricultural Economics* 31 (4): 31–53.

—. 1993. "Agricultural Policy: Prices and Public Distribution System – A Review." *Indian Journal of Agricultural Economics* 48 (2): 173–186.

Deaton, Angus. 2008. "Height, Health and Inequality: The Distribution of Adult Heights in India." *American Economic Review* 98 (2): 468–474.

—. 2013. *The Great Escape: Health, Wealth, and the Origins of Inequality*. Princeton: Princeton University Press.

Deaton, Angus, and Jean Drèze. 2009. "Food and Nutrition in India: Facts and Interpretations." *Economic & Political Weekly* 44 (7): 42–65.

Delhi Rozi Roti Adhikar Abhiyan and Satark Nagrik Sangathan. 2017. "Peoples' Assessment of the Implementation of Transparency, Grievance Redress and Accountability Measures of the National Food Security Act in Delhi." http://snsindia.org/wp-content/uploads/2018/03/Report-13-with-annexures-FINAL.pdf.

Desai, Sonalde, and Reeve Vanneman. 2015. "Enhancing Nutrition Security via India's National Food Security Act: Using an Axe Instead of a Scalpel?" *India Policy Forum (India Policy Forum)* 11: 67–113. https://www.ncbi.nlm.nih.gov/pmc/articles/PMC4811376/pdf/nihms-758663.pdf.

Drèze, Jean, Nazar Khalid, Reetika Khera, and Anmol Somanchi. 2017. "Aadhaar and Food Security in Jharkhand: Pain without Gain?" *Economic & Political Weekly* 52 (50): 50–59.

Drèze, Jean, and Amartya Sen. 1989. *Hunger and Public Action*. Oxford: Clarendon Press.

—. 2013. *An Uncertain Glory: India and Its Contradictions*. Princeton: Princeton University Press.

—. 2015. "Understanding Leakages in the Public Distribution System." *Economic & Political Weekly* 50 (7): 39–42.

George, P. S. 1984. "Some Aspects of Public Distribution of Foodgrains in India." *Economic & Political Weekly* 19 (39): A106–A110.

Gopalan, C., B.V. Rama Sastri, and S. C. Balasubramanian. 1991. *Nutritive Value of Indian Foods*. Hyderabad: National Institute of Nutrition, Indian Council of Medical Research.

Himanshu, and Abhijit Sen. 2011. "Why Not a Universal Food Security Legislation?" *Economic & Political Weekly* 46 (12): 38–47.

—. 2013a. "In-Kind Food Transfers – I: Impact on Poverty." *Economic & Political Weekly* 48 (45–46): 46–54.

—. 2013b. "In-Kind Food Transfers – II: Impact on Nutrition and Implications for Food Security and its Costs." *Economic & Political Weekly* 48 (47): 60–73.

Howes, Stephen, and Shikha Jha. 1992. "Urban Bias in Indian Public Distribution System." *Economic & Political Weekly* 27 (19): 1022–1030.

IFPRI/Welthungerhilfe/ Concern Worldwide. 2009. *Global Hunger Index: The Challenge of Hunger: Focus on Financial Crisis and Gender Inequality*. Washington, DC, Bonn, Dublin: International Food Policy Research Institute (IFPRI)/Welthungerhilfe/Concern Worldwide.

—. 2017. *Global Hunger Index: The Inequalities of Hunger*. Washington, DC, Bonn, Dublin: International Food Policy Research Institute (IFPRI)/Welthungerhilfe/Concern Worldwide.

IIPS and ICF. 2017. *National Family Health Survey (NFHS-4), 2015–16: India*. Mumbai: International Institute for Population Sciences (IIPS).

IIPS and Macro International. 2007. *National Family Health Survey (NFHS-3), 2005–06: India: Volume I*. Mumbai: International Institute for Population Sciences (IIPS).

Kaul, Tara. 2014. *Household Response to Food Subsidies: Evidence from India*. Working Paper. College Park: University of Maryland.

Kaushal, Neeraj, and Felix M Muchomba. 2015. "How Consumer Price Subsidies Affect Nutrition." *World Development* 74: 25–42.

Khera, Reetika. 2011a. "Revival of the Public Distribution System: Evidence and Explanations." *Economic & Political Weekly* 46 (44 & 45): 36–50.

—. 2011b. "Trends in Diversion of Grain from the Public Distribution System." *Economic & Political Weekly* 46 (21): 106–114.

Kjelsrud, Anders, and Rohini Somanathan. 2017. *Food Security and Child Malnutrition in India. Reference number F-35125-INC-1*. International Growth Centre. https://www.theigc.org/wp-content/uploads/2017/10/IGC_Final-report_Food-security-and-child-malnutrition-in-India-cover.pdf.

Kochar, Anjini. 2005. "Can Targeted Food Programs Improve Nutrition? An Empirical Analysis of India's Public Distribution System." *Economic Development & Cultural Change* 54 (1): 203–235.

Krishnamurthy, Prasad, Vikram Pathania, and Sharad Tandon. 2014. "Public Distribution System Reforms and Consumption in Chhattisgarh: A Comparative Empirical Analysis." *Economic & Political Weekly* 49 (8): 74–81.

Kumar, Anjani, Shinoj Parappurathu, Suresh C. Babu, and P. K. Joshi. 2017. "Can Better Governance Improve Food Security? An Assessment of the Public Food Distribution System in Odisha, India." *Food Security* 9: 1433–1445.

Menon, Purnima, Anil Deolalikar, and Anjor Bhaskar. 2009. *Comparisons of Hunger across States: India State Hunger Index*. Washington, DC, Bonn, Riverside: International Food Policy Research Institute.

MHFW. 2017. *NFHS-4 Factsheet*. Ministry of Health and Family Welfare (MHFW). http://rchiips.org/nfhs/pdf/NFHS4/India.pdf.

—. 2020. *NFHS-5, Key Indicators –22 States/ UTs from Phase-I*. Ministry of Health and Family Welfare (MHFW). http://rchiips.org/NFHS/NFHS-5_FCTS/NFHS-5%20State%20Factsheet%20Compendium_Phase-I.pdf.

Mittal, Surabhi. 2007. "What Affects Changes in Cereal Consumption?" *Economic & Political Weekly* 42 (5): 444–447.

Pandey, Prashant. 2017. "Jharkhand 'Starvation' Death: How Santoshi's Village Makes It to Two Meals a Day." *The Indian Express*, 29 October. http://indianexpress.com/article/india/santoshis-plate-jharkhand-starvation-death-aadhaar-pds-link-scheme-village-4911306/.

Patnaik, Utsa. 2010. "A Critical Look at Some Propositions on Consumption and Poverty." *Economic & Political Weekly* 45 (6): 74–80.

Planning Commission. 2008. "Nutrition and Social Safety Net." In *Eleventh Five-Year Plan 2007-12*, Volume II, 128–161. New Delhi: Oxford University Press.

Puri, Raghav. 2012. "Reforming the Public Distribution System: Lessons from Chhattisgarh." *Economic & Political Weekly* 47 (5): 21–23.

Radhakrishna, Rokkam, Kalanidhi Subbarao, Sulibhavi Indrakant, and Chagant Ravi. 1997. *India's Public Distribution System: A National and International Perspective.* Discussion Paper No. 380. Washington, DC: The World Bank.

Rahman, Andaleeb. 2014. "Revival of Rural Public Distribution System: Expansion and Outreach." *Economic & Political Weekly* 49 (20): 62–68.

—. 2016. "Universal Food Security Program and Nutritional Intake: Evidence from the Hunger Prone KBK Districts in Odisha." *Food Policy* 63: 73–86.

Ramachandran, V. K. 1997. "Kerala's Development Achievements." In *Indian Development: Selected Regional Perspectives*, edited by Jean Drèze and Amartya Sen, pp. 205–356. New Delhi: Oxford University Press.

Ramalingaswami, Vulimiri, Urban Jonsson, and Jon Rohde. 1996. *Commentary: The Asian Enigma.* The Progress of Nations 1996. UNICEF. https://www.unicef.org/pon96/nuenigma.htm.

Rao, C. H. Hanumantha. 2000. "Declining Demand for Foodgrains in Rural India: Causes and Implications." *Economic & Political Weekly* 35 (4): 201–206.

Right to Food Campaign. 2018. "Starvation Deaths." *Letters, Economic & Political Weekly* 53 (28): 4.

—. 2020. "Hunger Watch." 9 December. https://docs.google.com/document/d/1b3JgelVeO40TYfc-TujtJoE42FKea5vADJhEu8RGGog/edit.

Singh, Abhijeet, Albert Park, and Stefan Dercon. 2014. "School Meals as a Safety Net: An Evaluation of the Mid-Day Meal Scheme in India." *Economic Development and Cultural Change* 62 (2): 275–306.

Smith, Lisa C. 2015. "The Great Indian Calorie Debate: Explaining Rising Undernourishment during India's Rapid Economic Growth." *Food Policy* 50: 53–67.

Spears, Dean. 2013. *How Much International Variation in Child Height Can Sanitation Explain?* Policy Research Working Paper 6351. Washington, DC: World Bank. http://documents.worldbank.org/curated/en/449651468191643600/pdf/wps6351.pdf.

Suryanarayana, M. H. 1995. "PDS: Beyond Implicit Subsidy and Urban Bias – The Indian Experience." *Food Policy* 20 (4): 259–278.

Swaminathan, Madhura. 2000. *Weakening Welfare.* New Delhi: LeftWord Books.

Tarozzi, Alessandro. 2005. "The Indian Public Distribution System as Provider of Food Security: Evidence from Child Nutrition in Andhra Pradesh." *European Economic Review* 49: 1305–1330.

Thampi, Anjana. 2017. "The Impact of the Public Distribution System in India." *Indian Journal of Human Development* 10 (3): 353–365.

—. 2019. "Has the Economy Left the Children Behind? Nutritional Immiserization in India." In *Immiserizing Growth: When Growth Fails the Poor*, edited by Ravi Kanbur, Richard Sandbrook and Paul Shaffer, 176–202. Oxford: Oxford University Press.

Vollmer, Sebastian, Kenneth Harttgen, Malavika A. Subramanyam, Jocelyn Finlay, Stephan Klasen, and Sankaran V. Subramanian. 2014. "Association Between Economic Growth and Early Childhood Undernutrition: Evidence from 121 Demographic and Health Surveys from 36 Low-Income and Middle-Income Countries." *Lancet Global Health* 2 (4): e225–e234.

WHO. 2017. *Global Targets Tracking Tool, Version 2.3.* World Health Organization (WHO). https://www.who.int/tools/global-targets-tracking-tool

21

PUBLIC DISTRIBUTION SYSTEM IN THE POST-REFORM PERIOD

A comparative study of Tamil Nadu and West Bengal

Marina Rai

An overview of the Public Distribution System (PDS) in India

The Public Distribution System (PDS) is the vital policy affecting the food security of the people in India. According to Swaminathan (2000, p. 14), 'The PDS is a rationing mechanism that entitles households to specified quantities of selected commodities at subsidized prices'. Bapna (1990) has stated the historical objectives of PDS as maintaining price stability, increasing the welfare facilities for the poor (by providing access to basic food at reasonable prices), rationing during situations of scarcity and keeping a check on private trade. The first two objectives remain very important even in the post-liberalisation period, as domestic prices are easily affected by international price fluctuations, and in a situation of widespread malnutrition and inflation in food prices, access to basic food at reasonable prices has continued to remain a very important policy intervention (Swaminathan 2009). Mooij (1998) observed that the development of PDS has been influenced by the specific political–economic context in which it was shaped. The PDS food policy has played a vital role in establishing political legitimacy not only at the national level but also in the international arena.

The PDS in India has evolved through various phases from 1939 till now (Swaminathan 2009). The period after 1991, considered as the fourth phase, started when India adopted the Structural Adjustment Programme (SAP) in 1991, which imposed stress on the reduction of government subsidy and targeting was portrayed as a solution. The PDS since then has been a universal one which included the whole population and made no exclusion on the basis of income criteria and no differentiation in terms of pricing and quantity of entitlement. Thus the most significant change made after 1991 was the replacement of the Universal Public Distribution System (UPDS) by a targeted policy with the objectives of economic liberalisation when orthodox changes in the form of targeting led to price hikes of PDS commodities and exclusions of large sections of the population. The government of India introduced the Targeted Public Distribution System (TPDS) in 1997 in order to curtail food subsidy. The income poverty line was used to demarcate 'poor' and 'non-poor' households on the basis of which the targeting of poor households was initiated. Targeted PDS differs from the earlier version of PDS with respect to targeting and dual pricing (Swaminathan 2000). Dual pricing involved dividing

DOI: 10.4324/9780367855741-21

the entire population into Below Poverty Line (BPL) and Above Poverty Line (APL) categories based on the poverty line and treating the two groups differently in terms of quantities and prices. The BPL population were entitled to higher quantities at lower prices and the APL population were entitled to lower quantities at higher prices.

However, there have been further changes in the policy of entitlement and distribution of foodgrains. The National Food Security Act (NFSA) was implemented with effect from 5 July 2013, which brought changes to various key issues such as the categorisation of beneficiaries, cash transfers and cost sharing between the centre and states. The civil society groups and food activists of the Right to Food Campaign dissented on several grounds. They stated that instead of moving forward the recommendations were a leap backwards, as the existing entitlements were also removed. The Right to Food Campaign states that 'PDS is the backbone of food security in India and introducing any cash component in it would severely undermine most people's food security, particularly of the poor and other vulnerable groups' (Right to Food Campaign 2013).

The debate on whether the PDS should be 'universal' or 'targeted' has been one of the widely discussed issues in the context of food security policies in India.

An influential study by World Bank during 1996 and some other researches (Nawani, 1994, Dev and Suryanarayana, 1991) provided a strong argument for the implementation of targeted PDS in India instead of a universal program. The efficient utilisation of food subsidy which will not burden fiscal resources of government was presumed to be the benefit of targeting in PDS. Universal PDS was found to be fiscally costly and market distorting. Transfer cost of subsidy was also found to be very high. When targeting is done, then a large proportion of household requirement of the target population can be fulfilled by enhancing the scale, which would also generate a commitment on the part of card holders. The diversion was huge and the non-poor were also getting unnecessary benefits.

Dev and Suryanarayana (1991) studied the utilisation of PDS using the NSS data for the year 1986–87 and found that PDS was no longer urban biased except for West Bengal but the poorest sections were not protected effectively by PDS. Nawani (1994) observed that universal coverage provided grounds for the main weakness of PDS, i.e. not reaching the poor effectively. The World Bank (1991) highlighted the urgent need for short-term restraint in food subsidy and improving the impact of food distribution programmes through targeting of PDS.

Bhagwati and Srinivasan (1993) advocated for reforms in favour of targeting to protect the poor effectively during macroeconomic adjustments. They argued that the inefficiencies on the delivery side are due to poor targeting. They suggested alternatives for better targeting of the poor through a means test, through entrusting the task to local bodies and social action groups at the block or village level and through commodity-based targeting by confining the PDS to coarse cereals and excluding sugar and vegetable oil from the PDS.

Jha and Srinivasan (2001) examined how the benefit–cost ratio for PDS increases when subsidies are targeted at the poor, using counter-factual simulations. However, targeted PDS also has several problems. Hence they supported geographical targeting, which involves universal coverage of areas with a high concentration of poverty, especially smaller administrative units such as villages. On a similar note, Kochar (2005) analysed that a universal programme is difficult to sustain because of the magnitude of income transfers required for effective implementation. So, if poverty is regionally concentrated, then regional targeting would be effective.

However, the implementation of TPDS proved to be difficult with institutional constraints and vested interests which were overlooked by the politicians and policy makers (Mooij 1999). Increased errors of wrong exclusion, i.e. the needy population not being covered by the PDS, have been highlighted by several case studies (Swaminathan 2009; Swaminathan and Mishra 2001; Khera 2009; Dreze 2004).

Dreze (2004) argued that the official distribution of 'BPL' and 'APL' households for PDS benefits reduces direct incentives to correctly monitor the PDS, where local monitoring authorities usually belong to an APL group. Thus it raises the importance of universalisation of PDS. He found that effective implementation of food security programmes was dependent on the vigilance of the public perception of rights and their participation. He observed that endemic corruption has badly affected PDS and it is rampant especially in the northern states like Bihar and Jharkhand. Dreze gave examples of low corruption/leakages in grains of PDS in South India compared to North India; where there is sharp awareness of their entitlements and of the redressal mechanism, corruption and leakages are found to be very low.

Khera (2009) argued that if PDS is not universal then exclusion errors are unavoidable. The costs associated with correct identification of households are also large, and universal PDS can thrive as it improves the financial viability of fair price shops which in turn can possibly help in reducing leakages from the PDS.

Ghosh (2010) suggested that the benefit of universalisation of a public food programme will outweigh its economic cost. According to her it provides the economies of scale, it reduces transaction cost and administrative inconvenience and associated errors; it gives incentive to politically influential better off groups to provide adequate vigilance for well-functioning of the system. She rejected the popular notion of high cost of food subsidies associated with a universal scheme providing empirical observation on it.

Himanshu and Sen (2011) put forth their arguments on the National Advisory Council's final proposal on NFSA, arguing that the shift from universal to targeted PDS has in fact increased inefficiency and leakages and a universal NFSA is not only desirable, it is also a more efficient and feasible way to ensure food security for all.

India has witnessed various modifications in the PDS policies and its changing objectives complying with the necessity of the socio-political and economic situation since its inception in 1939. However, ensuring food security to the poor and vulnerable section has remained one of the important objectives at all times. The NFSA, which targets only two-thirds of the population (75 per cent of the rural population and 50 per cent of the urban population), is also a form of TPDS, except that the dual pricing system is forgone. And this process of the identification of the two-thirds population is susceptible to targeting errors. Hence the debate on Universal PDS versus Targeted PDS still remains pertinent in terms of assessing the food security policy. However, there is a lack of an exhaustive comparative study for an extended time period between the two policies, UPDS and TPDS, in two states which had similar stature in terms of access to PDS when PDS was universal in nature.

Objectives

The study is intended mainly to determine which policy, whether the 'Universal' or the 'Targeted' policy is better for a public distribution system in India. Keeping it as the broad objective of the study, first a comparison of the coverage provided by the Public Distribution System in two states as well as all of India is done in terms of participation and percentage of households benefitting from PDS in both the rural and urban sector. Secondly, targeting errors of coverage are determined and an assessment is made for the two states and for the all India level. The last objective is to compare the effectiveness of the Universal PDS in Tamil Nadu and Targeted PDS in West Bengal, as a measure of food security. In this paper, a comparative study of the policy of UPDS and TPDS is done by evaluating the performance of these policies in Tamil Nadu and West Bengal, respectively

In the context of changing PDS policies, Tamil Nadu was the only state in India which had gone against the central government policy of targeting and maintaining a system of Universal

PDS even after 1997. Later, on 1 November 2016, Tamil Nadu became the last state of the country to implement the NFSA after resisting it for three years (Govindarajan 2016). However, the act has been modified for Tamil Nadu specifically to ensure unfettered supply of rice to rice card holders, thereby maintaining the universal feature of PDS in the state.

West Bengal is chosen among all the other states implementing TPDS for comparison with Tamil Nadu because before the implementation of TPDS, West Bengal and Tamil Nadu were in a similar position in terms of state distribution of PDS foodgrains and poverty. Mooij (1999) represented the data for state distribution of PDS foodgrains and poverty, providing figures for different states. From the table provided by Mooij (1999), from 1986 to 1996, the average annual lifting of PDS foodgrains was higher for West Bengal (1454 thousand tonnes) than Tamil Nadu (1011 thousand tonnes), which can be attributed to the higher population of West Bengal. However, the per capita distribution of foodgrains in 1993–94 was the same, which is 19 kilograms per year in both Tamil Nadu and West Bengal. At the same time, the percentage of people below the poverty line was also the same at 35 per cent both in West Bengal and Tamil Nadu. Such similar statistics for the two states is also evident from the data and observations for the year 1993–94, used in the analysis later. Hence the differences thereafter in participation in PDS and the share of benefits to the poor can be subjected to the pursuance of the respective policies. Another similarity between Tamil Nadu and West Bengal is that both states are rice-growing states and rice forms the staple diet in both states. Hence, West Bengal would be an appropriate representative state among various other states with TPDS to analyse how the policies affected the food security situation. It would therefore be possible to analyse the specific impacts of targeting policy and draw conclusions on how effective the policy is in terms of participation or coverage, targeting errors as well as effectiveness in ensuring food security with respect to the universal policy.

Data and methodology

The evaluation of PDS policies is done taking three different time periods: 1993–94, which is before the implementation of TPDS, 2004–05 and 2009–10, after the implementation of the policy. National Sample Survey Organisation (NSSO) 50th Round (1993–94), 61st Round (2004–05) and 66th Round (2009–10) 'Household Consumer Expenditure' unit-level data have been used in the analysis. The data have been computed and tabulated at the household level for Tamil Nadu, West Bengal and all India, separately for both rural and urban sectors according to social groups and monthly per capita consumer expenditure (MPCE) decile classes. Data from reports of the National Family Health Survey; NFHS-2 (1998–99) and NFHS-3 (2005–06) are also used in the analysis.

Tables, line charts and bar diagrams are used in this analysis. A comparison of participation in PDS according to income deciles and social group between the two states as well as with 'all India' is done for rural and urban sectors separately. The measurement of targeting errors in PDS is done for the two states and all India, following the method used by Cornia and Stewart (1993) which is discussed later in detail in the analysis of targeting errors. An evaluation of the effectiveness of PDS is done by comparing input and outcome indicators used by the reports on food insecurity.

The MPCE decile classes in consideration are formed with reference to the NSS division of MPCE separately for rural and urban sectors. Each NSS Round divides the rural/urban population into 12 classes according to their MPCE. The class limits are so chosen that the two pairs of classes, one each at the ends, i.e. the lower two classes and the upper two classes, approximately contain an estimated 5 per cent of the population. Each of the remaining eight classes at the mid-

Table 21.1 MPCE decile class limits (URP)

MPCE Decile	*1993–94*		*2004–05*		*2009–10*	
	Rural	*Urban*	*Rural*	*Urban*	*Rural*	*Urban*
1	0–140	0–190	0–270	0–355	0–450	0–642
2	140–165	190–230	270–320	355–485	450–537	642–797
3	165–190	230–265	320–365	485–580	537–613	797–945
4	190–210	265–310	365–410	580–675	613–685	945–1114
5	210–235	310–355	410–455	675–790	685–765	1114–1307
6	235–265	355–410	455–510	790–930	765–853	1307–1543
7	265–300	410–490	510–580	930–1100	853–974	1543–1843
8	300–355	490–605	580–690	1100–1380	974–1144	1843–2303
9	355–455	605–825	690–890	1380–1880	1144–1477	2303–3166
10	455 & above	825 & above	890 & above	1880 & above	1477 & above	3166 & above

Source: NSSO Reports, 50th Round (1993–94), 61st Round (2004–05) and 66th Round (2009–10).

dle approximately contains an estimated 10 per cent of the rural/urban population. However, in this analysis, the lower end two classes are combined as one class, so that the lowest class also has approximately 10 per cent of the population and the same is done for the upper two classes. This results in the formation of ten classes or deciles, each class containing approximately an estimated 10 per cent of the rural/urban population. The decile classes are in ascending order such that the lowest decile 1 corresponds to the lowest income group and decile 10 indicates the 10 per cent population with the highest income. The MPCE decile classes are formed according to the class limits provided by the three NSS Rounds in consideration as shown in Table 21.1.

The reference period for the data used in tabulation and analysis is taken as 'last 30 days', i.e. the Uniform Reference Period (URP), in order to facilitate comparison between the three rounds, as the data for the 50th Round is recorded only for a 30-day period. The study is exclusively focused on the public distribution of food; hence the commodities under consideration are rice, wheat/atta and sugar.

Participation of households in PDS

The distribution of subsidised foodgrains through fair price shops is carried out on account of the ration cards issued by the government to the beneficiary households. No household was excluded from the rationing scheme prior to 1997; however, after 1997 households were issued ration cards on the basis of income criteria. The NSSO 61st Round (2004–05) provides the data for possession of a ration card, i.e. whether a household possess a ration card or not. The distribution of households by types of ration card possessed (supply and issue prices of subsidised foodgrains varied for each category), viz. Antyodaya Anna Yojana (AAY), Above Poverty Line (APL) and Below Poverty Line (BPL) are also available for 2004–05. However, such information is not available for the other two time periods in consideration. It should be noted that Tamil Nadu issues Rice cards, AAY cards, Sugar cards and No Commodity Cards. But NSSO (2004–05) provides data on the type of ration card possessed according to AAY, BPL and Others category for Tamil Nadu also.

Tables 21.2 and 21.3 show the percentage distribution of households by type of ration card possessed for the year 2004–05 in the rural and urban sectors, respectively. 'Others' category in the table refers to the households with an APL card.

Table 21.2 Distribution of households by type of ration card possessed in 2004–05 according to MPCE class for rural sector (%)

Rural	*Antyodaya*			*BPL*			*Others*		
MPCE Class	*Tamil Nadu*	*West Bengal*	*All India*	*Tamil Nadu*	*West Bengal*	*All India*	*Tamil Nadu*	*West Bengal*	*All India*
01	1.78	8.73	8.99	26.82	47.27	52.11	71.41	44.00	38.90
02	2.27	9.31	6.49	34.18	42.91	44.51	63.54	47.77	49.00
03	1.92	2.92	4.64	28.03	38.66	42.55	70.05	58.42	52.81
04	0.71	1.93	3.61	26.16	34.68	37.30	73.13	63.39	59.09
05	2.35	6.21	4.00	21.10	37.02	35.95	76.55	56.78	60.05
06	2.83	3.91	3.69	24.36	34.86	33.26	72.80	61.23	63.05
07	1.40	2.08	2.49	19.51	28.41	28.85	79.08	69.50	68.67
08	1.90	1.70	2.28	15.69	22.84	26.19	82.41	75.46	71.53
09	0.69	3.03	1.61	13.55	18.73	22.43	85.77	78.23	75.97
10	0.93	0.74	1.13	11.06	12.46	16.17	88.01	86.80	82.70
All Classes	1.65	3.48	3.62	21.17	29.80	32.64	77.18	66.72	63.74

Source: Calculated from unit level record NSSO 61st Round (2004–05).

Table 21.3 Distribution of households by type of ration card possessed in 2004–05 according to MPCE class for urban sector (%)

Urban	*Antyodaya*			*BPL*			*Others*		
MPCE Class	*Tamil Nadu*	*West Bengal*	*All India*	*Tamil Nadu*	*West Bengal*	*All India*	*Tamil Nadu*	*West Bengal*	*All India*
01	5.50	4.29	5.35	33.60	32.00	39.01	60.91	63.71	55.65
02	0.99	2.96	2.33	33.53	30.66	32.76	65.49	66.38	64.90
03	1.52	0.21	2.33	22.55	16.12	25.55	75.93	83.67	72.12
04	0.86	1.91	1.48	21.23	16.52	22.89	77.91	81.57	75.63
05	0.88	0.00	0.80	15.33	12.86	16.34	83.78	87.14	82.86
06	0.00	1.45	0.44	18.38	18.85	14.06	81.62	79.70	85.50
07	0.00	0.25	0.66	11.39	5.12	9.58	88.61	94.63	89.75
08	0.00	0.00	0.16	10.56	1.19	6.37	89.44	98.81	93.47
09	0.00	0.45	0.16	8.32	1.33	3.35	91.68	98.22	96.48
10	0.00	0.33	0.12	3.09	0.66	2.00	96.91	99.01	97.87
All Classes	0.74	0.97	1.22	16.45	10.98	15.71	82.81	88.05	83.07

Source: Calculated from unit level record NSSO 61st Round (2004–05).

It is evident from Tables 21.2 and 21.3 that even the higher MPCE class (from 6 to 10) households possess the Antyodaya and BPL ration cards in both rural and urban sectors of Tamil Nadu, West Bengal and All India, except for urban Tamil Nadu where the higher MPCE decile class households do not possess AAY ration cards. On the other hand, it is also worth noting that the lowest MPCE decile households also fall in the 'Others' category instead of possessing AAY or BPL ration cards. This indicates the failures in the identification and issuance of ration cards to eligible households in both urban and rural sectors.

Table 21.4 Percentage of households possessing ration card and percentage of households purchasing from PDS in 2004–05.

2004–05	*Rural*		*Urban*	
	Possess ration card	*Purchase from PDS*	*Possess ration card*	*Purchase from PDS*
All India	81.44	31.31	67.03	18.71
Tamil Nadu	89.24	88.16	77.58	70.95
West Bengal	91.65	24.25	80.43	13.32

Source: Calculated from unit level record NSSO 61st Round (2004–05).

Possession of a ration card endows a household the right to buy subsidised foodgrains or allows participation in PDS. But mere possession of a ration card does not imply benefitting from the PDS. There are other factors which have to be taken into account like household income, tastes, local availability of ration shops, ease of obtaining ration cards, the issue price, prices of market goods that are close substitutes e.g. market price of rice, wheat (Dutta and Ramaswami 2001). Since we are considering the public distribution of food, the households actually benefitting from PDS can be taken as the households consuming rice, wheat/atta and sugar (either one or two or all of them) from PDS. Hence, the juxtaposition of the percentage of households possessing a ration card and the percentage of households consuming from PDS in the same time period is shown in Table 21.4 to facilitate comparison between the two.

Table 21.4 shows a significant difference between the percentages of households possessing ration cards and households actually using the ration card to purchase from PDS in West Bengal and all India, both for the rural and urban sectors. As such, in rural West Bengal, 91.5 per cent of households possess a ration card out of total rural households but only 24.5 per cent purchased from PDS out of total rural households. A similar difference can be seen in the case of urban West Bengal and at the all-India level. However, such difference is negligible in the case of Tamil Nadu, as 89.24 per cent and 77.58 per cent of total households possess a ration card and 88.24 per cent and 70. 95 per cent of total households purchased from PDS in rural and urban sectors respectively. Such higher utilisation of PDS in Tamil Nadu can be attributed to its implementation of inclusive universal PDS. But the gap is substantial in the case of West Bengal and all India. Hence, possession of a ration card does not imply participating in PDS and realising its benefit. Thus to determine the households acquiring benefit through PDS, taking account of mere possession of ration cards by households would be inappropriate. Hence 'participation' would imply a household actually utilising PDS. To compare the PDS participation across three different time periods, the percentage of households consuming rice, wheat/atta and sugar (either one or two or all of them) from PDS has been taken under consideration.

Figure 21.1 shows the percentage of households purchasing from PDS for three time periods in Tamil Nadu, West Bengal and all India for both the rural and urban sectors. It can be seen from Figure 21.1 that, before the implementation of PDS, i.e. 1993–94, the participation in PDS in West Bengal was higher in comparison to Tamil Nadu and all India in the rural sector. In the case of the urban sector, participation was also greater than all India level and slightly lower than that of Tamil Nadu. However, as TPDS was implemented in West Bengal and all India in 1997, excluding Tamil Nadu, the figures for 2004–05 reveal that participation of households in West Bengal and all India declined sharply in both rural and urban sectors. In contrast to this, participation of households in Tamil Nadu increased in 2004–05 in both sectors. The policy

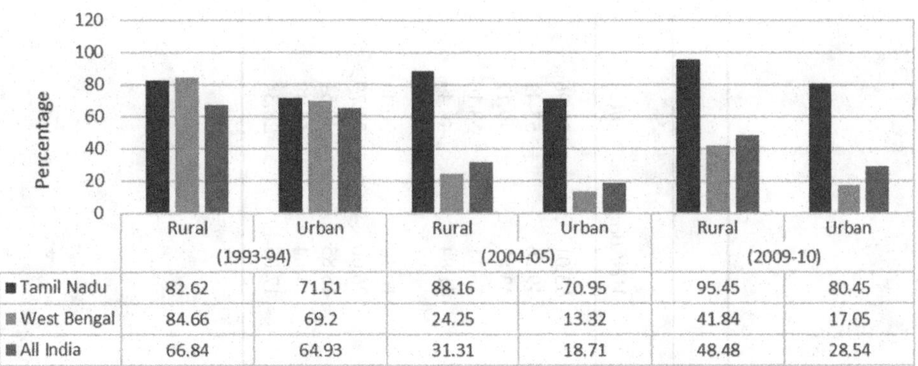

	Rural (1993-94)	Urban (1993-94)	Rural (2004-05)	Urban (2004-05)	Rural (2009-10)	Urban (2009-10)
■ Tamil Nadu	82.62	71.51	88.16	70.95	95.45	80.45
■ West Bengal	84.66	69.2	24.25	13.32	41.84	17.05
■ All India	66.84	64.93	31.31	18.71	48.48	28.54

Figure 21.1 Percentage of households consuming from PDS. *Source*: Calculated from unit level record NSSO 50th (1993–94), 61st (2004–05) and 66th Round (2009–10).

differences, i.e. Tamil Nadu being the only state resorting to UPDS even after 1997, accounts for this vast difference in the percentage of participation of households. This is mainly because UPDS in Tamil Nadu is more inclusive, unlike TPDS in West Bengal and other states excluding a large section of the population by dividing into APL and BPL categories with different issue prices for each category. Even though in 2009–10, the participation in PDS increased for both West Bengal and All India, the participation in Tamil Nadu was very high.

A distinctive feature of Indian society is the existence of social institutions like caste, religion and the socio-cultural customs and practices associated with it. The caste system practised for centuries has segregated the Indian society since its inception, as the higher castes enjoyed higher social status and economic prosperity whereas the lower castes were treated as 'untouchables', preordained to serve the higher castes. In many cases the caste hierarchy is reflected in the discrimination faced by the Dalits or Scheduled Castes (SC) and the Adivasis or Scheduled Tribes (ST). Thorat and Lee (2005) observed that the patterns of exclusion and caste discrimination also afflict food security programmes like PDS and Mid-day Meal Scheme (MDMS). In case of PDS, the main hindrance for Dalit access to PDS, have been discrimination in quantity and price, caste-based favouritism and 'untouchability' practices of the PDS dealer. In this backdrop it becomes necessary to perceive the pattern of participation of households in PDS according to social groups.

Table 21.5 shows the percentage of participation of households in rural and urban sectors for three time periods according to social groups. In the year 1993–94, the participation of Others (general) social group households was higher than that of SC/ST households, but in the latter two periods the participation of SC/ST households was higher than that of 'Others' category households for Tamil Nadu, West Bengal and all India for both sectors. This suggests that the overtime exclusion on the basis of caste in terms of access to PDS decreased to some extent in Tamil Nadu and West Bengal as well as on an all-India level. However, in 2004–05 the consumption from PDS by all social categories declined, with a sharper decline in the case of SC/ST households in West Bengal and all India, which can be a consequence of TPDS. In 2009–10, the condition improved slightly – however, they lagged far behind Tamil Nadu.

To evaluate the PDS policy, it is important to examine whether the benefits of the programme are accruing to the target population or not. The main target of PDS is the population with low incomes or low MPCE classes; as such the participation in PDS should be higher for the low income households. Figures 21.2 to Figure 21.5 are PDS usage curves displaying the

Table 21.5 Percentage of households consuming from PDS by social group

Social Group	*1993–94*			*2004–05*			*2009–10*		
Rural	*Tamil Nadu*	*West Bengal*	*All India*	*Tamil Nadu*	*West Bengal*	*All India*	*Tamil Nadu*	*West Bengal*	*All India*
ST	84.75	73.80	60.68	80.65	31.60	39.98	100.00	53.01	58.96
SC	79.85	85.93	62.05	91.26	33.27	35.81	95.96	49.56	53.41
OBC	–	–	–	87.81	23.91	31.06	95.25	43.87	49.17
Others	83.55	85.65	69.47	64.67	18.29	24.31	92.94	36.11	38.10
Total	82.62	84.66	66.84	88.16	24.25	31.32	95.45	41.84	48.49
Urban									
ST	66.04	67.66	52.75	56.20	23.70	18.84	89.72	16.12	30.40
SC	66.12	58.77	60.49	77.44	17.86	22.65	89.09	26.06	35.79
OBC	–	–	–	72.17	25.46	29.26	80.69	18.85	40.54
Others	72.55	71.49	66.17	52.93	11.22	9.40	59.51	14.64	15.48
Total	71.51	69.20	64.93	70.95	13.30	18.71	80.45	17.05	28.54

Source: Calculated from unit level record NSSO 50th (1993–94), 61st (2004–05) and 66th Round (2009–10).

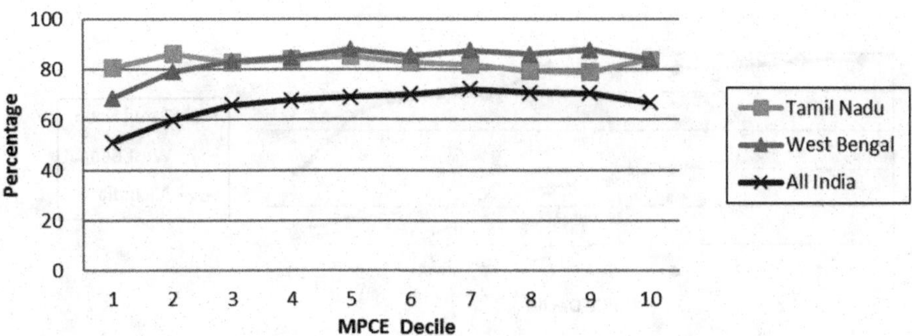

Figure 21.2 PDS use by decile group in rural sector, 1993–94. *Source*: Data calculated from unit level record NSSO 50th Round (1993–94).

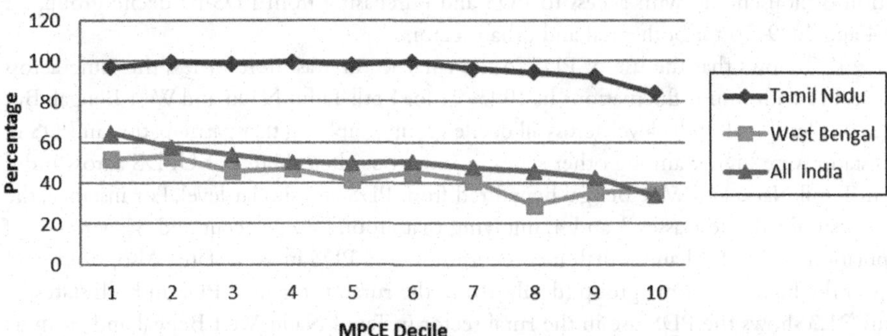

Figure 21.3 PDS use by decile group in rural sector, 2009–10. *Source*: Data calculated from unit level record NSSO 66th Round (2009–10).

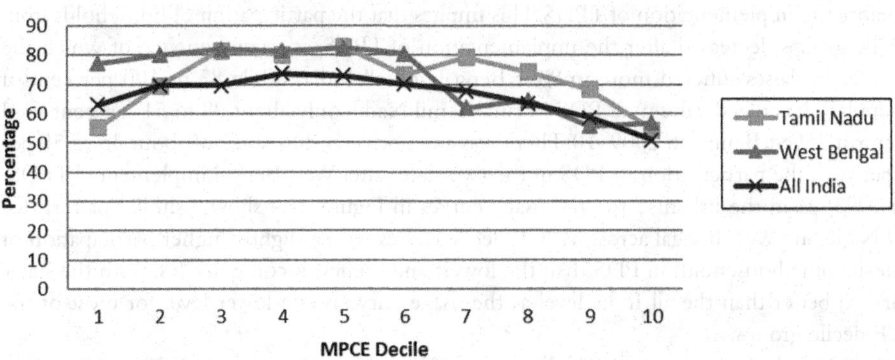

Figure 21.4 PDS use by decile group in urban sector, 1993–94. *Source*: Data calculated from unit level record NSSO 50th Round (1993–94).

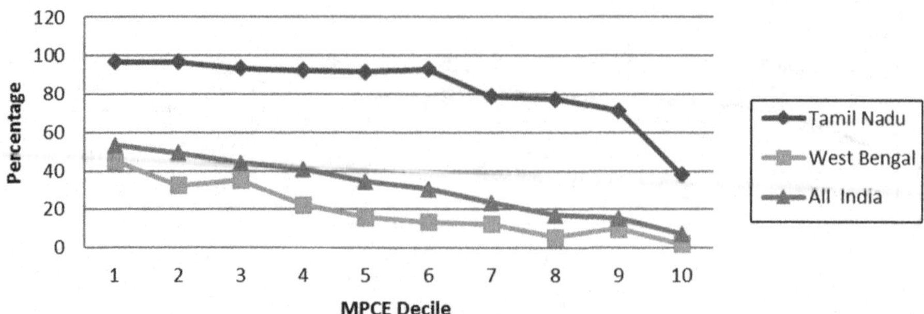

Figure 21.5 PDS use by decile group in urban sector, 2009–10. *Source*: Data calculated from unit level record NSSO 66th Round (2009–10).

proportion of households, with access to PDS and purchasing from PDS by decile group, for 1993–94 and 2009–10 for both rural and urban sectors.

Figure 21.2 shows that the use of PDS in the rural sector was more or less the same across MPCE deciles with minor fluctuations in 1993–94 for both Tamil Nadu and West Bengal. But the usage was less for all India level across all decile groups implying that participation in PDS in the two states were higher among other states in India. So when there was UPDS across India, people in Tamil Nadu and West Bengal benefitted from PDS at a similar level. For instance, the curves overlap for decile classes 3 and 4, implying that around 83 per cent and 85 per cent of the population in the third and fourth income groups used PDS in both states. Also, around 84 per cent of the highest income group (decile 10) of the rural sector used PDS in both states.

Figure 21.3 shows the PDS use in the rural sector in Tamil Nadu, West Bengal and all India in 2009–10. Since TPDS was implemented in 1997, this figure can be interpreted as the effect of change in the PDS policy across India except for Tamil Nadu. It is evident from Figure 21.3 that, over time, almost 100 per cent of the lowest income groups up to decile 6 in Tamil Nadu benefitted from the universal PDS. However, for West Bengal and all India there was a sharp downward shift of the usage curves for all decile classes in 2009–10 compared to 1993–94, which was before the implementation of TPDS. This implies that the participation of households from all decile groups decreased after the implementation of TPDS, as a consequence of which the lowest decile classes suffered more in West Bengal and all India. While 83 to 100 per cent of the population across deciles used PDS in rural Tamil Nadu, only about 28 to 51 per cent used PDS in rural West Bengal in 2009–10. There was an enormous difference of about 35 to 50 per cent between the participation in PDS in the two states after West Bengal implemented TPDS.

In 1993–94 in the urban sector, the usage curves in Figure 21.4 show a similar pattern for Tamil Nadu and West Bengal across MPCE decile classes with a slightly higher participation of middle-income households in PDS than the lowest and highest income deciles. Both the states performed better than the all India level as the usage curve is at a lower level for most of the MPCE decile groups.

Figure 21.5 depicts the pattern of the use of PDS in the urban sector in 2009–10, that is, after more than a decade of the implementation of TPDS. It can be seen that a huge difference emerged in PDS use between Tamil Nadu and West Bengal. PDS use in West Bengal went down even below the all India level for all decile groups from the lowest to the highest. In the case of Tamil Nadu, the entire PDS use curve is on a much higher level than that of West Bengal and all India. It falls from decile 6 as it approaches towards higher income groups and it is at its lowest in decile 10 (highest income group) implying that the poor section reaped maximum benefit from PDS in Tamil Nadu and the rich decile classes were benefitted less. So the PDS in urban Tamil Nadu which retained the UPDS was actually able to maximise benefits for the poor while reducing the benefits going to the rich decile classes.

Targeting errors

Targeting errors occur when a programme does not benefit the target group for whom it is intended. The estimation of targeting errors is done following the method used by Cornia and Stewart (1993), for both rural and urban sectors of Tamil Nadu, West Bengal and all India for 1993–94, 2004–05 and 2009–10. They defined targeting errors as 'F'-mistake, i.e. failure to reach the target population and 'E'-mistake i.e. excessive coverage of the non-target population. The total household is considered to be 'N' which constitutes poor households 'P' and non-poor households 'NP'. One of the main objectives of the PDS in India is to provide food security to the poor, i.e. the households falling within the lowest MPCE deciles. Here, the lowest four deciles (1–4) or approximately 40 per cent of households falling in the lowest income groups in the three time periods are considered as the target group 'P' or poor households, constituting the vulnerable section genuinely needing subsidised food. And the remaining 60 per cent (decile 5–10), having higher MPCE are considered to be non-poor 'NP' households. Table 21.6 illustrates the format for E and F mistakes in this specific case of PDS.

In Table 21.6, $P + NP = N^c + N^{nc} = P^c + P^{nc} + NP^c + NP^{nc} = N$

According to Cornia and Stewart (1993), an ideal situation is where the E- and F-mistakes are zero, i.e. $P^c + NP^{nc} = N$. In this situation all the poor are covered by PDS and the non-poor are not covered. In contrast to this, the case of total mistargeting occurs when the entire poor population is left out and all the non-poor are covered by PDS, i.e. $NP^c + P^{nc} = N$. In this case, F-mistakes are calculated as P^{nc}/P, i.e. the poor households not covered by PDS (P^{nc}) as a proportion of the total target households (P). Similarly, the E-mistakes are calculated as NP^c/NP i.e. all the non-poor households covered by PDS (NP^c) as a proportion of the total non-target households (NP).

Table 21.7 shows the estimated targeting errors for both rural and urban sectors of Tamil Nadu, West Bengal and all India for 1993–94, 2004–05 and 2009–10. For all three time periods Tamil Nadu had very low F-mistakes (ranging from 0.01 to 0. 17) in comparison to West Bengal and all India in both sectors, except for 1993–94 in the urban sector, which was 0.29. It implies that Tamil Nadu had almost covered the target population for PDS. As untargeted programmes are more likely to encompass E-mistakes, the errors of excessive coverage were higher in Tamil Nadu compared to West Bengal and all India in both sectors. However, it was successful in fulfilling its objective of providing subsidised food to the poor. In 1993–94, F-mistakes were relatively lower than E- mistakes in both sectors for Tamil Nadu, West Bengal and all India. After

Table 21.6 E- and F-mistakes in the coverage of PDS

	Poor	*Non-poor*	*Total*
All covered by PDS	P^c	NP^c (E-mistakes)	N^c
All not covered by PDS	P^{nc} (F-mistakes)	NP^{nc}	N^{nc}
Total	P	NP	N

Where ^{c} implies covered by PDS and ^{nc} implies not covered by PDS.

Table 21.7 Targeting errors in coverage of PDS

Targeting errors in coverage of PDS		*F-mistakes*		*E-mistakes*	
		Rural	*Urban*	*Rural*	*Urban*
1993–94	All India	0.39	0.31	0.70	0.63
	Tamil Nadu	0.17	0.29	0.82	0.72
	West Bengal	0.19	0.20	0.87	0.65
2004–05	All India	0.65	0.64	0.29	0.13
	Tamil Nadu	0.09	0.15	0.87	0.64
	West Bengal	0.69	0.78	0.21	0.09
2009–10	All India	0.44	0.53	0.44	0.20
	Tamil Nadu	0.01	0.05	0.94	0.73
	West Bengal	0.51	0.67	0.38	0.10

Source: Calculated from unit level record NSSO 50th (1993–94), 61st (2004–05) and 66th Round (2009–10).

implementation of TPDS, F-mistakes for West Bengal and all India were high ranging from 0.44 to 0.78 and relatively lower E-mistakes ranging from 0.13 to 0.44 in both rural and urban sectors in 2004–05 and 2009–10. Higher F-mistakes for West Bengal and all India suggest that the TPDS was not effective in covering and benefitting the target population and the values for E-mistakes signify that even the TPDS could not totally do away with the excessive coverage of non-poor households. Hence the higher errors of failing to cover the target population and non-negligible errors of excessive coverage manifest that TPDS was barely able to realise its intended objective.

Effectiveness of PDS as a measure for food security

Food access and food absorption are the most important aspects of food security that have to be considered to evaluate how far the PDS has been effective in curbing food insecurity. The food security statuses of Tamil Nadu, West Bengal and all India are compared with the help of some indicators used by the Food Insecurity Atlas of Urban India (FIAUI 2002) Report on the State of Food Insecurity in Rural India (RSFIRI 2008) and Report on the State of Food Insecurity in Urban India (RSFIUI 2010) that are directly related to PDS.

The important role of PDS in improving access to food has been identified by FIAUI (2002) as it used the per capita consumption of grains from PDS as an indicator in the sense of affordability. Since the study is based on the household level, the data for monthly average household consumption from PDS and other sources are compared for Tamil Nadu, West Bengal and all India, across three time periods, separately for the rural and urban sectors.

Figures 21.6 and 21.7 show the monthly average household consumption of rice in Tamil Nadu, West Bengal and all India rural and urban sectors, respectively. The monthly average household consumption of rice from PDS was the highest in rural Tamil Nadu in comparison to West Bengal and all India level for all three periods in consideration, which is evident from Figure 21.6. Even though the consumption of rice from PDS increased slightly over time for West Bengal and all India in the rural sector, it remained far below the monthly average house-

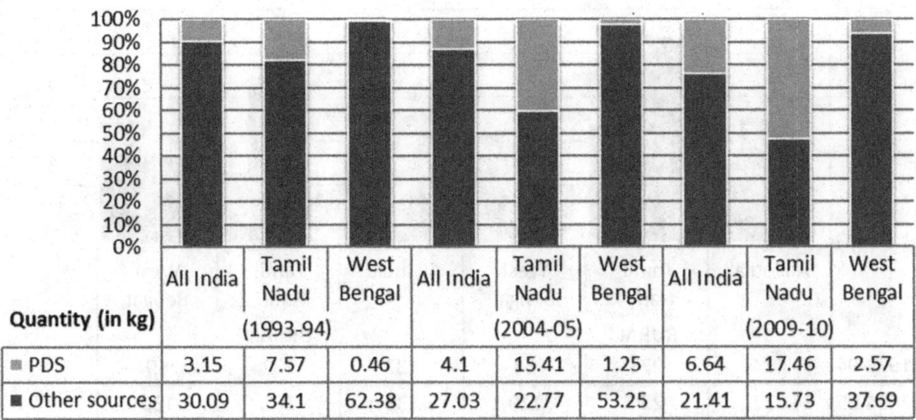

Figure 21.6 Monthly average household consumption of rice from PDS and other sources (rural). *Source*: Calculated from unit level record NSSO 50th (1993–94), 61st (2004–05) and 66th Round (2009–10).

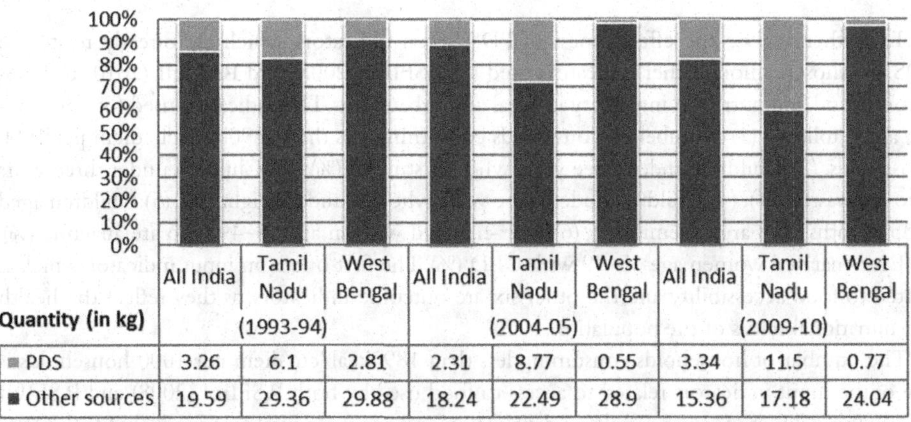

Figure 21.7 Monthly average household consumption of rice from PDS and other sources (urban). *Source*: Calculated from unit level record NSSO 50th (1993–94), 61st (2004–05) and 66th Round (2009–10).

hold consumption from PDS in Tamil Nadu. The PDS fulfilled more than 50 per cent of the monthly household need of rice in Tamil Nadu in 2009–10.

The monthly average household consumption of rice from PDS declined in the urban sector after the implementation of TPDS in West Bengal and all India as shown in Figure 21.7 for 2004–05, after which it increased marginally in 2009–10. Even in the urban sector, the consumption of rice from PDS in Tamil Nadu is much higher than that of West Bengal and all India. The highest proportion of consumption of rice from 'other sources' was for West Bengal in all three periods for both sectors. The proportion of household consumption met by PDS is abysmally low after the implementation of TPDS in urban West Bengal.

Hence in the case of both sectors, UPDS in Tamil Nadu provided better access to food than TPDS in West Bengal and all India. The lower proportions of monthly average consumption of rice from PDS in West Bengal and all India indicate low access to food in the case of TPDS.

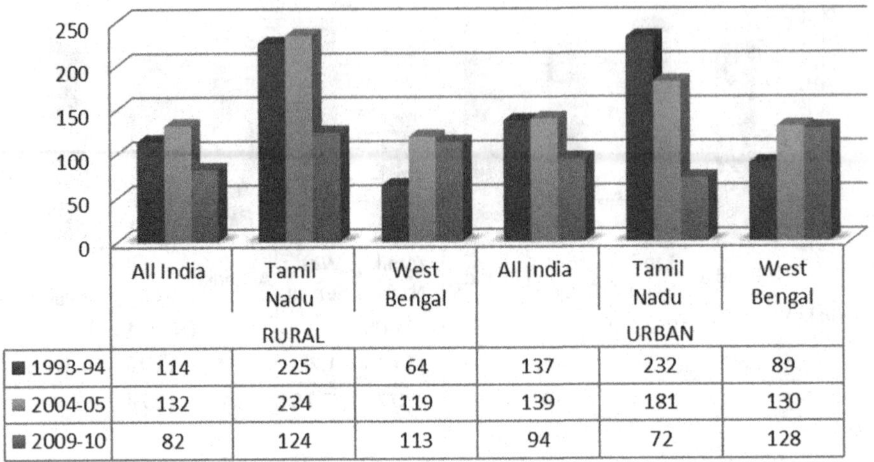

	All India	Tamil Nadu	West Bengal	All India	Tamil Nadu	West Bengal
	RURAL			URBAN		
1993-94	114	225	64	137	232	89
2004-05	132	234	119	139	181	130
2009-10	82	124	113	94	72	128

Figure 21.8 Number of households consuming less than 1890kcal/cu/diem per 1000 households. *Source:* NSSO 50th (1993–94), 61st (2004–05) and 66th Round (2009–10) Reports.

To further analyse the effectiveness of PDS, seven indicators which are directly related to PDS are chosen among other indicators used by RSFIRI (2008) and RSFIUI (2010) to assess chronic food and nutrition insecurity in rural and urban areas. The indicators used for comparison are as follows: (1) Number of households consuming less than 1890kcal/cu/diem per 1000 households, (2) Children under three years who are stunted (%), (3) Children under three years who are wasted (%), (4) Children under three years who are underweight (%), (5) Children aged 6–35 months who are anaemic (%), (6) Ever-married women age 15–49 who are anaemic (%), (7) Ever-married women age 15–49 with CED (%). The first one is an input indicator which is related to food accessibility and the other six are outcome indicators, as they reflect the health and nutritional status of the population.

The number of households consuming less than 1890kcal/cu/diem per 1000 households is one of the input indicators related to access to food used by both RSFIRI (2008) and RSFIUI (2010). It is a direct measure of calorie deprivation and adequate intake of food (RSFIUI 2010).

Figure 21.8 shows that in 1993–94, Tamil Nadu had the highest and West Bengal had the lowest number of households consuming less than 1890 kcal/cu/diem per 1000 households in both rural and urban sectors. In 2004–05, the number of households consuming less than 1890 kcal/cu/diem per 1000 households increased for Tamil Nadu, West Bengal as well as all India in the rural sector but in 2009–10, it decreased for all. The most significant decline was observed for Tamil Nadu with a decrease of about 50 per cent in the number of households consuming less than 1890 kcal/cu/diem from 2004–05 to 2009–10. In case of the urban sector, all India follows a similar pattern as the rural sector. But over the years such households decreased in Tamil Nadu and increased in West Bengal. The most notable fact is that Tamil Nadu had the highest, i.e. 232 households consuming less than 1890 kcal/cu/diem per 1000 households in 1993–94 and at the same time West Bengal had only 89 such households, but in the year 2009–10 Tamil Nadu had the lowest, 72 households, and West Bengal had the highest, i.e. 128 households consuming less than 1890 kcal/cu/diem per 1000 households. A substantial decrease in the number of households consuming less than 1890 kcal/cu/diem per 1000 households in both rural and urban sectors implies improvement of the food security situation in Tamil Nadu.

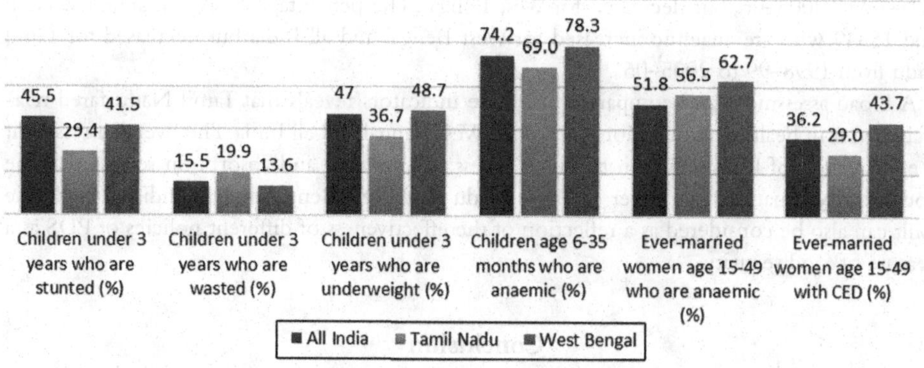

Figure 21.9 Food insecurity outcome indictors (1998–99). *Source*: NFHS-2 (1998–99) Report.

The other six indicators used for comparison are outcome indicators, as they reflect the health and nutritional status of the population. The data for outcome indicators are taken from NFHS reports and a comparison is done for the period 1998–99 and 2005–06.

Figure 21.9 and 21.10 show the food insecurity outcome indicators in Tamil Nadu, West Bengal and all India for two time periods, 1998–99 and 2005–06, respectively. It can be seen that in both 1998–99 and 2005–06, out of six indicators, Tamil Nadu had the lowest percentage for four indicators, namely, children under three years who are stunted, children under three years who are underweight, children aged 6–35 months who are anaemic, and ever-married women aged 15–49 with CED. West Bengal had the lowest percentage of children less than three years who are wasted and all India percentage of ever-married women aged 15–49 who are anaemic was the lowest. The percentage of children under three years who are stunted, children under three years who are underweight and ever-married women aged 15–49 with CED decreased from 1998–99 to 2005–06 for Tamil Nadu, West Bengal and all India which signifies an improvement in the overall health and nutrition status. The percentage of children less than three years who are wasted increased for all from 1998–99 to 2005–06. In case of children aged 6–35 months who are anaemic, the percentage increased for Tamil Nadu and all India from

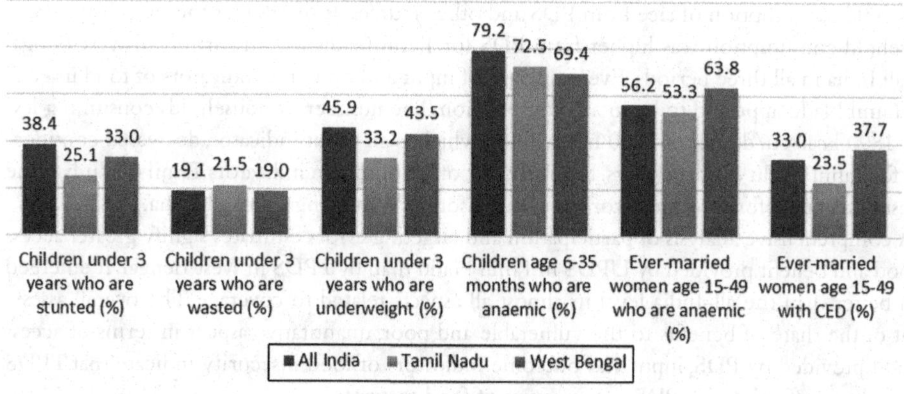

Figure 21.10 Food insecurity outcome indictors (2005–06). *Source*: NFHS-3 (2005–06) Report.

1998–99 to 2005–06, but decreased for West Bengal. The percentage of ever-married women aged 15–49 who are anaemic increased for West Bengal and all India but decreased for Tamil Nadu from 1998–99 to 2005–06.

A broad assessment and comparison of these indicators reveals that Tamil Nadu fared relatively better in health and nutrition status than West Bengal and all India. The overall assessment of effectiveness of PDS policy in terms of access, affordability and absorption reveals that the food security situation was better in Tamil Nadu than West Bengal and all India; as such, the result can also be considered as a reflection of the effectiveness of different policies of PDS as a measure of food security.

Conclusion

Targeted PDS was introduced in 1997, so the selected period of study 1993–94 was prior to the implementation of TPDS and the other two periods 2004–05 and 2009–10 are post TPDS. However, NFSA, a new food security policy was implemented in 2013, which exhibits the characteristics of both universal (same price) and targeted PDS (identification of certain percentage as a target group). Such dual nature of NFSA complicates any comparison of targeted system vis-à-vis universal PDS and the inclusion of the post NFSA period in the analysis may confound the results. Besides, there has been no significant structural change in the policy of PDS even after 2013 as targeting as a policy continues to date with only changes in the percentage of targeted beneficiaries. Hence the validity of the conclusion drawn from the current study remains relevant even in the post-NFSA phase.

A comparative assessment of the participation in PDS on account of the possession of a ration card, type of ration card and households actually purchasing from PDS or using the PDS, according to Social Groups and MPCE decile classes for both rural and urban sectors, is done. The data analysis reveals that the PDS of Tamil Nadu served larger beneficiaries than TPDS in West Bengal and in 2009–10 Tamil Nadu covered almost the whole of its rural population with the scheme. Targeting errors calculated for both the states and all India suggest that F-mistakes, i.e. the failure of reaching the target population was very low for Tamil Nadu in comparison to West Bengal and all India, or the target population is almost covered. Even though there were errors of excessive coverage in Tamil Nadu, such errors were also present in the case of West Bengal and all India. Hence, TPDS hardly achieved its foremost objective of providing food to the most vulnerable.

The quantitative aspect of access to food is analysed by comparing the monthly average household consumption of rice from PDS and other sources. It shows that the monthly average household consumption was higher from PDS for Tamil Nadu in comparison to West Bengal and all India in all three periods. Even in terms of input and outcome indicators of food insecurity, Tamil Nadu appeared to be in a better position. The number of households consuming less than 1890 kcal/cu/diem per 1000 households, which is an input indicator, decreased considerably for Tamil Nadu over the years. Similarly, out of six outcome indicators Tamil Nadu had the lowest percentage for four indicators in comparison to West Bengal and all India.

A comprehensive analysis of participation and targeting errors estimates signify greater access to food and benefit provided by UPDS in Tamil Nadu than by TPDS in West Bengal. It emerged even better than the all-India level in almost all aspects related to coverage. The overall assessment of the share of benefits to the vulnerable and poor, quantitative aspect in terms of access to food provided by PDS, input and outcome indicators of food insecurity indicate that TPDS has not been effective as UPDS as a measure of food security.

It is worth noting that Tamil Nadu is the only state which has managed to maintain the universalisation of PDS through certain modifications even after the implementation of NFSA. In the post-liberalisation period, the PDS in Tamil Nadu was found to be more successful than West Bengal and all India with respect to various aspects. Therefore, it can be concluded that the pursuit of the policy of TPDS in the post-reform period has hardly succeeded in improving the welfare of the most vulnerable section of society. As such, if the state government takes initiative to reform the PDS and make it universal then it is likely to give better outcomes like higher participation, lower targeting errors of excluding the needy, greater benefits to the poor, which in turn gets reflected in a better food security situation and nutritional outcomes.

Acknowledgment

I am thankful to my MPhil supervisor Dr Himanshu for his suggestions as this paper is a part of my MPhil dissertation submitted to the Centre for the Study of Regional Development, Jawaharlal Nehru University. I am solely responsible for any errors and opinions expressed.

References

Bapna, S. L. (1990): "Food Security through the PDS: The Indian Experience", in Davendra Singh Tyagi and Vijay Shankar Vyas (eds), *Increasing Access to Food: The Asian Experience*, New Delhi: Sage Publications.

Bhagwati, Jagdish, and Thirukodikaval Nilakanta Srinivasan (1993): *India's Economic Reforms*, New Delhi: Ministry of Finance, Government of India.

Cornia, Giovanni Andrea, and Frances Stewart (1993): *Two Errors of Targeting*, Innocenti Occasional Papers Economic Policy Series, No. 36. Florence: International Child Development Centre, UNICEF.

Dev, S. Mahendra, and M. H. Suryanarayana (1991): "Is PDS Urban Biased and Pro-Rich? An Evaluation", *Economic and Political Weekly*, Vol. 26, No. 41, pp. 2357–2366, October 12.

Dreze, Jean (2004): "Democracy and Right to Food", *Economic and Political Weekly*, Vol. 39, No. 17, pp 23–31, April 24.

Dutta, Bhaskar, and Bharat Ramaswami (2001): "Targeting and Efficiency in the Public Distribution System: Case of Andhra Pradesh and Maharashtra", *Economic and Political Weekly*, Vol. 36, No. 18, pp. 1524–1532, May 5–11.

Ghosh, Jayati (2010): "The Political Economy of Hunger in 21st Century India", *Economic and Political Weekly*, Vol. XLV, No. 44, pp. 33–38, October 30.

Govindarajan, Vinita (2016): "Tamil Nadu Finally Adopts Food Security Act, by Adding Crores to Its Subsidy Bill", https://scroll.in/article/820604/tamil-nadu-finally-adopts-food-security-act-by-adding-crores-to-its-subsidy-bill, November 5.

Himanshu, and Abhijit Sen (2011): "Why not a Universal Food Security Legislation?", *Economic and Political Weekly*, Vol. 46, No. 12, pp 38–47, March 19.

Jha, Sikha, and P. V. Srinivasan (2001): "Taking the PDS to the Poor: Directions for Further Reform", *Economic and Political Weekly*, Vol. 36, No. 39, pp. 3779-3786.

Kochar, Anjini (2005): "Can Targeted Food Programs Improve Nutrition? An Empirical Analysis of India's Public Distribution System", *Development and Cultural Change*, Vol. 54, No. 1, pp 203–235, October.

Khera, Reetika (2009): "Right to Food Act: Beyond Cheap Promises", *Economic and Political Weekly*, Vol. 44, No. 29, pp 40–44, July 18.

Mooij, Jos (1998): "Food Policy and Politics: The Political Economy of the Public Distribution System in India", *Journal of Peasant Studies*, Vol. 25, No. 2, pp 77–101.

——— (1999): "Dilemmas in Food Policy: About Institutional Contradictions and Vested Interests", *Economic and Political Weekly*, Vol. 34, No. 52, pp. A114–A117+A119–A120.

MSSRF-WFP (2002), *Food Insecurity Atlas of Urban India*, Chennai: M. S. Swaminathan Research Foundation.

——— (2008): *Report on the State of Food Insecurity in Rural India*, Chennai: M. S. Swaminathan Research Foundation.

——— (2010): *Report on the State of Food Insecurity in Urban India*, Chennai: M. S. Swaminathan Research Foundation.

National Family Health Survey (1998–99), (2005–06): *India, Report NFHS-2,3*, Mumbai: International Institute for Population Studies.

Nawani, N. P. (1994): "Indian Experience on Household Food and Nutrition Security", Paper presented in *Regional Expert Consultation of the Asia-Pacific Network for Food and Nutrition on Household Food Security with Respect to Desirable Dietary Pattern*, Bangkok, Thailand, FAO August 8–11, 1994.

Right to Food Campaign (2013): "Why the Parliament Should Reject the Standing Committee's Recommendations on the Food Security", January 27, viewed on www.kafila.org.

Swaminathan, Madhura (2000): *Consumer Food Subsidies: What Needs to Be Done in India*, ARC Working Paper No. 2, Asia Research Centre, London School of Economics and Political Science, London.

——— (2009): "Neo-Liberal Policy and Food Security in India: Impact on the Public Distribution System", Paper presented in the International Conference on "The Crisis of Neo-liberalism in India: Challenges and Alternatives" organised by TISS, Mumbai and IDEAs, March 13–15.

Swaminathan, Madhura, and Neeta Mishra (2001): "Errors of Targeting: Public Distribution of Food in a Maharashtra Village, 1995–2000", *Economic and Political Weekly*, Vol. 36, No. 26, pp. 2447–2454.

Thorat, Sukhdeo, and Joel Lee (2005): "Caste Discrimination and Food Security Programmes", *Economic and Political Weekly*, Vol. 40 , No. 39, pp. 4198–4201.

The World Bank (1991): *India: 1991 Country Economic Memorandum, Volume II: Agriculture: Challenges and Opportunities*. Report No. 9412-IN, Washington, DC: World Bank Group.

22
MARKET IN EDUCATION IN THE POST-REFORM ERA
A case study of private tuition in India

Indrani Sengupta

Introduction

Economic Reform in India in 1991 under the policy framework of the Washington Consensus has led to a number of changes in the domain of trade, industry, agriculture and social sectors like education and health (Williamson, 1990). In order to manage fiscal crises several clauses were made by the World Bank and the IMF against structural loans which had been made before (Williamson 2003). In social sectors like health and education, a market system has been created where the State acted as a mediator in providing fertile ground for the entry of private players and their smooth functioning. This is symptomatic of the neoliberal agenda which swept the country after reform. It has far-reaching implications on education, especially the elementary education sector which needs funds from the government to ensure equity and education for all sections of society, i.e., to fulfil goals set by the Right to Education Act, 2009. What is mainly observed is that when the finances of the government are dwindling, there is an attempt to cut down expenditure in social sectors, education being one of them. According to Venkatanarayanan (2015), the share of expenditure on education increased only from 10.4% in 1990–91 to 11.4 % in 2011–12 which is low compared to the increase in student population. The percentage of total expenditure by the government (both Central and State) on education fell from 10.4% in 1990–91 to 9.7% in 2016–17 (Economic Survey 2002–03; 2017–18). On the other hand, there is rhetoric of fall in the quality of government schools which has been documented in some studies (Kingdon 1996; Muralidharan and Kremer 2006). In several states, this has led to a surge in the demand for private schools and the proliferation of low fee private schools which are affordable for the poor (Srivastava 2007). In some states like West Bengal, Tripura, Orissa and Bihar there is a high prevalence of private tuition. While privatization has taken various forms in different states of India in the form of private schools for the poor to public–private partnership, what has not received much attention is the phenomenon of private tuition or coaching which is gradually making its presence felt in some Indian states. This has created a market for education where the idea of 'common school system' gets threatened because the market for education will be based on the 'ability to pay' and this would lead to 'cream skimming' where the marginalized section of the society will be left behind. These events are the result of various forces at play of which a fall in the government's stake in education is one.

 DOI: 10.4324/9780367855741-22

The chapter draws attention to the fact that if the government were to withdraw from education, we might have a market which will function like the tuition market which benefits only the privileged section and poses a threat to the idea of equity. Also, an individual effort to gain education stands in contrast with the notion that education is a 'merit' good and has to be provided by the government. The dependence on private tuition suggests that something is wrong with the school system which calls for more attention from the government.

This chapter also sets the ground for an analysis of the emergence of the market in education by looking at the private tuition market which highlights how parents are seeking a 'private' solution for the poor functioning of schools. A market which epitomizes education as a private investment has implications for the society which is hierarchized on the basis of class, caste and gender. The fact that education yields positive externality which hints at the greater role of the government gets undermined when people invest privately for gaining quality education.

Against this background, the chapter seeks to understand the prevalence of private tuition by first looking at the evolution of the market from a pre-reform period 1986–87 to 2017–18, using NSSO data in India, focusing only on school-going children up to higher secondary level. Here, we particularly look at the determinants of private tuition using a Probit model in the two periods: 1986–87 (pre reform) and 2017–18 (post reform) to analyse how factors affecting the demand for private tuition have changed. This chapter argues that the phenomenon of tutoring increases the cost of education which pinches the poor as the burden of education falls heavily on them. Thus, the idea of 'free' education at the elementary level becomes a myth in this scenario. The chapter is organized as follows: in the next section we show the changing role of the government through various reports of the government followed by a brief literature review on private tuition. The focus then shifts to the Indian context where we tried to ascertain the pattern of participation and expenditure, keeping in mind social groups, gender and income. The paper concludes by prescribing a greater role of the government not only to improve quality but also to improve governance and regulatory mechanism to tap private tuition.

Withdrawal of the government from education in the post-reform period

The priorities in the post-reform period (after 1991) of the government shifted towards 'prudent macroeconomic policies, outward orientation and free market capitalism' as Williamson (1990) puts it. It was argued that market principles would work best for the economy and the economy would benefit if the government were to intervene at the minimum. The role assigned to the government under the Structural Adjustment Programme (SAP) is that of a 'facilitator' to ensure the smooth functioning of the market. Social sectors also appeared as a priority area in the Washington Consensus as it suggested public expenditure should switch from non-merit subsidies to merit goods (Williamson 2003). But contrary to the objectives laid out in the reform policies India's performance in the social sector has not been satisfactory (Dreze and Sen 1995) and is far from meeting the target of 6% of GDP as laid down in the Kothari Commission (1966). There is also a variation across States as well as the education expenditure incurred by States (State governments). We observe that in the post-reform period, i.e. after 1990 till 1998, there is a continuous fall in education expenditure (Figure 22.1). Although expenditure picked up after 1998, it fell again to 3.09% in 2011. According to the Economic Survey Report (2016–17), the percentage education expenditure to GDP is 2.9% (budget estimate) which is much lower than in many other developing countries in the world. We also observe that education expenditure shows a decreasing trend in the composition of social services expenditure in both revenue and capital accounts (Figure 22.2). The figure went down far below 50%, i.e., 39.7% in 2017–18 (revised estimate) as compared to the period 1990–1995. This reflects that education

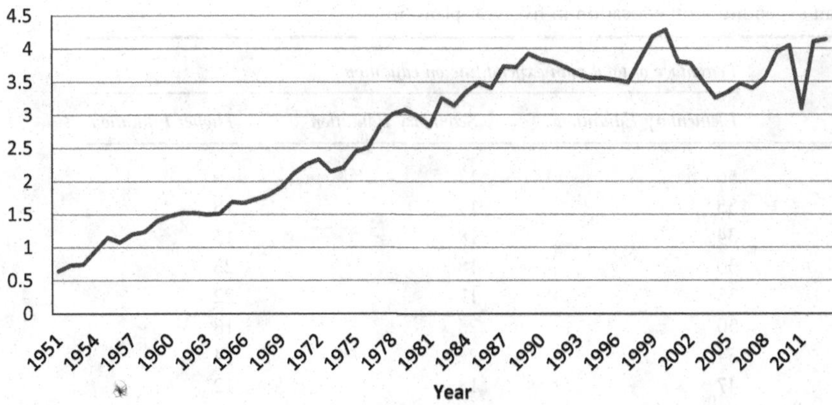

Figure 22.1 Expenditure on education as percentage of GDP in various plan periods (1951–2011). *Source*: GDP figures are taken from CSO. Budgeted expenditure on education taken from Department of Higher Education (MHRD).

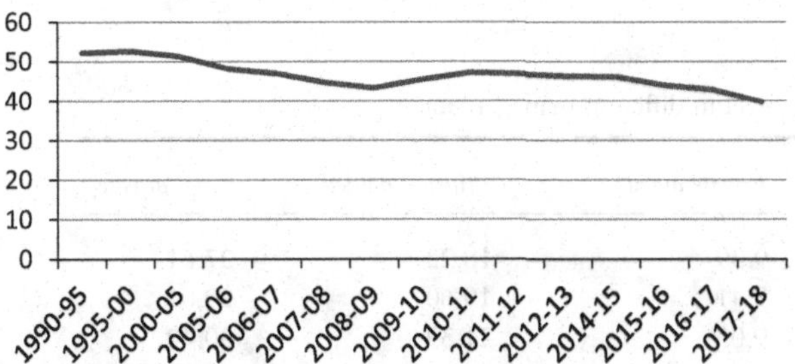

Figure 22.2 Education expenditure on total social service expenditure (revenue and capital accounts, in %). *Source*: RBI (2007–08 to 2009–10 and 2018–19).

has not been accorded primacy over the years although expenditure on education increased in absolute terms (CBGA Report 2013).

If we focus on the expenditure allocated to education in each plan period, we find that in each five-year plan period starting from 1992–1997, percentage of total plan expenditure on education increased from 4.9% to 19.4% in 2007–2012 but the share of elementary education in total plan expenditure on education fell from 47% in 1992–97 to 43% in 2007–2012 (Venkatarayanan 2015). There also exists a huge difference in the allocation of resources at various levels of education. If we look at the secondary level, the share of plan expenditure on education is showing a decreasing trend in several plan periods as more expenditure allocation is needed at the elementary level for universalization of education as mandated in RTE, 2009 (Table 22.1). Secondary education in India has not received attention from the government which is also reflected in a high drop-out rate at the secondary level as compared to other levels of education. The average annual drop-out rate at the secondary level is 17.86% which is higher than primary (4.34%) and upper primary level (3.77%), according to DISE (2013–14).

Indian school education is also beset with conundrums. On one hand, 8 million children are out of school (*The Economic Times* May 11 2014), and on the other hand, there is a shift towards fee-charging private schools (low fee schools) by the lower income group from government schools which provide almost free schooling. Certainly, parents show a desire for quality educa-

Table 22.1 Plan expenditure on education in five-year plans (in %)

Five-year plan	*Percentage of total plan expenditure on education*		
	Elementary Education	*Secondary Education*	*Higher Education*
1951–1956	56	13	9
1956–1961	35	19	18
1961–1966	34	18	15
1969–1980	30	18	25
1974–1979	35	17	22
1980–1985	30	25	18
1985–1990	34	22	14
1992–1997	47	18	12
1997–2002	57	21	10
2002–2007	66	10	13
2007–2012	47	20	11

Source: Centre for Budget and Governance Accountability (2011, 2013), GOI (1966), GOI (2002), GOI (2008).

Table 22.2 Enrolment (%) at elementary level in different managements

Years	*Government*	*Private aided*	*Private unaided*	*Total private*
2007–08	72.23	9.39	18.22	27.61
2008–09	70.96	9.41	19.60	29.01
2009–10	69.51	9.03	21.39	30.42
2010–11	67.39	8.64	21.98	30.62
2011–12	65.01	8.30	24.28	32.59
2012–13	62.62	8.28	26.65	34.92
2013–14	61.32	8.02	27.80	35.81
2014–15	60.18	7.54	29.67	37.21
2015–16	59.44	7.78	30.17	37.95

Source: DISE Flash Statistics of various years (2007–08 to 2014–15).

tion which they believe is achieved through private schooling. There is thus a surge in private schools all over the country, i.e., the number of schools rose by 71,360 in the major 20 states of India over the four year period from 2010–11 to 2014–15 (Kingdon 2017).

Enrolment in government schools fell from 72.23% in 2007–08 to 60.18% in 2014–15 and there was a subsequent rise in the enrolment of private schools from 27.61% to 37.95% in 2007–08 and 2015–16, respectively (Table 22.2). Within the private schools, private unaided showed a significant increase in enrolment for the same period.

In secondary education, private school enrolment stands at 54.39% (DISE, 2015–16) which is higher than the elementary level. Thus the shift towards the 'private' is seen mostly at the secondary level. The unsatisfactory expenditure pattern of the government over the years as reflected in the Budget figures and different plan period along with the increasing private participation in school education point towards the fact that the government need to address the systemic imbalance. In a situation where the government is facing fiscal challenges, it has made room for private participation to ensure efficiency in education. This comes out clearly in the twelfth five-year plan document (Planning Commission, 2013) where the government underscored public–private partnership to strengthen the ailing system of education. The draft mentions:

> the role of the private sector in secondary schooling can further be strengthened through right policies, proper regulation, innovative public private partnership and a variety of demand side financing measures that improve accountability and enhance parental choice, thereby achieving all three objectives of access, quality and equity in secondary education. (GOI, 2013, pp. 73)

Clearly, the role of the State in the neoliberal regime is restructured towards providing fertile grounds for private players through partnering. This also means providing 'private solutions to public deficiencies' as Majumdar (2012) calls it which is driven towards the creation of a form of market in education fostered by the government. In recent years, the National Education Policy 2020 which has garnered attention in the education policy debate also highlights the importance of 'philanthropic' private in the provision of education which is intended towards building more private schools and colleges. Apart from this, one can find a vehement emphasis on the idea of 'choice' vis-à-vis the question of right hinting at the triumph of the market in education.

This section presented how the government is gradually taking a backseat in school education through reduced public spending and by promoting private–public partnership. We observe that there is an attempt to look for an alternative in the form of private schooling to lower cost and gain efficiency and in the process the State assumes a new role of 'facilitator'. The implications for such market-based reform are questioned and open to debate on equity grounds which are beyond the scope of this article. There is another manifestation of privatization, i.e., the phenomenon of tutoring which has lost sight in policy discussion needs to be scrutinized. We particularly focus on the private tuition market which is growing parallel to the mainstream education market based on 'ability to pay' to establish the role of the government in education. The private tuition market act as a prism to show inequalities that the market generates which aggravate existing social inequality. In the next sections that follow, we discuss the emergence of private tuition in India and find the socioeconomic determinants of demand.

Private tuition: the 'shadow' of the mainstream education market

The private tuition market is often referred to as the 'shadow' education market because its existence is dependent on mainstream education. According to Stevenson and Baker (1992), shadow education is defined as a 'set of educational activities outside formal schooling that are designed to improve a student's chances of successfully moving through the allocation process'. It has certain features which make it distinct from the formal education market. The activities are mostly hidden and the curriculum in the tuition may not mimic that taught in schools. For instance, coaching centres operate independently of school curriculum as they prepare children for examinations like Olympiad, entrance for IIT JEE and medical and other competitive examinations.[1] There is also an underlying assumption about the poor functioning of government schools in developing countries in some studies (Baker et al. 2001; Dang and Rogers 2008; Kim and Lee 2010; Safarzynska 2013) that gives rise to the demand for private tuition among government school students. This might not be true in the Indian context as private school students too avail private tuition and whether the apparent private school effect (i.e. private schools performing better than government schools) is the true effect of attending private schools or a private tutoring effect has not been investigated in most studies (Aslam and Atherton 2014). Also, the quality of low fee private schools is no different from the poor quality of schooling provided by state schools (Andrabi et al. 2002). Thus, we cannot assume that government school students only avail private tuition. These issues raised in the literature suggest that one needs to contextualize the private tuition market to understand the dynamics of decision making. Dang and Rogers (2008) point out that the market is more flexible than the school education market. This might be because of the ease with which a parent can change one type of tutor over the other. Private tuition can be more perilous for the school system as a whole as it can completely wipe out learning in schools by making students less attentive in class. This can also be seen as a disincentive for schoolteachers to teach in the class (Biswal 1999; Jayachandran 2014). The idea that low salaries in developing countries are a reason to engage in private tuition by school teachers may be challenged in the Indian context. The ratio of teacher's salary to per capita GDP was much higher in India (around 3) in 2009 as compared to countries like China, Indonesia and Japan which were less than 1 (Dreze & Sen 2013). It has been argued that there exists a 'culture' of tuition (Majumdar 2014) which is further making the phenomenon more pervasive in certain parts than in others. In East Asian countries, the phenomenon is so deeply rooted that government policies to ban private tuition have failed (Dierkes 2008). In India, the phenomenon is becoming visible with quite a number of coaching institutes in various metro cities and home-based tutoring in others. The city of Kota in India has gained popularity as a coaching hub because of the concentration of various coaching centres. In India, there is no data available to document the supply side of tuition but there exists supply side aggression that is pointed out by Majumdar (2014). Azam (2016) highlighted various determinants of demand for private tuition in India which showed the importance of household specific factors in sending a child to tuition. Our analysis also highlights the demand side of tuition by comparing the pre-reform with post-reform period to situate informal privatization within the context of economic reform.

Data

The National Sample Survey Organization (NSSO) which is a nationally representative survey collects information on 'participation and expenditure on education' from households and individuals. The data provides information on the participation of individuals aged 5–29 years who are in some form of educational institute and the expenditure they incur. Total households surveyed in the 42nd Round (1986–87), 64th Round (2007–08) and 75th Round (2017–18) are 77,011, 100,581 and 513,426, respectively. We have confined the study in school education by considering those attending schools up to the higher secondary level. The number of individuals attending school up to the higher secondary level in 2017–18 was 76,278. We have focused on three types of institutions in this study – government, private aided and private unaided, and have not considered unrecognized schools for 2007–08 and 2014–15. However, the 42nd Round does not differentiate between private aided and unaided and uses the umbrella term 'private' to include both categories. For the years 1986–87 and 2007–08, we have considered individuals incurring positive expenditure on private coaching[2] as attending private tuition. We have made an attempt to understand the decision to take private tuition with the help of a Probit model. Detailed methodology for this part is provided in a later section.

The private tuition story in India

In India, private tuition enrolment gradually increased from 18.09% in 1995–96 to 18.81% in 2007–08 to 21.41% in 2017–18 (NSSO, 1992–96, 2007–08 and 2017–18). In the pre-reform era, the enrolment was 15.34% (NSSO 1986–87). The data suggests that the growth in enrolment pattern is gradual in India but in some states like West Bengal, Tripura, Orissa and Bihar, enrolment is more than the national average according to NSSO (2017–18). There are various reasons that are attributable to the demand for tuition, of which competition is one. The increasing reliance on private tuition in schools is also driven by an obsession with 'first boys', what Sen (2015) coins as the 'first boy syndrome' where there is a celebration of getting high scores in examinations. So it is a common observation that students are in a 'rat race' trying to secure more marks in examinations.

Table 22.3 shows the percentage of students availing tuition categorized by different types of institutions – government, private aided and private unaided schools; grade – primary, upper primary, secondary and higher secondary; gender; social group – SC, ST, OBC and Others. We have also divided the students on the basis of income quintile. Monthly consumption expenditure is taken as a proxy for monthly income. Quintile 1 represents the poorest 20% of the population whereas quintile 5 represents the richest 20% of the population. Comparing the data on the basis of the above categories for the period 1986–87 to 2007–08 spanning almost two decades, we find that the proportion of students across all categories increased within this period. In 2017–18, the percentage of students attending private tuition, however, showed a decline under some categories. For instance, as compared to 2007–08, the percentage of students attending tuition from private schools fell which might be due to better schooling options in the differentiated private school market with branded private schools providing remedial facilities within schools. On the other hand, government school goers attending tuition increased in both rural and urban sectors from 1986–87 to 2017–18, implying that parents rely less on the functioning of government schools.

The increase in the percentage of students going to private tuition from 1986–87 to 2017–18 was very small in the rural areas, i.e. from 18.36% to 18.40% as compared to the urban areas, i.e. from 25.14% to 29.86%. This implies that over a span of three decades, the demand for private tuition increased in the urban areas which might be due to supply-side push as more and more coaching centres are targeting the urban sectors. If we look at the stages of schooling, enrolment in private tuition increases with the level of education but for both the years 1986–87 and 2017–18, students took private tuition more at the secondary level than at the higher secondary. This implies that as examinations draw nearer, the incidence of tuition increases. The secondary and higher secondary levels determine a student's chances of getting into good colleges and it is the score in these examinations which signal whether the student is capable or not of achieving the later stages. This private effort appears to be skewed in favour of males with larger numbers of males availing tuition in both years in both sectors than females. However, in the rural areas, there was a fall in the percentage of male tutees in 2017–18 as compared to 2007–08, implying the presence of alternative forms of 'private' in terms of private schools which might have led to the substitution of private tuition with better private schooling for male children.

When we look at the social group, we find that the distribution of opportunity gets reflected in the differential participation of backward social groups. In both periods, the proportion of students belonging to the ST category is the lowest in both rural and urban sectors followed by SC and OBC. This figure indicates caste privileges by 'other' castes in the sample which makes it easier for them to invest privately in education. On the other hand, if we look solely at the income quintile, we find that across each quintile in each sector (rural and urban) percentage of students going to tuition has increased, but quintile 1 has shown the highest increase from 7.52% to 17.49% from the year 2007–08 to 2017–18 which shows some form of private tuition is available to people from low income groups. It is interesting to note that in the highest quintile, there is a drop in the percentage of tutees from 2007–08 to 2017–18 which is to be

Table 22.3 Proportion of students attending tuition in school up to Higher Secondary level

	Rural			*Urban*			*Rural+Urban*		
	1986–87	*2007–08*	*2017–18*	*1986–87*	*2007–08*	*2017–18*	*1986–87*	*2007–08*	*2017–18*
School type									
Government	10.29	15.61	19.84	19.29	27.21	30.63	12.41	17.32	21.43
Private: aided		19.71	16.52		33.15	34.48		25.78	24.76
unaided	18.36	14.58	13.63	25.14	27.30	27.18	21.81	20.35	19.83
Grade									
Primary	7.46	10.06	13.75	16.54	20.48	24.58	9.87	12.24	16.44
Upper Primary	13.69	18.60	19.38	22.25	29.21	29.36	16.61	21.23	21.93
Secondary	25.82	26.59	27.20	33.91	40.25	38.32	28.78	30.47	30.21
Higher Secondary	22.65	25.64	23.09	27.25	42.37	36.78	24.97	31.95	27.47
Gender									
Male	12.60	26.29	19.11	23.61	29.85	30.66	15.77	19.57	22.17
Female	10.86	14.10	17.52	19.93	26.17	28.84	14.17	17.13	20.46
Social group									
SC	10.07	14.18	17.17	15.38	25.02	26.93	11.41	16.16	19.00
ST	5.33	7.92	9.29	16.51	19.78	19.73	7.00	9.01	10.45
OBC		15.66	16.95		25.43	24.11		16.17	18.79
Others	12.98	26.85	28.73	23.10	36.21	39.55	16.40	30.31	33.01
Income quintile									
Quintile-1	7.05	11.03	17.11	13.24	18.73	21.73	7.52	11.73	17.49
Quintile-3	11.72	15.43	19.94	24.03	32.00	33.32	13.86	18.12	21.04
Quintile-5	21.65	26.10	19.38	27.61	37.77	36.48	26.75	35.21	33.46

Source: Author's calculation based on NSSO 1986–87, 2007–08 and 2017–18. NSSO 42nd Round (1986–87) does not make distinction between private aided and unaided. Therefore, private unaided is taken as private under this Round.

understood in terms of facilities provided in schools. It might be because parents belonging to the higher income strata are sending their children to schools with tuition facilities, and hence, they do not require out of school tuition.

Quintile 3 represents the middle class whose presence is being felt in the education system as they are the ones who raise their voice. Middle-class aspiration in the sphere of education has been documented by many (Nambissan 2012). What we thus observe is that a market for private tuition narrates the story of caste, class, gender and space (rural and urban) in India. Thus an education system which is based on 'ability to pay' creates a new form of inequality over and above existing inequality of opportunities. The comparison between the pre-reform period (1986–87) with the post-reform period (2007–08 and 2017–18) enabled us to understand how the demand for tuition increased across all categories and how the existence of this form of market created a rift between various sections of the society.

Table 22.4 provides us another picture of inequality in terms of expenditure. The average expenditure for the year 1986–87 and 2007–08 has been adjusted with the Consumer Price Index of the year 2017–18 to make it comparable with the expenditure of 2017–18. Across all the years, there is a stark difference in expenditure between rural and urban. The average expenditure shows a larger increase for male students than for female students during the years 1986–87 to 2017–18. If we compare the expenditure in each year separately, the bias against females is clear from the table. In 2007–08, expenditure on males is 6.9% higher than on females in rural and 5.78% in the urban areas. The chances of a girl child going to school in a rural set up is bleak where social norms discriminating against girls operate more than in the urban areas. Thus, we find discrimination against girls both in participation and expenditure in private investment like tuition.

If we look at the social group, we find that the increase in expenditure in a 30-year period has been the highest for 'other' castes as compared to SC and ST, showing predominance of the upper castes over the years. While in 2017–18 the expenditure across different social groups was more compared to 1986–87 and 2007–08, the pattern of discrimination is similar. In 1986–87, average expenditure of SC and ST groups was 49.6% and 69% lower than Other caste. In

Table 22.4 Average expenditure (in Rs) in current academic year on private tuition up to Higher Secondary level

	1986–87			*2007–08*			*2017–18*		
	Rural	*Urban*	*Combined*	*Rural*	*Urban*	*Combined*	*Rural*	*Urban*	*Combined*
Male	246	844	413	1168	1711	1399	1370	4742	2332
Female	192	656	357	1087	1612	1337	1213	3914	1963
SC	173	370	221	948	1285	1012	1221	3194	1625
ST	82	454	136	930	1472	962	596	2560	837
OBC	–	–	–	1060	1172	1069	1204	3303	1742
Others	251	824	440	1318	2082	1779	1897	5993	3609
Government	172	591	269	1359	1423	1033	1260	3602	1626
Private aided				1765	2010	2133	1814	5767	3807
Private unaided	431	958	686	1326	1735	1808	1260	4441	2890

Source: Author's calculation based on NSSO 1986–87, 2007–08 and NSSO 2017–18. Data on OBC is not available for the 42nd Round.

2007–08 average expenditure by SC, ST and OBC was lower than Other caste by 43.1%, 45.9% and 39.9% respectively whereas in 2017–18 average expenditure by SC, ST and OBC was lower than Other caste by 54.97%, 76.80% and 51.70% respectively. Comparing 1986–87 figures with 2017–18 figures, we observe that the gap between backward castes and Other caste in terms of expenditure on private tuition increased. The figures clearly indicate that the people belonging to forward castes are spending more than the backward castes implying that some type of tutoring options are available at higher cost and this might be of better quality than those availed by backward castes. Thus, we observe that the average expenditure pattern shows the stark differences among the social group than what the participation data showed (Table 22.3).

Observing the average expenditure by type of management, we find that the overall expenditure increased for the students in government schools from 1986–87 to 2017–18. But in the rural sector government school students spent less in 2017–18 as compared to 2007–08. It is interesting to note that over the span of 30 years starting from 1986–87, government school students showed a higher percentage increase in expenditure (83%) as compared to private unaided students (76%). This phenomenal increase in private tuition expenditure in both types of schools shows how education has become expensive over the years and how the informal form of market increasingly plays a significant role in education. Students in private aided schools spend more on tuition than other types of schools and the increase in expenditure for the students in private aided schools was the highest for 2007–08 and 2017–18. On the other hand, the gap between expenditure by government school students and private (both aided and unaided together) students has decreased over the years indicating that students of government schools are availing some form of expensive tutoring which was earlier availed by only private school students. We can therefore conclude that although government schools provide free education, the out of pocket expenditure is much higher for the government school goers which poses a challenge for low income students.

The NSSO data 2014–15 collected information on the reasons for taking private tuition. The reasons are grouped into four categories – augmenting basic education, preparation for getting a job, preparation for getting into an institute and others. It has been found that 90.1% cited 'augmenting basic education' as a reason for attending private tuition. This implies that there is a belief that schools are not able to deliver basic quality education due to which students opt for tuition (Figure 22.3). It has been found that 90.1% cited 'augmenting basic education' as a reason for taking tuition.

Determinants of demand for tuition

Dang and Rogers (2008) suggested that demand for tuition should be analysed in the light of micro and macro factors. In this article, we focus on micro factors, i.e. household and child-specific factors to understand how they drive demand for tuition.

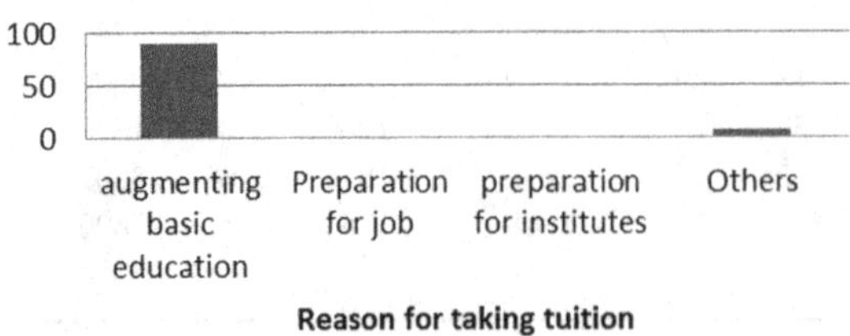

Figure 22.3 Reasons for taking private tuition in India. *Source*: Author's calculation based on NSSO 2014–15.

The decision that the household faces at the onset is whether to send a child to tuition or not. For this, we have used Probit Model in which decisions are based on two outcomes. In this case we have a decision variable – to go for private tuition which takes the value 1 if a person decides to go for tuition and value 0 if a person does not. The participation equation is given as follows:

$$DP_i = \alpha + \beta X_i + \epsilon_i$$

Where, DP_i is the binary choice variable indicating whether the *ith* child is taking private tuition or not. It takes the value 1 if the child is taking tuition; otherwise it takes the value 0. X_i denotes the vector of explanatory variables, described in Table 22.5. ϵ_i is an identically independently distributed error term.

We estimate three separate Probit models (Table 22.6) for both the pre-reform (1986–87) and post-reform period (2017–18). We find that income has a positive significant influence in all models. The effect of income is stronger in the post-reform period where a 1% increase in per capita household expenditure increases the probability of attending private tuition by 6.0 percentage points as compared to 5.8 percentage points in the pre-reform period. The influence of income is much higher in urban than in rural areas. If we consider occupation status, we find that as compared to a salaried person, casual labourers and others have a lower probability (5.6% in 2017–18) of sending the child to tuition and the probability has gone down in the post-reform period indicating greater bias in favour of salaried persons. Similar observations can be drawn by looking at the social group category where both scheduled caste and scheduled tribes are at a disadvantageous position in 2017–18 as compared to 1986–87. The probability of STs (SCs) going to private tuition is 8.2% (2%) lower than the other caste in 2017–18 whereas in 1986–87 the figures are 6.5% and 2.1% for STs and SCs. The locational disadvantage remains almost similar in both years where a parent located in a rural

Table 22.5 List of explanatory variables for the Probit model

List of explanatory variables	*Description of variables*
Log of per capita consumption expenditure	Calculated from household's usual consumption Expenditure (monthly)
Education of Head	Primary = 1, Upper Primary = 2, Secondary + Diploma = 3, Higher Secondary + Diploma= 4, Graduate = 5, Post Graduate and above = 6
Female-headed household	Male head = 0, Female head = 1
Social group	Other caste = 1 (base), Scheduled tribe ST = 1, SC = 2
Sector	Rural = 1 and Urban = 0
Gender	Male = 0, Female = 1
Number of siblings	For children who are in primary stage or above
Distance to nearest school(d)	d < 1 km = 1, 1 km ≤ d < 2 = 2, 2kms ≤ d < 3 = 3, 3kms ≤ d < 5 = 4, d ≥ 5 = 5
Level of current attendance	Primary = 1, Upper Primary = 2, Secondary + Diploma = 3, Higher Secondary + Diploma = 4
Occupation	Salaried or regular wage earner = 0, self-employed = 1, casual labour and others = 2
Type of school	Government = 1, Private = 2 (for 1986–87); private aided = 2 and private unaided = 3 (for 2017–18)

Source: NSSO 1986–87, 2017–18.

Table 22.6 Probit estimation result

Dependent variable: Private tuition status (Attend tuition=1, Not attend tuition=0)

Independent variables	*All India*		*Rural India*		*Urban India*	
	1986–87	*2017–18*	*1986–87*	*2017–18*	*1986–87*	*2017–18*
log per capita monthly household expenditure	0.058***	0.060***	0.063***	0.054***	0.060***	0.067***
	(0.003)	(0.003)	(0.004)	(0.004)	(0.005)	(0.005)
Self employed	–0.001	–0.010***	–0.007*	–0.009***	0.007	–0.001
	(0.003)	(0.003)	(0.004)	(0.004)	(0.005)	(0.005)
Casual labour and others	–0.034***	–0.035***	–0.030***	–0.022***	–0.040***	–0.056***
	(0.004)	(0.004)	(0.005)	(0.005)	(0.007)	(0.006)
Scheduled tribe	–0.065***	–0.082***	–0.060***	–0.071***	–0.064***	–0.093***
	(0.005)	(0.003)	(0.004)	(0.004)	(0.012)	(0.008)
Scheduled caste	–0.021***	–0.020***	–0.021***	–0.022***	–0.025***	–0.013**
	(0.004)	(0.003)	(0.004)	(0.003)	(0.007)	(0.006)
Female head	0.001	0.004	–0.002	0.008	0.009	0.002
	(0.005)	(0.004)	(0.005)	(0.005)	(0.009)	(0.007)
Education of head: Upper Primary	0.026***	0.034***	0.021***	0.018***	0.030***	0.029***
	(0.003)	(0.004)	(0.004)	(0.003)	(0.006)	(0.007)
Secondary	0.031***	0.024***	0.036***	0.018***	0.027***	0.036***
	(0.004)	(0.003)	(0.006)	(0.004)	(0.007)	(0.006)
Higher Secondary	0.016***	0.016***	0.020**	0.016***	0.015	0.020***
	(0.006)	(0.004)	(0.009)	(0.005)	(0.009)	(0.007)
Graduation	0.001	0.019***	0.029***	0.014***	–0.007	0.030***
	(0.005)	(0.004)	(0.009)	(0.006)	(0.008)	(0.007)
Post Graduation and above	–0.017**	0.036***	0.014	0.070***	–0.024**	0.037***
	(0.008)	(0.008)	(0.017)	(0.015)	(0.012)	(0.011)
Number of siblings	–0.001***	–0.005***	–0.000	–0.004***	–0.004***	–0.008**
	(0.000)	(0.000)	(0.000)	(0.001)	(0.001)	(0.002)
Private school	0.007***	0.070***	0.004	0.064***	0.010**	0.079***

	(0.003)	(0.003)	(0.004)	(0.003)	(0.005)	(0.005)
Female	–0.032***	–0.012***	–0.024***	–0.011***	–0.045***	–0.015***
	(0.002)	(0.002)	(0.003)	(0.002)	(0.004)	(0.004)
Level of schooling: Upper	0.046***	0.049***	0.047*** (0.003)	0.043***	0.044***	0.061***
Primary	(0.003)	(0.027)		(0.003)	(0.005)	(0.005)
Secondary	0.135***	0.123***	0.133***	0.109***	0.137***	0.152***
	(0.004)	(0.003)	(0.005)	(0.004)	(0.006)	(0.006)
Higher Secondary	0.078***	0.105***	0.084***	0.091***	0.079***	0.136***
	(0.005)	(0.003)	(0.008)	(0.004)	(0.008)	(0.006)
Distance from school: 1–2	0.002	–0.009***	0.002 (0.004)	–0.009**	–0.003	–0.011***
km	(0.003)	(0.003)		(0.003)	(0.005)	(0.005)
2–3 km	0.013***	–0.017***	0.013***	–0.013***	0.011	–0.019
	(0.004)	(0.004)	(0.005)	(0.005)	(0.007)	(0.009)
2–5 km	0.010**	–0.012**	0.013***	0.018***	–0.000	0.016
	(0.004)	(0.005)	(0.004)	(0.007)	(0.009)	(0.015)
Distance >5km	–0.012***	–0.039***	0.023***	–0.035**	–0.039***	0.013
	(0.004)	(0.004)	(0.005)	(0.004)	(0.008)	(0.019)
Rural	–0.059***	–0.060***				
	(0.003)	(0.028)				
Constant	–2.122***	–3.117***	–2.823***	–3.721***	–1.762***	–2.789***
	(0.079)	(0.107)	(0.126)	(0.165)	(0.102)	(0.144)
Pseudo likelihood	–34284.985	–39196.818	–17552.79	–20693.286	–16519.039	–18174.571
Pseudo R-square	0.1449	0.2724	0.1700	0.3122	0.0944	0.2013
Wald chi2	10404.29***	20026.56***	6104.19***	13527.11***	3170.57***	6518.92***
Correctly predicted	84.13%	78.41%	87.37%	82.95%	78.85%	71.99%
Observations	89,113	102128	54,202	64824	34,387	37,304
State dummy	YES	YES	YES	YES	YES	YES

Robust standard errors in parentheses. Average marginal effects are reported.
*** p<0.01, ** p<0.05, * p<0.1

area has a lower probability (6.0% in 2017–18 and 5.9% in 1986–87) of sending his child to private tuition. The education of the household head has a significant positive impact on the decision to go for tuition but the impact varies in the two time periods, i.e., 1986–87 and 2017–18. As compared to a primary educated household head, household heads who are educated up to higher secondary level are more likely to send a child to private tuition in both the periods, showing greater concern for education of the child. The coefficient is higher in 2017–18 indicating that over the years parents have become more concerned about the education of their child. We observe that in 2017–18, a postgraduate head is more likely (by 3.7%) to send a child to private tuition than a primary level educated head. On the other hand, we find that in 1986–87, a postgraduate household head is less likely (by 1.7%) to send a child to private tuition. Therefore, we observe a certain change in the attitude regarding education over the years based on the educational qualification of the head.

The number of siblings enrolled in schools has more impact on the probability of attending private tuition in the pre-reform period. This implies as the number of siblings increases, the probability of going to private tuition falls as there is a lot of bargaining that happens within the family arising out of family resource constraints. Turning our focus on the child level factors like the type of school, gender of the child and stages of schooling, we find that all these factors are significant in the decision making of the parent. If a child is in a private unaided school, he has more probability of attending tuition than a child at a government school. The probability of a child in private unaided school attending private tuition increased from 0.7% in 1986–87 to 7.9% in 2017–18 which is much higher than in the pre-reform period. One explanation of this could be that parents who demand private schools are also in an advantageous position to demand supplementary education and therefore consider sparing an extra amount for tuition to gain an edge over others. This finding corroborates with Azam (2016). The probability of attending tuition is much higher in urban than in rural areas and this difference is higher in the post reform period. The gender of the child also decides who goes to tuition. As private tuition is a private investment it is more likely in developing countries like India to prefer boys. This gets reflected in the models where girls are less likely to attend tuition than boys. Interestingly, drawing a comparison between the two periods, we find that in 1986–87, a girl child is less likely to attend tuition by 3.2 percentage points than a boy whereas in 2017–18, a girl child is less likely to attend tuition by 1.2 percentage points. Although girls have a lower probability than boys to attend tuition, the probability of attending tuition has increased over the years. As compared to the primary level, students enrolled in the upper primary, secondary and higher secondary levels are more likely to attend tuition. This is because of the curriculum pressure as the child moves up the ladder of grades. Also, at the secondary and higher secondary level, students face board examination and credentials become important for later stages of their career. In the pre-reform period, the coefficients were higher implying that as compared to the primary level, a child studying at higher stages of schooling was more likely to attend tuition. But, in the post-reform period the probability has fallen in comparison to the base category implying that private tuition is being demanded at all stages of schooling. Thus the market also selects children on the basis of caste in the sense that backward castes are underrepresented in the tuition market.

Distance of home from school also plays a role. If the distance from the school is more than 5 km we find that the probability of going to tuition decreases in 1986 as compared to a distance of less than 1 km. This pattern is different for the year 2017–18, where we find as the distance from school increases, the probability of attending private tuition decreases. This might be because of the time taken to commute in schools which reduces the time for attending tuition.

To sum up, the Probit estimation suggests that the decision to attend tuition depends on socioeconomic variables. We find that the gap between different categories increased over the years. The probability of attending tuition is higher for more advantaged people in terms of income, caste, occupation status and location. This also shows how an informal market is gaining visibility and creating a rift between the haves and the have nots. The comparison between these two periods helped us in understanding how the perception of education towards a new alternative, i.e. in the form of private tuition has taken shape in recent years. This change in the favour of an informal market which is fee based needs to be taken on board as this can pose a threat to the existing education policies aimed at serving the poor. This merits attention from the government which would require enhancing the quality of school education as well as some regulatory mechanisms to check the supply side of the tuition market. These observations vehemently put forth that if education is solely based on the 'ability to pay', existing inequality will be reinforced. In other words, the government must assume a greater role in education to ensure equity; otherwise education as a means of social mobility would be a distant dream for the underprivileged section of society.

Conclusion

The chapter makes an argument for a greater role of government in school education by looking at an alternative form of market in education which is based only on 'ability to pay'. In a neoliberal era, the role of the government has been shaped by market ideologies of efficiency where the role of the private sector is recognized. Education, which is considered to be a 'positional good' for backward social groups, will gradually become out of reach for the underprivileged section if market mechanisms were to operate fully in education. This has been shown by taking the case of private tuition. The chapter looks at the role of the government through various reports and traces the changes that have taken place over the years in the way the State is being envisioned. In the latter sections, we have made an attempt to find the determinants of private tuition at two time periods: pre reform (1986–87) and post reform (2017–18) based on NSSO data to make a comparison between the change in each of the factors over the span of 20 years. We observe that there has been a significant change in the demand for private tuition over the years where the gap between underprivileged (in terms of caste, occupation status and income) and privileged has increased. The chapter establishes that the market tells the tale of inequality of class, caste and gender. As the market is based on the 'ability to pay' it filters only those who are able to pay for the service. This has serious implications for the universalization goal of education which aims at equity. In the context of privatization, where the government's role is shrinking, it is important that we do not lose sight of this market which reinforces inequality. Thus if the government were to withdraw completely from education and encourage a fee-based market system in education we might have a market which is akin to the private tuition market. This essentially establishes that the government's role in education is indispensable especially in recent years where private solutions are much in vogue in education.

Notes

1 Information gathered from websites of coaching centres.
2 Coaching and tuition has been used interchangeably.

References

Andrabi, T., Das, J., and Khwaja, A. (2002): *The Rise of Private Schooling in Pakistan: Catering to the Urban Elite or Educating the Rural Poor?*, Cambridge: Government Innovators Network, Harvard Kennedy School.

Aslam, M., and Atherton, P. (2014): "Shadow Education Sector in India and Pakistan", in I. Macpherson, S. Robertson, and G. Walford (Eds.), *Education Privatisation and Social Justice: Case Studies form Africa, South Asia and South East Asia*, Oxford: Symposium Books, pp. 137–158.

Azam, M. (2016): "Private Tutoring: Evidence from India", *Review of Development Economics*, Vol. 20, No. 4, pp. 739–761.

Baker, D. P., Akiba, M., LeTendre, G. K., and Wiseman, A. W. (2001): "Worldwide Shadow Education: Outside-School Learning, Institutional Quality of Schooling, and Cross-National Mathematics Achievement", *Educational Evaluation and Policy Analysis*, Vol. 23, pp. 1–17.

Biswal, B. P. (1999): "Private Tutoring and Public Corruption: A Cost-effective Education System for Developing Countries", *The Developing Economies*, Vol. 37, No. 2, pp. 222–240.

Centre for Budget and Governance Accountability (2011): *Reclaiming Public Provisioning: Priorities for the 12th Five Year Plan*, New Delhi.

——. (2013): *How Has the Dice Rolled? - Response to Union Budget 2013–14*, New Delhi .

Dang, H.-A., and Rogers, F. H. (2008): "The Growing Phenomenon of Private Tutoring: Does It Deepen Human Capital, Widen Inequalities, or Waste Resources?", *The World Bank Research Observer*, Vol. 23, No. 2, pp. 161–200.

Dierkes, J. (2008): "Japanese Shadow Education: The Consequences of School Choice", in Forsey, M., Davies, S., and Walford, G. (Eds.), *The Globalisation of School Choice?*, Oxford: Symposium Books, pp. 231–248.

Drèze, J., and Sen, A. (1995): *Economic Development and Social Opportunities*, New Delhi: Oxford University Press.

——. (2013): *An Uncertain Glory: India and Its Contradictions*, Princeton: Princeton University Press.

Government of India (1966): *Education and National Development*, New Delhi: Ministry of Education.

Government of India (2002): *Tenth Five Year Plan (2002–2007)*, New Delhi: Planning Commission.

——. (2008): *Eleventh Five Year Plan (2007–2012)*, New Delhi: Planning Commission, Government of India.

——. (2013): *Twelfth Five Year Plan (2012–2017)*, Social Sectors Vol. III, New Delhi: Planning Commission, SAGE Publications India.

Jayachandran, S. (2014): "Incentives to Teach Badly: After-School Tutoring in Developing Countries", *Journal of Development Economics*, Vol. 108, pp. 190–205.

Kim, S., and Lee, J. (2010): "Private Tutoring and Demand for Education in South Korea", *Economic Development and Cultural Change*, Vol. 58, No. 2, pp. 259–296.

Kingdon, G. G. (1996): "The Quality and Efficiency of Private and Government Education: A Case Study of Urban India", *Oxford Bulletin of Economics and Statistics*, Vol. 58, No. 2, pp. 57–81.

——. (2017): "Private Schooling Phenomenon in India : A Review", *IZA Paper Discussion* No. 10612.

Majumdar, M. (2012): "In Defence of Public Education: Voices from Bengal", *Economic and Political Weekly*, Vol. 47, No. 40, pp. 50-55.

Majumdar, M. (2014): "The Shadow School System and New Class Divisions in India", TRG Poverty and Education Working Paper Series Paper 2, Max Weber Stiftung.

Muralidharan, K., and Kremer, M. (2006): "Public and Private Schools in Rural India", in R. Chakrabarty and P. Peterson (Eds.), *School Choice International: Exploring Public-Private Partnership*, Cambridge, MA: MIT press, pp. 91–110.

Nambissan, G. (2012): "Private Schools for the Poor: Business as Usual?", *Economic and Political Weekly*, Vol. 47, No. 41, pp. 51–58.

Safarzyńska, K. (2013): "Socio-Economic Determinants of Demand for Private Tutoring", *European Sociological Review*, Vol. 29, No. 2, pp. 139–154.

Sen, A. (2015): *The Country of First Boys*, New Delhi: Oxford University Press.

Srivastava, P. (2007): "Low-Fee Private Schooling: Challenging an Era of Education for All and Quality Provision?", in G. Verma, C. Bagley, and M. M. Jha (Eds.), *International Perspectives on Educational Diversity and Inclusion: Studies from America, Europe and India*, New York: Routledge, pp. 138–161.

Stevenson, D. L., and Baker, D. P. (1992): "Shadow Education and Allocation in Formal Schooling: Transition to University in Japan", *American Journal of Sociology*, Vol. 97, No. 6, 1639–1675.

Venkatnarayanan, S. (2015): "Economic Liberalization in 1991 and Its Impact on Elementary Education in India", *Sage Open*, Vol. 5, No. 2, pp. 1–13.

Williamson, J. (1990): *Latin American Adjustment: How Much Has Happened?*, Washington, DC: Institute for International Economics.

——. (2003): "The Washington Consensus and Beyond", *Economic and Political Weekly*, Vol. 38, No. 15, pp. 1475–1481.

23

INDIA'S HUMAN DEVELOPMENT INDEX

Components, methodological issues and forecasting[1]

Gaurang Rami

Introduction

Human development[2] is about the realization of human potential. It is about what people can do and become – their capabilities – and about the freedom they have to exercise real choices in their lives. This framework is based on the 'capabilities' and 'functioning' approach. Not only is it important to achieve more 'functioning', but it is essential for people to have the 'capabilities' or the freedom to achieve these. Human development is a development paradigm that is much more than the rise or fall of national incomes. It is about creating an environment in which people can develop their full potential and lead productive, creative lives in accord with their needs and interests. People are the real wealth of nations. Development is about expanding the choices people have to lead lives that they value. It is much more than economic growth, which is only a means – if a very important one – of enlarging people's choices. Fundamental to enlarging these choices is building human capabilities – the range of things that people can do or be in life. The most basic capabilities for human development are to lead long and healthy lives, to be knowledgeable, to have access to the resources needed for a decent standard of living and to be able to participate in the life of the community. Without these, many choices are simply not available, and many opportunities in life remain inaccessible (Sen, 1993).

The term human development[3] was the result of criticisms of the approach that was taken in early 1980 on development. At that time, it was believed that there was a close link between a country's economic growth and the expansion of individual choices of human beings.

The work of Mahbub ul Haq, Amartya Sen and others laid the foundations for a different approach and broader human development. The latter was defined as the process of enlarging people's choices and improving human capabilities (the range of things that they can do or be in life) and freedoms so they can live a long and healthy life, have access to education and a decent standard of living, participate in their community and the decisions that affect their lives.

Drawing on this, it is undeniable that people are the real wealth of nations, so that human development involves expanding the opportunities and capacities to enable them to live a creative and productive life according to their needs and interests.

DOI: 10.4324/9780367855741-23

For this reason, development is focused on expanding the choices human beings have in order to have the life they value. In this sense, it is essential to work on building capacities for human development that are sustainable over time.

These core capacities[4] for human development are: (1) enjoying a long and healthy life; (2) being educated; (3) access to resources that enable people to live in dignity; and (4) being able to participate in decisions that affect their community. If people are not offered the opportunity to develop these capacities, many of the opportunities for obtaining a better quality of life are unavailable or simply do not exist for them. For it is said that human development is the development of the people, for the people and by the people.

Therefore, human development considers the six main factors integral:

1. **Equity:** Equal opportunities for all. Special emphasis is placed on equity of human development between men and women and various social groups.
2. **Empowerment:** Freedom of the people to influence, as the subjects of development, decisions that affect their lives.
3. **Cooperation:** Participation and belonging to communities and groups as a means of mutual enrichment and a source of social meaning.
4. **Sustainability:** Meeting the needs of today without compromising the ability to satisfy the same by future generations.
5. **Security:** Exercise development opportunities freely and safely with confidence that they will not disappear suddenly in the future.
6. **Productivity:** Full participation of people in the process of income generation and gainful employment.

To enhance these factors, countries or regions should guide their development strategies towards the gradual creation of an economic, social, political and cultural environment which enhances individual and social capabilities.

Origins of the human development approach

The human development[5] approach arose in part as a result of growing criticisms of the leading development approach of the 1980s, which presumed a close link between national economic growth and the expansion of individual human choices. Many, such as Mahbub ul Haq, who played a key role in formulating the human development paradigm, came to recognize the need for an alternative development model due to many factors, including:

- Growing evidence that did not support the then prevailing belief in the 'trickle down' power of market forces to spread economic benefits and end poverty;
- The human costs of Structural Adjustment Programmes became more apparent;
- Social ills (crime, weakening of social fabric, HIV/AIDS, pollution, etc.) were still spreading even in cases of strong and consistent economic growth;
- A wave of democratization in the early 1990s raised hopes for people-centred models.

As of 1990, the human development concept was applied to a systematic study of global themes, as published in the yearly global Human Development Reports (HDR) under the auspice of the United Nations Development Programme (UNDP). The work of Amartya Sen and others provided the conceptual foundation for an alternative and broader human development approach defined as a process of enlarging people's choices and enhancing human capabilities (the range of things people can be and do) and freedoms, enabling them to live a long and healthy life, have access to knowledge and a decent standard of living, and participate in the life of their community and decisions affecting their lives.

Human development has always been flexible and 'open-ended' with respect to more specific definitions. There can be as many human development dimensions as there are ways of enlarging people's choices. The key or priority parameters of human development can evolve over time and vary both across and within countries.

Literature review

A relevant review of literature helps to understand the existing body of literature along with research gaps. Following a selected review of literature helps to understand the concept of human development along with its components. It also discusses the conceptual and methodological issues involved in measuring human development (HD) and calculating Human Development Indices (HDI).

Human capital concentrates on skill knowledge and productivity while human capability helps individuals to live the lives they choose and increases the choices they have. Both are concerned with human beings. Human capital need not be understood in the form close to physical capital. Education, health care and other factors enrich economic prosperity along with the freedom people wish for. Human beings are not just means of production. They are the ends of production. Human capabilities promote wellbeing and freedom of the people along with production; they influence social changes (Sen, 1977).

In the First Global Human Development report, it is concluded that people are the real wealth of a nation. Human development is all about the 'process of enlarging people's choices'. It mainly focused on building human capabilities, enhancement of freedom and the process of achieving outcomes. The report treats human beings primarily as inputs in the production process. Education, skill formation and health are means for enhancing the quality of human capital. Further, the report also addressed how economic growth translates into human development. The report strongly recommends the restructuring of budgetary expenditures, including military expenditures, and creating an international economic and financial environment conducive to human development (UNDP, 1990).

Income is not only the source of wellbeing; other factors (i.e. education and health) are also important because one would be important for one itself and not for the other, it looked up that on averaging the income and life expectancy the result could not be concluded properly. On the other hand, literacy and education are defined by 0 or 1 that also do not come up with the basic factor that was used for measurement (Anand & Sen, 1997).

Human development is more than GNP growth, more than income and wealth and more than producing commodities and accumulating capital. A person's access to income may be one of the choices, but it is not the sum total of human endeavour. People are the real wealth of the nation. The basic capabilities for human development consist of health, education, access to resources and community participation. Without these, many choices are simply not available, and many opportunities in life remain inaccessible (Haq, 1997).

Society's standard of living should be judged not by the average level of income, but by people's capabilities to lead the lives they value. Nor should commodities be valued in their own right; instead, they should be seen as ways of enhancing such capabilities as health, knowledge, self-respect and the ability to participate actively in community life. Therefore, the expansion of human capabilities implies greater freedom of choice (Sen, 2000).

The concept of human development can be traced to oriental societies as Kautilya's Arthasastra and Adam Smith's Wealth of Nations refer to the good of the common man. Methodological issues, weights and the like in the construction of HDI are questioned. They have worked out Human Development Indices with alternative methods. The authors suggest that the researchers and academicians better use alternate data sources and methodology to build up a vision. Planning bodies, policy framers and academicians are to interact among themselves. It is also stated that no single method of HDI construction is superior or inferior. HDI depends on the conditions of development of the region choice of indicators and methodology. The planning commission and other bodies should obtain larger acceptability in the selection of indicators and methodology (Kundu, Sheriff, & Ghosh 2002).

Socio-economic development, emancipative cultural change and democratization constitute a human development of social progress. Socio-economic development increases individual resources, emancipative values leads to choice, democratization provides freedom rights (Welzel, Inglehart, & Klingemann, 2003).

It is not only per capita income that measures the wellbeing of human development, other factors are there such as access to health, education and goods (Elizabeth, 2007).

India is in 127th position with a HDI score of 0.602 among 177 countries as estimated by the HDR of UNDP for 2006. The chapter examines the level of human development in comparison with other countries between 1975 and 2005 by taking different points of time. It also makes an assessment of the variations in human development across the states. The chapter focuses on the health care scenario both in the country and major states to identify the determining factors and the study finds wide disparity in human development across the states. Health infrastructure, safe drinking water and sanitation besides maternal and child health care are not effective in some states. Health care, if neglected can lead to adverse effects on education and level of poverty which are determining factors of HDI and the authors conclude that the governments suffer from a funds crunch to increase expenditure on the social sector including health care. They suggest a public–private partnership in promoting health infrastructure (Mahapatra and Raj, 2009).

Education, health and income are the three dimensions to measure human progress. In this report, the indicators of education and income are modified. Knowledge dimension earlier was measured with literacy and gross enrolment. This has been replaced by expected years of schooling and mean years of schooling. GDP per capita to measure the standard of living is replaced by GNI as there are international remittances from and by the citizens along with the flow of aid from abroad. Life expectancy at birth is retained as a health indicator, as a better alternative is not identified. The method of aggregation also changed from 2010. The geometric mean of the three indicators is introduced to ascertain the performance indicator-wise. Based on the suggestions it has received, HDI computation is modified, keeping the basic elements in fact (UNDP, 2010).

The Human Development Index was created to emphasize that expanding human choices should be the ultimate criterion for assessing development results. Economic growth is a means to that process, but is not an end by itself. It was found that, as per the new methodology, the value of India's HDI increased from 0.362 to 0.629 from 1980 to 2016; while as per the old methodology, India's HDI value increased from 0.427 to 0.612 from 1980 to 2007. The new methodology was found to be superior compared to the old methodology as far as the concern for the determination of the goalposts, capturing knowledge and use of an appropriate mean i.e. geometric mean to calculate the value of the HDI. Based on the deterministic model of the Human Development Index for India, it was found that, relatively, the Education Index (EI) contributes more to the increasing value of India's Human Development Index compare to the Health Index (HI) and Income Index (II) using data from 1990 to 2014. Brown (ARIMA

(0,2,2)) model predicts the value of HDI from 1980 to 2016 with more than 99% accuracy as the value of residuals for all years from 1980 to 2016 is almost zero (0). Based on our sample forecast, it was found that India's value of HDI will be greater than 0.8 by 2037 and greater than 0.9 by 2048. Hence, India will have HHDI by 2037 and VHHDI by 2048 (Rami, 2020).

Research problem

Based on the review of literature, it is observed that UNDP has tried to improve and enhance its methodology for calculating the value of HDI from time to time. In this direction from 1990 to 2009 UNDP has used a different methodology for calculating the value of HDI and from 2010 onward UNDP has changed its methodology for calculating the value of HDI. These changes in the methodology were due to several criticism and weaknesses of methodology adopted by UNDP prior to 2009. Changes in the methodology for calculating HDI has a significant impact on the value of HDI and policy implications related to enhancing human development in general and value of HDI in particular. It describes the methodologies for calculating the value of HDI using examples along with their calculations, goalposts, classification, interpretations and criticism. The deterministic regression model is applied to estimate the contribution of a long and healthy life captured through the Health Index (HI), being knowledgeable measured through the Education Index (EI) and having a decent standard of living calculated using the Income Index (II) in HDI. This will help policymakers to formulate an appropriate policy to increase the value of India's HDI. It will also help policymakers to decide among health, education and income, where more interventions are required to improve India's performance in HDI. The paper also estimates and forecasts in which year India will enter the High Human Development Index (HHDI) and Very High Human Development Index (VHHDI). For the purpose of the forecasted value of HDI (in sample and out sample), time series analysis with a sophisticated forecasting model like Auto Regressive Integrated Moving Average (ARIMA) has been applied using data from 1980 to 2018.

Objectives of the study

(1) To understand the value of India's Human Development Index
(2) To estimate the contribution of each separate index, i.e. Health Index (HI), Education Index (EI) and Income Index (II) in India's Human Development Index (HDI)
(3) To determine the year in which India will enter into High Human Development Index (HHDI) and Very High Human Development Index (VHHDI)

Research Methodology and Sources of Data

The study utilized secondary data and employs a descriptive research methodology. Data on the value of HDI from 1980 to 2018 has been taken from various published issues of the Human Development Report (HDR) by the United Nations Development Programme (UNDP). For forecasting the value of HDI, a time series analysis with sophisticated forecasting model like Auto Regressive Integrated Moving Average (ARIMA) has been applied.

Measurement of Human Development Index (HDI)

The HDI is a composite index measuring average achievement in three basic dimensions of human development – a long and healthy life, being knowledgeable and a decent standard of living.

HDI is calculated by UNDP and has been made available under the Human Development Report (HDR) every year since 1990. From 1990 to 2009 UNDP used different methods for calculating the value of HDI and from 2010 onward UNDP changed its methods for calculating the value of HDI. Details of the methodology adopted for HDI calculation by the UNDP from 1990 to 2009 along with goalposts (i.e. minimum and maximum values) for calculating HDI (Table 23.1), classification of value of HDI (Table 23.2), interpretation and criticism are as follows:

HDI calculation (from 1990 to 2009): old methodology

$$\text{X-Index}=\frac{X-\text{Min}(X)}{\text{Max}(X)-\text{Min}(X)}$$

1. $\text{Life Expectancy Index}=\frac{LE-25}{85-25}$

2. $\text{Education Index} = 2/3^{*}\text{ALI}+1/3^{*}\text{GEI}$

$$\text{Adult Literacy Index}(\text{ALI})=\frac{\text{ALR}-0}{100-0}$$

$$\text{Gross Enrolment Index}(\text{GEI})=\frac{\text{CGER}-0}{100-0}$$

3. $\text{GDP Index}=\frac{\log(\text{GDPpc})-\log(100)}{\log(40000)-\log(100)}$

Example: For some country 'X' following information is available.

Indicator	*Value*
Life expectancy at birth	81.1
Adult literacy rate	98.9
Gross enrolment ratio	91.8
GDP per capita measured in $	30353

Table 23.1 Goalposts for calculating the HDI (1990 to 2009)

Indicator	*Minimum value*	*Maximum value*
Life expectancy at birth	25 years	85 years
Adult literacy rate	0%	100%
Gross enrolment ratio	0%	100%
GDP per capita	100 (PPP US$)	40,000 (PPP US$)

Source: Human Development Report (2009), UNDP

Table 23.2 Classification of value of HDI

Value of index	*Classification of human development*	*Classification of nation*
Over 0.800	High Human Development (HHD)	Developed Nation
0.500 to 0.800	Medium Human Development (MHD)	Developing Nation
Below 0.500	Low Human Development (LHD)	Underdeveloped / Poor Nation

Source: Human Development Report (2009), UNDP and Author's classification

1. **Health Index**

$$H1=\frac{\text{Actual value}-\text{minimum value}}{\text{maximum value}-\text{minimum value}}$$

$$=\frac{81.1-25}{85-25}$$

$$=\frac{56.1}{60}$$

$$=0.935$$

2. **Education Index**

$$\text{E.I.}=\frac{2}{3}\text{ALR}+\frac{1}{3}\text{GER}$$

$$\text{ALRI}=\frac{\text{Actual value}-\text{minimum value}}{\text{maximum value}-\text{minimum value}}$$

$$=\frac{98.9-0}{100-0}$$

$$=0.989$$

$$\text{GERI}=\frac{\text{Actual value}-\text{minimum value}}{\text{maximum value}-\text{minimum value}}$$

$$=\frac{91.8-0}{100-0}$$

$$=0.918$$

$$\text{E.I.}=\frac{2}{3}\text{ALR}+\frac{1}{3}\text{GER}$$

$$=\frac{2}{3}0.989+\frac{1}{3}0.918$$

$$=0.965$$

3. **Income Index**

$$\text{II}=\frac{\log(\text{Actual value})-\log(\text{minimum value})}{\log(\text{maximum value})-\log(\text{minimum value})}$$

$$= \frac{\log(30353) - (100)}{\log(40000) - \log(100)}$$

$$= 0.954$$

4 **Human Development Index**

$$\text{HDI} = \frac{\text{HI+EI+II}}{3}$$

$$= \frac{(0.935 + 0.965 + 0.954)}{3}$$

$$= 0.951$$

HDI for 'X' country is 0.951; the HDI indicates that 'X' country comes under the High Human Development (HHD).

Criticisms of HDI calculation method from 1990 to 2009

- Goalposts were arbitrarily determined by UNDP
- Use of Arithmetic Mean is not advisable to calculate HDI index based on LI, EI and II
- Knowledge is not appropriately captured using Adult Literacy Rate and Gross Combined Enrolment Ratio.

Considering the above criticism and weaknesses for calculating the value of HDI, UNDP made the following modifications in indicators, goalposts and methods for calculating the value of HDI from 2010 onwards.

Goalposts for calculating the value of HDI from 2010: new methodology

To determine a maximum and minimum value for different dimensions of HDI; UNDP has used 30 years data from 1980 to 2010.

Table 23.3 Goalposts for calculating value of HDI from 2010 – new methodology

Dimension	*Observed maximum*	*Minimum*
Life expectancy at birth	83.2 (Japan, 2010)	20.0
Mean years of schooling (MYS[6])	13.2 (United States, 2000)	0
Expected years of schooling (EYS[7])	20.6 (Australia, 2002)	0
Combined Education Index (CEI)	0.951 (New Zealand, 2010)	0
Per Capita Income (PPP US$)	108,211 (United Arab Emirates, 1980)	163 (Zimbabwe, 2008)

Source: Human Development Report (2010), UNDP

Table 23.4 Classification of value of HDI – new methodology

Value of index	*Classification of human development*	*Classification of nation*
Over 0.900	Very High Human Development (VHHD)	Highly Developed Nation
0.800 to 0.900	High Human Development (HHD)	Developed Nation
0.500 to 0.800	Medium Human Development (MHD)	Developing Nation
Below 0.5	Low Human Development (LHD)	Underdeveloped / Poor Nation

Source: Human Development Report (2010), UNDP and Author's classification

Example: For some countries 'Y' following information is available

Indicator	*Value*
Life expectancy at birth (years)	77.7
Mean years of schooling (years)	9.3
Expected years of schooling (years)	13.4
GNI per capita (PPP US$)	21,673

Source: Human Development Report (2010), UNDP

$$\textbf{Life Expectancy Index} = \frac{\text{Actual value} - \text{Minimum value}}{\text{Maximum value - Minimum value.}}$$

$$= \frac{77.7 - 20}{83.2 - 20}$$

$$= 0.912975$$

Education Index:

$$\text{Mean years of schooling} = \frac{\text{Actual value} - \text{Minimum value}}{\text{Maximum value - Minimum value.}}$$

$$= \frac{9.3 - 0}{13.2 - 0}$$

$$= 0.704545$$

$$\text{Expected years of schooling} = \frac{\text{Actual value} - \text{Minimum value}}{\text{Maximum value - Minimum value.}}$$

$$= \frac{13.4 - 0}{20.6 - 0}$$

$$= 0.650485$$

$$\text{Education Index} = \frac{\sqrt{\text{MYSI} \cdot \text{EYSI}} - 0}{\text{Combine Education-0}}$$

$$\frac{\sqrt{0.704545 \cdot 0.650485} - 0}{0.951 - 0}$$

$$= 0.711857$$

$$\text{Income Index}=\frac{\ln(\text{GNP})-\ln(163)}{\ln(108211)-\ln(163)}$$

$$=\frac{\ln(21{,}673)-\ln(163)}{\ln(108211)-\ln(163)}$$

$$= 0.75254$$

The HDI is the geometric mean of the three dimension indices:

$$\text{HDI} = \left(I_{\text{life}}^{1/3} \cdot I_{\text{education}}^{1/3} \cdot I_{\text{income}}^{1/3}\right)$$

$$\text{Human Development Index} = \text{HDI} = \left(I_{\text{life}}^{1/3} \cdot I_{\text{education}}^{1/3} \cdot I_{\text{income}}^{1/3}\right)$$

$$= 0.787881$$

HDI for 'Y' country is 0.787; the HDI indicates that 'Y' country comes under the Medium Human Development (MHHD).

In 2010,[8] the geometric mean was introduced to compute the HDI. Poor performance in any dimension is directly reflected in the geometric mean. That is to say, a low achievement in one dimension is not anymore linearly compensated for by high achievement in another dimension. The geometric mean reduces the level of substitutability between dimensions and at the same time ensures that a 1% decline in index of, say, life expectancy has the same impact on the HDI as a 1% decline in education or income index. Thus, as a basis for comparisons of achievements, this method is also more respectful of the intrinsic differences across the dimensions than a simple average.

Advantages of new methodology (post-2010 report):

- Maximum value in Goalpost was determined based on observed value using 30 years of data by UNDP
- Knowledge is captured through MYS and EYS
- Use of Geometric Mean to calculate the value of HDI instead of Arithmetic Mean

Significance of the Human Development Index[9]:

- 'Human Development' is an index indicating the development of the country.
- It views human progress and the composite relationship between income and wellbeing.
- Governments often obtain it as an instrument for measuring their performance against that of neighbouring countries.
- A preview of standard national performance in human development.
- Useful access point into the affluent information enclosed in the consequent display tables on different aspects of human development.

Human Development Index of India

India ranked 129 among 188 countries in 2018 as per the Human Development Report 2019 released by the United Nations Development Programme (UNDP). India's HDI value was 0.647

Table 23.5 India's HDI using old and new methodology

Year	*New methodology (post 2010)*	*Old methodology (pre 2009)*
1980	0.362	0.427
1985	0.397	N.A.
1990	0.428	N.A.
1995	0.462	0.513
2000	0.496	N.A.
2005	0.539	0.596
2007	0.557	0.612*
2010	0.586	
2015	0.627	
2018	0.647	

Source: Human Development Report (various issues), UNDP
* (as per 2009 report), N.A. – not available

for the year 2018 which puts the country in the Medium Human Development Index (MHDI) category. From 1980 to 2018, India's HDI value increased from 0.362 to 0.647. Life expectancy at birth increased to 69.4 years in 2018 which was 53.9 years in 1980. Gross National Income (GNI) per capita (2011 PPP $) was $6,829 in 2018 up from $5,180 in 2013 and $1,255 in 1980. The expected years of schooling increased up to 12.3 years which had been stagnant at 11.7 years since 2011. Also, mean years of schooling increased up to 6.5 years which has not changed since 2010.

It can be seen from Table 23.5 that as per the new methodology the value of India's HDI increased from 0.362 to 0.647 during the period from 1980 to 2018. While as per the old methodology, India's HDI value increased from 0.427 to 0.612 during the period from 1980 to 2007. New methodology was found to be superior compared to old methodology as far as a concern to the determination of goalposts, capturing knowledge and the use of an appropriate mean, i.e. geometric mean to calculate the value of HDI. However, the use of the new methodology reduces India's value of HDI significantly and brings back the progress of HDI by around one decade.

Deterministic regression model of Human Development Index (HDI) for India

As described earlier, the HDI is a composite index measuring average achievement in three basic dimensions of human development – a long and healthy life captured through the Health Index (HI), being knowledgeable measured through the Education Index (EI) and having a decent standard of living calculated using the Income Index (II). To estimate the contribution of each separate index i.e. HI, EI and II in HDI, the following deterministic regression model is applied for India using data from 1990 to 2014. Results of this model will be useful for policymakers to formulate an appropriate policy to increase the value of India's HDI. It will also help the policymakers to decide among health, education and income, where more interventions are required to improve India's performance in HDI.

Human Development Index (HDI) = Health Index (HI)
+ Education Index (EI) + Income Index (II)

Since the deterministic model is applied, no residual or error term is incorporated in the model. Following are the results of the above regression model.

Table 23.6 Model summary

Model	*R*	*R square*	*Adjusted R square*	*Std. error of the estimate*
1	1.000[a]	1.000	1.000	.000491

Source: Author's calculation

In the deterministic model, expected value of R square and Adjusted R square is 1. This has reflected from Table 23.6 in model summary. As the value of HDI is derived using value of HI, EI and II. Hence, these three variables explain 100% variations in HDI.

[a]Predictors: (Constant), Education Index, Income Index, Health Index

Table 23.7 ANOVA[b]

Model	*Sum of squared*	*Df*	*Mean square*	*F*	*Sig.*
Regression	.058	3	.019	80151.44	.000[a]
Residual	.000	9	.000		
Total	.058	12			

Source: Author's calculation

[a]Predictors: (Constant), Education Index, Income Index, Health Index

[b]Dependent Variable: HDI

Table 23.8 Coefficients[a]

Model	*Unstandardized coefficients*		*Standardized coefficients*	*t*	*Sig.*
	B	*Std. Error*	*Beta*		
(Constant)	−.006	0.15		−.383	.711
Health Index	.257	.043	.202	5.918	.000
Income Index	.330	.020	.323	16.680	.000
Education Index	.446	.020	.478	22.185	.000

Source: Author's calculation

[a]Dependent variable: HDI

In ANOVA Table 23.7, the calculated value of F-statistics is 80151.44 and its associated significance value is 0.000 which is lower compare to 0.01. This indicates that the model is specified correctly at a 99% confidence level and all three explanatory variables, i.e. HI, EI and II are important variables and they explain 100% variations in the dependent variable, i.e. HDI.

Table 23.8 provides details of estimated coefficients. Using unstandardized coefficients, the following model is estimated for India.

$$\mathbf{HDI = -0.006 + 0.257\,HI^{***} + 0.330\,II^{***} + 0.446\,EI^{***}}$$

*** indicates significant at 0.01

Interpretation of estimated coefficients and policy recommendation:

(1) Holding Income Index and Education Index constant, one unit increase in Health Index will increase the value of HDI by 0.257 units.

(2) Keeping Education Index and Health Index constant, one unit increase in Income Index will increase the value of HDI by 0.330 units.
(3) When Health Index and Income Index remain constant, one unit increase in Education Index will increase the value of HDI by 0.446 units.
(4) Estimated coefficients of Health Index, Income Index and Education Index are statistically significant at a 99% confidence level.
(5) Among health, income and education, relatively education contributes more in human development compared to health and income in India.
(6) As far as policy recommendation is concerned, for improvement in the value of human development index, education should be given the highest priority followed by income generation and providing health-related services.

Forecasting of India's HDI

To have a better and appropriate forecasting value of HDI; time series analysis with sophisticated forecasting model like Auto Regressive Integrated Moving Average (ARIMA) has been applied.

Model description

Among different ARIMA models, ARIMA (0,1,0) model was found to be the most suitable for forecasting the value of HDI (for both, in-sample and out-sample). Following are the results of model fit and model statistics.

Model Fit

The estimated mean value of R-square, RMSE, MAPE, MaxAPE, MAE and MaxAE for ARIMA (0,1,0) model as given in Table 23.9 is given as Model Fit. The mean value of R-square is 1.00, which indicates that on average this estimated model through the ARIMA procedure has the capacity to explain about 100% variations in HDI. The mean value of Stationary R-squared[10] is 0.232, indicating that the model under consideration is better than the baseline model. The mean of MAPE is 0.259, which is less than 1%. The mean of MaxAPE is 0.590, which is also less than 1%. This indicates that the maximum mean absolute percentage error is 0.590, which is very small, so one can rely on the forecasting. This model gives even at MaxAPE level more than 99% accuracy in forecasting.

Model Statistics

Table 23.10 of Model Statistics suggests that there is one outlier in the data. The calculated value of Ljung-Box Q[11] is 17.233 and its associated significance value is 0.507 which is greater compared to 0.01 (at 99% confidence level); this means residuals are normally distributed.

Table 23.11 provides information on actual and predicted value of HDI along with its residuals based on results obtained using ARIMA (0,1,0) model for the period 1980–2018. The ARIMA (0,1,0) model predicts the value of HDI during 1980 to 2018 with more than 99% accuracy as value of residual (gap between actual value of HDI and predicted value of HDI) for all years during 1980 to 2018 as almost zero (0). Hence one can rely on this model for out sample forecast. India has Lower Human Development Index (LHDI) up to year 2000. From

Table 23.9 Model fit

Fit statistic	*Mean*	*Minimum*	*Maximum*	*Percentile*						
				5	*10*	*25*	*50*	*75*	*90*	*95*
Stationary R-squared	.232	.232	.232	.232	.232	.232	.232	.232	.232	.232
R-squared	1.000	1.000	1.000	1.000	1.000	1.000	1.000	1.000	1.000	1.000
RMSE	.002	.002	.002	.002	.002	.002	.002	.002	.002	.002
MAPE	.259	.259	.259	.259	.259	.259	.259	.259	.259	.259
MaxAPE	.590	.590	.590	.590	.590	.590	.590	.590	.590	.590
MAE	.001	.001	.001	.001	.001	.001	.001	.001	.001	.001
MaxAE	.004	.004	.004	.004	.004	.004	.004	.004	.004	.004
Normalized BIC	−12.574	−12.574	−12.574	−12.574	−12.574	−12.574	−12.574	−12.574	−12.574	−12.574

Source: Author's calculation
RMSE: Root Mean Square Error, MAPE: Mean Absolute Percentage Error, MAE: Mean absolute error, MaxAPE: Maximum Absolute Percentage Error, MaxAE: Maximum Absolute Error

Table 23.10 Model statistics

Model	*Number of predictors*	*Model fit statistics*				*Ljung-Box Q(18)*			*Number of outliers*
		Stationary R-squared	*R-squared*	*MAPE*	*MaxAPE*	*Statistics*	*DF*	*Sig.*	
HDI_Value_ INDIA-Model_1	0	.232	1.000	.259	.590	17.233	18	.507	1

Source: Author's calculation

2001 onwards India enters in to Medium Level Human Development Index (MHDI) as India's value of HDI is greater than 0.5.

Out sample forecasting of India's HDI value

To get the answer for which year India will enter the High Human Development Index (HHDI) and Very High Human Development Index (VHHDI), out sample forecasting has been done using the ARIMA (0,1,0) model. Table 23.12 provides result of the out sample forecasting value of India's HDI from 2019 to 2055.

It was found that India's value of HDI will be greater than 0.8 by 2039 and greater than 0.9 by 2053. Hence, India will have HHDI by 2039 and VHHDI by 2053. Figure 23.1 describes the observed, fitted and forecasted value of India's HDI from 1980 to 2018.

Observations about HDI

The following five observations are quite pertinent about the HDI (Selim, 2015):

1. *First*, the HDI is not a comprehensive measure of human development. It just focuses on the basic dimensions of human development and does not take into account a number of other important dimensions of human development.
2. *Second*, it is composed of long-term human development outcomes. Thus it does not reflect the input efforts in terms of policies nor can it measure short-term human development achievements.
3. *Third*, it shares all the limitations of composite measures. But it is important to keep it simple with minimum variables to ensure its acceptability, understanding and predictability.
4. *Fourth*, the HDI is an average measure and thus masks a series of disparities and inequalities within countries. Disaggregation of the HDI in terms of gender, regions, races and ethnic groups can unmask the HDI and can be and has been used widely for policy formulation.
5. *Fifth*, income enters into the HDI not in its own right, but as a proxy for resources needed to have a decent standard of living. The issue with regard to income is how it is transformed into the health and education dimensions of the HDI. Thus between income and the other two dimensions of the HDI, the issue is that of *transformation*, and not of *substitution*.

Conclusion

The Human Development Index was created to emphasize that expanding human choices should be the ultimate criterion for assessing development results. Economic growth is a mean

Table 23.11 Actual and forecasted value of HDI for India (1980 to 2018)

Year	*HDI actual*	*Forecasted HDI using ARIMA (0,1,0)*	*Residual (forecasted – actual)*
1980	0.362	–	–
1981	0.369	0.369	.000
1982	0.376	0.376	.000
1983	0.383	0.383	.000
1984	0.390	0.390	.000
1985	0.397	0.397	.000
1986	0.403	0.404	–.001
1987	0.409	0.411	–.001
1988	0.416	0.417	–.001
1989	0.422	0.423	–.001
1990	0.431	0.429	.002
1991	0.436	0.438	–.002
1992	0.442	0.443	–.001
1993	0.449	0.449	.000
1994	0.456	0.456	.000
1995	0.463	0.463	.000
1996	0.471	0.470	.001
1997	0.477	0.478	–.001
1998	0.484	0.484	.000
1999	0.492	0.491	.001
2000	0.497	0.499	–.002
2001	0.502	0.504	–.002
2002	0.508	0.509	–.001
2003	0.521	0.521	.000
2004	0.530	0.528	.002
2005	0.539	0.537	.002
2006	0.548	0.546	.002
2007	0.558	0.555	.003
2008	0.565	0.565	.000
2009	0.571	0.572	–.001
2010	0.581	0.578	.003
2011	0.590	0.588	.002
2012	0.600	0.597	.003
2013	0.607	0.607	.000
2014	0.618	0.614	.004
2015	0.627	0.625	.002
2016	0.637	0.634	.003
2017	0.643	0.644	–.001
2018	0.647	0.650	–.003

Source: Author's calculation.

to that process, but is not an end by itself. It was found that as per the new methodology, the value of India's HDI increased from 0.362 to 0.647 during the period from 1980 to 2018. While as per the old methodology, India's HDI value increased from 0.427 to 0.612 from 1980 to 2007. The new methodology is found to be superior compared to the old methodology in terms of the determination of goalposts, capturing knowledge and use of an appropriate mean, i.e. geo-

Table 23.12 Out sample forecasting of India's HDI value

Year	*Forecasted HDI*	*Year*	*Forecasted HDI*
2019	0.654	2038	0.794
2020	0.662	**2039**	**0.801**
2021	0.669	2040	0.809
2022	0.676	2041	0.816
2023	0.684	2042	0.823
2024	0.691	2043	0.831
2025	0.698	2044	0.838
2026	0.706	2045	0.845
2027	0.713	2046	0.853
2028	0.721	2047	0.860
2029	0.728	2048	0.868
2030	0.735	2049	0.875
2031	0.743	2050	0.882
2032	0.750	2051	0.890
2033	0.757	2052	0.897
2034	0.765	**2053**	**0.904**
2035	0.772	2054	0.912
2036	0.779	2055	0.919
2037	0.787		

Source: Author's calculation.

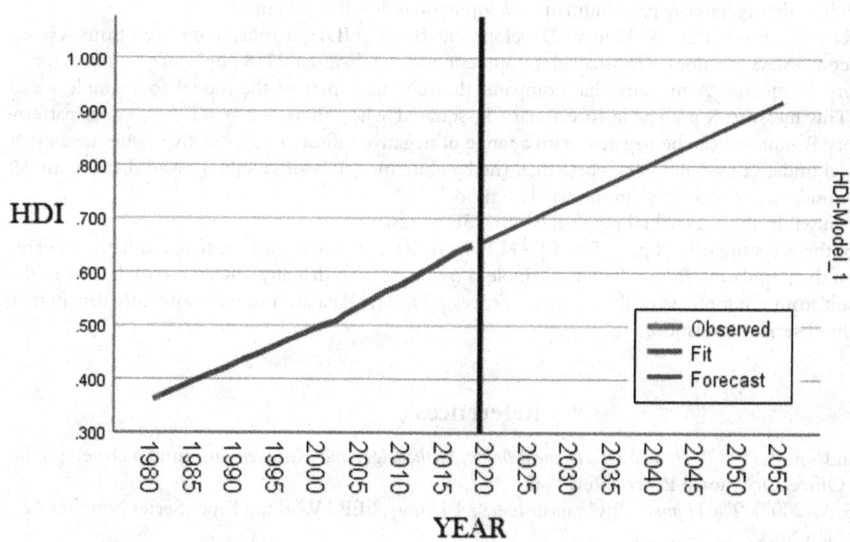

Figure 23.1 Observed, fit and forecasted value of India's HDI from 1980 to 2018

metric mean to calculate the value of HDI. Based on the deterministic model of the Human Development Index for India, it was found that relatively the Education Index (EI) contributes more in increasing the value of India's Human Development Index compared to the Health Index (HI) and Income Index (II), using data from 1990 to 2014. The ARIMA (0,1,0) model predicts the value of HDI from 1980 to 2018 with more than 99% accuracy as the value of residuals for all years from 1980 to 2018 is almost zero (0). Based on our sample forecast, it was found that India's value of HDI will be greater than 0.8 by 2039 and greater than 0.9 by 2053. Hence, India will have HHDI by 2039 and VHHDI by 2053. The HDI has limited scope. It cannot provide a complete picture of human development in any situation. It has to be supplemented with other useful indicators in order to get a comprehensive view. Thus, it is human development accounting, not the HDI, which can portray the complete picture of the country's development.

Notes

1 The present chapter is a revised version of the paper entitled 'Determinants and Prediction of Human Development Index (HDI) in India: Measurements and Methodological Issues' presented in the National Seminar on *India after a Quarter Century of Economic Reforms: The Benefits and Costs*, organized by Department of Economics, Sikkim University, Gangtok, India during 5–6 October 2018 and the paper entitled 'Human Development Index (HDI) of India: Methodological Issues for Measurement and Forecasting' in an edited book entitled 'Bettering Indian Economy: A Global Perspective' published by N.S. Patel Arts College: Anand (Gujarat).

2 http://hdr.undp.org/en/media/Primer_complete.pdf

3 www.undp.org.bz/human-development/what-is-human-development/

4 www.ijsret.org/pdf/rahul_bhardwaj.pdf

5 http://terpconnect.umd.edu/~dcrocker/Courses/Docs/Scott%20-%20Human%20Development%20Briefing%20Note.pdf

6 MYS: Mean years of schooling (years that a 25-year-old person or older has spent in schools).

7 EYS: Expected years of schooling (years that a 5-year-old child will spend with his education in his whole life).

8 http://hdr.undp.org/en/faq-page/human-development-index-hdi#t292n50

9 Essays, UK. (November 2013). Human Development Index (HDI) of India. Retrieved from www.ukessays.com/essays/economics/human-development-index-hdi-india-2718.php?vref=1

10 Stationary R-squared: A measure that compares the stationary part of the model to a simple mean model. This measure is preferable to ordinary R-squared when there is a trend or seasonal pattern. Stationary R-squared can be negative with a range of negative infinity to 1. Negative values mean that the model under consideration is worse than the baseline model. Positive values mean that the model under consideration is better than the baseline model.

11 https://en.wikipedia.org/wiki/Ljung%E2%80%93Box_test

Hypothesis testing using Ljung-Box Q – H_0: The data are independently distributed (i.e. the correlations in the population from which the sample is taken are 0, so that any observed correlations in the data result from randomness of the sampling process), H_a: The data are not independently distributed; they exhibit serial correlation.

References

Anand, S., and Sen, A. (1997). *Human Development Index, Methodology and Measurement*, Human Development Report Office, Occasional Paper., New York

Elizabeth, E. A. (2007). *The Human Development Index: A History*, PERI Working Paper Series Number 127, UNDP, New York.

Haq, M. (1997). *Reflection of Human Development*, Oxford University Press, New York.

Kundu, A., Shariff, A., and Ghosh, P. (2002). *Indexing Human Development in India: Indicators, Scaling and Composition*, Working Paper Series Number 83, National Council of Applied Economic Research (NCAER), New Delhi.

Mahapatra, M., and Raj, R. (2009). *Human Development in India: Issues and Challenges*, New Century Publications, New Delhi.

Rami, G. (2020). Human Development Index (HDI) of India: Methodological Issues for Measurements and Forecasting, in A. A. Shaikh and P. Brijen (eds.), *Bettering Indian Economy: A Global Perspective*, N.S. Patel Arts College, Anand, pp. 175–200.

Selim, J. (2015). The Human Development Index – What It Is and What It Is Not, Retrieve from http://hdr.undp.org/en/hdi-what-it-is

Sen, A. (1977). *Human Capital and Human Capacity*, Oxford University Press, New York.

Sen, A. (1993). Capability and Well-Being, in M. Nussbaum and A. Sen (eds.), *The Quality of Life*, Clarendon Press, Oxford, pp. 30–53.

Sen, A. (2000). A Decade of Human Development, *Journal of Human Development*, Vol. 1, No. 1, pp. 17–24.

UKEssays. (2013). Human Development Index (HDI) of India, Retrieved from http://www.ukessays.com/essays/economics/human-development-index-hdi-india-2718.php?vref=1

UNDP (1990). *Human Development Report*, Oxford University Press, New York.

UNDP (2009). *Human Development Report*, Oxford University Press, New York.

UNDP (2010). *Human Dev elopement Report*, Oxford University Press, New York.

UNDP (2019). *Human Development Report*, Oxford University Press, New York.

Welzel, C., Inglehart, R., and Klingemann, H. (2003). The Theory of Human Development: A Cross-Cultural Analysis, *European Journal of Political Research*, Vol. 42, pp. 341–379.

PART VI

Sectoral and regional issues

24

THE DYNAMICS OF ECONOMIC GROWTH IN INDIA'S NORTH-EASTERN REGION IN THE PRE- AND POST-REFORM PERIODS

Komol Singha and Rajesh Raj S. N.

Introduction

In economic parlance, the concept of 'development' refers to a dynamic process, which transforms an economy from a relatively backward to an advanced level. In short, economic development encompasses growth with institutional changes. The New Economic Policy 1991 (NEP or economic reform) has been an important landmark in India's economic reform history. Under this policy, India's economy has undergone a drastic transformation by giving markets more leverage and lifting restrictions which were embedded in various sectors of the economy. The country's north-eastern region (NER or simply region hereafter)[1] is no exception in this regard. In the post-reform period, a huge amount of funds has been pumped into this region through the Ministry for Development of North Eastern Region (DoNER) for speedy development, especially for the basic physical infrastructural projects. At the same time, the Look East Policy (LEP) was framed in 1991 for greater economic integration of the country with the ASEAN nations through NER, albeit the modalities of the policy (LEP) were not very clear. There is some evidence of disappointment over the LEP to capture nuances of India's post-cold war re-engagement with South Asia (Bajpaee 2017). In 2014, the policy was renamed as Act East Policy (AEP) for strengthening greater economic cooperation with the Asia-Pacific region beyond the ASEAN. India's NER being the gateway to these nations, growth of this region, especially the basic physical infrastructures, is essential and hence given top priority in this policy. Recently, NITI Aayog has also outlined five major sectors for the speedy development of this region. They are horticulture, tourism, handicraft (bamboo-based), food processing and medium-scale industries with a mission to 'Make in North-East' (*The Times of India* 2018).

In conventional wisdom, the ideal form of a pro-poor economic development process begins with an objective to transform its economy via investment in the agriculture sector (Roumasset 2004). This idea of pro-poor economic development is widely prevalent in most of the developing countries in the world, where agriculture provides livelihood to around 70 per cent of the poor, either directly or indirectly (Wik et al. 2008). Due to its ability to provide a livelihood to the rural poor, this sector is considered a driving force for the development of the rural economy. However, for achieving sustained and long-term development, an economy cannot entirely

 DOI: 10.4324/9780367855741-24

depend on just agriculture. After a certain stage of development, growth in the industrial and manufacturing sector is equally essential (Kniivila 2007). This idea was also reflected in Rostow's stages of growth. According to a study by Rondinelli, Johnson and Kasarda (1998), the tertiary sector may turn out to be the best option for speedy development in the twenty-first century as it encompasses high-technology industries and information-based services.[2] Nevertheless, to date, there is still no consensus, either from theoretical formulation or empirical analysis, on whether any developed nation started with the agriculture sector or the economic development stimulated the agriculture sector (Beckford 1965).

Against this backdrop, it is important to investigate the forces that actually drive the economy of NER, both in pre- and post-reform periods. Since NER is considered a vital cog in India's Act East Policy, it is therefore essential to study the economic growth dynamics of the region. From a policy perspective too, it is indispensable to know the sectoral contributions, inter-state growth trends and other growth dynamics in the region's economy. Some of the major research questions that have been raised in this study are: (1) Does this region continue to remain at the pre-traditional stage of growth? (2) Has the NEP enhanced the region's economy, especially in the post-reform period? (3) Which sector is acting as a driving force for economic growth in the region? (4) Has the growth trend been quite smooth and uniform across the states of NER in the last three decades?

Conceptual framework and literature

Kaldorian growth theory hinges around four fundamental dimensions: (1) economic development requires industrialisation, (2) industrialisation in turn stimulates agricultural revolution, (3) development needs global market and requires a certain level of protection for the newly established industries and (4) the state must encourage export-led growth policies (Targetti 2005). Therefore, a synergetic approach is necessary for sustainable development. With the development and popularity of technological innovations, the importance of growth theory developed by Robert Solow has now been felt by many growth economists who have tried to endogenise his concept, 'Solow residual' by using technological changes in the long run. Similarly, Ayres (1998) felt a need to reflect the existence of some 'growth engines' in the development process, apart from the population and traditional saving investment mechanism. In this manner, the modern world economies have developed from the stages that built on the extraction of raw materials for consumption and sale to those that are more dependent on the revenue from services. Such economic shift is important not only to understand from a sector in isolation but also to look from an integrated manner, including the primary, secondary and tertiary sectors. It is quite contextual in nature that rapid global economic development is made up of complex country-specific or region-specific problems. Rostow (1959) believes that modern economic growth theory cannot bypass any one of the stages of growth that encompass five sequential stages – traditional society, preconditions for take-off, take-off, drive to maturity and age of high mass consumption.

While analysing the drivers of growth in the Malaysian context, Cheen (2005) explored that more than agriculture or manufacturing, the service sector has been identified as highly dependent on the abilities and know-how of people. While understanding Africa's growth momentum, the role of its rich natural resources was widely recognised. But, the institutional and other service sectors were not much talked about. On the other hand, the McKinsey Global Institute's research report showed that the role of natural resources in enhancing economic development in Africa accounted for only about one-third of the new-found growth since the 2000s and the rest of it resulted from the internal structural changes that spurred the broader domestic economy (Leke et al. 2010). In India, a study by Kathuria and Raj (2013) found that manufacturing has been the engine of growth, supported by the ICT-induced service sector. Using vector auto-regression analysis, Chakravarty and Mitra (2009) also explored and found more or less the same result. However, some other studies (e.g. Thomas 2009; Dasgupta and Singh 2006) found the service sector to be the prime mover of growth resurgence in India since the 1990s.

Apart from the agriculture sector's serious implication of 'inclusiveness' on the growth dynamics for the long term, the synergistic linkage among various sectors and the forces of globalisation, especially the financial development, have focused more on achieving higher inclusive growth (Nayak et al. 2010). As per a report of DoNER (2013), in NER, primary and tertiary sectors have been the main drivers of growth, and the same has also been reflected in the 11th Five Year Plan document. But, these days, growing activities like transport and communication, banking and insurance, trade and commerce, hotel and restaurant, real estates and others seem to generate more employment both in the public and private sectors in the region. Another study by Debnath and Roy (2012) explored how the growth of the region's economy depends largely on the degree of sectoral interdependence. Income generated from the services sector is one of the drivers of growth and this, in turn, depends on the growth of agriculture and industry. According to Singha (2010), with the emergence of globalisation and liberalisation, the opportunities for economic development by integrating and participating the region with the neighbouring markets has been realised. But the trade policies linking NER with ASEAN markets under LEP/AEP must be reformulated to fit the global trade environment. However, Menon (2007) lamented that even after the country's 60 years of planned economic strategy the isolated region (NER) is still lagging behind other major states of the country in different economic parameters. The region is seemingly missing economic opportunities of globalisation and economic reform opportunities due to its imbalanced basic economic structure. According to Nayak and Mishra (2013), though the states of Tripura and Assam have done well in the wake of industrialisation and privatisation, the major impact of it is not much visible in the region as a whole. Investment from the private sector was still negligible in the post-reform era. Loitongbam (2018) focused more on the regional trade and investment promotion agencies for the speedy development of the region. In this manner, the inconclusive findings and conflicting study results in terms of the factors or the sectors influencing the region's economic growth in the long run drew attention for the scholars and academia to re-examine the issue scientifically.

Objectives and methodology

Using secondary data, the present paper attempts to assess the growth and trend of the region's (NER) economy in the last three decades. The sector-wise and state-wise contributions within the region are also discussed with an objective to identify the best performing sector and state. The paper further tries to examine the long-run impact of the new economic policy or reform in NER, especially in the post reform era. It also attempts to assess inter-state inequality and decadal growth level.

In order to measure decadal growth trends, the study period from 1981 to 2012 has been decomposed into three: 1981–1991 (henceforth 1980s), 1991–2001 (henceforth 1990s) and 2001–2012 (henceforth 2000s). Due to lack of appropriate and consistent time series data across the states, data analysis on the post-reform period is restricted up to 2012–13. Hence, the impacts of policy changes introduced by the NDA government from 2014 onwards are not covered. Similarly, due to lack of consistent time series data, the state of Mizoram has been excluded, hence only seven states of the region – Assam, Arunachal, Manipur, Meghalaya, Nagaland, Sikkim and Tripura – have been included in this study. While treating the dataset, the issue of non-stationarity has been tackled by employing Augmented Dickey-Fuller (ADF) technique. The study has also employed Gini Co-efficient to estimate inter-state disparity within the region. For simplification of the general readers, the sectors have been classified into three broad categories:

(1) Primary sector that includes agriculture, fishing, forestry and logging, (2) Secondary sector that includes manufacturing overall, mining and quarrying and (3) Tertiary/service sector that includes banking, real estate, ownership of dwellings and business services, trade, hotels and restaurants, transport, storage and communication, and others. Further, to capture economic growth in NER, the study relies on two basic indicators – Gross State Domestic Product (GSDP) and Per Capita GSDP. Data used in this study have been mainly drawn from the EPW Research Foundation (EPWRF) and Central Statistical Organisation (CSO). Since the GSDP values were expressed on different base years, they were arithmetically brought to a common base year, 2004–05, so as to make the figures comparable over time and across the states. Both regression and elasticity analyses have been employed to identify the drivers of economic growth in the region.

GSDP growth performance

The annual average growth rates of GSDP in NER during the period from 1981 to 2012 are presented in Table 24.1. By comparing average GSDP growth in the last three decades, it gives us an impression that the region experienced a slow growth during the 1990s and a sharp increase in the 2000s. The combined GSDP growth of the entire region was registered at 4.4 per cent compound annual growth rate (CAGR) in the 1980s. But, in the 1990s, the region experienced a slight slowdown in the growth rate, which dropped to 4 per cent. Interestingly, in the 2000s, the growth rate witnessed a significant upsurge at an annual compound growth rate of 6.4 per cent. Further, the study also found a considerable disparity in growth performance across the states in the 1980s and 1990s. However, in the 2000s, the degree of growth disparity in the region was found to be declining drastically. It is well reflected by the coefficient of variation (CV) values in Table 24.1. The CV values increased from 0.22 in the 1980s to 0.43 in the 1990s, and sharply declined to 0.04 in the 2000s. If we assess the overall growth trend from 1981 to 2012, the annual average GSDP growth in NER was estimated at 4.7 per cent, which is lower than the national level of 5.7 per cent. It is clear that the region's decadal GSDP growth rate has been lower than that of the national level throughout the study period.

Table 24.1 Decadal growth rate of GSDP/GDP (in %)

State	*1981–91*	*1991–2001*	*2001–12*	*1981–2012*
Arunachal	6.2	0.5	6.1	3.6
Meghalaya	3.4	5.3	6.2	4.7
Sikkim	4.1	5.0	6.7	5.3
Assam	4.5	3.0	6.4	4.5
Nagaland	5.0	4.9	6.7	6.1
Tripura	3.8	4.8	6.7	5.2
Manipur	3.6	4.7	6.2	3.6
NER	4.4	4.0	6.4	4.7
India	4.7	4.7	7.6	5.7
CV	0.22	0.43	0.04	0.19

Source: Authors' calculations from CSO and EPWRF data.
Note: NER excludes Mizoram; India covers an average of 15 major states and Assam is also included in it; CV implies Coefficient ofVariation.

When we look at the state-wise growth trend, in the 1980s, the annual GSDP growth rate of the states within the region ranges as low as 3.4 per cent in Meghalaya to the highest rate of 6.2 per cent in Arunachal Pradesh. In the 1990s, Arunachal Pradesh registered the lowest rate at 0.5 per cent and the state of Meghalaya turned out to be the best performer during the decade in NER, with registered growth rate at 5.3 per cent. In the 2000s, there was a drastic increase in the GSDP growth trend across the states in the region. In fact, all seven states included in the present study registered an average annual GSDP growth rate above 6 per cent, ranging from as low as 6.1 per cent in Arunachal Pradesh to as high as 6.7 per cent in each of Sikkim, Tripura and Nagaland. However, one must note that the average GSDP growth rate for the states in NER was still less than that of the all India GDP average during the study period (1981–2012).

While analysing the two geographically bigger states within the region, Arunachal Pradesh and Assam, a drastic fall in GSDP growth trend in the 1990s was observed. Fortunately, all the states in NER performed well in the 2000s, with the states of Sikkim, Nagaland and Tripura registering growth rates higher than the region's overall average rate. Whether the NEP has driven this economic growth in the region requires a thorough investigation.

Per capita GSDP growth

For a better understanding of the intra-regional disparities in the region, an analysis of the growth of per capita GSDP has been made. Figure 24.1 portrays the income per capita growth rates for the seven states for two decades of pre reform periods – 1981–1991 on the horizontal axis and 1991–2001 on the vertical axis. Three out of the seven states lie above the 45 degree line. They are Manipur, Meghalaya and Tripura. This implies that these three states substantially enhanced their GSDP per capita income in the 1990s. The average annual GSDP per capita growth of the region registered at 3.5 per cent in the 1980s, but declined to 2.6 per cent in the 1990s (see Table 24.2).

For easy comparison of the growth between the pre and post reform periods, a similar exercise but for different decades (post reform periods) has been done and depicted in Figure 24.2. The growth trends of per capita income for six states for the period 1991–2001 are given on the horizontal axis and for 2001–2011 are depicted on the vertical axis. The annual average GSDP per capita growth rates for the six states lie above the 45 degree line. This indicates that there has been a substantial growth in GSDP per capita in the region in the post reform period. In

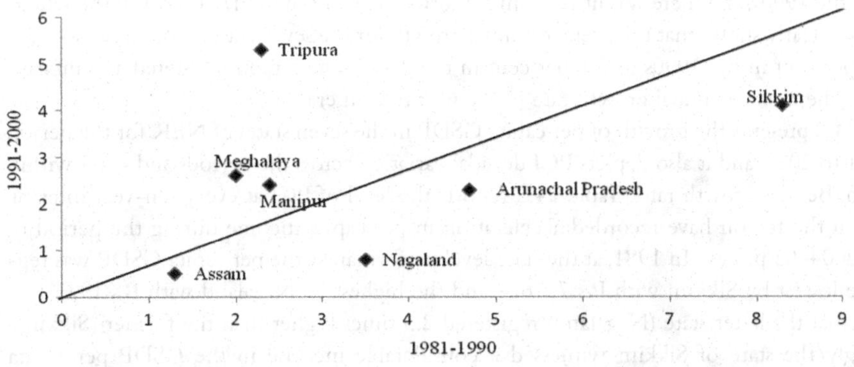

Figure 24.1 Annual average growth rate of GSDP per capita (in 1981–90 and 1991–2000) Source: Authors' calculations from CSO and EPWRF data.

Table 24.2 Annual growth rate of GSDP/GDP per capita

State	*Per capita GSDP level (in Rs)*				*Per capita GSDP growth (in % per year)*			
	1981	*1991*	*2001*	*2012*	*1981–90*	*1991–2000*	*2001–12*	*1981–2012*
Arunachal	9317	15971	21431	40556	4.7	2.3	5.6	4.4
Meghalaya	13019	17400	22523	42003	2.0	2.6	6.0	3.8
Sikkim	7516	16484	24458	68826	8.3	4.1	7.6	6.2
Assam	12946	15638	16762	26037	1.3	0.5	4.1	1.8
Nagaland	19091	26485	29885	46546	3.5	0.8	4.1	2.2
Tripura	9359	12071	20018	42968	2.3	5.3	6.7	5.4
Manipur	11532	14527	17464	26692	2.4	2.4	4.0	2.6
NER	11826	16939	21792	44052	3.5	2.6	5.4	3.8
India	13514	17341	23244	45177	2.5	2.8	6.0	3.8
CV	0.32	0.27	0.21	0.44	0.68	0.66	0.26	0.44

Source: Authors' calculations from CSO and EPWRF data.

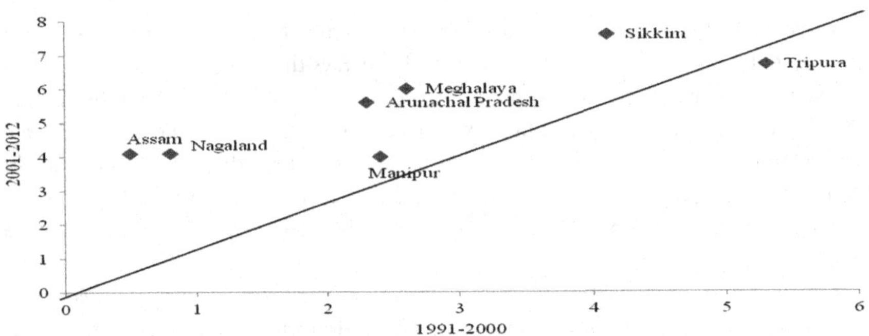

Figure 24.2 Annual average growth rate of GSDP per capita (in 1991–2000 and 2001–12) Source: Authors' calculations from CSO and EPWRF data.

the case of Tripura, one must argue that the state had already exhibited a substantial per capita growth in the 1990s, and there was little room for further expansion in the 2000s. On the whole, our analysis clearly shows that the average annual growth for the seven states more than doubled from 2.6 per cent in the 1990s to 5.4 per cent in the 2000s. The region registered a significant increase in the average annual growth rate in the post reform era.

Table 24.2 presents the growth of per capita GSDP in the seven states of NER for the period from 1981 to 2012, and it also depicts PCI decadal variation across the periods and states within the region. Besides growth rates, Table 24.2 reports the level of PCI at every ten-year interval. All states in the region have recorded acceleration in per capita income during the period of study (at 2004–05 prices). In 1981, at the state level performance, the per capita GSDP was registered the lowest by Sikkim with Rs 7516/– and the highest by Nagaland with Rs 19,091/–. It implies that the latter state (Nagaland) registered 2.5 times higher than the former (Sikkim). Interestingly, the state of Sikkim witnessed a considerable increase in the GSDP per capita growth after economic reform policy in the country, and recorded the highest in the region with per capita income of Rs 68,826/– in 2012.

In terms of growth rate, we find a considerable variation in PCI across the states, especially in the 1980s and 1990s. If we go by the coefficient of variation value reported in Table 24.2, it is clearly indicated that the regional disparity in terms of standard of living, as measured by per capita GSDP at constant prices, barely changed during the 1980s and 1990s. In the 1980s, Assam recorded the lowest per capita GSDP growth to the tune of 1.3 per cent per annum and Sikkim recorded the highest with 8.3 per cent. Three states, namely Sikkim, Arunachal Pradesh and Nagaland recorded significantly higher growth rates than the average annual GDP growth rate of the country as a whole (average of 15 major states of India including Assam). Though there had been an evidence of a marginal slowdown in PCI (2.6 per cent per annum) in the 1990s, it increased sharply in the 2000s at the rate of 5.4 per cent. Nevertheless, NER was able to catch up with the national average of 3.8 per cent in terms of average annual growth rate of GSDP per capita during the period 1981 to 2012.

When we look closely across the states in the region, a wide variation of PCI growth rate was found in the 1990s, ranging from as low as 0.5 per cent in Assam to 5.3 per cent in Tripura. It is evident from the CV value that there was a considerable decline in inter-regional PCI growth disparity in the 2000s.[3] During 2001 to 2012, Manipur registered the lowest annual growth rate (4 per cent), while Sikkim registered the highest (7.6 per cent). During the same period, in the region, the states of Sikkim, Tripura and Meghalaya registered relatively higher growth rates, which even exceeded the national average. More importantly, the growth performance of Sikkim and Tripura was very impressive as their growth rates jumped significantly from 4.1 per cent and 5.3 per cent respectively in the 1990s to 7.6 per cent and 6.7 per cent respectively in the 2000s. The performance of some other states, which had initially lagged far behind the national and regional average, have now improved in the latter stages. As a result of which, the overall average annual growth rate of GSDP per capita in NER has increased from 2.6 per cent in the 1990s to 5.4 per cent in the 2000s. We have already witnessed a significant improvement in terms of PCI in most of the states in the 2000s. In totality, the region has been remarkably successful in registering significant growth rates both in terms of GSDP and PCI during the study period.

Figure 24.3 shows the growth of GSDP per capita in seven states in four different quadrants: (1) Quadrant I: higher growth both in the 1980s and 1990s, (2) Quadrant II: higher growth in the 1990s, but lower in the 1980s, (3) Quadrant III: lower growth both in the 1980s and 1990s, (4) Quadrant IV: higher growth in the 1980s, but lower in the 1990s. For

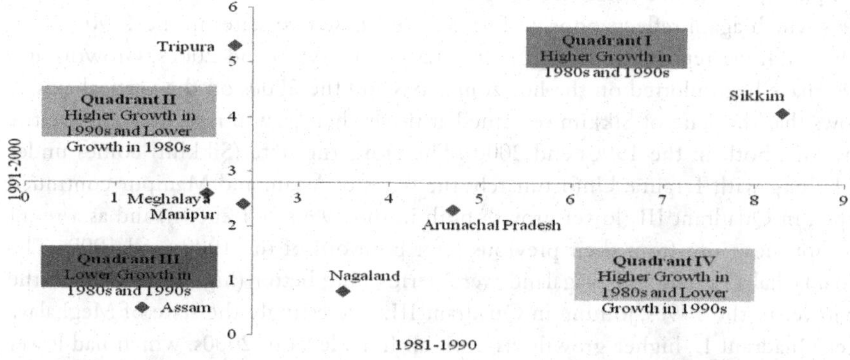

Figure 24.3 Performers' and non-performers' PCI growth in the 1980s and 1990s Note: The origin represents all India average growth rates for the 1980s and 1990s. Source: Authors' calculations from CSO and EPWRF data.

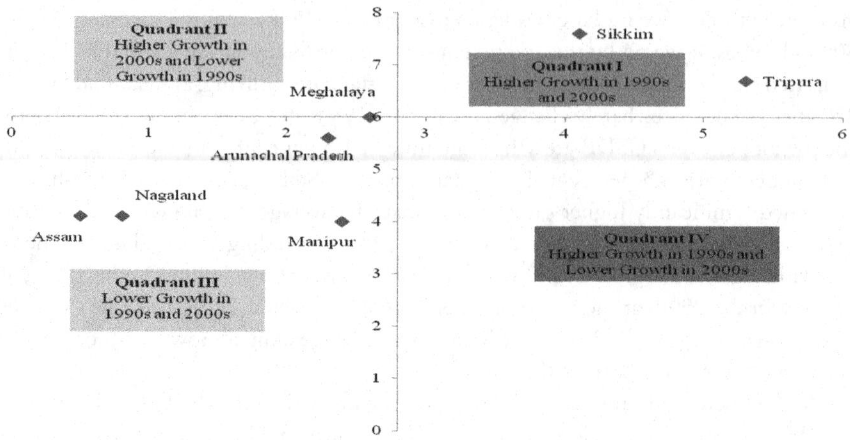

Figure 24.4 Performers' and non-performers' PCI growth in the 1990s and 2000s Note: The origin represents all India average growth rates for the 1990s and 2000s. Source: Authors' calculations from CSO and EPWRF data.

categorising these four quadrants, the all India annual average growth of PCI in the 1980s and 1990s are recorded and found at 2.5 per cent and 2.8 per cent, respectively, and taken as origin or base value. In Figure 24.3, the origin in the scatter plot corresponds to all India growth rates with 2.5 per cent and 2.8 per cent of the 1980s and 1990s respectively. Growth rates of the 1980s have been plotted on the horizontal axis and the 1990s on the vertical axis. From this exercise, in Quadrant I, we observe that the state of Sikkim recorded a higher growth both in the 1980s and 1990s. This gives an impressive picture that the state of Sikkim is the least populated and the smallest state in terms of the geographical area in the entire region and the second smallest state in India (Census of India, 2011). In quadrant II, the state of Tripura recorded a higher growth in the 1990s, but lower in the 1980s. In Quadrant III, the states of Assam, Meghalaya and Manipur have been mapped and registered lower growth, both in the 1980s and 1990s. It is unfortunate that only three states out of the seven in Quadrant III were mapped, but this explains a poor economic performance of the states during the period. In Quadrant IV, the states of Nagaland and Arunachal Pradesh have been figured, and hence these states registered higher growth in the 1980s, but lower in the 1990s which again reflects poor performance of these two states in the 1990s.

In Figure 24.4, we report the PCI growth rates of the 1990s and 2000s. Growth rates of the 1990s have been plotted on the horizontal axis and the 2000s on the vertical axis. It clearly shows that the state of Sikkim remained at the higher growth rate, much above the all India average both in the 1990s and 2000s. Therefore, the state (Sikkim) comes under Quadrant I along with Tripura. Unfortunately, the states of Assam and Manipur continued to be trapped in Quadrant III (lower growth both in the 1990s and 2000s), and as a result they could not move out from their previous poor positions of the 1980s and 1990s. The states of Arunachal Pradesh and Nagaland were performing better (higher growth) in the 1980s but lower in the 1990s, joining in Quadrant III. Interestingly, the state of Meghalaya came under Quadrant II, higher growth vis-à-vis all India level in 2000s, which had lower performance in the 1990s. Fortunately, no state was found to be trapped in Quadrant IV. From this exercise, we can say that the performance of Sikkim has been quite commendable and the growth rate was higher than that of the all India level throughout the period of study. In the case of Tripura, in the 1990s and 2000s, the state improved strikingly, albeit it was found to be quite lacklustre in the 1980s.

Inter-state inequality

Regional differences in terms of per capita income level have long been a matter of concern in India (Ahluwalia 2000). In this section, an attempt has been made to investigate whether there has been any convergence in the growth of per capita GSDP among the states in the region over time. To assess inequality, a popular measure, the Gini Coefficient, has been constructed for the total population of the seven states. It has been constructed with an assumption that all individuals within a state have a gross income equal to the per capita GSDP and it is also assumed that the Gini Coefficient takes care of the inequality emerging from the differences in per capita GSDP growth across the states of the region.

As evident from Figure 24.5, the inter-state inequality depicted by the Gini Coefficient trend line is found to be declining all through the 1980s and 1990s but began to increase in the 2000s. The saddest part in this context is that the rise in inequality in the 2000s even surpassed the inequality level that persisted in the 1980s. This indicates that the states in the region are doing well at the macro level. It is also evident from the statistics given in the previous sections that the increase in income has not been uniformed across the states, mainly going to a few states and this has led to a greater inequality among the states in the region. This further indicates that the number of hitherto poor states during the pre-reform periods either remained poor in the post reform period as well or the hitherto poor states during the pre-reform periods might have been replaced by others in post reform periods within the region, leaving the number of poor states in the region unchanged. It is also possible that a few sections in the society might have enjoyed the benefits/opportunities created by the reform policy in the region. Of course, the region's economy is believed to have been enhanced in the post–economic reform era. For further investigating whether it is merely a natural growth process or driven by the NEP of the country, we need to look at the sectoral contribution in the region.

Sectoral contribution

In order to analyse sectoral share and contribution in the region's economy, the GSDP data have been divided into three major sectors: primary, secondary and tertiary. Further, the share

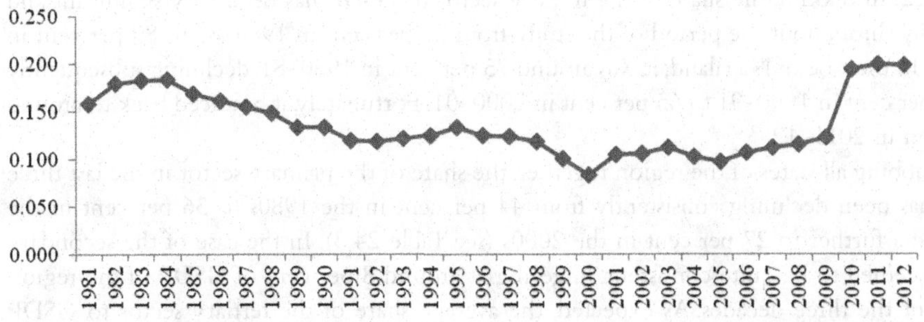

Figure 24.5 Inter-state inequality in NER (Gini-Coefficient) Source: Authors' calculations from CSO and EPWRF data.

Table 24.3 Sectoral share to GSDP in different decades (in %)

Sector	*Year*	*Arunachal*	*Assam*	*Manipur*	*Meghalaya*	*Nagaland*	*Sikkim*	*Tripura*	*NER*
Primary	1980s	76.03	46.06	46.10	43.77	23.74	41.10	57.66	43.59
	1990s	71.19	38.01	35.68	29.26	25.76	35.68	44.46	36.38
	2000s	56.25	31.00	28.88	24.66	33.58	22.36	27.10	27.47
	2011–12	29.98	21.97	26.71	16.26	28.10	13.46	24.69	–
Secondary	1980s	1.77	14.23	6.18	4.04	1.29	7.18	4.66	7.64
	1990s	4.90	18.76	8.12	13.36	4.60	6.63	5.62	8.30
	2000s	5.02	17.02	5.62	10.67	1.74	5.04	9.15	7.50
	2011–12	5.11	13.27	5.00	14.65	2.66	4.40	4.61	–
Tertiary	1980s	22.19	39.70	47.72	52.19	74.97	51.72	37.68	47.97
	1990s	23.91	43.23	56.20	57.38	69.64	57.68	49.92	55.32
	2000s	38.72	51.98	65.50	64.67	64.69	72.60	63.74	64.59
	2011–12	64.91	64.76	68.29	69.09	69.25	82.15	70.71	–

Source: Authors' calculations from CSO and EPWRF data.

of these sectors to total GSDP in different decades is presented across the states of the region in Table 24.3.

From Table 24.3, we can see the growth trend and structure of the sectoral contribution in the economy of NER. Barring Nagaland, the share of the primary sector to GSDP has declined gradually in the region from 1980–81 to 2011–12. The share of the primary sector in the state of Nagaland increased from 24 per cent in 1980–81 to 26 per cent in 1990–91 and further shot up to 34 per cent in 2000–01. However, it started declining thereafter, reached 28 per cent in 2011–12. In the case of the secondary sector, it was quite confusing and inconsistent across the states in the region. The share of the secondary sector to GSDP of Meghalaya and Assam was found to be slightly higher than the other states in the region. Apart from the secondary sector's inconsistent growth pattern over the years, its share to GSDP in five states of the region – Arunachal Pradesh, Manipur, Nagaland, Sikkim and Tripura – have been meagre, as low as below 10 per cent. However, in Assam, the sector's share to GSDP has ranged between 13 and 19 per cent in the last three decades, while it was 11 to 15 per cent in Meghalaya during the same period. With regard to the tertiary sector, it was the opposite of the primary sector. Barring Nagaland, the states of NER increased their share of the tertiary sector to GSDP to a great extent over the three decades. In Arunachal Pradesh, the share of the tertiary sector to GSDP in 1980–81 was hardly registered at 22 per cent, but rose consistently and reached 65 per cent in 2011–12. In Sikkim, the share of the tertiary sector to GSDP has been very significant and rose rapidly throughout the period of the study from 52 per cent in 1980–81 to 82 per cent in 2011–12. In the case of Nagaland, it was around 75 per cent in 1980–81, declining subsequently from 70 per cent in 1990–91 to 65 per cent in 2000–01. Fortunately, it bounced back to around 70 per cent in 2011–12.

On clubbing all states of the region together, the share of the primary sector in the last three decades has been declining consistently from 44 per cent in the 1980s to 36 per cent in the 1990s, and a further to 27 per cent in the 2000s (see Table 24.3). In the case of the secondary sector, it seemed to be quite consistent, lingering at around 8 per cent of GSDP of the region throughout the three decades. As expected, the average share of the tertiary sector to GSDP increased consistently from 48 per cent in the 1980s to 55 per cent in the 1990s, and further rose to 65 per cent in the 2000s (see Table 24.3). This clearly shows that the sectoral growth and share

Table 24.4 Average decadal sectoral growth rate (in %)

Sector	*Decades*	*Arunachal*	*Assam*	*Manipur*	*Meghalaya*	*Nagaland*	*Sikkim*	*Tripura*
Primary	1980s	4.9	1.9	2.0	–0.5	5.1	7.8	1.0
	1990s	–4.9	0.8	1.8	3.8	6.2	1.6	2.6
	2000s	0.7	2.5	6.0	3.0	4.7	2.3	6.6
Secondary	1980s	22.3	4.7	7.6	11.4	3.1	11.7	3.5
	1990s	1.0	2.7	–1.8	3.6	3.3	3.4	5.8
	2000s	6.5	2.1	6.1	9.6	10.8	9.0	3.2
Tertiary	1980s	7.8	4.2	6.5	6.0	4.9	11.2	7.0
	1990s	6.4	3.8	7.1	5.9	4.6	9.0	8.6
	2000s	9.1	7.7	6.4	8.1	7.8	8.9	8.5

Source: Authors' calculations from CSO and EPWRF data.

to GSDP in the region as well as individual states have been more or less the same. However, in terms of the tertiary sector, we observe a consistent rise in its share to GSDP. From this analysis, we further infer that the performance of the secondary sector in the region is still very weak, albeit a marginal growth was witnessed in Assam and Meghalaya.

From Table 24.4, we can find average decadal sectoral growth rates across the states of NER. In the 1980s, Sikkim registered the highest average decadal growth of the primary sector at 8 per cent, followed by Nagaland and Arunachal Pradesh with 5 per cent each, while the state of Meghalaya registered at the bottom with a negative growth rate. In the 1990s, the average decadal growth rate of the primary sector in Sikkim fell drastically to 2 per cent. The situation of the sector was more or less the same in the 2000s as well. Unfortunately, the state of Arunachal Pradesh, one of the second best performers in the 1980s, had even fallen to negative (–5 per cent) growth rate. The states of Manipur, Nagaland and Tripura performed well in the 2000s.

As for the secondary sector, the state of Arunachal Pradesh performed the best with 22 per cent of average decadal growth in the 1980s. It was followed by the states of Sikkim, Meghalaya and Manipur with 12 per cent, 11 per cent and 8 per cent respectively. In the 1990s, the growth rate of the secondary sector in Manipur had fallen drastically, reaching negative growth (–2 per cent). The best performer in the 1980s, Arunachal Pradesh, witnessed a drastic fall in the 1990s to 1 per cent, but, it recovered to 7 per cent in the 2000s. The growth rate of the secondary sector in all states of the region, barring Assam and Tripura, was found to be impressive, ranging from 6 to 11 per cent in the 2000s. However, the average decadal growth rate of the tertiary sector across time and space has been very positive. The growth rates have been more or less consistent, ranging from 4 to 11 per cent across the states in the 1980s and 1990s. However, in the 2000s, the average decadal growth rate of the tertiary sector was lingering at around 6 to 9 per cent across the states of the region.

Sectoral impact on GSDP growth

In this section, it is intended to identify the sector that contributes more to the overall economic growth in NER. In short, we try to identify the drivers of economic growth in the region's economy. To do this, we rely on the Kaldorian framework and by using this model we test each sector's role on the growth performance of the region. Originally, the Kaldorian framework was used to examine the relationship between manufacturing and GDP growth performance, argu-

Table 24.5 Regression result for relationship between sectoral and GSDP growth (1980–81 to 2011–12)

Sectors	*(1)*	*(2)*	*(3)*	*(4)*	*(5)*	*(6)*
Primary	0.605*** (0.125)	0.538*** (0.138)				
Secondary			0.191* (0.112)	0.182** (0.082)		
Tertiary					0.886*** (0.159)	0.755*** (0.161)
Decadal dummies	N	Y	N	Y	N	Y
R^2	0.51	0.62	0.17	0.36	0.47	0.54
F	23.31***	9.30***	2.91*	4.52**	31.08***	8.69***
No. of observation	21	21	21	21	21	21

Note: ***, ** and * stand for significance at 1 per cent, 5 per cent and 10 per cent level or more respectively. *N=No, Y=Yes.*

ing that a faster growth rate of manufacturing output leads to higher growth in GDP. Following Felipe et al. (2007) and Dasgupta and Singh (2006), the analogous relationships with two other sectors – agriculture and services sectors – have also been examined. As already mentioned in the methodology section, an empirical analysis is carried out for the states of NER from 1981–82 to 2011–12. We performed this analysis for the overall period and separately for the three decades – the 1980s, 1990s and 2000s.

Table 24.5 reports the regression analysis result for the overall period (1980–81 to 2011–12). The model has been estimated with and without state dummies. The inclusion of state dummies control is for state-specific factors that are likely to affect the relationship between GSDP growth and sectoral growth.[4] The summarised estimation result for Table 24.5 is presented in Figure 24.6. The summarised estimation results basically show the estimated long-run elasticity of GSDP with respect to the output in each sector. As expected, the tertiary sector is identified as the best/largest engine of growth elasticity for the NER economy (Table 24.5 and Figure 24.6),

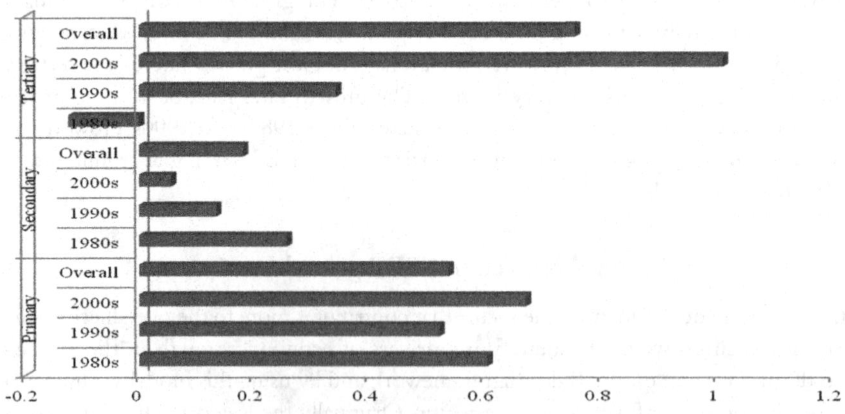

Figure 24.6 Engine of growth effects (elasticities). Source: Authors' calculations from CSO and EPWRF data.

followed by the primary and secondary sectors. This implies that the region's economy is mainly driven by the tertiary sector and supported sequentially by the primary and secondary sectors.

We further delve into knowing whether there exists any variation in the sectoral contribution to GDP growth in the NER economy across the decades. In other words, we are interested to examine whether there occurs any variation in the elasticity of the sectors across the three decades. It is very likely that the sector that dominated in a particular decade (in terms of its contribution to GDP growth) is replaced by another sector in the following decade. For example, it is possible that the primary sector might have had the largest elasticity in the 1980s and been replaced by the tertiary sector in the 1990s. Therefore, in order to have a better and clearer understanding of the sectoral contribution in the region, we repeat our analysis, which has already been presented in Table 24.5, decade-wise separately in the following Tables: Table 24.6 for the 1980s, Table 24.7 for the 1990s and Table 24.8 for the 2000s. Again, the model has been estimated with and without state dummies for the above-cited reason. The results clearly point to the decade-wise relationship between sectoral contribution and GDP.

Looking at this relationship across the three decades – 1980s, 1990s and 2000s – an interesting trend can be discerned. In the 1980s and 1990s, the primary/agriculture sector appears to have driven the region's economic growth process, but a shift in favour of the services sector (tertiary) can be observed during the 2000s. In spite of a larger role taken by the services sector, the primary/agriculture sector still appears to have contributed significantly to the region's overall economic growth process. In essence, these results indicate that both primary/agriculture and service sectors have acted as engines of growth in the region's economy during the period analysed – 1980–81 to 2011–12. Our analysis also brought out the role of the secondary/industrial sector that has been very insignificant in the region's economic growth process. The outcome of this study has been in line with the researchers' rational expectation, because the industrial development is still at the nascent stage in the region.[5]

Table 24.9 reports the sectoral contribution to GSDP growth in each state in the NER.[6] The findings of the individual states are in line with the result for the north-east economy as a whole. From Table 24.9, it is again evident that the service sector exhibits the highest growth elasticity across all the states, barring Arunachal Pradesh. In Arunachal Pradesh, the agricultural

Table 24.6 Regression results for relationship between sectoral and GSDP growth (1980s)

Sectors	*(1)*	*(2)*	*(3)*	*(4)*	*(5)*	*(6)*
Primary	0.604***	0.604***				
	(0.056)	(0.062)				
Secondary			0.258**	0.258**		
			(0.088)	(0.094)		
Tertiary					–0.016	–0.125
					(0.278)	(0.288)
State dummies	N	Y	N	Y	N	Y
R^2	0.821	0.825	0.217	0.255	0.0001	0.05
F	116.5***	15.23***	8.64**	2.01*	0.00	0.79
No. of Observation	63	63	63	63	63	63

Source: Authors' calculations from CSO and EPWRF data.
Note: ***, ** and * stand for significance at 1 per cent, 5 per cent and 10 per cent level or more respectively. *N=No, Y=Yes.*

Table 24.7 Regression results: relationship between sectoral and GSDP growth, 1990s

Sectors	*(1)*	*(2)*	*(3)*	*(4)*	*(5)*	*(6)*
Primary	0.511*** (0.084)	0.522*** (.081)				
Secondary			0.132** (0.049)	0.134** (0.053)		
Tertiary					0.353** (0.173)	0.344 (0.185)
State dummies	N	Y	N	Y	N	Y
R^2	0.68	0.72	0.12	0.15	0.093	0.11
F	36.88***	12.89***	7.39**	4.84***	4.19*	6***
No. of observations	70	70	70	70	70	70

Source: Authors' calculations from CSO and EPWRF data.
Note: ***, ** and * stand for significance at 1 per cent, 5 per cent and 10 per cent level or more respectively.
N=No, Y=Yes.

Table 24.8 Regression results: relationship between sectoral and GSDP growth, 2000s

Sectors	*(1)*	*(2)*	*(3)*	*(4)*	*(5)*	*(6)*
Primary	0.613** (0.215)	0.670** (0.249)				
Secondary			0.073 (0.124)	0.055 (0.124)		
Tertiary					0.972** (0.334)	1.010** (0.351)
State dummies	N	Y	N	Y	N	Y
R^2	0.24	0.27	0.01	0.03	0.41	0.44
F	8.13**	3.36**	0.34	2.3**	8.39**	4.39***
No. of observations	91	91	91	91	91	91

Source: Authors' calculations from CSO and EPWRF data.
Note: ***, ** and * stand for significance at 1 per cent, 5 per cent and 10 per cent level or more respectively.
N=No, Y=Yes.

sector appears to have a larger impact on GSDP growth, followed by the industrial sector. In terms of growth elasticity, the tertiary sector turns out to be the highest contributor in Sikkim (1.23), followed by Nagaland (0.91). In totality, the region's economy is largely driven by the tertiary sector, followed by the primary sector. Understandably, the secondary sector trailed at the bottom in the growth impetus. Within the region, the state of Sikkim out-performed all other states, followed by Nagaland and Tripura.

Concluding remarks

From the above analysis, it can be inferred that the GSDP growth of the region (NER) in the last three decades was found to be lower than that of the national average. The overall inter-state inequal-

Table 24.9 Growth elasticities of the three sectors by states

State	*Primary*	*Secondary*	*Tertiary*
Arunachal Pradesh	0.70	0.40	–0.17*
Assam	0.53	0.15	0.60
Manipur	0.32	0.06*	0.68
Meghalaya	0.37	0.13	0.59
Nagaland	0.39	0.08	0.91
Sikkim	0.62	0.13*	1.23
Tripura	0.45	0.02*	0.77

Source: Authors' calculations from CSO and EPWRF data.
Note: * indicates the CV is not significant at 10 per cent level or above.

ity in the region witnessed a rather slow decline in the 1990s and reached the lowest level ever in the 2000s. Though it showed some signs of revival in the following few years, the inequality level touched the highest mark ever in 2010 and has remained stable at that rate since then. Analysis of the economic growth pattern of the individual states revealed that the state of Sikkim has been the best performing state in terms of GSDP per capita growth throughout the period of study. The states of Tripura and Meghalaya have been picking up lately. The last decade i.e., 2000–2012 was very promising in terms of the region's economic growth. The average annual GSDP growth trend of the region more than doubled in the last decade, i.e., from 2.6 per cent in the 1990s to 5.4 per cent in the 2000s. Again, in terms of the average annual growth rate of GSDP per capita, the region was able to catch up with the national average of 3.8 per cent during the period from 1981 to 2012. In terms of PCI too, the region showed remarkable improvement. Again, all the states of NER performed well in the 2000s. The PCI growth rate for the few states of the region like Sikkim, Nagaland and Tripura was much higher than that of the regional average. Undoubtedly, the region registered a significant increase in the average annual growth rate in the post reform era. However, the increasing inequality in the reason has been a matter of concern.

A consistent rise in the share of the tertiary sector and the fall in the share of the primary sector was observed over the decades. The tertiary sector was identified as the better engine of growth elasticity in the region's economy. However, in the initial period of the study (1980s), the picture was quite gloomy. In fact, there existed variations with respect to the sectoral contribution to GSDP growth across the decades. While the primary sector seemed to have driven the region's economy in the 1980s and 1990s, the services sector emerged as a driver of growth in the 2000s. In totality, despite a great role occupied by the service sector in the region's economy, the agriculture sector still appears to have contributed significantly in the region's overall economic growth process. It is also evident that the secondary sector is still very weak with no sign of improvement over the last three decades. Looking at the present state of the secondary sector, it is imperative to recommend that the region's economic policies must put more emphasis on the secondary sector, which is believed to be the driver of growth in the bigger states of the country.

Notes

1 NER consists of eight states – Assam, Arunachal Pradesh, Manipur, Meghalaya, Mizoram, Nagaland, Sikkim and Tripura.
2 This context was employed on urban development in the USA.

3 Fall in CV value does not necessarily imply an evidence of convergence. Proper testing of convergence would require estimating marginal impact of the initial income level (negative value implies convergence) on the subsequent period's growth level, which is not done in this study due to an insignificant number of observations.
4 As a robustness test, we have also carried out a panel data analysis so as to skirt the problem of cyclical changes. The results, which are not reported here, clearly suggest that our findings are robust to alternate specifications and methodology.
5 Available evidence shows that the region contributes a little over 1 per cent to the value of output of the manufacturing sector of India.
6 The state-wise exercise carried out acts as a robustness check and further strengthens our claims.

References

Ahluwalia, M. S. (2000). "State level performance under economic reforms in India", *Presented at the Centre for Research on Economic Development and Policy Reform Conference on Indian Economic Prospects: Advancing Policy Reform*, Stanford, CA, Stanford University.

Ayres, R. U. (1998). "Theoretical growth models vs real world evidence – Implications for greenhouse gas policy", *Working Paper No.* 97/67/EPS, Fontainebleau, France: INSEAD, *Centre for the Management of Environmental Resources*.

Bajpaee, C. (2017). "Dephasing India's look east/act east policy", *Contemporary Southeast Asia*, 39(2): 348–372.

Beckford, G. L. F. (1965). "Agriculture and economic development", *Caribbean Quarterly*, 11(1/2): 50–63.

Cheen, L. C. (2005). "Malaysia–strategies for the liberalization of the services sector", Case Study No. 25, Managing the Challenges of WTO Participation: World Trade Organisation. Accessed: https://www.wto.org/ENGLISH/res_e/booksp_e/casestudies_e/case25_e.htm.

Chakravarty, S. and Mitra, A. (2009). "Is industry still the engine of growth? An econometric study of the organized sector employment in India", *Journal of Policy Modelling*, 31: 22–35.

Dasgupta, S., and Singh, A. (2006). "Manufacturing, services and premature deindustrialization in developing countries: A Kaldorian analysis", *Research Paper No.2006/49*, Helsinki, Finland: UNU-WIDER.

DoNER (2013). *8th north-east business summit*, January 9, 2013. New Delhi: Ministry for Development of North-East Region, Government of India.

Debnath, A. and Roy, N. (2012). "Structural change and inter-sectoral linkages–The case of North-east India", *Economic and Political Weekly*, 47(6): 72–76.

Felipe, J., et al., (2007). "Sectoral engines of growth in developing Asia: Stylized facts and implications", *Working Paper No.* 107, Manila, Philippines: Economics and Research Department, Asian Development Bank.

Kathuria, V. and Raj, R. S. N. (2013). "Is manufacturing an engine of growth in India in the post-nineties?" *Journal of South Asian Development*, 8(3): 385–408.

Kniivila, M. (2007). "Industrial development and economic growth: Implications for poverty reduction and income inequality", in United Nations (ed.), *Industrial Development for the 21st Century: Sustainable Development Perspectives* (pp. 295–332). New York: Department of Economic and Social Affairs, United Nations.

Loitongbam, B. S. (2018). "The potential of participation in global value chains development of North East India", *Economic and Political Weekly*, 73(39): 76–82.

Leke, A., et al., (2010). "What's driving Africa's growth". Accessed 26 February 2015: http://www.mckinsey.com/insights/economic_studies/whats_driving_africas_growth.

Menon, S. (2007). "Northeast India and globalization: The way ahead". Accessed 12 January 2019: https://dlc.dlib.indiana.edu/dlc/bitstream/handle/10535/4016/Northeast_the_way_ahead.pdf?sequenc.

Nayak, P. K., et al., (2010). "Inclusive growth and its regional dimension", *Reserve Bank of India Occasional Papers*, 31(3): 91–156.

Nayak, P., and Mishra, S.K. (2013). "Status of development of NE states in India in the national perspective". Accessed 24 January 2019: https://mpra.ub.uni-muenchen.de/48441/MPRAPaperNo.48441,posted27July201304:52UTC.

Rostow, W. W. (1959). "The stages of economic growth", *The Economic History Review*, 12(1): 1–16.

Rondinelli, D. A., Johnson, J. H. and Kasarda, J. D. (1998). "The changing forces of urban economic development – Globalization and city competitiveness in the 21st century", *Cityscape*, 3(3): 71–105.

Roumasset, J. (2004). "Rural institutions, agricultural development and pro-poor economic growth", *Asian Journal of Agriculture and Development*, 1(1): 61–82.

Singha, K. (2010). "Globalization and economic development: A study of Nagaland", *Journal of Global Economy*, 6(3): 199–211.

Targetti, F. (2005). "Nicholas Kaldor – Key contributions to development economics", *Development and Change*, 36(6): 1185–1199.

Thomas, J.J. (2009). *Why is manufacturing not the engine of India's economic growth, examining trends, 1959–60 to 2008–09*, Mimeo, Singapore: National University of Singapore.

The Times of India (2018). "NITI outlines five development missions for Northeast". Accessed 14 January 2019: https://timesofindia.indiatimes.com/india/niti-outlines-five-development-missions-for-northeast/articleshow/63697974.cms.

Wik, M., Pingali, P. and Broca, S. (2008). "Global agricultural performance: Past trends and future prospects", *Background Paper of the World Development Report 2008*. Washington, DC: World Bank.

25

QUARTER CENTURY OF ECONOMIC REFORMS

Transformation of the occupational structure in rural India

Aparajita Dhara

Introduction

The post-reform years in India have witnessed a rapid transition from agriculture to the services sector and this has been accompanied by a decline in the agricultural workforce. Since agriculture has traditionally been the mainstay of the rural economy this has led to livelihood diversification towards non-agricultural activities and a transformation of the occupational structure in rural areas. The share of workers engaged in non-agricultural activities as their main occupation increased from 21.8% to 23.7% during the 1990s and to 32.1% in 2010 (NSSO reports).

Rural Non-Farm Employment (RNFE) helps farm-based households to spread their risks, offers more remunerative activities to supplement or replace agricultural income during lean seasons and provides means to cope when farming fails. This in turn has the potential of reducing rural poverty levels and distress-led migration to urban areas. But these positive developments will be taking place when the occupational shift happens due to the maturing of growth-led forces in the economy and not as a result of demographic pressure on cultivable land or due to adverse trends in the agrarian sector. It is therefore important to identify the reasons behind the changes in the rural occupational structure, in order to determine whether the growth in RNFE is driven by growth and prosperity-related 'pull' factors or due to distress-driven 'push' factors.

This chapter focuses on the forces behind the livelihood diversification in rural India across industrial sub-sectors and genders and tries to ascertain whether the growth phenomenon is inclusive of the different sections of the workforces or not. The major research questions addressed are:

a) *How has the rural workforce in India changed during the post-reform decades, with respect to industrial sub-sectors and gender?*
b) *Is the growth in rural non-farm employment during the post-reform period 'distress-driven' or 'growth-driven'?*

We begin with a brief survey of literature on the determinants of rural non-farm employment in the next section and discuss some major hypotheses put forward by researchers regarding the

DOI: 10.4324/9780367855741-25

growth of RNFE. The third section introduces the data used in our analysis and the fourth section gives a macroeconomic overview of the data. In the fifth section we undertake a regression analysis on the data set, to ascertain the determinants of rural non-farm employment. The sixth section finally concludes the paper with some policy suggestions.

Brief survey of literature

The factors identified in the literature regarding the growth of rural non-farm employment can broadly be grouped into two categories:

(i) Determinants concerned with the business environment, policies and other region-level variables affecting the growth of the non-agricultural sector (macro level demand side factors) and
(ii) Determinants which enable an individual rural worker or a rural household to take part in the non-farm sector job market (micro level supply side factors).

The macro-factors can further be separated as

(a) Agricultural growth led diversification,
(b) Distress led diversification,
(c) Factors external to agriculture but within the rural economy (such as rural infrastructure, rural literacy and per-capita public expenditure on rural development) and
(d) Factors external to the rural economy (such as growth in urban areas).

We discuss here some of the studies that have been carried out in this regard.

In the early 1970s, it was postulated that with increase in levels of agricultural income the relative share of consumption expenditure on non-food items tends to increase and this in turn stimulates the growth of rural non-farm employment. Moreover, agricultural growth leads to an increased demand by the agriculturalists for inputs such as fertilisers, tools, machinery and their repairing services, as well as an increase in the demand for processing of the agricultural products. These backward and forward production linkages also lead to the growth of non-farm sector employment in the rural areas. This theory of '*inter-sectoral linkage hypothesis*' was put forward by Mellor (1976) and several empirical studies (Johnston and Kilby 1975; Haggblade, Hazell and Brown 1989; Hazell and Haggblade 1991; Shukla 1991, 1992; de Janvry and Sadoulet 1993; Srivastav and Dubey 2002) have documented the power of these farm–nonfarm linkages in Asia, Africa and Latin American countries. But some other studies (Sankaranarayanan 1980; Vaidyanathan 1986; Jayaraj 1989; Dev1990; Unni 1991; Narayanmoorthy, Rodrigues and Phadnis 2002) did not find any strong association between consumption–linkage and rural non-farm employment. Region level studies have shown that the impact of agricultural growth on the rural non-agricultural sector depends on the stage of agricultural prosperity and that correlation was not monotonic. Studies undertaken in the different states of India by Harris (1987), Chandrasekhar (1993), Eapen (1994, 1995), Verma and Verma (1995), Chand (1996), Basant and Parthasarathy (1998), Mecharla (2002) did not find any significant correspondence between agricultural growth and rural non-farm employment either and they argued that the growth of the non-farm sector was driven by factors outside of agriculture, like degree of urbanisation, population density, rural infrastructure, market integration and allocation of public sector resources.

A different set of literature argues that due to lack of employment opportunities in agriculture a large section of rural labourers gets 'pushed' into low-productive casual activities in the non-agricultural sector and the growth in rural non-farm employment can thus be seen as distress diversification. Vaidyanathan (1986) observed a strong positive relationship between unemployment rate and rural non-farm employment and formulated this spill-over of the labour force from agriculture to the non-agricultural sector as the '*Residual Sector Hypothesis*'. The hypothesis received considerable attention from many scholars like Dev (1990), Unni (1991), Bhalla (1997), Parthasarathy, Shameem and Reddy (1998), Kaur (2002) and Srivastav and Dubey (2002), especially regarding the choice of 'unemployment rate' as the measurement of 'distress in agriculture'. Dev (1990) found a positive association between agricultural prosperity and rural unemployment rate, whereas Unni (1991) and Biradar and Bagalkoti (2001) argued that higher unemployment rate should have reduced both agricultural and non-agricultural wage rates as an indication of excess supply of labour. If the excess labour from agriculture moves to the non-agricultural sector, then non-agricultural wages should have been lower than the agricultural wage rate, but this was not the case observed. Still, the distress movement of the labour force into non-agricultural activities from agriculture cannot completely be ruled out and alternative distress causes like population density, proportion of marginal land-holdings and casualisation of the agricultural labour force were suggested. They were found to have a positive impact on rural non-farm employment in the studies by Verma and Verma (1995), Eapen (1995), Kaur (2002), Biradar (2007), and Mecharla (2002).

The growth of rural non-farm employment was also found to be determined by factors external to agriculture but within the rural economy, like rural infrastructure (particularly road density, telecommunications, banking facilities and electricity consumption), human capital and government programmes as observed in the studies by Oshima (1994), Lane (1996), Islam (1997), Shukla (1991), Singh (1994), Mecharla (2002), Narayanmoorthy et al. (2002) and Kaur (2002). On the other hand, ease of transport between rural and urban areas also confronts rural enterprises with increased competition from urban areas and imports, especially for the small-scale and cottage industries that face competition from cheaper products produced by urban-based large-scale industries or imported from outside the state or country. It also affects the taste and preferences of rural households and orients them towards urban products, especially in the case of richer households (Islam 1997). Taking literacy rate as a proxy for human capital, Chadha in his studies (2001, 2004) found that at the all India level the proportion of illiterate workers was higher in agriculture than in non-agriculture, the participation in non-farm activities tended to increase with an increase in the level of education and there was a shift from casual non-agricultural jobs to regular employment. Jayaraj (1989), Singh (1994), Eapen (1994), Mecharla (2002), Biradar (2007), Narayanmoorthy et al., (2002) and Kaur (2002) all found a strong positive association between literacy rate and rural non-farm employment, especially for the male workforce. Moreover, the earning level of the workers in the non-farm sector was also found to depend on the level and quality of education. Scholars like Jayaraj (1989), Unni (1991) and Parthasarathy et al. (1998) attempted to understand the role of factors external to the rural economy like degree of urbanisation, size of nearby villages/cities, macro-level policy environment and the like in influencing the growth of rural non-agricultural employment.

For our study we will be focusing on such macro-level determinants to estimate their impact on the growth of rural non-farm employment in India during the post-reform period.

Data source

The study is based on official secondary data published by the National Sample Survey Office (NSSO) under the Ministry of Statistics and Programme Implementation, Government of India (MOSPI, GOI), the Central Statistical Office (CSO) (under MOSPI, GOI) and the National Accounts Statistics (NAS), Government of India.

The NSSO has been carrying out detailed sample surveys on the 'Employment and Unemployment Situation in India' every five years since 1972–73 and the analysis is based extensively on unit-level data-files for the 43rd, 50th, 55th, 61st and 66th rounds of these quinquennial surveys covering the time period 1987–88 to 2009–10. The population figures have been interpolated from the decennial census reports for 1981, 1991, 2001 and 2011. The data on value-added in terms of Net State Domestic Product at Factor Cost (NSDP) has been obtained from the National Accounts Statistics and converted to constant 2004–05 base-year prices to arrive at comparable figures. Any other data used or mentioned in the analysis have also been taken from different official government sources.

The analysis covers the 16 major states of India which account for 89.27% of India's rural area and 97.66% of India's rural population. These states are – Andhra Pradesh (AP), Assam (ASM), Bihar (BHR), Gujarat (GUJ), Haryana (HRY), Himachal Pradesh (HP), Karnataka (KNT), Kerala (KER), Madhya Pradesh (MP), Maharashtra (MHA), Orissa (ODS), Punjab (PUN), Rajasthan (RAJ), Tamil Nadu (TN), Uttar Pradesh (UP) and West Bengal (WB). The newly formed states of Jharkhand, Chhattisgarh and Uttarakhand have been merged with their parent states Bihar, Madhya Pradesh and Uttar Pradesh respectively to maintain data comparability over the period.

The activity status of a person during the reference period of 365 days preceding the date of survey, on which the person spent relatively long time is defined by the NSSO as Usual Principal Status (UPS) of a person, and we have taken the UPS workforce for our analysis, and segregated them by a 1-digit Industrial Classification Code, gender and castes for detailed probing. The study covers all workers residing in rural areas, irrespective of their place of work, which may be within the village, outside the village but within rural areas, in urban areas or without any fixed location.

The author would like to mention here the following notations which will be used subsequently – RNFE for Rural Non-Farm Employment, AGRI for Agriculture and Allied activities, NONAGRI for Non-Agricultural activities, MFG for Manufacturing activities, CON for Construction, TRD for Trade, Hotel and Restaurant activities, TRA for Transport, Storage and Communication, SVS for All Other Service Sector activities (Banking, Finance, Public Administration, Community Services etc.), OTH for Mining–Quarrying–Electricity etc. (which have been deliberately left out from detailed study as they employ only around 1% of the total workforce).

Growth of output and employment during the first two decades of economic reforms

Data on the Indian Economy (Figure 25.1 and Figure 25.2) show that the share of Non-Agriculture in Total Value Added increased from 69.5% to 84.8% from 1988 to 2010, while its share in employment increased from 33.8% to 48.8% during the same period. At the same time India's population grew at an average annual rate of 2.3%, resulting in approximately 6.9% average annual rate of growth in per capita national output. What needs to be analysed is how this growth rate is getting translated into productive employment of the labour force, which is growing at a rate of approximately 1.9% per annum.

At a rural–urban disaggregated level, one finds that the ratio of % change in employment and % change in output (which can be termed as employment elasticity of output) was greater for the urban non-agricultural workforce than their rural counterpart. But during the second decade we find that the elasticity of the rural non-agricultural workforce became greater than the urban workforce, indicating a higher growth of rural non-farm sector employment in the later years.

Probing into the growth of rural non-farm employment one finds that rural–urban ratios for the rates of growth of the rural population and rural workforce have been less

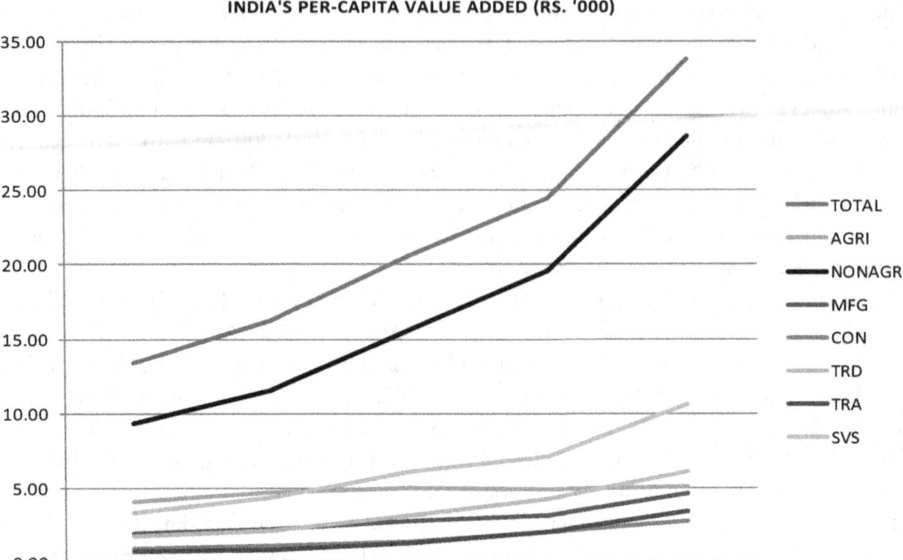

Figure 25.1 India's per-capita value added from 1988 to 2010 sub-sector-wise Source: Author's calculations based on CSO data.

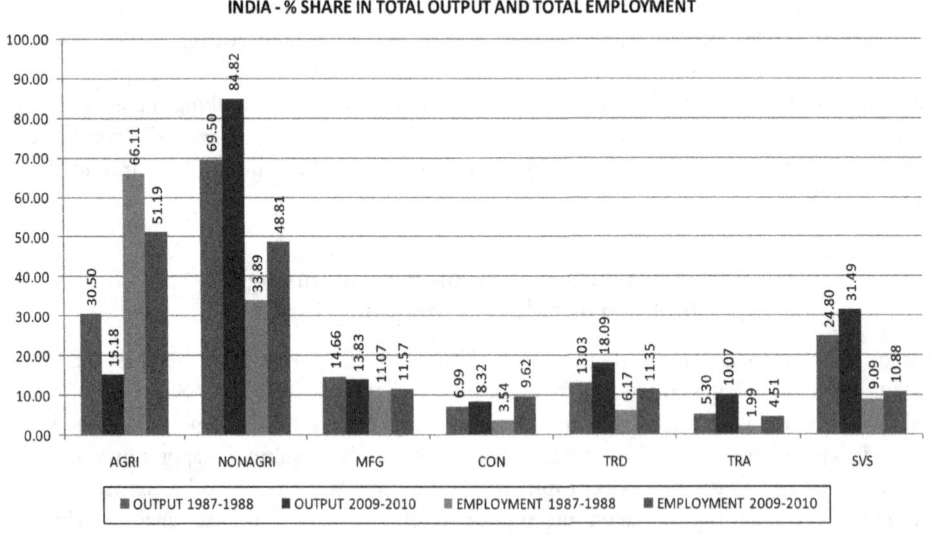

Figure 25.2 Share of sub-sectors in output and employment in India from 1988 to 2010 Source: Author's calculations based on NSSO, CSO and population census data.

than those of the urban population and urban workforce. This is due to the process of urbanisation of the country – the percentage of population living in urban areas has been rising continuously with the development process and many rural areas are getting re-designated as urban areas. But at the same time we find that for the non-agricultural workforce, the ratio is greater than 1, and that was through the CON, TRD and TRA sectors during

2000–10. This indicates that a high proportion of the rural workforce is getting absorbed in these three sectors.

Further calculations reveal that while the rural agricultural workforce was growing at an average rate of 1.4%, the rural non-agricultural workforce was increasing at 4.2%, with the figures for CON, TRA and TRD being 12.8%, 11.4% and 5.9% respectively. This reflects the occupational transformation in the rural areas of India during the post-reform decades, especially for the later period, when 1.12% of the net addition to the rural workforce diversified towards non-agricultural employment.

Disaggregation of the rural workforce in India by gender (Figure 25.3) shows that for the male workforce (which accounts for 72% of rural workers) the share of agriculture fell from

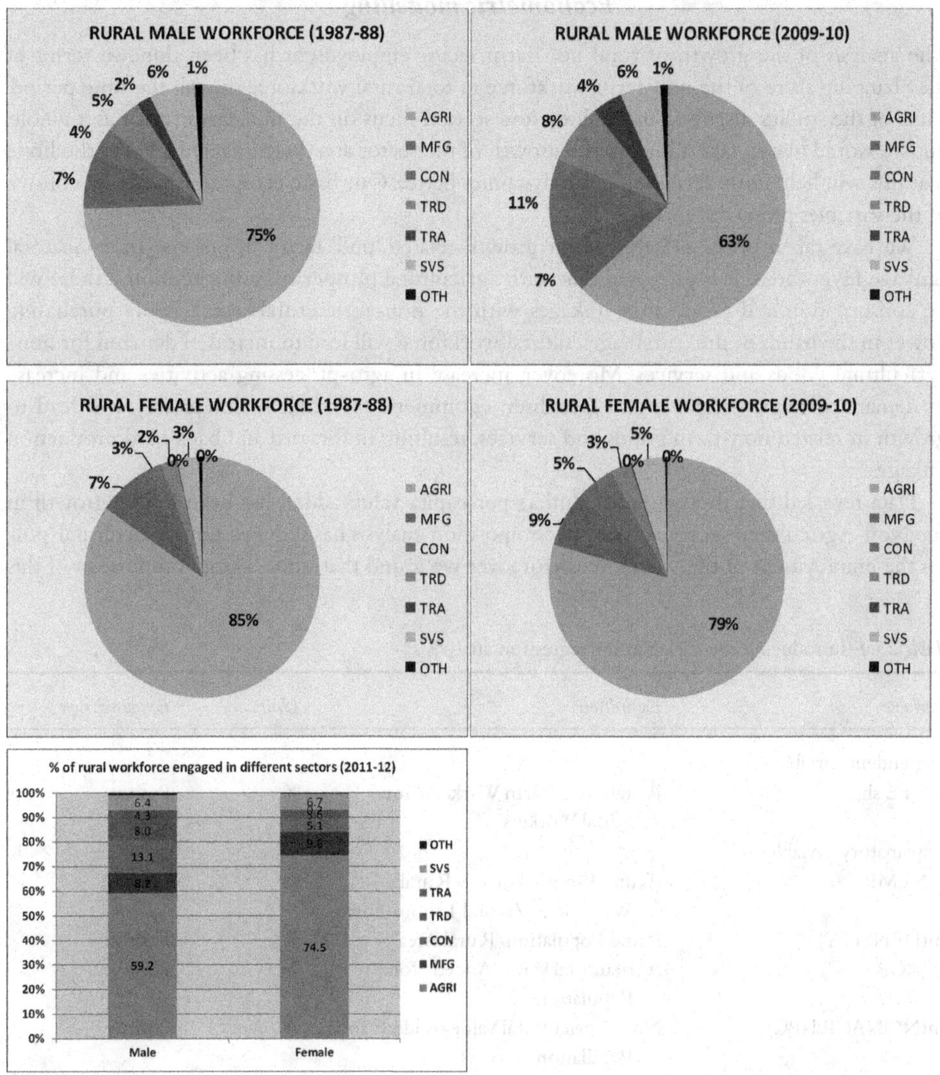

Figure 25.3 Composition of rural workforce segregated by gender Source: Data from 43rd, 66th and 68th Round of NSSO survey reports

75% to 63% and most have gone towards CON, TRA and TRD. On the other hand, for the female workforce the share of agriculture fell from 85% to 79% during the same period, with CON, MFG and SVS being the major attractors. (One can observe that the trend continued during 2011–12.)

Thus in this section we addressed our first research question regarding the growth trend of Rural Non-Farm employment segregated by industrial sub-sectors and gender. We now move on to our empirical analysis in the following section, where we would like to analyse the determinants of this livelihood diversification in rural India to answer our second research question.

Empirical analysis

Econometric modelling

The analysis of the growth of rural non-farm sector employment has been done in terms of the changing share of the non-farm workforce in total rural workforce during the time period. Most of the studies discussed in the literature section focus on the non-farm sector as a whole, but we would like to take a look at the growth of the sector at a disaggregated level in the hope that this will help in understanding the dynamics better. Our basic econometric model consists of the variables presented in Table 25.1.

We have taken up AGRI-PC as our growth-related 'pull' factor as per the Inter-Sectoral Linkage Hypothesis. It is proposed that with agricultural prosperity in the economy, there will be consumption and production linkages with the non-agricultural sector. More purchasing power in the hands of the (rural) agricultural workforce will lead to increased demand for non-agricultural goods and services. Moreover, increase in agro-processing activities and increase in demand for agricultural inputs (fertiliser, equipment and their maintenance) will lead to growth in related non-farm goods and services, resulting in forward and backward production linkages.

Data revealed that the growth in India's per-capita value-added has been led by growth in the Non-Agricultural sector, and our decomposition analysis has shown a non-agricultural 'pull' on the employment of the workforce. Moreover we found that quite a large proportion of this

Table 25.1 Introducing the variables for regression analysis

Variable	*Definition*	*Unit*	*Expected sign*
Dependent variable			
RNFE share	Rural Non-Farm Workers/Total Rural Workers	%	Positive
Explanatory variables			
UNEMP	(Rural Labour Force – Rural Workforce)/Rural Labour Force	%	Positive
In(DENSITY)	Rural Population/Rural Area	%	Positive
In(AGRI-PC)	Agricultural Value-Added/Total Population	%	Positive
In(NONAGRI-PC)	Non-Agricultural Value-Added/Total Population	%	Positive
URBAN	Urban Population/Total Population	%	Positive
LITERACY	Rural Literates/Rural Population	%	Positive

addition to the non-farm workforce has gone to the rural sector. Thus with non-agricultural prosperity also there are consumption and production linkages with the rural non-farm workforce. So we also include a variable NONAGRI-PC as another explanatory variable.

On the other hand, distress in agriculture will be reflected in an increase in unemployment among the rural workforce, due to lack of opportunities in the agricultural sector. In such a situation, the unemployed labour force will be forced to take up non-farm activities out of duress, even at a lower wage rate. So as per the Residual-Sector Hypothesis, we have taken up UNEMP as the 'push' factor.

As for the factors external to agriculture but within the rural economy, the important determinants are population pressure on land, development of a human–capital base and infrastructural development (electricity, road density, telecommunication, banking system etc.), and from here we have taken DENSITY and LITERACY as our determinants. Degree of urbanisation, presence of urban agglomeration and governmental policies are other important determining factors external to the rural economy, and we have taken URBAN from this set.

Thus in our model UNEMP and DENSITY represent the distress-driven factors, AGRI-PC and NONAGRI-PC represent the growth-related factors, LITERACY is the proxy for human capital and URBAN is the extra-rural influence.

The pair-wise correlation matrix and the variance inflation factors show the presence of a high degree of multicollinearity if we use all the explanatory variables together in our multiple regression equations, and so we estimate the determinants by two separate models:

Model – 1 (with distress factors and growth factors)
RNFE-SHARE = f (UNEMP, Ln(DENSITY), Ln(AGRI-PC), Ln(NONAGRI-PC))
and
Model – 2 (with distress factors and other factors)
RNFE-SHARE = f (UNEMP, Ln(DENSITY), URBAN, LITERACY)
The models have been checked for multicollinearity and endogeneity problems.

However, it is to be noted that due to lack of appropriate instrumental variables we could not merge these two models together and there exists the problem of omitted variable biases in each model. One needs to take into account broader considerations in formulating policies, drawing on wider literature.

Methodology

The data that we will be working with covers 16 states of India over five NSSO rounds. This makes the data set possess some characteristics of both the cross-sectional studies and time-series studies. We can pool the data to arrive at a bigger data set and run a simple OLS linear regression. But since here we are dealing with the same set of entities over the time points we can attempt to utilise the panel regression methods also, which examine individual specific effects, time effects or both, in order to deal with observed or unobserved heterogeneity, which are not captured by the explanatory variables of our model. These effects are either fixed or random effects.

A *fixed effect model* examines whether intercepts vary across group or time period, whereas a *random effect model* explores differences in error variance components across individual or time period. For this modelling we have referred to Greene (2008).

If individual effect u_i (cross-sectional or time-specific effect) does not exist (i.e. u_i=0), ordinary least squares (OLS) produces efficient and consistent parameter estimates.

OLS model: $y_{it} = \alpha + \beta X_{it} + \varepsilon_{it}$, $(u_i = 0)$

If individual effect u_i is not zero in longitudinal data, heterogeneity may influence some of the core assumptions of OLS estimation. Then panel data models provide a way to deal with these problems.

The functional forms of one-way fixed and random effect models are as follows:

Fixed effect model (FE): $y_{it} = (\alpha + u_i) + \beta X_{it} + v_{it}$
Random effect model (RE): $y_{it} = \alpha + \beta X_{it} + (u_i + v_{it})$,

where u_i is a fixed or random effect specific to individual (group) or time period that is not included in the regression, and errors are *independent identically distributed*, $v_{it} \sim IID\,(0, \sigma v^2)$.

Fixed effects are tested by the F test, while random effects are examined by the Lagrange multiplier (LM) test (Breusch and Pagan 1980). If the null hypothesis is not rejected in either test, the pooled OLS regression is favoured. The Hausman specification test (Hausman 1978) compares a random effect model to its fixed counterpart. If the null hypothesis, that the individual effects are uncorrelated with the other regressors, is not rejected, a random effect model is favoured over its fixed counterpart.

Results

Table 25.2 gives the summary statistics of the variables used in the models and the results of the panel data regression analysis are presented in Table 25.3 and Table 25.4.

Table 25.2 Summary statistics of the dependent and independent variables of the models

Table of summary statistics				
Dependent variables	Mean	Std. dev.	Min.	Max.
RNFE-M	33.31	11.25	13.00	68.20
RNFE-F	22.29	15.35	4.00	70.00
MFG-M	7.49	2.80	2.10	13.80
MFG-F	8.90	7.92	1.20	35.80
CON-M	7.07	5.49	0.80	24.90
CON-F	2.43	2.97	0.00	20.30
TRD-M	7.21	2.86	2.20	16.30
TRD-F	2.70	1.59	0.20	7.20
TRA-M	3.55	1.97	0.60	10.20
TRA-F	0.23	0.40	0.00	2.40
SVS-M	6.83	2.46	3.70	17.20
SVS-F	7.75	3.47	1.92	18.44
Independent variables	Mean	Std. dev.	Min.	Max.
UNEMP	2.02	2.14	0.23	11.46
Ln(DENSITY)	5.53	0.59	4.38	6.60
Ln(AGRI-PC)	3.93	0.38	3.12	4.77
Ln(NONAGRI-PC)	4.96	0.56	4.02	6.21
URBAN	26.38	10.26	8.37	47.89
LITERACY	53.22	13.98	24.99	86.60
No. of observations=80				

Source: Author's calculations from NSSO, CSO and NAS data.

Table 25.3 Regression results for rural MALE workforce

No. of observations=80 (n=16, t=5)
MALE

Dependent variables		Share of rural workforce in different sub-sectors					
Model 1		RNFE	MFG	CON	TRD	TRA	SVS
Explanatory variables							
UNEMP	coeff.	–0.20	0.32***	0.15	0.08	–0.02	–0.45***
	robust SE	0.53	0.12	030	0.11	0.09	0.07
Ln(DENSITY)	coeff.	14.39	0.95	-0.18	6.27 ***	0.10	0.67
	robust SE	8.60	0.75	2.50	1.77	127	1.85
Ln(AGRI-PC)	coeff.	-8.49*	-1.01	-4.38	-0.42	0.25	0.62
	robust SE	4.51	0.79	2.77	024	0.56	0.94
Ln(N0NAGRI - PC)	coeff.	8.71**	0.49	7.13***	1.43 **	2.30***	-1.52*
	robust SE	3.01	0.41	1.43	0.51	0.47	0.77
constant	coeff.	-55.54	2.91	-10.51	-33.10***	-9.36*	9.36
	robust SE	40.34	4.09	14.50	7.00	529	8.48
Breusch Pagan Test	chi bar2	49.37	65.25	60.63	15.96	21.21	14.20
	prohnhi hart	0.00	0.00	0.00	0.00	0.00	0.00
Hausman Test	chit	19.97	3.67	7.00	15.98	12.06	58.14
	prohnhi 2	0.00	0.45	014	0.00	0.02	0.00
Model		FE	RE	RE	FE	FE	FE
Dependent variables		Share of rural workforce in different sub-sectors					
Model		RNFE	MFG	CON	TRD	TM	SVS
Explanatory variables							
UNEMP	caeff.	0.17	0.47 ***	-0.16	0.13	–0.03	–0.51**
	robust SE	0.45	0.12	034	012	0.06	0.23
Ln(DENSITY)	caeff.	2.40	1.22	-199	8.11*	3.31	0.64
	robust SE	4.01	0.89	225	3.96	332	4.25
URBAN	caeff.	0.15	0.13***	0.04	0.12	016**	-0.12
	robust SE	0.28	0.04	0.15	0.08	0.06	0.14
UTERACY.	caeff	0.52 ***	-0.03	0.34 ***	0.01	0.03	-0.04
	robust SE	0.16	0.02	0.07	0.08	0.08	0.09
	constant caeff.	-16.72	-2.40	-3.50	–41.73 **	-20.51	10.35
	robust SE	19.43	4.59	11.35	18.77	15.21	20.85
Breusch Pagan Test	chi bar2	66.03	75.34	61.10	16.11	29.15	12.59
	Prob>chibar 2	0.00	0.00	0.00	0.00	0.00	0.00
Hausman Test	chit	6.86	4.47	8.72	9.50	10.82	54.65
	Prob>chi 2	0.14	0.35	0.08	0.05	0.03	0.00
Model		RE	RE	RE	FE	FE	FE

',",'" denotes significance levels of 20%, 5% and 1% respectively.

Source: Panel data regression on data from NSSO, CSO and NAS.

The Breusch-Pagan Lagrange multiplier test indicates the presence of state-specific unobserved heterogeneity for all the sub-sectors of RNFE in all of our four models. The Hausman-Specification test (which checks whether the unobserved heterogeneity is correlated with our explanatory variables or not) shows that the omitted variables are sometimes correlated and sometimes non-correlated for the different industrial sub-sectors and also for the different

Table 25.4 Regression results for rural FEMALE workforce

No. of observations=80 (n=16, t=5)							
FEMALE							
Dependent variables		Share of rural workforce in different sub-sectors					
Model 1		RNFE	MFG	CON	TRD	TRA	SVS
Explanatory variables							
UNEMP.	coeff	0.31**	0.05	-0.02	0.03	0.07 ***	0.25***
	robust SE	0.12	0.09	0.05	0.02	0.02	0.07
In(DENSITY).	coeff	11.35	10.23***	1.64	150 ***	0.81*	−0.18
	robust SE	9.36	2.15	3.61	029	0.40	5.86
Ln(AGRI-PC).	coeff	−11.68	−0.49	−11.35*	0.66	0.03	−0.45
	robust SE	7.72	1.60	5.44	0.55	0.16	2.30
Ln(NONAGRI-PC).	coeff	5.42*	−1.82*	2.86**	0.34	-0.01	3.76
	robust SE	3.00	1.05	1.13	030	0.10	2.24
constant	coeff.	−22.80	−36.87 ***	23.84	−9.95 ***	−4.66 **	-9.30
	robust SE	4526	11.13	24.04	2.01	1.75	25.33
Breusch Pagan Test	chi bar2	29.57	113.48	1.89	16.67	0.04	15.51
	prob>chi bar2	0.00	0.00	0.05	0.00	0.04	0.00
Hausman Test	chi2	14.46	2.10	12.42	4.79	21.56	13.55
	prob,chi 2	0.01	0.72	0.02	031	0.00	0.01
Model		FE	RE	FE	RE	FE	FE
Dependent Variables		Share of rural workforce in different sub-sectors					
Model 2		RNFE	MFG	CON	TRD	TRA	SVS
Explanatory Variables							
UNEMP.	coeff	0.31**	0.06	−0.03	−0.01	0.07 ***	0.37***
	robust SE	0.12	0.09	−0.04	0.02	0.02	0.06
In(DENSITY).	coeff	7.42	9.95***	-0.77	0.74	1.06	3.96***
	robust SE	23.08	2.54	0.90	1.75	0.62	1.50
URBAN.	coeff	0.47	−0.04	0.02	0.12 ***	0.01	0.21
	robust SE	0.49	0.10	0.04	0.03	0.01	0.17
LITERACY.	coeff	0.08	−0.06	0.03	−0.01	−0.01	0.06
	robust SE	0.29	0.05	0.03	0.03	0.01	0.04
	constant coeff.	−36.12	−42.90 ***	5.04	−4.46	−6.06 *	−23.93***
	robust SE	125.49	11.99	5.58	8.74	320	9.33
Breusch Pagan Test	chi bar2	37.01	107.96	2.47	17.87	2.07	55.81
	Prob>chibar 2	0.00	0.00	0.05	0.00	0.04	0.00
Hausman Test	chi2	10.30	4.70	17.29	10.69	25.88	7.75
	Prob>chi 2	0.04	0.32	0.00	0.03	0.00	0.10
Model		FE	RE	FE	FE	FE	RE

". ", "' denotes significance levels *of* 10%, 5% and 1% respectively

Source: Panel data regression on data from NSSO, CSO and NAS.

sections of the workforce, and we have taken the robust fixed effect and random effect results accordingly.

The regression results show that the MFG sector jobs are often distress driven, for both the genders while a higher density of population leads to a higher participation in trading activities. Agricultural prosperity seems to lower female CON-sector participation whereas non-agricultural growth seems to emerge as the major 'pull' factor, especially for CON, TRD and TRA sector employment for rural male workers. Rising urbanisation increases the demand for male MFG and TRA workers and widens the scope of TRD among rural females.

From the results one thus finds a validity of both 'Residual Sector Hypothesis' and 'Inter-sectoral Linkage Hypothesis' and the results show the existence of both distress-driven 'Push' factors and growth-driven 'Pull' factors in the economy, but the factors are affecting the different sections in somewhat different ways. It can be observed that the push factors are more dominant for female workforces while pull factors are more significant for male workforces. Population density emerges as an important determinant for increase in female non-farm activities while non-agricultural prosperity seems to drive the male workforce. Moreover female MFG workforce is mostly driven by distress-related factors, and one can separate female SVS activities into two types – low-end and high-end – since it is found to get affected by both distress and growth factors.

The NSS reports reveal a high degree of self-employment among the rural manufacturing sector and it might be that distress driven diversification is towards the self-employment in home-based jobs work in the manufacturing sector. Some distress diversification is also towards the transport activities, where we found a positive and significant impact of the unemployment rate. But it is not that the rural non-farm sector is acting as a 'sponge' or 'sink' for the low-skilled labour displaced from agriculture. The ratio of the non-farm wage rates to agricultural wage rate in rural India is found to be greater than unity (almost 1.5 times) for the male workforce in all 16 major states of India. So we cannot say that the average wage rate in non-agricultural activities is lower than that in agriculture, especially for male workers. It might be that better wages are encouraging the workers to shift towards non-farm activities if they possess the required skills. There may always exist some 'residual-ness' in the non-farm sector in the form of 'low-productive' 'dead-end' jobs, but those are not very effective in lowering the average wage in non-farm activities below that of agriculture. For the rural female workers, however, the non-farm sector shows some sign of being a 'residual sector' in some of the states. The average wage rate in the non-farm activities undertaken by female workers is lower than the prevailing agricultural wage rate and the ratio is found to have decreased between 1993–94 and 2004–05. So the 'Residual Sector Hypothesis' cannot be completely ruled out, especially for the female non-farm workforce.

The other distress factor – low land-man ratio or high population density – has emerged as an important determinant of rural non-farm employment, especially for the trade related workforce, but apart from being just a 'push factor', high population density seems to facilitate trading activities by lowering the transaction cost.

A rising trend in the share of non-food expenditure in a household's average monthly consumption expenditure in rural areas indicates a rise in the demand for non-agricultural goods and services by a rural household. There will be a corresponding rise in the demand for non-agricultural labour also, which will be met by rural and/or urban workforces. The inter-sectoral linkages through agricultural prosperity lead to such increase in the demand for non-farm activities through consumption linkages. But our regression results do not show much positive impact of agricultural growth on the growth of non-farm employment in rural areas, except for male transport workers in India. It seems that the rural demand for non-farm goods is mostly supplied by the urban sector. So the 'Inter-Sectoral Linkage Hypothesis' led by agricultural prosperity in the economy is not supported much by our data set as the linkages are not found to be that particularly significant. However the linkages are growing within the non-agricultural sector itself due to the growth in non-agricultural output, and these are spreading among the rural workforce too to a large extent.

Conclusion

By analysing the major determinants behind the growth of rural non-farm employment, one can thus conclude that there exist both 'push' and 'pull' factors in the dynamics behind the growth of rural non-farm employment in India, but the factors vary over gender and sectors.

When we divide the workforce by male–female grouping, the results indicate that while the shift in the male workforce from agriculture towards non-agricultural employment is driven mostly by growth-related forces – especially a 'non-agricultural pull' – for females it is mostly the distress forces that are behind their occupational decision to take up non-farm employment over agriculture. This might be attributed towards limited mobility possibility among the female workforce, who have to take care of their household commitments along with their occupational requirements.

Policymakers should attempt to take these aspects of rural occupational transformation into account for a better utilisation of the economy's labour force and for making the growth process more inclusive in nature. Suitable schemes may be undertaken to tap rural female labour more effectively.

The author acknowledges certain limitations of this chapter, especially regarding lack of comparable data since the 2011–12 NSSO 68th Round after which the quinquennial surveys were discontinued. Considering the importance of data availability at more frequent time intervals, at present Periodic Labour Force Surveys are being conducted with the hope that a more dynamic picture will emerge for proper policy implementation and monitoring.

References

Basant, R, B.L. Kumar and R Parthasarathy (1998): *Non-Agricultural Employment in Rural India*, Rawat Publications, Jaipur.

Bhalla, S. (1997): The Rise and Fall of Workforce Diversification Process in Rural India. In G.K. Chadha and A.N. Sharma (eds.), *Growth, Employment and Poverty: Change and Continuity in Rural India*, pp. 145–183, Vikas Publishing House, New Delhi.

Biradar, R.R. (2007): Growth of Rural Non-Farm Activities in Karnataka: Emerging Issues and Prospects. In Jayasheela (ed.), *Rural Karnataka*, Serial Publications, New Delhi.

Biradar, R.R. and S.T. Bagalkoti (2001): Changing Facets of Employment in Rural India: Emerging Issues and Challenges. *Indian Journal of Agricultural Economics*, 56(3): 538–552.

Breusch, T.S. and A.R. Pagan (1980): The Lagrange Multiplier Test and Its Applications to Model Specification in Econometrics. *Review of Economic Studies*, 47(1): 239–253.

Chadha, G.K. (2001): Impact of Economic Reforms on Rural Employment: No Smooth-Sailing is Anticipated. *Indian Journal of Agricultural Economics*, 56(3): 491–525.

Chadha, G.K. (2004): Human Capital Base of the Indian Labour Market: Identifying Worry Spots. *The Indian Journal of Labour Economics*, 47(1): 3–38.

Chand, R. (1996): Agricultural Diversification and Farm and Non-Farm Employment in Himachal Pradesh. *The Indian Journal of Labour Economics*, 39(4): 841–851.

Chandrasekhar, C.P. (1993): Agrarian Change and Occupational Diversification: Non-Agricultural Employment and Rural Development in West Bengal. *The Journal of Peasant Studies*, 20(2): 205–270.

de Janvry A. and E. Sadoulet (1993): Rural Development in Latin America: Re-Linking Poverty to Growth. In M. Lipton and J. van dir Gaag (eds.), *Including the Poor*, World Bank, Washington, DC.

Dev, M.S. (1990): Non-Agricultural Employment in Rural India: Evidence at a Disaggregated Level. *Economic and Political Weekly*, 26(28): 1526–1536.

Eapen, M. (1994): Rural Non-Agricultural Employment in Kerala: Some Emerging Tendencies. *Economic and Political Weekly*, 29(21): 1285–1296.

Eapen, M. (1995): Rural Non-Agricultural Employment in Kerala: Inter-District Variations. *Economic and Political Weekly*, 30(12): 634–638.

Greene, W.H. (2008): *Econometric Analysis*, 6th ed. Prentice Hall, Hoboken.

Haggblade, S., P. Hazell and J. Brown (1989): Farm–Non Farm Linkages in Sub-Saharan Africa. *World Development*, 17(8): 1173–201.

Harris, B. (1987): Regional Growth Linkages from Agriculture and Resource Flows in the Non-Farm Economy. *Economic and Political Weekly*, 22(1–2): 31–46.

Hausman, J. A. (1978): Specification Tests in Econometrics. *Econometrica*, 46(6):1251–1271.

Hazell, P.B.R. and S. Haggblade (1991). Rural–Urban Growth Linkages in India. *Indian Journal of Agricultural Economics*, 46(4): 515–529.

Islam, N. (1997): The Non-Farm Sector and Rural Development: Review of Issues and Evidence. *Food Agriculture and Environment* Discussion Paper 22. International Food Policy Research Institute, Washington, DC.

Jayaraj, D. (1989): *Determinants of Rural Non-Agricultural Employment.* Working Paper No. 90, Madras Institute of evelopment Studies, Madras.

Johnston, B.F. and P. Kilby (1975): *Agriculture and Structural Transformation: Economic Strategies for Late Developing Countries*. Oxford University Press, London.

Kaur, K. (2002): Determinants of Rural Non-Agricultural Employment: An Inter-State Analysis. *The Indian Journal of Labour Economics*, 45(4).

Lane, D.W. (1996): Political Base and Rural Industrialisation: Korea and Taiwan. In *Towards the Rural-Based Development of Commerce and Industry: Selected Experience from East Asia*, World Bank, Washington, DC.

Mecharla, P.R. (2002): Determinants of Inter-District Variations in Rural Non-Farm Employment in Andhra Pradesh. *The Indian Journal of Labour Economics*, 45(4): 807–820.

Mellor, J. (1976): *The New Economics of Growth: A Strategy for India and the Developing World*. Cornell University Press, Ithaca, New York.

Narayanamoorthy, A., Q. Rodrigues and A. Phadnis (2002): Determinants of Rural Non-Farm Employment: An Analysis of 256 Districts. *The Indian Journal of Labour Economics*, 45(4): 759–769.

Oshima, H.T. (1994): *The Significance of Off-Farm Employment and Incomes in Post-War East-Asian Growth*, Asian Development Bank, Manila.

Parthasarathy, G., and B.S. Reddy (1998): Determinants of Rural Non-Agricultural Employment: The Indian Case. *Indian Journal of Agricultural Economics*, 53(2), 139–54.

Shankaranarayanan, V. (1980): *Inter-Sate Variation in Rural Non-Agricultural Employment: Some Tentative Results*. Working Paper No. 104, Centre for Development Studies, Trivandrum.

Shukla, V. (1991): Rural Non-Farm Activity: A Regional Model and Its Empirical Application to Maharashtra. *Economic and Political Weekly*, 26(45): 2587–2595.

Shukla, V. (1992): Rural Non-Farm Employment in India: Issues and Policy. *Economic and Political Weekly*, 27(28): 1477–1488.

Singh, A.K. (1994): Changes in the Structure of Rural Workforce in Uttar Pradesh: A Temporal and Regional Study. In P. Visaria and R. Basant (eds.), *Non-Agricultural Employment in India: Trends and Prospects*, Sage Publications, New Delhi.

Srivastav, N. and A. Dubey (2002): Rural Non-Farm Employment in India: Spatial Variations and Temporal Change. *The Indian Journal of Labour Economics*, 45(4): 745–758.

Unni, J. (1991): Regional Variations in Rural Non-Agricultural Employment: An Exploratory Analysis. *Economic and Political Weekly*, 26(3): 109–122.

Vaidyanathan, A. (1986): Labour Use in Rural India: A Study of Spatial and Temporal Variations. *Economic and Political Weekly*, 21(52): 130–146.

Verma, B.N. and N. Verma (1995): Distress Diversification from Farm to Non-Farm Employment in Rural Sector in the Eastern Region. *Indian Journal of Agricultural Economics*, 50(3): 422–429.

26

OIL PRICES AND EMPLOYMENT IN THE TRANSPORT SECTOR

Evidence from India

Saibal Kar and Sweta Lahiri

Introduction

The implications of energy price shocks are varied. The developing and transition countries around the world have previously been negatively affected by the waves of oil-price shocks far more than any other exogenous crisis of similar magnitudes. However, the global recessions of 1973–75, 1978–80 and 1990–1993 caused predominantly by the Organization of Petroleum Exporting Countries (OPEC)-led high prices of crude oil have not recurred in recent years despite its higher prices following the two Gulf wars. Instead, Nordhaus (2007) points out that output grew, unemployment fell and inflation remained moderate while cohabiting with oil prices three times as high as those prevalent in the pre-war years. It is not automatic, however, that other sectors adjust quickly and favorably. During economic downturns, which might accompany an oil price shock, some sectors and some locations may be more affected than others (Fields 1988). How does the transport sector itself, especially in the urban areas, and their workers, cope with this? It is also important to inquire whether the observed adjustments are outcomes of a more liberal regime and would have been negligible if India maintained the same policy structures as in the pre-reform era. We discuss briefly how the previous attitude towards gradualist economic reforms allowed the country to maintain a relative stability even during the epitome of first generation reforms. Naturally, with lesser controls adopted by the government, the transfer of economic shocks would be direct. Under the circumstances, if the benefits of exposing the internal economies to external forces outweigh the costs, which may happen due to strong institutional characteristics of a country, then the subject remains wide open for empirical verifications.

This chapter explores the wage and employment conditions of transport sector workers in India, the larger proportion of which is engaged predominantly in the informal sector (ILO 1972; NCEUS 2007; Chaudhuri and Mukhopadhyay 2009; Marjit and Kar 2011). Do the relatively high oil prices observed in the last few years (notwithstanding the all-time low prices in the last few months of 2015–16) affect the wages and employment of informal transport workers adversely? To the best of our knowledge, this question remains unanswered in the concerned literature. The flipside of the problem is that, during historically low prices, should wages and employment of such workers then receive unprecedented impetus? The welfare implications

DOI: 10.4324/9780367855741-26

of such impact on a sizable section of the labor force associated with transport services in developing countries is unmistakable. Presently, we address this question empirically by drawing on the primary survey data available from the National Sample Survey of India and offer a general equilibrium model in order to generalize these results. The analytical section shows that the informal sector contracts and faces lower nominal and real wages when the oil price rises. Interestingly, in our model the traded sectors expand and leave the effect of oil price shock on national income, ambiguous. We are nonetheless aware of the fact that the sectoral or regional impact on the income of the poor may be quite deterministic as many of them depend on urban transport. This has been distinctly taken up earlier by Glaeser, Kahn and Rappaport (2008).

Indeed, the impact of oil price shock as a trigger for economic crisis is much more common for countries that use lesser administrative controls internally. India, for example, has practiced price control on essential items including petroleum since independence even going a few years into the economic reforms of the 1990s. The gradualist approach to economic reforms that India adopted over a sustained period of time helped internal adjustments much better than rapid transitions into uncharted territories that disrupted economic and social circumstances in more recent times. Importantly, India also practiced a managed float exchange rate system during the early reforms and did not allow full convertibility of the capital accounts. Both of these required continuous monitoring and intervention by the central bank. In fact, the economic reforms of the 1990s not only raised economic growth to an unprecedented level, but also managed to maintain relative economic stability – of course, not without the costs that any reform brings about. The government control on capital account has been especially favorable for protecting India from the Asian financial crisis (see Marjit and Kar, 1998). Unlike, the East and South-East Asian countries, allowing short-term foreign portfolio investments to leave the countries at short notice, thus bringing about the crisis, India preferred long-term foreign investments and disallowed dollar-for-dollar repatriation to the source. In other words, India used several monetary and fiscal instruments to insulate itself from various external sources of crisis, and even a globally spread out oil-price rise would make a limited impact owing to partial pass-through on to the local markets.

In addition, it is argued that the 'Great Moderation' in macroeconomic shocks consequent primarily on reduced volatility is the driving force behind this unexpected non-crisis. Some of the earlier contributions (viz. Nordhaus 2007; Segal 2011) suggest that the oil price shocks have fairly limited impact on the growth and distribution in most countries, because the earlier tradition of reorienting the monetary policy to allow a dollar-to-dollar pass-through of oil price shocks have of late been replaced. In fact, the usual monetary policy response to oil price pass-through had so far been a rise in the interest rate, which in turn slowed growth. In recent times, the reactions from the central banks have been moderate in the face of oil price shocks because the monetary policy seems to be more concerned with core inflation, which excludes the energy component. Nevertheless, possible impact in sectors directly dependent on the consumption of oil can hardly be ignored. The price of crude oil increased in India from USD 32.37 in April 2004 to 132.47 in July 2008. It fell sharply for six months following that and rose to USD 123.67 in March 2012 (see Figure 26.1). This upward trend continued until August 2013 and since then the oil price has started falling significantly and stayed at the USD 40 mark in March 2016 (see Figure 26.2).

To reiterate, the extant literature, dealing with energy prices and sectoral readjustments, does not discuss the pass-through of oil prices on to wages, viz. in the domestic transport services. The transport services we deal with in the empirical section include both formal and informal activities. This seems to be an appropriate depiction of the range of activities in the transport sector in developing countries and is also formalized in the empirical model we develop next. We categorically estimate

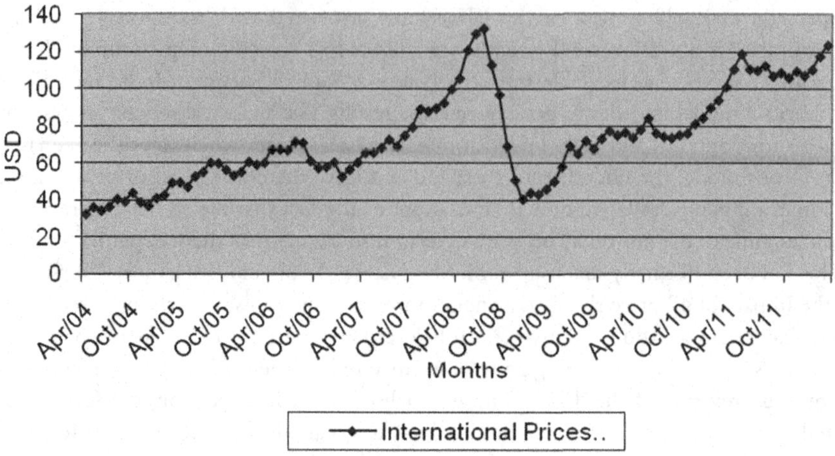

Figure 26.1 International price of crude oil per barrel (US$) Source: Ministry of Petroleum, Government of India.

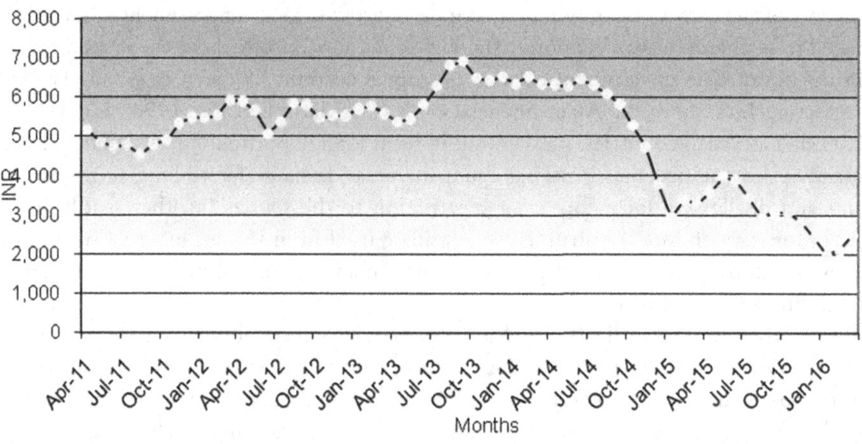

Figure 26.2 Crude oil (petroleum) monthly price (Rupees Indian) Source: World Bank.

the wage impact of switching from the formal to the informal sector – a plausible feature of this labor market associated with rising oil prices. The presence of an urban informal sector has several implications associated with use of fuel and impact on the environment, largely because they are often outside the monitoring circuit of the local governments (Kahn and Pfaff 2000). While we discuss the scope in detail shortly, to clear any confusion presently, the idea is to observe whether the formal transport fails to cope with rising oil prices and contracts employment, leading to relocation of workers to the informal sector. Does it lead to a definitive fall in real wages when workers move from the formal to the informal transport services? This is what we estimate, with rising oil price as the source of change. We accommodate a number of other variables to substantiate this effect calculated between 2004–05 and 2011–12.[1] The fall in real wage of transport workers is a testable proposition because the switch from formal to informal also implies that the service provider would no longer have to bear the 'institutional costs' (including adherence to labor laws, environmental strictures, various taxes, etc.) of running formal services and therefore, the workers need not necessarily settle for a lower real wage.[2] In the related literature, Radchenko (2014) offers an interesting technique to identify the heterogeneity of labor markets in poor countries. The proposition that the displaced lose out is similar in spirit to the 'movers and stayers' hypothesis in Davidson and Matusz (2006).

In the next section we offer the data and scope of the empirical investigation. In the third section we determine the impact of oil price rise on the wages of workers that switch jobs, and the fourth section concludes.

Empirical observations

Data and methodology

This section investigates the impact of sectoral mobility of workers on the real wage. Based on the National Industry Code (NIC1998; 2004; 2008) classification we can broadly divide employment in the transport sector in India into four categories (at the 4-digit level). Since the classifications changed from one year to another, they were not comparable. Therefore, we used concordance tables to convert them all into the latest NIC classification.[3] In addition, the classifications are further disaggregated depending on whether they are formal or informal. We consider a broader definition of the term 'formal' sector that employs more than ten people. We focus on the real wage of the road–transport industry worker. Our analysis leaves out railways transport since Indian Railways is still fully under the public sector. The categories of interest are therefore, 'urban or suburban passenger land transport – formal (USF)', 'urban or suburban passenger land transport – informal (USI)', 'other passenger land transport – formal (OF)', 'other passenger land transport – informal (OI)', 'freight transport by road – formal (FF)' and 'freight transport by road – informal (FI)'. Dependence of these sectors on fossil fuel and diesel is very high. Given these categories, we investigate the wage response when workers from the urban or suburban passenger land transport (formal) potentially move to any of the other five categories.

The data is collected from two major sources for calculation of our dependent variable (real wage). We have collected information on nominal wage of the transport sector workers from the latest Employment Unemployment Surveys of the National Sample Survey Organization (NSSO). It is the primary source of data on various indicators of labor force at national and state level and provides a vast set of information on each individual of the households selected in the sample. First, we identify individuals working in the land transport industry and calculate their nominal wages from 61st (2003–04), 66th (2009–10) and 68th (2011–12) round surveys on employment unemployment using NSSO usual principal activity status, respectively. In order to calculate the real wage of these workers (nominal wage deflated by the price level of the corresponding year), information on the price level has been collected from the All India Price Index (General) for Industrial Workers (CPIIW, Base-1982=100) of the Labor Bureau of the Government of India. Further, we have collected information on age, sex, highest levels of completed education of individual workers and area of residence (rural or urban) from the same source as mentioned earlier. Before testing empirical association, we offer a framework which enables us to shed some light on the methodology we have adopted. To briefly apprise of the subsequent information on transport and communication services as available from the 73rd round of sample survey by the NSSO (see note 1), we present Table 26.1. The table clearly shows that between 2011–12 and 2015–16, both the number of enterprises engaged with transport and communication belonging to the unorganized sector, and the employment of workers in such organizations, fell. Indeed, the direction of change corroborates our findings further, even though this information is not part of the final set of regressions.

We have considered three land transport industries with their formal–informal divisions. There are 3,294, 2,936 and 3,070 observations in the sample for workers who belong to these

Table 26.1 Changes in the number of enterprises and number of workers in the transport and communication services between 2011–12 and 2015–16

Industrial sector	*67th Round: 2011–12*			*73rd Round: 2015–16*			*Growth rate*		
	Rural	*Urban*	*Rural+Urban*	*Rural*	*Urban*	*Rural+Urban*	*Rural*	*Urban*	*Rural+Urban*
Transport and communication: number of enterprises ('00)	31449	26698	58147	32021	25941	57962	1.8	−2.8	−0.3
Transport and communication: number of workers ('000)	4027	3602	7628	4003	3521	7524	−0.6	−2.2	−1.4

Source: NSS Report No.581: Operational Characteristics of Unincorporated Non-Agricultural Enterprises (Excluding Construction) in India

transport sectors according to the three rounds specified above. We provide a descriptive analysis on the distribution of the workers for these industries with respect to their levels of education and age groups in Appendix 26A.1. We also provide summary statistics on the daily wage rate of these workers. The analysis is done for rural and urban areas, separately, in order to understand regional variation in the possible outcomes. The reason behind this is also direct. The rural to urban migration is the well-known progenitor of the vast informal sector in the urban space of the developing world in general (see Harris and Todaro, 1970 and several works thereafter). The rural sector itself also has a large informal counterpart, and the low productivity of agricultural workers is primarily responsible for such outcomes. Thus, if the wage of informal transport workers in the urban area (as one form of informal jobs) is adversely affected by an external factor, but the rural informal worker is differently affected, the migration pattern and consequently the wages may also respond to that.

Most of the rural transport workers are concentrated in the informal sector of 'Freight transport industry' followed by 'Other passenger land transport'. This is also true for the urban sample and for all the rounds we have considered. Table 26A.1 gives the distribution of the workers in these six different industries with respect to their levels of education. Three major columns are representative of the three NSS rounds. We find that with education up to the secondary level, the transport workers are more likely to be in the informal sectors of these two sub-sectors. The percentage concentration of these workers in these sub-sectors has in fact increased over the last two rounds. For higher levels of education, participation in the formal sector of urban or suburban passenger land transport rises irrespective of the residential area. However, for education level of twelfth standard and above the concentration in this sector falls between the 61st and the 66th round, but increases thereafter.

We have also grouped the transport industry workers according to their age groups into three cohorts, Youth (15–29), Adult (30–49) and Elderly (50 and above), respectively. Table 26A.2 shows that youth transport workers are mostly concentrated in the informal sector of 'Freight transport by road' followed by the informal sector of the 'Other passenger land transport' industry. Concentration in the formal sector of the urban or suburban is highest among the older cohorts. However, in case of the formal sectors of the other two industries, participation is very low and almost similar among the three age cohorts. This in general is true for the three NSS rounds and for both areas.

Table 26A.3 offers the daily wage distribution of these workers for the rural and urban areas, separately. We see that the transport industry wage is positively skewed. The variation in the wage rate is higher for rural areas compared to their urban counterparts and it has also increased over the consecutive rounds. However, after deflating the wage by CPIIW, the variance falls. Subsequently, we take the log transformation of the real wage and obtain a normal distribution amenable to empirical investigation.

Empirical analysis

Ordinary least square (OLS) specifications

We aim to investigate empirically how different informal and formal transport service providing sectors influence change in the prevailing real wage when workers switch sectors.

$$\left(\frac{W}{P}\right)_i = \alpha + \beta_j \text{transport}_{ji} + \gamma \text{age}_i + \delta \text{age}^2_i + \mu \text{sex}_i + \theta_k \text{edu}_{ki} + \vartheta_1 \text{district}_{li} + \varepsilon_i \quad (26.1)$$

Equation (26.1) is the conventional Mincer equation, which estimates the wage rate with inclusion of standard variables like age, age squared (measuring experience), levels of education, etc. $\left(\frac{W}{P}\right)_i$ represents real wage of ith worker in the transport industry; $transport_{ji}$ is a categorical variable, which can be represented by a dummy. It can assume six categories depending on the sectors (formal/informal) we have classified earlier. The first one (USF) is treated as our base category. Therefore β_j measures the effect of movement from the base to the jth category by the ith individual, on the real wage.

Depending on the highest level of education, we convert education into a categorical variable also. The categories are 'no elementary education', 'primary education (up to)', 'secondary education (up to)', 'higher secondary education' and 'tertiary education (more than twelfth standard)', respectively. The coefficient θ_k measures the impact of movement from no elementary (our base category) education to k^{th} level on the real wage. In order to take into account local labor market conditions, we have controlled for the district specific heterogeneities; $district_{li}$ measures district-specific fixed effect. Finally, ε_i is the error term. The estimation has been considered for rural and urban areas separately and for three different time points (2004–05, 2009–10 and 2011–12). Interestingly, the high crude oil prices reported for India largely coincide with the rounds under consideration (Figure 26.1). Table 26.1 contains the result of the OLS estimation. There are three major columns and sub columns corresponding to three different time points and the areas of residences respectively.

Table 26.1 offers a number of noteworthy features. First, regardless of what sector a formal transport worker moves into during the period when the crude oil prices were high, the real wage outcome is usually negative and significant. This implies that change of sector has largely been unrewarding for the workers in the transport sector, unless the education level cushions the potential fall in real wage. Indeed, even workers with some education received the benefit of education while moving between the formal sector (USF) and any other sector. Education above twelfth standard leads to an almost 40% gain in real wage if the worker relocates from the USF to any city-based transport service facility. However, it may not be enough to reverse the strong negative effects arising from spread and depth of such activities in the various cities and towns of India. The fall in real wage particularly in the 61st and 66th rounds were generally larger compared to the 67th round. Movement of workers from the formal to the urban informal affects wages by a larger magnitude in more recent rounds. However, if the worker moved from USF to another formal sector in the rural area, the loss of real wage is stronger as compared to moving into the urban area in the same sub-sector (OF). If the worker moves to another informal sector, the fall in real wage is rather high for both rural and urban areas. It seems that on the one hand, the lack of opportunities in the rural areas for transport sector workers could be a potential reason for causing a steep decline in the real wage, and on the other hand, oversupply of such workers in the urban area is responsible for an almost equivalent fall in real wage. It is expected that most such workers are male and therefore sex has a weak impact on the observed change, although the age factor seems to have a positive impact on the real wage in the earlier rounds, but the effect has dampened in the 68th round. More experience on the job still cannot reverse the loss in real wage completely, but the effect of job switching becomes rather small. The results are supported by adequate goodness of fit for the econometric model.

Concluding remarks

This chapter dealt with the wage response of a typical transport worker in a developing country that allows cohabitation of both formal and informal modes of transport. The

Table 26.2 Ordinary least square estimates

	61st (2004–05)		*66th (2009–10)*		*68th (2011–12)*	
	Rural	*Urban*	*Rural*	*Urban*	*Rural*	*Urban*
Variables	*Real wage*	*Real wage*	*Real wage*	*Real wage*	*Real wage*	*Real wage*
USI	–0.698***	–0.686***	–0.444***	–0.617***	–0.425***	–0.469***
	(0.073)	(0.075)	(0.099)	(0.100)	(0.074)	(0.075)
OF	–0.396***	–0.256***	–0.117	–0.333***	–0.358***	–0.144*
	(0.103)	(0.085)	(0.104)	(0.097)	(0.083)	(0.083)
OI	–0.824***	–0.718***	–0.598***	–0.725***	–0.633***	–0.552***
	(0.060)	(0.057)	(0.072)	(0.076)	(0.059)	(0.065)
FF	–0.582***	–0.508***	–0.509***	–0.576***	–0.566***	–0.299***
	(0.081)	(0.074)	(0.094)	(0.088)	(0.0790	(0.083)
FI	–0.786***	–0.689***	–0.559***	–0.664***	–0.572***	–0.536***
	(0.057)	(0.054)	(0.072)	(0.075)	(0.057)	(0.065)
Age	0.0629***	0.0629***	0.0427***	0.0653***	0.0207**	0.0350***
	(0.008)	(0.008)	(0.008)	(0.009)	(0.008)	(0.009)
Age 2	–0.00064***	–0.000637***	–0.000439***	–0.000698***	–0.000123	–0.00031***
	(0.0001)	(0.0001)	(0.0001)	(0.0001)	(0.0001)	(0.0001)
Sex	–0.318*	–0.428***	–0.369***	–0.229	–0.390***	–0.0619
	(0.168)	(0.123)	(0.112)	(0.142)	(0.137)	(0.195)
Primary	0.172***	0.0719	0.0832*	0.121**	–0.0920**	–0.00283
	(0.042)	(0.046)	(0.047)	(0.059)	(0.044)	(0.057)
Secondary	0.219***	0.218***	0.145***	0.300***	0.0739**	0.0962**
	(0.037)	(0.038)	(0.041)	(0.047)	(0.036)	(0.046)
Higher secondary (HS)	0.276***	0.418***	0.251***	0.334***	0.133**	0.272***

(*Continued*)

Table 26.2 (*Continued*)

	61st (2004–05)		*66th (2009–10)*		*68th (2011–12)*	
	Rural	*Urban*	*Rural*	*Urban*	*Rural*	*Urban*
Variables	*Real wage*	*Real wage*	*Real wage*	*Real wage*	*Real wage*	*Real wage*
	(0.067)	(0.066)	(0.068)	(0.071)	(0.056)	(0.067)
More than HS	0.257***	0.543***	0.322***	0.581***	0.223***	0.436***
	(0.079)	(0.066)	(0.082)	(0.0809)	(0.074)	(0.0713)
						(0.507)
Constant	–1.770***	–2.331***	–1.993***	–2.293***	–1.597***	–2.141***
	(0.535)	(0.513)	(0.528)	(0.452)	(0.514)	(0.302)
Observations	1,738	1,556	1,667	1,269	1,696	1,374
R-squared	0.601	0.636	0.513	0.610	0.563	0.575

Source: Own calculations.
Standard errors in parentheses. *** $p<0.01$, ** $p<0.05$, * $p<0.1$.

underlying source of change in this chapter arises from international oil prices. It has been duly argued in the macroeconomics literature that rising oil prices coexist with growth in most economies in recent times and do not cause the economic crises observed in previous decades. The alignment of international oil prices with domestic prices without artificial buffers and the non-interference of monetary policy to counter oil price shocks have led to such outcomes in most countries. The literature does not, however, discuss other ensuing adjustments, namely those in the factor markets. This chapter showed through an empirical exercise and an analytical model closely resembling the developing country structure that oil price rise is quite likely to affect the wages of the transport sector workers negatively. In the empirical section, it was shown that the negative effect on workers' wage is a result of potential mobility of such workers from the formal to the informal sub-sectors within the transport sector at large. The workers nevertheless get the benefit of educational capital when they might be forced to move from the formal sector to the informal sector due to looming job losses following a steep rise in oil prices, which the formal transport sector often cannot cope with due to other institutional inflexibilities. Notwithstanding, the possibility of wage loss is still rather compelling for transport workers in India. The three rounds of survey under consideration strictly coincided with the periods of high oil prices prevailing in India.

Indeed, the coexistence of high oil prices, high inflation and reasonable economic growth could be a realistic feature of the developing economies, although in terms of the internal readjustments, the wage of workers seems to bear a disproportionate burden of the negative impacts. Clearly, more research is needed to understand whether the initial negative adjustments faced by the workers turn into permanent disadvantages for a large mass of the population. The relationship with poverty and inequality is almost integral to such issues, which needs careful reconsideration.

Appendix 26 A

Table 26A.1 Transport industry participation rate by general education

Area of residence	*NSS rounds*	*61st*					
		Urban or suburban passenger land transport		*Other passenger land transport*		*Freight transport by road*	
	General education	*Formal*	*Informal*	*Formal*	*Informal*	*Formal*	*Informal*
Rural	Below primary	2	3	1	21	7	66
	Up to primary	3	7	2	34	5	49
	Secondary	11	9	2	35	4	40
	Higher secondary	28	14	5	27	3	22
	more than HS	45	9	11	17	6	12
	Total	9	8	2	30	5	46
Urban	Below primary	1	4	2	32	6	55
	Up to primary	4	7	3	38	7	41
	Secondary	11	9	3	35	7	34
	Higher secondary	30	9	5	27	8	21
	more than HS	50	6	16	11	6	11
	Total	12	8	4	33	6	38
					66th		
Rural	Below primary	1	3	2	22	8	64
	Up to primary	2	2	1	37	4	53
	Secondary	4	5	3	40	5	43
	Higher secondary	13	4	9	35	3	35
	more than HS	32	5	12	29	5	17
	Total	5	4	3	35	6	47
Urban	Below primary	1	3	2	22	8	64
	Up to primary	2	2	1	37	4	53
	Secondary	4	5	3	40	5	43
	Higher secondary	13	4	9	35	3	35
	more than HS	32	5	12	29	5	17
	Total	5	4	3	35	6	47
					68th		
Rural	Below primary	1	3	2	26	6	62
	Up to primary	2	8	2	33	4	51
	Secondary	7	9	4	34	4	41
	Higher secondary	23	10	5	30	5	27
	more than HS	34	2	14	27	6	17
	Total	7	7	4	32	5	46

Source: Own calculations.

Table 26A.2 Transport industry participation rate by age group

Area of residence	*NSS rounds*	*61st*					
		Urban or suburban passenger land transport		*Other passenger land transport*		*Freight transport by road*	
	Age group	*Formal*	*Informal*	*Formal*	*Informal*	*Formal*	*Informal*
Rural	15–29	2	8	1	36	4	49
	30–49	14	8	3	25	6	44
	50 & above	30	3	6	13	5	44
Urban	15–29	4	8	1	42	6	39
	30–49	13	7	5	29	7	39
	50 & above	33	8	9	18	4	27
					66th		
Rural	15–29	1	4	2	37	5	51
	30–49	6	4	4	35	6	45
	50 & above	23	3	3	25	4	41
Urban	15–29	2	4	4	41	9	39
	30–49	7	6	7	37	7	36
	50 & above	16	6	5	23	10	40
					68th		
Rural	15–29	2	8	2	37	5	46
	30–49	9	7	4	30	5	46
	50 & above	17	9	8	20	5	42
Urban	15–29	4	13	3	39	5	36
	30–49	9	11	6	32	7	35
	50 & above	26	12	8	21	6	27

Source: Own calculations.

Table 26A.3 Wage distribution of the transport workers

Area of residence	*NSS rounds*	*61st*					
	variable	*Number of observations*	*Mean*	*Median*	*SD*	*Skewness*	*Kurtosis*
Rural	wage	1738	99	79	76	3	27
	realwage	1738	0.189	0.150	0.145	3.379	26.878
	log_realwage	1738	−1.883	−1.899	0.660	−0.107	3.843
Urban	wage	1556	115.634	85.714	94.839	2.822	17.308
	realwage	1556	0.220	0.163	0.181	2.822	17.308
	log_realwage	1556	−1.754	−1.812	0.677	0.222	3.318
					66th		
Rural	wage	1667	153.825	128.571	106.028	2.854	15.929
	realwage	1667	0.200	0.167	0.138	2.854	15.929
	log_realwage	1667	−1.788	−1.791	0.590	−0.135	4.448
Urban	wage	1269	176.615	142.857	147.520	4.227	34.420
	realwage	1269	0.229	0.185	0.191	4.227	34.420
	log_realwage	1269	−1.693	−1.686	0.642	0.133	4.044
					68th		
Rural	wage	1696	214.8079	178.5714	141.4818	2.164318	9.163108
	realwage	1696	0.23	0.19	0.15	2.16	9.16
	log_realwage	1696	−1.63	−1.65	0.58	−0.03	3.98
Urban	wage	1374	243.39	200.00	210.48	5.02	47.89
	realwage	1374	0.26	0.22	0.23	5.02	47.89
	log_realwage	1374	−1.55	−1.53	0.63	0.14	4.70

Source: Own calculations.

Notes

1 It is unfortunate that the data and report of the NSSO on Unorganized Enterprise Survey was published after this chapter was completed. Importantly, the data is unlikely to display considerable changes since it was collected within one year of the term of the government formed in 2014, and would have shown substantial fall in employment and wages if the survey covered the period of demonetization in November 2016. Nevertheless, we have included some indicators of the transport sector enterprises and employment over the two rounds, below.

2 See, 'Man with a Van' written by John Tierney, *New York Times Magazine*, August 10, 1997 and reproduced in *Economics: Principles and Applications*, (Ch. 15, Monopoly) by G. Mankiw (2007), Cengage Publishing. According to this article the state council of New York prevents private van operators from running transport services, simply by declining their licenses. The state transport service maintains a monopoly (veiled under the pretext that private van operators are more accident prone owing to competition for passengers) and charges a higher price by disallowing private operators, who nonetheless operate informally in specific locations, such as the 'curbs' near shopping centers. Here informal operation is synonymous with illegal operations. The developing countries like India on the other hand have institutionalized private informal service providers and the status of such facilities is not necessarily illegal. Also see Rizzo (2011) for Tanzania.

3 To make the NIC-1998 and NIC-2004 comparable with NIC-2008 we have transferred some industries based on their four-digit classification from one broad group to another or isolated them to form

a new group as per the latest classification with the help of the concordance tables published by Central Statistical Organisation (CSO) of the Government of India.

References

Cervero, R. (2000): *Informal transport in the developing world*, United Nations Centre for Human Settlements (Habitat), Nairobi.

Chaudhuri, S. (2016): 'Trade unionism and welfare consequences of trade and investment reforms in a developing economy', *Metroeconomica* 67, 1, 152–171.

Chaudhuri, S. and Mukhopadhyay, U. (2009): *Revisiting the informal sector: a general equilibrium approach*, Springer, New York.

Combes P. P. and Lafourcade M. (2004): 'Transport costs: measures, determinants, and regional policy implications for France', *Journal of Economic Geography* 5, 3, 319–349.

Davidson, C. and S. Matusz, (2006): 'Trade liberalization and compensation', *International Economic Review* 47, 723–747.

Fields, G. (1988): 'Employment and economic growth in Costa Rica', *World Development* 16, 12, 1493–1509.

Goodwin P. B., Dargay J. and Hanly M. (2004): 'Elasticities of road traffic and fuel consumption with respect to price and income: a review', *Transport Reviews* 24, 3, 275–292.

Glaeser, E., Kahn, M. and Rappaport, J. (2008), 'Why do the poor live in cities? the role of public transportation,' *Journal of Urban Economics* 63, 1, 1–24.

Graham, D. and Glaister S. (2002): 'The demand for automobile fuel: a survey of elasticities', *Journal of Transport Economics and Policy* 36, 1, 1–25.

Ihara, R. (2008), 'Transport costs, capital mobility and the provision of local public goods,' *Regional Science and Urban Economics*, 38, 1, 70–80.

International Labour Organisation (ILO). (1972): *Employment, Incomes and Equality: A Strategy for Increasing Productive Employment in Kenya*, ILO, Geneva.

Kahn, M. and Pfaff, A. (2000), 'Informal economies, information and the environment,' *Journal of International Affairs*, 53, 2, 525–544.

Kennedy D. and Wallis I. (2007): *Impacts of fuel price changes on New Zealand transport*, Land Transport New Zealand Research Report 331, Booz Allen Hamilton (NZ) Ltd., Wellington, DC.

Mankiw, G. (2007): *Economics: principles and applications*, Cengage Publishing, New York.

Marjit, S. and Kar, S. (1998): 'Financial volatility and convertibility- some methodological issues', *Economic and Political Weekly* XXXIII, 8, 401–406.

Marjit, S. and Kar, S. (2011): *The outsiders: economic reform and informal labour in a developing economy*, Oxford University Press, New Delhi.

Mussoa, A., Piccionia, C., Tozzia, M. Godard, G., Lapeyre, A. and Papandreou, K. (2013): 'Road transport elasticity: how fuel price changes can affect traffic demand on a toll motorway', *Procedia – Social and Behavioral Sciences* 87, 85–102.

National Industrial Classification (NIC). (1998, 2004, 2008): *Ministry of Statistics and Programme Implementation*, Govt. of India, New Delhi.

NCEUS. (2007): *Conditions of Work and Promotion of Livelihood in the Unorganised Sector*, National Commission for Enterprises in the Unorganised Sector, Government of India, New Delhi.

Nordhaus, W. (2007): 'Who's afraid of a big bad oil shock?', *Brookings Papers on Economic Activity* 2, 1–20.

Radchenko, N. (2014): 'Heterogeneity in informal salaried employment: evidence from the Egyptian labor market survey', *World Development* 62, 169–188.

Rizzo, M. (2011): 'The struggles of informal transport workers in Tanzania: debunking the myth of micro solutions', *Development viewpoint*, SOAS, London, Number 68.

Segal, Paul. (2011): 'Resource rents, redistribution, and halving global poverty: the resource dividend', *World Development*, 39 (4). doi:10.1016/j.worlddev.2010.08.013.

27

NEXUS BETWEEN TRADE LIBERALIZATION, GENDER AND EMPLOYMENT – WITH A SPECIAL REFERENCE TO INDIA'S PLANTATION SECTOR

Malini L. Tantri

Introduction

Being desirable from an efficiency perspective, gender equality is in itself a legitimate policy goal, as better opportunities for women foster human development. Initially, governments and the United Nations made commitments in the Beijing Platform for Action (1995) towards bringing the gender issue under the mainstream policy and development related debate. This was subsequently followed by the inclusion of the goal of gender equality and the empowerment of women in the Millennium Development Goals (MDGs) and the Task Force on Education and Gender Equality of the United Nations Millennium Project. Despite all these commitments and efforts at the international level, its awareness at the grassroots level continues to be very low. As a result, gender as an issue is generally side-lined in discussions that centre around economic and development policy, more specifically, in the case of trade policy formulation. However, given the fact that trade has more far-reaching effects on redistribution through various channels, it becomes imperative to understand its possible implications for gender as an issue. While analysing the effects of trade on gender, two specific issues need to be considered (UNCTAD 2009): the extent to which trade policies affect women's empowerment and well-being; and the impact that trade policies have on the level of inequality between men and women. Regarding the gender wage gap, while trade is not the underlying cause of gender income inequality, it can magnify or reduce the existing disparities. Fontana (2009) points out that it is due to the gender difference in access and control over resources and the different roles played in the markets that trade reform is more likely to bring about gender differentiated effects, leading to gender inequality and thereby limiting the potential gains from trade. The empirical literature on the relation between trade and gender, however, gives very inconclusive evidence. In fact, these diverse findings across nations could be due to the pre-existing socioeconomic setups in each country and the policy framework adopted which, perhaps, recognize and alter the pre-existing gender inequality and the level of trade openness itself. In the Indian context, very few studies have attempted to capture the gender element of trade expansion. Thus, this particular paper

DOI: 10.4324/9780367855741-27

attempts to explore gender relations with respect to trade liberalization in the context of India's plantation sector.

The reason for choosing the plantation sector for a comprehensive analysis lies in its export potential as well as its importance in meeting domestic requirements. In the process, it acts as a major channel for employment generation and poverty alleviation programmes in the rural sector. To be precise, as per one estimation, the plantation crops in India account for nearly 5 per cent of the net sown area and about 10 per cent of the income from agriculture and about 13 per cent of agricultural exports (Joseph 2010). Further, female labour accounts for a substantial share in the total employment in the plantation sector. In fact, it increased from being a little over 50 per cent in 1958–59 to 53.5 per cent in 2006 (ibid.). In the case of tea, women labour force accounted for almost 54 per cent in 2006 (ibid., p. 12). In addition to this, historically, the plantation sector has been a major source of export earnings for the country ever since colonial times. Tea, coffee and spices together constituted about 51 per cent of India's total agricultural export earnings during 1970–71. In fact, this trend remained more or less undisturbed until the mid-1980s when the share of these three plantation products constituted almost 47 per cent of India's export earnings during 1985–86. However, post 1990s, India's plantation sector has been experiencing two issues: a steep fall in domestic prices has caused tremendous pressures on the production sector, raising questions regarding the economic viability and profitability of plantation crops (Viswanathan 2007); second, the loss of conventional exports markets (Viswanathan and Shah 2012). As a result, the plantation sector is seen to adopt a coping mechanism in the form of cost cutting and layoffs affecting the workers. With respect to the direction of plantation trade, while India's export is mainly concentrated to the developed nations, the Asian markets act as a major source of import for India (Smitha 2011). In this context, it becomes very interesting to locate changing composition of the workforce based on gender differences across the plantation industries and across occupations of the plantation sector with a greater focus on the post-liberalization period. The analysis is based largely on data collected through occupational wage surveys of the plantation industry, which consist of seven rounds (first round, 1958; second round, 1963; third round, 1974; fourth round, 1985; fifth round, 1992, sixth round, 2006 and seventh round, 2016) and statistical profiles of women's labour, (2004, 2007 and 2013), Labour bureau – Ministry of Labour, Government of India.[1] The next section outlines how the relation between trade and gender is perceived in a theoretical construct. The third section provides an overview of India's plantation sector. The fourth section outlines, post 1990s, what kind of changes are noticed with respect to the employment pattern, wage structure and working conditions across the plantation sector. The last section summarizes the paper.

Trade liberalization and gender: a theoretical perspective

Recently, gender has come to be looked at as a macroeconomic variable, which can affect the country's growth, productivity and international trade. But although there exist a lot of empirical studies that consider gender as an important variable in explaining economic growth, the theoretical research on international trade is seldom concerned with gender as an important component in economic growth (Zhang 2008). In fact, gender has always taken a back seat in mainstream economics – be it macroeconomics, international trade, investment and/or finance (Cagaty 2005). Thus, the gender aspect finds itself completely ignored in international trade theories.

However, with growing inequality in gender, especially in developing nations where female labourers form a major portion of the workforce, it was imperative to comprehend gender implications in trade and growth. As a result, the New Trade Theory (NTT) tried to establish this through extending the factor price equalization model of Hecksher-Ohlin-Samuleson (H-O-S) theorem, thereby claiming that the trade openness would reap benefits for women as gender wages and employment gaps would be reduced due to trade. Subsequent literature further substantiated this by stating gender equality would be promoted as international trade would correct market imperfections and reduce the gender wage gap.[2] This idea of gender equality through trade was further proposed by Toulemonde (2014) with the notion that the trading of unskilled labour-intensive products, which are mainly produced by unskilled women in developing nations, should be emphasized, so as to promote gender equality.

However, trade openness was criticized by economists from the non-neoclassical school of thought (Darity and Williams 1985; Williams 1987) as they believed that, given the lower bargaining power of female workers, trade openness would further aggravate gender inequality. Meanwhile, feminist economists too reject the neoclassical economist view on the basis that it does not consider the social sphere which forms the major part of factor endowment and derives theories considering perfect competition which in the real world is unrealistic.[3] Further, the endogenous growth theories have highlighted that innovation would benefit only skilled labour and not the vast unskilled female labourers and the engagement of unskilled labour by export companies would only decrease their wages. Thus, on the whole, there seems to be ambiguity with respect to whether or not trade promotes gender quality. Moreover, many of these theoretical studies fail to accommodate/explain how trade liberalization can change the consumption pattern, asset holding, and dissemination of power in relation to gender. Given this, the next section explores whether India's plantation sector in the post-liberalization period supports NTT or endogenous growth theory construct in shaping female employment and earning is concerned.

An overview of India's plantation sector

As per the Plantation Labour Act (PLA) 1951, a plantation is defined as a piece of land of 5 hectares (15 acres) or more being used for the cultivation of tea, coffee, rubber, cinchona, cocoa, oil palm and cardamom with 15 or more persons being employed on any day of the preceding 12 months (Tantri, 2017). Among these, tea is an important crop with a history spanning more than 160 years. With respect to ownership pattern, the bulk production of tea (80 per cent) is accounted for by the corporate sector or by large estates, whereas, the bulk production of rubber (87 per cent) and coffee (60 per cent) is accounted for by small holdings (GoI, 2008–09). With respect to geographical spread, the plantation crops in India cover a minuscule area. Within that, spices occupy the major plantation area, covering 52 per cent of the cultivable plantation area (Figure 27.1). Although tea plantations provide major employment opportunities, they cover only 9 per cent of the total plantation area, followed by rubber (8 per cent) and coffee (only 7 per cent) of the plantation area. The plantation area again varies across regions, with south India covering 77 per cent of the plantation area and the remaining in the rest of the nation (Figure 27.2). The major plantation state are Karnataka with a plantation area of 25 per cent, followed by Kerala with 24 per cent and Tamil Nadu with 18 per cent, while Assam, which is mainly known for tea plantation, covers only 3 per cent of the total plantation area (Figure 27.3).

Employment, wage structure and working conditions in the plantation sector

As discussed in the previous section, post 1990s has had significant impacts on the export performance of plantation products. In this context, it becomes very interesting to locate the changes in employment, wage and working conditions of plantation labour in general and

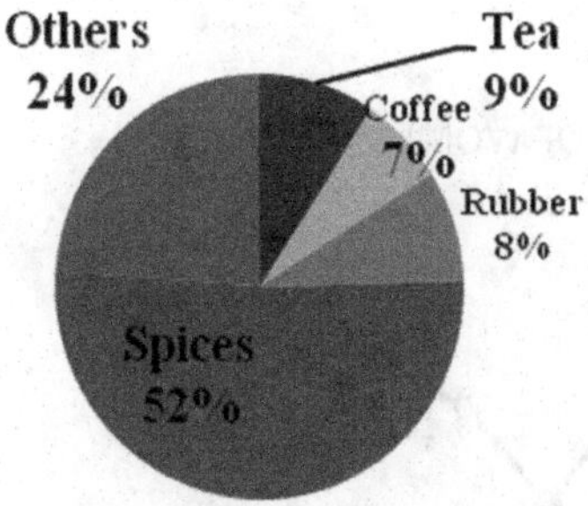

Figure 27.1 A crop-wise size and spread of the plantation sector in India (2013–14) Source: EPW Research Foundation.

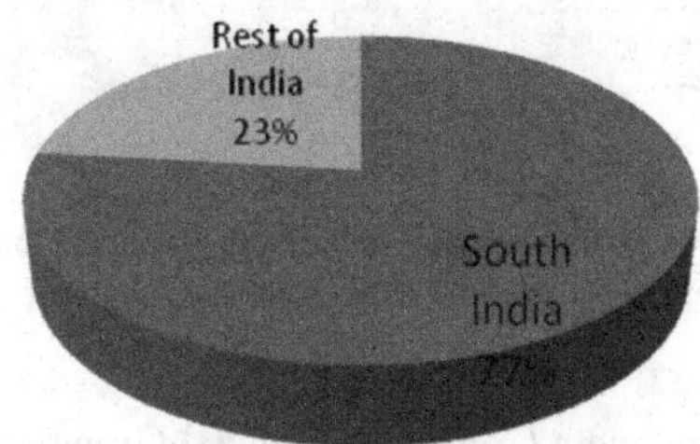

Figure 27.2 Total area spread of the plantation sector – South India and Rest of India (2014–15)* Source: Ministry of Agriculture, GoI.

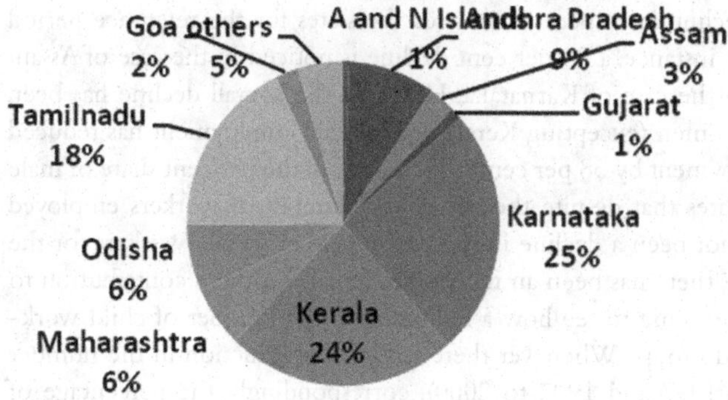

Figure 27.3 State-wise spread of the total plantation area (2014–15) Source: Ministry of Agriculture, GoI.

women in particular. As this sector among others, is known for the feminization of employment, an attempt is made in this section to examine/analyse the composition of the working force based on gender differences across the plantation industries and across occupations of the plantation sector with a greater focus on the post-liberalization period.

With respect to trends in employment, on an average, daily employment in the plantation industry shows a decrease in the post-reform period from 10.85 lakhs in 1990 to 6.63laks in 2010 (Figure 27.4), thereby revealing a negative growth rate of −2.31 per cent. In fact, a declining trend seems quite obvious post 2000. For the same period (1990–2010), there has been a decline in absolute numbers of the total average daily employment of women from

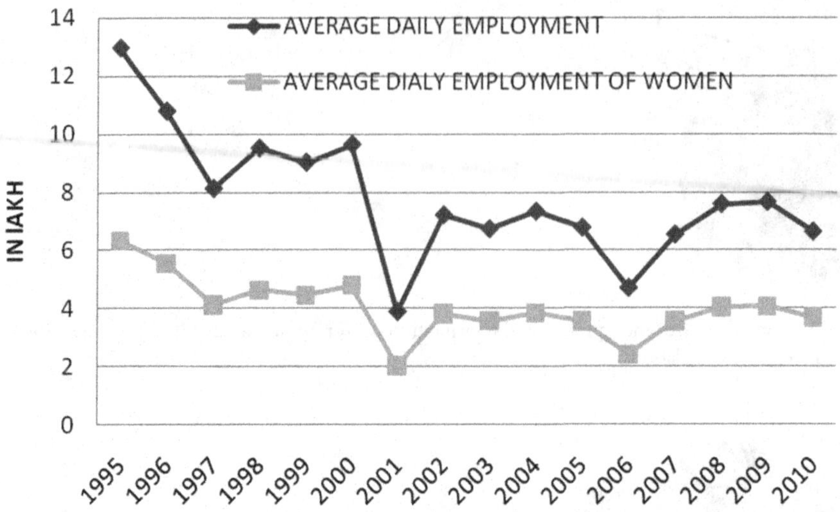

Figure 27.4 Average daily employment and women's share of average daily employment in the plantation sector/industry Source: Statistical Profile on Women's Labour 2004, 2007 and 2013. Labour Bureau – Ministry of Labour.

558,016 in 1990 to 370,619 in the year 2010, thereby revealing a Compound Annual Growth Rate (CAGR) of −1.93 per cent. However, at the same time, the percentage share of women's employment shows an increasing trend from 51.45 per cent to 55.86 per cent for the same period, thereby representing a case of dominance of female workers in the plantation industry.

As against the national trend, at the disaggregate level, female employment (in the total plantation employment) shows a decline in respect of most of the states for the reference period 1990–2010 (see Table 27.1). For instance, a 26 per cent decline is noticed in the case of Assam and a 37.60 per cent decline in the case of Karnataka. However, the overall decline has been more in the case of men than women (excepting Kerala where male employment has reduced by 36 per cent and female employment by 38 per cent). An analysis of the per cent share of male and female adult workers indicates that despite the decreasing number of workers employed in most of the states, there has not been a decline in the percentage of female workers for the respective years; on the contrary, there has been an increase in female worker's contribution to the total employed. It is also interesting to see how a reduction in the number of child workers has shifted to other sexes and groups. Whenever there has been a reduction in the number of children employed (1995 to 1997 and 1997 to 2000), correspondingly the percentage of adolescents' contribution to the workforce shows an increase. For instance, in Assam, during 1996, child workers fell to nil from 30,873 male children and 41,539 female children in 1995. The year 1996 showed an increase in the number of adolescent workers as compared to the corresponding previous years, despite a reduction in the overall number of workers employed. Male adolescents increased by 78 per cent in 1996 as compared to 1995 and females by 112 per cent. Similarly, whenever there was a decrease in the number of adolescent workers over the period 2000–05, the female workers' contribution shows an increasing trend. Further, there has been a regional difference i.e., states such as Karnataka, Kerala and Tamil Nadu pay much higher wages as compared to West Bengal (Bhowmik, 2005). The employment rates of the plantation sector across Indian states, such as Assam, West Bengal and Kerala with a substantial tea production show fluctuation, thereby pointing to a decline in the number of female workers employed (Table 27.1).

Table 27.1 State-wise and gender-wise average daily employment of adults and children in plantations

Sl. No.	States	Year	Gender				Adolescents		Children		Total
			Male	Percentage of male workers to the total	Female	Percentage of female workers to the total	Male	Female	Male	Female	
1	Karnataka	1990	11576	43.89	14008	53.11	408	355	0	29	26376
		1995	13880	55.79	10901	43.81	39	41	11	9	24881
		2000	9145	45.69	10789	53.91	35	45	0	0	20014
		2005	6916	39.1	10772	60.9	0	0	0	0	17688
		2010	5752	39.68	8740	60.3	2	1	0	0	14495
2	Kerala	1990	42473	47.74	45399	51.03	477	614	0	0	88963
		1995	44359	49.24	45616	50.63	66	49	0	0	90090
		2000	36509	45.13	43987	54.37	120	280	0	0	80896
		2005	28983	48.88	30317	51.12	0	0	0	0	59300
		2010	27004	48.89	28233	51.11	0	0	0	0	55237
3	Tamil Nadu	1990	35483	43.22	46555	56.71	19	11	12	12	82092
		1995	29829	44.91	36449	54.87	62	82	0	0	66422
		2000	31251	46.04	36628	53.96	0	0	0	0	67879
		2005	22531	41.13	32252	58.87	0	0	0	0	54783
		2010	N/A	N/A	N/A	N/A	N/A	N/A	N/A	NA	N/A
4	Andaman & Nicobar Islands	1990	479	81.32	110	18.68	0	0	0	0	589
		1995	492	82	108	18	0	0	0	0	600
		2000	340	71.58	135	28.42	0	0	0	0	475
		2005	N/A	N/A	N/A	N/A	N/A	N/A	N/A	N/A	N/A
		2010	272	75.56	88	24.44	0	0	0	0	360

(Continued)

Table 27.1 (Continued)

Sl. No.	*States*	*Year*	*Gender*				*Adolescents*		*Children*		*Total*
			Male	*Percentage of male workers to the total*	*Female*	*Percentage of female workers to the total*	*Male*	*Female*	*Male*	*Female*	
5	Himachal Pradesh	1990	158	44.13	193	53.91	2	0	0	5	358
		1995	110	57.29	82	42.71	0	0	0	0	192
		2000	116	45.49	139	54.51	0	0	0	0	255
		2005	49	34.51	93	65.49	0	0	0	0	142
		2010	69	34.85	129	65.15	0	0	0	0	198
6	Tripura	1990	1963	53.87	1473	40.42	0	0	181	27	3644
		1995	3265	53.07	2600	42.26	65	11	134	77	6152
		2000	7153	51.56	6495	46.82	0	0	178	47	13873
		2005	4225	56.5	3253	43.5	0	0	0	0	7478
		2010	5585	45.23	6762	54.77	0	0	0	0	12347
7	Uttar Pradesh	1990	N/A	N/A	N/A	N/A	N/A	N/A	N/A	NA	N/A
		1995	86	33.99	167	66.01	0	0	0	0	253
		2000	53	30.64	120	69.36	0	0	0	0	173
		2005	N/A	N/A	N/A	N/A	N/A	N/A	N/A	N/A	N/A
		2010	N/A	N/A	N/A	N/A	N/A	N/A	N/A	N/A	N/A
8	Uttarakhand	1990	N/A	N/A	N/A	N/A	N/A	N/A	N/A	NA	N/A
		1995	N/A	N/A	N/A	N/A	N/A	N/A	N/A	NA	N/A
		2001	52	31.52	113	68.48	N/A	N/A	N/A	N/A	165
		2008	463	35.24	851	64.76	N/A	N/A	N/A	N/A	1314
		2009	263	31.01	585	68.99	N/A	N/A	N/A	N/A	848
		2010	N/A	N/A	N/A	N/A	N/A	N/A	N/A	N/A	N/A

9	West Bengal	1990	98148	46.42	100187	47.38	2618	1987	4407	4090	211437
		1995	100024	46.74	103628	48.42	5129	5241	N/A	N/A	214022
		2000	96620	47.31	102888	50.38	2549	2186	N/A	N/A	204243
		2005	71785	46.61	79568	51.67	1234	1415	N/A	N/A	154002
		2010	73542	44.71	90006	54.71	481	472	N/A	N/A	164501
10	Assam	1990	276181	41.17	290117	43.24	3979	6083	48080	46442	670882
		1995	419765†	46.99	369659	41.38	14222	17234	30873	41539	893292
		1996	317961	45.7	315840	45.39	25333	36687	N/A	N/A	695821
		1997	206799	45.74	200181	44.27	12930	7137	8520	15981	452148
		2000	272820	47.22	263839	45.66	28502	12644	N/A	N/A	577805
		2005	178353	46.45	186175	48.49	7571	11578	148	159	383984
		2010	177404	42.61	213951	51.38	12108	12906	N/A	N/A	416369

Data source: Statistical profile on women labour, 2004 and 2013, Labour Bureau, Ministry of Labour.
† = includes artisans and clerical staff also.

Table 27.2 Trends in the composition of workers across industries by sex/age

Sl. No.	*Industry/ OWS round no./ reference year*	*Estimated total number of workers*	*Percentage of workers by sex/age group*			
			Men	*Women*	*Adolescent*	*Children*
1	*2*	*3*	*4*	*5*	*6*	*7*
I.	Coffee plantations					
	First round (1958)	95700	48.60	45.70	1.60	4.10
	Second round (1963)	87324	46.10	47.80	N/A	6.10
	Third round (1974)	26317	46.60	48.70	3.10	1.60
	Fourth round (1985)	66721	39.47	57.35	2.05	1.13
	Fifth round (1992)	70998	43.94	55.30	0.49	0.27
	Sixth round (2006)	105288	44.83	54.71	0.46	N/A
	Seventh round (2016)	31256	43.41	56.59	–	–
II.	Rubber plantations					
	First round (1958)	11900	74.40	25.6	N/A	N/A
	Second round (1963)	20581	71.20	28.3	N/A	0.50
	Third round (1974)	24824	63.70	36.1	0.20	N/A
	Fourth round (1985)	35947	66.02	33.98	N/A	N/A
	Fifth round (1992)	34123	60.20	39.8	N/A	N/A
	Sixth round (2006)	61270	57.70	42.3	N/A	N/A
	Seventh round (2016)	26702	52.58	47.42	–	–
III.	Tea plantations					
	First round (1958)	766500	43.20	51.30	0.40	5.10
	Second round (1963)	788469	43.30	49.90	N/A	6.80
	Third round (1974)	612079	41.20	49.10	0.60	9.10
	Fourth round (1985)	917965	40.67	49.41	1.06	8.86
	Fifth round (1992)	927069	43.97	51.16	0.43	4.44
	Sixth round (2006)	811854	44.36	54.24	1.40	N/A
	Seventh round (2016)	1159527	40.24	59.40	0.36	–

Source: Occupational Wage Survey, Seventh Round (2016).

Until 2006, the total number of workers employed in three major plantation industries shows an increasing trend (Table 27.2). However, for the latest available data, except for tea plantation, there seems to be a dip in the total workers employed. The 2016 survey indicates women constituting 56.59 per cent and 59.40 per cent of the total employment in the coffee and tea industries respectively.

Historically, the rubber industry has been dominated by men, in view of the physical exertion involved in rubber tapping. However, over the years, feminization has shown an increasing trend in the rubber industry as compared to the tea and coffee industries, engaging women more in activities other than plantation labour; these are activities involving weeding, fertilizer application, etc. (Viswanathan and Amita 2012). As per the occupational wage survey report of 2006, these jobs are classified under 'field worker' with women accounting for 40.68 per cent in the rubber industry. The rubber industry has been badly hit by the crashing of global prices since

2011–12. However, even prior to this, there was a constant reduction observed in the number of workers employed in all the rubber growing states of the south, including U/T Andaman and Nicobar Islands, where rubber is the only plantation activity listed in the above survey. Tripura, however, reveals a positive trend. Despite a fall in the total employment, the production of rubber reveals a positive trend. This is specifically due to a surge in the number of small growers who have continued to dominate the production of rubber (90.5 per cent) (Rubber Board, 2013) However, the tea industry happens to be the largest employer of workers across the plantation sector as a whole. With just a small dip in the third round (1974), the number of tea workers employed shows a fair recovery. However, with multiple closures (135 gardens in 1999–2005, Tea Board 2007), the situation seems to be bleak. With the introduction of the Child Labour (Prohi bition and Abolition) Act, 1986 and an amendment effected to the Plantations Labour Act, 1951, child labour has totally been abolished, as per records, across all three sectors. But still children above 14 years and less than 18 years under adolescent category continue to be employed on a small scale in the tea industry.

A state-wide analysis of trends in employment across major Indian states and also major plantation crops reveals a very interesting picture, in that states engaged predominantly in tea cultivation such as Assam, Kerala, Tamil Nadu, Karnataka and West Bengal witnessed a major decrease in the employment rate for the year 2010 as against the 1990s (Table 27.3), and especially Assam, effecting a reduction in its workforce in the tea plantation industry in the year 2010 as compared to 1990. Of an overall reduction in workers, the percentage decline of male workers is more than female workers. This is seen in respect of all the tea producing states except Kerala where the percentage decline of female workers (–37.03 per cent) is more than that of male workers (–26.04 per cent). A pronounced feminization of the workforce is seen in the coffee plantation industry too. Tamil Nadu has seen an increase in the number of workers employed in the coffee industry where female workers have more than tripled. But the other two coffee producing states, Karnataka and Kerala, have witnessed a decline in female workers' employment. However, the rate of decline of female workers is less than that of male workers. It is interesting to note that states such as Himachal Pradesh, Tripura, Uttarakhand and Uttar Pradesh (data for UP state as in the year 2002), which are not traditional growers of tea, fare better in terms of labour employment vis-à-vis the traditional growing states (Table 27.3).

In fact, a reduction in the total number of workers employed has been observed despite an increase in and the constant value of area under tea cultivation.[4] The area under cultivation since 1995 has seen an increase in both the traditional tea growing states and non-traditional growers (Table 27.4). In respect of states like Assam, West Bengal, TN and Kerala, this may have happened due to cost cutting measures followed by big plantations and/or labour shortages.

From colonial times there has been a practice of employing entire local resident families as a workforce. However, with a growing seasonal demand and the availability of cheap labour, another category of workers has been noticed in the plantation sector. Based on the tea statistics data, we can observe that the annual compound growth rate of outside workers (2.80 per cent) is much higher than the growth rate of resident workers. Further, there has been an increasing trend in the employment of workers from outside on a temporary basis rather than on a permanent basis (Thapa 2012). Tea plantations are found to engage the highest number of permanent workers as compared to other plantation crops. This could also be due to the fact that tea plantations happen to be a big grower phenomenon and other crops are largely dominated by small growers. The highest percentage of female temporary employment is found in respect of the rubber industry.

Table 27.3 State-wise average daily employment in major plantations by sex

Sl. No.	State/Union territory	Year	*Average daily employment in plantations*											
			Tea			*Coffee*			*Rubber*			*Other plantation*		
			Male	*Female*	*Total*	*Male*	*Female*	*Total*	*Male*	*Female*	*Total*	*Male*	*Female*	*Total*
1	Assam	1995	464860	428432	893292	N/A	N/A	N/A	N/A	N/A	N/A	N/A	N/A	N/A
		2000	301322	276483	577805	N/A	N/A	N/A	N/A	N/A	N/A	N/A	N/A	N/A
		2005	186072	197912	383984	N/A	N/A	N/A	N/A	N/A	N/A	N/A	N/A	N/A
		2010	189152	226857	416369	N/A	N/A	N/A	N/A	N/A	N/A	N/A	N/A	N/A
	Total		1141406	1129684	2271450	N/A	N/A	N/A	N/A	N/A	N/A	N/A	N/A	N/A
2	Himachal Pradesh	1995	110	82	192	N/A	N/A	N/A	N/A	N/A	N/A	N/A	N/A	N/A
		2000	116	139	255	N/A	N/A	N/A	N/A	N/A	N/A	N/A	N/A	N/A
		2005	49	93	142	N/A	N/A	N/A	N/A	N/A	N/A	N/A	N/A	N/A
		2010	69	129	198	N/A	N/A	N/A	N/A	N/A	N/A	N/A	N/A	N/A
	Total		344	443	787	N/A	N/A	N/A	N/A	N/A	N/A	N/A	N/A	N/A
3	Karnataka	1995	1465	1250	2715	11231	8340	19571	1234	1361	2595	N/A	N/A	N/A
		2000	694	1141	1835	7111	7794	14905	1375	1899	3274	N/A	N/A	N/A
		2005	951	1394	2345	5046	8084	13130	914	1294	2208	N/A	N/A	N/A
		2010	587	748	1335	4378	6926	11304	789	1067	1856	N/A	N/A	N/A
	Total		3697	4533	8230	27766	31144	58910	4312	5621	9933	N/A	N/A	N/A
4	Kerala	1995	24870	34384	59254	1027	1208	2235	17240	8314	25554	1280	1759	3039
		2000	23567	32706	56273	974	1317	2291	15627	2978	18605	1461	2266	3727
		2005	15359	19152	34511	1335	1615	2950	11011	7706	18717	1278	1844	3122
		2010	18288	21650	39938	683	929	1612	6395	3819	10214	1638	1835	3473
	Total		82084	107892	189976	4019	5069	9088	50273	22817	73090	5657	7704	13361
5	Tamil Nadu	1995	24870	34384	59254	1027	1208	2235	17240	8314	25554	1280	1759	3039
		2000	23567	32706	56273	974	1317	2291	15627	2978	18605	1461	2266	3727
		2005	18127	28400	46527	2530	3031	5561	1812	781	2593	634	451	1085
		2009	14803	26082	40885	2125	3945	6070	2010	937	2947	35	48	83
		2010	N/A	N/A	N/A	N/A	N/A	N/A	N/A	N/A	N/A	N/A	N/A	N/A
	Total		81367	121572	202939	6656	9501	16157	36689	13010	49699	3410	4524	7934

6	Tripura	1995	2061	2242	4303	N/A	N/A	N/A	1403	446	1849	N/A	N/A	N/A
		2000	6072	6213	12285	N/A	N/A	N/A	1259	329	1588	N/A	N/A	N/A
		2005	2166	3026	5192	N/A	N/A	N/A	2059	227	2286	N/A	N/A	N/A
		2010	3710	5697	9407	N/A	N/A	N/A	1875	1065	2940	N/A	N/A	N/A
	Total		14009	17178	31187	N/A	N/A	N/A	6596	2067	8663	N/A	N/A	N/A
7	Uttarakhand	2001	52	113	165	N/A	N/A	N/A	N/A	N/A	N/A	N/A	N/A	N/A
		2003	49	103	152	N/A	N/A	N/A	N/A	N/A	N/A	N/A	N/A	N/A
		2006	46	84	130	N/A	N/A	N/A	N/A	N/A	N/A	N/A	N/A	N/A
		2009	263	585	848	N/A	N/A	N/A	N/A	N/A	N/A	N/A	N/A	N/A
	Total		410	885	1295	N/A	N/A	N/A	N/A	N/A	N/A	N/A	N/A	N/A
8	West Bengal	1995	103894	108413	212307	N/A	N/A	N/A	N/A	N/A	N/A	1359	456	1815
		2000	97485	103832	201317	N/A	N/A	N/A	N/A	N/A	N/A	1679	1247	2926
		2005	72673	80719	153392	N/A	N/A	N/A	N/A	N/A	N/A	346	264	610
		2010	73043	89705	162748	N/A	N/A	N/A	N/A	N/A	N/A	980	773	1753
	Total		347095	382669	729764	N/A	N/A	N/A	N/A	N/A	N/A	4364	2740	7104
9	Andaman & Nicobar Islands	1995	N/A	N/A	N/A	N/A	N/A	N/A	492	108	600	N/A	N/A	N/A
		2000	N/A	N/A	N/A	N/A	N/A	N/A	340	135	475	N/A	N/A	N/A
		2006	N/A	N/A	N/A	N/A	N/A	N/A	272	89	361	N/A	N/A	N/A
		2009	N/A	N/A	N/A	N/A	N/A	N/A	272	88	360	N/A	N/A	N/A
	Total		N/A	N/A	N/A	N/A	N/A	N/A	1376	420	1796	N/A	N/A	N/A
10	Uttar Pradesh	1995	86	167	253	N/A	N/A	N/A	N/A	N/A	N/A	N/A	N/A	N/A
		2000	53	120	173	N/A	N/A	N/A	N/A	N/A	N/A	N/A	N/A	N/A
		2001	3388	2803	6191	N/A	N/A	N/A	N/A	N/A	N/A	N/A	N/A	N/A
		2002	3185	2726	5911	N/A	N/A	N/A	N/A	N/A	N/A	N/A	N/A	N/A
		2005	N/A	N/A	N/A	N/A	N/A	N/A	N/A	N/A	N/A	N/A	N/A	N/A
		2010	N/A	N/A	N/A	N/A	N/A	N/A	N/A	N/A	N/A	N/A	N/A	N/A
	Total		6712	5816	12528	N/A	N/A	N/A	N/A	N/A	N/A	N/A	N/A	N/A

Source: Data Source: Statistical Profile on Women's Labour 2004, 2008 and 2013, Labour Bureau, Ministry of Labour.

Table 27.4 Total area under tea cultivation in India (area in hectares)

State	*1995*	*2000*	*2001*	*2002*	*2003*	*2004*	*2005*	*2006*	*2007*	*2008*	*2009*	*2010*	*2011*	*2012*
Assam	226280	266512	269154	270683	271589	271768	0502	311822	321319	322214	322214	322214	322210	322210
West Bengal	101190	107479	110820	113113	113351	114003	14525	114788	115095	115095	115095	115095	115100	115100
Kerala	36775	36940	36940	36967	36967	37107	36772	36236	37137	37137	37137	37137	37140	37140
Tamil Nadu	48958	74398	75625	75619	75619	75978	80939	81276	80462	80462	80462	80462	80460	80460
Tripura	5952	6623	7200	7591	8268	8268	8710	8710	8962	N/A	N/A	N/A	N/A	N/A
Himachal Pradesh	2312	2325	2312	2312	2348	2348	2348	2348	2348	N/A	N/A	N/A	N/A	N/A
Utter Pradesh	1068	1068	1068	N/A	N/A	N/A	N/A	N/A	N/A	N/A	N/A	N/A	N/A	N/A
Uttaranchal	1068	1068	1068	1068	1471	1446	1456	1456	1585	N/A	N/A	N/A	N/A	N/A

Source: Data compiled from Tea Statistics (1995–2004) and The India Tea Association (2005–12).

Wages

Wages in the plantation industry are subject to the Minimum Wage Act, 1948 and Equal Remuneration Act, 1976. However, these laws are often not followed, as workers do not demand for it or, they themselves are not aware of their rights. A Labour Bureau report on the socioeconomic conditions of women workers in the plantation sector points out that only 34.7 per cent of women workers are aware of the Minimum Wage Act and 18.5 per cent of women workers are aware of the Equal Remuneration Act, 1976. (GoI 2008–09). A quick survey of wages across gender and major plantation crops reveals that, over the decades, the average daily wage rates have been increasing in respect of all three plantations, but in order to arrive at a logical judgement, these wages are deflated to the 1960 base year for calculating the real wage rates (Table 27.5). Real wages in the coffee and rubber industries have seen a gradual increase, while the tea industry, on the other hand, has seen many fluctuations with real wages reported in the third round (1974) and fifth round (1992) being less than those of 1963 wages. An increase in real wages in percentage terms is found second highest in respect of the tea industry with coffee being first and rubber last. It is interesting to note that while all three plantations have experienced a slump in both absolute and real wages post the fourth round (1985), the tea industry has suffered majorly with real wages falling drastically (–7.10 per cent) as compared to the previous round data. The average daily wages are found to be lowest in the tea industry, as compared to coffee and rubber. With respect to gender-based wage differential it is seen that there is a difference between adult male and female workers in terms of the wages they receive in all three industries. However, these are absolute numbers representing the overall wage rates of various occupations; in order to comprehend the issue of discrimination, a classification has been made in terms of occupation and wage rate for all three industries (Table 27.6).

Plantation is mainly a feminized activity, but still certain occupations such as drivers and supervisors are occupied by men. Driver occupation is occupied 100 per cent by men in all the plantations. The Supervisor level jobs too are predominantly occupied by men in coffee, rubber and tea plantations (94.64, 97.68 and 98.68 per cent, respectively) (Table 27.7). This explains the occupational differences where skilled jobs like supervising have been predominantly occupied by men with females dominating only unskilled jobs which require more manual labour. This reflects a very clear case of gender discrimination through occupational a disaggregation followed by wage discrimination. Even in occupations where women workers are employed in relatively large numbers, they do not seem to enjoy a major difference in terms of daily earnings (Table 27.7). In the tea industry, especially, there exists a huge wage differential as women supervisors are paid much less than male supervisors.

Working conditions

Despite many statutory provisions of the Plantation Labour Act (PLA) in place, a quick survey of working conditions in the plantation industry reveals a gloomy picture and thereby questions whether or not these statutory provisions are implemented in its true spirit. The conditions of tea garden workers, both in terms of work and living, have been neglected since colonial times. Workers initially in the 19th century used to migrate from non-plantation regions to plantation regions as a way of escaping from poverty. The immigration of such workers, oppression and low wages in the name of productivity were considered the main components of the colonial times tea plantations (Bhowmik 1980). These plantations, merging over the years, even after the independence of India, continued to operate as an

Table 27.5 Trends in the average daily wage rates

Sl. No.	*Industry/OWS Round no./ Reference year*	*Average daily wage rates (Rs) of workers*						*Percentage change in wages*	
		By sex/age groups				*Overall*	*Real wage rate(Rs.)*	*Wage rate at current prices*	*Real wage rate*
		Men	*Women*	*Adolescents*	*Child*				
I	Coffee plantations								
	First round (1958)	N/A	N/A	N/A	N/A	1.34	1.34	N/A	N/A
	Second round (1963)	1.93	1.32	1.01	0.96	1.58	1.17	17.98	–12.36
	Third round (1974)	4.25	3.55	2.59	1.90	3.82	1.16	142.54	–0.75
	Fourth round (1985)	11.52	10.98	8.30	6.48	11.09	1.68	190.18	38.95
	Fifth round (1992)	26.61	25.48	20.76	18.62	25.93	2.04	133.92	26.97
	Sixth round (2004)	73.20	70.52	58.03	N/A	71.66	2.60	176.36	41.95
	Seventh round (2016)	277.57	257.93	–	–	266.46	3.92	271.83	50.77
II	Rubber plantations								
	First round (1958)	N/A	N/A	N/A	N/A	2.17	2.17	N/A	N/A
	Second round (1963)	1.96	1.47	1.15	1.05	1.82	1.35	–15.94	–37.64
	Third round (1974)	7.95	7.51	5.99	N/A	7.79	2.36	328.02	46.65
	Fourth round (1985)	21.40	19.38	N/A	N/A	20.71	3.13	165.85	35.56
	Fifth round (1992)	41.37	39.29	N/A	N/A	40.53	3.19	95.70	2.77
	Sixth round (2004)	91.43	87.50	N/A	N/A	89.77	3.26	121.49	3.24
	Seventh round (2016)	428.46	408.77	–	–	419.13	6.17	366.89	89.26
III	Tea plantations								
	First round (1958)	N/A	N/A	N/A	N/A	2.26	2.26	N/A	N/A
	Second round (1963)	3.16	1.81	2.02	2.06	3.05	2.26	35.03	0.22
	Third round (1974)	4.74	5.00	3.35	2.75	4.67	1.41	53.37	–37.69
	Fourth round (1985)	13.65	14.22	9.83	7.26	13.33	2.02	185.44	27.05
	Fifth round (1992)	24.21	24.29	18.71	11.94	23.68	1.86	77.61	–7.10
	Sixth round (2004)	55.76	53.62	32.45	N/A	54.27	1.97	129.23	4.88
	Seventh round (2016)	149.56	139.26	127.00	–	141.57	2.08	160.86	5.58

Source: Occupational Wage Survey, Seventh Round (2016).
Note: Average daily wage rates up to fifth round correspond to mean of the average daily minimum and max wage rates.
$: Percentage increase has been measured with respect to that of the previous year.

Table 27.6 Average daily earning of workers across industries by occupation, sex and age

Sl. no.	*Industry/ OWS round no./Reference year*	*Average daily earnings (Rs)*				
		Men	*Women*	*Adolescent*	*Children*	*Overall*
I	Coffee plantations	277.77	257.93	–	–	266.46
1	Driver	320.64	–	–	–	320.64
2	Supervisor	381.59	384.57	–	–	381.74
3	Watchmen	258.18	–	–	–	258.18
4	Plantation labour	253.75	257.33	–	–	255.75
5	Miscellaneous	702.47	–	–	–	702.49
II	Rubber plantations	439.12	427.50	–	–	433.85
1	Driver	637.96	–	–	–	637.96
2	Supervisor	501.61	438.18	–	–	500.14
3	Watchmen	486.53	–	–	–	486.53
4	Rubber tapper	391.26	419.25	–	–	404.98
5	Field worker	464.89	361.51	–	–	398.42
6	Miscellaneous	367.61	329.54	–	–	358.44
III	Tea plantations	149.56	136.26	127.0	–	141.57
1	Driver	352.10	–	–	–	352.10
2	Supervisor	264.03	259.86	–	–	263.97
3	Watchmen	185.47	–	–	–	185.4
4	Plantation labour	140.88	136.20	127.0	–	137.93
	All plantation industry	160.99	144.05	127	–	150.87

Source: Occupational wage survey, Seventh Round – Report on plantation industry.

enclave sector with workers found themselves at the mercy of planters. Besides, over the years, plantation owners have failed to provide even the basic amenities such as better toilets and clean drinking water. With respect to housing facilities, only 64.17 per cent of the total eligible (411,831) workers have been provided with housing. West Bengal, despite being a traditional plantation growing state, is the least among all the states providing just 3.36 per cent of the total eligible 98,729 workers with housing (Labour Bureau 2012). Although Assam has covered 83.05 per cent of eligible workers, it is faced with a shortage of 37,893 houses. Overall, in the nine plantation states of India, only 64.17 per cent of the total, that is, 264,254 workers have been provided with housing, with a shortage of 147,577 houses. As per the government maternity benefit report, during the year 2011, out of 3119 plantations, 51.94 per cent submitted returns with daily women workers numbering 793,360. Out of which, 29,123 (3.67 per cent) women workers claimed their maternity benefits. In fact, in a separate survey by the government, it was found that only 43.5 per cent of women workers of the plantation sector were aware of Maternity Benefits Act, 1961. It was noted that out of the 42 tea units taken into consideration, 89 per cent of them were providing medical facilities to workers and their family members. Coffee units, on the other hand, performed poorly in that out of 22 units surveyed in Karnataka, only 4.5 per cent provided medical facilities and shockingly only one medical officer was reported to have been deputed

Table 27.7 Distribution of plantation workers by occupation, sex and age

Sl. No.	*Industry/Occupation*	*Percentage of workers*	
		Men	*Women*
I	**Coffee plantations**	43.41	56.59
	Driver	100	–
	Supervisor	94.64	5.36
	Watchman	100	–
	Plantation labour	38.42	61.58
	Miscellaneous	100	–
II	**Rubber plantations**	52.58	47.42
	Driver	100	–
	Supervisor	97.68	2.32
	Watchman	100	–
	Rubber tapper	50.99	49.01
	Field worker	35.70	64.30
	Miscellaneous	75.91	24.09
III	**Tea plantations**	40.24	59.40
	Driver	100	–
	Supervisor	98.68	1.32
	Watchman	100	–
	Plantation labour	37.80	61.82
	All plantation industries	40.59	59.06

Source: Occupational Wage Survey, Seventh Round (2016).
Note: Wherever the percentage has not added up to 100, it indicates a contribution by adolescent workers of both sexes.

for the entire 22 units. A study with respect to Assam and West Bengal by Bhowmik et al. (1996) argues that not much has changed in these two states since the introduction of the PLA. The Government survey reported that only 10.6 per cent out the 47 tea plantation units surveyed provided urinal facilities. In respect of the coffee plantation industry, only 2.9 per cent out of 33 units provided a urinal facility. Even trade unions have been ineffective; the presence of multiple trade unions was being seen as a reason for poor bargaining power in West Bengal, while in the case of Assam, the main trade union, Indian National Trade Union Congress (INTUC) was reported to be leaning towards employers (Bhowmik 2015). Further, trade unions did not represent the societal problems nor did they take into consideration women's role in them. Such marginalization apart, over the years, the living conditions became so deteriorating that plantation women workers in Kerala went on strike urging for decent work and their rights (Bhowmik 2015). Starvation deaths and malnutrition were still prevailing in the plantation area. Deaths occurred due to the closure of many of the tea plantations as they were not able to cope with competition and also due to increasing costs involved in running estates and joblessness and lack of other sources of income. Apart from this, there were high costs associated with working in the plantation industry, especially post liberalization. For example, with an increase in the amount of fertilizers used in rubber and spice cultivation there were adverse effects on the health of workers.

Summary

Following the introduction of trade reforms, India's plantation sector has been experiencing two major challenges: first, a steep fall in the domestic prices and the loss of conventional markets caused by global market integration. This, however, has led to major changes in the pattern of women's employment and wages. Nevertheless, to date, the plantation industry has been mainly dominated by female workers, despite a fall in the total number of workers. The feminization of the workforce is also increasing in the rubber industry, which, historically, has been mainly dominated by males. However, the post-reform period has witnessed the plantation owners changing the nature of employment from a residential permanent workforce to an outside temporary workforce, specifically as a cost cutting strategy. Gender discrimination is seen in both occupational disaggregation and wage discrimination. Among others, the tea industry has a high margin of difference vis-à-vis coffee. On the one hand, our analysis does not support the new trade theory's theoretical construct that trade openness promotes better employment opportunities for women, while on the other, it supports the endogenous growth model viewpoint that trade liberalization may further widen the gap between males and females in relation to equality and wages. Further, it is important to note that many of the statutory requirements are not being fully adhered to, which means that there is a need for improving the work and living conditions of the plantation workers. Thus, on the whole, the analysis helps us to argue that the impact of trade liberalization on gender is highly sector specific and that preparedness at the national and regional levels may arrest the adverse impacts of trade liberalization on women, in particular.

Notes

1 The updates of the analysis to examine the impact of policy changes introduced by the current NDA government from 2014 onwards are not covered due to binding constraints of data availability.
2 For a detailed discussion on this refer to: Becker 1957; Black and Brainerd 2004; Cagatay 2005 and others.
3 For detailed discussion please refer to: Cagaty 2005; William 2002; Ozler 2000 and 2001 and others.
4 A caveat to this argument could be the employment data under analysis represents only the case of big estates, whereas, area under cultivation includes both STGs and big estates.

Acknowledgement

This research paper is part of Indian Council of Social Science Research (ICSSR), New Delhi, India Sponsored research Project on Trade, Gender and Food Security with a special reference to Tea Plantation in the Nilgiris. In this connection, Author acknowledges with gratitude ICSSR for the facilitation of this study through financial support and also all stakeholders who participated in the survey.

References

Alarcón-González, Diana, and Terry McKinley. "The adverse effects of structural adjustment on working women in Mexico." *Latin American Perspectives* 26.3 (1999): 103–117.

AlAzzawi, Shireen. "Trade liberalization, industry concentration and female workers: The case of Egypt." *IZA Journal of Labor Policy* 3.1 (2014): 20.

Artecona, Raquel, and Wendy Cunningham. *Effects of trade liberalization on the gender wage gap in Mexico*. World Bank, Washington, DC (2002).

Chaudhuri, Bivas, A. K. Panigrahi. "Gender bias in Indian industry." *The Journal of Industrial Statistics* 2.1 (2013): 108–127.

Banerjee, Purna, and C. Veeramani. *Trade liberalisation and women's employment intensity: Analysis of India's manufacturing industries.* Working Papers 2015-018, Indira Gandhi Institute of Development Research, Mumbai, India (2015).

Becker, Gary. *The Economics of Discrimination*, University of Chicago, Chicago (1957).

Bhattacharya, Debapriya, and Mustafizur Rahman. *Female employment under export propelled industrialization: Prospects for internalizing global opportunities in the apparel sector in Bangladesh.* Occasional Paper No. 10. United Nations Research Institute for Social Development (UNRISD), Geneva (1999).

Bhowmik, Sharit Kumar. "The plantation as a social system." *Economic and Political Weekly*, 50.36 (1980): 1524–1527.

Bhowmik, Sharit K. "Tea plantation workers' strike: Workers lose out on wages." *Economic and Political Weekly*, 40. 32 (2005): 4103–4105.

Bhowmik, Sharit K. "Living conditions of tea plantation workers." *Economic and Political Weekly*, 50. 46/47 (2015) 46–47.

Bhowmik, Sharit, V. Xaxa, and M. K. Kalam. *Tea Plantation Labour in India*, Friedrich Ebert Foundation, New Delhi (1996).

Black, Sandra E., and Elizabeth Brainerd. "Importing equality? The impact of globalization on gender discrimination." *Industrial & Labor Relations Review*, 57.4 (2004): 540–559.

Black, S. E., and A. Spitz-Oener. "Explaining women's success: Technological change and the skill content of women's work." *The Review of Economics and Statistics*, 92.1 (2010): 187–194.

Bøler, Esther Ann, Beata Smarzynska Javorcik, and Karen Helene Ulltveit-Moe. *Globalization: A woman's best friend? Exporters and the gender wage gap.* CESifo Working Paper Series 5296, CESifo (2015).

Boserup, Ester. *Woman's role in economic development*, George Allen & Unwin, London (1970).

Braunstein, Elissa, and Mark Brenner. "Foreign direct investment and gendered wages in urban China." *Feminist Economics*, 13.3–4 (2007): 213–237.

Çağatay, N. Gender Inequalities and International Trade: Theoretical Considerations. Paper Presented at the LA-IGTN and International Development Research Centre Workshop on "Trade, Gender and Equity in Latin America: Knowledge Creation for Political Action". Montevideo, Uruguay (2005).

Darity W, Williams R: Peddlers forever? Culture, competition, and discrimination. *Am Econ Rev*, 75.2 (1985): 256–261.

Deepika, M. G. *Export performance and factors affecting competitiveness of plantation commodities in India.* NRPPD Discussion Paper 45, Centre for Development Studies, Trivendrum (2015).

Ding, Sai, Xiao-Yuan Dong, and Shi, Li. "Women's employment and family income inequality during China's economic transition." *Feminist Economics*, 15.3 (2009): 163–190.

Fernandes, Walter, Sanjay Barbora, and Gita Bharali. *Children of the plantation labourers and their right to education*, North Eastern Social Research Centre, Guwahati (2003).

Fontana, Marzia. *Gender justice in trade policy: The gender effects of economic partnership agreements.* One World Action, London (2009).

Francis, Smitha. "The ASEAN-India free trade agreement: A sectoral impact analysis of increased trade integration in goods." *Economic and Political Weekly*, 46.2 (2011): 46–55.

Gaddis, Isis, and Janneke Pieters. *Trade liberalization and female labor force participation: Evidence from Brazil.* IZA Discussion Papers 6809, Institute of Labor Economics (IZA) (2012).

Gobillon, Laurent, Dominique Meurs, and Sébastien Roux. "Estimating gender differences in access to jobs." *Journal of Labor Economics* 33.2 (2015): 317–363.

Goldar, Bishwanath. *Impact on India of tariff and quantitative restrictions under WTO.* No. 172. Indian Council for Research on International Economic Relations, New Delhi, India (2005).

Government of India. *Socio-economic conditions of women workers in plantation industry.* Ministry of Labor & Employment Labor Bureau, Chandigarh (2008–2009).

Government of India*Report on the working of the plantations labour act 1951 for the year*, Ministry of Labor & Employment Labour Bureau, Chandigarh (2012).

Government of India. *Ministry of commerce and industry annual report.* New Delhi (2012–13).

Government of India. *Ministry of commerce and industry annual report.* New Delhi (2015–16).

Government of India. *Ministry of commerce and industry, ASEAN-India trade in goods agreement.* New Delhi (2010).

Government of India. *Ministry of commerce and industry, department of industrial policy and promotion.* Consolidated FDI Policy , New Delhi (2015).

High Commission of India *Handbook on the India-Sri Lanka free trade agreement*, High Commission of India, Colombo, Sri Lanka (2013).

Harilal, K. N., N. Kanji, J. Jeyaranjan, M. Eapen, and P. Swaminathan. *Power in global value chain: Implication of employment and livelihood in the cashew nut industry in India*, IIED Working Paper No. 2, London (2006).

Hayashi, Michiko. *Trade in textiles and clothing priority issues for women in post ATC division of international trade in goods and services and commodities*, UNCTAD, Geneva (2004).

IANWGE. *Gender equality and trade policy resource paper.* United Nations Inter-Agency Network on Women and Gender Equality, New York (2011).

Joseph, K. J., *Towards a new paradigm for plantation development in India: An analysis of the system of production and innovation from an inclusive growth perspective.* NRPPD Discussion Paper 1, Centre for Development Studies, Trivendrum (2010).

Joseph, K. J., and P. S. George. *Structural infirmities in India's plantation sector: Natural rubber and spices.* NRPPD Report, Centre for Development Studies, Trivendrum (2010).

Juhn, Chinhui, Gergely Ujhelyi, and Carolina Villegas-Sanchez. "Men, women, and machines: How trade impacts gender inequality." *Journal of Development Economics*, 106 (2014): 179–193.

Juhn, Chinhui, Gergely Ujhelyi, and Carolina Villegas-Sanchez. "Trade liberalization and gender inequality." *The American Economic Review*, 103.3 (2013): 269–273.

Kelegama, Saman, and Chandana Karunaratne. *Experiences of Sri Lanka in the Sri Lanka–India FTA and the Sri Lanka–Pakistan FTA*, BACKGROUND PAPER NO. RVC-10. UNCATD, Geneva (2013).

Kochhar, Kalpana, Utsav Kumar, Raghuram Rajan, and Arvind Subramanium. "India's pattern of development: What happened, what follows?" *Journal of Monetary Economics*, 53.5 (2006): 981–1019.

Li, Haizheng, and Jeffrey Zax. "Economic transition and labor supply in China." In *China's labor market and problems of employment*, edited by Y. Wang and A. Chen. Southwest University of Economics and Finance Press, Chengdu, China (2000), pp. 217–233.

Mahmud, Simeen, and Naila Kabeer. *Compliance versus accountability: Strug igration and international trade.* World Bank Discussion Papers, Washington, DC (1995).

Mahmud, Simeen, and Naila Kabeer. "Compliance versus accountability: Struggles for dignity and daily bread in the Bangladesh Garment Industry." *The Bangladesh Development Studies*, 29.3/4 (2003): 21–46.

Mahmud, Simeen, and Naila Kabeer. "Compliance versus accountability: Struggles for dignity and daily bread in the Bangladesh Garment Industry." *The Bangladesh Development Studies*, 29.3/4 (2003): 21–46.

Markusen, James R. "Factor movements and commodity trade as complements." *Journal of International Economics*, 14.3–4 (1983): 341–356.

Mahbub ul Haq Human Development Centre. *Human development in South Asia 2009: Trade and Haman Development.* The Mahbub ul Haq Human Development Centre. Oxford University Press, Pakistan (2009).

Melitz, Marc J. "The impact of trade on intra-industry reallocations and aggregate industry productivity." *Econometrica*, 71.6 (2003): 1695–1725.

Mengesha, Emezat. "Rethinking the rules and principles of the international trade regime: Feminist perspectives." *Agenda*, 22.78 (2008): 13–26.

Menon, Nidhiya, and Yana Van der Meulen Rodgers. "International trade and the gender wage gap: New evidence from India's manufacturing sector." *World Development*, 37.5 (2009): 965–981.

Government of India *Occupation wage survey sixth round*, GOI Labour Bureau , Chandigarh (2006).

Oostendorp, Remco H.. "Globalization and the gender wage gap." *The World Bank Economic Review*, 23.1 (2009): 141–161.

Ozler, Sule. "Export orientation and female share of employment: Evidence from Turkey." *World Development*, 28.7 (2000): 1239–1248.

Ozler, Sule. "Export led industrialization and gender differences in job creation and destruction: Micro evidence from the Turkish manufacturing sector." *Economic Research Forum Working Papers*. No. 0116 (2001).

Panagariya, A. *India: The emerging giant*, New York: Oxford University Press. (2008).

Paul-Majumder, Pratima. "Health impact of women's wage employment: A case study of the garment industry of Bangladesh." *The Bangladesh Development Studies*, 24.1/2 (1996): 59–102.

Pieters, Janneke. *Trade liberalization and gender inequality*, IZA World of Labor, Bonn, Germany (2015).

Ramessur, Taruna Shalini, and Sanjeev K. Sobhee. "Impact of trade liberalisation on labour conditions on the textile sector of Mauritius: The fate of female workers." *Regional and Sectoral Economic Studies*, 9.2 (2009): 69-84.

Richards, David L., and Ronald Gelleny. "Women's status and economic globalization." *International Studies Quarterly*, 51.4 (2007): 855–876.

Rubber Board. *Indian Rubber Statistics*, Vol 34, Rubber Board, Kottayam, India (2013): 68.

Russell, Sharon Stanton, and Teitelbaum, Michael S. *International migration and international trade*, World Bank, Washington, DC (1992).

Sajhau, Jean-Paul, and Jürgen Von Muralt. *Plantations and plantation workers*, ILO (1987).

Seguino, Stephanie. "Gender wage inequality and export-led growth in South Korea." *Journal of Development Studies*, 34.2 (1997): 102–132.

Segupta, Ranja, and Abhilash Gopinath. *The current trade frame work and gender linkage in developing economies: An introduction survey of issues with special reference to India*, CENTAD, New Delhi (2009).

Shu, Xiaoling, Yifei Zhu, and Zhanxin Zhang. "Global economy and gender inequalities: The case of the urban Chinese labor market." *Social Science Quarterly*, 88.5 (2007): 1307–1332.

Sinha, Nistha, Dhushyanth Raju, and Andrew Morrison. *Gender equality, poverty and economic growth.* World Bank Policy Research Working Paper No. 4349. World Bank, Washington, DC (2007).

Sutradhar, Ruman. "What caused marginalization: A study of the tea plantation women of Cachar." *International Journal of Science and Research* 6.14 (2013): 2771–2775.

Tantri, Malini L.. *A critique on India's plantation labour act*, ISEC Working Paper No. 398, Institute for Social and Economic Change (ISEC), Bangalore (2017).

Thapa, Namrata. *Employment status and human development of tea plantation workers in West Bengal.* NRPPD Discussion Paper, CDS, Trivendrum (2012).

The Cotonou Agreement. *Multiannual financial framework*, European Commission, Brussels and Luxembourg (2014–20).

Toppo, Toppo. "Violation of human rights in the tea plantations of Assam and West Bengal." In *Identity of adivasis in Assam*, edited by T. Pullopillil. Indian Publishers and Distributors, Delhi (1999), pp. 129–156.

UNCTAD. "Mainstreaming gender in trade policy." *Trade and Development Commission Expert Meeting on Mainstreaming Gender in Trade Policy, First Session*, Geneva, 10–11 March, 2009 (2009).

UNCTAD. "Mainstreaming gender in trade policy." *Trade and Development Commission Expert Meeting on Mainstreaming Gender in Trade Policy, First Session*, Geneva, 10–11 March, 2009 (2009).

Veeramani, C. "Anatomy of India's merchandise export growth 1993–94 to 2010–11." *Economic and Political Weekly*, 47.1 (2012): 94–1014.

Veeramani, C., and Gordhan K. Saini. "Impact of ASEAN-India preferential trade agreement on plantation commodities: A simulation analysis." *Economic and Political Weekly*, 46.10 (2011): 83–92.

Villarreal, Andrés, and Wei-hsin Yu. "Economic globalization and women's employment: the case of manufacturing in Mexico." *American Sociological Review*, 72.3 (2007): 365–389.

Viswanathan, P. K. *People's planning and Kerala's agriculture: The missed linkages.* Local Governance in India: Ideas Challenges and Strategies, Concept Publishing Company, New Delhi (2007), pp. 342–359.

Viswanathan, P. K., and Amita Shah. *Challenges, opportunities and imperatives for techno-economic and institutional reforms under trade liberalization: case studies of tea and rubber plantation sectors in India.* Report submitted to The South Asia Network of Economic Research Institutes (SANEI), Islamabad, Pakistan (2009).

Viswanathan, P. K., and Amita Shah. *Gender impact of trade reforms in Indian plantation sector: An exploratory analysis.* NRPPD Discussion Paper 17. CDS, Trivendrum (2012).

Viswanathan, P. K., and Amita Shah. "Gender impacts of trade reforms in India: An analysis of tea and rubber production sector." In *Globalization, development and plantation labour in India*, edited by K. J. Joseph and Viswanathan, P. K., Routledge (2016).

Weinberg, Bruce A. "Computer use and the demand for female workers." *Industrial and Labor Relations Review*, 53.2 (2000): 290–308.

Williams R: Capital, competition, and discrimination: a reconsideration of racial earnings inequality. *Rev Radic Polit Econ* 19.2 (1987):1–15.

Williams, Mariama. *The Political Economy of Tourism, Liberalization, Gender and the GATS.* Center of Concern-Global Women's Project, International Gender and Trade Network-Secretariat, Brighton, UK (2002).

Yahmed, Sarra Ben. *Gender wage gaps across skills and trade openness*, No. 1232, Aix-Marseille School of Economics, Marseille, France (2012).

Yao, Shujie. *Economic growth, income distribution and poverty reduction in contemporary China*, Routledge, London (2005).

Zaki, Chahir. "On trade, employment and gender: Evidence from Egypt." *ICITE 3rd Regional Conference: Trade, Jobs and Inclusive Development in Africa*, Tunisia (2011).

Zhang, Wei-Bin. *A theory of International Trade: capital, Knowledge and Economic Structure.* Springer-verlag Berlin Heidelberg (2008).

INDEX

Page numbers in italic indicate a figure and page numbers in bold indicate a table on the corresponding page.

Printed in the United States
by Baker & Taylor Publisher Services